CoreMacroeconomics

Gerald

Metropolitan State C

Worth Publishers

To Josephine and Sheila

Senior Publisher: Craig Bleyer
Acquisitions Editor: Sarah Dorger
Development Editor: Bruce Kaplan
Development Editor, Media and Supplements: Marie McHale
Director of Market Development: Steven Rigolosi
Consulting Editor: Paul Shensa
Senior Marketing Manager: Scott Guile
Associate Managing Editor: Tracey Kuehn
Project Editors: Dana Kasowitz
              Jennifer Carey, Matrix Publishing Services
Art Director: Babs Reingold
Senior Designer: Kevin Kall
Cover and Interior Designer: Karen Quigley
Illustrations: Matrix Publishing Services
Photo Editor: Cecilia Varas
Production Manager: Barbara Anne Seixas
Composition: Matrix Publishing Services
Printing and Binding: RR Donnelley

Library of Congress Control Number: 2007938459

ISBN-13: 978-1-4292-0622-8
ISBN-10: 1-4292-0622-5

First printing 2007

Worth Publishers
41 Madison Avenue
New York, NY 10010
www.worthpublishers.com

Gerald W. Stone is Emeritus Professor of Economics at Metropolitan State College of Denver. He has taught principles of economics to over 10,000 students throughout his career, and he has also taught courses in labor economics and law and economics. He has authored or coauthored over a half dozen books and numerous articles that have been published in economic journals such as the *Southern Economic Journal* and the *Journal of Economics and Sociology.* He earned his Bachelor's and Master's degrees in economics at Arizona State University, his Ph.D. in economics at Rice University, and a J.D. in law at the University of Denver.

Whoa. Not another principles of macroeconomics book. How could it offer anything new? Hasn't everything been done by now? I hope you will answer *no* to both questions after you see what is available to you and your students with *CoreMacroeconomics*.

I sought to write a textbook that is interesting and usable for instructors. I also wanted to give students extra help to learn the material. My experience with my students at Metropolitan State College of Denver, who come from wide backgrounds in an urban setting, led me to produce a unique student supplement (*CourseTutor*) that is integrated with the text. Together, the textbook and unique supplement provide instructors and students something that no one else provides.

What Does *Core* Mean?

My students complained continually that their textbooks were too expensive, too long, and too encyclopedic, and as a result, one-third or more of the material in the text wasn't covered in the course. They often resented paying for this unused extra material.

CoreMacroeconomics is not an encyclopedic offering. It does not cover every topic, but is partly based on a survey of economics professors to determine what they actually covered in their courses. Two important points emerged from this survey:

- **One chapter per week.** Instructors typically cover one chapter per week, or 15 chapters in a 15-week semester.
- **The majority of instructors teach roughly the same two-thirds of a standard economics textbook.** The overwhelming majority of instructors covers the same chapters in their course and then spends minimal time covering additional chapters. Over 90% of instructors cover roughly 15 chapters in their macroeconomics text, which typically includes 19–22 chapters.

In this sense, *core* does not mean brief or abridged. Rather, it means that the textbook contains the chapters that most instructors need, and very few additional chapters or special-interest topics.

The Core Text

The organization is traditional and the coverage concise. Concepts are thoroughly explained and illustrated with contemporary examples and issues integrated seamlessly into the text with the aim of enhancing the reading–learning experience. A conscious effort has been made to resist putting too much information – more than students need and unnecessary detail – to keep students honed in on the most important concepts. The goal has been to give students what is needed and no more.

The text incorporates the historical development of macroeconomics so students see how ideas and theories evolve over time. A dozen historical figures are highlighted in biographies and, in addition, the biographies of particular Nobel Prize winners are included when their contributions are of particular importance to the material covered in the chapter.

The text is loaded with applications that I think instructors and students will find interesting. These applications are not boxed off – they appear seamlessly throughout. Here are a few of them:

- In Chapter 6, we look at the different unemployment and job creation numbers given by the Establishment (payroll) Survey as opposed to the Household Survey. We show how a simple measurement issue has important policy ramifications.
- In Chapter 7, we look at innovation waves. The pace of technological change is speeding up. It took 50 years to go from steam power to electricity, and in 40 years digital devices, software, and the Internet have replaced electrical equipment. Today computers are speeding up developments in biotechnology on a decade timescale. What does this imply for economic growth?
- In Chapter 13, we look at the fiscal sustainability of the federal budget and intergenerational burdens. Are we headed for a fiscal train wreck? If so, what needs to be done?

I have sought to make the end of chapter questions interesting by basing many of them on recent issues, quotes, and articles, extending the analysis in unique ways. These questions should make good lecture starters to get students involved in the chapter material. Sample answers are included in the Instructor's Manual.

The text is written with beginning students in mind. I set out to provide a text that reduced student anxiety and made the material more accessible and interesting.

What Is *CourseTutor?*

For many years I taught two classes that met only on Saturday for three hours each. It soon became clear that students needed more feedback than what a once-a-week meeting could provide. I gave short quizzes on Saturday, analyzed each student's responses on Sunday, and sent each student a personalized set of study suggestions and additional exercises on Monday. *CourseTutor* evolved from this approach and is intended to help students who need something more than just a traditional study guide.

CourseTutor is divided into two basic sections: tutorial and study guide. The tutorial section guides students through each section of each chapter, while the study guide provides traditional study guide material. Both sections are designed for interactivity.

Each section in *CourseTutor* begins with frequently ask questions (FAQs) with extensive answers. This helps students to see what is really important in this section. This is followed by a Quick Check (five to ten questions). Their results on the quiz are diagnosed and suggestions for additional study, if needed, are provided. These suggestions are backed up with solved problems, exercises, and an explanation of core graphs, equations, and formulas. Those students who traditionally become frustrated or have trouble with economics will find *CourseTutor* helpful and hopefully improve their attitude and interest in economics.

Following the tutorial section is a brief section called "Hints, Tips, and Reminders" that I have found helpful for students over my career. Also included for each chapter is a single-sheet exam preparation guide (ExamPrep) where the important concepts are boiled down to one sheet that students must complete. The Exam-Prep sheets typically have enough space for students to add concise summaries of class notes. Also included for each chapter is a single-sheet homework assignment that you can require students to hand in, or students can complete online at the Worth online learning center and have their grades e-mailed directly to you.

Students learn by many different methods. *CourseTutor* addresses this by providing a buffet of learning choices. Students select those methods that best help them learn. Students having problems with specific material can turn to that particular section in *CourseTutor* for help. But, it is important to note that students are not expected to work through all of the material unless they absolutely need this level of additional help.

The remainder of each chapter in *CourseTutor* is standard study guide material including chapterwide matching, true-false, fill-in, multiple choice, essay questions, and problems for students to practice.

CourseTutor should save you time if students work through the tutorial before they come to see you; they should have fewer unfocused questions when they show up at your office for help. I believe you will find *CourseTutor* a worthwhile addition for your students.

Together, I think *CoreMacroeconomics* and *CourseTutor* provide something for you and your students that no one else in the market provides.

Outline of the Book

CoreMacroeconomics follows a traditional organizational sequence.

Students are introduced to economics in the first four chapters that focus on the nature of economics, trade, markets, supply, and demand. Chapters 1 and 2 provide a foundation for the study of economics along with a brief look at production and trade. Chapter 3 lays out supply, demand, and market equilibrium and details the efficiency of markets. Chapter 4 provides a balance to Chapter 3 by introducing the requirements for efficient markets, what happens when markets fail and how they tend to fail, and what government can do, in addition to a discussion of the impacts of price ceilings and floors. These two chapters give students a good foundation in the benefits of markets along with some of the caveats.

Macroeconomic coverage begins with Chapter 5 that introduces students to macroeconomic issues and GDP accounting. Chapter 6 follows with its attention on measuring inflation and unemployment. These two chapters give students the background needed for our discussion of macroeconomic theory in the next three chapters.

Chapter 7, 8, and 9 contain the core of macroeconomic theory. Chapter 7 introduces students to a brief overview of classical theory before the 1930s and an expanded discussion of the importance and sources of economic growth. Keynesian macroeconomics with its focus on aggregate expenditures is covered in Chapter 8. The last chapter in this sequence, Chapter 9, introduces students to the modern macroeconomics of aggregate supply and demand. One important note: These three chapters can be read or studied in any sequence adding flexibility for instructors who prefer to include or exclude one chapter or another.

Fiscal and monetary policy is the focus of Chapters 10 to 12. Discretionary fiscal policy, automatic stabilizers, and how fiscal policy affects aggregate supply constitute most of Chapter 10. Money—its nature, measurement, and creation by banks—and the institutional aspects of the Federal Reserve are the focus of Chapter 11. Monetary theory and policy are covered in Chapter 12, with an emphasis on how money and monetary policy affect interest rates, investment, and the economy.

Chapters 13 and 14 cover federal deficits and the public debt and macroeconomic challenges facing policymakers. Chapter 13 discusses deficits and the public debt, how they are financed, their burden on future generations, and their implications for macroeconomic policy in an open economy. Philips curves, inflationary expectations, and the implications of rational expectations on macroeconomic policy are the main issues presented in Chapter 14. In addition, an extended discussion of the problems associated with the "jobless recovery" aspects of the last two recessions is included.

The final two chapters of the book are devoted to the international economy. Chapter 15 covers the classical issues of international trade including the gains from trade (the Ricardian perspective), the terms of trade, along with a discussion of the impacts of tariffs and quotas, and an expanded discussion and evaluation of the arguments against trade. The last chapter (Chapter 16) examines the traditional topics of international finance (the balance of payments and exchange rates) along with an examination of fixed and flexible exchange rate systems. The final section of this chapter looks at the effect of these exchange rate systems on monetary and fiscal policy in an open economy.

Supplements

A useful and seamless supplements package has been developed to accompany this textbook. The package was crafted to help instructors teach their principles course, with both the experienced and novice instructors in mind. Along with the accompanying *CourseTutor* the additional ancillaries have been designed to help students work through the Core topics and to more readily grasp these key concepts. The entire package has been coordinated to guarantee uniformity and has been designed to work with the content, examples, and style of the Core text and *CourseTutor*.

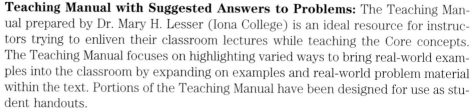

For Instructors

Teaching Manual with Suggested Answers to Problems: The Teaching Manual prepared by Dr. Mary H. Lesser (Iona College) is an ideal resource for instructors trying to enliven their classroom lectures while teaching the Core concepts. The Teaching Manual focuses on highlighting varied ways to bring real-world examples into the classroom by expanding on examples and real-world problem material within the text. Portions of the Teaching Manual have been designed for use as student handouts.

Every chapter of the Teaching Manual includes:

- *Chapter Overview:* A brief summary of the main topics covered in each chapter is provided.
- *Ideas for Capturing Your Classroom Audience:* Written with both the experienced and novice instructor in mind, this section provides ideas for introducing the chapter material. The suggestions provided can be used in a number of ways; they can be in-class demonstrations or enrichment assignments, and can be used in on-site, distance-learning, or hybrid course formats.
- *Chapter Checkpoints:* Each chapter of the text has Chapter Checkpoint sections that provide both bulleted review points and questions designed to assess whether students have mastered the main points of the section material. The Teaching Manual provides the instructor with suggested answers to those questions, notations about points to emphasize, and suggestions about reinforcing the assessment of student learning.
- *Extended Examples in the Chapter:* The Teaching Manual reproduces the extended examples used in each chapter and provides a discussion of these exam-

ples. As with the Chapter Checkpoint material, teachers will find that these sections delineate points to emphasize and provide additional resources for spurring student interest.

■ *Examples Used in the End-of-Chapter Questions:* A number of the End-of-Chapter Questions refer to specific articles in major newspapers or specific real-world examples. The Teaching Manual provides the instructor with a succinct overview of those questions and cites additional resources that can be used to develop more in-depth analysis of the topics covered. Note that this is in addition to the sample answers that are also provided.

■ *For Further Analysis:* Each Teaching Manual chapter contains an additional extended example that can be used in a variety of ways. Formatted as a one-page handout, it can be duplicated and distributed in class (or posted online), and is designed for use either as an in-class group exercise or as an individual assignment in both the on-site and online class format. Asking students to document research allows the instructor to use the example as a case study or group project as well. Learning objectives are specified and a one-page answer key is also available for reference or distribution.

■ *Web-Based Exercise:* Each Teaching Manual chapter includes a Web-Based Exercise that requires students to obtain information from a web site and use it to answer a set of questions. This Web-Based Exercise can be used in a variety of ways as in-class group exercises or as individual assignments. Learning objectives are specified and suggested answers to questions are provided that can be used for reference or distribution.

■ *Tips from a Colleague:* Each chapter of the Teaching Manual concludes with a "tips" section that shares ideas about classroom presentation, use of other resources, and insights about topics that students typically find difficult to master.

Test Bank: *Coordinator and Contributor:* Richard Croxdale (Austin Community College). *Test Bank Contributors:* Emil Berendt (Siena Heights University), Dennis Debrecht (Carroll College), Elizabeth J. Wark (Springfield College). The Test Bank contains nearly 2,500 carefully constructed questions to help you assess your students' comprehension, interpretation, analysis, and synthesis skills. Questions have been checked for this continuity with the text content and reviewed extensively for accuracy.

The Test Bank features include the following:

■ To aid instructors in building tests, each question has been categorized according to their general *degree of difficulty*. The three levels are: easy, moderate, or difficult. *Easy* questions require students to recognize concepts and definitions. These are questions that can be answered by direct reference to the textbook. *Moderate* questions require some analysis on the student's part. These questions may require a student to distinguish between two or more related concepts, to apply a concept to a particular situation, or to use an economic model to determine an answer. *Difficult* questions will usually require more detailed analysis by the students.

■ To further aid instructors in building tests, each question is referenced by the page number and specific topic heading in the textbook. Questions are presented in the order in which concepts are presented in the text.

■ Questions have been designed to correlate with the questions and problems within the text and *CourseTutor*. A beginning set of Objectives Questions are available within each chapter. These questions focus directly on the key concepts from the text that students should grasp after reading the chapter. These questions can be used easily for brief in-class quizzes.

■ The test bank includes questions with tables that students must analyze to solve for numerical answers. It contains questions based on the graphs that appear in the book. These questions ask students to use the graphical models developed in the textbook and to interpret the information presented in the graph. Selected questions are paired with scenarios to reinforce comprehension.

Computerized Test Bank: Diploma was the first software for PCs that integrated a test-generation program with grade book software and an online testing system. Diploma is now in its fifth generation. The printed Test Banks for *CoreMacroeconomics* are available in CD-ROM format, powered by Brownstone, for both Windows and Macintosh users.

With Diploma, you can easily create and print tests and write and edit questions. You can add an unlimited number of questions, scramble questions, and include figures. Tests can be printed in a wide range of formats. The software's unique synthesis of flexible word processing and database features creates a program that is extremely intuitive and capable.

Instructor's Resource CD-ROM: Using the Instructor's Resource CD-ROM, instructors can easily build classroom presentations or enhance online courses. This CD-ROM contains all text figures (in JPEG and GIF formats), PowerPoint Lecture slides, and detailed solutions to all End-of-the-Chapter Questions. You can choose from the various resources, edit, and save for use in your classroom.

PowerPoint Lecture Presentation: PowerPoint slides provide graphs from the textbook, data tables, and bulleted lists of key concepts suitable for lecture presentation. Key figures from the text are replicated and animated to demonstrate how they build. The Checkpoints from the text have been included to facilitate a quick review of key concepts. These slides may be customized by instructors to suit individual needs. These files may be accessed on the instructor's side of the web site or on the Instructor's Resource CD-ROM.

For Instructors and Students

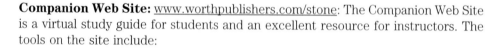

Companion Web Site: www.worthpublishers.com/stone: The Companion Web Site is a virtual study guide for students and an excellent resource for instructors. The tools on the site include:

Student Resources

- Self-Test Quizzes: This quizzing engine provides a set of quiz questions for each chapter with appropriate feedback and page references to the textbook. All student answers are saved in an online database that can be accessed by instructors.
- Key Term Flashcards: Students can test themselves on the key terms with these popup electronic flashcards.

Instructor Resources

- Quiz Gradebook: The site gives you the ability to track students' work by accessing an online gradebook. Instructors have the option to have student results emailed directly to them.
- PowerPoint Lecture Presentations: These PowerPoint slides are designed to assist instructors with lecture preparation and presentation by providing bulleted lecture outlines suitable for large lecture presentation. Instructors can customize these slides to suit their individual needs.
- Textbook Illustrations: A complete set of figures and tables from the textbook in JPEG and PowerPoint format is available.

▧ End-of-Chapter Problems: The text's End-of-Chapter Problems have been posted here in an electronic format for instructors to incorporate into assignments or in-class quizzes.

***CourseTutor* Online Study Center:** This dynamic site enables students to gauge their comprehension of concepts and provides a variety of resources to help boost their performance within the course. This Online Study Center provides an alternative to the pen and paper version of *CourseTutor*. Instead students can work through *CourseTutor* content online. In this online format, students can follow their own pace and complete any or all steps of *CourseTutor*. All of this is possible with or without instructor involvement.

The Online Study Center contains an electronic version of the *CourseTutor* authored by Gerald W. Stone. Content is organized and accessible through the major headings within the *CourseTutor*. The Quick Checks and Homework are available in an online quizzing engine for automatic grading. Answers to the Homework and End-of-Chapter Questions will be posted on the instructor side. Students will find the additional Interactive Resources where appropriate within the body of *CourseTutor*. The interactive resources may also be accessed under the resources tab within the Online Study Center.

CourseTutor Online Study Center includes the following Interactive Resources:

▧ *Solved Problems:* Problems designed for this online environment using a graphing and assessment engine. Students may be asked to draw, interpret, or interact with a graph to provide an answer. Students will receive detailed feedback and guidance on where to go for further review.
▧ *Core Graphs:* Animated versions of these key graphs.
▧ *Audio Summaries*

STUDENTS: What can they do with the Online Study Center?

▧ Test mastery of important concepts from the text.
▧ Improve understanding of difficult topics by working with interactive tutorials and flashcards, along with an electronic version of your *CourseTutor*.
▧ Take notes on any of the resources and add them to a collection of favorites.
▧ Browse by chapter or search by topic if they need quick information about a specific concept.

INSTRUCTORS: What can you do with the Online Study Center?

▧ Interact with your students as little or as much as you like! You can assign the exercises as out-of-class activities, or encourage your students to work independently.
▧ If you so desire, monitor your students' progress within the Online Study Center using a sophisticated online gradebook.
▧ Export grades to your current Course Management System.
▧ Create customized web pages for your students.

Additional Online Offerings

Aplia—Integrated Textbook Solution: Aplia, founded by Paul Romer (Stanford University), is the first web-based company to integrate pedagogical features from a textbook with interactive media. Specifically designed for use with the Stone text, textbook resources have been combined with Aplia's interactive media to save time for professors and encourage students to exert more effort in their learning.

The integrated online version of the Aplia media and the Stone text will include:

- extra problem sets suitable for homework and keyed to specific topics from each chapter
- regularly updated news analyses
- real-time online simulations of market interactions
- interactive tutorials to assist with math
- graphs and statistics
- instant online reports that allow instructors to target student trouble areas more efficiently

With Aplia, you retain complete control and flexibility for your course. You choose the topics you want students to cover, and you decide how to organize it. You decide whether online activities are practice (ungraded or graded). You can even edit the Aplia content—making cuts or additions as you see fit for your course.

For a preview of Aplia materials and to learn more, visit http://www.aplia.com.

The Stone WebCT & Blackboard EPacks enable you to create a thorough, interactive, and pedagogically sound online course or course web site. The EPacks provides you with cutting-edge online materials that facilitate critical thinking and learning, including Test Bank content, preprogrammed quizzes, links, activities, animated graphs, and an array of other materials. Best of all, this material is preprogrammed and fully functional in the WebCT & Blackboard environment. Prebuilt materials eliminate hours of course-preparation work and offer significant support as you develop your online course. The result: an interactive, comprehensive online course that allows for effortless implementation, management, and use. The files can be easily downloaded from our Course Management System site directly onto your department server.

Package Options

i-clicker is a new 2-way radio-frequency classroom response solution developed by educators for educators. University of Illinois physicists Tim Stelzer, Gary Gladding, Mats Selen, and Benny Brown created the i-clicker system after using competing classroom response solutions and discovering they were neither classroom appropriate nor student friendly. Each step of i-clicker's development has been informed by teaching and learning. i-clicker is superior to other systems from both a pedagogical and technical standpoint. To learn more about packaging i-clicker with this textbook, please contact your local sales rep or visit www.iclicker.com.

***Wall Street Journal* Edition:** For adopters of the Stone text, Worth Publishers and the *Wall Street Journal* are offering a 10-week subscription to students at a tremendous savings. Professors also receive their own free *Wall Street Journal* subscription plus additional instructor supplements created exclusively by the *Wall Street Journal*. Please contact your local sales rep for more information or go to the *Wall Street Journal* online at www.wsj.com.

***Financial Times* Edition:** For adopters of the Stone text, Worth Publishers and the *Financial Times* are offering a 15-week subscription to students at a tremendous savings. Professors also receive their own free *Financial Times* subscription for one year. Students and professors may access research and archived information at www.ft.com.

Acknowledgements

No project of this scope is accomplished alone. Many people have helped make this package a better resource for students, and I sincerely appreciate their efforts. These include reviewers of blocks of manuscript chapters, focus group participants, reviewers of single chapters and its accompanying *CourseTutor* chapter, accuracy reviewers, and the production and editorial staff of Worth Publishing.

First, I want to thank those reviewers who read through blocks of chapters in manuscript form and offered many important suggestions that have been incorporated into this project. They include:

Dwight Adamson, South Dakota State University

Norman Aitken, University of Massachusetts, Amherst

Fatma Wahdan Antar, Manchester Community College

Anoop Bhargava, Finger Lakes Community College

Craig Blek, Imperial Valley College

Mike W. Cohick, Collin County Community College

Kathleen Davis, College of Lake County

Dennis Debrecht, Carroll College

Christopher Erickson, New Mexico State University

Shaikh M. Ghanzanfar, University of Idaho

Lowell Glenn, Utah Valley State College

Jack Hou, California State University, Long Beach

Charles Kroncke, College of Mount St. Joseph

Laura Maghoney, Solano Community College

Pete Mavrokordatos, Tarrant County College

Philip Mayer, Three Rivers Community College

John McCollough, Penn State University, Lehigh

Pat Mizak, Canisius College

Jay Morris, Champlain College

Jennifer Offenberg, Loyola Marymount University

Joan Osborne, Palo Alto College

Diana Petersdorf, University of Wisconsin, Stout

Oscar Plaza, South Texas Community College

Mary Pranzo, California State University, Fresno

Mike Ryan, Gainesville State College

Supriya Sarnikar, Westfield State College

Lee Van Scyoc, University of Wisconsin, Oshkosh

Paul Seidenstat, Temple University

Ismail Shariff, University of Wisconsin, Green Bay

Garvin Smith, Daytona Beach Community College

Gokce Soydemir, University of Texas, Pan America

Martha Stuffler, Irvine Valley College

Ngoc-Bich Tran, San Jacinto College

Alan Trethewey, Cuyahoga Community College

Chad Turner, Nicholls College

Va Nee L. Van Vleck, California State University, Fresno

Dale Warnke, College of Lake County

Second, I would like to take this opportunity to thank those focus group participants who devoted a lot of time and effort to discussing the elements of this project. Their thoughts and suggestions (and criticisms) contributed immensely to the development of this project. They include:

Emil Berendt, Friends University

Harmanna Bloemen, Houston Community College, Northeast

Mike Cohick, Collin County Community College

Rohini Divecha, San Jacinto College, South

Bob Francis, Shoreline Community College

John Kane, State University of New York, Oswego

Sukanya Kemp, University of Akron

Charlene Kinsey, Houston Community College, Northwest

Delores Linton, Tarrant Community College, Northwest

Fred May, Trident Tech

Saul Mekies, Kirkwood Community College

Diego Mendez-Carbajo, Illinois Wesleyan

Cyril Morong, San Antonio College

Oscar Plaza, South Texas Community College

Michael Polcen, Northern Virginia Community College

Jaishankar Raman, Valparaiso University

Belinda Roman, Palo Alto College

Ted Scheinman, Mt. Hood Community College

Marianna Sidoryanskaya, Austin Community College, Cypress

Lea Templer, College of the Canyons

Ngoc-Bich Tran, San Jacinto College, South

Don Weimer, Milwaukee Area Technical College, Downtown

Third, my thanks go out to those who took the time to review single chapters of the text and the *CourseTutor* together, and to those who class-tested single chapters. Thanks for the reviews and the suggestions. These reviewers included:

Shawn Abbott, College of the Siskiyous

Roger Adkins, Marshall University

Richard Agesa, Marshall University

Ali Akarca, University of Illinois, Chicago

Frank Albritton, Seminole Community College

Anca Alecsandru, Louisiana State University

Innocentus Alhamis, Southern New Hampshire University

Basil Al-Hashimi, Mesa Community College

Samuel Andoh, Southern Connecticut State University

William Ashley, Florida Community College at Jacksonville

Rose-Marie Avin, University of Wisconsin, Eau Claire

Sukhwinder Bagi, Bloomsburg University

Dean Baim, Pepperdine University

Joanne Bangs, College of St. Catherine

Abby Barker, University of Missouri, St. Louis

Perry Barrett, Chattahoochee Technical College

David Bartram, East Georgia College

Robert Beekman, University of Tampa

Emil Berendt, Siena Heights University

Gerald Bialka, University of North Florida

Paul Biederman, New York University

Richard Bieker, Delaware State University

Tom Birch, University of New Hampshire, Manchester

John Bockino, Suffolk Community College

Orn Bodvarsson, St. Cloud State University

Antonio Bos, Tusculum College

Laurette Brady, Norwich University

Bill Burrows, Lane Community College

Rob Burrus, University of North Carolina, Wilmington

Tim Burson, Queens University of Charlotte

Dean Calamaras, Hudson Valley Community College

Charles Callahan, State University of New York, Brockport

Colleen Callahan, American University

Dave Cauble, Western Nebraska Community College

Henrique Cezar, Johnson State College

Matthew Chambers, Towson University

Lisa Citron, Cascadia Community College

Ray Cohn, Illinois State University

Kevin Coyne, Southern New Hampshire University

Tom Creahan, Morehead State University

Richard Croxdale, Austin Community College

Rosa Lea Danielson, College of DuPage

Amlan Datta, Cisco Junior College

Helen Davis, Jefferson Community & Technical College

Susan Davis, Buffalo State College

Dennis Debrecht, Carroll College

Robert Derrell, Manhattanville College

Julia Derrick, Brevard Community College

Jeffrey Dorfman, University of Georgia

Justin Dubas, St. Norbert College

Harold Elder, University of Alabama

G. Rod Erfani, Transylvania University

William Feipel, Illinois Central College

Rick Fenner, Utica College

James Ford, San Joaquin Delta College

Marc Fox, Brooklyn College

Lawrence Fu, Illinois College

Mark Funk, University of Arkansas, Little Rock

Mary Gade, Oklahoma State University

Khusrav Gaibulloev, University of Texas, Dallas

Gary Galles, Pepperdine University

Lara Gardner, Florida Atlantic University

Kelly George, Florida Community College at Jacksonville

Lisa George, Hunter College

JP Gilbert, Mira Costa College

Chris Gingrich, Eastern Mennonite University

James Giordano, Villanova University

Susan Glanz, St. John's University

Devra Golbe, Hunter College

Michael Goode, Central Piedmont Community College

Gene Gotwalt, Sweet Briar College

Glenn Graham, State University of New York, Oswego

David Gribbin, East Georgia College

Phil Grossman, St. Cloud State University

Marie Guest, North Florida Community College

J. Guo, Pace University

N.E. Hampton, St. Cloud State University

Deborah Hanson, University of Great Falls

Virden Harrison, Modesto Junior College

Fuad Hasanov, Oakland University

Scott Hegerty, University of Wisconsin, Milwaukee

Debra Hepler, Seton Hill College

Jim Henderson, Baylor University

Jeffrey Higgins, Sierra College

Jannett Highfill, Bradley University

Harold Hotelling, Lawrence Technological University

Wanda Hudson, Alabama Southern Community College

Terence Hunady, Bowling Green University

Mitchell Inman II, Savannah Technical College

Anisul Islam, University of Houston, Downtown

Eric Jamelske, University of Wisconsin, Eau Claire

Russell Janis, University of Massachusetts, Amherst

Andres Jauregui, Columbus State University

Jonathan Jelen, The City College of New York

George Jouganatos, California State University, Sacramento

David Kalist, Shippensburg University

Jonathan Kaplan, California State University, Sacramento

Nicholas Karatjas, Indiana University of Pennsylvania

Janis Kea, West Valley College

Deborah Kelly, Palomar College

Kathy Kemper, University of Texas, Arlington

Brian Kench, University of Tampa

Mariam Khawar, Elmira College

Young Jun Kim, Henderson State University

TC Kinnaman, Bucknell University

Paul Koch, Olivet Nazarene College

Andy Kohen, James Madison University

Lea Kosnik, University of Missouri, St. Louis

Charles Kroncke, College of Mount Saint Joseph

Craig Laker, Tri-State University

Carsten Lange, California Polytechnic State University, Pomona

Gary Langer, Roosevelt University

Leonard Lardaro, University of Rhode Island

Daniel Lawson, Drew University

Bill Lee, St. Mary's College

Mary Jane Lenon, Providence College

Mary Lesser, Iona College

Bozena Leven, The College of New Jersey

Ralph Lim, Sacred Heart University

Anthony Liuzzo, Wilkes University

Jennifer Logan, Southern Arkansas University

Dening Lohez, Pace University

Ellen Magenheim, Swarthmore College

Y. Lal Mahajan, Monmouth University

Mary Ellen Mallia, Siena College

Don Mathews, Coastal Georgia Community College

Phil Mayer, Three Rivers Community College

Norman Maynard, University of Oklahoma

Kimberly Mencken, Baylor University

John Messier, University of Maine, Farmington

Randy Methenitis, Richland College

Charles Meyer, Cerritos College

David Mitchell, Missouri State University

Ilir Miteza, University of Michigan, Dearborn

Jay Morris, Champlain College

Charles Myrick, Dyersburg State Community College

Natalie Nazarenko, State University of New York, Fredonia

Tim Nischan, Kentucky Christian University

Tom Odegaard, Baylor University

Jennifer Offenberg, Loyola Marymount University

Jack Peeples, Washtenaw Community College

Don Peppard, Connecticut College

Elizabeth Perry, Randolph-Macon Women's College

Dean Peterson, Seattle University

John Pharr, Cedar Valley College

Chris Phillips, Somerset Community College

Mary Pranzo, California State University, Fresno

Joseph Radding, Folsom Lake College

Jaishankar Raman, Valparaiso University

Donald Richards, Indiana State University

Bill Ridley, University of Oklahoma

William Rieber, Butler University

Dave Ring, State University of New York, Oneonta

Paul Robillard, Bristol Community College

Denise Robson, University of Wisconsin, Oshkosh

Rose Rubin, University of Memphis

Chris Ruebeck, Lafayette University

Randy Russell, Yavapai College

Marty Sabo, Community College of Denver

Hedayeh Samavati, Indiana University-Purdue University, Fort Wayne

Julia Sampson, Malone College

Paul Schoofs, Ripon College

Peter Schwarz, University of North Carolina, Charlotte

Paul Seidenstat, Temple University

T.M. Sell, Highline Community College

Chad Settle, University of Tulsa

Bill Seyfried, Rollins College

Maurice Shalishali, Columbus State

R. Calvin Shipley, Henderson State University

William Simeone, Providence College

Geok Simpson, University of Texas, Pan American

Noel Smith, Palm Beach Community College

Phil Smith, Georgia Perimeter College, Lawrenceville

Dennis Spector, Naugatuck Valley Community College

Todd Steen, Hope College

Richard Stratton, University of Akron

Stuart Strother, Azusa Pacific University

Martha Stuffler, Irvine Valley College

Boo Chun Su, Santa Monica Community College

Della Lee Sue, Marist College

Abdulhamid Sukar, Cameron University

Thomas Swanke, Chadron State College

Thomas Sweeney, Des Moines Area Community College

Michael Tansey, Rockhurst University

Henry Terrell, University of Maryland

Thomas Tiemann, Elon College

Dosse Toulaboe, Fort Hays State University

Christine Trees, State University of New York, Cobbleskill

Andrew Tucker, Tallahassee Community College

David Tufte, Southern Utah University

Jennifer VanGilder, Ursinus College

Yoav Wachsman, Coastal Carolina University

Craig Walker, Oklahoma Baptist University

Elizabeth Wark, Springfield College

Jonathan Warner, Dordt College

Roger White, Franklin & Marshall College

Jim Wollscheid, Texas A&M University, Kingsville

John Yarber, NE Mississippi Community College

Haichun Ye, University of Oklahoma

Anne York, Meredith College

Nazma Zaman, Providence College

Madeline Zavodny, Agnes Scott College

Fourth, I owe a special debt and want to give a special thanks to Eric Chiang of Florida Atlantic University, Garvin Smith of Daytona Beach Community College, and Ngoc-Bich Tran from San Jacinto College for their tireless effort at accuracy checking. Together, they caught errors that none of us want to see. Thanks again!

Fifth, a huge debt of gratitude is owed to Marie McHale and the supplements authors. Marie coordinated the development of the supplements and our online presence. She did a remarkable job and was able to get some great people to author the supplements. They include Mary H. Lesser from Iona College who authored the Teaching Manual. Among other things, she did a wonderful job of adding real-world examples designed for use as student handouts. My thanks to Richard Croxdale from Austin Community College who coordinated the development of the Test Bank along with creating questions. Emil Berendt of Siena Heights University, Dennis Debrecht of Carroll College, and Dr. Elizabeth J. Wark from Springfield College all contributed questions. Thanks to all of you for creating a Test Bank with nearly 2,500 questions.

Sixth, the production team at Worth is outstanding. My thanks to the entire team including Kevin Kall, Senior Designer, for a great set of interior and cover designs; Dana Kasowitz the Project Editor who kept the project on a strict time-line; Tracey Kuehn, the Associate Managing Editor; Babs Reingold, the Art Director; and Barbara Anne Seixas, the Project Manager—all who made sure each part of the production process went smoothly. A special thanks to both Jennifer Carey who worked tirelessly to see that we went smoothly from manuscript to book (one tough job) and Carol Gilbert at Matrix Publishing Services who flooded me with beautiful book pages. Thanks for a job well done.

I want to thank Charlie Van Wagner for signing this project and Sarah Dorger for smoothly picking it up and moving it along when he left. Thanks to Paul Shensa for his support and ideas on editorial changes and marketing; he is a valuable resource for any author. I really appreciate Craig Bleyer's many suggestions for the project, the way he kept the project moving along, and his faith in my vision for *CoreEconomics*. There is no way that I can thank Bruce Kaplan enough for what he has meant to this project and me. He has kept me focused and has suggested so many good ideas that I could fill several pages with his contributions. Thanks Bruce, you are the best!

You couldn't ask for a better marketing manager than Scott Guile. His enthusiasm is infectious and I appreciate the huge effort he has put into this project. Todd Elder's design for the marketing brochure was stunning. Steve Rigolosi created an extensive pre-launch marketing campaign that was second to none. Also I want to thank Tom Kling for helping sales reps see many of the benefits of this project. He is an incredible personality and I appreciate his efforts. Also, I want to thank Christine Ondreicka for handling the Fall, 2006 reviewing program.

I am also indebted to Andrew Carlson for his editing and suggested rewrites of the first draft of this project and to Michael McGrath for drafts of many of the historical and Nobel biographies.

Finally, I am grateful to my wife, Sheila, for putting up with the forgone vacations given the demands a project like this requires. I hope it lives up to her expectations.

Gerald W. Stone

Exploring Economics

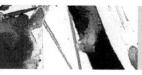

Production, Economic Growth, and Trade   2

Supply and Demand   3

SUPPLY   60

MARKET EQUILIBRIUM   64

PUTTING SUPPLY AND DEMAND TO WORK   73

Market Efficiency, Market Failure, and Government Intervention

4

MARKETS AND EFFICIENCY   82

Introduction to Macroeconomics   5

Measuring Inflation and Unemployment   6

INFLATION   140

UNEMPLOYMENT   149

UNEMPLOYMENT AND THE ECONOMY   154

Economic Growth   7

THE CLASSICAL MODEL   167

SOURCES OF LONG-RUN ECONOMIC GROWTH   172

INFRASTRUCTURE AND ECONOMIC GROWTH   177

Keynesian Macroeconomics

8

Aggregate Demand and Supply

Fiscal Policy

FISCAL POLICY AND AGGREGATE SUPPLY   243

IMPLEMENTING FISCAL POLICY   248

The Monetary System

WHAT IS MONEY?   258

MONEY: DEMAND AND SUPPLY   262

THE FEDERAL RESERVE SYSTEM   268

Monetary Policy   12

MONETARY THEORIES   280

MONETARY POLICY LAGS   291

IMPLEMENTING MONETARY POLICY   293

Federal Deficits and Public Debt

Macroeconomic Policy Challenges

International Trade 15

Open Economy Macroeconomics 16

1 Exploring Economics

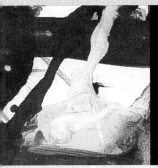

deas are important. They change civilizations. Most of the world in the last two decades has renewed its interest in economic ideas. The phrase "It's the economy, stupid" became the political mantra of the Clinton administration. Britain in the 1980s turned to markets to bring the economy out of the doldrums. Both the former Soviet Union and China have looked to economic incentives and markets to help spur their economies. China has had remarkable success. While the economy is improving in Russia, it is still a work in progress.

Why are governments so preoccupied with economic growth? Does it really matter that much? Answering the last question answers the first. Our level of economic growth today largely determines the standards of living for our children, and their children, and then their children.

How important is economic growth, really? To put this in perspective, let's conduct the following experiment. Today, our real gross domestic product (GDP; it represents all the goods and services produced annually, or you can think of it as our income) is roughly $12 trillion (that's a 12 with 12 zeros—a very big number). The United States has the largest economy in the world, with the European Union a close second. To see the importance of economic growth rates on our standard of living, let's assume that from 1930 to today our growth rate was just *1 percentage point* less every year. So, for example, if our economy grew at a 7% rate between 1953 and 1954, we will assume that it really only grew at a 6% rate.

What would be the impact of lowering our growth rate just 1 percentage point every year over the last 75 years? Simply subtracting 1 percentage point *would cut in half the size of our economy today.* Since we have removed the effects of inflation from our estimates, this small adjustment in economic growth rates each year would give us real (adjusted for inflation) aggregate income of less than $6 trillion today—not the $12 trillion we actually have.

While real GDP for the total economy is not a perfect measure of our standard of living, real GDP per capita, a better measure, would also roughly be cut in half. So, toss out half your stuff and move to an apartment half the size you are in today. Note that we have *ignored* a bunch of complementary impacts like reduced education, as well as reduced research and development, that are closely associated with lower incomes. These impacts probably would have reduced these numbers and our standard of living even further. If we were to conduct this little experiment going back to the beginning of the century rather than from 1930, we would likely have the standard of living of Mexico today.

This calculation shows that economic growth is crucial if we are to make this world a better place to live. This example leads to an obvious question: What causes economic growth? Why have some countries leaped ahead, while others have made little progress at all?

John Kay[1] examined 19 highly productive countries with the highest living standards in the world. He found that they were distinguished from the other countries in the world by numerous complex relationships. Highly productive countries have the following characteristics:

- Most are democracies.
- Most have high environmental standards.
- Most have cool climates.
- Most enjoy freedom of expression.
- Women's rights and freedoms are better protected.
- Most enjoy better health.
- Population is taller.
- Government is less corrupt.
- Income inequality is lower.
- Inflation is lower.
- Population is more literate.
- Most have fewer restrictions on trade (more open).
- Population growth is lower.
- Property rights are more secure.

John Kay noted that "correlation does not imply causation." Some of these characteristics follow from a nation being more productive and rich; some, like literacy and health, help promote productivity. These are clearly complex relationships. As Jared Diamond[2] has argued, development in Europe and the United States benefited from immense luck with the weather and the types of flora and fauna native to our regions. Without all three, he argued we would probably not have seen the high level of economic growth that has transpired.

That is why the structure of the society and the economy are so important, and why politicians and governments focus so much of their attention on economic issues. Economies do not develop overnight; it can take 50 years or more to produce modern living standards. For many countries of the world, even beginning today with the right economic programs and policies might mean it would not be until the end of this century before their living standards reach our standards of today. And by that time, much of the world will have moved on.

Today, some people are concerned about outsourcing, globalization, and international trade. Look at this from an undeveloped country's point of view. These things can help them rise from abject poverty to attain modern living standards.

---

[1]John Kay, *The Truth About Markets: Their Genius, Their Limits, Their Follies* (London: Allen Lane), 2003, pp. 27–31. The highly productive countries are United States, Singapore, Switzerland, Norway, Canada, Denmark, Belgium, Japan, Austria, France, Hong Kong, Netherlands, Germany, United Kingdom, Finland, Italy, Australia, Sweden, and Ireland.
[2]Jared Diamond, *Guns, Germs, and Steel: The Fates of Human Societies* (New York: WW Norton), 1999.

After all, the United States was once underdeveloped, and trade with richer nations like France and Britain helped us develop.

Modern technologies and improvements in computing, transportation, and communications all are accelerating the development process. For example, cellular phone infrastructure is so much cheaper to install than the landline technology of the past. This has meant that developing nations can now get a state-of-the-art communications network at a fraction of the price that the United States paid to lay and string cables over the last century. Future communications will undoubtedly be wireless, so many developing nations will be up to speed in a decade. We will see early in this book what countries can do to accelerate their economic growth.

This is the broad picture. Living standards are important, and economic growth improves living standards. Certain programs and policies can foster economic growth. So far, so good. But you are probably asking: What is in it for me? Why should I study economics if I am never going to be an economist? Probably the best reason is that you will spend roughly the next 40 years working in an economic environment. You will have a job; you will pay taxes; you will see the overall economy go from recession to a growth spurt and then maybe stagnate; you will have money to invest; and you will have to vote on economic issues affecting your locality, your region, and your country. It will benefit you to know how the economy works, what to expect in the future, and how to correct the economy's flaws.

But more than that—much more, in fact—economic analysis gives you a structure from which you can make decisions in a more rational manner. This course may well change the way you look at the world. It can open your eyes to how you make everyday decisions from what to buy to whom to marry. It may even make you reconsider your major.

Notice that we have just talked about economic analysis as a way of analyzing decisions that are not "economic" in the general sense of the term. That is the benefit of learning economic analysis. It can be applied all over the map. Sure, learning economic thinking may change your views on spending and saving, on how you feel about government deficits and public debt, and on your opinion of globalization and international trade. You may also reflect differently on environmental policies and what unions do. But you also may develop a different perspective on how much time to study each of your courses this term, or how much to eat at an all-you-can-eat buffet. Such is the broad scope of economic analysis.

In this introductory chapter, we will look at what economics is about. We take a brief look at a key method of economic analysis: model building. Economists use stylized facts and the technique of holding some variables constant to develop testable theories about how consumers, businesses, and government act. Second, we turn to a short discussion of some key principles of economics to give you a sense of the guiding concepts you will meet throughout this book.

The purpose of this introductory chapter is just that: introductory. It seeks to give you a sense of what economics is, what concepts it uses, and what it finds to be important. Do not go into this chapter thinking you have to memorize these concepts. You will be given many opportunities to understand and use these concepts throughout this course. Rather, use this chapter to get a sense of the broad scope of economics. Then return to this chapter at the end of the course and see if everything has now become crystal clear.

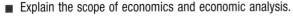

After studying this chapter
you should be able to

- Explain the scope of economics and economic analysis.
- Differentiate between microeconomics and macroeconomics.

- Describe how economists use models.
- Describe the *ceteris paribus* assumption.
- Discuss the difference between efficiency and equity.
- Describe the key ideas in economics.

What Is Economics About?

Economics is a very broad subject, and often it seems that economics has something important to say about almost everything.

For example, economics has some important things to say about crime and punishment. On first glance, you might think we are talking about the cost of a prison system when we apply economic analysis here. But if we categorize economics as a way of thinking about how people make rational decisions, we can broaden the discussion. Economics considers criminals and potential criminals as rational people who follow their incentives. Criminals are concerned with getting caught and being punished: That is their cost. Longer prison sentences potentially raise the cost of committing a crime. Possibly more important than longer prison sentences is the probability of being convicted for an offense: A long sentence is not an effective incentive if it is rarely used. This is why wounding or killing police officers is prosecuted aggressively and publicized: Potential criminals know they will pay a high cost if a police officer is harmed. Thus, economics looks at all of those factors that raise the cost of crime to criminals. Economics is a way of thinking about an issue, not just a discipline that has money as its chief focus.

Economists tend to put a rational spin (or analysis if you prefer) on nearly everything. Now all of this "analysis/speculation" may bring only limited insight in some cases, but it gives you some idea of how economists think. We look for rational responses to incentives. We begin most questions by considering how rational people would respond to the incentives that specific situations provide. Sometimes (maybe even often) this analysis leads us down an unexpected path. Be prepared to go down some unexpected avenues during your semester in this course.

Microeconomics Versus Macroeconomics

Microeconomics
Microeconomics focuses on decision making by individuals, businesses, industries, and government.

Economics is split into two broad categories: microeconomics and macroeconomics. **Microeconomics** deals with decision making by individuals, business firms, industries, and governments. It is concerned with issues such as which orange juice should you buy, which job to take, and where to go on vacation; which products a business should produce and what price it should charge; and whether a market should be left on its own or be regulated.

We will see that markets—from flea markets to real estate markets to international currency markets—are usually efficient and promote competition. This is good for society. The opposite of competitive markets—monopoly, where one firm controls the market—leads to high prices, and it is bad for society. There is also a vast middle between the extremes of competition and monopoly. Economists analyze the various forms that markets take when they look at market structure.

Microeconomics extends to such things as labor markets and environmental policy. Labor market analysis looks at both the supply (how much we as individuals are willing to work and at what wage) and demand (how much business is willing to hire and at what wage) of labor to determine market salaries. Designing policies to mitigate environmental damage uses the tools of microeconomics.

Adam Smith (1723–1790)

When Adam Smith was a 4-year-old boy, he was kidnapped by gypsies and held for ransom. Had the gypsies not taken fright and returned the boy unharmed, the history of economics might well have turned out differently.

Born in Kirkaldy, Scotland, in 1723, Smith graduated from the University of Glasgow at age 17. He then spent 6 years at Oxford—time he considered to be largely wasted, given the deplorable state of English education at the time. Returning to Scotland in 1751, Smith was named Professor of Moral Philosophy at the University of Glasgow.

After 12 years at Glasgow, Smith began tutoring the son of a wealthy Scottish nobleman. This job provided him with a lifelong income, as well as the opportunity to spend several years touring the European continent with his young charge. In Paris, Smith met some of the leading French economists of the day, which helped stoke his own interest in "political economy." The question that fundamentally guided Smith, as with all the other economists of his time, was, "How best to increase the wealth of the nation?"

Returning to Kirkaldy in 1766, Smith spent the next decade writing *The Wealth of Nations.* This seminal work of free market economic theory actually contained few new ideas. Smith's genius rather was in taking the disparate forms of economic analysis his contemporaries were then developing and putting them together in systematic fashion, thereby making sense of the national economy as a whole. Smith further demonstrated numerous ways in which individuals left free to pursue their own economic interests end up acting in ways that enhance the welfare of all. This is Smith's famous "invisible hand." In Smith's words: "By directing that industry in such a manner as its produce may be of the greatest value, he intends only his own gain, and he is in this, as in many other cases, led by an invisible hand to promote an end which was no part of his intention."

Macroeconomics, on the other hand, focuses on the broader issues we face as a nation. Most of us could care less whether you buy Nike or Merrell shoes. But whether prices of *all* goods and services rise is another matter. Inflation—a general increase in prices economy-wide—affects all of us. And as we have already seen, economic growth is a macroeconomic issue that affects everyone.

Macroeconomics uses microeconomic tools to answer some questions, but its main focus is on the broad aggregate variables of the economy. Macroeconomics

Macroeconomics
Macroeconomics is concerned about the broader issues in the economy such as inflation, unemployment, and national output of goods and services.

has its own terms and topics: business cycle fluctuations such as recessions and depressions, unemployment rates, job creation rates, policies that increase economic growth rates, the impact of government spending and taxation, the effect of monetary policy on the economy, and inflation. Further, macroeconomics looks closely at theories of inflation, international trade, and international finance. All of these topics have broad impacts on our economy and our standard of living.

Although we break economics into microeconomics and macroeconomics, there is considerable overlap in the analysis. We use simple supply and demand analysis to understand both individual markets and the general economy as a whole. You will find yourself using concepts from microeconomics to understand fluctuations in the macroeconomy.

Economic Theories and Reality

If you are like me, the first thing you do when you buy a book is flip through the pages to see what's inside. If the number of charts and graphs in this book, along with the limited number of equations, started to freak you out, relax. All of the charts and graphs become relatively easy to understand since they all basically read the same way. The few equations in this book stem from fifth- or sixth-grade algebra. Once you get through one equation, the rest are similar.

Economics is a social science that uses many facts and figures to develop and express ideas. After all, economists try to explain the behavior of the economy and its participants. This inevitably involves facts and numbers. For macroeconomics, this means getting used to talking and thinking in huge numbers: billions (9 zeros) and trillions (12 zeros).

Graphs, charts, and equations are often the simplest and most efficient ways to express data and ideas. Simple equations are used to express relationships between two variables. Complex and wordy discussions can often be reduced to a simple graph or figure. These are efficient techniques for expressing economic ideas.

Model Building

As you study economics this semester or quarter, you will encounter stylized approaches to a number of issues. By *stylized,* we mean that economists boil down facts to their basic relevant elements and use assumptions to develop a stylized (simple) model to analyze the issue. While there are always situations that lie outside these models, they are the exception. Economists generalize about economic behavior and reach generally applicable results.

We begin with relatively simple models, then gradually build in more difficult issues. For example, in the next chapter we introduce one of the simplest models in economics, the production possibilities frontier that illustrates the limits of economic activity. This simple model has profound implications for the issue of economic growth. We can add in more dimensions and make the model more complex, but often this complexity does not provide any greater insight than the simple model.

Ceteris Paribus: All Else Held Constant

Ceteris paribus
Assumption used in economics (and other disciplines as well), where other relevant factors or variables are held constant.

To aid in our model building, economists use the **ceteris paribus** assumption: "Holding all other things equal" means we will hold some important variables constant. For example, to determine how many music CDs you might be willing to purchase in any given month, we would hold your monthly income constant. We then would change the prices of music CDs to see the impact on the number purchased (again holding your monthly income constant). Music labels use this information to set what they hope is an optimum price.

Though model building can lead to surprising insights into how economic actors and economies behave, it is not the end of the story. Economic insights lead to economic theories, but these theories must then be tested. We will see many instances where economic predictions turned out to be false. One of the major errors was the classical notion that economy-wide contractions would be of short duration. The Great Depression turned this notion on its head. New models were then developed to explain what had happened. So it may be best to think of model building as a *process* of understanding economic actors and the general economy: Models are created and then tested; if they fail to explain, new models are constructed. Some models have met the test of time. Others have had to be corrected or discarded. Progress, however, has been made.

Efficiency Versus Equity

Efficiency deals with how well resources are used and allocated. No one likes waste. Much of economic analysis is directed toward ensuring that the most efficient outcomes result from public policy. *Production efficiency* occurs when goods are produced at the lowest possible cost, and *allocative efficiency* occurs when individuals who desire a product the most (as measured by their willingness to pay) get those goods and services. It would not do for society to allocate to me a large amount of cranberry sauce—I would not eat the stuff. Efficient policies are generally good policies.

Efficiency
How well resources are used and allocated. Do people get the goods and services they want at the lowest possible resource cost? This is the chief focus of efficiency.

The other side of the coin is **equity** or fairness. Is it fair that the CEOs of large companies make hundreds of times more money than rank-and-file workers? Many think not. Is it fair that some have so much and others have so little? Again, many think not. There are many divergent views about fairness until we get to extreme cases. When just a few people earn nearly all of the income and control nearly all of a society's wealth, most people agree that this is unfair.

Equity
The fairness of various issues and policies.

Throughout this course you will see instances where efficiency and equity collide. You may agree that a specific policy is efficient, but think it is unfair to some group of people. This will be especially evident when you consider tax policy and its impact on income distribution. Fairness or equity is a subjective concept, and each of us has different ideas about what is just and fair. Economists generally stay out of discussions about fairness, leaving that issue to philosophers and politicians. When it comes to public policy issues, economics will help you see the tradeoffs between equity and efficiency, but you will ultimately have to make up your own mind about the wisdom of the policy given these tradeoffs.

In summary, the scope of economics is unusually broad, from decision making by individuals to businesses and large markets. In microeconomics, it looks at individual economic actors; in macroeconomics, it focuses on the economy at large. Economists use stylized models to understand economic activity and predict likely outcomes of various policies, but models are tested and refined or discarded as necessary. And economists tend to focus on matters of efficiency and avoid making sweeping judgments about equity, leaving each one of us to decide what is fair. Even so, the bottom line is that economics has much to say about many things.

Checkpoint

What Is Economics About?

REVIEW

- Economics is separated into two broad categories: microeconomics and macroeconomics.
- *Microeconomics* deals with individuals, firms, and industries and how they make decisions.
- *Macroeconomics* focuses on broader economic issues such as inflation, employment and unemployment, and economic growth.

■ Economics uses a stylized approach, creating simple models holding all other relevant factors constant (*ceteris paribus*).

■ Economists and policymakers often confront the tradeoff between efficiency and equity. Economists have much to say about efficiency.

QUESTIONS

In each of the following situations, determine whether it is a microeconomic or macroeconomic issue.

1. Hewlett-Packard announces that it is lowering the price of printers by 15%.

2. The president proposes a tax cut.

3. You decide to look for a new job.

4. The economy is in a recession, and the job market is bad.

5. Enron falsifies its accounting books and goes bankrupt.

6. The Federal Reserve announces that it is raising interest rates because it fears inflation.

7. You get a nice raise.

8. Average wages grew by 2% last year.

Answers to the Checkpoint questions can be found at the end of this chapter.

Key Ideas of Economics

Economics has a set of key principles that show up continually in economic analysis. Some are more restricted to specific issues, but most apply universally. As mentioned earlier, these principles should give you a sense of what you will learn in this course. Do not try to memorize these principles at this juncture. Rather, read through them now, and return to them later in the course to assess your progress. By the end of this course, these key principles should be crystal clear.

Choice and Scarcity Force Tradeoffs

Wouldn't it be grand if we all had the resources of Bill Gates or if nanotechnology developed to the point where any product could be made with sand and thus was virtually costless? But we don't, and it hasn't, so back to reality.

We all have limited resources. Some of us are more limited than others, but each of us has time limitations: There are only 24 hours in a day, and some of that must be spent in sleep. Our wants are always greater than our resources. Therefore, we face **scarcity**.

The fact that we have limited resources (scarcity) means that we must make tradeoffs in nearly everything we do. In fact, *economics is often defined as the study of the allocation of scarce resources to competing wants*. We have to decide between alternatives.

Such decisions as which car to buy, which school to attend (this may be constrained by factors other than money), and whether to study or party all involve tradeoffs. We cannot do everything we would like if for no other reason than our time on earth is limited.

Scarcity
Our unlimited wants clash with limited resources, leading to scarcity. Everyone faces scarcity (rich and poor) because, at a minimum, our time is limited on earth. Economics focuses on the allocation of scarce resources to satisfy unlimited wants.

Nobel Prize Paul A. Samuelson

n 1970, Paul Samuelson became the first American to win the Nobel Prize in Economics. One might say that Paul Samuelson literally wrote the book on economics. When he was a young professor at the Massachusetts Institute of Technology, the university asked him to write a standard text for the required junior year course in economics, no satisfactory alternative being available at the time. More than 4 million copies of his textbook, *Economics,* have been sold since it was first published in 1948. The book has been translated into 41 different languages.

Samuelson once described himself as one of the last "generalists" in economics. His interests are wide ranging, and his contributions include everything from the highly technical and mathematical to a popular column for *Newsweek* magazine, which ran from 1966 to 1981. As a scholar, he made original contributions in consumer theory, welfare economics, international trade, finance theory, capital theory, dynamics and general equilibrium, and macroeconomics.

Born in Gary, Indiana, in 1915, Samuelson attended the University of Chicago as an undergraduate. At graduate school at Harvard, where his thesis advisor was Joseph Schumpeter, he was considered something of a prodigy. When he was 21 and still working on his Ph.D., he published his first important contribution to economic theory, "A Note on the Measurement of Utility." In another article in 1938, he introduced the concept of "revealed preference," a breakthrough in the understanding of consumer choice involving the integration of empirical studies of observable behavior with theoretical constructs.

He began teaching at MIT in 1940 and was made a full professor after 6 years. In 1947, he published his magnum opus, the *Foundations of Economic Analysis,* a major contribution to the area of mathematical economics.

Samuelson introduced the concept of neoclassical synthesis, a synthesis of neoclassical microeconomics with Keynesian macroeconomics. Samuelson believed that government intervention through fiscal and monetary policy was sometimes necessary to achieve full employment. Once it reached that level, however, the market functioned well.

Samuelson was an advisor to President John F. Kennedy. In 1960, Samuelson warned of the danger of future inflation. He urged increased spending on defense, foreign aid, educational programs, welfare, unemployment programs, public works, and highway construction. A prolific writer, he averaged one technical paper each month during his active career.

Opportunity Costs Dominate Our Lives

Opportunity costs
The next best alternative; what you give up to do something or purchase something. For example, to watch a movie at a theater, there is not just the monetary cost of the tickets and refreshments, but the time involved in watching the movie. You could have been doing something else (knitting, golfing, hiking, or studying economics).

Economics is often categorized as the discipline that always weighs benefits against costs. This is straightforward enough. What makes this harder is that economists use a special concept: **opportunity costs**. If we undertake to do one activity, some other highly valued activity must be given up. For example, going to a movie requires buying a ticket and giving up our next highest valued activity that takes roughly two hours to perform. Economists refer to the *full costs* of attending the movie (ticket plus time) as *opportunity costs.*

We have limited resources. College students have limited budgets. Say we can purchase that new music CD we want or have ice cream for a week, but not both. Ice cream for a week is the opportunity cost of purchasing that music CD.

Every activity we do involves opportunity costs. Sleeping, eating, studying, partying, running, hiking, and so on, all require that we spend resources that could be used in another activity. This other activity represents the opportunity costs of the current activity chosen. Opportunity costs apply to us as individuals and to societies as a whole. The next chapter focuses on this issue in detail.

Rational Behavior Requires Thinking at the Margin

Have you ever noticed that when you eat at an all-you-can-eat buffet, you always go away fuller than when you order and eat at a normal restaurant? Is this phenomenon unique to you, or is there something more fundamental? Remember, economists look at facts to find incentives to economic behavior.

In this case, people are just rationally responding to the price of *additional* food. They are thinking at the margin. In a restaurant, dessert costs extra, and you make a decision as to whether the dessert is worth the extra cost. At the buffet, dessert is free. So now you don't have to ask yourself if dessert is worth the extra money since it costs nothing. Where you might be nearly full and decline dessert in a restaurant, you will often have dessert in the buffet even if you are stuffed afterwards.

Throughout this book, we will see examples of thinking at the margin. Businesses use marginal analysis to determine how much of their products they are willing to supply to the market. People use marginal analysis to determine how many hours to work. And governments use marginal analysis to determine how much pollution should be permitted.

People Follow Incentives

Tax policy rests on the idea that people follow their incentives. Do we want to encourage people to save for their retirement? Then let them deduct a certain amount that they can put in an individual retirement account (IRA), and let this money compound tax free. Do we want businesses to spend more to stimulate the economy? Then give them tax credits for new investment. Do we want people to go to college? Then give them tax advantages for setting up education savings accounts when children are young, and provide tuition tax credits.

Tax policy is an obvious example in which people follow incentives. But this principle can be seen in action wherever you look. Want to encourage people to use commuter trains during non-rush-hour times? Provide an off-peak discount. Want to spread out the dining time at restaurants? Give Early-Bird Special discounts for those willing to consider a 5:00 P.M. dinner time slot rather than a more popular 8:00 P.M. slot. Want to fill up airplanes during the slow days of Tuesday and Wednesday? Offer price discounts or additional frequent flyer miles for flying on those days.

Note that in saying that people follow incentives, economists do not claim that everyone follows each incentive at every time. You may not want to eat dinner at

4:30 P.M. But there might be a sufficient number of people who are willing to accept an earlier time slot in return for a cheaper meal.

Markets Are Efficient

Private markets and the incentives they provide are the best mechanisms known today for providing products and services. There is no government food board that makes sure that bread, cereal, coffee, and all the other food products you demand are on your plate in the evening. The vast majority of products we consume are privately provided, assuming, of course, that we have the money to pay for them.

Markets bring buyers and sellers together. Competition for the consumer dollar forces firms to provide products at the lowest possible price, or some other firm will undercut their high price. New products enter the market and old products die out. Such is the dynamic characteristic of markets. Starbucks has made latte drinkers of us all, whereas just a short time ago, few of us could even spell the word.

What drives and disciplines markets? Prices and profits are the keys. Profits drive entrepreneurs to provide new products (think of pharmaceutical firms or dot-coms) or existing products at lower prices (think of Wal-Mart). When prices and profits get too high in any market, new firms jump in with lower prices to grab away customers. This competition, or sometimes even the threat of competition, keeps markets from exploiting consumers.

Government Must Deal with Market Failure

As efficient as markets usually are, there are some products and services that markets fail to provide efficiently. Where consumers have no choice but to buy from one firm (local utility, telephone, or cable companies), the market will fail to provide the best solution, and government regulation is often used to protect consumers. Another example is pollution: Left on their own, companies will pollute the air and the water supplies—we will see why later in this book. Governments then intervene to deal with this market failure.

Information Is Important

Markets are efficient because people tend to make rational choices. To help make these choices, people rely on information. Each of us has to decide when we have enough information: Complete information may not be possible to obtain, and too much information can be debilitating. Some decisions require little information: What brand of table salt should you buy? Other decisions require more information: What type of automobile should you buy? Information is valuable.

As we will see before long, strange things happen to markets when one side of a transaction has a consistently superior information advantage. Martha Stewart was convicted of lying about selling stock based on insider information. The top officials of a business know much more quickly than anyone else if their company is developing business problems. These problems might lead to a fall in the price of the company's stock. If the officials act on this inside information while it is still secret, they can sell their stock before the price dips. This information gives them an unfair advantage over the other stockholders or people who may want to own the stock. That is why there are laws preventing insiders from taking undue advantage of their privileged position.

Markets work best when both sides of a transaction can weigh carefully the costs and benefits of goods and services. Superior information can provide significant advantages. We will see what markets can do to correct for information problems, and what government can do when the market cannot provide an acceptable solution.

Specialization and Trade Improve Our Lives

Trading with other countries leads to better products for consumers at lower prices. David Ricardo laid out the rationale for international trade almost two centuries ago, and it still holds true today. We will expand on this in the next chapter.

As you will learn, economies grow by producing those products where they have an advantage over other countries. This is why few of us grow our own food, sew our own clothes, make our own furniture, or write the books we read. We do those things we do best and let others do the same. In nearly all instances, they are able to do it cheaper than we can. The next time you come back from a shopping trip, look closely to discover where every product was made. More than likely, over half will have come from another country.

Productivity Determines Our Standard of Living

> You can see the computer age everywhere but in the productivity statistics.
>
> *Robert Solow*

> If you want jobs for jobs' sake, trade in bulldozers for shovels. If that doesn't create enough jobs, replace shovels with spoons. Heresy! But there will always be more work to do than people to work. So instead of counting jobs, we should make every job count.
>
> *Robert McTeer, Jr.*[3]

Imagine you need to hire someone in your own business (You've finished college and you are now an entrepreneur). You have narrowed the field down to two candidates who are equal in all respects except two. One person can do twice as much as the other (assume you can accurately measure these things), and this same person wants a salary that is 50% higher. Other than that they are equal. Whom should you hire?

The answer is obvious in this situation, because the more productive person is actually the best buy since she produces twice as much as the other candidate, but only wants half again as much pay. In this case, you would be willing to pay even more to get this person. Productivity and pay go together. Highly paid movie stars get high pay because they are worth it to the movie producer. The same is true of professional athletes, corporate executives, rocket scientists, and heart surgeons.

The same is true for nations. Those countries with the highest average per capita income are also the most productive. Their labor forces are highly skilled, and firms are willing to place huge amounts of capital with these workforces because this results in immense productivity. In turn, these workers earn high wages. So, high productivity growth results in solid economic growth, high wages and income, and large investments in education and research. All of this leads to higher standards of living.

Government Can Smooth the Fluctuations in the Overall Economy

All of us have heard of recessions and depressions. These terms refer to downturns in the general economy. The general movement of the economy from good times to bad and back again is called the business cycle.

Classical economic theory viewed the overall economy as a self-correcting mechanism that would quickly adjust to disturbances in the business cycle if only it was left to itself. Along came the Great Depression of the 1930s, which showed that the overall economy could get stuck in a downturn. The solution was government inter-

---

[3]Past president of the Federal Reserve Bank of Dallas.

vention. Just as government can intervene successfully in individual markets when market failure occurs, so too can government intervene successfully when the overall economy gets stuck in a downturn. You can observe this principle at work when you hear discussions of using a tax cut (or increased government spending) to pull an economy out of a recession.

The intricacies of what government can do to smooth out the business cycle are a major part of your study of macroeconomics. Remember that saying the government *can* successfully intervene does not mean it *always* successfully intervenes. The macroeconomy is not a simple machine. Successful policymaking is a tough task.

You will learn more about these important ideas as the semester progresses. For now, realize that economics rests on the foundation of a limited number of important concepts.

Key Ideas of Economics

REVIEW

- Choice and scarcity force tradeoffs.
- Opportunity costs dominate our lives.
- Rational thinking requires thinking at the margin.
- People follow incentives.
- Markets are efficient.
- Government must deal with market failure.
- Information is important.
- Specialization and trade improve our lives.
- Productivity determines our standard of living.
- Government can smooth the fluctuations in the overall economy.

QUESTION

McDonald's has recently introduced a premium blend of coffee that sells for more than its standard coffee. How does this represent thinking at the margin?

Answers to the Checkpoint question can be found at the end of this chapter.

Key Concepts

Microeconomics, p. 4
Macroeconomics, p. 5
Ceteris paribus, p. 6
Efficiency, p. 7

Equity, p. 7
Scarcity, p. 8
Opportunity costs, p. 10

Chapter Summary

What Is Economics About?

Economics is about almost everything. Economic analysis can be usefully applied to topics as diverse as how businesses make decisions and how college students allocate their time between studying and relaxing, how individuals determine whether to "invest in themselves" by taking additional courses while on the job, and how government deals with electric utilities that pollute nearby rivers.

Economics is separated into two broad categories: microeconomics and macroeconomics. *Microeconomics* deals with individual, firm, industry, and public decision making. For example, microeconomics deals with issues such as whether you should go to the movies or study, and if you study, how you allocate your study time between all of your courses. Business firms consider issues such as how much output to produce and how many people to hire to sell the output.

Macroeconomics, on the other hand, focuses on the broader economic issues confronting the nation. Issues such as inflation (a general increase in prices economy-wide), employment and unemployment, and economic growth affect all of us.

Economics uses a *stylized* approach to a number of issues. Stylized models boil issues and facts down to their basic relevant elements. Then, using assumptions, stylized (simple) models are developed. Not all situations are covered by the models, because economists seek to generalize about economic behavior and reach generally applicable results.

To build models means that we make use of the *ceteris paribus* assumption and hold some important variables constant. This useful device often provides surprising insights about economic behavior.

Economists and policymakers often confront the tradeoff between efficiency and equity. Efficiency reflects how well resources are used and allocated; economic analysis often focuses on ensuring that efficient outcomes result from public policy. Sometimes the equity (or fairness) of the outcome is questioned. Because fairness is a subjective matter, there are differences of opinion about fairness except in extreme cases where people tend to come to a general agreement. For public policy issues, economics illuminates the tradeoffs between equity and efficiency. Economists have much to say about efficiency; they tend to keep quiet on the subjective issue of equity.

Key Ideas of Economics

Economics rests on some basic ideas. These are ideas that will be met again and again throughout this course.

Our economy has limited resources. Our wants are limitless. This means that we face scarcity and must make tradeoffs in nearly everything we do. Economics is often defined as the study of the allocation of scarce resources to competing wants.

Everything we do involves opportunity costs. All activities require that we spend resources (e.g., time and money) that could be used in another activity. This other activity represents the opportunity cost of the current activity chosen. Opportunity costs apply to us as individuals and to societies as a whole.

Rational thinking requires that you think and make decisions at the margin. Businesses use marginal analysis to determine how much output to produce. People use marginal analysis to determine which products to buy. And governments use marginal analysis to determine which tracts of land to allow oil leases on.

People follow their incentives. If society wants to discourage some behavior, it can tax it, punish it, or do a host of other things that increases its costs. Conversely, society can provide incentives such as tax benefits for behaviors it wishes to encourage.

Markets bring buyers and sellers together. Competition for the consumer's dollar forces firms to provide products at the lowest possible price, or some other firm will undercut the price. New products are introduced to the market and old products disappear. This dynamism makes markets efficient.

Though markets are usually efficient, there are recognized times when they are not. Pollution is an example of this. Government can provide a solution to problems of market failure.

Information is important. Superior information gives economic actors a decided advantage. Sometimes this is simply a fact of life. At other times, information advantages can result in dysfunctional markets.

Trading with other countries leads to better products for consumers at lower prices. Economies grow by producing those products where they have an advantage over other countries. This is why much of what we buy today comes from other countries. Specialization leads to tangible benefits.

Countries with the highest average per capita income are also the most productive. Their labor forces are highly skilled, and firms place huge amounts of capital with these workforces. This results in immense productivity and correspondingly high wages for the workers. High productivity growth results in high economic growth, which leads to high wages and high incomes, which stimulate large investments in education and research. All of this activity leads to higher standards of living.

The overall economy moves from growth spurts to recessions, then back to growth spurts. Economists have been unable to tame this business cycle, though government has been successful at smoothing the fluctuations in the overall economy.

Questions and Problems

1. *The Wall Street Journal* recently noted that bachelor's degrees in economics were up 40% between 1999 and 2004 and "There is a clear explosion in economics as a major," and "the number of students majoring in economics has been rising even faster at top colleges." What might be some reasons for this now? (Jessica E. Vascellaro, "The Hot Major for Undergrads is Economics," *Wall Street Journal*, July 5, 2005, p. A11.)

2. Gregg Easterbrook, in his book, *The Progress Paradox* (New York: Random House, 2003) noted that life in the United States is significantly better today than in the past and provided many statistical facts, including:
   a. Nearly a quarter of households (or 60+ million people) have incomes of at least $75,000 a year.
   b. Real (inflation adjusted) per capita income has more than doubled since 1960—people on average have twice the real purchasing power now as in 1960.
   c. In 1956, the typical American had to work 16 weeks for each 100 square feet of new housing. Today that number is 14 weeks, and new houses are considerably more luxurious.
   d. The United States accepts more legal immigrants than all other nations of the world combined.
   e. The quality of health care improved substantially over the last half century, and life spans have grown dramatically.
   This is just a sampling of the improvements in living standards Easterbrook catalogued. However, his book is subtitled *How Life Gets Better While People Feel Worse*, and this is a paradox he set out to explain. What reasons might explain why even though our lives have improved, people feel that life was better in an earlier time?

3. In 2001 Nobel Prize winner Robert Solow noted that "the computer age is seen everywhere except in productivity data." More recent studies suggest that it takes roughly seven years for investment in computers to have an impact on productivity. Why do you think this is the case?

4. The Black rhinoceros is extremely endangered. Its horn is considered a powerful aphrodisiac in many Asian countries, and a single horn fetches many

thousands of dollars on the black market, creating a great incentive for poachers. Unlike other stories of endangered species, this one might have a simple solution. Conservationists could simply capture as many rhinos as possible and remove their horns, reducing the incentive to poach. Do you think this will help reduce poaching? Why or why not?

5. In contrasting equity and efficiency, why do high-tech firms seem to treat their employees better (better wages, benefits, working environments, vacations, etc.) compared to how landscaping or fast-food franchises treat their employees? Is this fair? Is it efficient?

6. Does your going to college have anything to do with expanding choices or reducing scarcity? Explain.

7. With higher gasoline prices, the U.S. government wants people to buy more hybrid cars that use much less gasoline. Unfortunately, hybrids are approximately $4,000 to $5,000 more expensive to purchase than comparable cars. If people follow incentives, what can the government do to encourage the purchase of hybrids?

8. You normally stay at home on Wednesday nights and study. Next Wednesday night, the college is having a free concert on the main campus. What is the opportunity cost of going to the free concert?

9. People talk about a boom in the housing market. Who specifically is helped by this boom? Consider real-estate agents, current homeowners, home builders, banks or financing institutions, and newly married couples who want to buy a home. Now consider what happens if the economy is booming, but the housing market starts to stumble. What happens to the groups you discussed earlier? Assume the housing market is booming, but the economy starts to go into a recession. What groups would be hurt by this? What would this likely do to the housing market?

10. In 2006 the Nobel Peace Prize went to economist Muhammad Yunus and the Grameen Bank "for their efforts to create economic and social development from below." Yunus led the development of micro loans to poor people without financial security: loans of under $200 to people so poor they could not provide collateral, to use for purchasing basic tools or other basic implements of work. This helped to pull millions of people out of poverty. Discuss how economic prosperity and security for everyone can result in a more peaceful planet.

Answers to Checkpoint Questions

CHECKPOINT: WHAT IS ECONOMICS ABOUT?

(1) microeconomics, (2) macroeconomics, (3) microeconomics, (4) macroeconomics, (5) microeconomics, (6) macroeconomics, (7) microeconomics, (8) macroeconomics.

CHECKPOINT: KEY IDEAS OF ECONOMICS

McDonald's is adding one more product (premium coffee) to its line. Thinking at the margin entails thinking about how you can improve an operation (or increase profits) by adding to your existing product line or reducing costs.

Appendix: Working with Graphs and Formulas

You can't watch the news on television or read the newspaper without looking at a graph of some sort. If you have flipped through this book, you have seen a large number of graphs, charts, and tables, and a few simple equations. This is the language of economics. Economists deal with data for all types of issues. Just looking at data in tables often doesn't help you discern the trends or relationships in the data.

Economists develop theories and models to explain economic behavior and levels of economic activity. These theories or models are simplified representations of real-world activity. Models are designed to distill the most important relationships between variables, and then these relationships are used to predict future behavior of individuals, firms, and industries, or to predict the future course of the overall economy.

In this short section, we will explore the different types of graphs you are likely to see in this course (and in the media) and then turn to an examination of how graphs are used to develop and illustrate models. This second topic leads us into a discussion of modeling relationships between data and how to represent these relationships with graphs and simple equations.

After studying this appendix you should be able to

- Describe the four simple forms of data graphs.
- Make use of a straightforward approach to reading graphs.
- Read linear and nonlinear graphs and know how to compute their slopes.
- Use simple linear equations to describe a line and a shift in the line.
- Explain why correlation is not the same as causation.

Graphs and Data

The main forms of graphs of data are time series, scatter plots, pie charts, and bar charts. Time series, as the name suggests, plots data over time. Most of the figures you will encounter in publications are time series graphs.

Time Series

Time series graphs involve plotting time (minutes, hours, days, months, quarters, or years) on the horizontal axis and the value of some variable on the vertical axis. Figure APX-1 illustrates a time series plot for civilian employment of those 16 years and older. Notice that since the early 1990s, employment has grown by almost 20 million for this group. The vertical strips in the figure designate the last two recessions. Notice that in both cases when the recession hit, employment fell, then rebounded after the recession ended.

FIGURE APX-1

Civilian Employment, 16 Years and Older

This time series graph shows the number of civilians 16 years and older employed in the United States since 1990. Employment has grown steadily over this period, except in times of recessions, indicated by the vertical strips. Note that employment fell during the recessions, and then bounced back after each recession ended.

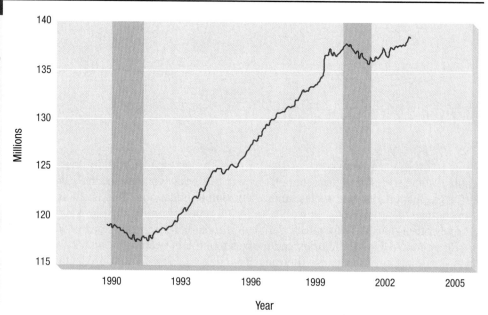

Scatter Plots

Scatter plots are graphs where two variables (neither variable is time) are plotted against each other. Scatter plots often give us a hint if the two variables are related to each other in some consistent way. Figure APX-2 plots one variable, the number of strikes, against another variable, union membership as a percent of total employment.

Two things can be seen in this figure. First, these two variables appear to be related to each other in a positive way. A rising union membership as a percent of employment leads to a greater number of strikes. It is not surprising that greater union membership and more strikes are related, because greater union membership means more employees are covered by collective bargaining agreements, and thus we would expect more strikes. Also, greater union membership means that unions would be more powerful, and strikes represent a use of this power. Second, given that the years for the data are listed next to the dots, we can see that union representation as a percent of total employment has fallen significantly over the last half century. From this simple scatter plot, we get a lot of information and ideas of how the two variables are related.

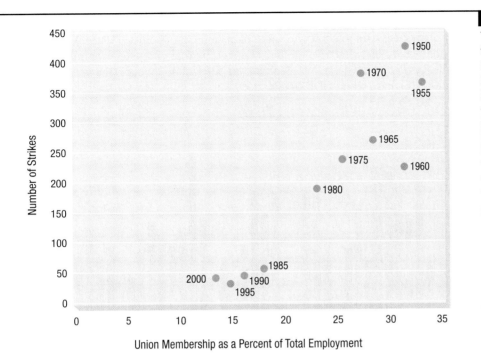

FIGURE APX-2

The Relationship between the Number of Strikes and Union Membership as a Percent of Total Employment

This scatter diagram plots the relationship between the number of strikes and union membership as a percentage of total employment. The number of strikes increased as union membership became a larger percentage of those employed. Note that union membership as a percentage of those employed has fallen in the last half century.

Pie Charts

Pie charts are simple graphs that show data that can be split into percentage parts that combined make up the whole. A simple pie chart for the relative importance of components in the consumer price index (CPI) is shown in Figure APX-3. It reveals how the typical urban household budget is allocated. By looking at each slice of the pie, we get a picture of how typical families spend their income.

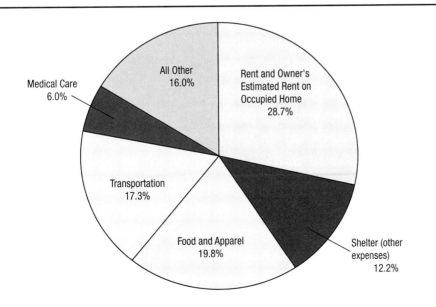

FIGURE APX-3

Relative Importance of Consumer Price Index (CPI) Components (2003)

This pie chart shows the relative importance of components of the consumer price index, showing how typical urban households spend their income.

Bar Charts

Bar charts use bars to show the value of specific data points. Figure APX-4 is a simple bar chart showing the annual changes in real (adjusted for inflation) gross domestic product (GDP). Notice that over the last 40+ years the United States has had only 5 years when GDP declined.

FIGURE APX-4

Percentage Change in Real (Inflation Adjusted) GDP

This bar chart shows the annual percentage change in real (adjusted for inflation) gross domestic product (GDP) over the last forty years. Over this time period, GDP has declined only five times.

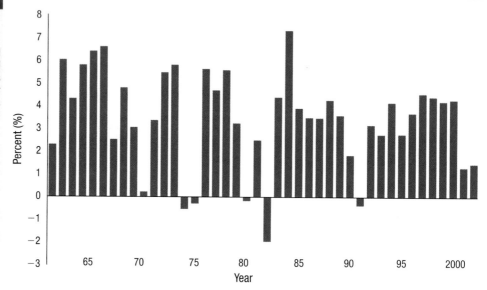

Simple Graphs Can Pack a Lot of Information

It is not unusual for graphs and figures to have several things going on at once. Look at Figure APX-5, illustrating the yield curve for government bonds. On the horizontal axis are years to maturity for the existing government bonds. At matu-

FIGURE APX-5

Yield Curve

This yield curve for government bonds shows that interest rates fell between the middle of 2002 and the middle of 2003, shown by each point on the August 2003 curve being below the corresponding point on the July 2002 curve. Also, this figure shows that the yield (rate of return) for each bond grew as the time to maturity grew. This is due to higher risk associated with longer term bonds.

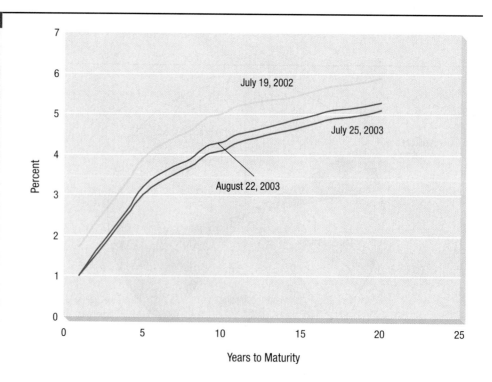

rity, the federal government must pay to the bond holders the principal amount of the bond (more about this in later chapters). On the vertical axis is the yield for each bond in percent. This is the monetary return to the bond expressed as a percent of the bond's price. Figure APX-5 shows three different yield curves for different periods. They include the most recent period shown (August 2003), a month previous (July 2003), and a year before (July 2002).

You should notice two things in this figure. First, at this time the yield curves sloped upward (they do not always do this). This meant that bonds that had a longer time to mature had higher yields; bonds with longer maturity periods are riskier and usually require a higher return. Second, interest rates fell over this period (July 2002 to August 2003) as shown by the position of the curves. Each point on the August 2003 curve is below the corresponding point on the July 2002 curve.

A Few Simple Rules for Reading Graphs

Looking at graphs of data is relatively easy if you follow a few simple rules. First, read the title of the figure to get a sense of what is being presented. Second, look at the label for the horizontal axis (x axis) to see how the data are being presented. Make sure you know how the data are being measured. Is it months or years, hours worked or hundreds of hours worked? Third, examine the label for the vertical axis (y axis). This is the value of the variable being plotted on that axis; make sure you know what it is. Fourth, look at the graph itself and see if it makes logical sense. Are the curves (bars, dots) going in the right direction?

Look the graph over and see if you notice something interesting going on. This is really the fun part of looking closely at figures both in this text and in other books, magazines, and newspapers. Often simple data graphs can reveal surprising relationships between variables. Keep this in mind as you examine graphs throughout this course.

One more thing. Graphs in this book are always accompanied by explanatory captions. Examine the graph first, making your preliminary assessment of what is going on. Then carefully read the caption, making sure it accurately reflects what is shown in the graph. If the caption refers to movement between points, follow this movement in the graph. If you think there is a discrepancy between the caption and the graph, reexamine the graph to make sure you have not missed something.

Graphs and Models

Let's now take a brief look at how economists use graphs and models, also looking at how they are constructed. Economists use what are called *stylized graphs* to represent relationships between variables. These graphs are a form of modeling to help us simplify our analysis and focus on those relationships that matter. Figure APX-6 is one such model.

Linear Relationships

Figure APX-6 on the next page shows a linear relationship between average study hours and your grade point average (GPA). The more you study, the higher your GPA (duh!). By a linear relationship, we mean that the "curve" is a straight line. In this case, if you don't study at all, we assume you are capable of making Ds and your GPA will equal 1.0, not enough to keep you in school for long. If you hit the books for an average of 10 hours a week, your GPA rises to 2.0, a C average. Studying for additional hours raises your GPA up to its maximum of 4.0.

The important point here is that the curve is linear; any hour of studying yields the same increase in your grade point. All hours of studying provide equal yields from beginning to end. This is what makes linear relationships unique.

Studying and Your GPA

This figure shows a hypothetical linear relationship between average study hours and grade point average. Without studying, a D average results, and with 10 hours of studying, a C average is obtained, and so on.

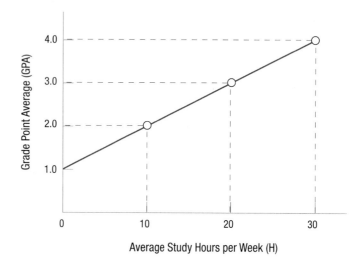

Computing the Slope of a Linear Line

Looking at the line in Figure APX-6, we can see two things: The line is straight, so the slope is constant, and the slope is positive. As average hours of studying increase, GPA increases. Computing the slope of the line tells us how much GPA increases for every hour that studying is increased. Computing the slope of a linear line is relatively easy and is shown in Figure APX-7.

Computing Slope for a Linear Line

Computing the slope is based on a simple rule: rise over run (rise divided by run). In the case of this straight line, the slope is equal to 0.1 because every 10 additional hours of studying yields a 1.0 increase in GPA.

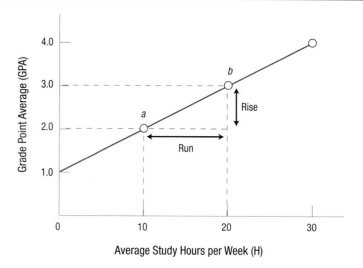

The simple rule for computing slope is: Slope is equal to rise over run (or rise ÷ run). Since the slope is constant along a linear line, we can select any two points and determine the slope for the entire curve. In Figure APX-7 we have selected points a and b where your GPA moves from 2.0 to 3.0 when studying increases from 10 to 20 hours per week.

Your GPA increases (rises) by 1.0 for an additional 10 hours of study. This means that the slope is equal to 0.1 (1.0 ÷ 10 = 0.1). So for every additional hour of studying you add each week, your GPA will rise by 0.1. Thus, if you would like to improve your grade point average from 3.0 to 3.5, you would have to study 5 more hours per week.

Computing slope for negative relations that are linear is done exactly the same way, except that when you compute the changes from one point to another, one of the values will be negative, making the relationship negative.

Nonlinear Relationships

It would be nice for model builders if all relationships were linear, but that is not the case. It is probably not really the case with the amount of studying and your GPA either. Figure APX-8 depicts a more realistic nonlinear and positive relationship between studying and GPA. Again, we assume that you can get a D average (1.0) without studying and reach a maximum of straight As (4.0) with 30 hours per week.

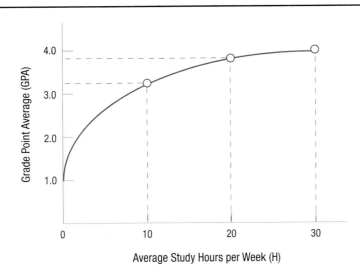

FIGURE APX-8

Studying and Your GPA (nonlinear)

This nonlinear graph of study hours and GPA is probably more typical than the one shown in Figures 6 and 7. Like many other things, studying exhibits diminishing returns. The first hours of studying result in greater improvements to GPAs than further hours of studying.

Figure APX-8 suggests that your first few hours of study per week are more important to raising your GPA than are the others. Your first 10 hours of studying yields more than the last 10 hours: You go from 1.0 to 3.3 (a gain of 2.3), as opposed to going only from 3.8 to 4.0 (a gain of only 0.2). This curve exhibits what economists call diminishing returns. Just as the first bite of pizza tastes better than the one-hundredth, so the first 5 hours of studying brings a bigger jump in GPA than the 25th to 30th hours.

Computing the Slope of a Nonlinear Curve

As you might suspect, computing the slope of a nonlinear curve is a little more complex than for a linear line. But it is not that much more difficult. In fact, we use essentially the same rise over run approach that is used for lines.

Looking at the curve in Figure APX-8, it should be clear that the slope varies for each point on the curve. It starts out very steep, then begins to level out above 20 hours of studying. Figure APX-9 on the next page shows how to compute the slope at any point on the curve.

Computing the slope at point a requires drawing a line tangent to that point, then computing the slope of that line. For point a, the slope of the line tangent to it is found by computing rise over run again. In this case, it is length $dc \div bc$ or $[(3.8 - 3.3) \div (10 - 7)] = .5 \div 3 = 0.167$. Notice that this slope is significantly

Computing Slope for a Nonlinear Curve

Computing the slope of a non-linear curve requires that you compute the slope of each point on the curve. This is done by computing the slope of a tangent to each point.

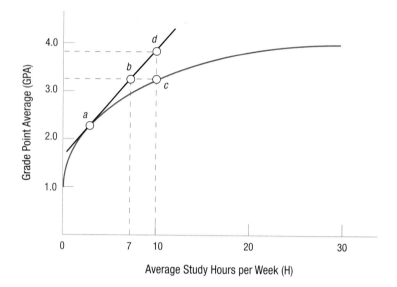

larger than the original linear relationship of 0.1. If we were to compute the slope near 30 hours of studying, it would approach zero (the slope of a horizontal line is zero).

Ceteris Paribus, Simple Equations, and Shifting Curves

Hold on while we beat this GPA and studying example into the ground. Inevitably when we simplify analysis to develop a graph or model, important factors or influences must be controlled. We do not ignore them, we hold them constant. These are known as *ceteris paribus* assumptions.

Ceteris Paribus: All Else Equal

By *ceteris paribus* we mean other things being equal or all other relevant factors, elements, or influences are held constant. When economists define your demand for a product, they want to know how much or how many units you will buy at different prices. For example, to determine how many DVDs you will buy at various prices (your demand for DVDs), we hold your income and the price of movie tickets constant. If your income suddenly jumped, you would be willing to buy more DVDs at all prices, but this is a whole new demand curve. *Ceteris paribus* assumptions are a way to simplify analysis; then the analysis can be extended to include those factors held constant, as we will see next.

Simple Linear Equations

Simple linear equations can be expressed as: $Y = a + bX$. This is read as, Y equals a plus b times X, where Y is the variable plotted on the y axis and a is a constant (unchanging), and b is a different constant that is multiplied by X, the value on the x axis. The formula for our studying and GPA example introduced in Figure 6 is shown in Figure APX-10.

The constant a is known as the vertical intercept because it is the value of your GPA when study hours (X) is zero, and therefore when it cuts (intercepts) the vertical axis and is equal to 1.0 (D average). Now each time you study another hour on average, your GPA rises by 0.1, so the constant b (the slope of the line) is equal to 0.1. Letting H represent hours of studying, the final equation is: GPA = 1.0 +

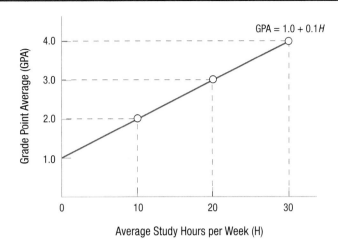

FIGURE APX-10

Studying and Your GPA: A Simple Equation

The formula for a linear relationship is $Y = a + bX$, where Y is the y axis variable, X is the x axis variable, and a and b are constants. For the original relationship between study hours and GPA, this equation is $Y = 1.0 + 0.1X$.

$0.1H$. You start with a D average without studying and as your hours of studying increase, your GPA goes up by 0.1 times the hours of studying. If we plug in 20 hours of studying into the equation, the answer is a GPA of 3.0 ($1.0 + (0.1 \times 20) = 1.0 + 2.0 = 3.0$).

Shifting Curves

Now let's introduce a couple of factors we have been holding constant (the *ceteris paribus* assumption). These two elements are tutoring and partying. So, our new equation now becomes GPA $= 1.0 + 0.1H + Z$, where Z is our variable indicating whether you have a tutor or whether you are excessively partying. When you have a tutor, $Z = 1$, and when you party too much, $Z = -1$. Tutoring adds to the productivity of your studying (hence $Z = 1$), while excessive late night partying reduces the effectiveness of studying; you are always tired (hence $Z = -1$). Figure APX-11 shows the impact of adding these factors to the original relationship.

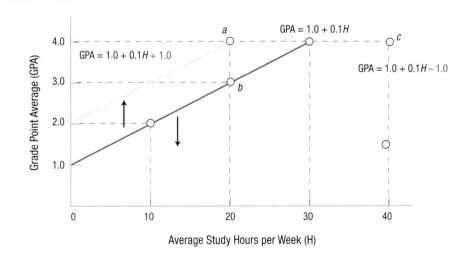

FIGURE APX-11

The Impact of Tutoring and Partying on Your GPA

The effect of tutoring and partying on our simple model of studying and GPA is shown. Partying harms your academic efforts and shifts the relationship to the right, making it harder to maintain your previous average (you now have to study more hours). Tutoring, on the other hand, improves the relationship (shifts the curve to the left).

With tutoring, your GPA-studying curve has moved upward and to the left. Now, because $Z = 1$, you begin with a C average (2.0), and with just 20 hours of studying (because of tutoring) you can reach a 4.0 GPA (point a). Alternatively, when you don't have tutoring and you party every night, your GPA-studying relationship has worsened (shifted downward and to the right). Now you must study 40 hours (point *c*) to accomplish a 4-point GPA. Note that you begin with failing grades.

The important point here is that we can simplify relationships between different variables and use a simple graph or equation to represent a model of behavior. In doing so, we often have to hold some things constant. When we allow those factors to change, the original relationship is now changed and often results in a shift in the curves. You will see this technique applied over and over as you study economics this semester.

Correlation Is Not Causation

Just because two variables seem related or appear related on a scatter plot does not mean that one causes another. Economists a hundred years ago correlated business cycles (the ups and downs of the entire economy) with sunspots. Because they appeared related, some suggested that sunspots caused business cycles. The only rational argument was that agriculture was the dominant industry and sunspots affected the weather; therefore, sunspots caused the economy to fluctuate.

Another example of erroneously assuming that correlation implies causality is the old Wall Street saw that related changes in the Dow Jones average to women's hem lines. Because two variables appear to be related does not mean that one causes the other to change.

Understanding graphs and using simple equations is a key part of learning economics. Practice helps.

Production, Economic Growth, and Trade

2

e live in a consumer world. Everywhere you look, people are purchasing and consuming things. Everything from plastic wrap to baseballs, from artichokes to cellular phones, gets produced, traded, and consumed. Whether an economy is a capitalistic market economy as in the United States, a capitalist marketplace with a strong touch of socialism as in many European countries, or a predominately communist economy as is true of many of China's markets, goods and services must change hands. Several centuries ago, individuals produced most of what they consumed. Today, most of us produce little of what we consume. Instead, we work at specialized jobs, then use our wages to purchase the goods we need. And purchase we do.

Though newspapers frequently report consumption excesses—and these excesses occur in rich *and* poor countries around the globe—we should not let these excesses obscure the fact that consumption is a great driver of economic growth. In many respects, consumption is simply a way for people to better themselves, to make their lives less of a drudgery, or to enrich their lives. Farmers in poor countries move from a precarious existence as subsistence farmers to producers of cash crops—keeping enough to live on but generating a surplus to sell—to obtain those consumption goods that better their lives.

Another great driver of economic growth is technological change. In 1950, only a small minority of households had television sets. Today, nearly every home has at least one color television set, and the average home has nearly three! In response to the resulting change in demand for programming, channels have multiplied; programming choices are almost limitless. But what brought about these changes in the first place? Technological advances from 1950 through the present day have led to cheaper, higher-performance television sets. This has allowed more families to afford not just one TV but also flat-screen HDTVs with huge screens and theater quality surround sound that are a fraction of the weight and size of older sets. New devices permit viewers to record and watch programs at their leisure.

27

Technological advances have similarly led to a telecommunications industry that simply was not dreamed of 50 years ago. In 1950, long distance phone calls were placed with the assistance of live operators, every minute costing the average consumer several hours' worth of pay. Today, fiber-optic cables allow thousands of calls to be made on one cable, thus drastically reducing the cost of telephone service. Cell phones, meanwhile, have become business necessities because of their convenience and productivity. The globe is shrinking as communications bring us closer together.

Another factor reducing the size of the world is airline travel. Fifty years ago, few people flew cross-country or overseas. Jets were nonexistent, tickets were expensive—the equivalent of a month's wages to fly coast to coast—and flights took forever. Today, because of technological change, jet aircraft can whisk us across the country or overseas at a price well within the budgets of most Americans.

A further driver of economic growth—trade—is less obvious. Yet its effect is clear. Nearly every country engages in commercial trade with other countries to expand the opportunities for consumption and production by its people. As products are consumed, new products must be produced, so increased consumption in one country can spur economic growth in another. Given the ability of global trade to open economic doors and raise incomes, it is vital for growth in developing nations.

In the previous chapter, we noted that a reduction in America's growth rate of only *1 percentage point* each year since 1930 would have significant consequences today. Figure 1 shows real (adjusted for inflation) gross domestic product (GDP) since 1930 and real GDP if the rate of growth was just 1 percentage point less. As the graph shows, real GDP would be roughly half today. One important point to get from the graph is that the 1 percentage point reduction had minimal impact for the first 20 years or so, but the impact widened as time marched forward. Policies that affect economic growth today will have their biggest impact several generations later.

This chapter will give you a framework for understanding economic growth. It provides a simple model for thinking about production, then applies this model to economies at large so you will know how to think about economic growth and its determinants. It then goes on to analyze international trade as a special case of economic growth. By the time you finish this chapter, you should understand the impor-

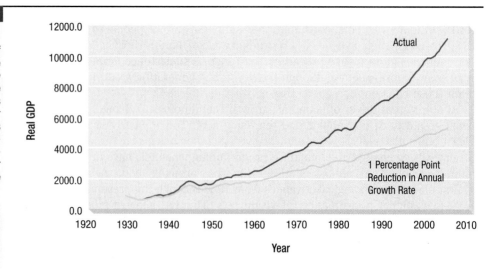

FIGURE 1

Real GDP Growth

This figure shows the impact of reducing the annual growth rate of real GDP by *1 percentage point.* Thus if the growth rate between 1953 and 1954 was 7%, we assume in the lower curve that the growth rate was actually 6%. As the figure illustrates, the impact of the reduction in growth had only a minor impact early on, but became more important over time.

tance of economic growth and what drives it. To start, we turn to an examination of the three basic questions that every economy, no matter how it is organized, must solve.

- Describe the three basic questions that must be answered for any economy.

- Describe production and the factors that go into producing various goods and services.

- Describe the opportunity cost an economy incurs to increase the production of one product.

- Use a production possibilities frontier (PPF) or curve to analyze the limits of production.

- Describe economic growth and the impacts of expanding resources through increasing human resources, capital accumulation, and technological improvements.

- Describe the concepts of absolute and comparative advantage and explain what they tell us about the gains from trade when countries specialize in certain products.

- Describe the practical constraints on free trade and how some industries might be affected.

Basic Economic Questions and Production

Regardless of the country, its circumstances, or its precise economic structure, every economy must answer three basic questions.

Basic Economic Questions

The three basic economic questions that each society must answer are:

- What goods and services are to be produced?
- How are these goods and services to be produced?
- Who will receive these goods and services?

The response an economy makes to the first question—What to produce?—depends on the goods and services a society wants. In a communist state, the government will decide what a society wants, but in a capitalist economy, consumers are allowed to signal what products they want by way of their demands for specific commodities. In the next chapter, we will investigate how the consumer demand for individual products is determined and how markets meet these demands. For now, we will assume that consumers, individually and as a society, are able to decide on the mix of goods and services they most want, and that producers supply these items at acceptable prices.

Once we know what goods a society wants, the next question its economic system must answer is how these goods and services are to be produced. In the end, this problem comes down to the simple question of how labor, capital, and land should be combined to produce the desired products. If a society demands a huge amount of corn, say, we can expect its utilization of land, labor, and

Friedrich von Hayek

Gunnar Myrdal

Nobel Prize Friedrich von Hayek and Gunnar Myrdal

*a*ll societies have to answer the three basic economic questions. The 1974 Nobel Prize winners Friedrich von Hayek and Gunnar Myrdal proposed very different answers.

Friedrich von Hayek was the foremost advocate of free markets and classical economics during the heyday of the Keynesian revolution. Born in 1899, von Hayek was the son of a botanist. After serving in World War I, he studied law and political science at the University of Vienna, later joining a group of young academics in a private seminar conducted by the eminent economist Ludwig von Mises. From 1932 until his death in 1992, von Hayek taught at several schools including the London School of Economics and the University of Chicago.

Von Hayek's early work was primarily concerned with business cycles. Von Hayek argued that economic booms could lead to financial conditions in which investment exceeded savings, resulting in a mismatch between consumption and output and, consequently, an economic contraction while a balance between the two was being achieved. Von Hayek viewed this "concertina effect" as the primary explanation for business cycles. He was one of the few economists of his era to predict the Great Depression.

After the mid-1930s, von Hayek focused on critiques of socialism and centralist economic planning. His impassioned defense of libertarian economics in the *Road to Serfdom* is, if anything, more widely read today than it was in 1940, the year of publication. Von Hayek attributed failures in socialism to an inefficient use of knowledge and information. Central planners, in his view, were no match for the pricing mechanism as a means of communicating information. The pricing system evolved spontaneously from the interplay of individuals with limited and particular information. A decentralized system with competition and price freedom, therefore, was the most efficient and socially beneficial way to organize an economy. He also saw markets as advancing human liberty and freedom.

In contrast to von Hayek, Swedish economist and sociologist Gunnar Myrdal argued for a different way to organize an economy. He advocated a more active role for government. Myrdal established his reputation with the 1944 publication of his book on race relations in the United States, *An American Dilemma.* Considered a classic of social scientific literature, the work has been compared to Alexis de Tocqueville's *Democracy in America.* Myrdal's criticisms of the doctrine of "separate but equal" had a major influence on the 1954 Supreme Court ruling in *Brown v. Board of Education,* which outlawed segregation in public schools.

Born in Sweden in 1898, Myrdal received his degree in law and economics in 1927 from Stockholm University. He later served in the Swedish senate and as Minister of Commerce after World War II. In 1957, he undertook a comprehensive study of economic trends and policies in Asia for the Twentieth Century Fund, which led to the book, *Asian Drama: An Inquiry into the Poverty of Nations and the Challenge of World Poverty,* where he advocated a major role for government in directing economies. Myrdal died in 1987.

capital will be different from a society that demands digital equipment. But even an economy devoted to corn production could be organized in different ways, perhaps relying on extensive use of human labor, or perhaps relying on automated capital equipment.

Once an economy has determined what goods and services to produce and how to produce them, it is faced with the distribution question: Who will get the resulting products? *Distribution* refers to the way an economy allocates the goods and services it produces to consumers. In a capitalist economy, most products are distributed through private markets. In a socialist economy, many goods are produced in state-owned facilities. Theoretically, governments in socialist economies use tax monies to subsidize producers, while governments in capitalist economies leave producers free to survive or perish based on their efficiency and the quality of their products.

Resources, Production, and Efficiency

Having answered the three basic economic questions, let's take a look at the production process. **Production** involves turning **resources** into products and services that people want. Let's begin our discussion of this process by examining the scarce resources used to produce goods and services.

Land

For economists, the term **land** includes both land in the usual sense, but it also includes all other natural resources that are used in production. Natural resources like mineral deposits, oil and natural gas, and water are all included by economists in the definition of land. Economists refer to the payment to land as *rents*.

Labor

Labor as a factor of production includes both the mental and physical talents of people. Few goods and services can be produced without labor resources. Improvement to labor capabilities from training, education, and apprenticeship programs, typically called human capital, all add to labor's productivity and ultimately to a higher standard of living. Labor is paid *wages*.

Capital

Capital includes all manufactured products that are used to produce other goods and services. This includes equipment such as drill presses, blast furnaces for making steel, and other tools used in the production process. It also includes trucks and automobiles used by business as well as office equipment such as copiers, computers, and telephones. Any manufactured product that is used to produce other products is included in the category of capital. Capital earns *interest*.

Production
The process of converting resources (factors of production)—land, labor, capital, and entrepreneurial ability—into goods and services.

Resources
Productive resources include land (land and natural resources), labor (mental and physical talents of people), capital (manufactured products used to produce other products), and entrepreneurial ability (the combining of the other factors to produce products and assume the risk of the business).

Land
Includes natural resources such as mineral deposits, oil, natural gas, water, and land in the usual sense of the word. The payment to land as a resource is called rents.

Labor
Includes the mental and physical talents of individuals that are used to produce products and services. Labor is paid wages.

Capital
Includes manufactured products such as welding machines, computers and cellular phones that are used to produce other goods and services. The payment to capital is referred to as interest.

Note that the term *capital* as used by economists refers to real capital—actual manufactured products used in the production process—not money or financial capital. Money and financial capital are important in that they are used to purchase the real capital that is used to produce products.

Entrepreneurial Ability

Entrepreneurs
Entrepreneurs combine land, labor, and capital to produce goods and services. They absorb the risk of being in business, including the risk of bankruptcy and other liabilities associated with doing business. Entrepreneurs receive profits for this effort.

Entrepreneurs *combine* land, labor, and capital to produce goods and services, and they assume the *risks* associated with running the business. Entrepreneurs combine and manage the inputs of production, and manage the day-to-day marketing, finance, and production decisions. Today, the risks of running a business are huge, as the many bankruptcies and failures testify to; and globalization has opened many opportunities as well as risks. For undertaking these activities and assuming the risks associated with business, entrepreneurs earn *profits*.

Production and Efficiency

Production turns *resources*—land, labor, capital, and entrepreneurial ability—into products and services. The necessary production factors will vary for different products. To produce corn, for instance, one needs arable land, seed, fertilizer, water, farm equipment, and the workers to operate that equipment. Farmers looking to produce corn would need to devote hundreds of acres of open land to this crop, plow the land, plant and nurture the corn, and finally harvest the crop. Producing digital equipment, in contrast, requires less land but more capital and highly skilled labor.

As we have seen, every country has to decide what to produce, how to produce it, and decide who receives the output. Countries desire to do the first two as efficiently as possible, but this leads to two different aspects of efficiency.

Production efficiency
Goods and services are produced at their lowest resource (opportunity) cost.

Production efficiency occurs when the mix of goods society decides to produce is produced at the lowest possible resource or opportunity cost. Alternatively, production efficiency occurs when as much output as possible is produced with a given amount of resources. Firms use the best technology available and combine the other resources to produce products at the lowest cost to society.

Allocative efficiency
The mix of goods and services produced are just what individuals in society desire.

Allocative efficiency occurs when the mix of goods and services produced are the most desired by society. In capitalist countries this is determined by consumers and businesses and their interaction through markets. The next chapter explores this interaction in some detail. Needless to say, it would be inefficient (a waste of resources) to be producing 45 rpm records in the age of the iPod, XM radio, and other digital music players. Allocative efficiency requires that the right mix of goods be produced at the lowest cost.

Every economy faces constraints or limitations. Land, labor, capital, and entrepreneurship are all limited. No country has an infinite supply of available workers or the space and machinery that would be needed to put them all to work efficiently; no country can break free of these natural restraints. Such limits are known as production possibilities frontiers (PPFs), and they are the focus of the next section.

Checkpoint
Basic Economic Questions and Production

REVIEW

■ Every economy must decide what to produce, how to produce it, and who will get what is produced.

- Production is the process of converting factors of production (resources)—land, labor, capital, and entrepreneurial ability—into goods and services.
- Land includes land and natural resources. Labor includes the mental and physical resources of humans. Capital includes all manufactured products used to produce other goods and services. Entrepreneurs combine resources to produce products, and they assume the risk of doing business.
- Production efficiency requires that products be produced at the lowest cost. Allocative efficiency occurs when the mix of goods and services produced is just what society wants.

QUESTION

The one element that really seems to differentiate entrepreneurship from the other resources is the fact that entrepreneurs shoulder the *risk* of failure of the enterprise. Does this seem right? Explain.

Answers to the Checkpoint question can be found at the end of this chapter.

Production Possibilities and Economic Growth

As we discovered in the previous section, all countries, and all economies, face constraints on their production capabilities. Production can be limited by the quantity of the various factors of production in the country and its current technology. Technology includes such considerations as the country's infrastructure, its transportation and education systems, and the economic freedom it allows. Though perhaps going beyond the everyday meaning of the word *technology,* for simplicity, we will assume all of these factors help determine the state of a country's technology.

To further simplify matters, production possibilities analysis assumes that the quantity of resources available and the technology of the economy remain constant. Moreover, all economic agents—workers and managers—are assumed to be technically efficient, meaning that no waste will occur in production. Finally, we will examine an economy that produces only two products. While keeping our analysis simple, altering these assumptions will not fundamentally change our general conclusions.

Production Possibilities

Assume our sample economy produces leather jackets and microcomputers. Figure 2 with its accompanying table on the next page shows the production possibilities frontier for this economy. The table shows seven possible production levels (*a–g*). These seven possibilities, which range from 12,000 leather jackets and zero microcomputers to zero jackets and 6,000 microcomputers, are graphed in Figure 2.

When we connect the seven production possibilities, we delineate the **production possibilities frontier (PPF)** for this economy (some economists refer to this curve as the production possibilities curve). All points on the PPF curve are considered *attainable* by our economy. Everything to the left of the PPF curve is also attainable, but is an inefficient use of resources—the economy can always do better. Everything to the right of the curve is considered *unattainable.* Therefore, the PPF maps out the economy's limits; it is impossible for the economy to produce at levels beyond the PPF. What the PPF in Figure 2 shows is that, given an efficient use of limited resources and taking technology into account, this economy can produce any of the seven combinations of microcomputers and leather jackets listed. Also, the economy can produce any combination of the two products on or within the PPF, but not any combinations beyond it.

Production possibilities frontier (PPF)
Shows the combinations of two goods that are possible for a society to produce at full employment. Points on or inside the PPF are feasible, and those outside of the frontier are unattainable.

FIGURE 2

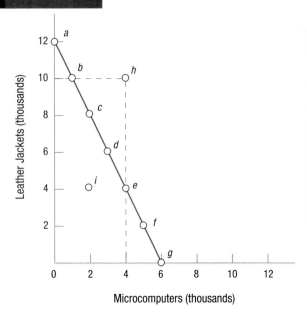

	(In thousands)	
Possibility	**Leather Jackets**	**Microcomputers**
a	12	0
b	10	1
c	8	2
d	6	3
e	4	4
f	2	5
g	0	6

Production Possibilities Frontier

Using all of its resources, this stylized economy can produce many different mixes of leather jackets and microcomputers. Production levels on, or to the left of, the resulting PPF are attainable for this economy. Production levels to the right of the PPF curve are unattainable.

Full Employment

As Figure 2 further suggests, all of the points along the PPF represent points of maximum output for our economy, that is, points at which all resources are being fully used. Therefore, if the society wants to produce 1,000 microcomputers, it will only be able to produce 10,000 leather jackets, as shown by point *b* on the PPF curve. Should the society decide Internet access is important, it might decide to produce 4,000 microcomputers, which would force it to cut leather jacket production down to 4,000, shown by point *e*.

Contrast points *c* and *e* with production at point *i*. At point *i* the economy is only producing 2,000 microcomputers and 4,000 jackets. Clearly some resources are not being used—unemployment exists. When fully employed, the economy's resources could produce more of both goods (point *d*).

Because the PPF represents a maximum output, the economy could not produce 4,000 microcomputers and still produce 10,000 leather jackets. This situation, shown by point *h*, lies to the right of the PPF and hence outside the realm of possibility. Anything to the right of the PPF is impossible for our economy to attain; all points along the curve represent full employment.

Opportunity Cost

Opportunity cost
The cost paid for one product in terms of the output (or consumption) of another product that must be foregone.

Whenever a country reallocates resources to change production patterns, it does so at a price. This price is called **opportunity cost**. Opportunity cost is the price an economy or an individual must pay, measured in units of one product, to increase its production (or consumption) of another product. In moving from point *b* to point *e* in Figure 2, microcomputer production increases by 3,000 units, from 1,000 units to 4,000 units. In contrast, our country must forego producing 6,000 leather jackets because production falls from 10,000 jackets to 4,000 jackets. Giving up 6,000 jackets for 3,000 more computers represents an opportunity cost of 6,000 jackets, or of two jackets for each microcomputer.

Opportunity cost thus represents the tradeoff required when an economy wants to increase its production of any single product. Governments must choose between guns and butter, or between military spending and social spending. Since there are limits to what taxpayers are willing to pay, spending choices are necessary. Think of opportunity costs as what you or the economy must give up to have more of a product or service.

Every day, everyone faces tradeoffs based on opportunity cost. A day has only 24 hours: You must decide how much time to spend eating, watching movies, going to class, sleeping, playing golf, partying, or studying—more time partying means less time for study. And if you set aside a certain amount of time for studying, more time studying biology means less time studying history. But time is not the only constraint we face. Money restricts our choices as well. Should you buy a new computer, move to a nicer apartment, or save up for next semester's tuition? Indeed, virtually every choice in life involves tradeoffs or opportunity costs.

Increasing Opportunity Costs

In most cases, land, labor, and capital cannot easily be shifted from producing one good or service to another. You cannot take a semitruck and use it to plow a farm field, even though the semi and a top-notch tractor cost about the same money. The fact is that some resources are suited to specific sorts of production, just as some people seem to be better suited to performing one activity over another. Some people have a talent for music or art, and they would be miserable—and inefficient—working as accountants or computer programmers. Some people find they are more comfortable working outside, while others require the amenities of an environmentally controlled, ergonomically correct office.

Thus, a more realistic production possibilities frontier is shown in Figure 3. This PPF curve is bowed out from the origin, since opportunity costs rise as more factors are used to produce increasing quantities of one product. Let us consider why this is so.

Let's begin at a point where the economy's resources are strictly devoted to leather jacket production (point *a*). Now assume that society decides to produce

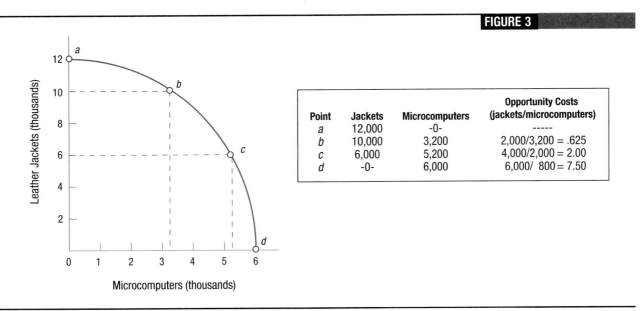

FIGURE 3

Point	Jackets	Microcomputers	Opportunity Costs (jackets/microcomputers)
a	12,000	-0-	-----
b	10,000	3,200	2,000/3,200 = .625
c	6,000	5,200	4,000/2,000 = 2.00
d	-0-	6,000	6,000/ 800 = 7.50

Production Possibilities Frontier (increasing opportunity costs)

This figure shows a more realistic production possibilities frontier for an economy. This PPF curve is bowed out from the origin since opportunity costs rise as more factors are used to produce increasing quantities of one product or the other.

3,200 microcomputers. This will require a move from point *a* to point *b*. As we can see, 2,000 leather jackets must be given up to get the added 3,200 microcomputers. This means the opportunity cost of 1 microcomputer will be 0.625 leather jackets (2,000 ÷ 3,200 = 0.625). This is a low opportunity cost, because those resources that are better suited to producing microcomputers will be the first ones shifted into this industry, resulting in rapidly increasing returns from specialization.

But what happens when this society decides to produce an additional 2,000 computers, or moves from point *b* to point *c* on the graph? As Figure 3 illustrates, each additional computer costs 2 leather jackets since producing 2,000 more computers requires the society to sacrifice 4,000 leather jackets. Thus, the opportunity cost of computers has more than tripled due to diminishing returns on the computer side, which arise from the unsuitability of these new resources as more resources are shifted to microcomputers.

To describe what has happened in plain terms, when the economy was producing 12,000 leather jackets, all its resources went into jacket production. Those members of the labor force who are engineers and electronic assemblers were probably not well suited to producing jackets. As the economy backed off jackets to start producing microcomputers, the opportunity cost of computers was low, since the resources first shifted, including workers, were likely to be the ones most suited to computer production and least suited to jacket manufacture. Eventually, however, as computers became the dominant product, manufacturing more computers required shifting leather workers to the computer industry. Employing these less suitable resources drives up the opportunity costs of computers.

You may be wondering which point along the PPF is the best for society. Economists have no grounds for stating unequivocally which mixture of goods and services would be ideal. The perfect mixture of goods depends on the tastes and preferences of the members of society. In a capitalist economy, resource allocation is determined largely by individual choices and the workings of private markets. We will consider these markets and their operations in the next chapter.

Economic Growth

We have seen that PPFs map out the maximum that an economy can produce: Points to the right of the PPF curve are unattainable. But what if that PPF curve can be shifted to the right? This shift would give economies new maximum frontiers. In fact, we will see that economic growth can be viewed as a shift in the PPF curve outward. In this section, we will use the production possibilities model to determine some of the major reasons for economic growth. Understanding these reasons for growth will enable us to suggest some broad economic policies that could lead to expanded growth.

The production possibilities model holds resources and technology constant to derive the PPF. These assumptions suggest that economic growth has two basic determinants: expanding resources and improving technologies. The expansion of resources allows producers to increase their production of all goods and services in an economy. Specific technological improvements, however, often affect only one industry directly. The development of a new color printing process, for instance, will directly affect only the printing industry.

Nevertheless, the ripples from technological improvements can spread out through an entire economy, just like ripples in a pond. Specifically, improvements in technology can lead to new products, improved goods and services, and increased productivity.

Sometimes, technological improvements in one industry allow other industries to increase their production with existing resources. This means producers can produce more output without using added labor or other resources. Alternately, they can get the same production levels as before while using fewer resources than before. This frees up resources in the economy for use in other industries.

When the electric lightbulb was invented, it not only created a new industry (someone had to produce lightbulbs), but it also revolutionized other industries. Factories could stay open longer since they no longer had to rely on the sun for light. Workers could see better, thus improving the quality of their work. The result was that resources operated more efficiently throughout the entire economy.

The modern day equivalent to the lightbulb might be the cellular phone. Widespread use of these devices enables people all across the world to produce goods and services more efficiently. Insurance agents can file claims instantly from disaster sites, deals can be closed while one is stuck in traffic, and communications have been revolutionized. Thus, this new technology has ultimately expanded time, the most finite of our resources. A similar argument could be made for the Internet. It has profoundly changed how many products are bought, sold, and delivered, and has expanded communications and the flow of information.

Expanding Resources

The PPF represents the constraints on an economy at a specific time. But economies are constantly changing, and so are PPFs. Capital and labor are the principal resources that can be changed through government action. Land and entrepreneurial talent are important factors of production, but neither is easy to change by government policies. The government can make owning a business easier or more profitable by reducing regulations, or by offering low-interest loans or favorable tax treatment to small businesses. However, it is difficult to turn people into risk takers through government policy.

Increasing Labor and Human Capital. A clear increase in population, the number of households, or the size of the labor force will shift the PPF outward, as shown in Figure 4. With added labor, the production possibilities available to the economy expand from PPF_0 to PPF_1. Such a labor increase can be caused by higher birthrates, increased immigration, or an increased willingness of people to enter the labor force. This last type of increase has occurred over the past several decades as more women have entered the labor force on a permanent basis. America's high immigration (legal and illegal) fuels our strong rate of economic growth.

Rather than simply increasing the number of people working, however, the labor factor can also be increased by improving workers' skills. Economists refer to this as *investment in human capital.* Activities such as education, on-the-job training, and other professional training fit into this category. Improving human capital

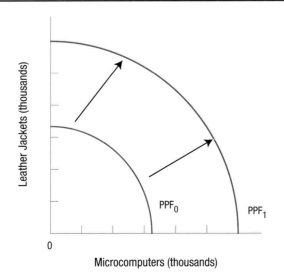

Leather Jackets (thousands)

PPF_0 PPF_1

0

Microcomputers (thousands)

FIGURE 4

Economic Growth by Expanding Resources

A clear increase in population, the number of households, or the size of the labor force will shift the PPF outward. In this figure, a rising supply of labor expands the economy's production possibilities from PPF_0 to PPF_1.

FIGURE 5

Consumption and Capital Goods and the Expansion of the Production Possibilities Frontier

If a nation selects a product mix where the bulk of goods produced are consumption goods, it will initially produce at point *b*. The small investment made in capital goods has the effect of expanding the nation's productive capacity only to PPF$_b$ over the following decade. If the country decides to produce at point *a*, however, devoting more resources to producing capital, its productive capacity will expand much more rapidly, pushing the PPF curve out to PPF$_a$ over the following decade.

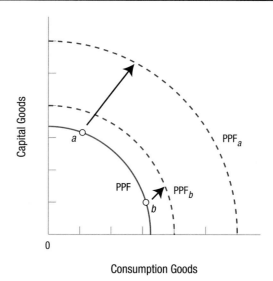

means people are more productive, resulting in higher wages, a higher standard of living, and an expanded PPF for society.

Capital Accumulation. Increasing the capital used throughout the economy, usually brought about by investment, would similarly shift the PPF outward, as shown in Figure 4. Additional capital makes each unit of labor more productive and thus results in higher possible production throughout the economy. Adding robotics and computer-controlled machines to production lines, for instance, means each unit of labor produces many more units of output.

The production possibilities model and the economic growth associated with capital accumulation suggest a tradeoff. Figure 5 illustrates the tradeoff all nations face between current consumption and capital accumulation.

Let's first assume a nation selects a product mix where the bulk of goods produced are consumption goods, that is, goods that are immediately consumable and have short life spans, such as food and entertainment. This product mix is represented by point *b* in Figure 5. Consuming most of what it produces, a decade later the economy will face PPF$_b$. Little growth has occurred, since the economy has done little to improve its productive capacity—the present generation has essentially decided to consume rather than to invest in the economy's future.

Contrast this decision to one where the country at first decides to produce at point *a*. In this case, more capital goods such as machinery and tools are produced, while fewer consumption goods are used to satisfy current needs. Selecting this product mix results in the much larger PPF curve a decade later (PPF$_a$), since the economy steadily built up its productive capacity during those 10 years.

Technological Change

Figure 6 illustrates what happens when an economy experiences a technological change in one of its industries, in this case the microchip industry. As the diagram shows, the economy's potential output of microcomputers expands greatly, though its maximum production of leather jackets remains unchanged. The area between the two curves represents an improvement in the society's standard of living. People produce and consume more of both goods than before: more microcomputers because of the technological advance, and more jackets because some of the resources once devoted to microcomputer production can be shifted to leather jacket production, even as the economy is turning out more computers than before.

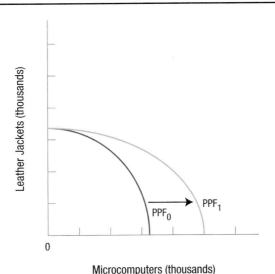

FIGURE 6

Technological Change and Expansion of the Production Possibilities Frontier

In this figure, an economy's potential output of microcomputers has expanded greatly, while its maximum production of leather jackets has remained unchanged. The area between the two curves represents an improvement in the society's standard of living, since more of both goods can be produced and consumed than before. Some of the resources once used for microcomputer production are diverted to leather jackets, even as the number of microcomputers increases.

This example reflects the United States today, where the computer industry is exploding with new technologies. Intel Corporation, the leading microprocessor manufacturer in the world, leads the way. Intel relentlessly develops newer, faster, and more powerful chips, setting a target time of 18 months for the development, testing, and release of each new generation of microprocessors. Consequently, consumers have seen home computers go from clunky conversation pieces to powerful, fast, indispensable machines. Today's microcomputers are more powerful than the mainframe supercomputers of just a few decades ago! The latest developments include PDAs and cell phones that surf the Web and download and play music, videos, and current TV programs.

Besides new products, technology has dramatically reduced the cost of microprocessor production. These cost reductions have permitted the United States to produce and consume more of other products as our consumption of high-tech items has soared. Our whole PPF has expanded outward.

But technological improvements result not only in smaller and cheaper microchips. An economy's technology also depends on how well its important trade centers are linked together. If a country has mostly dirt paths rather than paved highways, you can imagine how this deficiency will affect its economy: Distribution will be slow, and industries will be slow to react to changes in demand. In such a case, improving the roads might be the best way to stimulate economic growth.

As you can see, there are many ways to stimulate economic growth. A society can expand its output by using more resources, perhaps encouraging more people to enter the workforce or raising educational levels of workers. The government can encourage people to invest more, as opposed to devoting their earnings to immediate consumption. The public sector can spur technological advances by providing incentives to private firms to do research and development or underwrite research investments of its own.

Estimating the Sources of Economic Growth

But just how important are each of these factors? A recent study by the Organisation for Economic Co-operation and Development (OECD)[1] focused on what has been driving economic growth in 21 nations over the last several decades. The study

Adrian Hillman

---

[1]*The Sources of Economic Growth in the OECD Countries* (Paris: Organisation for Economic Co-operation and Development), 2003.

first looked at contribution to economic growth from the macroeconomic perspective of added resources and technological improvements as we have been discussing in this chapter. It then looked at some benefits from good government policies that stimulate growth and finally examined the industry and individual firm level for clues to the microeconomic sources of growth. Some of the findings include:

■ A 1 percentage point increase in business investment as a percent of gross domestic product (GDP) leads to an increase in per capita GDP of 1.3%.
■ An additional 1-year increase in average education levels increases per capita GDP by 4 to 7%.
■ A 0.1 percentage point increase in research and development as a percent of GDP increases per capita GDP by 1.2%.
■ Reducing both the level and variability of inflation by 1 percentage point leads to an increase in per capita GDP of 2.3%.
■ A 1 percentage point decrease in the tax burden as a percent of GDP leads to a 0.3% increase in per capita GDP.
■ An increase in trade exposure (a combined measure of imports and exports as a percent of GDP) of 10 percentage points increases per capita GDP by 4%.

In less numerical terms, greater investment by business (physical capital), higher levels of education (human capital), high levels of research and development, lower inflation rates, reduced tax burdens, and greater levels of international trade all result in higher standards of living (per capita GDP). One important point to take away from this discussion is that our simple stylized model of the economy using only two goods gives you a good first framework upon which to judge proposed policies for the economy. While not overly complex, this simple analysis is still quite powerful. Trying to discover why some countries grow and others do not is a complex undertaking and has occupied economists for several centuries. But as this study illustrates, a country can achieve greater economic growth and raise its standard of living by expanding trade with other countries. This is the subject of the next section.

Checkpoint
Production Possibilities and Economic Growth

REVIEW

■ A production possibilities frontier (PPF) depicts the different combinations of goods that a fully employed economy can produce, given its available resources and current technology (both assumed fixed in the short run).
■ Production levels inside and on the frontier are possible, but production mixes outside the curve are unattainable.
■ Because production on the frontier represents the maximum output attainable when all resources are fully employed, reallocating production from one product to another involves *opportunity costs:* The output of one product must be reduced to get the added output of the other. The more of one product that is desired, the higher its opportunity costs because of diminishing returns and the unsuitability of some resources for producing some products.
■ The PPF model suggests that economic growth can arise from an expansion in resources or improvements in technology. Economic growth is a shift out of the PPF curve.
■ Economic growth can be enhanced by increasing the quantity or quality of labor.

QUESTION

Having abundant resources such as oil or diamonds would seem to be a benefit to an economy, yet some people have considered it a curse. Why would plentiful resources like these be a curse?

Answers to the Checkpoint question can be found at the end of this chapter.

Specialization, Comparative Advantage, and Trade

As we have seen, economics is all about voluntary production and exchange. People and nations do business with one another because all expect to gain from the transactions. Centuries ago, European merchants ventured to the Far East to ply the lucrative spice trades. These days, American consumers buy wines from Italy, cars from Japan, electronics from Korea, and millions of other products from countries around the world.

Many people assume that trade between nations is a zero-sum game—a game in which, for one party to gain, another party must lose. This is how poker games work. If one player walks away from the table a winner, someone else must have lost money. But this is not how voluntary trade works. Voluntary trade is a positive-sum game: Both parties to a transaction score positive gains. After all, who would voluntarily enter into an exchange if he or she did not believe there was some gain from it? To understand how all parties to an exchange (whether individuals or nations) can gain from it, we need to consider the concepts of absolute and comparative advantage developed by David Ricardo roughly 200 years ago.

David Ricardo (1772–1823)

*d*avid Ricardo's rigorous, dispassionate evaluation of economic principles influenced generations of theorists, including such vastly different thinkers as John Stuart Mill and Karl Marx. The son of Dutch-Jewish immigrants, Ricardo was born in London in 1772. As a teenager, he joined his father's business on the London Stock Exchange, but after marrying and converting to Christianity, Ricardo broke with his family and started his own business. Within 5 years, he amassed a small fortune as a stockbroker and devoted his energies to politics and writing. As a member of the British Parliament, Ricardo was an advocate of sound monetary policies and an outspoken critic of the Corn Laws, which placed high tariffs on imported grain to protect British landowners. His political views would figure prominently in his economic writings. In 1817, Ricardo published the *Principles of Political Economy and Taxation,* in which he made two of his most important contributions to economics, "the iron law of wages" and the "labor theory of value."

Ricardo believed that increasing wages would only lead to population increases among workers and, eventually, to falling wages. He linked the value of exchange goods to the labor needed to produce them. Protectionism for domestic agriculture, he reasoned, would lead to higher rents for landowners, higher prices for food, and higher subsistence wages for workers, which in turn would depress the rates of profit for capitalists and discourage economic development. Despite a pessimistic streak, Ricardo was an optimist when it came to free trade. His theory of "comparative advantage" suggested that countries would mutually benefit from trade by specializing in export goods they could produce at a lower opportunity cost than another country. His classic example was trade between Britain and Portugal. If Britain specialized in producing cloth, and Portugal in exporting wine, each country would gain from a free exchange of goods. Ricardo died in 1823, leaving an enduring legacy of classical economic analysis.

Absolute and Comparative Advantage

Absolute advantage
One country can produce more of a good than another country.

Figure 7 shows hypothetical production possibilities curves for the United States and Mexico. Both countries are assumed to produce only crude oil and microcomputer chips. Given the PPFs in Figure 7, the United States has an **absolute advantage** over Mexico in producing both products. An absolute advantage exists when one country can produce more of a good than another country. In this instance, the United States can produce 4 times more oil (40 million vs. 10 million barrels) and 10 times as many microcomputer chips (40 million vs. 4 million microchips) as Mexico.

At first glance you might wonder why the United States would even consider trading with Mexico. The United States has so much more productive capacity than Mexico, so why wouldn't it just produce all of its own crude oil and microcomputers? The answer lies in comparative advantage.

Comparative advantage
One country has a lower opportunity cost of producing a good than another country.

One country has a **comparative advantage** in producing a good if its opportunity cost to produce that good is lower than the other country's. In Figure 7, Mexico has a comparative advantage over the United States in producing oil. For the United States to produce an additional million barrels of crude oil, the *opportunity cost* is one million microcomputer chips. Each barrel of oil therefore costs the American economy one computer chip.

Contrast this with the situation in Mexico. For every microchip Mexican producers forgo, they are able to produce an additional 2.5 barrels of oil. This means one barrel of oil costs the Mexican economy only 0.4 computer chip. Therefore, Mexico has a comparative advantage in the production of crude oil, since a barrel of oil costs Mexico only 0.4 microchip, but to produce the same barrel of oil costs one microchip in the United States.

Conversely, the United States has a comparative advantage over Mexico in producing computer chips: Producing a microchip in the United States costs one barrel of oil, whereas the same chip in Mexico costs 2.5 barrels of oil. These relative costs suggest that the United States should pour its resources into producing computer chips, while Mexico specializes in crude oil. The two countries can then engage in trade to their mutual benefit.

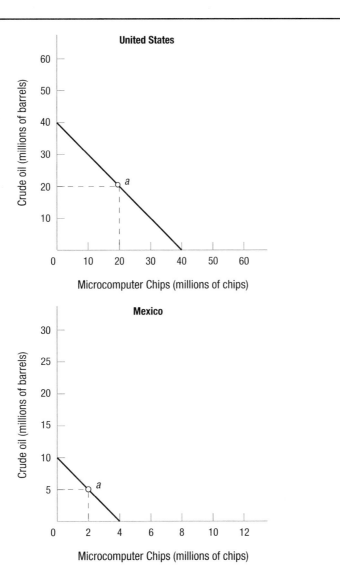

FIGURE 7

Production Possibilities for the United States and Mexico

One country has an absolute advantage if it can produce more of a good than the other country. In this case, the United States has an absolute advantage over Mexico in producing both microchips and crude oil—it can produce more of both goods than Mexico can. Even so, Mexico has a comparative advantage over the United States in producing oil, since it can increase its output of oil at a lower opportunity cost than can the United States. This comparative advantage leads to gains for both countries from specialization and trade.

The Gains from Trade

To see how specialization and trade can benefit both trading partners, even when one has the ability to produce more of both goods than the other, assume each country is at first (before trade) operating at point a in Figure 7. At this point, both countries are producing and consuming only their own output; the United States produces and consumes 20 million barrels of oil and 20 million computer chips; Mexico, 5 million barrels of oil and 2 million computer chips. Table 1 summarizes these initial conditions.

Table 1	Initial Consumption-Production Pattern		
	United States	**Mexico**	**Total**
Oil	20	5	25
Chips	20	2	22

Now assume Mexico focuses on oil, producing the maximum it can: 10 million barrels. We will assume both countries want to continue consuming 25 million barrels of oil between them. So the United States only needs to produce 15 million barrels of oil since Mexico is now producing 10 million barrels. For the United States, this frees up some resources that can be diverted to producing computer chips. Since each barrel of oil in the United States costs one microchip, reducing oil output by 5 million barrels means that 5 million more microcomputer chips can be produced.

Table 2 shows each country's production after Mexico has begun specializing in oil production.

Table 2	Production after Mexico Specializes in Producing Crude Oil		
	United States	**Mexico**	**Total**
Oil	15	10	25
Chips	25	0	25

Notice that the combined production of crude oil has remained constant, but the total output of computer chips has risen by 3 million chips. Assuming the two countries agree to share the added 3 million computer chips between them equally, Mexico will now ship 5 million barrels of oil to the United States in exchange for 3.5 million computer chips. From the 5 million additional computer chips the United States produces, Mexico will receive 2 million (its original production) plus 1.5 million for a total of 3.5 million, leaving 1.5 million additional chips for U.S. consumption. The resulting mix of products consumed in each country is shown in Table 3. Clearly, both countries are better off, having engaged in specialized production and trade.

Table 3	Final Consumption Patterns after Trade		
	United States	**Mexico**	**Total**
Oil	20	5	25
Chips	21.5	3.5	25

The important point to remember here is that even when one country has an absolute advantage over another country, both countries will still benefit from trading with one another. In our example, the gains were small, but such gains can grow; as two economies become more equal in size, the benefits of their comparative advantages grow.

Ancient Humans and Trade

Neanderthals *(Homo neanderthalensis)* lived 200,000 years before *Homo sapiens* arrived on the scene. Both species then lived together in roughly the same ranges for another 10,000 years, at which time the Neanderthals died out. Modern evidence suggests that Neanderthals were roughly as intelligent, stronger, and also capable of speech. Until recently, the generally accepted reason for the Neanderthals' extinction was that *Homo sapiens* had more sophisticated tools, developed modern symbolic thinking, and created a more sophisticated language.

Digging in prehistoric *Homo sapiens'* caves has uncovered such items as paintings, spear points, stone tools made from materials not found in the same location, and seashell jewelry found in inland locations far from the ocean. These discoveries have produced a new theory of why *Homo sapiens* came to dominate the land: They were trading with other colonies of humans.[2] The theory is that trade led to specialization, whereby the best hunters hunted, and the others made weapons, clothes, and other necessities.

To test this theory, several anthropologists created a computer population simulation model that included such variables as rates of fertility and mortality, specialization and trade, hunting ability, and the same number of skilled hunters and craftsmen in each population. They gave *Homo sapiens* an edge in the ability to specialize and trade. As the model ran, *Homo sapiens* had superior hunting success, giving them more meat and driving up fertility and population. The model assumed the number of animals was fixed, so the available meat for the Neanderthals declined, and so did their population. Depending on the model's parameters, the time it took for Neanderthals to die out roughly coincided with that estimated by other anthropologists. Ancient humans may have known the benefits of trade long before David Ricardo developed his theory of absolute and comparative advantage.

Limits on Trade and Globalization

Before leaving the subject of international trade, we should take a moment to note some practical constraints on trade. First, every transaction involves costs, including transportation, communications, and the general costs of doing business. Even so, over the last several decades, transportation and communication costs have been declining all over the world, resulting in growing global trade.

Second, the production possibilities curves for nations are not linear, but rather governed by increasing costs and diminishing returns. Therefore, it is difficult for countries to specialize in producing one product. Complete specialization would be risky, moreover, since the market for a product can always decline, perhaps because the product becomes technologically obsolete. Alternately, changing weather patterns can wreak havoc on specialized agriculture products, adding further instability to incomes and exports in developing countries.

Finally, though two countries may benefit from trading with one another, expanding this trade may well hurt some industries and individuals within each country. Notably, industries finding themselves at a comparative disadvantage may be forced to scale back production and lay off workers. In such instances, the government may need to provide workers with retraining, relocation, and other help to ensure a smooth transition to the new production mix.

When the United States signed the North American Free Trade Agreement (NAFTA) with Canada and Mexico, many people experienced what we have just been discussing. Some American jobs went south to Mexico because of low production costs. By opening up more markets for American products, however, NAFTA did stimulate economic growth, such that retrained workers may end up with new and better jobs.

Before ending this chapter, let's take a moment to review what we have learned, then apply it briefly. We listed the three basic questions that any economy has to answer and discussed production. We used the production possibilities frontiers (PPF) model to understand what economic growth is. We then looked at the determinants of economic growth. Finally, we examined trade as a driver of economic growth. Now let's apply this growth framework.

---

[2]For a more detailed discussion of this issue, see "Human Evolution: Homo Economicus?" *The Economist,* April 9, 2005, pp. 67–68; and "Mrs. Adam Smith," *The Economist,* December 9, 2006, p. 85.

Economic growth in the United States has slowed over the second half of the 20th century, but our standard of living has nonetheless risen dramatically. Expansion of our resources and technological progress has driven this growth—just as our growth framework suggests. Women have entered the workforce in droves, immigration has expanded, and technology has advanced by leaps and bounds, thus spurring the production of more goods and services. Expanding global trade has opened up new markets for our products and increased imports from areas with lower production costs. These developments have contributed to America's economic growth and improved the economic welfare of its people.

Is There a Moral Dimension to Economic Growth?

Why do we care so much about economic growth? When we talk about microeconomic issues in economics, the conversation boils down to efficiency: How can we best organize economic activity—production, buying, selling, consuming—in order to keep the economy as close as possible to the frontier that represents the maximum possible production and satisfaction of the desires of all.

Benjamin M. Friedman

Robin Jareaux/Getty Images

Clearly, economic growth expands the economy's production possibilities frontier and improves our standard of living, but does it improve the quality of life? Benjamin Friedman[3] made a compelling argument that we also care so much about growth because there are moral consequences to growth. This is the other side of the coin that is rarely discussed.

Looking back at two centuries of historical evidence of our country and others, he found that when the economy is growing and the general population feels they are getting ahead, they are more likely to protect and enhance their basic moral values. These, he argued, include providing greater opportunity for all; expanding tolerance for people of other races, ethnic groups, and religions; and improving our sense of fairness to those in need. As a result, we become more committed to our democratic institutions.

His analysis also brings a warning: When economic growth stagnates for an extended period, the evidence suggests that "predictable pathologies have flourished in American society in ways that we all regret." Friedman's analysis of the moral implications provides another dimension of economic growth to add to our toolbox.

How about around the globe? While poverty and starvation exist and are constant challenges to policymakers, there has been a clear trend of progress, spurred by international trade and technological advances. Cell phones are one simple example. Thirty years ago, policymakers focused on developing infrastructure such as roads and telephones to improve communication. These were not trivial tasks. To improve telephone usage, massive capital and labor outlays (think of putting up telephone poles and stringing the telephone wires) were needed. It was a huge, almost impossible, task. In this new century, countries have leaped beyond this because of technological breakthroughs in telecommunications: It is much less expensive to put up cell phone towers than put down the standard telephone pole infrastructure. Just as the United States has witnessed an explosion in cell phone usage, so have other places around the globe—with more dramatic results. Technology truly has improved communication almost overnight, and in its wake has come economic growth.

From this framework for understanding economic growth, especially trade, we turn to a discussion of the market system. The following chapter will look at how individual consumers and firms operate through markets to solve the three basic economic questions of what to produce, how to produce it, and who will ultimately consume the goods and services produced.

---

[3]Benjamin M. Friedman, *The Moral Consequences of Economic Growth* (New York: Knopf), 2005.

Specialization, Comparative Advantage, and Trade

REVIEW

- An absolute advantage exists when one country can produce more of some good than another.
- A comparative advantage exists if one country has lower opportunity costs of producing a good than another country. Both countries gain from trade if each focuses on producing those goods at which it has a comparative advantage.
- Thus, voluntary trade is a positive-sum game, because both countries benefit from it.

QUESTION

Unlike most people, why do Hollywood stars (and many other rich people) have full-time personal assistants who manage their personal affairs?

Answers to the Checkpoint question can be found at the end of this chapter.

Key Concepts

Production, p. 31
Resources, p. 31
Land, p. 31
Labor, p. 31
Capital, p. 31
Entrepreneurs, p. 32

Production efficiency, p. 32
Allocative efficiency, p. 32
Production possibilities frontier (PPF), p. 33
Opportunity cost, p. 34
Absolute advantage, p. 42
Comparative advantage, p. 42

Chapter Summary

Basic Economic Questions and Production

Every economy must decide what to produce, how to produce it, and who will get the goods produced. How these questions are answered depends on how an economy is organized (capitalist, socialist, or communist), but in the end, all three questions must somehow be addressed.

Production is the process of converting factors of production—land, labor, capital, and entrepreneurial ability—into goods and services. Production processes can be labor- or capital-intensive depending on the available resources. Production efficiency occurs when goods and services are produced at the lowest possible resource cost. Allocative efficiency occurs when the mix of goods and services produced is that desired by society.

Production Possibilities and Economic Growth

The PPF curve shows the different combinations of goods that a fully employed economy can produce, given its available resources and current technology (both assumed to be fixed in the short run). Production levels inside and on the frontier are possible, but production mixes lying outside the curve are unattainable.

Production on the frontier represents the maximum output attainable by the economy when all resources are fully employed. At full employment, reallocating production from one product to another involves opportunity costs: The output of one product must be reduced to get the added output of the other. As an economy desires more of one product, the opportunity costs for this product will rise because of diminishing returns and the unsuitability of some specialized resources to be devoted to producing some products.

The production possibilities model suggests that economic growth can arise from an expansion in resources or from improvements in technology. Expansions in resources expand the production possibilities frontier for all commodities. Technological advances in one industry directly expand production only in that industry, but nonetheless allow more of all types of goods to be produced. The new technology allows previous output to be produced using fewer resources, thus leaving some resources available for use in other industries.

Economic growth can be enhanced by increasing the quantity or quality of labor available for production. Population growth, caused by higher birthrates or immigration, will increase the quantity of labor available. Investments in human capital will improve labor's quality. Greater capital accumulation will further improve labor's productivity and thus increase growth rates.

Specialization, Comparative Advantage, and Trade

An absolute advantage exists when one country can produce more of some good than another. A country has a comparative advantage if its opportunity costs to produce this good are lower than in the other country. Countries gain from voluntary trade if each focuses on producing those goods at which it enjoys a comparative advantage. Voluntary trade is thus a positive-sum game: Both countries stand to benefit from it.

Questions and Problems

1. When can an economy increase the production of one good without reducing the output of another?

2. The "Rule of 72" permits you to quickly determine how fast an economy can double by dividing 72 by the growth rate. For example, if the growth rate is 1%, an economy will double in size in 72 years; if the growth rate is 7%, it will double in roughly 10 years; and so on. In the table below assume that the economy starts with income of $100. When the growth rate equals 2%, income will double every two generations (consider a generation to be 18 years), as shown in the third column. In 36 years, income grows to $200, and 36 years later it is $400. Compute the doubling in the fourth column when growth rates rise to 4%. Are these different growth rates really so important? Who is most affected?

Generation	Years	2% Growth	4% Growth
1	18		_____
2	36	200	_____
3	54		_____
4	72	400	_____

3. Explain the important difference between a straight line PPF and the PPF that is concave (bowed out) to the origin.

4. The table on the next page shows the potential output combinations of oranges and jars of prickly pear jelly (from the flower of the prickly pear cactus) for Florida and Arizona.
   a. Compute the opportunity cost for Florida of oranges in terms of jars of prickly pear jelly. Do the same for prickly pear jelly in terms of oranges.

b. Compute the opportunity cost for Arizona of oranges in terms of jars of prickly pear jelly. Do the same for prickly pear jelly in terms of oranges.

c. Would it make sense for Florida to specialize in producing oranges and for Arizona to specialize in producing prickly pear jelly and then trade? Why or why not?

Florida		Arizona	
Oranges	Prickly Pear Jelly	Oranges	Prickly Pear Jelly
0	10	0	500
50	8	20	400
100	6	40	300
150	4	60	200
200	2	80	100
250	0	100	0

5. Complete the following based on the figure below where three different production possibilities curves are shown.

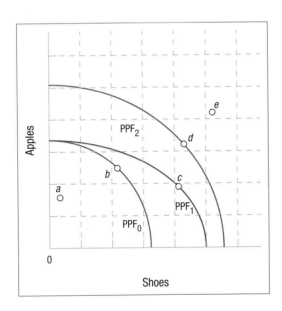

a. If the production possibilities frontier for this nation is PPF_0, then point a represents _____.

b. If the production possibilities frontier for this nation is PPF_0, then point e represents _____.

c. Production possibilities PPF_1 represents _____.

d. If the initial production possibilities frontier is PPF_0, then PPF_2 represents _____ and is caused by _____.

6. Describe how a country producing more capital goods rather than consumer goods ends up in the future with a PPF that is larger than a country that produces more consumer goods and fewer capital goods.

7. List the way an economy can grow given the discussion in this chapter.

8. Describe how opportunity cost is shown on a PPF.

9. The United States has an absolute advantage in making many goods, such as short-sleeve cotton golf shirts. Why do Costa Rica and Bangladesh make these shirts and export them to the United States?

10. In which of the three basic questions will technology play the greatest role?

11. As individuals, we all know what scarcity means: not enough time (even the rich face a scarcity of time); insufficient income so we are unable to buy that new car, vacation home, or water-ski boat we want. But for nations as a whole, what does it mean to face scarcity?

12. Why is it that America uses heavy street cleaning machines driven by one person to clean the streets, while China and India use many people with brooms to do the same job?

13. How would unemployment be shown on the PPF?

14. China has experienced levels of economic growth in the last decade that have been two to three times that of the United States (10% versus 3–4% per year in the U.S.). Has China's high growth rate eliminated scarcity in China?

15. If specialization and trade as discussed in this chapter lead to a win-win situation where both countries gain, why is there often opposition to trade agreements and globalization?

Answers to Checkpoint Questions

CHECKPOINT: BASIC ECONOMIC QUESTIONS AND PRODUCTION

Typically, entrepreneurs put their personal money into the business and often pledge private assets as collateral for loans. Should the business fail, they stand to lose more than their jobs, rent from the land, or interest on capital loaned to the firm. Workers can get other jobs, land owners can rent to others, and capital can be used in other enterprises. But the entrepreneur must suffer the loss of personal assets and move on.

CHECKPOINT: PRODUCTION POSSIBILITIES AND ECONOMIC GROWTH

Abundant resources like oil or diamonds can be a curse because the economy often depends only on these resources for income and develops little else in terms of commerce. Many of the countries in the Middle East and Africa face this situation. Because their major source of income is concentrated in one resource, corruption often results, harming development in other sectors of the economy.

CHECKPOINT: SPECIALIZATION, COMPARATIVE ADVANTAGE, AND TRADE

For Hollywood stars and other rich people, the opportunity cost of their time is high. As a result, they hire people at lower cost to do the mundane chores that each of us is accustomed to doing because our time is not as valuable.

Supply and Demand

Imagine you are going to build a house. Your plans are drawn up, the land is purchased, and you are all set to begin construction. What is the first thing you do? Do you immediately start putting up walls or set the painters to work? Of course not! Before you can build any walls, much less start painting, you must lay a foundation. The same is true in economics: Before you can understand more complex economic concepts, you need a foundation. This chapter provides the basic foundation on which all other economic theory rests. This foundation—supply and demand analysis—explains how market economies operate. In the previous chapter on economic growth, we took markets for granted. Here we start examining markets in detail.

In our economy, most goods and services (including labor) are bought and sold through private markets. These products include everything from iPods to airline flights, from haircuts to new homes. Most markets offer consumers a wide variety of choices. The typical Wal-Mart, for instance, features over a half million different items, while even a small town has numerous competing choices of hair salons, movie theaters, and shoe stores.

In any given market, prices are determined by "what the market will bear." But which factors determine what the market will bear, and what happens when events that occur in the marketplace cause prices to change? For answers to these questions, economists turn to supply and demand analysis. The basic model of supply and demand presented in this chapter will allow you to determine why product sales rise and fall, what direction prices move in, and how many goods will be offered for sale when certain events happen in the marketplace. Later chapters will use this same model to explain complex phenomena such as how personal income is distributed.

This chapter introduces some of the basic economic concepts you will need to know to understand how the forces of supply and demand work. These concepts include markets, the law of demand, demand curves, the determinants of demand, the law of supply, supply curves, the determinants of supply, equilibrium, surpluses, and shortages.

After studying this chapter you should be able to

- Describe the nature and purposes of markets.
- Describe the nature of demand, demand curves, and the law of demand.
- Describe the determinants of demand and be able to forecast how a change in one or more of these determinants will change demand.
- Describe the difference between a change in demand and a change in quantity demanded.
- Describe the nature of supply, supply curves, and the law of supply.
- Describe the determinants of supply and be able to forecast how a change in one or more of these determinants will change supply.
- Describe the difference between a change in supply and a change in quantity supplied.
- Determine market equilibrium price and output.
- Determine and predict how price and output will change given changes to supply and demand in the market.

Markets

Markets
Institutions that bring buyers and sellers together so they can interact and transact with each other.

A **market** is an institution that enables buyers and sellers to interact and transact with one another. A lemonade stand is a market because it allows people to exchange money for a product, in this case lemonade. Ticket scalping, though illegal in many states, similarly represents market activity since it leads to the exchange of money for tickets. As Chris Anderson pointed out in his recent book, *The Long Tail*,[1] the Internet, without a physical location, permits firms and individuals to sell a large number of low-volume niche products and still make money. This includes students who resell their textbooks on Amazon.com and Half.com.

Even though all markets have the same basic component—the transaction—they can differ in a number of ways. Some markets are quite limited because of their geographical location, or because they offer only a few different products for sale. Other markets, like the Wal-Mart superstore, feature literally thousands of items. The New York Stock Exchange serves as a market for just a single type of financial instrument, stocks, but it facilitates exchanges worth billions of dollars daily. Compare this to the neighborhood flea market, which is much smaller and may operate only on weekends, but offers everything from food and crafts to T-shirts and electronics. Cement manufacturers are typically restricted to local markets due to high transportation costs, whereas Internet firms can easily do business with customers around the world.

The Price System

When buyers and sellers exchange money for goods and services, accepting some offers and rejecting others, they are also doing something else: They are communi-

---

[1]Chris Anderson, *The Long Tail: Why the Future of Business is Selling Less of More* (New York: Hyperion), 2006.

cating their individual desires. Much of this communication is accomplished through the prices of items. If buyers sufficiently value a particular item, they will quickly pay its asking price. If they do not buy it, they are indicating they do not believe the item to be worth its asking price.

Prices also give buyers an easy means of comparing goods that can substitute for each other. If margarine falls to half the price of butter, this will suggest to many consumers that margarine is a better deal. Similarly, sellers can determine what goods to sell by comparing their prices. When prices rise for tennis rackets, this tells sporting goods stores that the public wants more tennis rackets, leading these stores to order more. Prices, therefore, contain a huge amount of useful information for both consumers and sellers. For this reason, economists often call our market economy the **price system**.

Price system
A name given to the market economy because prices provide considerable information to both buyers and sellers.

Markets

REVIEW

- Markets are institutions that enable buyers and sellers to interact and transact business.
- Markets differ in geographical location, products offered, and size.
- Prices contain a wealth of information for both buyers and sellers.
- Through their purchases, consumers signal their willingness to exchange money for particular products at particular prices. These signals help businesses decide what to produce, and how much of it to produce.
- The market economy is also called the price system.

QUESTION

What are the important differences between the markets for financial securities such as the New York Stock Exchange and your local flea market?

Answers to the Checkpoint question can be found at the end of this chapter.

Demand

Whenever you purchase a product, you are voting with your money. You are selecting one product out of many and supporting one firm out of many, both of which signal to the business community what sorts of products will satisfy your wants as a consumer.

Economists, incidentally, typically focus on wants rather than needs because it is so difficult to determine what we truly need. Theoretically, you could survive on tofu and vitamin pills, living in a lean-to made of cardboard and buying all your clothes from thrift stores. Most people in our society, however, choose not to live in such austere fashion. Rather, they want something more, and in most cases they are willing and able to pay for more. These wants—the desires consumers have for particular goods and services, which they express through their purchases—are known as demands.

Demand
The maximum amount of a product that buyers are willing and able to purchase over some time period at various prices, holding all other relevant factors constant (the *ceteris paribus* condition).

The Relationship between Quantity Demanded and Price

Demand refers to the goods and services people are willing and able to buy during a certain period of time. Given the current popularity of television, most people would probably love to own a flat panel HDTV with surround sound and hook it to a digital satellite or cable system that features hundreds of channels. And, indeed, if the products needed for such a setup were priced low enough, virtually everyone owning a television would opt for this system.

As your television gets bigger, and as you upgrade from basic television to cable or digital satellite, the cost of your home entertainment system increases. Yet, as the price of these services increases, the quantity demanded will decrease, since fewer and fewer people will be willing to spend their money on such luxuries, if they even have the money.

Thus, in a survey of households with television sets, we would expect to find a few people with virtually no service, perhaps receiving only network broadcasts through rabbit-ear antennas. A few people would have digital satellite hookups giving them access to sports channels, movie channels, and every other channel imaginable. The vast majority of consumers, however, would fall between these two categories, receiving some, but not all, of the services and channels available, in accord with their tastes and means.

In a market economy, there is a negative relationship between price and quantity demanded. This relationship, in its most basic form, states that as price increases, the quantity demanded falls, and conversely, as prices fall, the quantity demanded increases.

The Law of Demand

Law of demand
Holding all other relevant factors constant, as price increases, quantity demanded falls, and as price decreases, quantity demanded rises.

This principle, that as price increases, quantity demanded falls, and as price decreases, quantity demanded rises—all other factors held constant—is known as the **law of demand**. The law of demand states that the lower a product's price, the more of that product consumers will purchase during a given time period. This straightforward, commonsense notion happens because, as a product's price drops, consumers will substitute the now-cheaper product for other, more expensive products. Conversely, if the product's price rises, consumers will find other, cheaper products to substitute for it.

To illustrate, when videocassette recorders first came on the market 30 years ago, they cost $3,000, and few homes had one. As VCRs became less and less expensive, however, more people bought them, and others found more uses for them. Today, DVD players and digital video recorders (DVRs) are everywhere, and VCRs are essentially consigned to museums. A similar battle is now brewing around the format for high-definition DVDs, and digital cameras have largely replaced 35mm film cameras.

Time is an important component in the demand for many products. Consuming many products—watching a movie, eating a pizza, playing tennis—takes some time. Thus, the price of these goods includes not only their money cost, but also the opportunity cost of the time needed to consume them. It follows that, all other things being equal, including the cost of a ticket, we would expect more consumers to attend a 2-hour movie than a 4-hour movie. The shorter movie simply requires less of a time investment.

The Demand Curve

Several decades ago, computers filling entire air-conditioned rooms laboriously churned out data. Now, inexpensive laptop computers, PDAs, and cellular phones can perform even more complex operations in a fraction of the time. This advance in computer technology has led to the widespread use of computers for both business and pleasure. Once offering only Pong, game companies now take millions of players a year into mythical adventures, space battles, military campaigns, and rounds of championship golf. Indeed, games on the three main platforms—Sony's

Playstation 3, Microsoft's XBox 360, and Nintendo's Wii—are a driving force behind the development of faster microprocessor technology because games are voracious users of speed.

The law of demand states that as price decreases, quantity demanded increases. When we translate demand information into a graph, we create a **demand curve**. This demand curve, which slopes down and to the right, graphically illustrates the law of demand.

Demand curve
Demand schedule information translated to a graph.

For example, consider Betty and her demand for computer games. Figure 1 depicts her annual demand in both table (the demand schedule) and graphical (the demand curve) form. Looking at the table and reading down Betty's demand schedule, we can see that Betty is willing to buy more computer games as the price decreases, from zero games at a price of $100 to 20 games at a price of $20. It makes sense that Betty will buy more computer games as the price decreases.

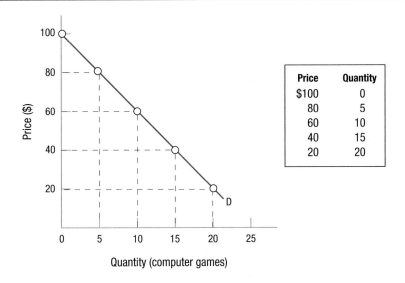

Price	Quantity
$100	0
80	5
60	10
40	15
20	20

FIGURE 1

Betty's Demand for Computer Games

This figure shows Betty's demand schedule (the table) and her demand curve (the graph) for computer games over a year. Betty will purchase 5 computer games when the price is $80, buy 10 when the price falls to $60, and buy more as prices continue to fall. The demand curve D is Betty's demand curve for computer games.

We can take the values from the demand schedule in the table and graph them in a figure, with price as the vertical axis and computer games as the horizontal axis, following the convention in economics of always placing price on the vertical axis and quantity demanded on the horizontal axis. This line is the demand curve. Comparing the table with the graph, we can see that they convey the same information. For instance, find the price of $60 on the vertical axis in the graph and look to the right to the point on the curve; then look down to locate the quantity of 10 computer games. This is the same information conveyed in the table: locating a price of $60 and looking to the right gives you the quantity of 10 computer games demanded.

Both the table and the graph portray the law of demand. As the price decreases, Betty demands more computer games. If the price of each game is $100, Betty will not purchase any games; they are just too expensive. Let the price drop to $40, however, and she will buy 15 games during the year.

Market Demand Curves

Though individual demand curves, like the one showing Betty's demand for computer games, are interesting, market demand curves are far more important to economists, as they can be used to predict changes in product price and quantity. Market demand is the sum of individual demands. To calculate market demand, economists simply add together how many units of a product all consumers will purchase at each price. This process is known as **horizontal summation**.

Horizontal summation
Market demand and supply curves are found by adding together how many units of the product will be purchased or supplied at each price.

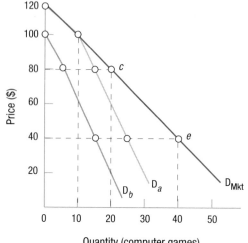

FIGURE 2

Market Demand: Horizontal Summation of Individual Demand Curves

Individual demand curves D_a and D_b are horizontally summed to get market demand, D_{Mkt}. Horizontal summation involves adding together the quantities demanded by each individual at each possible price.

Price	Abe	Betty	Market
$120	0	0	0
100	10	0	10
80	15	5	20
60	20	10	30
40	25	15	40
20	30	20	50

Figure 2 shows an example of horizontal summation of individual demand curves to obtain a market demand curve. Two individual demand curves for Abe and Betty, D_a and D_b, are shown. For simplicity, let's assume they represent the entire market, but recognize this process would work for a larger number of people. Note that at a price of $100 a game, Betty will not buy any, though Abe is willing to buy 10 games at $100. Above $100, therefore, the market demand is equal to Abe's demand. At $100 and below, however, we add both Abe's and Betty's demands at each price to obtain market demand. Thus, at $80, individual demand is 15 for Abe and 5 for Betty, so the market demand is equal to 20 (point c). When the price is $40 a game, Abe buys 25 and Betty buys 15, for a total of 40 games (point e). The heavier curve, labeled D_{Mkt}, represents this market demand; it is a horizontal summation of the two individual demand curves.

This all sounds simple in theory, but in the real world estimating market demand curves is a tricky business, given that many markets contain millions of consumers. Marketing professionals use sophisticated statistical techniques to estimate the market demand for particular goods and services.

The market demand curve shows the maximum amount of a product consumers are willing and able to purchase during a given time period at various prices, all other relevant factors being held constant. Economists use the term **determinants of demand** to refer to these other, nonprice factors that get held constant. This is another example of the use of *ceteris paribus:* holding all other relevant factors constant.

Determinants of demand
Other nonprice factors that affect demand including tastes and preferences, income, prices of related goods, number of buyers, and expectations.

Determinants of Demand

Up to this point, we have discussed only how price affects the quantity demanded, but several other factors also affect demand, including what people like, what their income is, and how much related products cost. More specifically, in addition to the price of the product, there are five determinants of demand: (1) tastes and preferences; (2) income; (3) prices of related goods; (4) the number of buyers; and (5) expectations regarding future prices, income, and product availability.

Tastes and Preferences

How many times have you heard the phrase, "It depends?" This phrase is often a shortened version of "It depends on whether I like it or not." We all have preferences for certain products instead of others, easily perceiving subtle differences in styling and quality. Automobiles, cellular phones, fashions, and music are just a few of the products that are subject to the whims of the consumer.

Businesses devote substantial resources to studying changes in consumer tastes and reacting to them, bringing out new products and casting away outdated items. They also spend considerable sums of money trying to influence consumer tastes and preferences through a barrage of media advertising. It is impossible to predict changes in tastes and preferences perfectly, but businesses use sophisticated market research techniques to try to gauge whether particular advertisements will increase or decrease the demand for their products.

Income

Income is another important factor influencing consumer demand. Generally speaking, as income rises, demands for most goods will likewise increase. Get a raise, and you are more likely to buy a nice car. Products for which demand is positively linked to income—when income rises, demand for the product also rises—are called **normal goods**.

Normal goods
A good where an increase in income results in rising demand.

But there are also some products for which demand declines as income rises. Economists call these products **inferior goods**. As your income grows, for instance, your consumption of public transportation will likely fall since you will probably own a car. Similarly, when you graduate from college and your income rises, your consumption of ramen noodles will fall as you begin dining in better restaurants.

Inferior goods
A good where an increase in income results in declining demand.

Prices of Related Goods

Though product price is the most important factor influencing quantity demanded, the prices of related commodities also affect consumer decisions. You may be an avid concert-goer, but with concert ticket prices often topping $50, if your local movie theater drops its ticket price to $5, you will probably end up seeing more movies than concerts. Movies, concerts, plays, and sporting events are good examples of **substitute goods**, since consumers can substitute one for another depending on their respective prices.

Substitute goods
Goods consumers will substitute for one another depending on their relative prices.

Movies and popcorn, on the other hand, are examples of **complementary goods**. These are goods that are generally consumed together, such that an increase or decrease in the consumption of one will similarly result in an increase or decrease in the consumption of the other—see fewer movies, and your consumption of popcorn will decline. Other complementary goods include cars and gasoline, hot dogs and mustard, and Windows Vista and DRAM (dynamic random access memory).

Complementary goods
Goods that are typically consumed together.

The Number of Buyers

Another factor influencing market demand for a product is the number of potential buyers in the market. Clearly, the more consumers there are who are likely to buy a particular product, the higher its market demand will be. As our average life span steadily rises, the demands for medical services, rest homes, and retirement communities will likewise increase.

Expectations about Future Prices, Incomes, and Product Availability

The final factor influencing demand involves consumer expectations. If consumers expect shortages of certain products or increases in their prices in the near future, they tend to rush out and buy these products immediately, thereby increasing the present demand for the products. During the Florida hurricane season, when a large storm forms and begins moving toward the coast, the demands for plywood, nails, water, and batteries quickly rise in Florida.

The expectation of a rise in income, meanwhile, can lead consumers to take advantage of credit to increase their present consumption. Department stores, electronics shops, and furniture stores often run "no payments until next year" sales designed to attract consumers who want to "buy now, pay later." These consumers expect to have more money later, when they can pay, so they go ahead and buy what they want now, thereby increasing the present demand for the sale items.

To cite one more example, when mortgage interest rates hit rock bottom in late 2001 and 2002, many potential homeowners decided to buy before rates went back up, thus increasing the demand for new construction. This increase in home purchases has been credited with making the 2001–02 recession a relatively mild one. It also left many apartments vacant, resulting in great deals for new renters.

Changes in Demand Versus Changes in Quantity Demanded

When the price of a product rises, consumers simply buy fewer units of that product. This is a movement along an existing demand curve. However, when one or more of the determinants change, the entire demand curve is altered. Now, at any given price consumers are willing to purchase more or less depending on the nature of the change. This section focuses on this important distinction between a change in demand versus a change in quantity demanded.

Changes in Demand

Change in demand
Occurs when one or more of the determinants of demand changes, shown as a shift in the entire demand curve.

Changes in demand occur whenever one or more of the determinants of demand change and demand curves shift. When demand changes, the demand curve shifts either to the right or to the left. Let us look at each shift in turn.

Demand increases when the entire demand curve shifts to the right. At all prices, consumers are willing to purchase more of the product in question. We can see this with each of the determinants of demand. Changes in consumer preferences will change demand. Consumer preferences can be changed through advertising. Another way to increase demand is to tie a product in with another, more popular product. Walt Disney's animated feature films are often marketed along with stuffed animals, books, computer games, and CDs. These products sell well because young movie fans want to purchase everything associated with their favorite movies. Panel A of Figure 3 shows how demand increases for a computer game when it gets tied in with a movie; the demand curve shifts from D_0 to D_1. Notice that more of these "tied-in" computer games will be purchased at all prices along D_1 as compared to D_0.

FIGURE 3

Changes in Demand Versus Change in Quantity Demanded

A shift in the demand curve from D_0 to D_1 in Panel A indicates an *increase in demand* since consumers will buy more of the product at each price. A shift from D_0 to D_2 reflects a decrease in demand. A movement along D_0 from point *a* to point *c* in Panel B indicates an *increase in quantity demanded;* this type of movement can only be caused by a change in the price of the product.

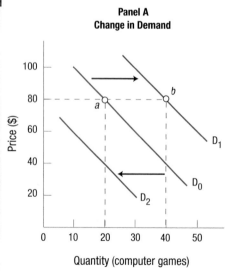

Panel A
Change in Demand

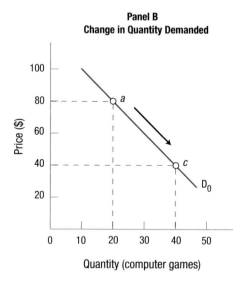

Panel B
Change in Quantity Demanded

Another cause of an increase in demand is an increase in consumer income. For most products (at least for normal goods), people are inclined to buy more of them as their incomes rise. Thus, for these products, a rise in consumer income will cause an increase in demand. We also know that expectations of future price hikes cause demand to grow, shifting the demand curve to the right, and the presence of more buyers in the market will increase demand.

Now let us look at a decrease in demand, when the entire demand curve shifts to the left. At all prices, consumers are willing to purchase less of the product in question. A drop in consumer income will normally be associated with a decline in demand (the demand curve shifts to the left). This decrease in demand is shown in Panel A of Figure 3 as the demand curve shifting from D_0 to D_2. A decrease in demand can also arise from variations in the price or availability of related products. The advent of digital satellite television has made an amazingly broad range of programming available to homes. The demand for cable television will undoubtedly decline as many homes decide to shift to digital satellite systems. Current demand shrinks if prices are expected to fall in the near future, if the number of buyers falls, or if the price of a complementary product rises. All of these will shrink demand, resulting in a shift in the demand curve to the left.

Changes in Quantity Demanded

Whereas a change in demand can be brought about by many different factors, a **change in quantity demanded** can be caused by only one thing: *a change in product price.* This is shown in Panel B of Figure 3 as a reduction in price from $80 to $40, resulting in sales (quantity demanded) increasing from 20 to 40 games annually. This distinction between a change in demand and a change in quantity demanded is important. Reducing price to increase sales is different from spending a few million dollars on Super Bowl advertising to increase sales at all prices!

These concepts are so important that a quick summary is in order. As Figure 3 illustrates, given the initial demand D_0, increasing sales from 20 to 40 games can occur in either of two ways. First, changing a determinant (say, increasing advertising) could shift the demand curve to D_1 in Panel A so that 40 games would be sold at $80 (point *b*). Alternatively, 40 games could be sold in Panel B by reducing price to $40 (point *c*). Selling more by increasing advertising causes an increase in demand, or a shift in the whole demand curve that brings about a movement from point *a* to point *b* in Panel A. Simply reducing the price, on the other hand, causes an increase in quantity demanded, or a movement along the existing demand curve, D_0, from point *a* to point *c* in Panel B.

Change in quantity demanded
Occurs when the price of the product changes, and is shown as a movement along an existing demand curve.

REVIEW

- Demand refers to the quantity of products people are willing and able to purchase at various prices during some specific time period, all other relevant factors being held constant.
- Price and quantity demanded have an inverse (negative) relation: As price rises, consumers buy fewer units; as price falls, consumers buy more units. This inverse relation is known as the law of demand. It is depicted as a downward-sloping (from left to right) demand curve.
- To find market demand curves, simply horizontally sum all of the individual demand curves.

- Demand curves shift when one or more of the determinants of demand change.
- The determinants of demand are consumer tastes and preferences, income, prices of substitutes and complements, the number of buyers in a market, and expectations about future prices, incomes, and product availability.
- A shift of a demand curve is a *change in demand.* An increase in demand is a shift to the right. A decrease in demand is a shift to the left.
- A *change in quantity demanded* occurs only when the price of a product changes, leading consumers to adjust their purchases along the existing demand curve.

QUESTIONS

Sales of hybrid cars are on the rise. The Toyota Prius, while priced above comparable gasoline-only cars, is selling well. Other manufacturers are adding hybrids to their lines as well. What has been the cause of the rising sales of hybrids? Is this an increase in demand or an increase in quantity demanded?

Answers to the Checkpoint questions can be found at the end of this chapter.

Supply

As mentioned earlier, the analysis of a market economy rests on two foundations: supply and demand. So far, we've covered the demand side of the market. The present section focuses on the decisions businesses make regarding production numbers and sales. These decisions cause variations in product supply.

The Relationship between Quantity Supplied and Price

Supply
The maximum amount of a product that sellers are willing and able to provide for sale over some time period at various prices, holding all other relevant factors constant (the *ceteris paribus* condition).

Supply is the maximum amount of a product that producers are willing and able to offer for sale at various prices, all other relevant factors being held constant. The quantity supplied will vary according to the price of the product.

What explains this relationship? As we saw in the previous chapter, businesses inevitably encounter rising opportunity costs as they attempt to produce more and more of a product. This is due in part to diminishing returns from available resources, and in part to the fact that, when producers increase production, they must either have existing workers put in overtime hours (at a higher hourly pay rate) or hire additional workers away from other industries (again at premium pay).

Producing more units, therefore, makes it more expensive for producers to produce each individual unit. These increasing costs give rise to the positive relationship between product price and quantity supplied to the market.

The Law of Supply

Law of supply
Holding all other relevant factors constant, as price increases, quantity supplied will rise, and as price declines, quantity supplied will fall.

Unfortunately for producers, they can rarely charge whatever they would like for their products; they must charge whatever the market will permit. But producers can decide how much of their product to produce and offer for sale. The **law of supply** states that higher prices will lead producers to offer more of their products for sale during a given period. Conversely, if prices fall, producers will offer fewer products to the market. The explanation is simple: The higher the price, the greater the potential for higher profits and thus the greater the incentive for businesses to produce and sell more products. Also, given the rising opportunity costs associated with increasing production, producers need to charge these higher prices to profitably increase the quantity supplied.

The Supply Curve

Just as demand curves graphically display the law of demand, **supply curves** provide a graphical representation of the law of supply. The supply curve shows the maximum amounts of a product a producer will furnish at various prices during a given period of time. While the demand curve slopes down and to the right, the supply curve slopes up and to the right.[2] This illustrates the positive relationship between price and quantity supplied: the higher the price, the greater the quantity supplied.

Supply curve
Supply schedule information translated to a graph.

Market Supply Curves

As with demand, economists are more interested in market supply than in the supplies offered by individual firms. To compute market supply, you use the same method used to calculate market demand, horizontally summing the supplies of individual producers. A hypothetical market supply curve for computer games is depicted in Figure 4.

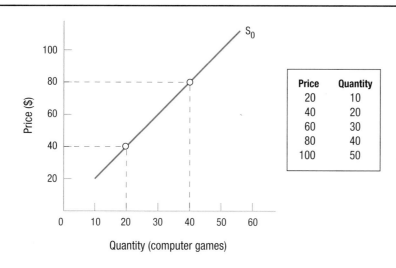

Price	Quantity
20	10
40	20
60	30
80	40
100	50

FIGURE 4

Supply of Computer Games

This supply curve graphs the supply schedule and shows the maximum quantity of computer games that producers will offer for sale over some defined stretch of time. The supply curve is positively sloped, reflecting the law of supply. In other words, as prices rise, quantity supplied increases; as prices fall, quantity supplied falls.

Determinants of Supply

Like demand, several factors other than price help to determine the quantity of a product supplied. Specifically, there are six **determinants of supply**: (1) production technology, (2) costs of resources, (3) prices of other commodities, (4) expectations, (5) the number of sellers (producers) in the market, and (6) taxes and subsidies.

Determinants of supply
Other nonprice factors that affect supply including production technology, costs of resources, prices of other commodities, expectations, number of sellers, and taxes and subsidies.

Production Technology

Technology determines how much output can be produced from given quantities of resources. If a factory's equipment is old and can turn out only 50 units of output per hour, then no matter how many other resources are employed, those 50 units are the most the factory can produce in an hour. If the factory is outfitted with newer, more advanced equipment, however, capable of turning out 100 units per hour, the firm can supply more of its product at the same price as before, or often even at a lower price.

Technology further determines the nature of products that can be supplied to the market. A hundred years ago, the supply of computers on the market was zero,

---

[2]There are some exceptions to positively sloping supply curves. But for our purposes, we will ignore them for now.

because computers did not yet exist. More recent advances in microprocessing and miniaturization brought a wide array of products not available just a few years ago to the market, including MP3 players, auto engines that go 100,000 miles between tune-ups, and constant monitoring insulin pumps that automatically keep a diabetic patient's glucose levels under control.

Costs of Resources

Resource costs clearly affect production costs and supply. If resources such as raw material or labor become more expensive, production costs will rise and supply will be reduced; the reverse is true if resource costs drop. The growing power of microchips along with their falling cost has resulted in cheap and plentiful electronics and microcomputers. Nanotechnology—manufacturing processes that fashion new products through the combination of individual atoms—may soon usher in a whole new generation of inexpensive products made from atoms of sand, an obviously cheap and plentiful resource. Some futurists even suggest that nanotechnology will one day end scarcity as we know it. (What would economists do then?)

On the other hand, if the cost of petroleum goes up, the cost of products using petroleum in their manufacture will go up, leading to the supply being reduced. If labor costs rise because immigration is restricted, this drives up production costs of California vegetables (fewer farm workers) and software in Silicon Valley (fewer software engineers from abroad) and leads to a decrease in supply.

Prices of Other Commodities

Most firms have some flexibility in the portfolio of goods they produce. A vegetable farmer, for example, might be able to grow celery, radishes, or some combination of the two. Given this flexibility, a change in the price of one item may influence the quantity of other items brought to market. If the price of celery should rise, for instance, most farmers will start growing more celery. And since they all have a limited amount of land on which to grow vegetables, this reduces the quantity of radishes they can produce. Hence, in this case, the rise in the price of celery may well cause a reduction in the supply of radishes brought to market.

Expectations

The effects of future expectations on market supplies can be complicated, and it is often difficult to generalize about how future supplies will be affected. When producers expect the prices of their goods to rise in the near future, they may react by increasing production immediately, causing current supply to increase. Yet, expectations of price cuts can also temporarily increase the supply of goods on the market as producers try to sell off their inventories before the price cuts hit. In this case, it is only over the long term that price reductions result in supply reductions, as we would expect.

Number of Sellers

Everything else being held constant, if the number of sellers in a particular market increases, the market supply of their product increases. It is no great mystery why: 10 shoemakers can produce more shoes in a given period than five shoemakers.

Taxes and Subsidies

To business, taxes and subsidies are costs. An increase in taxes (property, excise, or other fees) will reduce supply. Subsidies are the opposite of taxes. If the government subsidizes the production of a product, supply will rise. A luxury tax on power boats in the 1990s reduced supply (the tax was the equivalent of an increase in production costs), while today's subsidies to ethanol producers are expanding production.

Changes in Supply Versus Changes in Quantity Supplied

A **change in supply** results from a change in one or more of the determinants of supply; it causes the entire supply curve to shift. An increase in supply of a product, perhaps because advancing technology has made it cheaper to produce, means that more of the commodity will be offered for sale at every price. This causes the supply curve to shift to the right, as illustrated in Panel A of Figure 5 by the shift from S_0 to S_1. A decrease in supply, conversely, shifts the supply curve to the left, since fewer units of the product are offered at every price. Such a decrease in supply is here represented by the shift from S_0 to S_2.

Change in supply
Occurs when one or more of the determinants of supply change, shown as a shift in the entire supply curve.

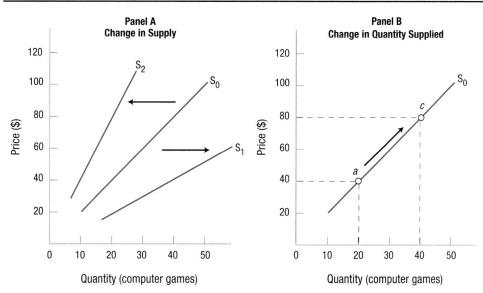

Panel A
Change in Supply

Panel B
Change in Quantity Supplied

FIGURE 5

Changes in Supply Versus Changes in Quantity Supplied

A shift in the supply curve from S_0 to S_1 in Panel A indicates an *increase in supply* since businesses are willing to offer more of the product to consumers at every price. A shift from S_0 to S_2 reflects a decrease in supply. A movement along S_0 from point *a* to point *c* in Panel B represents an *increase in quantity supplied;* it results from an increase in the product's market price from \$40 to \$80.

A change in supply involves a shift of the entire supply curve. In contrast, the supply curve does not move when there is a **change in quantity supplied**. Only a change in the price of a product can cause a change in the quantity supplied; hence, it involves a movement along an existing supply curve rather than a shift to an entirely different curve. In Panel B of Figure 5, for instance, an increase in price from \$40 to \$80 results in an increase in quantity supplied from 20 to 40 games, represented by the movement from point *a* to point *c* along S_0.

Change in quantity supplied
Occurs when the price of the product changes, and is shown as a movement along an existing supply curve.

In summary, a change in supply is represented in Panel A by the shift from S_0 to S_1 or S_2, and this involves a shift in the entire supply curve. A change in quantity supplied is shown in Panel B and is a movement along an existing supply curve caused by a change in price of the product.

As on the demand side, this distinction between change in supply and change in quantity supplied is crucial. It means that when a product's price changes, only quantity supplied changes—the supply curve does not move.

Checkpoint

Supply

REVIEW

■ Supply is the quantity of a product producers are willing and able to put on the market at various prices, all other relevant factors being held constant.

- The law of supply reflects the positive relationship between price and quantity supplied: the higher the market price, the more goods supplied, and the lower the market price, the fewer goods supplied.
- As with demand, market supply is arrived at by horizontally summing the individual supplies of all of the firms in the market.
- A change in supply occurs when one or more of the determinants of supply change.
- The determinants of supply are production technology, the cost of resources, prices of other commodities, expectations, the numbers of sellers or producers in the market, and taxes and subsidies.
- A *change in supply* is a shift in the supply curve. A shift to the right reflects an increase in supply, while a shift to the left represents a decrease in supply.
- A *change in quantity supplied* is only caused by a change in the price of the product; it results in a movement along the existing supply curve.

QUESTION

What has been the impact of the iPod, iTunes, and MP3 players in general on high-end stereo equipment production?

Answers to the Checkpoint question can be found at the end of this chapter.

Market Equilibrium

Before considering the concept of market equilibrium, let's take a quick look back at what we've covered so far. Demand and supply are both relationships between the price and quantity of some product over a given period of time, all other determinants being held constant. The quantity of a product supplied or demanded changes only when the product's price changes. Accordingly, changes in quantity supplied and quantity demanded cause movements along supply curves and demand curves, respectively. When one or more of the determinants of supply or demand changes, however, the curves themselves shift. This leads to more or less of the product being supplied or demanded at the current price. A summary of how the determinants impact both supply and demand is shown in Figure 6. You will find this a good reference when solving problems where supply and demand change.

Supply and demand together determine the prices and quantities of goods bought and sold. Neither factor alone is sufficient to determine price and quantity; it is through their interaction that supply and demand do their work, just as two blades of a scissors are required to cut paper.

Equilibrium
Market forces are in balance where the quantities demanded by consumers just equal quantities supplied by producers.

Equilibrium price
Market equilibrium price is the price that results when quantity demanded is just equal to quantity supplied.

Equilibrium quantity
Market equilibrium quantity is the output that results when quantity demanded is just equal to quantity supplied.

A market will determine the price at which the quantity of a product demanded is equal to the quantity supplied. At this price, the market is said to be cleared or to be in **equilibrium**, meaning the amount of the product that consumers are willing and able to purchase is matched exactly by the amount that producers are willing and able to sell. This is the **equilibrium price** and the **equilibrium quantity**. The equilibrium price is also called the market-clearing price.

Figure 7 puts together Figures 2 and 4, showing the market supply and demand for computer games. It illustrates how supply and demand interact to determine equilibrium price and quantity. Clearly, the quantities demanded and supplied equal one another only where the supply and demand curves cross, at point *e*. Alternatively, you can see this in the table that is part of the figure: Quantity demanded and quantity supplied are the same at only one particular point. At $60 a game, sellers are willing to provide exactly the same quantity as consumers would like to

FIGURE 6

Changes in Demand and
Supply and Their
Determinants

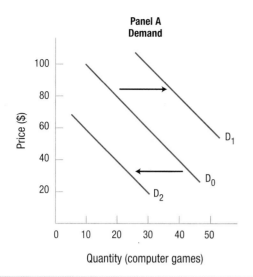

Panel A
Demand

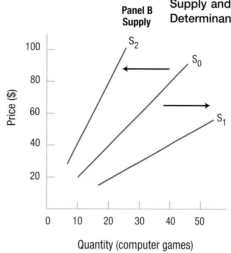

Panel B
Supply

Determinants of Demand		Determinants of Supply	
Decrease in Demand	**Increase in Demand**	**Decrease in Supply**	**Increase in Supply**
Tastes and preferences decline (less advertising, out of fashion).	Tastes and preferences grow (more advertising, fad).	Technology harms productivity (unusual).	Technology improves productivity (production robots in factories increase productivity and supply).
Income falls (economy is in a recession).	Income rises (economy is booming).	Resource costs rise (tough collective bargaining by unions could lead to higher labor costs and reduce supply).	Resource costs fall (large discoveries of natural resources such as oil, natural gas, would reduce world prices, increasing supply of products using these resources).
Price of substitute falls (price of tea falls, coffee demand declines). Price of complement rises (price of gasoline rises, demand for big SUVs drops).	Price of substitute rises (chicken prices rise, demand for beef increases). Price of complement falls (price of DVD players falls, demand for DVD movies increases).	Price of a production substitute rises (cucumber prices rise, reducing the supply of radishes as more cucumbers are planted).	Price of a production substitute falls (price of apples falls, landowners plant grapes instead and eventually the supply of wine rises).
Number of buyers falls.	Number of buyers grows.	Expectation of a rise in future price of product (unsettled world conditions lead to expectations that gold will jump in price, which may lead to a withholding of gold from the market, reducing current supply).	Falling future price expectations for product (if beef prices are expected to fall, producers may sell more cattle now).
Expecting future glut; expected surplus in future leads to lower prices so consumers hold off buying now (some consumers wait for after Christmas sales of unsold—surplus—merchandise).	Expecting future shortages; leads to stocking up now to avoid higher prices in future (predicted gasoline shortages lead to filling of tanks now—an increase in current demand).	Decreasing number of sellers	Rising number of sellers
		Increase in taxes or reduction in subsidies (increasing taxes on cigarettes or reducing subsidies for ethanol will reduce supplies of both products).	Decrease in taxes or an increase in subsidies (reductions in excise taxes on luxury vehicles and increases in subsidies to education will increase the supply of both).

FIGURE 7

Equilibrium Price and Quantity of Computer Games

Market equilibrium is achieved when quantity demanded and quantity supplied are equal. In this graph, that equilibrium occurs at point e, at an equilibrium price of $60 and an equilibrium output of 30. If the market price is above equilibrium ($80), a surplus of 20 computer games will result ($b - a$), automatically driving the price back down to $60. When the market price is too low ($40), a shortage of 20 computer games will result ($d - c$), and businesses will raise their offering prices until equilibrium is again restored.

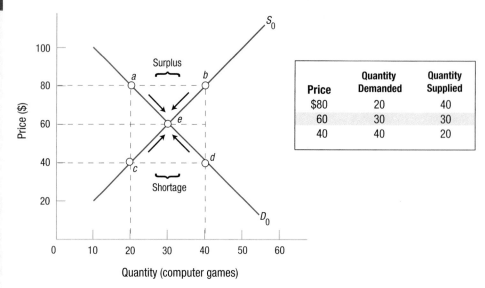

Price	Quantity Demanded	Quantity Supplied
$80	20	40
60	30	30
40	40	20

Surplus
Occurs when the price is above market equilibrium, and quantity supplied exceeds quantity demanded.

Shortage
Occurs when the price is below market equilibrium, and quantity demanded exceeds quantity supplied.

purchase. Hence, at this price, the market clears, since buyers and sellers both want to transact the same number of units.

The beauty of a market is that it automatically works to establish the equilibrium price and quantity, without any guidance from anyone. To see how this happens, let us assume that computer games are initially priced at $80, a price above their equilibrium price. As we can see by comparing points a and b, sellers are willing to supply more games at this price than consumers are willing to buy. Economists characterize such a situation as one of excess supply, or **surplus**. In this case, at $80, sellers supply 40 games to the market (point b), yet buyers want to purchase only 20 (point a). This leaves an excess of 20 games overhanging the market; these unsold games ultimately become surplus inventories.

Here is where the market kicks in to restore equilibrium. As inventories rise, most firms will cut production. Some firms, moreover, will start reducing their prices to increase sales. Other firms must then cut their own prices to remain competitive. This process will continue, with firms cutting their prices and production, until most firms have managed to exhaust their surplus inventories. This happens when prices reach $60 and quantity supplied equals 30, since consumers are once again willing to buy up the entire quantity supplied at this price, and the market is restored to equilibrium.

In general, therefore, when prices are set too high, surpluses result, which drive prices back down to their equilibrium levels. If, conversely, a price is initially set too low, say at $40, a **shortage** results. In this case, buyers want to purchase 40 games (point d), but sellers are only providing 20 (point c), creating a shortage of 20 games. Because consumers are willing to pay more than $40 to get hold of the few games available on the market, they will start bidding up the price of computer games. Sensing an opportunity to make some money, firms will start raising their prices and increasing production, once again until equilibrium is restored. Hence, in general, excess demand causes firms to raise prices and increase production.

When there is a shortage in a market, economists speak of a tight market or a seller's market. Under these conditions, producers have no difficulty selling off all their output. When a surplus of goods floods the market, this gives rise to a buyer's market, since buyers can buy all the goods they want at attractive prices.

We have now seen how changing prices naturally work to clear up shortages and surpluses, thereby returning markets to equilibrium. Some markets, once disturbed, will return to equilibrium quickly. Examples include the stock, bond, and money mar-

Alfred Marshall (1842–1924)

*b*ritish economist Alfred Marshall is considered the father of the modern theory of supply and demand—price and output are determined by both supply and demand. He noted that the two go together like the blades of a scissors that cross at equilibrium.

He assumed that changes in quantity demanded were only affected by changes in price, and that all other factors remained constant. Marshall also is credited with developing the ideas of the laws of demand and supply, and the concepts of price elasticity of demand, consumer surplus, and producer surplus—concepts we will study in the next two chapters.

In 1890, he published *Principles of Economics* at age 48. In it he introduced many new ideas for the first time, but as Ray Canterbery noted, "without any suggestion that they are novel or remarkable."[3] During his lifetime, the book went through eight editions. In hopes of appealing to the general populace, Marshall buried his diagrams in footnotes. And, although he is credited with many economic theories, he would always clarify them with various exceptions and qualifications. He expected future economists to flesh out his ideas.

John Maynard Keynes, the most influential economist of the last century and Marshall's student, wrote a 70-page, 20,000-word memorial to Marshall published in the *Economic Journal,* 3 months after his death in 1924.[4]

Marshall was an enormous figure in economics, but a disappointment to his father, because he went to study mathematics and physics at St. John's College, Cambridge, instead of joining the clergy, as was expected. But after long walks through the poorest sections of several European cities and seeing their horrible conditions, he decided to focus his attention on political economy. More than anyone else, Marshall is given credit for establishing economics as a discipline of study.

kets, where trading is nearly instantaneous and extensive information abounds. Other markets react very slowly. Consider the labor market, for instance. For various psychological reasons, most people have an inflated idea of their worth to both current and future employers. It is only after an extended bout of unemployment, therefore,

---

[3]E. Ray Canterbery, *A Brief History of Economics: Artful Approaches to the Dismal Science* (New Jersey: World Scientific), 2001, p. 139.
[4]Robert Skidelsky, *John Maynard Keynes: Volume Two The Economist as Saviour 1920–1937* (New York: Penguin), 1992, p. 181.

that many people will face reality and accept a position at a salary lower than their previous job. Similarly, real estate markets can be slow to adjust since sellers will often refuse to accept a price below what they are asking for, until the lack of sales over time convinces sellers to adjust the price downward.

These automatic market adjustments can make some buyers and sellers feel uncomfortable: It seems as if prices and quantities are being set by forces beyond anyone's control. In fact, this phenomenon is precisely what makes market economies function so efficiently. Without anyone needing to be in control, prices and quantities will naturally gravitate toward equilibrium levels. Adam Smith was so impressed by the workings of the market that he suggested it is almost as if an "invisible hand" guides the market to equilibrium.

Given the self-correcting nature of the market, long-term shortages or surpluses are almost always the result of government intervention. We will discuss such instances in the next chapter. First, however, we turn to a discussion of how the market responds to changes in supply and demand, or to shifts of the supply and demand curves.

Moving to a New Equilibrium: Changes in Supply and Demand

Once a market is in equilibrium and the forces of supply and demand balance one another out, the market will remain there unless an external factor changes. But when the supply curve or demand curve shifts (some determinant changes), equilibrium also shifts, resulting in a new equilibrium price and/or output. The ability to predict new equilibrium points is one of the most useful aspects of supply and demand analysis.

Predicting the New Equilibrium When One Curve Shifts

When only supply or only demand changes, the change in equilibrium price and equilibrium output can be predicted. We begin with changes in supply.

Changes in Supply. Figure 8 shows what happens when supply changes. Equilibrium initially is at point e, with equilibrium price and quantity at P_0 and Q_0, respectively. But let us assume a rise in wages or the bankruptcy of a key business in the market (the number of sellers declines) causes a decrease in supply. When supply

---

Equilibrium Price, Output, and Shifts in Supply

When supply alone shifts, the effects on both equilibrium price and output can be predicted. When supply grows (S_0 to S_1), equilibrium price will fall and output will rise. When supply declines (S_0 to S_2), the opposite will happen: Equilibrium price will rise and output will fall.

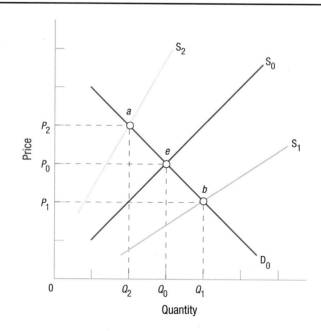

declines (the supply curve shifts from S_0 to S_2), equilibrium price rises to P_2, while equilibrium output falls to Q_2 (point a).

If, on the other hand, supply increases (the supply curve shifts from S_0 to S_1), equilibrium price falls to P_1, while equilibrium output rises to Q_1 (point b). This is what has happened in the electronics industry: Declining production costs have resulted in more electronic products being sold at lower prices.

Changes in Demand. The effects of demand changes are shown in Figure 9. Again, equilibrium is initially at point e, with equilibrium price and quantity at P_0 and Q_0, respectively. But let us assume the economy then enters a recession and incomes sink, or perhaps the price of some complementary good soars; in either case, demand falls. As demand declines (the demand curve shifts from D_0 to D_2), equilibrium price falls to P_2, while equilibrium output falls to Q_2 (point a).

During the same recession just described, the demand for inferior goods (beans and baloney) will rise, as declining incomes force people to switch to cheaper substitutes. For these products, as demand increases (shifting the demand curve from D_0 to D_1), equilibrium price rises to P_1, and equilibrium output grows to Q_1 (point b).

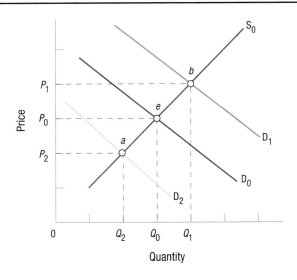

FIGURE 9

Equilibrium Price, Output, and Shifts in Demand

When demand alone changes, the effects on both equilibrium price and output can again be determined. When demand grows (D_0 to D_1), both price and output rise. Conversely, when demand falls (D_0 to D_2), both price and output fall.

Predicting the New Equilibrium When Both Curves Shift

When both supply and demand change, things get tricky. We can predict what will happen with price, in some cases, and output, in other cases, but not what will happen with both.

When Both Curves Shift in the Same Direction. Figure 10 on the next page portrays an increase in both demand and supply. Consider the market for corn. If government subsidizes the production of ethanol, demand for corn will increase. If bioengineering results in a new corn hybrid that uses less fertilizer and generates 50% higher yields, supply will increase. When demand increases from D_0 to D_1 and supply increases from S_0 to S_1, output clearly grows to Q_1. What happens to the price of corn, however, is not so clear. If demand grows relatively more than supply (Panel A), the new equilibrium price will be higher. Conversely, if demand grows relatively less than supply does (Panel C), the new equilibrium price will be lower.

In Figure 11 on the next page, supply and demand have declined to S_2 and D_2, respectively. If this is the cellular phone market, and cell phone use is shown to have serious detrimental health effects if used more than 10 minutes a day, the demand will decline. And if microchip production confronts the end of Moore's law

FIGURE 10

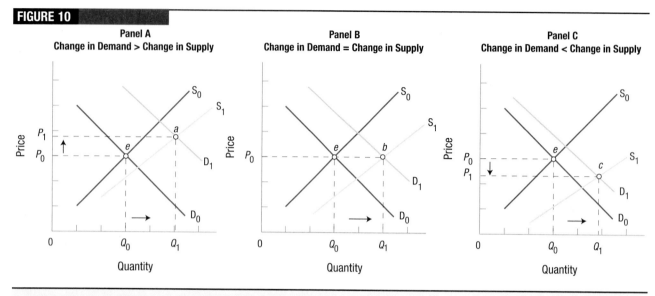

Panel A
Change in Demand > Change in Supply

Panel B
Change in Demand = Change in Supply

Panel C
Change in Demand < Change in Supply

Increase in Supply, Increase in Demand, and Equilibrium

When both demand and supply increase, output will clearly rise. What will happen to the equilibrium price is uncertain, however. If demand grows relatively more than supply (Panel A), price will rise, but if supply grows relatively more than demand (Panel C), price will fall.

(speed of micro chips doubles every 18 months at lower costs) and costs rise substantially, supply will decline. In this case, we can see that output will fall to Q_2. Again, however, what happens to price is ambiguous. If demand declines more than supply, price will fall. Alternatively, if supply declines more than demand, the new equilibrium price will be higher.

Thus, when supply and demand decline or rise together, we can forecast what will happen to output. In such cases, however, the change in price cannot be pre-

FIGURE 11

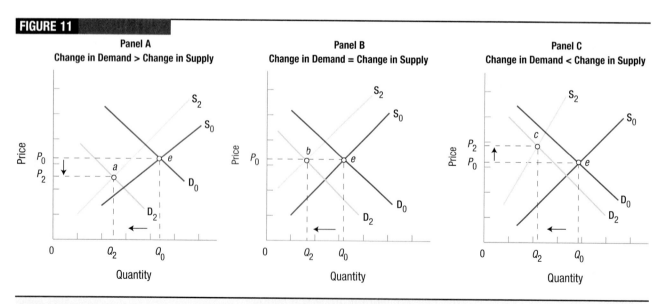

Panel A
Change in Demand > Change in Supply

Panel B
Change in Demand = Change in Supply

Panel C
Change in Demand < Change in Supply

Decrease in Supply, Decrease in Demand, and Equilibrium

When both demand and supply decrease, output will clearly fall, but what happens to the new equilibrium price is again uncertain. If demand falls relatively more than supply, the new equilibrium price will fall, and vice versa.

dicted without further information regarding the relative magnitudes of the changes in supply and demand.

When the Curves Shift in Opposite Directions. Figure 12 illustrates the case of rising demand and decreasing supply. This might represent the market for General Motors' cars if China offers high prices and absorbs most of the world's steel output for its own development efforts, increasing the price of a major input into GM's cars. Not to be deterred, GM develops a plug-in hybrid that averages over 75 miles per gallon and demand rises substantially. Demand increases to D_1 and supply decreases to S_2, thus clearly raising price to P_2. Still, what happens to equilibrium sales is ambiguous. If demand grows more than supply declines (Panel A), the new equilibrium output will be higher than before. But if supply declines more than demand grows (Panel C), the new equilibrium output will be lower.

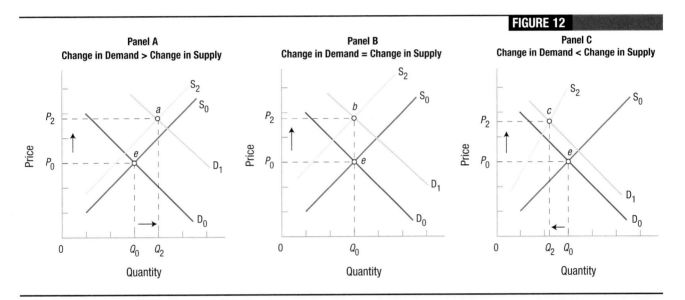

FIGURE 12

Panel A
Change in Demand > Change in Supply

Panel B
Change in Demand = Change in Supply

Panel C
Change in Demand < Change in Supply

Decrease in Supply, Increase in Demand, and Equilibrium
If demand grows and supply falls, equilibrium price will clearly rise, but now what happens to equilibrium output is indeterminate. If supply declines relatively more than demand grows, output will fall. If supply declines less than demand grows, output will rise.

In Figure 13 on the next page, we have the opposite case, where demand declines to D_2 and supply rises to S_1. This might represent the market for tape players and recorders and their decline in demand in the digital age. However, costs to manufacture these players have fallen given changing production technology. In this case, we can see that price will fall to P_2, but again, what happens with output is uncertain. If demand declines more than supply grows (Panel A), output will fall. Conversely, if supply grows more than demand falls (Panel C), the new equilibrium output will rise.

Thus, when supply and demand move in opposite directions, the resulting change in price can be predicted. Forecasting the accompanying change in output is impossible, however, without additional information concerning the relative strength of the changes in supply and demand.

Summarizing Shifts and Equilibrium

With these results in hand, a summary of what happens when both curves shift is in order. When demand and supply both increase or both decrease together (whenever they move in the same direction), the change in sales or output can be predicted. Specifically, when both curves rise, sales rise, and when both curves fall,

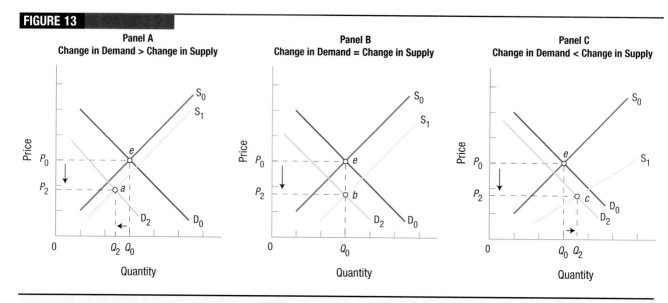

FIGURE 13

Increase in Supply, Decrease in Demand, and Equilibrium

When demand falls and supply grows, the new equilibrium price will clearly be lower than before, but the effect on output cannot be determined without further information. If supply grows relatively more than demand falls, output will rise. If supply grows relatively less than demand falls, output will fall.

sales fall. In neither case can we know what happens to price, however, without further information.

When supply and demand move in opposite directions, by contrast, the change in price can be forecasted. Specifically, when demand rises but supply falls—people want more of something that has become dearer—price will rise. Alternately, when demand falls but supply increases—there is more on the market of some good that people are less interested in—price will fall. Still, in both of these cases what happens to sales or output remains ambiguous without further information.

These results are summarized in Table 1. Where the table indicates that equilibrium price or quantity is indeterminate, it means that the change will depend on

Table 1	The Effect of Changes in Demand or Supply on Equilibrium Prices and Quantities			
Change in Demand	**Change in Supply**	**Change in Equilibrium Price**	**Change in Equilibrium Quantity**	**Figure Where Result is Shown**
No change	Increase	Decrease	Increase	8
No change	Decrease	Increase	Decrease	8
Increase	No change	Increase	Increase	9
Decrease	No change	Decrease	Decrease	9
Increase	Increase	Indeterminate	Increase	10
Decrease	Decrease	Indeterminate	Decrease	11
Increase	Decrease	Increase	Indeterminate	12
Decrease	Increase	Decrease	Indeterminate	13

the relative magnitudes of the shifts in supply or demand, and price or quantity can rise, fall, or remain the same. The last column in the table shows the figure where this result is shown.

Market Equilibrium

REVIEW

- Together, supply and demand determine market equilibrium.
- Equilibrium occurs when quantity supplied exactly equals quantity demanded.
- The equilibrium price is also called the market-clearing price.
- When supply and demand change, equilibrium price and output change.
- When only one curve shifts, the resulting changes in equilibrium price and quantity can be predicted.
- When both curves shift, we can predict the change in equilibrium price in some cases or the change in equilibrium quantity in others, but never both. We have to determine the relative magnitudes of the shifts before we can predict both equilibrium price and quantity.

QUESTIONS

As China and India (both with huge populations and rapidly growing economies) continue to develop, what do you think will happen to their demand for energy and specifically oil? What will suppliers of oil do in the face of this demand? Will this have an impact on world energy (oil) prices? What sort of policies or events could alter your forecast about the future price of oil?

Answers to the Checkpoint questions can be found at the end of this chapter.

Putting Supply and Demand to Work

Excess Grape Supply and Two-Buck Chuck

Let's apply these concepts to two short examples. The great California wines of the 1990s put California vineyards on the map. Demand, prices, and exports grew rapidly. Overplanting of new grape vines was a result. Driving along Interstate 5 or Highway 101 north of Los Angeles, grape vineyards extend as far as the eye can see, and most were planted in the mid to late 1990s. The 2001 recession reduced the demand for California wine, and a rising dollar made imported wine relatively cheaper. The result was a sharp drop in demand for California wine and a huge surplus of grapes.

Bronco Wine Company President Fred Franzia made an exclusive deal with Trader Joe's (an unusual supermarket that features exotic food and wine products), bought the excess grapes at distressed prices, and with his modern plant produced inexpensive wine under the Charles Shaw label. Selling for $1.99 a bottle, Two-Buck Chuck, as it is known, is available in chardonnay, merlot, cabernet sauvignon, shiraz, and sauvignon blanc. Consumers have flocked to Trader Joe's and literally haul cases of wine out by the carload. Today, Two-Buck Chuck sells well over a million cases a month. This is not rotgut: the 2002 shiraz beat out 2,300 other wines to win a double gold medal at the 28th Annual International Eastern Wine Competition in 2004.

Donald Gruener

Two-Buck Chuck was such a hit that other supermarkets were forced to offer their own discount wines. This good, low-priced wine has had the effect of opening up markets. As Figure 14 illustrates, people who previously avoided wine because of the cost have begun drinking more (demand curves do slope down and to the right). As *The Economist* has noted, the entire industry may benefit because "wine drinkers who start off drinking plonk often graduate to upmarket varieties."[5]

FIGURE 14

The Market for Wine

The glut of grapes and the subsequent reduction in grape prices caused the supply of wine to increase and the price to fall.

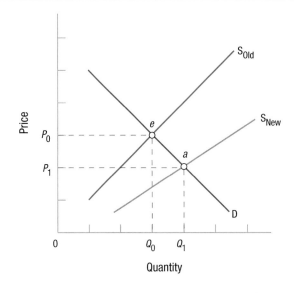

Trek Bicycles and Lance Armstrong

The second example deals with a growing demand but no change in supply. When Lance Armstrong won his seventh Tour de France cycling championship in July 2005, he rode a bicycle made by Trek of the United States.[6] So, on the demand side, we can expect demand for the victor's brand of bicycles to go up. This in fact happened, in both the United States and Europe. On the supply side, U.S. bicycle manufacturers such as Trek and Cannondale were willing to increase output, as shown in Figure 15 (note that the supply curve didn't change, only quantity supplied). This process worked well in the United States, but proved tougher in Europe, not so much in the actual production of the bicycles but in getting stores to stock them. Up until a few years ago, racing bicycles were almost exclusively made by European companies.

Using our supply and demand analysis, we see that demand increased. Since no determinant of supply changed, we know that output will increase, and prices for Trek bicycles will rise. Our supply and demand analysis gives us a useful framework for predicting how market participants will act, and what the resulting price and output might be.

You now have the fundamental tools of supply and demand analysis. In the next chapter, we will use these tools to analyze markets, policy choices, and government intervention.

---

[5]"California Drinking," *The Economist*, June 7, 2003, p. 56.
[6]See Ian Austen, "U.S. Bike Makers Seek Dominance in Europe," *New York Times*, December 30, 2003, p. W1.

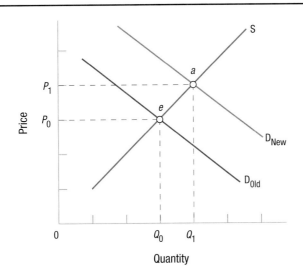

FIGURE 15

The Market for Bicycles

The demand for bicycles rose after Lance Armstrong won his seventh Tour de France, and as expected, prices of Trek bicycles rose.

Key Concepts

Markets, p. 52
Price system, p. 53
Demand, p. 53
Law of demand, p. 54
Demand curve, p. 55
Horizontal summation, p. 55
Determinants of demand, p. 56
Normal goods, p. 57
Inferior goods, p. 57
Substitute goods, p. 57
Complementary goods, p. 57
Change in demand, p. 58

Change in quantity demanded, p. 59
Supply, p. 60
Law of supply, p. 60
Supply curve, p. 61
Determinants of supply, p. 61
Change in supply, p. 63
Change in quantity supplied, p. 63
Equilibrium, p. 64
Equilibrium price, p. 64
Equilibrium quantity, p. 64
Surplus, p. 66
Shortage, p. 66

Chapter Summary

Markets

Markets are institutions that enable buyers and sellers to interact and transact business with one another. Markets differ in geographical location, products offered, and size. Prices contain an incredible amount of information for both buyers and sellers. Through their purchases, consumers signal their willingness to exchange money or other valuables for particular products at particular prices. These signals help businesses to decide what to produce and how much of it to produce. Consequently, the market economy is often called the price system.

Demand

Demand refers to the quantity of products people are willing and able to purchase during some specific time period, all other relevant factors being held constant. Price and quantity demanded stand in a negative (inverse) relationship: as price rises, consumers buy fewer units; and as price falls, consumers buy more units. This inverse relation is known as the law of demand. It is depicted in a downward-sloping demand curve.

Market demand curves are found by horizontally summing individual demand curves. We simply add the total quantities demanded by all consumers for each possible price.

The determinants of demand include (1) consumer tastes and preferences, (2) income, (3) prices of substitutes and complements, (4) the number of buyers in the market, and (5) expectations regarding future prices, incomes, and product availability. Demand changes (the demand curve shifts) when one or more of these determinants change.

A shift of the demand curve implies a change in demand. A shift to the right reflects an increase in demand, whereas a shift to the left represents a decline in demand. These shifts in demand are caused by changes in one or more of the determinants of demand. A change in quantity demanded occurs only when the price of a product changes, leading consumers to adjust their purchases along the existing demand curve.

Supply

Supply is the quantity of a product producers are willing and able to put on the market at various prices, all other relevant factors being held constant. The law of supply reflects the positive relationship between price and quantity supplied: The higher the market price, the more goods supplied; and the lower the market price, the fewer goods supplied. It is depicted in an upward-sloping supply curve. Market supply, as with market demand, is arrived at by horizontally summing the individual supplies of all of the firms in the market.

The six determinants of supply are (1) production technology, (2) the cost of resources, (3) prices of other commodities, (4) expectations, (5) the number of sellers or producers in the market, and (6) taxes and subsidies.

When one or more of the determinants of supply change, a change in supply results, causing a shift in the supply curve. A shift to the right reflects an increase in supply, whereas a shift to the left represents a decline in supply. A change in quantity supplied is only caused by a change in the price of the product; it results in a movement along the existing supply curve. A reduction in price results in a reduction of quantity supplied, whereas a price increase leads to an increase in quantity supplied.

Market Equilibrium

Supply and demand together determine market equilibrium. Equilibrium occurs when quantity demanded and quantity supplied are precisely equal. This means that producers are bringing precisely the quantity of some good to market that consumers wish to purchase, such that the market clears. The price at which equilibrium is reached is called the equilibrium price, or the market-clearing price.

If prices are set too high, surpluses result, which drive prices back down to equilibrium levels. If prices are set too low, a shortage results, which drives prices up until equilibrium is reached.

When supply and demand change (a shift in the curves), equilibrium price and output change. When only one curve shifts, then both resulting changes in equilibrium price and quantity can be predicted. For example, if demand increases, both equilibrium output and price will increase.

When the two curves both shift, the change in equilibrium price can be forecasted in some instances, and the change in equilibrium output in others, but never both. When both curves shift in the same direction, we can predict what will happen to output but not to price. When both curves shift in opposite directions, we can predict what will happen to price but not to output. We need more information on the relative magnitudes of the shifts in both curves before we can predict both equilibrium price and quantity.

Questions and Problems

1. Product prices give consumers and businesses a lot of information besides just the price. What are they?

2. Demand for tickets to sports events such as the Super Bowl has increased. Has supply increased? What does the answer to this tell you about the price of these tickets compared to a few years ago?

3. As the world population ages, the demand for cholesterol drugs will [increase/decrease/remain the same]? Assume there is a positive relationship between aging and cholesterol levels. Is this change a change in demand or a change in quantity demanded?

4. Describe some of the reasons why supply will change. Improved technology typically results in lower prices for most products. Why do you think this is true? Describe the difference between a change in supply and a change in quantity supplied.

5. In 2006 rental car companies often charged more to rent a compact car than an SUV or a luxury vehicle. Why do you think rental companies turned their normal pricing structure on its head?

6. Both individual and market demand curves have negative slopes and reflect the law of demand. What is the difference between the two curves?

7. Describe the determinants of demand. Why are they important?

8.

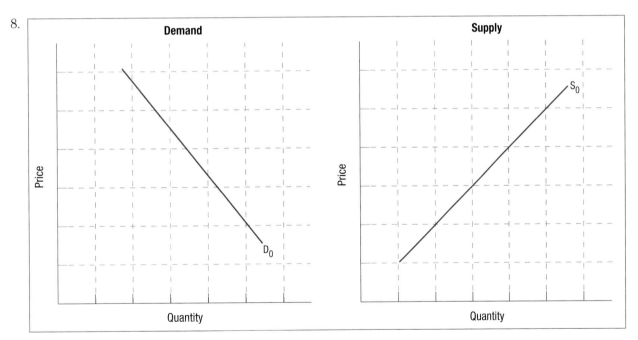

Using the figures above, answer the following questions:
a. On the Demand panel:
   - Show an increase in demand and label it D_1.
   - Show a decrease in demand and label it D_2.
   - Show an increase in quantity demanded.
   - Show a decrease in quantity demanded.
   - What causes demand to change?
   - What causes quantity demanded to change?

b. On the Supply panel:
   - Show an increase in supply and label it S_1.
   - Show a decrease in supply and label it S_2.
   - Show an increase in quantity supplied.
   - Show a decrease in quantity supplied.
   - What causes supply to change?
   - What causes quantity supplied to change?

9. Several medical studies have shown that red wine in moderation is good for the heart. How would such a study affect the public's demand for wine? Would it have an impact on the type of grapes planted in new vineyards?

10. Norrath is a place in the online game EverQuest II. It is a virtual world with roughly 350,000 players "arrayed over worlds that are tethered to dozens of servers." As Rob Walker noted, "EverQuest is filled with half-elves, castles, sword fights and such, and involves a fairly complex internal economy, whose currency is platinum pieces used to buy weapons, food and other goods." This virtual market, however, has led to a real-world market, with real dollars for virtual goods. Players sell weapons, complete characters, and other virtual items on EverQuest's internal market called Station Exchange and on eBay. Common items sell for $10 to $25, while extensive characters or weapons can fetch a thousand dollars or more. (Based on Rob Walker, "The Buying Game: A real market, overseen by a real corporation, selling things that don't really exist," *New York Times Magazine,* October 16, 2005, p. 28.)

    Why would someone buy virtual goods? Does supply and demand play any role in this real market for virtual goods? If there were virtual games similar to EverQuest II where everything is free, would any real markets exist for their virtual goods? How does paying for a virtual product differ from the situation where a buyer could purchase a nice watch for a reasonable price, but decides to buy a luxury brand for 10 to 20 times as much?

11. In December of 2005, the *Wall Street Journal* reported that Clark Foam, a major supplier of polyurethane cores (blanks) for hand-shaped surfboards, closed its plant and went out of business (Peter Sanders and Stephanie Kang, "Wipeout for Key Player in Surfboard Industry," *The Wall Street Journal,* December 8, 2005, p. B1). Clark Foam was the Microsoft of surfboard blank makers, and had been supplying foam blanks to surf shops for over 50 years. Polyurethane blanks, while light and sturdy, contain a toxic chemical, toluene diisocyanate (TDI). Over the last two decades the Environmental Protection Agency has increasingly been restricting the use of TDI. Clark Foam's owner Gordon "Grubby" Clark indicated in a letter to customers that he was tired of fighting environmental regulators, lawsuits over injury to employees, and fire regulations. Surf historian and author of *The Encyclopedia of Surfing,* Matt Warshaw said, "It's the equivalent of removing lumber for the housing industry."
    a. If you owned a retail surfboard shop and read this article in the *Wall Street Journal,* would you change the prices on the existing surfboards you have in the shop? Why or why not?
    b. If the demand for surfboards remains constant over the next few years, what would you expect to see happen on the supply side in this industry?

12. Polysilicon is used to produce computer chips and solar photovoltaics. Currently more polysilicon is used to produce computer chips, but the demand for ultra-pure polysilicon for solar panels is rising. According to a 2006 *Business Week* article (John Carey, "What's Raining on Solar's Parade," *Business Week,* February 6, 2006, p. 78), this has created a shortage, and prices have more than doubled between 2004 and 2006.

a. High oil and energy prices, along with subsidies from U.S. and European governments for solar power, has increased demand, but suppliers are reluctant to build new factories or expand existing facilities, because they fear governments can easily eliminate incentives and at this point they do not know if solar energy is just a fad as one executive suggested, "governments can take away incentives as easily as they put them in place," and asked "is the solar industry real or just a flash in the pan?" Are these legitimate concerns for business?

b. Given the uncertainty associated with building additional production capacity in the polysilicon industry, what might these manufacturers do to reduce the risk?

13. The table below represents the world supply and demand for natural vanilla in thousands of pounds. A large portion of natural vanilla is grown in Madagascar and comes from orchids that require a lot of time to cultivate. The sequence of events described below actually happened, but the numbers have been altered to make the calculations easier (See James Altucher, "Supply, Demand, and Edible Orchids," *Financial Times*, September 20, 2005, p.12). Assume the original supply and demand curves are represented in the table below.

Price ($/pound)	Quantity Demanded (thousands)	Quantity Supplied (thousands)
0	20	0
10	16	6
20	12	12
30	8	18
40	4	24
50	0	30

a. Graph both the supply (S_0) and demand (D_0) curves. What is the current equilibrium price? Label that point *a*.

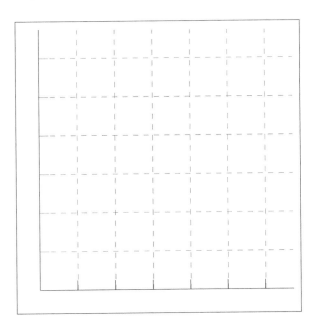

b. Assume that Madagascar is hit by a hurricane (actually occurred in 2000), and the world's supply of vanilla is reduced by 5/6, or 83%. Label the new supply curve (S_1). What will be the new equilibrium price in the market? Label that point *b*.

    c. Now assume that Coca-Cola announces plans to introduce a new "Vanilla Coke," and this increases the demand for natural vanilla by 25%. Label the new demand curve (D_1). What will be the new equilibrium price? Label this new equilibrium point c. Remember that supply of natural vanilla was reduced by the hurricane earlier.

    d. Growing the orchids that produce natural vanilla requires a climate with roughly 80% humidity, and the possible grower countries generally fall within 20° north or south of the equator. A doubling of prices encouraged several other countries (e.g., Uganda and Indonesia) to begin growing orchids or up their current production. Within several years, supply was back to normal (S_0), but by then, synthetic vanilla had replaced 80% of the original demand (D_0). Label this new demand curve (D_2). What is the new equilibrium price and output?

14. Assume initially that the demand and supply for premium coffees (one-pound bags) are in equilibrium. Now assume Starbucks introduces the world to premium blends, and so demand rises substantially. Describe what will happen in this market as it moves to a new equilibrium. If a hard freeze eliminates Brazil's premium coffee crop, what will happen to the price of premium coffee?

15. In late 2006 and early 2007, orange crops in Florida were smaller than expected, and the crop in California was put in a deep freeze by an Arctic cold front. As a result, the production of oranges was severely reduced. In addition, in early 2007, President George W. Bush called for the United States to reduce its gasoline consumption by 20% in the next decade. He proposed an increase in ethanol produced from corn and the stalks and leaves from corn and other grasses. What is the likely impact of these two events on food prices in the United States?

Answers to Checkpoint Questions

CHECKPOINT: MARKETS

The market for financial securities is a huge, well-organized, and regulated market compared to local flea markets. Trillions of dollars change hands each week in the financial markets, and products are standardized.

CHECKPOINT: DEMAND

Rising gasoline prices have caused the demand for hybrids to swell. This is a change in demand.

CHECKPOINT: SUPPLY

Since iPods and other MP3 players are substitutes for high-end stereo equipment, production and sales of high-end stereo equipment have declined.

CHECKPOINT: MARKET EQUILIBRIUM

Demand for both energy and oil will increase. Suppliers of oil will attempt to move up their supply curve and provide more to the market. Since all of the easy (cheap) oil has been found, costs to add to supplies will rise, and oil prices will gradually rise; in the longer term, alternatives will become more attractive, keeping oil prices from rising too rapidly.

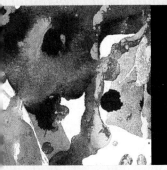

Market Efficiency, Market Failure, and Government Intervention

4

everywhere we look in the world there are markets, from the Tokyo fish markets, where every morning 20,000 flash-frozen tuna weighing 400–500 pounds each are auctioned off in a few hours; to Aalsmeer, Holland, where millions of fresh flowers are flown in from all over the world every day, auctioned off, then shipped to firms in other parts of the world; to Chicago, where billions of dollars of derivative securities and commodities are bought and sold on the futures market daily. Beyond these big markets, moreover, countless smaller markets dot our local landscapes, and many new virtual markets are springing up on the Internet.

Since the Soviet Union collapsed in 1989, markets and the market system have gained an even greater momentum as many countries have begun leaning more heavily on markets to allocate resources, products, and services. In earlier chapters, we saw that every economy faces tradeoffs in the use of its resources to produce various goods and services, as represented graphically by the production possibilities frontier (PPF). The last chapter considered how supply and demand work together to determine the quantities of various products sold and the equilibrium prices consumers must pay for them in a market economy. As we saw, Adam Smith's invisible hand works to ensure that, in a market society, consumers get what they want.

Thus far, the markets we have studied have been stylized versions of competitive markets: They have featured many buyers and sellers, a uniform product, consumers and sellers who have complete information about the market, and few barriers to market entry or exit.

In this chapter, we will consider some of the complexities inherent to most markets. The typical market does not meet all the criteria of a truly competitive market. That does not mean the supply and demand analysis you just learned will not be useful in analyzing economic events. Often, however, you will need to temper your analysis to fit the specific conditions of the markets you study. As we will find, some markets need constraints or rules to ensure that society gets the best results.

This chapter begins by considering the efficiency of the market system. We look at the conditions needed for a market to exist and be efficient. We also present a tool for determining economic efficiency. Efficient markets are rationing devices, ensuring that those who value a product the most are the ones who get it. Prices and profits help to carry out this rationing by serving as important market signals.

Markets rarely live up to our definition of the competitive market ideal. The second section of this chapter discusses markets in light of real-world experience, specifically focusing on market failures, or deviations from conditions of perfect competition. If a market is not competitive, this does not mean it collapses or is no longer a market. It just means that the market fails to contain the mechanisms for allocating resources in the best possible way, from the perspective of the larger society. In this section, we will also consider several of the common solutions to market failures. Some failures require just a minor fix, such as a new regulation or law, but others may require that the government take over and provide products.

In the final section of this chapter, we will consider what happens when markets work efficiently, but government intervenes by using price controls. The two most common examples of government price setting are rent controls (price ceilings) and minimum wage laws (price floors). You will see the price paid by society when government tampers with efficiently working markets.

After studying this chapter you should be able to

- Understand how markets allocate resources.
- Define the conditions needed for markets to be efficient.
- Understand how markets impose discipline on producers and consumers.
- Understand and be able to use the concepts of consumer and producer surplus.
- Understand what market failure is, and when it occurs.
- Describe the different types of market failure.
- Recognize why government may control prices.
- Understand the effects of price ceilings and price floors.
- Recognize that taxes lead to deadweight losses.

Markets and Efficiency

Markets are efficient mechanisms for allocating resources. Just think how much information a government bureaucrat would need to decide how many flat panel HDTVs should be produced, what companies should produce them, and who should get them. When you consider that our country has many millions of people who might want such televisions and several thousand possible suppliers, it becomes clear the likelihood of a lone bureaucrat or agency developing an efficient plan for HDTV production and distribution is extremely small. This was the problem the Soviet Union faced with virtually every good it produced, and it goes a long way toward explaining that nation's economic and political collapse.

The prices and profits characteristic of the market system provide incentives and signals that are nonexistent or seriously flawed in other systems of resource allocation. The old Soviet joke that "They pretend to pay us and we pretend to work" illustrates this problem. But efficient markets do not just spontaneously develop. They need reasonable laws and institutions to ensure their proper functioning.

Efficient Market Requirements

For markets to be efficient, they must have well-structured institutions. John McMillan[1] suggests five institutional requirements for workable markets: (1) Information is widely available, or in McMillan's words, "information flows smoothly"; (2) property rights are protected; (3) private contracts are enforced such that "people can be trusted to live up to their promises"; (4) spillovers from other actors are limited, or "side effects of third parties are curtailed"; and (5) competition prevails. Let's discuss each of these requirements in greater detail.

Accurate Information Is Widely Available

For markets to work efficiently, transactions costs must be kept low. One factor that reduces transactions costs is accurate and readily available information. Negotiations between the parties will be smoother if each party has adequate information about the product. Without good information, one party will not have the confidence needed to value the product so that party will be reluctant to enter into a transaction. Many products today are highly sophisticated, and consumers need high-quality information for good choices. As we will see, this is important for buyers and sellers.

When products are similar, such as oranges, coal, or blank CDs, informational requirements are easily satisfied. In other cases, where a product is extremely complex or conducive to fraud, governments often require that information be public. Securities markets, for instance, have statutory reporting requirements that help to ensure that investors have adequate and comparable information on which to base their investment decisions. This regulation creates the presumption of a fair market.

Property Rights Are Protected

"Imagine a country where nobody can identify who owns what, addresses cannot be easily verified, people cannot be made to pay their debts, resources cannot be conveniently turned into money, ownership cannot be divided into shares, descriptions of assets are not standardized and cannot be easily compared, and the rules that govern property vary from neighborhood to neighborhood or even from street to street."[2] These are the conditions Hernando de Soto found throughout most of the developing world.

Most of us are accustomed to elaborate title and insurance provisions that govern the transfer of automobiles, real estate, and corporate shares in this country. In many developing nations, however, no such provisions exist. When a government fails to establish and protect **property rights**, more informal economic mechanisms will evolve. But, as de Soto writes, these informal mechanisms often vary "from neighborhood to neighborhood or even from street to street." Thus, even though the poor in many developing countries often hold considerable assets, these assets are usually untitled, and this prevents them from being used as capital. You cannot borrow against your home, for instance, to purchase the sewing machine needed to

Property rights
The clear delineation of ownership of property backed by government enforcement.

[1]John McMillan, *Reinventing the Bazaar: A Natural History of Markets* (New York: WW Norton), 2002.
[2]Hernando de Soto, *The Mystery of Capital: Why Capitalism Triumphs in the West and Fails Everywhere Else* (New York: Basic Books), 2000, p. 15.

start a small tailoring business if your family's long-standing ownership of this home has never been legally documented. And this problem, according to de Soto, goes a long way toward explaining why much of the world is mired in poverty.

To see the importance of well-defined property rights, consider the following. Since the discovery of petroleum, whale oil has lost its economic importance, yet some countries and cultures still use whale products. But what if you were to gain ownership of all the whales in the world? How would you use your newly acquired resource? Would your ownership interest affect how whales are harvested? Of course it would. You would hire a marine biologist, for instance, to tell you the best harvest rate. You would not allow your valuable asset to be overharvested into extinction.

Property rights provide a powerful incentive for the optimal use of resources: With ownership comes the incentive not to waste. When property ownership is fuzzy or resources are owned in common by the whole society, the incentives to waste are much stronger. There will be more about this issue later in this chapter.

Contract Obligations Are Enforced

A well-functioning legal system makes doing business easier, and it is absolutely essential for large-scale business activity. Without the safeguards of a legal system, firms must rely on discussions with one another to determine whether customers are credit-worthy, or whether a customer's production order is trustworthy. The risk a seller can reasonably take on a given buyer depends on such information, yet getting information in this fashion is a costly process; it can prevent businesses from growing much larger.

Still, even when a legal system is operating well, markets require some informal rules to create the general presumption that bargains will be kept. Most civil court systems in developed nations take several years to hear and decide disputes. Lawsuits, moreover, are never cheap. You can only imagine the delays in some developing nations. For example, the average case in India may take a decade to litigate because too few resources are devoted to the courts. These problems mean informal arrangements develop, and this can mean that commercial development is severely restricted.

The more valuable the contract, the more a legal instrument is needed to ensure that it is honored. Business relationships involving small amounts can usually rely on simple honesty. But cheating on a large loan, contract, or shipment might be worth the sacrifice of one's reputation, so something more than a handshake is needed to ensure compliance. Large and complex markets need a well running legal system that enforces contracts and agreements.

There Are No External Costs or Benefits

When you drive your car on a crowded highway, you are inflicting *external costs* on other drivers and the larger society by adding to congestion and pollution. By attending a private college, conversely, you are conferring *external benefits* on the rest of us. You are more likely to become a better citizen, be less likely to commit a crime, and will probably pay a greater share of the tax bill. Thus, we all benefit from your education. These external costs and benefits are called *externalities*.

Markets operate most efficiently when externalities are minimized. As we will see later, markets tend to overproduce those commodities with external costs and underproduce those with external benefits. A product's market price reflects its value to consumers and its cost to producers most accurately when the product does not involve third-party costs or benefits.

Competitive Markets Prevail

When a market has many buyers and sellers, no one seller has the ability to raise its price above that of its competitors. To do so would mean losing most of its business. In competitive markets, products are close substitutes, so an increase in price by one firm would simply lead consumers to shift their purchases to other firms.

Competitive markets, moreover, tend to aggregate individual appraisals of value into market information. Without a market, values are determined in one-on-one encounters between buyer and seller. Competitive bargaining between many buyers and sellers gives rise to aggregate market prices and values much as prices are set in an auction.

To illustrate, the price for airing sports programming has skyrocketed in recent years, reflecting aggregate values and the power of competitive bidding. Early on, sports insiders knew that sports programming was valuable, but it took years before all the networks saw its real potential. When they finally did, market prices skyrocketed. Today, the National Football League's annual revenue from the sale of broadcast rights totals several billion dollars. In the beginning, only ABC, CBS, and NBC vied for the rights to broadcast games; today the three networks must compete with Fox, ESPN, pay-per-view, and several other cable channels. Competitive bidding has driven the price of carrying games through the roof.

Competitive markets must be open to entry and exit. If government regulations or private barriers restrict entry, higher prices will prevail. Restricted entry creates monopoly power in markets and leads to higher prices for consumers. If easy exit from a business is important for an efficient allocation of resources, the possibility of entry ensures that monopoly power cannot last for long. Restricted entry into the New York cab business, licenses for cornrow wrapping, and street vending permits do little but to protect existing firms, who lobby hard for such restrictions on the grounds of protecting consumers. The real reason for most regulations of this type is to protect incumbent firms.

Good information, protection of property rights, an efficient and fair legal system, the absence of externalities, and competition are all required if society is to get the best from its markets. These elements all work together to make markets efficient, as we will now see.

The Discipline of Markets

Markets impose discipline on consumers and producers. Sellers would like to get away with charging higher prices while producing shoddier goods, thereby earning greater profits. Few manufacturers or service providers turn out terrific goods and services simply to feel good. Rather, their economic survival depends on it. Markets can be brutal; just ask the former executives of Montgomery Ward and a whole host of dot-com firms.

As for us consumers, we all would like to drive better cars, wear nothing but designer clothes, drink the finest wines, and smoke Cuban cigars. (Well, some of us would like the cigars.) For the superrich, such consumption is not only possible but also commonplace. For the rest of us, however, the market rations us out of such goods, except on very special occasions. This is another function of the market: rationing. Given our limited resources, each of us must decide which products are most important to us, since we cannot have unlimited quantities. Everyone chooses based on their tastes, preferences, and limited incomes.

High prices in a market indicate that consumers value a product highly. Higher prices are usually accompanied by higher profits, and these higher profits will attract new firms into the market. These new firms will increase supply, and this reduces prices. The solution for high prices is high prices. As we will see later, however, if something keeps above-market prices from falling, surpluses will accrue. Conversely, if something keeps low prices from rising to their equilibrium level, shortages will result.

Markets can also be useful tools for the government, since markets allocate resources to those individuals or firms that are most efficient. For example, the government uses markets to allocate the radio and cellular spectrum, to supply the nation's electricity, and to reduce pollution. Central planning is difficult for governments, but private firms can use planning effectively, since a firm's management and stockholders have a vested interest in the firm's success. Product and financial markets, moreover, force a discipline on private firms that is absent when governments centrally plan. If a firm fails to innovate, or if it cooks its books as Enron, the British bank Barings, or the Italian firm Parmalat did, consumers will quit buying its products, financial markets will reduce or call in its loans, and stock markets will decimate its shares.

Consumer and Producer Surplus: A Tool for Measuring Economic Efficiency

Markets determine equilibrium prices and outputs. But both consumers and businesses get extra benefits economists call consumer and producer surplus.

Figure 1 illustrates both through a simple diagram. In both panels, the market determines equilibrium price to be $6 (point e), at which 6 units of output are sold when S_0 and D_0 are the original curves. Assume that each point on the demand curve represents an individual consumer. Some people value the product highly. For instance, the consumer at point a in Panel A thinks the product is worth $11. This consumer clearly gets a bargain, for although she would be willing to pay $11 for the product, the market determines that $6 will be the price everyone pays. Economists refer to this excess benefit that these consumers get ($11 − $6) as

FIGURE 1

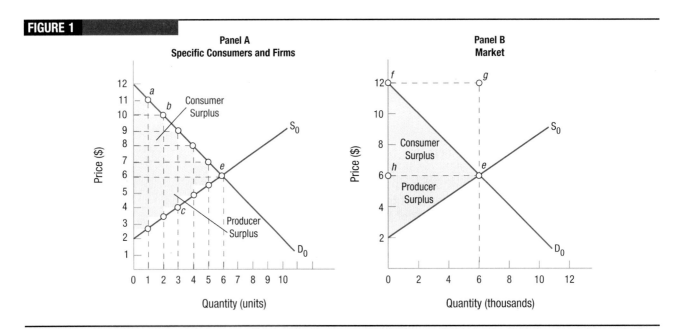

Consumer and Producer Surplus

Panel A shows a market with specific consumers and firms. This small market determines equilibrium price to be $6 (point e), at which 6 units of output are sold. Each point on the demand curve represents a specific consumer, and some people value the product highly. In Panel A, for instance, the consumer at point a thinks the product is worth $11. This consumer clearly gets a bargain, for although she would be willing to pay $11 for the product, she must pay only $6. This difference of $5 is *consumer surplus*. In Panel A, consumer surplus for this market is equal to the sum of individual surpluses. If each point on the supply curve represents a specific supplier, then for similar reasons, producer surplus is the sum of individual firms' producer surplus. Panel B shows how consumer surplus is computed when the market is huge. Consumer surplus is equal to the area under the demand curve but above the equilibrium price of $6. Thus, total market consumer surplus is equal to half of the rectangle *fgeh*, or [($12 − $6) × 6,000] ÷ 2 = ($6 × 6,000) ÷ 2 = $18,000. Producer surplus is the area under equilibrium price but above the supply curve and is computed in a similar fashion, and is equal to [($6 − $2) × 6,000] ÷ 2 = ($4 × 6,000) ÷ 2 = $12,000.

consumer surplus. So, for the consumer who purchases the first unit of output, consumer surplus is equal to $5 ($11 − $6). For the consumer purchasing the second unit (point *b*), consumer surplus is a little less, $4 ($10 − $6). And so on for buyers of the third though fifth units of output. Total consumer surplus for the consumers in Panel A is found by adding all of the individual consumer surpluses for each unit purchased. Total consumer surplus in Panel A is equal to $5 + $4 + $3 + $2 + $1 = $15.

In a similar way, assume that each point on the supply curve represents a specific firm. Notice at point *c* that this supplier is willing to provide the third unit to the market at a price of $4. Fortunately for them, equilibrium price is $6, so they receive a **producer surplus** equal to $6 − $4 or $2. Total producer surplus in Panel A is equal to the sum of each firm's producer surplus.

Panel B illustrates consumer and producer surplus for an entire market. For convenience we have simply assumed that the market is 1,000 times larger than that shown in Panel A so the *x* axis is output in thousands. Whereas in Panel A we had discrete individuals and firms, we now have a big market, so consumer surplus is equal to the area under the demand curve above equilibrium price or the area of the shaded triangle labeled "Consumer Surplus."

To put a number to the consumer surplus triangle in Panel B, we can compute the value of the rectangle *fgeh* and divide it in half. Thus total market consumer surplus in Panel B is [($12 − $6) × 6,000] ÷ 2 = ($6 × 6,000) ÷ 2 = $18,000. The shaded area labeled "Producer Surplus" is found in the same way and is equal to [($6 − $2) × 6,000] ÷ 2 = ($4 × 6,000) ÷ 2 = $12,000.

Markets are efficient from the standpoint that all consumers willing to pay $6 or more got the product from those firms willing to supply it for $6 or less. For demand and supply curves D_0 and S_0, total consumer and producer surplus is maximized. To see why, pick any price other than $6, and you will see that total consumers' and producers' surplus is less.

These two concepts are important to help us understand the impacts of market shocks and policy changes on consumer and producer well-being. We will use consumer and producer surplus as a way to evaluate the efficiency of policies throughout the remainder of the book.

The vast bulk of economic analysis focuses on questions of efficiency. Economic analysis is good at telling us the costs and benefits associated with various possible courses of action. And this analysis can help us resolve policy disputes that hinge on considerations of equity (or fairness) versus efficiency. If a policy creates considerable unfairness, for instance, while spurring only a small gain in efficiency, some other policy might be better. Still, economists have no more to say about fairness than other people. One person's view of what is fair is just as good as anyone else's. In the end, fairness always comes down to a value judgment.

Consumer surplus
The difference between market price and what consumers (as individuals or the market) would be willing to pay. It is equal to the area above market price and below the demand curve.

Producer surplus
The difference between market price and the price that firms would be willing to supply the product. It is equal to the area below market price and above the supply curve.

Checkpoint

Markets and Efficiency

- Markets are efficient mechanisms for allocating resources. Prices are signals of potential profit.
- For markets to be efficient, information must be widely available, property rights must be protected, private contracts must be enforced, spillovers should be minimal, and competition should prevail.
- Markets impose discipline on producers and consumers.
- Consumer surplus occurs when consumers would have been willing to pay more for a good or service than the going price. Producer surplus occurs when businesses would have been willing to provide products at prices lower than the going

price. Together, consumer and producer surplus can be used to understand the effects of public policies.

QUESTIONS

Business corporations are a basic form of entrepreneurship. When you think of a corporation, do you think of a big bureaucratic organization or a nimble company? Think of new and revolutionary products. For example, consider the Windows operating system produced by Microsoft: Was Microsoft a small or large company when this product was introduced? Do you consider Microsoft to be an entrepreneurial company now?

Answers to the Checkpoint questions can be found at the end of this chapter.

Market Failures

We have seen that for markets to be efficient, they must operate within robust institutional structures. These institutional requirements include accurate information for buyers and sellers, protection of property rights, a legal system that enforces private contracts, an absence of externalities or spillovers, and a fostering of competition. This is a tall order, and many markets do not meet these requirements. When one or more of these conditions are not met, the market is said to fail. Market failure does not mean a market totally collapses or stops existing as a market, but that it fails to provide the socially optimal amount of goods and services. As we will see later, there is one exception: when no goods whatsoever will be provided by private markets. In this section, we will examine market failures that arise from a failure to meet each of the requirements just listed, and suggest some possible solutions.

Accurate Information Is Not Widely Available: Asymmetric Information

One economist tells the story of a friend who for 10 years owned a house near a stream. Neighboring homes were plagued by rats and mice, but not the friend's house. When his neighbors complained about the infestation, the friend would profess never to having seen a rodent in his house. Then, as Todd Sandler tells it, "On the day before he was to sell his house, he was awakened in the middle of the night by a weird sound coming from the attic. Thinking that he would come face to face with his first rat, he went with a flashlight to inspect the attic. When he opened the trap door and stuck in his head, he let out a scream and dropped the light. The 10-year-old mystery had been solved—a large beady-eyed snake stared at him with a rat in its coils."[3]

Asymmetric information
Occurs when one party to a transaction has significantly better information than another party.

    This is a perfect example of **asymmetric information**, assuming the friend goes ahead and sells the house without mentioning anything about his rodent control secret. In this case, the seller knows more about the house than the buyer. To some, whether this information should properly be divulged in a real estate agreement is arguable. Some people would be unwilling to live in, or perhaps even purchase, a house in which they knew a snake was loose, while others would be happy know-

---

[3]Todd Sandler, *Economic Concepts for the Social Sciences* (Cambridge: Cambridge University Press), 2001, p. 110.

ing that the rodent problem was solved. For months my uncle would not visit our home because my son's boa was loose in the house.

It was suggested earlier that for markets to operate efficiently, accurate information must be widely available. But in many markets, one party to a transaction will almost always have better information than the other. Many buyers at garage sales have more information about the value of antiques being sold than their sellers. My brother-in-law earns a tidy living buying "junk" at weekend flea markets, then reselling it (at greatly increased prices) in his space in an antique mall.

More often, however, it is sellers who have the superior knowledge. Let us consider the used car market, which Nobel Prize winner George Akerlof studied many years ago.[4] Professor Akerlof wondered why the price of a new car drops so significantly once it is driven off the lot. Put five hundred miles on a car, then list it for sale, and the market price will be 10–20% less than the new-car price.

Let us first look at Figure 2, which assumes that all buyers and sellers have accurate information about used cars. We will divide the market into high-quality cars and low-quality cars, or lemons. For simplicity, we will also assume that sellers are willing to part with high-quality cars for $10,000 along supply curve S_{High}, and that sellers of lemons are willing to let them go for $5,000 along supply curve S_{Low}. Demand curve D_{UCars} shows the demand for used cars.

If we assume that the demand curve represents a ranking of consumers based on the prices they are willing to pay for cars, then length *ca* on the demand curve represents those people who are willing to pay $10,000 or more for a high-quality

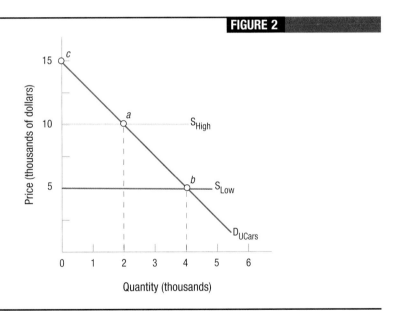

FIGURE 2

The Market for Used Cars

The market for used cars is divided into high- and low-quality cars (lemons). Sellers are willing to sell high quality cars for $10,000 along supply curve S_{High}, and others will sell lemons for $5,000 along supply curve S_{Low}. Demand curve D_{UCars} is the demand for used cars. If buyers and sellers have equal information, 2,000 high-quality cars are sold for $10,000 (point *a*), and 2,000 lemons are sold for $5,000 (point *b* minus point *a*). When sellers have better information than buyers, buyers cannot distinguish good from bad, so 4,000 lemons are sold at $5,000 each (point *b*), and high-quality cars go unsold in the market. To avoid this lemon problem, sellers of high-quality cars will give warranties and use other methods to signal to buyers that their cars are not lemons.

[4]George Akerlof, "The Market for Lemons: Quality, Uncertainty and the Market Mechanism," *Quarterly Journal of Economics*, 1970, pp. 488–500.

Nobel Prize George Akerlof, A. Michael Spence, and Joseph Stiglitz

George Akerlof

A. Michael Spence

Joseph Stiglitz

*g*eorge Akerlof, Michael Spence, and Joseph Stiglitz won the Nobel Prize in Economic Sciences in 2001 for their ideas on the economics of information, providing important insights into everything from used car sales to insurance to sharecropping.

George Akerlof attended Yale University and earned his Ph.D. in economics from MIT. Shortly after joining the faculty at the University of California at Berkeley, he published "The Market for Lemons," which explored the impact of asymmetric information between buyers and sellers in the used car industry.

In his "Lemons" essay, Akerlof introduced the concept of "adverse selection," which suggested that inadequate information for a buyer might result in an industry-wide selling of low-quality products. Based on his experiences in India, Akerlof explored the impacts of information asymmetries in developing economies. He used the example of rural India, where lenders charged interest rates that were twice as high as those in urban areas. Akerlof laced his economic work with insights from sociology and anthropology, noting, for example, that social conventions like the caste system could have adverse impacts on economic efficiency.

Michael Spence did graduate work at Harvard University, where he studied mathematical economics and equilibrium theory from another Nobel laureate, Kenneth Arrow. In 1971, he began teaching analytic methods at Harvard's Kennedy School of Government.

Spence provided important ideas about how well-informed individuals in a market can "signal" their information to lesser informed individuals to prevent the problems associated with adverse selection. Spence explored the question of education as a signal for participants in the labor markets. He also examined the question of different "expectations-based" equilibria for education and wages.

Joseph Stiglitz attended Amherst College and earned his Ph.D. in economics from MIT in 1967. During the Clinton Administration, he served on the Council of Economic Advisors and was the World Bank's chief economist between 1997 and 2001, resigning after his pointed criticisms of the actions of the World Bank during the Asian economic crisis. In 2001, he joined the faculty of Columbia University.

Stiglitz coauthored a classic paper on how information problems can be resolved in the insurance industry when companies do not have adequate information on the risk situations of their clients. Stiglitz has suggested that economic models may be misleading if they disregard the asymmetry of information between the various actors.

In a paper with Andrew Weiss, Stiglitz argued that bankers might reduce losses from bad loans by limiting the number of loans rather than raising the lending rates. Stiglitz has made important contributions to the field of international development: One study focused on sharecropping as an optimal relationship in agriculture, given the asymmetric information between landowner and tenant about harvest conditions and the level of the labor effort.

used car. Given the supply, we can see that 2,000 high-quality cars will be sold. The remaining segment *ab* represents the demand by people who are willing to pay $5,000 or more for a lemon. These people would prefer to purchase high-quality used cars for this price, but that is impossible, given the limited supply. Assuming accurate information, 4,000 used cars will be sold, evenly split between high- and low-quality cars.

But what happens when sellers have better information than buyers? Now buyers cannot differentiate good cars from lemons. The sellers of high-quality automobiles will still not sell their cars for anything less than $10,000. But since buyers cannot tell lemons from good cars, they must assume that each car is a lemon. More specifically, if buyers offer anything less than $10,000 but more than $5,000, they know that only lemons will be offered, and thus they will end up overpaying by the difference between the sales price and $5,000. But if buyers offer $10,000 or more, many of the cars they purchase will still be lemons, even if they also get a few high-quality cars. Hence, paying anything more than $5,000 for a car turns out to be a crapshoot.

This analysis suggests that high-quality used cars will be driven from the market, and that 4,000 lemons will be sold. Before this happens, however, dealers will start offering warranties in an attempt to get higher prices for their used cars and to assure buyers that their cars are not lemons. Consumers can then be more confident of getting high-quality used cars from a dealer, since offering a warranty on lemons would be a losing proposition for dealers.

For private sellers of used cars, this means they must accept less for their cars, or at least do something to convince buyers they are not selling lemons. Some car owners keep scrupulous records of oil changes and repairs or else get their cars detailed so that they "show well." Buyers, trying to reduce their risk, may take used cars to mechanics for inspection before agreeing to purchase them. The lemons problem explains why many high-quality used cars are bought by the friends of the people who sell them: Sometimes only personal trust can overcome asymmetric information.

Adverse Selection

Adverse selection occurs when products of different qualities are sold at the same price because of asymmetric information. Adverse selection is most apparent in insurance markets. People who purchase health insurance or life insurance know far more about their lifestyles and general states of their health than can an insurance company, even if the insurance company requires a physical.

Insurance rates are determined using averages, but the market includes some people who are higher than average risks and some people who are below average. Who do you think is more likely to purchase insurance? Overwhelmingly, it is those people above the average risk level who will buy insurance, while those below the average risk level are more likely to self-insure. The insurance pool therefore tends to be filled with higher-risk individuals, which can lead to payouts exceeding projections and insurance companies losing money. In this case, then, adverse selection skews the insurance pool, giving it a risk level higher than the social average.

Adverse selection
Occurs when products of different qualities are sold at the same price because of asymmetric information. Insurance is a typical example because people know far more about their health and risk levels than the companies insuring them.

How can insurance underwriters deal with this problem? The answer is that they offer policies at different prices to different groups. Health insurance companies, for instance, use deductibles and copayments to attract low-risk individuals. A deductible means that you must pay the first, say, $1,000 in medical expenses, then the insurance company begins covering a part, or even all, of the remaining costs. Copayments are small cash payments paid for each visit to the doctor. These policies are attractive to low-risk clients since they have lower monthly premiums. For low-risk people, the likelihood of their needing to cover copayments or pay their full deductible is low.

Conversely, a high-deductible policy is not attractive to high-risk individuals, since they can project that the cost of the policy will be too high. They know they will probably have to pay all their monthly premiums, many copayments, and their full deductible. These people will tend to opt for policies with higher premiums but lower deductibles. Thus, people who are high risk will select policies that accurately reflect their true state of health and lifestyle.

As a thought experiment, ask yourself why private unemployment insurance is not offered on the market? Who would most want to buy such insurance? How would an insurance company deal with slackers? Recently Robert Shiller[5] has suggested "livelihood insurance," which would create a futures market with trading based on forecasts of average incomes in various professions. Many of us choose our profession based on its expected future income. Technology introduces considerable uncertainty into many professions—just ask those computer professionals who were getting high wages in telecommunications. This market would permit people to hedge against future displacements. To reduce shirking and adverse selection, Shiller suggests that people whose pay is below a profession's average would not be reimbursed.

Moral Hazard

Moral hazard
Asymmetric information problem that occurs when an insurance policy or some other arrangement changes the economic incentives and leads to a change in behavior.

Moral hazard occurs when an insurance policy or some other arrangement changes the economic incentives we face, thus leading us to change our behavior, usually in a way that is detrimental to the market. Think about what happens when you get comprehensive coverage, which includes theft insurance, on your car. Does this affect how scrupulously you lock your car doors? Of course it does. The moral hazard occurs because the insurance policy, which compensates you in case of loss, changes your behavior to make loss *more* (not *less*) likely.

Insurance companies place restrictions on individual behavior in some contracts. For example, insurance designed to protect the ability of professional athletes to honor multiyear contracts often prohibits dangerous activities such as skiing, inline skating, hang gliding, and mountain climbing. In this way they reduce the moral hazard aspects of the policy. Some rental car companies, knowing that you won't check the oil in a rental car, rarely rent cars for more than a month at a time. They want to get their cars back into the shop to ensure all is well.

When high-quality information is not equally available to buyers and sellers, markets must adapt. The less complex the product and the better the information, the more efficient the market will be.

Information Markets: The Wisdom of Crowds

> Things sometimes work better than we had a right to expect from our abstract interpretations of theory.
>
> *Vernon Smith (2002 Nobel Prize winner)*

Will we land astronauts on Mars by 2015? Will Osama bin Laden be caught? Will an Asian flu pandemic reach the United States? The probabilities associated with

---

[5]Robert Shiller, *The New Financial Order: Risk in the 21st Century* (Princeton, NJ: Princeton University Press), 2003.

all of these questions are being forecasted every day by information (or prediction) markets. Some of these markets are small and just for fun, while others are large and have hundreds of millions of dollars at stake. Information markets have proved highly accurate with both real and virtual money.

Information markets began in 1988 at the University of Iowa. The Iowa Electronic Market, a real money market where participants are limited to an investment of $500, has done a better job of forecasting U.S. presidential election results than popular polls. Examples of other information markets include The Hollywood Stock Exchange (www.hsx.com), which focuses on the box office gross of newly released movies and the future success of stars, and TradeSports (www.tradesports.com), a site that has a huge set of sports, political, and entertainment futures contracts. The large-scale economic derivatives used to forecast the likely outcome of future economic data releases (www.economicderivatives.com) permit firms and financial institutions to hedge their portfolios against adverse macroeconomic data (e.g., consumer price index [CPI], gross domestic product [GDP], and employment) that are released on a regular basis. The release of disappointing economic numbers often plays havoc with large portfolios.

Before 9/11/2001, intelligence in the United States was decentralized among many agencies including the Defense Department, the CIA, the National Security Agency, and the FBI. As the 9/11 Commission discovered, many of these agencies were not sharing information with each other, some because of the law, and others because of interagency competition. This resulted in the knowledge gaps and a failure to "connect the dots." Information markets tend to aggregate this information in one spot. The Policy Analysis Market (PAM) program instituted by the Defense Advanced Research Projects Agency (DARPA) in 2003 was going to be a public market that would be used to predict terrorist activities and other important political events in the Middle East. Many critics suggested that it might suffer from foul play from terrorists driving up the market price of an event and profiting from an attack, or using the market to mislead intelligence authorities. This market was scrapped, yet the intelligence services now have internal markets that are used to aggregate information and aid their forecasts of world events. As James Surowiecki[6] noted,

> *PAM would have helped break down the institutional barriers that keep information from being aggregated in a single place. Since traders in a market have no incentive other than making the right prediction—that is, there are no bureaucratic or political factors influencing their decision—and since they have that incentive to be right, they are more likely to offer honest evaluations, rather than tailoring their opinions to fit the political climate or satisfy institutional demands.*

Information is important to the efficient functioning of markets and good public policy. Paradoxically, markets are good mechanisms to aggregate information for policymakers. Information markets can be used to reduce market failures due to incomplete information.

Problems with Property Rights

We saw earlier that property rights provide a powerful incentive to use resources wisely. We noted that incentives to waste are much stronger when property

---

[6]James Surowiecki, *The Wisdom of Crowds: Why the Many Are Smarter Than the Few and How Collective Wisdom Shapes Business, Economics, Societies, and Nations* (New York: Doubleday), 2004, pp. 91–92. For a more detailed discussion of these issues, see Robert Hahn and Paul Tetlock (eds.), *Information Markets: A New Way of Making Decisions* (Washington, DC: AEI-Brookings Joint Center for Regulatory Studies), 2006.

ownership is fuzzy or resources are owned in common. Here we want to look at these cases in detail, discussing two general instances of market failure caused by property right issues: public goods and common property resources.

Public Goods

Most of the goods we deal in are private goods: airline seats, meals at restaurants, songs on iTunes, bicycles, and the like. When we purchase such goods, we consume them, and no one else can benefit from them. To be sure, when you buy an airline ticket, other passengers will be on the same flight, but no one else can sit in your seat for that flight; only you can enjoy its benefits. Thus, private goods are those the buyer consumes, and this precludes anyone else from similarly enjoying them.

Public goods
Goods that, once provided, no one person can be excluded from consuming (nonexclusion), and one person's consumption does not diminish the benefit to others from consuming the good (nonrivalry).

Contrast private goods with **public goods**, goods that one person can consume without diminishing what is left for others. My watching PBS does not mean that there is less PBS for you to watch. Economists refer to such a situation as one of *nonrivalry*. Public goods are also *nonexclusive*, meaning that once such a good has been provided for one person, others cannot be excluded from enjoying it. Normally, public goods are both nonrival and nonexclusive, whereas private goods are rival and exclusive.

Free rider
When a public good is provided, consumers cannot be excluded from enjoying the product, so some consume the product without paying.

Public goods give rise to the **free rider** problem. Once a public good has been provided, other consumers cannot be excluded from it, so many people will choose to enjoy the benefit without paying; they will free ride. National Public Radio (NPR) and PBS are public goods. They exist because they receive donations from individuals, foundations, and governments, but their weeklong begging and guilt-transference sessions notwithstanding, most listeners and viewers (maybe as high as 90%) still choose to enjoy their services without pledging support.

Other public goods include weather forecasts, national defense, lighthouses, flood control projects, GPS satellites, World Court rulings, and mosquito eradication. Because these goods are nonrival and nonexclusive, they invariably end up being provided by governments.

Public goods are the one case where market failure typically leads to no goods at all being provided by private markets. Government must step in. Who would contribute—or contribute adequately—to the costs of providing accurate weather forecasts if your neighbors were free riders? Contributions would soon dry up, and the public good in question would not be provided at all.

Knowledge, too, can be a public good. As a result, markets need ways of protecting intellectual property if its development is not to be discouraged. These days, this protection is more crucial than ever with digital information technologies and the Internet. Digital files can fly around the world and be reproduced for nearly nothing. If work can be copied so quickly, what is the incentive to produce it in the first place? Protections and incentives are needed to ensure that individuals and companies continue to produce such products. Still, some compromise is needed between absolute protection and no protection to strike a balance between producer incentives and consumer interests. Patents, trademarks, and copyrights all convey some monopoly power, so their protections must have limits; otherwise, producers could take advantage of consumers.

Drug innovations take on public good aspects when intellectual property rights—in this case patents—are not enforced internationally. The Indian government does recognize patents with varying degrees for food and drugs, which helps explain why India has over 20,000 drug manufacturers. These companies can copy drugs patented in the United States and Europe, paying only their production costs, since their research and development costs are zero. As a result, Indian drugs cost only pennies on the dollar compared to prices in the United States and in Europe.

Similarly, Brazil encouraged drug manufacturers to copy American antiviral drugs for AIDS sufferers. The government then bought these drugs at greatly reduced prices and distributed them to patients. Brazilian AIDS sufferers could not afford the expensive drug cocktail American drug companies were offering, so the Brazilian government felt compelled to ignore the patents on these medicines.

Private research and development efforts by medical and drug companies in the United States and Europe, and the resulting drugs, often become public goods in much of the rest of the world. The developing world is free riding, with higher American insurance and prescription drug costs subsidizing the rest of the world.

To a lesser extent, European nations have engaged in similar free riding at the expense of American drug companies, but a recent study commissioned in Europe concluded that this may be costing Europe more than it helps. Keeping drug prices artificially low through price controls and government negotiations with drug companies has resulted in research and development funds, and scientists, flowing from Europe to the United States. Today, over 60% of all drug research and development in the world is done in the United States.

The other side of this issue is that few highly priced drugs would be sold in the developing world anyway. Poor people living on a dollar or two a day simply cannot afford to buy high-cost, high-tech drugs, so American and European pharmaceutical companies lose little revenue when these people are provided with cheap imitations of their products. Indeed, because the cost to pharmaceutical firms is so small and the benefits to developing countries and their people are so great, some drug companies have even begun selling their own products to developing nations at reduced rates.

As this drug example shows, public goods can lead to market failure if the free rider problem is present. If drug companies reap profits, they will continue to invest in research and development. If foreign nations free ride, they diminish the incentives that drug companies have to invest in product innovation. The more that drugs become like public goods, the less likely that new drugs will be developed.

Common Property Resources

Another market failure caused by problems with property rights occurs when a good is a **common property resource** or open-access resource. The market failure associated with commonly owned properties is often referred to as "the tragedy of the commons,"[7] where the tendency is for commonly held resources to be overused and overexploited. Because the resource is held in common, individuals have little incentive to use them in a sustainable fashion, so each person races to "get theirs" before others can do the same.

Common property resources Resources that are owned by the community at large (parks, ocean fish, and the atmosphere) and therefore tend to be overexploited because individuals have little incentive to use them in a sustainable fashion.

Ocean fisheries are a good example. Fish in the ocean were once in excess supply; there was no need for use of this resource to be restricted. Very often people fished one species until it was exhausted, then moved on to fish another. Since the ocean was so big and fish species so plentiful, no one noticed. As the global demand for fish has risen, improved fishing technologies and boats have made it possible for fishing boats to increase their hauls and to range around the world. Because many of the world's fisheries are still unregulated, one population after another has been fished out, so much so that nearly 90% of the ocean's predators are gone. The situation is clearly unsustainable, and indeed, as fish populations have shrunk, so have fishing fleets.

The most recent example of overfishing is the Patagonian toothfish (Chilean Sea Bass).[8] It is a big, ugly, black fish from deep cold waters weighing 40–80 pounds. Chefs discovered its meat to be very forgiving when cooking: It is difficult to overcook and has a nice oily texture that accepts nearly all spices. Because of these qualities, it became a huge hit in the United States, and the fish has been hunted to extinction. Scientists estimate that 40% of the preexploitation species (biomass)

---

[7]Hardin, Garrett, "The Tragedy of the Commons," *Science,* 162, pp. 1243–48, 1968.
[8]See Paul Greenberg, "The Catch," *New York Times Magazine,* October 23, 2005, and G. Bruce Knecht, *Hooked: Pirates, Poaching and the Perfect Fish* (Rodale Books), 2006.

is needed for sustainable fishing, and environmental groups and governments in the southern waters are concerned that this critical number may have been breached. They have recently begun to set limits on the catch. This has led to the problem of poaching. The Australian Coast Guard recently chased a poacher through Antarctic waters during a storm with a catch worth one million dollars. The trawlers today have 15-mile-long lines with 15,000 hooks. No species can withstand this type of predation. Common property resources need government regulation ultimately to protect these assets.

In summary, when property rights are clearly defined, people have an incentive to use resources efficiently. But property rights are not always clearly defined, and this leads to market failure and waste. In the case of public goods, the free rider problem means that these goods may not be provided at all if left to private devices—government needs to step in. With common property resources, there is an incentive for each individual to grab as much as he or she can. Government regulation can protect these resources.

Contract Enforcement Is Problematical

When an efficient legal system for the enforcement of contracts is lacking, contracts will inherently be small, given that large contracts with complex financial provisions are difficult to enforce informally. Only if the parties to a contract have long histories together and want to continue doing business will an informal system work. Just as the corporate structure was pivotal in Western economic development, enforcement mechanisms for contracts are essential for widespread business and commercial expansion.

When public officials are corrupt, businesses will invest less. Corrupt officials are like people who fish: They know any funds they fail to squeeze out of a firm will be appropriated by the next corrupt bureaucrat, so they try to extort as much as possible, just as people who fish are afraid of leaving fish behind for anyone else to catch. It is not surprising that higher corruption in a country is associated with lower economic growth.

There Are Significant External Costs or Benefits: Externalities

Markets rarely produce the socially optimal output when external costs or benefits are present. The market tends to overproduce goods with external costs, providing them at too low a price. To see why, consider Figure 3, keeping in mind that an **external cost** is some socially undesirable effect of economic activity such as pollution, overfishing, or traffic congestion.

External cost
Occurs when a transaction between two parties has an impact on a third party not involved with the transaction. External costs are negative such as pollution or congestion. The market provides too much of the product with negative externalities at too low a cost.

Demand curve D_P and supply curve S_P represent the private demand and supply for some product. Market equilibrium is at point a. Assume this good's production creates pollution—an external cost. If its producer were forced to clean up its production process, the firm's costs would rise, and the supply curve would decrease to $S_{P+Cleanup\ Costs}$. The result is a new equilibrium at point b with a higher price and lower output.

Output Q_1 is the socially desirable output for this product. But left on its own, this market will produce at Q_0 because consumers and producers of this product will not take this pollution (and cleanup costs) into consideration. The larger society bears the brunt of the pollution. Markets fail because they do not contain mechanisms forcing firms to eliminate external costs. Left unregulated, the firm in this example will produce more of its product than the society wants, pushing the increased costs of this production off onto the larger society as an undesirable externality.

External benefits
Positive externalities (also called spillovers) such as education and vaccinations. Private markets provide too little at too high a price of goods with external benefits.

In a similar way, markets tend to provide too little of products that have **external benefits**. Figure 4 depicts the market for college education with external ben-

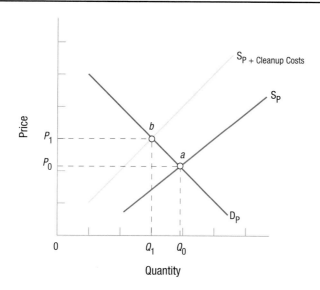

FIGURE 3

Markets with External Costs

Markets tend to overproduce goods with external costs. Demand curve D_P and supply curve S_P represent the private demand and supply. Market equilibrium is at point *a*. Assume this good's production creates pollution (an external cost). If the producer were forced to clean up the production process, the firm's costs would rise, and the supply curve would decrease to $S_{P+Cleanup\ Costs}$. The result is the socially optimal equilibrium at point *b* with a higher price and lower output. Now producers and consumers of this product are paying the full costs associated with the good's production. Markets do not inherently contain mechanisms that force firms to pay for external costs.

efits. Again, demand curve D_P and S_P represent private demand and supply, with equilibrium at point *a*.

Since education provides benefits not only to students but also to the society as a whole, the demand for college education is equal to the private demand plus external benefits, or $D_{P+Social\ Benefits}$. This moves the market equilibrium to point *b*, where more education, Q_1, is desired. The society can bring about this shift in equilibrium by subsidizing higher education to the tune of *bc*. (Perhaps the government pays part of students' tuition costs—does this sound familiar?) This lowers the price of higher education, which results in more people going to college, to the benefit of the larger society.

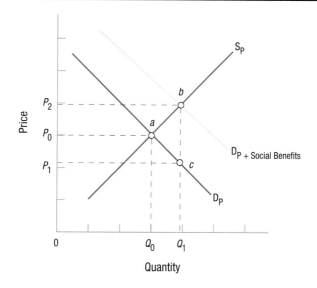

FIGURE 4

Markets with External Benefits

Private markets tend to provide too little of products that have external benefits (education). Curves D_P and S_P represent private demand and supply, with equilibrium at point *a*. Since education provides benefits not only to students but also to the society as a whole, the demand for college education is equal to the private demand plus external benefits, or $D_{P+Social\ Benefits}$. This moves the market equilibrium to point *b*, where more education, Q_1, is desired. By subsidizing higher education by an amount equal to *bc*, the price of higher education is lowered, resulting in more people going to college.

Externalities lead to market failure. To ensure that products are available at the socially desirable price and output, some government intervention may be required. Regulation or taxation can be used, for instance, to give markets the incentives they need to produce what society wants. Today, the government even uses the market as a mechanism to reduce pollution.

Originally, the government relied on command and control policies to reduce emissions from specific pollution sources. Using markets to achieve environmental goals seemed oxymoronic. Eventually the federal government began issuing marketable permits allowing limited emissions. Companies could then buy and sell these permits, thereby adjusting their pollution levels. And, wonder of wonders, it worked! Pollution levels were reduced more quickly and cheaply than anyone had thought possible.

Why did pollution permits work so well? Private firms and individuals are good at finding the most efficient solutions to problems. Sometimes, these solutions will produce externalities, but when market forces are properly harnessed, they can also be used to solve problems facing the entire society.

With the right regulatory incentives, markets can be used to reduce pollution at the least cost, remove trash efficiently, and confront such other problems as overfishing, road congestion, and the overuse of national parks. Some communities are looking at user fees for single passenger cars in underused HOV lanes. The revenue from these fares would expand highway funds and allocate scarce lane space to those who most value the resource.

When externalities are present, unregulated markets will fail to deliver socially optimal output. External costs, for example, are spread over the rest of society. Some form of governmental intervention is needed to ensure that markets provide what society wants. But market mechanisms can be used as part of a comprehensive plan to force markets to operate as desired.

Competitive Markets Do *Not* Prevail: Monopoly Power

In theory, a market left to itself should be competitive. In practice, however, the government must promote competition in the marketplace if it wants to see the most efficient outcomes. One problem is that some markets tend toward monopoly, and when a monopoly does control the market, prices go up. In the late 19th century, the monopolistic practices of the "robber barons" spurred passage of a series of antitrust laws that are still used today to promote competitive markets. The Department of Justice can block proposed mergers if they will harm competition in the marketplace. The Antitrust Division of the Department of Justice routinely files suit against companies deemed to be acting anticompetitively; the Microsoft case decided in 2000 is just one example of such a suit.

In all of these cases of market failure (except in the case of pure public goods), markets do not collapse. Rather, markets do not provide the most efficient distribution of goods and services. They need some ameliorative device, often something provided by government such as laws or incentives, but often provided by private firms and individuals acting on their own behalf (remember used car warranties). The important point to keep in mind is the need for correctives when market failure is present. We will have a lot more to say about these issues in a later chapter.

Market Failures

REVIEW

- When markets fail, they typically do not totally collapse (with the exception of public goods)—they simply fail to provide the socially optimal amount of goods and services.

- Asymmetric information—when one party to a transaction has better information than another—can lead to market failure.
- Adverse selection occurs when products of different qualities are sold at one price. Moral hazard occurs when an insurance policy or other arrangement changes the economic incentives people face and so leads them to change their behaviors.
- Private goods can be consumed only by the person who purchases them: They are rival and exclusive. Public goods are nonrival and nonexclusive: My consumption does not diminish your consumption, and others cannot be excluded from enjoying it.
- Public goods give rise to the free rider problem.
- Common property resources are typically subject to overexploitation.
- Markets rarely produce the socially optimal output when external benefits or costs are present.
- Monopoly markets result in prices higher than what is socially optimal.

QUESTION

One professor (who will go unnamed), wanting to remove the "grade grubbing" pressure from the classroom, announced to the class that all students who regularly attended his class would get an A, and all others in the class would receive Bs. Would this announcement create any moral hazard problems? Explain.

Answers to the Checkpoint question can be found at the end of this chapter.

Government-Controlled Prices

When competitive markets are left to determine equilibrium price and output, they clear. Businesses provide consumers with the quantity of goods they want to purchase at the established prices; there are no shortages or surpluses. When market failure occurs, individual or government action can improve the situation, bringing markets back to efficiency.

Problems arise because this bias toward government action (used to mitigate market failure) sometimes leads to government action when markets are efficient and doing what they are supposed to do. Why would government try to regulate freely working markets? In one word: fairness. There are times when the equilibrium price may not be what many people consider to be a desired or fair price. For political or social reasons—not economic ones—governments will intervene in the market by setting limits on such things as wages, apartment rents, electricity, or agricultural commodities. Government uses price ceilings and price floors to keep prices below or above market equilibrium. What happens when government meddles with efficiently working markets?

Price Ceilings

When the government sets a **price ceiling**, it is legally mandating the maximum price that can be charged for a product or service. This is a legal maximum; regardless of market forces, price cannot exceed this level.

Figure 5 on the next page shows an *effective* price ceiling, or one in which the ceiling price is set below the equilibrium price. In this case, equilibrium is at P_e, but the government has set a price ceiling at P_c. Quantity supplied at the ceiling price is Q_2, whereas consumers want Q_1, so the result is a shortage of $Q_1 - Q_2$ units of the product. Note that if the price ceiling is set above P_e, the market simply settles at P_e, and the price ceiling has no impact.

Price ceiling
A government-set maximum price that can be charged for a product or service. When the price ceiling is set below equilibrium, it leads to shortages. Rent control is an example.

Price Ceiling Below Equilibrium Price Creates Shortages

A price ceiling is a maximum sales price for a product. When the government enacts a price ceiling below equilibrium, it will create shortages. Consumers will demand Q_1 output at a price of P_c, but business will supply only Q_2, creating a shortage equal to $Q_1 - Q_2$. The product's price cannot rise to restore equilibrium because of the legal price ceiling.

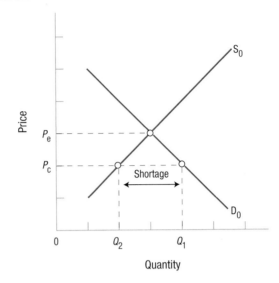

Rent controls are a classic example of price ceilings. Many local governments have decided affordable housing is a priority and that tenants need protection from high rental rates (presumably protection from greedy landlords). And in the short run, rent controls work. Landlords cannot easily convert apartment units to alternative uses, so they have little choice but to rent out these units at the lower rates. But as soon as they can, landlords will convert their real estate holdings to condominiums or offices. Other landlords, facing a ceiling on the rents they can charge, will not incur additional upkeep charges and so will let their properties deteriorate. Few landlords, meanwhile, will invest in more rental units. So the shortage we see in Figure 5 will come from a reduced number of rental units due to condo conversion and no new units, while current units are allowed to deteriorate.

Okay, you might say, there will be a shortage of rental units over time, but at least the rents charged will be "fairer." The question is, fairer to whom? The chief beneficiaries are the people already renting. Over time, their rents will be much lower than the equilibrium price. Sufferers include people moving to the area who cannot find a place to rent, or growing families that are trapped in small apartments. When these people do find a potential place, there is a huge incentive for landlords to ask for under-the-table payments, such as a $5,000 payment for keys to the apartment. In New York City, rent control instituted during Word War II is still in place: The beneficiary class is not the poor, but people lucky enough to be renters during the early phases of the rent control and who have passed on their apartments to their family. This has led to the gruesome habit of would-be renters reading obituaries to discover renters who died with no obvious heirs. This behavior is a far cry from the normal act of looking for an apartment when markets work freely.

More recently, the federal government has begun placing a form of price ceiling on the Medicare payments to doctors and hospitals. Doctors who accept Medicare patients are not allowed to charge patients more that what is allowed by Medicare for specific procedures. These maximum prices have been getting lower as the Medicare budget has been squeezed. As a result, some doctors no longer accept new Medicare patients, since the fees they can charge will no longer cover their costs. For some patients who are just retiring and joining Medicare, finding a doctor can be difficult. The price ceilings have created a shortage of doctors willing to treat Medicare patients.

Energy deregulation in California provides an example of how partial deregulation and price ceilings can go awry. In the early 1990s, California deregulated wholesale electricity prices, but not retail prices to end users. As a result, the market failed to function efficiently when it ran into a supply crisis. Wholesale electricity prices rose, but retail prices were prevented from rising to reduce the quantity demanded. Consumers thus continued to use as much electricity as before, resulting in rolling brownouts; not an efficient means of reducing usage, but one that worked. What the California energy market needed was flexible prices at the retail level to send signals to consumers to consume less, and profit signals to producers to produce more. Partial deregulation failed to provide this structure.

The key point to remember here is that price ceilings are intended to keep the price of a product below its market or equilibrium level. The ultimate effect of a price ceiling, however, is that the quantity of the product demanded exceeds the quantity supplied, thereby producing a shortage of the product in the market.

Price Floors

A **price floor** is a government-mandated minimum price that can be charged for a product or service. Regardless of market forces, product price cannot legally fall below this level.

Figure 6 shows the economic impact of price floors. In this case, the price floor, P_f, is set above equilibrium, P_e, resulting in a surplus of $Q_2 - Q_1$ units. At price P_f, businesses want to supply more of the product (Q_2) than consumers are willing to buy (Q_1), thus generating a surplus. Again, note that if the price floor is set below equilibrium, it has no impact on the market.

For over a half century, agricultural price supports or price floors have been used to try to smooth out the income of farmers, which often fluctuates wildly due to wide annual variations in crop prices. Government acts as a buyer of last resort, and if surpluses result, the government purchases these commodities. Since these price supports typically are above market equilibrium prices, frequent surpluses have resulted. These surpluses have been stored and earmarked for use in the event of future shortages, but few such shortages have arisen due to improvements in farm technology and rising crop yields. Consumers pay more for agricultural commodities, and surpluses arise and often rot, all in the expectation that the income of farmers will be steady. Despite their questionable economic justification, political pressures have ensured that agricultural price supports and related programs still command a sizable share of the discretionary domestic federal budget.

Price floor
A government-set minimum price that can be charged for a product or service. If the price floor is set above equilibrium price it leads to surpluses. Minimum wage legislation is an example.

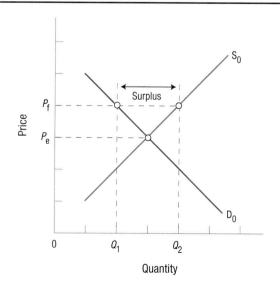

FIGURE 6

Price Floor Above Equilibrium Price Creates Surpluses

A price floor is the lowest price at which a product can be sold. When the government sets a floor above equilibrium, it creates surpluses. Businesses try to sell Q_2 at a price of P_f, but consumers are willing to purchase only Q_1 at that price. The result is a market surplus equal to $Q_2 - Q_1$. The price floor prevents the product's price from falling to equilibrium.

Another area in which price floors are used is the minimum wage. To the extent that the minimum wage is set above the equilibrium wage, unemployment—a surplus of labor—will result. The groups most affected by this unemployment tend to be low-skilled workers and teenagers, groups that already suffer high unemployment rates. Such people might have been able to find jobs had employers been allowed to pay them the equilibrium wage rate, but these jobs go uncreated when employers are forced to pay the higher minimum wage.

As these examples of price floors and price ceilings show, when government intervenes in functioning markets to promote fairness, problems occur. But we have also seen that government intervention can be useful in cases of market failure to promote economic efficiency. Markets require several institutions to ensure efficiency and socially desirable outcomes. These include good information, protection of property rights, contract enforcement, an absence of externalities, and commitment to competition. But many of these elements are not always present in markets, leading to market failure that often means government regulation of some aspects of production or distribution.

Some countries use extensive market regulation and public ownership to provide some goods and services. The United States has traditionally relied less on regulation, and increasingly uses market incentives to solve market failures.

Taxes and Deadweight Loss

As well as regulation and public ownership, government also affects economic efficiency through taxes. Governments need tax revenue to operate. Governments also use taxes to influence incentives. We have a large mix of taxes in the United States from income (both corporate and individual), excise (taxes on specific products such as cigarettes, alcohol, and luxury goods), to property and sales taxes. In this section we take a quick look at how taxes affect the market.

To keep our analysis simple, we will just consider the excise tax shown in Figure 7. The original supply and demand curves are D_0 and S_0, and the market is in equilibrium at $6 with 6,000 units sold (point e). Now assume that the government levies a $2 excise tax to be paid by suppliers. This in effect increases wholesale prices by $2 and results in supply shifting leftward to $S_{Tax\ (\$2)}$. Equilibrium moves up to point a and the new price is $7.25 and sales drop to 4,700 units. Several conclusions pop out from this analysis and Figure 7.

FIGURE 7

Taxes, Consumer and Producer Surplus, and Deadweight Loss

In this figure a $2 excise tax is levied on the producer. The result is that supply shifts leftward by the tax, resulting in lower output sold at a higher price (point a). Taxes drive a wedge between what consumers pay and what producers receive. Also, consumer and producer surpluses decline. The deadweight loss (loss of consumer surplus and producer surplus that evaporate) shown in the figure is the inefficiency associated with this tax.

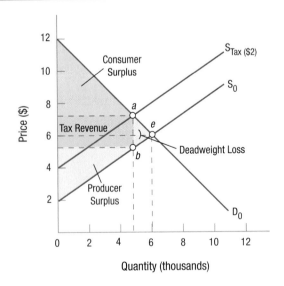

First, the excise tax has driven a \$2 wedge between what consumers pay and what producers receive. So, producers have to charge more (\$7.25 rather than \$6) but receive less (\$5.25 rather than \$6). Second, the government collects tax revenue (in this case revenue is equal to $\$2 \times 4,700 = \$9,400$). Third, both consumer and producer surplus have shrunk as shown in the figure.

And, fourth, and most interesting, there is an additional loss of consumer and producer surplus equal to the triangle labeled "Deadweight Loss" in the figure. Economists refer to this as a **deadweight loss** because it is the inefficiency costs of public policies (in this case, an excise tax) because the optimal level of price and output is disrupted. In this case, 1,300 units of this product $(6,000 - 4,700)$ are not traded in the market. This loss is dead weight because it is lost to all of society: not captured by consumers, not by producers, and not by society in the form of tax revenues.

Throughout the remainder of your study of economics, you will find the supply and demand model a good first approach to analysis. In addition, we will use producer and consumer surplus, and deadweight loss to evaluate the efficiency of various public policies. Economic and public policy questions are often amenable to this analysis, tempered by the considerations discussed in this chapter.

Deadweight loss
The loss in consumer and producer surplus due to inefficiency because some transactions cannot be made and therefore their value to society is lost.

Checkpoint — Government-Controlled Prices

REVIEW

- Competitive markets clear: Businesses provide consumers with the quantity of goods they want to purchase at the established price.
- People may ask government to intervene even when markets work because people may not think the equilibrium price is fair.
- Governments use price floors and price ceilings to intervene in markets.
- A price ceiling is a maximum legal price that can be charged for a product. Price ceilings set below equilibrium result in shortages.
- A price floor is the minimum legal price that can be charged for a product. Price floors set above market equilibrium result in surpluses.
- Deadweight losses often result from the inefficiencies inherent in public policies. But this has to be balanced against the benefits of the policies.

QUESTION

Rent controls are found in cities such as New York and Santa Monica, California, where land prices are at a premium and the city is relatively built-out (very little vacant land remains). Why is rent control not found in cities such as Phoenix, Arizona, or Denver, Colorado?

Answers to the Checkpoint question can be found at the end of this chapter.

Who Is Watching Your Money? Bank Regulation and Information Problems

Like most people, you probably have a bank account, maybe a checking and savings account. Who is watching your money? What do you know about your bank? Probably very little. The bank certainly knows much more about its business strength and viability than you do. Should you care about this information asymmetry? Probably not at this time, because of FDIC (Federal Deposit Insurance Corporation)

insurance: Your account is insured by a federal agency up to $100,000. So this federal insurance encourages you to put your savings in a bank. In other words, the FDIC insurance deals with the information problem that you really can not know very much about who is handling your money.

FDIC insurance did not stem from the Founding Fathers. It is a more recent thing. Federal deposit insurance grew out of the bank panics of the Great Depression.[9] These bank panics started in October of 1930, ebbing and flowing until 1933.

Consider a time without deposit insurance. You put your money in a local bank. How much do you really know about its financial strength? Not much. Let's see where this information problem led.

Say a bank in another locality nearby fails, meaning it closes its doors. People who had their savings in this bank cannot get them out—they will lose everything. You start to wonder whether the same thing will happen to your bank, so you decide to withdraw your money, just to be on the safe side. The next morning, you go to your bank, only to find a long line of like-minded savers. You wait in line. Meanwhile, people who pass by see this line and start to think that maybe their banks are not safe, so they go to withdraw their savings.

One factor that makes this process more dangerous is the fact that your bank never sits there with all of your savings gathering dust in a lockbox just waiting for you to come in and withdraw some. Your bank takes your money, keeps a small portion for everyday bank transactions, and loans out the rest. This means that a run on the bank—when people line up to take out their entire savings—is apt to cause problems for even a well-run solvent bank: How can it quickly turn its loans into cash during a bank run? If it cannot and receives no help from other financial institutions, the bank will have to close its doors. And when this happens, people at other banks will consider withdrawing their money, too.

This is precisely what happened during the Great Depression. One bank run led to another, leading to regional bank panics. Economic activity collapsed when savings could not go to potential business borrowers. To deal with this problem of asymmetric information—you know so little about your bank that it may be prudent to withdraw your money at the slightest whiff of trouble—the FDIC was created on January 1, 1934. Now you do not have to worry about withdrawing your money: You will recover your savings even if the bank fails. Since the creation of the FDIC, there have been no bank panics in the United States. Even during the failure of several savings and loans in the 1980s, bank runs were limited to the affected banks, and even here the bank runs soon dissipated when it became clear that savings were safe.

However, federal deposit insurance has not been an unqualified success. Solving one information problem has brought about another: a moral hazard problem. Without the insurance, there were information asymmetry problems, though at least there was a virtue in you knowing something about your bank. You would not want to lose your money, so you had to keep an eye on your bank to some degree. If you became nervous about your bank's financial strength, you would withdraw your savings. If enough people did this, it would be a signal that something might be amiss. This market action would then discipline the bank. With deposit insurance, you do not have to watch your bank, so the deposit insurance takes away this market discipline. It causes moral hazard: Without this potential market discipline, banks can engage in riskier loans where the payoff may be higher but the chance of success lower.

It turns out that financial institutions attract high-risk-taking individuals. Think of it: All of that money to play with, and not a penny of it the bank officer's. This is a key reason that financial institutions are so heavily regulated.

---

[9]See Milton Friedman and Anna Jacobson Schwartz, *A Monetary History of the United States, 1867–1960* (Princeton, NJ: Princeton University Press), 1963.

If information asymmetries led to bank runs and bank panics, and deposit insurance solved that problem but brought with it the problem of moral hazard, how has the federal government dealt with the problem of moral hazard? First, the federal government has to monitor financial institutions very closely. It is harder to take on high risks when you are watched all the time. Second, the federal government mandates specific capital requirements, limiting forays into risky loans. Third, financial institutions are forced to diversify their holdings among various asset classes. You can get a sense of these various requirements by reading a bank's annual report.

Do these requirements solve the problem of moral hazard? "Solve" is too strong a word. They make the problem less likely to occur, but as long as other people's money is involved, financial buccaneers will be attracted to it.

What does this response to information problems in the banking industry suggest? The proper course of action is to recognize the efficiency of markets and do what we can to get them to work. This approach may require adjustments and further adjustments. Deposit insurance may solve one problem while bringing about another problem, though of lesser scope. And the solution to the new problem may be less than perfect. But economic analysis provides us with a powerful set of tools to use in dealing with information problems.

Key Concepts

Property rights, p. 83
Consumer surplus, p. 87
Producer surplus, p. 87
Asymmetric information, p. 88
Adverse selection, p. 91
Moral hazard, p. 92
Public goods, p. 94

Free rider, p. 94
Common property resources, p. 95
External cost, p. 96
External benefits, p. 96
Price ceiling, p. 99
Price floor, p. 101
Deadweight loss, p. 103

Chapter Summary

Markets and Efficiency

Markets are efficient mechanisms for allocating resources. The prices and profits characteristic of market systems provide incentives and signals that are nonexistent or seriously flawed in other systems of resource allocation.

For markets to be efficient, they must have well-structured institutions. These include (1) information is widely available; (2) property rights are protected; (3) private contracts are enforced; (4) spillovers are minimal; and (5) competition prevails.

Markets impose discipline on producers and consumers. Producers would like to charge higher prices and earn greater profits. But their economic survival depends on turning out quality goods at reasonable prices. As consumers, we would all like to engage in frequent extravagant purchases. But given our limited resources, each of us must decide which products are most important to us. As a result, markets are also rationing devices.

Because many consumers are willing to pay more than market equilibrium prices for many goods and services, they receive a consumer surplus. In a similar way, since many businesses would be willing to provide products at prices below equilibrium prices, they receive a producer surplus. The concepts of consumer and producer surplus are helpful when we wish to examine the impacts of public policy.

Market Failures

For markets to be efficient, they must meet the five institutional requirements identified earlier. When one or more of these conditions is not met, the market is said to fail. Market failure usually does not mean that a market totally collapses or fails to exist, but that it fails to provide the socially optimal amount of goods and services.

In some markets, one party to a transaction may almost always have better information than the other. In this case, the market is said to fail because of asymmetric information. Asymmetric information can result in the inability of sellers to find buyers for the products, but it usually just involves adjustments in contracting methods.

Adverse selection occurs when products of different qualities are sold at one price and involve asymmetric information. Insurance customers, for instance, know far more about their own health than do insurance companies. And because high-risk individuals are most likely to purchase insurance, adverse selection skews the insurance pool, giving it a risk level higher than average.

Moral hazard occurs when an insurance policy or some other arrangement changes the economic incentives people face, leading people to change their behavior, usually in a way detrimental to the market. Theft insurance for cars, for instance, tends to make people less scrupulous about locking their car doors.

Private goods are those goods that can be consumed only by the individuals who purchase them. Private goods are rival and exclusive. Public goods, in contrast, are nonrival and nonexclusive, meaning my consumption does not diminish your consumption and that once such a good has been provided for one person, others cannot be excluded from enjoying it.

Public goods give rise to the free rider problem. Once a public good has been provided, other consumers cannot be excluded from it, so many people will choose to enjoy the benefit without paying for it: They will free ride. And because of the possibility of free riding, the danger is that no one will pay for the public good, so it will no longer be provided by private markets, even though it is publicly desired. Pure public goods usually require public provision.

Common property resources are owned in common by the community and are subject to the "tragedy of the commons" and overexploitation.

When an efficient legal system for the enforcement of contracts is lacking, contracts will be small because large contracts with complex financial provisions are difficult to enforce informally.

Markets rarely produce the socially optimal output when external costs or benefits are present. The market overproduces goods with external costs, selling them at too low a price. Conversely, markets tend to provide too little of products that have external benefits.

Some markets tend toward monopoly, and when a monopoly does control the market, prices go up. In the late 19th century, the monopolistic practices of the "robber barons" spurred passage of a series of antitrust laws that are still used today to promote competitive markets.

Government-Controlled Prices

When competitive markets are left to determine equilibrium price and output, they clear; businesses provide consumers with the quantity of goods they want to purchase at the established prices. Nevertheless, the equilibrium price may not be what many people consider fair. The government may then use price ceilings or price floors to keep prices below or above the market equilibrium.

A price ceiling is the maximum legal price that can be charged for a product. Price ceilings set below equilibrium result in shortages. A price floor is the minimum legal price that can be charged for a product. Price floors set above market equilibrium result in surpluses.

Questions and Problems

1. Many observers consider it a market failure when the pharmaceutical industry refuses to do research and development on what are known as neglected diseases: cures for malaria and tuberculosis and vaccines for other diseases in developing countries where the profit potential is small. Further, many drug firms are unwilling to make vaccines for illnesses such as influenza and other biohazards such as anthrax and small pox. Vaccines are especially prone to large lawsuits because when they are administered, they are administered to millions of people in an emergency, and if there are serious unanticipated side effects, settlement costs can be huge. With anthrax vaccine, ethical considerations prevent exposing someone to anthrax and then injecting the medicine, so these types of vaccines often are used in emergencies without sufficient testing.

   a. One of the solutions currently used for neglected diseases is the public–private partnership (PPP). Grants by the Bill & Melinda Gates Foundation currently fund most of the PPPs that are conducted on a "no profit, no loss" basis. The firm's research and development costs are covered, but firms must sell the drugs at cost to developing countries. Why would pharmaceutical firms be willing to spend time on these types of projects?

   b. Since lawsuits are an important impediment to research and development of vaccines, what policies could the government institute to solve this problem?

   c. Besides the use of the PPP, what other policies might the government introduce to encourage drug firms to do research and development on neglected diseases and orphan diseases (diseases that affect only a few people and thus have extremely limited markets)?

2. "If millions of people are desperate to buy and millions more desperate to sell, the trades will happen, whether we like it or not." This quote by Martin Wolf[10] refers to trades in illicit goods like narcotics, knockoffs (counterfeit goods), slaves, organs, and other goods we generally refer to as "bads." He suggests that the only way to eliminate traffic in these illicit goods is to eliminate their profitability. Do you agree? Why or why not?

3. Academic studies suggest that the amount people tip at restaurants is only slightly related to the quality of service, and that tips are poor measures of how happy people are with the service. Is this another example of market failure? What might account for this situation?

4. The U.S. Department of Labor reports that of the roughly 145 million people employed, just over half (73.9 million) are paid hourly, but less than 3% earn the minimum wage or less; 97% of wage earners earn more. And of those earning the minimum wage or less, 25% are teenagers living at home. If so few people are affected by the minimum wage, why does it often seem to be such a contentious political issue?

5. Adam Smith, in his famous book *The Wealth of Nations*, noted, "Every individual . . . neither intends to promote the public interest, nor knows how much he is promoting it. By preferring the support of domestic to that of foreign industry he intends only his own security; and by directing that industry in such a manner as its produce may be of the greatest value, he intends only his own gain, and he is in this, as in many other cases, led by an invisible hand to promote an end which was no part of his intention." What was he describing and what did it do?

---

[10]Martin Wolf, "The Profit Motive May Be Universal but Virtue Is Not," *Financial Times*, November 16, 2005, p.13.

6. When professors get tenure, essentially guaranteeing them lifetime jobs, does this affect the effort they expend on teaching and research? What concept might be used to explain your answer?

7. Are buying brands (e.g., Coke, Sony, and Dell) a way consumers compensate for asymmetric information? Explain.

8. What is the purpose of a warranty given by a used-car dealer? Evaluate one used-car warranty that gives your money back if not satisfied in a certain time period, and one that does not give you back your money but lets you put this money toward the purchase of another used car. Which warranty would you prefer?

9. Farm price supports (price floors) have been a part of the economic landscape for the better part of a century as farming has evolved from a way of life to today where most agricultural products are produced on large corporate farms. Stable farm prices are the benefit of these policies. What are the costs?

10. In 2006 Medicare recipients were permitted to sign up for a federally subsidized drug benefit plan. The sign-up phase had a May 15th deadline, and those signing up after that date faced a premium penalty. Does this deadline have anything to do with adverse selection? Explain.

11. Nobel Prize winner Gary Becker and Judge Richard Posner[11] suggested that "unions strongly favor the minimum wage because it reduces competition from low-wage workers (who, partly because most of them work part time, tend not to be unionized) and thus enhances unions' bargaining power." They further argued that "although some workers benefit—those who were paid the old minimum wage but are worth the new higher one to the employers—others are pushed into unemployment, the underground economy or crime. The losers are therefore likely to lose more than the gainers gain; they are also likely to be poorer people." Are both of these statements consistent with the model of price floors discussed in this chapter? Why or why not?

12. Describe consumer surplus. Describe producer surplus. Using the graph below show both. Now assume that a new technology reduces the cost of production. What happens to consumer surplus? Show the impact of the change in the graph.

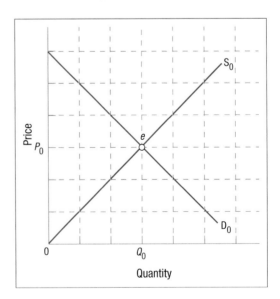

[11]Gary Becker and Richard Posner, "How to Make the Poor Poorer," *The Wall Street Journal*, January 26, 2007, p. A11.

13. Define public goods. What is the free rider problem? Give several examples of public goods.

14. Describe a price ceiling. What is the impact of an effective price ceiling? Show this on the figure below. Give an example. Describe a price floor. What is the impact of an effective price floor? Show this on the figure below. Give an example.

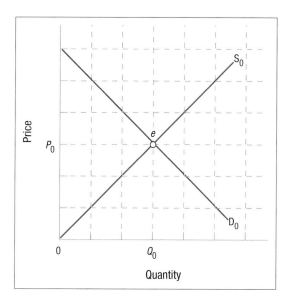

15. Describe the tragedy of the commons. Give some examples. How might this tragedy be avoided?

16. Professor Donald Boudreaux wrote (*Wall Street Journal*, 8/23/06, p. A11), that "There are heaps of bad arguments for raising the minimum wage. Perhaps the worst . . . is that a minimum wage increase is justified if a full-time worker earning the current minimum wage cannot afford to live in a city such as Chicago." He then asked "why settle for enabling workers to live only in the likes of Chicago? Why not raise the minimum wage so that everyone can afford to live in, say, Nantucket, Hyannis Port or Beverly Hills, within walking distance of Rodeo Drive?" Should the minimum wage be a "living wage," so a full-time worker can live comfortably in a given locale? What would be the impact if minimum wages were structured this way?

Answers to Checkpoint Questions

CHECKPOINT: MARKETS AND EFFICIENCY

Some large corporations are innovative and nimble (Google, Genentech, and Apple are examples), but most become bureaucratic and reactive to developments in their markets. Microsoft was a reasonably large firm when it produced Windows. Microsoft is less innovative today in that it spends so much time and effort defending its existing products. It is, however, spending huge sums on research and development.

CHECKPOINT: MARKET FAILURES

This approach to the class would and did alter student behavior. Once students understood that the professor intended to stand behind the offer (essentially made it a contract with students) attendance dropped off, and many settled for a grade of B. Even though he was a good professor, students, like many others, have commitments on their time and optimized by accepting a B instead of attending class and getting an A.

CHECKPOINT: GOVERNMENT-CONTROLLED PRICES

Cities with a lot of vacant land do not have rents high enough to support activists who try to get people to control rents. Only in cities with little vacant land and high population densities are rents high enough that enough people think it "unfair," resulting in rent controls. If rent controls are introduced where a lot of vacant land exists, the land simply remains vacant because development is stymied.

Introduction to Macroeconomics

5

"Imagine"[1]
(with apologies to John Lennon)

Imagine strong expansion,
It's easy if you try
There'd be no
unemployment,
Just think what you could
buy,
Imagine all the people
Living well today . . .

Imagine budget balance,
It isn't hard to do,
Adjust the rate of spending,
Adjust the revenue,
Imagine all the people
Living without debt . . .

Imagine there's no trade
gap,
I wonder if you can,
No need for strain with
China,
No need to peg the yuan,
Imagine all the people
Sharing all the world . . .

You may say I'm a
dreamer,
But I'm not the only one,
Price stability has
happened,
No one thought it could be
done.

n a market economy, some markets may be doing well even as others are in the dumps. Many firms are starting with the most optimistic of outlooks, while many other firms and individuals are going bankrupt. Changing consumer tastes, poor management, or bad timing can make even the most promising ventures unprofitable.

Because specific individuals, firms, and industries may do better or worse in any economic environment, some other measures are needed to gauge the state of the aggregate economy, or what is called the macroeconomy. Anecdotal evidence—such as Kodak laying off 15,000 workers in 2004 because of reduced demand for film and film cameras, or General Motors and Ford in 2005–06 each embarking on plans to eliminate 30,000 jobs from their respective workforces—may not be reflective of the economy as a whole. Such big layoffs by major firms make headlines, but the number of workers being added to payrolls of expanding small businesses can be just as economically significant, even if the media typically ignore that number. Huge disasters such as 9/11 and Hurricane Katrina can have major impacts on the macroeconomy.

Several times a week, the government announces the latest level of some macroeconomic variable or another. These data help firms, markets, and consumers gauge the general condition of the economy. Most data are released monthly, although some aggregate measures are released only quarterly. When a drop in the unemployment rate is reported, we all feel better and have more confidence in the economy, even if we know someone who has just lost a job. Every other year—during election years—even if the economy is doing well, the party out of power has every incentive to paint a bleak picture for voters: "It's the economy, stupid!"

Studying macroeconomics will let you distill the wheat from the chaff when you listen to politicians and watch news broadcasts. Once you have completed this course, you will often find yourself watching television and asking, "What are these

[1]From the Federal Reserve Board of Cleveland, *Economic Trends,* November 2003.

people talking about?" It is not that you will fail to understand the economics underlying the issues they are discussing. Rather, you will be able to see that the "experts" often do not! You will also be better able to determine what impact changes in various aggregate variables portend for the economy.

In the first section of this chapter, we will consider some of the major events that have accelerated the development of macroeconomic analysis. We then turn to the primary macroeconomic goals our nation has set for itself. Next we look at how business cycles are defined and measured.

The second major section of this chapter looks at the system of national income accounts. These accounts give us our primary measures of income, consumer and government spending, investment, and foreign transactions including exports and imports. To conclude the chapter, we will raise the question of how well these accounts measure our standard of living.

Together, these two sections will give you an introduction to the study of macroeconomics. The foundation established here will apply to the remainder of this course.

After studying this chapter you should be able to

- Describe the scope of macroeconomics.
- Describe the big events that shaped the study of macroeconomics.
- Describe the goals of macroeconomic policy.
- Describe the business cycle and some of the important macroeconomic variables that affect the level of economic activity.
- Describe the national income and product accounts (NIPA).
- Describe the circular flow of income and discuss why GDP can be computed using either income or expenditure data.
- Describe the four major expenditure components of GDP.
- Describe the major income components of national income.
- Describe the shortcomings of GDP as a measure of our standard of living.

The Scope of Macroeconomics

Macroeconomics studies economic activity from the broadest of perspectives, that of the entire economy. Macroeconomics focuses on such issues as economic growth, output of the economy (called gross domestic product [GDP]), inflation rates, employment, unemployment, and interest rates. These are the dominant variables that define our macroeconomy. They have come into prominence as several major events have shaped the way we study macroeconomics.

Major Events that Shaped Macroeconomic Ideas

The study of macroeconomics has developed out of a series of real-world experiences. To better understand these major economic events or catastrophes, economists have been forced to produce macroeconomic analysis that explains how the macroeconomy works. Three major events of the past century—the Great Depression, episodes of hyperinflation, and massive budget deficits—helped form much of the macroeconomic analysis presented in the following chapters.[2]

The Great Depression

The first and most important event—the event that really put macroeconomics on the map as a discipline of consideration and study—was the Great Depression of the 1930s. Between 1929 and 1933, a $1,000 investment in the stock market fell to a value of $150. Massive bank failures and unemployment rates approaching 25% devastated the American economy, with similar downturns spreading all over the world. Business investment dropped from nearly 18% of gross domestic product in 1929 to under 4% in 1933. Government spending doubled during this period, but it was still not enough to pull the economy out of the Depression.

The collapse of economies around the world during the Depression changed our whole approach to macroeconomics. Before the Depression, macroeconomics was regarded as an extension of the microeconomics of markets. It was assumed that labor, capital, and output markets would keep the economy near full employment, with small fluctuations in wages, prices, and interest rates helping the economy to adjust to disruptions. The Depression forced economists to reconsider—and for several decades to scrap—this earlier way of looking at the macroeconomy.

British economist John Maynard Keynes led the profession in providing an explanation for the Depression. He shifted the entire focus of economic analysis. He didn't begin by studying individual markets, then assuming the economy would behave in similar fashion. Instead, Keynes began by looking at the broader economy, focusing on such aggregate data as spending by consumers, business, and government. His analysis serves as the foundation of modern macroeconomics; it underlies much of what follows in the rest of this book. After Keynes, macroeconomics became a subject in its own right, not just a small extension of microeconomics.

Episodes of Hyperinflation

The second major event to influence macroeconomic analysis was episodes of extremely high inflation, or hyperinflation. These high inflationary episodes, which include the hyperinflation in Germany in the 1920s and the inflation crises many South American countries experienced during the last part of the 20th century, involved inflation rates of over 1,000% a year.

Episodes of high inflation cripple economies by forcing people to spend much of their time coping with rapidly changing prices, until finally the economy collapses. Hyperinflation is associated with a rapid increase in the money supply, usually because governments finance deficits by pulling out all the stops on the printing presses—printing more and more money. Periods of high inflation, therefore, tend to be associated with high budget deficits, which many governments finance by printing money. Several chapters in this book will consider the link between the quantity of money in the economy and changes in output and inflation.

These inflationary episodes and the havoc they wreaked have convinced monetary authorities such as the Federal Reserve to carefully manage the money supply. As you will see, nudging the growth rate of the money supply up can lead to short-term gains in employment and output, but increasing the money supply too rapidly simply leads to higher prices in the longer term, or inflation. Modern monetary theory and policy has developed out of this cauldron of past episodes of high inflation.

Budget Deficits

A third influence on macroeconomic analysis has been the huge swings in federal budget deficits over the past two or three decades. Massive deficits in many

---

[2]These three major events (and others) are described and analyzed in detail in Rudiger Dornbusch, et al., *Macroeconomics* (New York: McGraw-Hill Irwin), 2004, Chap. 18, p. 452.

developing countries devastated their economies, focusing attention on the long-run consequences of mismanaging the economy.

High budget deficits must be financed by either borrowing from the public or printing money. Borrowing huge sums of money in the capital markets drives up interest rates and often crowds out the private investment in new plants and equipment that must occur if the economy is to grow and prosper. Just as you are less likely to take out a mortgage when interest rates are 15% as compared to 6%, so businesses are far less likely to invest in production capacity when interest rates climb into double digits. And as noted earlier, running the printing presses to finance a deficit simply generates inflation. The higher the deficit relative to the size of the economy, the higher inflation rates go, and the more devastating the results.

It is not surprising that major economic problems such as a depression, hyper-inflation, and massive budget deficits should focus the attention of economists, much as a 1,000-foot drop straight down will focus the attention of the mountain climber. In times of economic trouble, economists are not just engaged in academic research. They desperately try to solve problems that, if not corrected, can bring massive hardship to millions of people and whole nations. Later, with the benefit of hindsight, economists can develop more complete explanations of what has happened. These theories help economists prevent the future occurrence of similar events. These theories also help achieve future macroeconomic goals.

Macroeconomic Goals

Before the Great Depression and World War II, no one talked about macroeconomic goals. Government policy revolved around a few limited responsibilities, such as national defense, tax and tariff collection, road building, and the maintenance of a stable legal environment. During the Depression, the Roosevelt administration expanded the role of government by enacting a wide variety of employment and spending programs, collectively known as "the New Deal," and establishing the Social Security Administration to ensure a minimal standard of living for the elderly.

Following World War II, many people assumed that the economy would shrink back to its prewar recession levels, possibly ushering in another depression. To avert such a downturn, Congress passed the Employment Act of 1946, which mandated a national goal of providing full employment to all Americans who are willing and able to work. Rationing and the focus on producing armaments during the war years left consumers with huge pent-up demands for cars, appliances, and housing. As a result, the economy mushroomed after the war, much to the surprise of many Americans.

Roughly 30 years later, Congress passed the Full Employment and Balanced Growth Act of 1978, also known as the Humphrey-Hawkins Act, to augment the original act. Besides full employment, this act directs the government to pursue policies designed to stimulate economic growth and reduce inflation. Because inflation had reached double digits by the 1970s, it was only natural that Congress should add price stability to the nation's economic goals.

Figure 1 shows how well these major macroeconomic goals have been met over the past four decades. The growth of GDP has varied from small negative numbers to over 7% in the early 1980s. Unemployment has hovered around the 5–6% range, with two major jumps in the 1970s and early 1980s. Inflation shot up in the 1970s and early 1980s because of worldwide oil price spikes and monetary accommodation, but it has since fallen steadily.

Budget deficits have been the norm across this period, with the notable exception of the late 1990s, when the economy was booming and Congress kept a tight reign on spending. A glance at these four variables in the early 2000s gives the impression of an economy that is sound, with unemployment and inflation low, and economic growth at over 5%. The only negative indicator is a rising budget deficit.

In summary, the major economic goals our nation has set for itself include full employment (defined roughly as 4% unemployment, as we will see in the next chap-

FIGURE 1

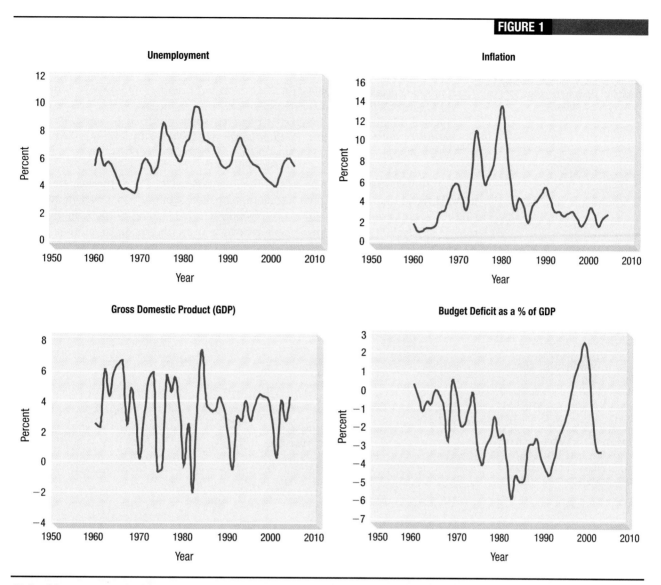

Major Macroeconomic Data

This graph shows the major macroeconomic variables over the past 4 decades. These include the percentage change in current dollar GDP, the inflation rate, the unemployment rate, and ratio of deficits to GDP. Note that the growth of GDP has varied from small negative numbers to over 7% in the early 1980s. Unemployment has hovered around the 5–6% range, with increases in the 1970s and early 1980s. Inflation shot up in the 1970s and early 1980s, but has since fallen steadily. Budget deficits have been the norm across this period, with the notable exception of the late 1990s.

ter), price stability, and high economic growth. Though 5% has become the standard measure of full employment, many economists see such a goal as unrealistic. As we will see, moreover, full employment and low inflation involve tradeoffs: It is difficult to have both for long. This issue, however, we will leave for a later chapter. Let's turn now to a brief look at business cycles.

Business Cycles

America's economic growth over the past century has been little short of phenomenal. Even so, the general upward rise in economic activity and standard of living has been punctuated by periods of downturn, recession, and one outright depression. These fluctuations around the long-run growth trend are called business cycles. Business cycles are a common feature of industrialized economies.

Defining Business Cycles

Business cycles are defined as alternating increases and decreases in economic activity. As economists Arthur Burns and Wesley Mitchell wrote,

> *Business cycles are a type of fluctuation found in the aggregate economic activity of nations that organize their work mainly in business enterprises: a cycle consists of expansions occurring at about the same time in many economic activities, followed by similarly general recession, contractions and revivals which merge into the expansion phase of the next cycle.*[3]

Figure 2 shows the four phases of the business cycle. These phases, around an upward trend, include the peak (sometimes called a boom), followed by a recession (often referred to as a downturn or contraction), leading to the trough or bottom of the cycle, finally followed by a recovery or an expansion to another peak.

FIGURE 2

Typical Business Cycle

The four phases of the business cycle are the peak or boom, followed by a recession (often called a downturn or contraction), leading to the trough or bottom of the cycle, followed by a recovery or an expansion leading to another peak. Note that although this diagram suggests business cycles have regular movements, in reality the various phases of the cycle vary widely in duration and intensity.

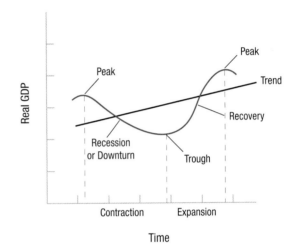

A peak in the business cycle usually means the economy is operating at its capacity. Peaks are followed by downturns or recessions. This change can happen simply because the boom runs out of steam and business investment begins to decline, thereby throwing the economy into a tailspin, as we will see in later chapters.

Once a recession is under way, business will react by curtailing hiring and perhaps even laying off workers, thus adding to the recession's depth. Eventually, however, a trough will be reached, and economic activity will begin to pick up as businesses and consumers become more enthusiastic about the economy. Often, the federal government or the Federal Reserve institutes fiscal or monetary policies to help reverse the recession. Again, this analysis is the focus of future chapters.

Figure 2 suggests that business cycles are fairly regular, but in fact the various phases of the cycle can vary dramatically in duration and intensity. As Table 1 shows, the recessions of the last half century have lasted anywhere from 6 months to 16 months. Expansions or recoveries have varied even more, lasting from 1 year to as many as 9 years. Some recessions, moreover, have been truly intense, bringing about major declines in income, while others have been little more than potholes in the road, causing no declines in real income.

---

[3]Arthur Burns and Wesley Mitchell, *Measuring Business Cycles* (New York: National Bureau of Economic Research), 1946, p. 3.

Table 1			Selected Data for U.S. Business Cycles Since 1950			
Years	Peak	Trough	Recession Length (months)	Expansion Length (months)	Percentage Change in Real GDP	Maximum Unemployment Rate
1953–54	Jul-53	May-54	10	39	−2.2	5.9
1957–58	Aug-57	Apr-58	8	24	−3.6	7.4
1960–61	Apr-60	Feb-61	10	106	−0.6	7.1
1969–70	Dec-69	Nov-70	11	36	+0.2	6.1
1973–75	Nov-73	Mar-75	16	58	−1.8	9.0
1980	Jan-80	Jul-80	6	12	−2.3	7.8
1981–82	Jul-81	Nov-82	16	92	−2.2	10.8
1990–91	Jul-90	Mar-91	8	108	−1.0	6.9
2001	Mar-01	Nov-01	8	—	+1.0	5.8

Unemployment has shown a similar variability: The more severe the recession, the higher the unemployment rate goes. In our last two recessions (1990–91 and 2001), the economy as a whole showed remarkable resiliency, but the recoveries were termed "jobless recoveries" because the early rate of employment increase was well below the average for past recoveries.

Dating Business Cycles

Business cycles are officially dated by the National Bureau of Economic Research (NBER), a nonprofit research organization founded in 1920. The NBER assigns a committee of economists the task of dating "turning points"—points at which the economy switches from peak to downturn or from trough to recovery. The committee looks for clusters of aggregate data pointing either up or down. Committee members date turning points when they reach a consensus that the economy has switched directions.

The committee's work has met with some criticism because their decisions rest on the consensus of six eminent economists, who often bring different methodologies to the table. The committee's deliberations, moreover, are not public; the committee announces only its final decision. Finally, the NBER dates peaks and troughs only after the fact: Their decisions appear several months after the turning points have been reached.[4] By waiting, the panel can use updated or revised data to avoid premature judgments. But some argue that the long lag renders the NBER's decisions less useful to policymakers.

The duration and intensity of business cycles are measured using data collected by the Bureau of Economic Analysis (BEA) and U.S. Department of Labor. These data for aggregate income and output come from the national income and product accounts (NIPA). We turn in a moment to see how these data are collected and analyzed and consider how well they measure our standard of living. Keep in mind that these data are the key ingredients economists use to determine the state of the macroeconomy and to decide whether our national macroeconomic goals are being met.

---

[4]Marcelle Chauvet and Jeremy Piger, "Identifying Business Cycle Turning Points in Real Time," *Review* (St. Louis: The Federal Reserve Bank of St. Louis), March/April 2003, pp. 47–61.

Is the New Economy Producing Micro Recessions?

Are U.S. recessions becoming milder and more spread out? Looking at the data, it certainly seems that way. Looking at Figure 3 and Table 2, you should get the impression that the macroeconomy is becoming less variable and more stable. First, Figure 3 shows that the percentage change in real GDP from roughly 1983 onward seems a lot less volatile. Second, Table 2 shows the data for the seven recessions between 1953 and 1982 and compares them to the two recessions since 1982.

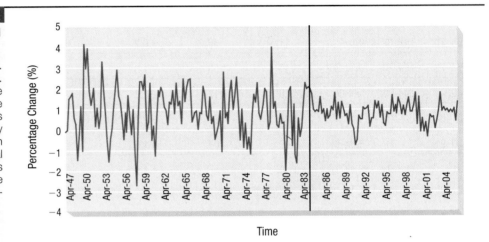

FIGURE 3

Percentage Change in Real GDP (quarterly)

Before roughly 1983, the U.S. economy was quite volatile. After 1983 the intensity of the business cycle seems to have been reduced. Several reasons might explain this change. They include better supply chain management, technological improvements in computers and communications, and the shift to more of a service economy.

Table 2	Comparing Data for Seven Recessions Before 1983 and the Two Recessions After 1983	
Variable	**1953–1982**	**Since 1982**
Number of years covered	30	25
Number of recessions	7	2
Average recession length	11 months	8 months
Average maximum unemployment rate	7.7%	6.3%
Average percentage drop in real GDP	−1.8%	0% (no change)
Average length of following expansion	39 months	85 months

In the 30 years between 1953 and 1982, there were seven recessions, lasting an average of 11 months accompanied by a reduction in real GDP of 1.8% and a maximum unemployment rate averaging 7.7%. The expansion period for these business cycles lasted an average of 39 months. In contrast, in the last 25 years, we have experienced two mild recessions lasting 8 months with an average of no drop in real GDP and a maximum unemployment rate of 6.3%. As of the end of 2006, the expansions have exceeded 85 months on average. There is quite a difference between the two periods.

All of this is the good news. The downside, as Figure 4 shows, is that while the last two recessions have been short and mild, the economy has also been slow to add new jobs and increase real output after the recession has reached its trough. Figure 4 compares the 1973–75 and 1981–82 recessions and subsequent recoveries to the last two recessions in 1990–91 and 2001. Note that the graph measures each recession from the trough and shows the percentage change in real GDP 2 years (8 quarters) before the trough and 4 years (16 quarters) after the trough. Notice that the real GDP decline before the trough is greater for the earlier recessions, but the growth in real GDP after the trough for these recessions is significantly greater. Although today's recessions are milder, they do not show as strong a recovery as previous downturns.

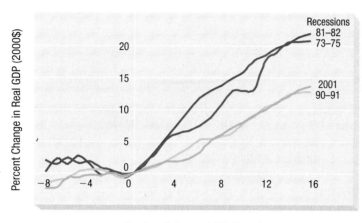

Quarters Before and After Trough

FIGURE 4

Comparison of the Percentage Change in Real GDP Over Four Recessions

The last two recessions have been minor compared to the previous recessions. The percentage drop in real GDP has been less during the recession, but the growth in real GDP has been muted after the trough in recent recessions. These mini-recessions may just reflect changes in the flexibility of the economy and its ability to quickly adapt to change.

What accounts for the fact that our last two recessions have been micro (or mini) recessions? Some of the possible reasons include the remarkable changes that have taken place in transportation and supply-chain management. First, firms today use FedEx, UPS, and the U.S. Postal Service to deliver high-value, important packages overnight, and a steady stream of container ships move cargo steadily across the ocean, reducing the need for firms to maintain huge inventories of products for retailing or manufacturing. Just-in-time (JIT) inventories have become commonplace today. This has made the economy more flexible. Second, the shift to more services in our economy has acted to diversify demand and stabilize output. Third, globalization has provided a form of diversification to our economy; if sales fall in one part of the world, often another part is growing. Fourth, technical advances in communications and computing have made many of these changes possible, along with many others that increase the flexibility of the economy to adapt to change. All of these factors seem to be providing a cushioning effect that not only buffers the downturn but also dampens the upswing.

As Princeton economist and former vice chairman of the Federal Reserve system, Alan Blinder, has noted, "In the classic old business cycle, there would be a diminution in sales; it would take a little while for this information to reach corporate headquarters, and there would be an inventory pileup. And then—bam—businesses would react, sometimes violently, by cutting production."[5] As we would expect, this would lead to layoffs, reducing income and consumer spending, and subsequently reducing investment by business, and the recession would feed on itself, reducing GDP further.

Given that in both of the last recessions, the unemployment rate remained around 6%, relatively close to full employment, it may not be surprising that subsequent employment and GDP growth was only modest. Clearly, 25 years with only two modest recessions is a remarkable record, but it does not mean the end of the business cycle.

---

[5]Quoted in David Leonhardt, "Have Recessions Absolutely, Positively Become Less Painful?" *New York Times*, October 8, 2005, p. C1.

The Scope of Macroeconomics

REVIEW

- Three major events have shaped macroeconomic ideas in the last century: the Great Depression, episodes of hyperinflation, and large budget deficits.
- The Great Depression and John Maynard Keynes completely changed the focus of macroeconomics from an extension of microeconomic theory to an analysis in its own right.
- The havoc from hyperinflation provided evidence of money's role and the need to carefully manage the money supply.
- High budget deficits illustrated the impact on inflation of deficits that are large relative to the economy.
- The Employment Act of 1946, later amended to become the Full Employment and Balanced Growth Act of 1978 (Humphrey-Hawkins Act), directs the government to pursue policies that generate full employment with economic growth while maintaining price stability.
- Business cycles are alternating increases and decreases in economic activity.
- The four phases of the business cycle include the peak, recession (or contraction), trough, and recovery (or expansion).
- Business cycles are dated by the National Bureau of Economic Research (NBER). Business cycles are usually dated some time after the trough and peak have been reached.

QUESTION

Do you think the business cycle has a bigger impact on automobile and capital goods manufacturers or on grocery stores?

Answers to the Checkpoint question can be found at the end of this chapter.

National Income Accounting

The National Income and Product Accounts (NIPA) let economists judge our nation's economic performance, compare American income and output to that of other nations, and track the economy's condition over the course of the business cycle. Many economists would say these accounts represent one of the greatest inventions of the 20th century.[6]

Before World War I, estimating the output of various sectors of the economy—and to an extent the output of the economy as a whole—was a task left to individual scholars. Government agencies tried to measure various sorts of economic activity, but little came of these efforts. When the Great Depression struck, the lack of reliable economic data made it difficult for the administration and Congress to design timely and appropriate policy responses. Much of the information that was available at the time was anecdotal: newspaper reports of plant shutdowns, stories of home and farm foreclosures, and observations of the rapid meltdown of the stock market.

In 1933, Congress directed the Department of Commerce to develop estimates of "total national income for the United States for each of the calendar years 1929,

---

[6]William Nordhaus and Edward Kokkelenberg (eds.), *Nature's Numbers: Expanding the National Economic Accounts to Include the Environment* (Washington, DC: National Academy Press), 1999, p. 12.

Nobel Prize Simon Kuznets and Richard Stone

Simon Kuznets

Richard Stone

Simon Kuznets and Richard Stone were each awarded the Nobel Prize for devising systematic approaches to the compilation and analysis of national economic data,. Kuznets, winning in 1971, is often credited with developing gross national product as a measurement of economic output. Stone, winning in 1984, created a system of "national accounts" that has been adopted by nations throughout the world.

Born in the Ukraine in 1901, Kuznets immigrated to the United States in 1922 to join his father. He earned a Ph.D. from Columbia University in 1926. Kuznets then worked at the National Bureau of Economic Research (NBER), conducting studies of national income and capital formation. During World War II, Kuznets served as associate director of the Bureau of Planning and Statistics of the War Production Board. Starting in 1931, he taught economics at the University of Pennsylvania, Johns Hopkins University, and Harvard University. When he died in 1985, economist Paul Samuelson called him "a giant in 20th century economics."

Kuznets developed methods for calculating the size and changes in national income. Caring little for abstract models, he sought to define concepts that could be observed empirically and measured statistically. Kuznets considered factors such as population growth, technology, industrial structures, and market growth in discerning patterns in growth and changes in business cycles.

Richard Stone was born in London in 1913, the son of a barrister. He showed little interest in school until he switched to economics as an undergraduate at Cambridge University, where he attended John Maynard Keynes's lectures. After Cambridge, he worked for Lloyds of London for several years but continued to do research in and writing on economics.

At the outbreak of World War II, he joined the British government, where he developed the statistical analysis for a survey on England's economic conditions that was shown to Keynes, who was then serving as chief advisor to the British Treasury. Working with fellow economist James Meade, Stone collected statistical information used to analyze potential imbalances in the British wartime economy. The systems they developed caused Keynes to exclaim: "We are in a new era of joy through statistics."

Stone's design of a national accounts system integrated different subsectors of the economy, measuring household expenditures, outlays by businesses, expenditures by the public sector, and interactions with other nations. After the war, Stone developed international norms for national accounts through his work with the United Nations. His models achieved wide acceptance, making it easier to derive comparisons of national economies. Stone died in 1991.

1930, and 1931, including estimates of the portions of national income originating from [different sectors] and estimates of the distribution of the national income in the form of wages, rents, royalties, dividends, profits and other types of payments." This directive was the beginning of the NIPA.

In 1934, a small group of economists working under the leadership of Simon Kuznets and in collaboration with the NBER produced a report for the Senate. The report defined many standard economic aggregates still in use today, including gross national product, gross domestic product, consumer spending, and investment spending. Kuznets was later awarded a Nobel Prize for his lifetime of work in this area.

Work continued on NIPA through World War II, and by 1947 the basic components of the present day income and product accounts were in place. Over the years, the Department of Commerce (DOC) has modified, improved, and updated the data it collects. These data are released on a quarterly basis, with preliminary data being put out in the middle of the month following a given quarter. By the end of a given quarter, the DOC will have collected about two thirds of the survey data it needs, allowing it to estimate the remaining data to generate preliminary figures.

The Core of NIPA

The major components of the NIPA can be found in either of two ways: adding up the income in the economy or adding up spending. A simple circular flow diagram of the economy shows why either approach can be used to determine the economy's level of economic activity.

The Circular Flow Diagram

Circular flow diagram
Illustrates how households and firms interact through product and resource markets and shows that economic aggregates can be determined by either examining spending flows or income flows to households.

Figure 5 is a simple **circular flow diagram** that shows how businesses and households interact through the product and resource markets.

Let us first follow the arrows that point in a clockwise direction. Begin at the bottom of the diagram with households. Households supply labor (and other inputs or factors of production) to the resource market; that is, they become employees of businesses. Businesses use this labor (and other inputs) to produce goods and services that are supplied to the product markets. Such products in the end find their way back into households through consumer purchases. The arrows pointing clockwise show the flow of real items: hours worked, goods and services produced and purchased.

The arrows pointing counterclockwise, in contrast, represent flows of money. Businesses pay for inputs (factors) of production: land, labor, capital, and entrepreneurship. Factors are paid rents, wages, interest, and profits. These payments become income for the economy's households, which use these funds to purchase goods and services in the product market. This spending for goods and services becomes sales revenues for the business sector.

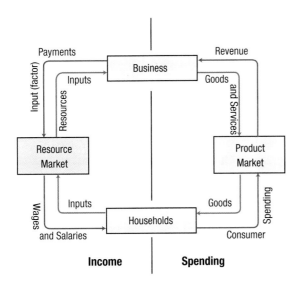

FIGURE 5

A Simple Circular Flow Diagram

Businesses and households interact through the product and resource markets. Households supply labor to input (factor) markets and businesses use this labor to produce products. These products find their way back into households through consumer purchases. Hence, the arrows pointing clockwise reflect the flow of real items including hours worked, and goods and services produced and purchased. The arrows pointing counterclockwise represent the money flows. Businesses pay rents, wages, interest, and profits to inputs (factors) of production. These payments become income for the economy's households, which use these funds to purchase goods and services. These payments for goods and services become revenues for the business sector.

This simple circular flow diagram illustrates why the economic aggregates in our economy can be determined in either of two ways. Spending flows through the right side of the diagram, while the left side of the diagram shows incomes flowing to households.

Spending and Income: Looking at GDP in Two Ways

This simple circular flow diagram illustrates why economic aggregates in our economy can be determined in either of two ways. The spending in the economy accrues on the right side of the diagram. In this simple diagram, all spending is assumed to be consumer spending for goods and services. We know, however, that businesses spend money on investment goods such as equipment, plants, factories, and specialized vehicles to increase their productivity. Also, government buys goods and services, as do foreigners. This spending shows up in the NIPA, though is not included in our simple circular flow diagram.

Second, similar income is generated equal to the spending in the product market. This is shown on the left side of the diagram. Wages and salaries constitute the bulk of income in our economy (roughly three quarters of it), with rents, interest, and profits comprising the rest. Everything that is spent on the right side represents income on the left side; all spending must equal input (factor) incomes. We now define the major aggregates in NIPA.

Gross Domestic Product

Gross domestic product (GDP) is a measure of the economy's total output; it is the most widely reported value in NIPA. Technically, the nation's *GDP is equal to the total market value of all final goods and services produced by resources in the United States.* A few points about this definition need to be noted.

Gross domestic product (GDP)
A measure of the economy's total output; it is the most widely reported value in the national income and product accounts (NIPA) and is equal to the total market value of all final goods and services produced by resources in the United States.

First, GDP reflects the *final* value of goods and services produced. So measurements of GDP do not include the value of intermediate goods used to produce other products. This distinction helps prevent what economists call "double counting," since a good's final value will include the intermediate values going into its production.

To illustrate, consider a box of toothpicks. The firm producing these toothpicks must first purchase a supply of cottonwood, let's say for $0.22 a box. The firm then mills this wood into toothpicks, which it puts into a small box purchased from another company at $0.08 apiece. The completed box is sold to a grocery store wholesale for $0.65. After a markup, the grocery retails the box of toothpicks for $0.89. The sale raises GDP by $0.89, *not* by $1.84 (0.22 + 0.08 + 0.65 + 0.89), since the values of the cottonwood, the box, and the grocery store's services are already included in the toothpicks' final sales price. Thus, by including only final prices in GDP, double counting is avoided.

A second point to note is that, as the term gross *domestic* product implies, GDP is a measure of the output produced by resources in the United States. It does not matter whether the producers are American citizens or foreign citizens as long as the production takes place using resources in this country. GDP does not include goods or services produced abroad, even if the producers are American citizens or companies.

In contrast to GDP is *gross national product* (GNP), the standard measure of output the DOC used until the early 1990s. GNP reflects the market value of all goods and services produced by resources supplied by U.S. residents. So GNP includes goods produced both at home and abroad, as long as the production involves resources owned by U.S. residents. The difference between GDP and GNP is small. The main reason the DOC switched its measurements was to ensure its data were more directly comparable to that collected by the rest of the world.

Third, note that whenever possible, NIPA uses market values, or the prices paid for products, to compute GDP. So even if a firm must sell its product at a loss, the product's final sales price is what figures into GDP, not the firm's production costs.

Fourth, the NIPA accounts focus on market-produced goods and services. The major exceptions to this approach include substituting payroll costs for the value of government services and estimating (imputing) the rental value of owner-occupied housing. This focus on market values has been criticized on the grounds that nanny services, for instance, are figured into GDP, while the values for these same services when performed by parents are not.

The Expenditures Approach to Calculating GDP

Again, GDP can be measured using either spending or income. With the expenditures approach, all spending on final goods and services is added together. The four major categories of spending are personal consumer spending, gross private domestic investment (GPDI), government spending, and net exports (exports minus imports).

Personal Consumption Expenditures

Personal consumption expenditures (PCE) are goods and services purchased by residents of the United States, whether individuals or businesses. Goods and services are divided into three main categories: durable goods, nondurable goods, and services. Durable goods are products that can be stored or inventoried; they have an average life span of 3 years. Automobiles, major appliances, books, CDs, and firearms are all examples of durable goods. Nondurable goods include all other tangible goods, such as canned soft drinks, frozen pizza, toothbrushes, and underwear (all of which should be thrown out before they are 3 years old). Services are commodities that cannot be stored and are consumed at the time and place of purchase, for example, legal, barber, and repair services. Table 3 gives a detailed account of

Personal consumption expenditures (PCE)
Goods and services purchased by residents of the United States, whether individuals or businesses; they include durable goods, nondurable goods, and services.

Table 3	The Expenditures Approach to GDP (2006)	
Category	**Billions of $**	**% of GDP**
Personal Consumption Expenditures	9,268.9	70.00
Durable goods	1,070.3	8.08
Nondurable goods	2,714.9	20.50
Services	5,483.7	41.40
Gross Private Domestic Investment	2,212.5	16.70
Fixed nonresidential	1,396.2	10.54
Fixed residential	766.7	5.79
Change in Inventories	49.6	0.37
Government Purchases of Goods and Services	2,527.7	19.08
Federal	926.6	7.05
State and local	1,601.1	12.09
Net Exports	−762.5	−5.76
Exports	1,466.2	11.07
Imports	−2,228.7	−16.82
Gross Domestic Product	13,246.6	100.00

Source: U.S. Department of Commerce, Bureau of Economic Analysis, www.bea.doc.gov.

U.S. personal consumption spending in 2006. Notice that personal consumption is 70% of GDP, far and away the most important part of GDP, and services are nearly 60% of personal consumption.

Gross Private Domestic Investment

The second major aggregate listed in Table 3 is **gross private domestic investment (GPDI),** which at over 16% of GDP, refers to *fixed investments,* or investments in such things as structures (residential and nonresidential), equipment, and software. It also includes changes in private inventories.

Residential housing represents about a third of GPDI, and nonresidential structures are just less than two thirds of investment. Nonresidential structures include such diverse structures as hotels and motels, manufacturing plants, mine shafts, oil wells, and fast-food restaurants. Improvements to existing business structures and new construction are counted as fixed investments.

A "change in inventories" refers to a change in the physical volume of the inventory a private business owns, valued at the average prices over the period. If a business increases its inventories, this change is treated as an investment since the business is adding to the stock of products it has ready for sale.

Private investment is a key factor driving economic growth and an important determinant of swings in the business cycle. Figure 6 on the next page tracks GPDI as a percentage of GDP since 1950. The last nine recessions are represented by vertical shaded areas, with business cycle peaks (P) and troughs (T) so labeled. Notice that just before each peak of the business cycle, GPDI turns down, and just before

Gross private domestic investment (GPDI)
Investments in such things as structures (residential and nonresidential), equipment, and software, and changes in private business inventories.

FIGURE 6

Gross Private Domestic Investment (GPDI) as a Percent of GDP

Private investment is a key factor driving economic growth and an important determinant of swings in the business cycle. This graph tracks gross private domestic investment (GPDI) as a percentage of GDP since 1950. The last nine recessions are represented by vertical shaded areas, with business cycle peaks (P) and troughs (T) shown. Notice that just before each peak of the business cycle, GPDI turns down, and just before each of the troughs, GPDI turns up.

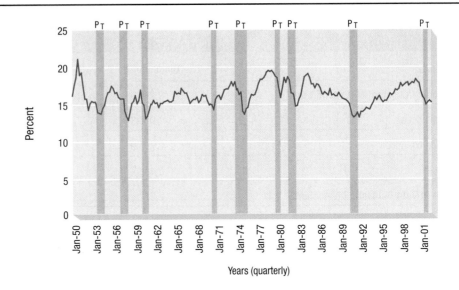

each of the recessions ends, GPDI turns up. Investment is, therefore, an important factor shaping the turning points of the business cycle, especially at the troughs, and an important determinant of how severe recessions will be.

Government Purchases

Government spending
Includes the wages and salaries of government employees (federal, state, and local); the purchase of products and services from private businesses and the rest of the world; and government purchases of new structures, equipment, and software.

The government component of GDP measures the impact **government spending** has on final demand in the economy. At nearly 19% of GDP, government spending is a relatively large and stable component of GDP. It includes the wages and salaries of government employees (federal, state, and local) and the purchase of products and services from private businesses and the rest of the world. Government spending also includes the purchase of new structures, equipment, and software.

Net Exports of Goods and Services

Net exports
Exports minus imports for the current period. Exports include all the items we sell overseas such as agricultural products, movies, and technology products, while imports are all those items we bring into the country such as vegetables from Mexico, wine from Italy, and cars from Germany.

Net exports of goods and services are equal to exports minus imports for the current period. Exports include all the items we sell overseas: items such as agricultural products, movies, and technology products such as computers and software. Our imports are all those items we bring into the country, including vegetables from Mexico, clothing from the Far East, and cars from Japan. Most years our imports exceed our exports, so net exports are a minus percentage of GDP.

Summing Aggregate Expenditures

The four categories just described are commonly abbreviated as C (consumption), I (investment), G (government), and X − M (net exports; exports minus imports). Together, these four variables constitute GDP. We often summarize this by the following equation:

$$GDP = C + I + G + (X - M)$$

Using the information from Table 3, we can calculate GDP for 2006 (in $ billion) as

$$13,246.6 = 9,268.9 + 2,212.5 + 2,257.7 + (-762.5)$$

The Income Approach to Calculating GDP

As we have already seen, spending that contributes to GDP provides an income for one of the economy's various inputs (factors) of production. And in theory, this is how this process works. In practice, however, the national income accounts need to be adjusted to fully account for GDP when we switch from the expenditures to the income approach. Let's work our way through the income side of NIPA, which Table 4 summarizes.

Table 4	The Income Approach to GDP (2006)	
Category	**Billions of $**	**% of GDP**
Compensation of Employees	7,498.4	56.61
Wages and salaries	6,043.6	45.62
Employer contribution for social insurance	462.1	3.49
Employer contribution to pensions and insurance	992.7	7.49
Proprietors' Income	1,015.1	7.66
Corporate Profits	1,615.7	12.20
Rental Income	77.4	.58
Net Interest	509.3	3.84
Taxes, Foreign Income, and Miscellaneous Adjustments	995.1	7.51
National Income	11,711.0	88.41
Adjustments to National Income		
Capital consumption allowance	1,576.9	11.90
Income payments to rest of world	−625.7	−4.80
Income payments from rest of world	665.6	5.02
Statistical discrepancy	−71.2	−0.54
Gross Domestic Product	13,246.6	100.00

Source: U.S. Department of Commerce, Bureau of Economic Analysis, www.bea.doc.gov.

Compensation of Employees

Compensation to employees refers to payments for work done, including wages, salaries, and benefits. Benefits include the social insurance payments made by employers to various government programs, such as Social Security, Medicare, and workers' and unemployment compensation. Some other benefits that count as labor income are employer-provided pensions, profit-sharing plans, group health insurance, and in-kind benefits such as day care services. Employee compensation is nearly 57% of GDP.

Proprietors' Income

Proprietors' income represents the current income of all sole proprietorships, partnerships, and tax-exempt cooperatives in the country. It includes the imputed (estimated) rental income of owner-occupied farm houses. Proprietors' income is adjusted by a capital consumption allowance to account for depreciating equipment (equipment that is used up while producing goods and services). Although there are a lot of proprietorships in the United States, their combined income is less than 8% of GDP.

Rental Income

Rental income, less than 1% of GDP, is the income that flows to individuals engaged in renting real property. This does not include the income of real estate agents or brokers, but it does include the imputed value of owner-occupied homes, along with royalties from patents, copyrights, and rights to natural resources.

Corporate Profits

Corporate profits are defined as the income that flows to corporations, as adjusted for inventory valuation and capital consumption allowances. Most corporations are private enterprises, although this category also includes mutual financial institutions, Federal Reserve banks, and nonprofit institutions that mainly serve businesses. Despite the huge profit figures reported in the news media, corporate profits are less than 13% of GDP.

Net Interest

Net interest is the interest paid by businesses less the interest they receive, from this country and abroad, and is under 4% of GDP. Interest expense is the payment for the use of capital. Interest income includes payments from home mortgages, home improvement loans, and home equity loans.

Taxes, Foreign Income, and Miscellaneous Adjustments

Both indirect business taxes (sales and excise taxes) and foreign income earned in the United States are part of GDP, but must be backed out of payments to factors of production in this country. Neither is paid to U.S. factors of production.

National Income

National income
All income including wages, salaries and benefits, profits (for sole proprietors, partnerships, and corporations), rental income, and interest.

National income is all income including wages, salaries, and benefits; profits (for sole proprietors, partnerships, and corporations); rental income; and interest. Pay to employees represents nearly two thirds of national income, whereas corporate profits compose nearly 14%, with rental income and interest making up the rest.

From National Income to GDP

National income is the income that accrues to U.S.-supplied resources, whether at home or abroad. Getting from national income to GDP requires a few adjustments. Specifically, three major items (and some minor ones that we will ignore) plus a statistical discrepancy must be added to national income to arrive at the GDP figures listed on the bottom of Table 4.

An allowance for the depreciation (or consumption) of fixed capital is added back, since gross domestic product is gross of depreciation to fixed capital. Second, the payments U.S. residents receive from foreign sources are added, and the payments U.S. corporations and residents send to foreign residents are subtracted out.

This adjusted sum is known as *gross domestic income*. Once a small statistical discrepancy has been corrected, it is equal to GDP. When these adjustments are completed, GDP is the same whether it is derived from spending or income.

Net Domestic Product

Net domestic product
Gross domestic product minus depreciation or the capital consumption allowance.

As firms and individuals generate GDP, they use up some capital, which must be replaced if future production is to continue at similar levels. A more realistic measure of sustainable output, **net domestic product,** is defined as GDP minus depreciation or the capital consumption allowance. Equipment wears out as output is produced. Motor graders, cranes, trucks, and automobiles do not last forever. Therefore, net domestic product represents the output the economy produced after adjusting for capital used up in the process.

Personal Income and Disposable Personal Income

Personal income includes all income including wages, salaries, and other labor income, proprietors' income, rental income, personal interest and dividend income, and transfer payments (welfare and Social Security payments) received, with personal contributions for social insurance subtracted out.

People can do three things with the money they receive as personal income: pay taxes, spend the money (engage in consumption), or put the money into savings. **Disposable personal income** is defined as personal income minus taxes. Disposable income (Y) can be either spent (C) or saved (S); thus,

$$Y = C + S$$

This simple equation, which you will see again, led John Maynard Keynes to some powerful ideas about the workings of our economy.

We have seen how the national income and product accounts determine the major macroeconomic aggregates. But what does NIPA tell us about our economy? When GDP rises, are we better off as a nation? Do increases in GDP correlate with a rising standard of living? What impact does rising GDP have on the environment and the quality of life? We conclude this chapter with a brief look at some of these questions.

GDP and Our Standard of Living

After World War II, GDP growth was viewed universally as a positive event for the economy. Today, Americans have become increasingly concerned with the impact economic activity has on the natural world. These days, it is difficult to watch a nightly newscast without seeing a report about some ecological disaster or looming environmental problem. Government, consumers, and businesses in the United States spend hundreds of billions of dollars annually to protect the environment at home and abroad. Surprisingly, however, our national income and production statistics do little to account for the environmental benefits or harmful impacts of economic activity.

In 1992, the Bureau of Economic Analysis (BEA) decided to develop an experimental set of economic accounts known as the Integrated Environmental and Economic Satellite Accounts (IEESA). Preliminary versions of these green GDP accounts were published in 1994, and later Congress directed the Department of Commerce to set up an outside panel of experts to study this issue in greater depth. DOC asked the National Academy of Sciences to look at green economic accounting, which it did, appointing a select panel that completed its report in 1999.

The DOC panel concluded that "extending the U.S. NIPA to include assets and production activities associated with natural resources and the environment is an important goal." The panel concluded, "Developing nonmarket accounts to address such concerns as environmental impacts, the value of nonmarket natural resources, the value of nonmarket work, the value of investments in human capital, and the use of people's time would illuminate a wide variety of issues concerning the economic state of the nation."[7]

The panel's recommendations highlight some of the broader shortcomings of NIPA. For example, the national accounts ignore nonmarket transactions. If a maid cleans your apartment, GDP rises, but if you did the same job yourself, GDP is unaffected. The same is true for babysitting, lawn care, and car maintenance. Nor is the notion of augmenting the national accounts to account for nonmarket activities anything new; NIPA already imputes (estimates) the rental value of owner-occupied homes and adds this to GDP. The panel proposed that further measures be developed to reflect "not merely what consumers buy in stores, but also what they

Personal income
All income including wages, salaries, and other labor income; proprietors' income; rental income; personal interest and dividend income; and transfer payments (welfare and Social Security payments) received, with personal contributions for social insurance subtracted out.

Disposable personal income
Personal income minus taxes.

---

[7]Nordhaus and Kokkelenberg, *Nature's Numbers*, pp. 2–3.

produce for themselves at home; the government services they 'buy' with their taxes; and the flow of services that are produced by environmental capital such as forests, national parks, and ocean fisheries."[8]

Many people believe NIPA should be an index of the well-being found within our economy. In that case, it would ideally need to take into account the implications of economic activity the DOC panel noted and more, perhaps including data on life expectancy, business spending on research and development, the stock of human capital including education and health, greenhouse gas emissions, income distribution, poverty rates, and unemployment rates.

It is important, however, to keep NIPA's original purpose in mind. As the DOC panel noted, "The modern national income and product accounts are among the great inventions of the twentieth century. Among other things, they are used to judge economic performance over time, to compare the economies of different nations, to measure a nation's saving and investment, and to track the business cycle. Much as satellites in space can show the weather across an entire continent, the national accounts can give an overall picture of the state of the economy."[9]

To be sure, NIPA has served us well. Still, adjusting the current accounts to account for various environmental and other nonmarket considerations might provide us with an even better picture of the health of our economy. But we must keep in mind that an aggregate measure of the economy cannot be all things to all people. As we add complexity to an already complex undertaking, the NIPA may lose some of their effectiveness as a measure of economic activity. This is a difficult balancing act facing policymakers.

The NIPA allow us to track business cycles, compare the domestic economy with that of other nations, and take a crude measure of our standard of living. In the next chapter, we will see how two other important policy variables, unemployment and inflation, are measured.

In the next several chapters, our focus will be on developing explanations of short-term movements in the business cycle and long-term economic growth (the trend line in Figure 2). If we can understand why upturns and downturns occur, we may be able to devise policies that reduce the severity of business cycle swings while promoting economic growth. These investigations and policy objectives form the essence of modern macroeconomic analysis.

National Income Accounting

REVIEW

- The circular flow diagram shows how households and firms interact through product and labor markets.
- GDP can be computed as spending or as income.
- GDP is equal to the total market value of all final goods and services produced by labor and property in the United States.
- Personal consumption expenditures are goods and services purchased by residents of the United States, both by individuals and businesses.
- Gross private domestic investment (GPDI) refers to fixed investments such as structures, equipment, and software.
- GDP is equal to consumer expenditures, investment expenditures, government purchases, and exports minus imports, in equation form: GDP = C + I + G + (X − M).

---

[8]Ibid., p. 22.
[9]Ibid., p. 12.

■ GDP can also be computed by adding all of the payments to factors of production. This includes compensation to employees, proprietors' income, rental income, corporate profits, and net interest, along with some statistical adjustments.

■ While not perfect, GDP is a good measure of economic activity in our economy.

QUESTIONS

Each individual has a sense of how the macroeconomy is doing. Is it a mistake to extrapolate from one's own experience what may be happening in the aggregate? How might individual experiences lead one astray in thinking about the macroeconomy? How might it help?

Answers to the Checkpoint questions can be found at the end of this chapter.

Technology and Schumpeter's Creative Destruction

As a final consideration of business cycles, consider Schumpeter's analysis (see Schumpeter biography). Schumpeter focused on the power of major innovations to form waves of growth throughout the macroeconomy. The United States may have witnessed such a wave in the 1990s. The innovation was computer technology and the Internet.

There is a general consensus that information technology played a major role in the economic boom of the 1990s.[10] At issue is whether or not this technology affected most parts of the economy and so was more like a Schumpeter innovation wave or not.

The effect of information technology on manufacturers is easy enough to see. It is obvious that computer-aided design has streamlined product creation in the automobile, airline, and heavy-machinery industry.

What have not been so obvious are the beneficial effects of information technology on the service part of the economy. In fact, economists have been surprised by these impacts. Preliminary studies have revealed that productivity in services grew at a greater rate than for goods-producing sectors. This is surprising because services are so labor-intensive.

This growth in services productivity due to information technology has been almost across the board. So far, 24 out of 29 service industries studied have witnessed growth in labor productivity after 1995. The service industry laggards were hotels, health, education, and entertainment, possibly because these industries are especially labor-intensive.

It is fairly clear how information technology has helped service industries that have seen significant growth. The telephone industry, wholesale and retail trade, and finance have all benefited from being better able to track inventory and communicate with customers. Think of bar-coded merchandise and scanners at grocery stores or retail stores. These stores know immediately what is selling, what is not, what stock is on hand, and what needs to be replenished quickly. And the ubiquity of bar codes on products and the plummeting cost of "smart" cash registers mean that your local 7-Eleven is practically as efficient in tracking customer demand and inventory as the big Wal-Mart down the road.

The preliminary view is that the rapid decline in the price of information technology in the 1990s brought this technology to medium- and small-size service enterprises. This led to productivity growth throughout most of the economy. So, the next time you order tickets from Ticketmaster over the Internet rather than the old way by telephone, consider how much easier and quicker it is for you, and how

---

[10]The information in the following paragraphs comes from the article by Hal R. Varian, "Economic Scene: Information Technology May Have Been What Cured Low Service-Sector Productivity," *New York Times,* February 12, 2004, p. C2.

Joseph Schumpeter (1883–1950)

*J*oseph Schumpeter drew attention to the critical role of the entrepreneur in the process of economic development. He famously coined the term "creative destruction" to describe the innovative dynamism of capitalism but came to the surprising conclusion that the system he exalted was ultimately doomed by the forces it helped create.

Born in Triesch, Moravia, in 1883, Schumpeter was the son of a cloth manufacturer. He attended an elite private school and then studied law and economics at the University of Vienna. After graduating, he practiced law in Cairo and provided financial advice to an Egyptian princess. In 1909 he returned to Europe and began teaching at the University of Czernowitz and later at the University of Graz. After an unsuccessful term as minister of finance for Austria, he took a position as bank president in Germany. In 1932, he immigrated to the United States, where he would finish his career as an influential economics professor at Harvard University.

Schumpeter was a confirmed elitist who suffered from self-doubt and depression. Although his career was in the shadow of the more famous John Maynard Keynes, he considered himself to be the greater economist.

In 1912, at the age of 28, he wrote his first important book, the *Theory of Economic Development,* in which he emphasized the importance of the innovator, as opposed to the inventor, in making use of the benefits of technology and scientific discovery to advance economic progress. Schumpeter criticized earlier economists for failing to distinguish the role of the entrepreneur from that of the capitalist.

In 1939, he published *Business Cycles,* which linked entrepreneurial activity to business cycles. He identified a first wave of innovation in the 1780s with the advent of steam power and textile manufacturing. The second wave of innovation came with railways and steel production. The third wave was concerned with electricity and the automobile. Paradoxically, Schumpeter connected innovation with the downturns or depressions in the business cycle, as new products competed with the old. Depressions, in his view, were part of the process of adapting to new innovations. As entrepreneurs spent their capital to pay off debts, the result was deflation. Economic recovery would come when adaptation was completed and the deflationary forces ended.

In 1942, Schumpeter published *Capitalism, Socialism and Democracy,* considered by many to be his masterpiece. He wrote about the future of capitalism, which he now described as creative destruction. In an odd exercise in devil's advocacy, he praised the economic thinking of Karl Marx and came to a similar conclusion about the ultimate fate of capitalism. In Schumpeter's view, however, it was the "bourgeoisie" and not the working class that would destroy the system, as the role of the individual entrepreneur was supplanted by the bureaucratic administration of large corporations.

much cheaper it is for the ticket provider. Then consider how this change might just be a good example of a Schumpeterian wave of innovation, a main driver of the ups and downs of business cycles.

Key Concepts

Business cycles, p. 116
Circular flow diagram, p. 122
Gross domestic product (GDP), p. 123
Personal consumption expenditures (PCE), p. 124
Gross private domestic investment (GPDI), p. 125

Government spending, p. 126
Net exports, p. 126
National income, p. 128
Net domestic product, p. 128
Personal income, p. 129
Disposable personal income, p. 129

Chapter Summary

The Scope of Macroeconomics

Macroeconomics is the study of economic activity from the perspective of the entire economy. It focuses on such issues as economic growth, output of the economy, employment levels, inflation, unemployment, and interest rates.

The study of macroeconomics was driven by three major events of the 20th century: the Great Depression, episodes of hyperinflation, and extensive budget deficits. In each case, major economic problems forced economists to focus their attention on the economy as a whole.

The study of macroeconomics has led policymakers to set several macroeconomic goals. In the United States, the Employment Act of 1946 mandated that the government pursue policies designed to ensure full employment. The Full Employment and Balanced Growth Act of 1978 further directs the government to pursue policies designed to stimulate economic growth and reduce inflation.

Business cycles are the alternating increases and decreases in economic activity typical of market economies. These fluctuations take place around a long-run growth trend.

Business cycles contain four phases: the peak or boom, followed by a recession or downturn, leading to the trough of the cycle, followed by a recovery leading to another peak. Although the business cycle has regularity in its movements, business cycles vary dramatically in duration and intensity.

Business cycles are officially dated by the National Bureau of Economic Research. The NBER assigns a committee of economists the task of dating "turning points," or points at which the economy switches from peak to downturn or from trough to recovery.

National Income Accounting

The national income and product accounts (NIPA) allow economists to judge our nation's economic performance, compare American income and output to that of other nations, and track the economy's condition over the course of the business cycle. The NIPA were first developed in the early 1930s by the Department of Commerce, which has refined them over the years.

The major components of NIPA can be constructed in either of two ways: by summing the income of the economy or by summing spending. A simple circular flow diagram of the economy shows why either approach can be used to determine the country's economic activity: All spending ultimately represents payments to the various inputs (factors) of production and income for whoever receives these payments.

Gross domestic product (GDP) is now the standard measure the Department of Commerce uses to gauge the economy's output. It is equal to the total market value of all final goods and services produced by resources in the United States.

Gross national product (GNP) was the standard measure of output the DOC used until the early 1990s. It measured the market value of all goods and services produced by resources supplied by U.S. residents. Thus, GNP includes goods produced here and abroad, as long as the production involves labor or property owned by U.S. residents. The difference between GDP and GNP is small.

GDP can be measured by adding together either spending or income. With the expenditures approach, all spending on final goods and services is added together. The four major categories of spending are personal consumer spending, gross private domestic investment, government spending, and net exports (exports minus imports).

Personal consumption expenditures (PCE) are goods and services purchased by residents of the United States, whether individuals or businesses. They are divided into three main categories: durable goods, nondurable goods, and services. Personal consumption expenditures account for 70% of GDP and are stable.

Gross private domestic investment (GPDI) includes fixed investments, or investments in residential and nonresidential structures, equipment, and software. GPDI also includes changes in private inventories. GPDI currently accounts for just over 16% of GDP, but it fluctuates significantly.

The government component of GDP measures the impact government spending has on final demand in the economy. It includes the wages and salaries of government employees and the purchase of products and services from private businesses and the rest of the world. Government spending currently accounts for almost 20% of GDP.

The net export of goods and services is equal to exports minus imports for the current period. Currently, net exports account for -5.8% of GDP (imports are greater than exports, hence the negative sign).

The four spending categories are commonly abbreviated as C (consumption), I (investment), G (government), and X − M (exports minus imports, or net exports). Together, these four variables constitute GDP:

$$GDP = C + I + G + (X - M)$$

Using the income approach to measure GDP, the major categories of income are compensation of employees, proprietors' income, rental income, corporate profits, and net interest. Several adjustments are required to the national accounts to fully account for GDP.

Compensation to employees refers to payments for work done, including wages, salaries, and benefits (57% of GDP). Proprietors' income (less than 8% of GDP) is the current income of all sole proprietorships, partnerships, and tax-exempt cooperatives. Rental income is the income that flows to individuals engaged in renting real property (less than 1% of GDP). Corporate profits (12% of GDP) are defined as the income that flows to corporations, as adjusted for inventory valuation and capital consumption allowances. Net interest is the interest paid by businesses less the interest they receive from this country and abroad and is less than 4% of GDP.

National income is the sum of all the income just listed. To get from national income to GDP requires adding an allowance for depreciation of fixed capital, and the payments U.S. residents receive from foreign sources minus the payments they send abroad. These adjustments yield gross domestic income, which is equal to GDP once a small statistical discrepancy is added.

Net national product (NNP) is defined as GDP minus capital consumption allowance (depreciation). Since some assets are used up in the production process, NNP is a better indicator of sustainable income or output.

Personal income includes all income including wages, salaries, and other labor income; proprietors' income; rental income; personal interest and dividend income; and transfer payments, with personal contributions for social insurance subtracted out.

Disposable personal income is defined as personal income minus taxes. Disposable income (Y) can be either spent (C) or saved (S), yielding the equation $Y = C + S$.

NIPA has some shortcomings. For instance, the national accounts ignore most nonmarket transactions: If a maid cleans your condo, GDP rises, but if you do the same job yourself, GDP is unaffected. And NIPA fail to account for the environmental impact of economic activity.

Questions and Problems

1. Describe why GDP can be computed using either expenditures or income.

2. Assume the federal government runs huge budget deficits today to finance, say, Social Security, Medicare, and other programs for the elderly, and finances these deficits by selling bonds that raises interest rates. Since business often borrows money to invest, and interest is the cost of borrowing, these higher interest rates will reduce investment. Describe why this scenario is likely to be bad for the macroeconomy.

3. Critics of the NIPA argue that they are outdated and fail to account for "intangibles" in our new knowledge economy. For example, many firms create copyrighted materials (movies, books, etc.) that when completed are much more valuable than just the value of the marketplace inputs that went into their production. What might be some of the problems associated with trying to include these intangibles in the NIPA?

4. What accounts for the difference between personal income and disposable personal income?

5. Assume that we are able to accurately account for environmental degradation in the NIPA. Rank the following countries by the percent reduction to their GDP (from least to most percentage reduction): the United States, China, and Norway.

6. Gross domestic product and its related statistics are published quarterly and are often revised in the following quarter. Do you think quarterly publication and revision in the next quarter would present problems for policymakers trying to control the business cycle? Why or why not?

7. Describe the three major goals of macroeconomics. How well has the United States economy performed in accomplishing these three goals in the last few years?

8. How are business cycles defined? Describe the four phases of business cycles. Business cycles are dated by which federal agency?

9. What is the difference between a recession and a depression?

10. Describe the circular flow diagram. Why must all income equal spending in the economy?

11. The table below lists gross domestic product (GDP), consumption (C), gross private domestic investment (I), government spending (G), and net exports (X − M). Compute each as a percent of GDP for the 5 years presented.

Year	GDP	C	I	G	X − M	C(%)	I(%)	G(%)	X − M(%)
1965	719.1	443.8	118.2	151.5	5.6	____	____	____	____
1975	1638.3	1034.4	230.2	357.7	16	____	____	____	____
1985	4220.3	2720.3	736.2	879	−115.2	____	____	____	____
1995	7397.7	4975.8	1144	1369.2	−91.4	____	____	____	____
2005	12455.8	8742.4	2057.4	2372.8	−716.7	____	____	____	____

   a. Which component of GDP is the most stable? Look for the smallest change from the year with the smallest contribution to GDP to the year with the largest contribution.
   b. Which is the most volatile as a percent of GDP?
   c. Ignoring net exports, which component has grown the fastest as a percent of GDP since 1965?

12. Why does GDP accounting only include the final value of goods and services produced? What would be the problem if intermediate products were included?

13. Gross private domestic investment (GPDI) includes new residential construction as investment. Why is new housing included? Isn't this just another consumer purchase of housing services? How would the sale of an existing house be treated in the GDP accounts?

14. What are some of the limitations of the national income accounts in how they represent our standard of living?

15. Using the data below, compute GDP, national income, and NNP.

Corporate profits	1,200
Gross private domestic investment	2,000
Nondurable goods	3,000
Exports	1,200
Proprietors' income	900
Taxes, imports, and miscellaneous adjustments	800
Services	4,000
Net interest	550
Compensation of employees	7,000
Change in inventories	80
Imports	1,800
Rental income	150
Government spending	2,000
Durable goods	1,000
Capital consumption allowance	1,500

CHECKPOINT: THE SCOPE OF MACROECONOMICS

Big-ticket (high-priced, high-margin) items like automobiles will be affected by a recession more than grocery stores where the margins are less and prices are lower. When the economy turns down, investment falls, so the capital goods industry will be one of the first to feel the pinch.

CHECKPOINT: NATIONAL INCOME ACCOUNTING

In general, it is probably a bad idea to extrapolate how the aggregate economy is doing by your personal situation. Just because you are having trouble finding a job, does not mean that everyone else is. The recent downsizing by General Motors, and Ford, and Countrywide Finance mean that auto workers and mortgage brokers are having problems, even though the rest of the economy seems to be growing steadily. There might be times when your situation (a layoff in an important industry such as the automotive layoff above) may be a leading indicator of what is coming for the economy as a whole. In general, anecdotal evidence is not particularly helpful in forecasting where the aggregate economy is going.

Measuring Inflation and Unemployment

6

wo primary goals of macroeconomic policy are full employment and low inflation. The past two decades have witnessed a steady decline in unemployment and inflation rates. Every month, the Department of Labor (DOL) through its Bureau of Labor Statistics (BLS) issues updates on unemployment and the price level. Both numbers are considered important indicators of how the economy is doing and where it is headed. Stock markets can immediately change direction on the release of this data.

Measures of employment, unemployment, consumer prices, and producer prices have been estimated on a monthly basis only since the Great Depression. The lack of historical and timely data in the early 1930s made it difficult to track the impact of fiscal and monetary policies during the Depression. At the time, the data produced on the severity of the Depression were anecdotal (newspaper accounts of layoffs, plant closings, and bankruptcies) that did not lend themselves to systematic analysis for policymakers.

Because economists and policymakers had so much trouble making sense of the economy during the Depression, the government began to systematically collect data on aggregate (economy wide) variables. The Departments of Commerce and Labor began tracking things such as aggregate output, unemployment, and inflation.

To understand changes that are happening to the economy and to make good policy, we must know just what these numbers represent and how they are calculated. Are they accurate? Are they biased? Do they reflect the political philosophy of the party holding the White House? Why do they sometimes seem to get better just before an election and get worse afterwards? How can these numbers be used for economic policymaking? These and other questions are the focus of this chapter. Let's begin with a look at the various measures of inflation, then go on to measures of unemployment.

- Define inflation and the various terms associated with inflation.
- Describe the methods for measuring inflation used by the Bureau of Labor Statistics.
- Describe the gross domestic product deflator.
- Use an escalator formula to determine future values.
- Convert a nominal value to a real or constant dollar value.
- Describe the economic consequences of the different forms of inflation.
- Describe the differences between the labor force, employment, unemployment, and under-employment.
- Describe the different forms of unemployment and their economic consequences.
- Define the phrase full employment.

Inflation

Inflation
A measure of changes in the cost of living. A general rise in prices throughout the economy.

Inflation is a measure of changes in the cost of living. In an economy like ours, prices are constantly changing. Some go up as others go down, and some prices rise and fall seasonally. What we need, however, is a measure of how the cost of living is changing.

Why do we need such a measure? Why is it such a big deal if the cost of living is changing? Everyone has some intuitive sense of the cost of unemployment, in the waste that occurs when people want to work but cannot find a job, or when there are huge layoffs in a time of recession. Inflation, however, is a little harder to grasp.

Here is a simple example of inflation's destructive effects in the hope this gives you some intuitive sense of why inflation is bad. Say you work hard at a job after graduation and after your first year, your effort is rewarded with a 3% raise when the average wage increase in your company is 2%. You feel happy, that is, until the government releases its inflation report and says that inflation is running at 5%. In effect, you have lost purchasing power. You may not consider the 2% difference to be much, but keep going like this for a few years, and you will see that inflation will take a big bite out of your standard of living. Inflation has many other bad effects, as we will see later in this chapter. At this point, you should have a preliminary, general sense of why inflation is bad.

Because inflation is bad, we need a precise measure of how the cost of living is changing. If gas prices rise, electronic components hold steady, and there is a decline in the price of donuts (a major component of some budgets), determining the overall change in consumer prices can be complicated. What follows is a description of how the Bureau of Labor Statistics collects and analyzes the prices of various products to construct an index that measures inflation in our economy.

Defining Inflation Terms

Around the middle of each month, the Bureau of Labor Statistics announces the change in retail prices over the previous month. These updates in the consumer price index (CPI) provide us with our principal measure of inflation. Before we discuss how this index is arrived at and used, however, let us briefly examine some of the terms often used to discuss inflation-related topics.

- *Price level:* The **price level** is the absolute level of a price index, whether this is the CPI (retail prices), the producer price index (PPI; wholesale prices), or the gross domestic product (GDP) deflator (average price of all items in GDP).
- *Inflation:* A general rise in prices throughout the economy. A rise in the CPI or GDP deflator is usually referred to as inflation.
- *Rate of Inflation:* The percentage increase in prices over a 12-month period. An inflation rate of 3% for 2008 means price levels increased by that rate in 2008 over 2007.
- *Disinflation:* A reduction in the rate of inflation. Note that an economy going through **disinflation** may still be facing inflation, but it will be at a declining rate. This was the case from the mid-1980s throughout the 1990s.
- *Deflation:* A decline in overall prices throughout the economy. **Deflation** is the opposite of inflation. During deflationary periods, such as the early 1930s, average prices in the economy fall.
- *Hyperinflation:* An extremely high rate of inflation. At first, **hyperinflation** was defined as an inflation rate of at least 50% a month. Today, most economists refer to inflation above 100% a year as hyperinflation. Hungary experienced the highest rate of inflation on record during World War II. By the end of the war, in August 1946, it took over 800 octillion (8 followed by 29 zeros) Hungarian pengos to equal 1 prewar pengo. We will discuss hyperinflation in greater detail later in this chapter.

Measuring Inflation

Measuring consumer spending and inflation is one of the oldest data-collection functions of the Bureau of Labor Statistics. Unlike today's monthly surveys, before the Depression these surveys were collected every decade or so. According to the *BLS Handbook of Methods*, "The first nationwide expenditure survey was conducted in 1888–91 to study workers' spending patterns as elements of production costs. With special reference to competition in foreign trade, it emphasized the worker's role as a producer rather than as a consumer."[1]

During World War I, several other economic surveys were conducted, including one that weighted various areas of consumer spending to compute a cost of living index. During the Great Depression, more extensive consumer surveys were used to study the welfare of selected groups, notably farmers, rural families, and urban families. The Bureau of Labor Statistics began regular reports of the modern CPI during the late 1930s. Today, the CPI is the measure of inflation with which the average American is most familiar. There are, however, four measures of inflation in use today.

The **consumer price index (CPI)** is a measure of the average change in prices paid by urban consumers for a typical market basket of consumer goods and services. The **personal consumption expenditures (PCE) index** measures changes in consumer prices by focusing on consumer expenditures in the GDP accounts. The **producer price index (PPI),** originally known as the wholesale price index (WPI), measures the average changes in the prices received by domestic producers for their output. A fourth index, the **GDP deflator,** is a measure of the average change in prices of the components in GDP. The GDP deflator is the broadest measure of inflation, but it is not as well known as the CPI.

Price level
The absolute level of a price index, whether the consumer price index (CPI; retail prices), the producer price index (PPI; wholesale prices), or the GDP deflator (average price of all items in GDP).

Disinflation
A reduction in the rate of inflation. An economy going through disinflation will typically still be facing inflation, but it will be at a declining rate.

Deflation
A decline in overall prices throughout the economy. This is the opposite of inflation.

Hyperinflation
An extremely high rate of inflation; above 100% a year.

Consumer price index (CPI)
A measure of the average change in prices paid by urban consumers for a typical market basket of consumer goods and services.

Personal consumption expenditures (PCE) index
A measure of the changes in consumer prices by focusing on consumer expenditures in the GDP accounts.

Producer price index (PPI)
A measure of the average changes in the prices received by domestic producers for their output.

GDP deflator
An index of the average prices for all goods and services in the economy, including consumer goods, investment goods, government goods and services, and exports. It is the broadest measure of inflation in the national income and product accounts (NIPA).

---

[1]U.S. Department of Labor, Bureau of Labor Statistics, *BLS Handbook of Methods,* 1997. Available at www.bls.gov

In what follows, we will discuss how each of these indexes is constructed and measured, how each is used to adjust nominal values of income and output, and some other conceptual issues surrounding indexes. We begin with the CPI.

The Consumer Price Index (CPI)

The CPI measures the average change in prices paid by urban consumers (CPI-U) and urban wage earners (CPI-W) for a market basket of consumer goods and services. The CPI-U covers roughly 87% of the population.

Cost-of-Living Versus Cost-of-Goods. The CPI is often referred to as a "cost-of-living" index, but the current CPI differs from a true cost-of-living measure. A cost-of-living index (COLI) compares the cost of maintaining the same standard of living in the current and base periods. It is a complex index that requires knowing a good deal more than just prices and quantities of products purchased in a market basket of goods and services. It also requires information on how consumers will respond to changes in product prices and income.

A cost-of-goods index (COGI), in contrast, merely measures the cost of a fixed bundle of goods and services from one period to the next. Such an index is calculated by dividing the market basket's cost in the current period by its cost in the base period. The current CPI is a cost-of-goods index, since it measures changes in the price of a fixed basket of goods. The reference or base period used today for the CPI is 1996, but any base year would work just as well. The index simply measures the percentage change from one period to the next, so the selection of the base year does not fundamentally alter the index.

How Bureau of Labor Statistics Measures Changes in Consumer Prices.[2] Measuring consumer prices requires the work of many people. Thousands of individuals complete household surveys and help collect retail prices in stores, the result of which BLS economists then analyze and publish. According to the BLS, the "cycle begins during the first week of the month when BLS data collectors (called economic assistants) gather price information from selected department stores, supermarkets, service stations, doctors' offices, rental units, and so on for the entire month, about 80,000 prices are recorded in 87 urban areas."

The BLS does not have enough resources to price all goods and services in all retail outlets, so it uses three scientifically selected sample groups to approximate the spending behavior of all urban consumers. These include a

Consumer Expenditure Survey from a national sample of over 30,000 families, which provides detailed information on spending habits. This information enables BLS to construct the CPI market basket of goods and services and to assign each item in the market basket a weight or importance based on total family expenditures. Another national sample of about 16,800 families serves as the basis for a Point-of-Purchase survey that identifies the places where households purchase various types of goods and services. Finally, BLS uses 1990 Census of Population data to select the urban areas where prices are collected, and to determine the housing units within each urban area that are eligible for use in the shelter (housing) component of the CPI.

Goods and services are divided into more than 200 categories, with each category specifying over 200 items for monthly price collection. After these data have been checked for accuracy, the data from the three surveys are combined, weighted, and used to compute the index. The result is the cost in the current period required

---

[2]The following is based on the BLS Web site. Material in quotation marks here comes directly from the site.

to purchase the fixed market basket of goods. This cost is then compared to the base period and put into percentage form using the following formula:

$$\text{CPI} = (\text{Cost in Current} \div \text{Cost in Base}) \times 100$$

For example, assume the market basket of goods cost \$5,000 in 1996, and that same basket of goods now costs \$5,750. The CPI for today, using 1996 for the base year, is 115.0 ([\$5,750 ÷ \$5,000] × 100). So the cost of goods has risen by 15%, since the index in 1996 was 100.0 ([\$5,000 ÷ \$5,000] × 100 = 1 × 100 = 100).

Given that this method is the way the Bureau of Labor Statistics collects and computes the CPI, how accurately does this index reflect the changes in our cost of living? As we have seen, the BLS has the establishment of a *cost-of-living* index as its ultimate measurement goal, yet the CPI is a *cost-of-goods* index. Indeed, crafting a true cost-of-living index is difficult. We now take a quick look at some of the problems inherent in the current approach to measuring the CPI.

Problems in Measuring Consumer Prices

The CPI is a *conditional* cost-of-goods index in that it measures only private goods and services; public goods and services are excluded. Other background environmental factors, meanwhile, are held constant. The current CPI, for instance, does not take into account such issues as the state of the environment, homeland security, life expectancy, crime rates, temperature changes, or other conditions affecting the quality of life. For these reasons alone, the CPI will probably never be a true cost-of-living index.

But even being free of the broader domain of environmental factors and public services, the CPI still has problems. The CPI uses a fixed market basket determined by consumer expenditures surveys that are often 3 to 5 years old. Inherent in a fixed-market-basket approach is the assumption that, as prices change, consumers will continue to purchase the same basket of goods as before. We know, however, that when the price of one good rises, consumers will substitute other goods that have fallen in price, or at least did not rise as much. To the extent that the CPI does not account for product substitution, it will overstate inflation.

In a given year, about 30% of the products in the market basket will disappear from store shelves.[3] Data collectors can directly substitute other products for roughly two thirds of these products. That means nearly a third of the dropped products, or 10% of the original market basket, must be replaced by products that have been improved or modified in some important way. Old and new products are often not directly comparable. Some adjustment must be made in the index to account for these changes in quality.

Adjusting the index to account for products that have undergone quality changes is difficult, but it is easier than accounting for new products. Cellular phones and the rapid conversion of taped content (video and audio) to CDs and DVDs are examples of the challenges facing BLS.

In some instances, a new product does not fit properly into any existing category, so it gets overlooked. Another question raised by new products is when to add them to the CPI product mix. New products at first often have high prices as producers "skim" the market for the most interested consumers. (Apple dropped the iPhone's price \$200 a couple of months after it was introduced.) Cell phones were expensive in the beginning, used only by some consumers, and available only in selected local markets. Only in the last few years have many people begun to replace their landlines with cell phones. Including cell phones in the index a decade

---

[3]National Research Council, *At What Price? Conceptualizing and Measuring Cost-of-Living and Price Indexes* (Washington, DC: National Academy Press), 2002, p. 28.

ago would have been premature, because the market was still small. As a result, the BLS will often wait until a product matures and is used by a significant number of consumers before including it in the market basket.

Another factor to consider is that stores, like goods, come and go. This means the BLS must adjust its selection of retail outlets frequently. Yet, even this adjustment presents problems. When consumers go shopping at an upscale department store such as Neiman Marcus, where prices are higher, the whole shopping experience is different from that of a discount store like Wal-Mart—at least, we would hope so. Thus, when a new retail store enters the sample, it may sell some product that the store it replaces sold at a different price. The BLS assumes this price difference reflects the differences in the quality of the shopping experience at the two stores and does not change the CPI. This assumption may not be completely accurate, but it does keep the CPI from showing a change in prices just because one firm left the sample.

One final difficulty to note has to do with measuring the changing costs of health care. The CPI looks only at consumers' out-of-pocket spending on health care. This number represents roughly 6% of total consumer spending. The current CPI does not track changes in medical costs paid by Medicare, Medicaid, or employer-financed health insurance policies. Yet, because total health care spending is roughly 18% of consumer spending, this means the CPI only considers about a third of the overall health care charges. To the extent that price changes are different in the two areas of health care spending, the CPI will be inaccurate.

Personal Consumption Expenditures (PCE) Index

The CPI does a good job of measuring inflation for urban consumers and is the most widely reported inflation measure. Policymakers, however, especially the Federal Reserve, have been focusing its attention on the personal consumption expenditures index (PCE). The PCE focuses on consumer expenditures in the GDP accounts and is a little broader index of consumer inflation than the CPI.

The major difference between the CPI and the PCE is the weighting of individual components. For example, the PCE has a heavier weighting on medical care, apparel, and recreation, but lighter weights on food and housing. The CPI is a fixed market basket that is updated every 2 years based on surveys, whereas the PCE, based on GDP components, is updated each period. The CPI reflects out-of-pocket expenses of households; the PCE includes expenditures made by businesses on behalf of households. For example, business spending on employee health care is included in the PCE, but only household out-of-pocket spending is included in the CPI.

The CPI is released about 2 weeks before the PCE, so it gets the most media attention. Which is best is up for debate, but the Federal Reserve has given the PCE a boost since it announced that Federal Reserve inflation policy will focus on the PCE as a key indicator of inflation.

Both price indexes are shown in Figure 1. They track each other fairly closely. Note that inflation trended downward in the 1990s, bumped up in the late 1990s, dropped back in the early part of the 2001 recession, and is now trending upward.

Finally, make a note that you will often see the "core" versions of both the CPI and the PCE reported in the press. The core CPI and core PCE indexes are just the respective indexes with food and energy costs removed. Since food and energy costs are quite volatile, the core indexes are considered more reflective of underlying inflationary trends. But keep in mind that if, for example, energy prices remain high or continue to grow, these prices will eventually filter back into the economy as a whole and increase inflationary pressures.

The Producer Price Index (PPI)

The producer price index (PPI) measures the average changes in the prices received by domestic producers for their output. Before 1978 this index was known as the

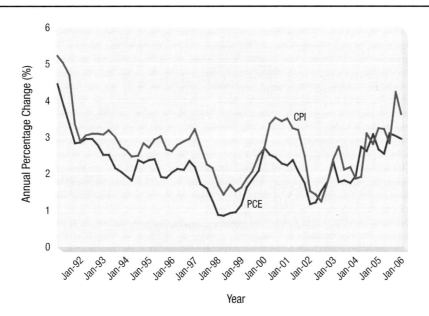

FIGURE 1

Comparing the Consumer Price Index and the Personal Consumption Expenditures Index

The CPI and PCE are indexes that both measure price changes in consumer spending. The CPI is a retail (out-of-pocket) price survey of a fixed market basket of goods and services each month. The PCE measures the changes in prices associated with consumer spending in GDP accounts including expenses by business on behalf of house-holds, such as employee health care and, thus, is a little broader index. As this figure shows, both indexes track quite closely.

wholesale price index (WPI). The PPI is compiled by doing extensive sampling of nearly every industry in the mining and manufacturing sectors of our economy.

The PPI contains the following:

- Price indexes for roughly 500 mining and manufacturing industries, including over 10,000 indexes for specific products and product categories
- Over 3,200 commodity price indexes organized by type of product and end use
- Nearly 1,000 indexes for specific outputs of industries in the service sector, and other sectors that do not produce physical products
- Several major aggregate measures of price changes, organized by stage of processing, both commodity based and industry based[4]

The PPI measures the net revenue accruing to a representative firm for specific products. Because the PPI measures net revenues received by the firm, excise taxes are excluded, but changes in sales promotion programs such as rebate offers or zero-interest loans are included. Since the products measured are the same from month to month, the PPI is plagued by the same problems discussed above for the CPI. These problems include quality changes, deleted products, and some manufacturers exiting the industry.

The GDP Deflator

The GDP deflator shown in Figure 2 on the next page is our broadest measure of inflation. It is an index of the average prices for all goods and services in the economy, including consumer goods, investment goods, government goods and services, and exports. The prices of imports are excluded. Note that *deflation* occurred in the Great Depression. The spike in inflation occurred just after the end of World War II, when price controls were lifted. Since the mid-1980s, the economy has witnessed disinflation where inflation was present but generally at a decreasing rate.

---

[4]This listing is excerpted from Chapter 14 of the *BLS Handbook of Methods,* 1997, found on the BLS Web site (www.bls.gov).

FIGURE 2

Inflation From 1930 to Today—GDP Deflator

The broadest measure of inflation, the GDP deflator, is used to graph inflation from 1930 to the present. From 1930 to 1950, the U.S. economy faced the extremes of deflation and a spike in inflation. Deflation occurred in the Great Depression. The spike in inflation occurred after World War II ended when price controls were lifted. Since then, inflation has existed in a 1–10% range. Since the mid-1980s, the U.S. economy has generally faced disinflation (inflation, but generally at a decreasing rate).

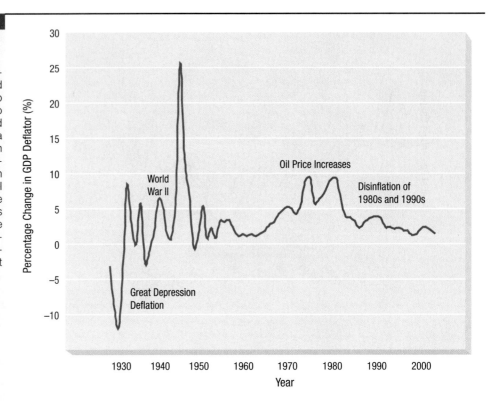

Adjusting for Inflation: Escalation and Deflation

Price indexes are used for two primary purposes: escalation and deflation. An escalator agreement modifies future payments, usually increasing them, to take the effects of inflation into account. Deflating a series of data with an index involves adjusting some *nominal value* for the impact of inflation, thereby creating what economists call a *real value*. Using the GDP deflator, for instance, to deflate annual GDP involves adjusting nominal GDP to account for inflation, thereby yielding real GDP, or GDP adjusted for inflation.

Escalator Clauses

Many contracts, including commercial rental agreements, labor union contracts, and Social Security payments are subject to escalator clauses. An escalator clause is designed to adjust payments or wages for changes in the price level. Social Security payments, for example, are adjusted upward every year to account for the rate of inflation. The general formula for an escalator clause adjustment is

New = Original × (Current Year Index ÷ Original Year Index)

To see how escalators work, let us assume your wages are tied to the CPI in such a way that your current wage is automatically adjusted by last year's inflation rate every April 1. (Can you guess why I chose this date?) Assume that you are earning $45,000 per year and that the CPI went from 115.0 to 118.5 last year. This means that the inflation rate for last year was about 3.0%:

(118.5 − 115) ÷ 115 = 0.0304

To calculate your new salary, simply divide the current year's CPI figure by the previous year's figure, and multiply this ratio by your current salary; thus, (118.5/115) × $45,000 = $46,369. Alternately, if the inflation rate is already known, just multiply the sum of 1 and this figure by your current salary to produce the same result: $45,000 × 1.0304 = $46,369. Note that we are simply increasing your current salary by a little over 3%.

Escalator clauses become important in times of rising or significant inflation. These clauses protect the real value of wages. For example, a 10% pay raise is great when there is little inflation, but if the inflation rate is 12%, you are worse off than before even with your 10% raise. In times of low inflation, as in the United States in the past 10 years, escalator clauses have been used infrequently.

Deflating Series: Nominal Versus Real Values

If GDP grows 10% in 1 year, and inflation as measured by the GDP deflator grows by 10% over the same period, how much has real output—output adjusted for inflation— increased? The answer is that real output has not grown at all. The entire change in GDP can be traced back to the change in prices. But how is real GDP computed?

First, remember that every index is grounded on a base year, and that the value for this base year is always 100. The base year used for the GDP deflator, for instance, is 2000. The formula for converting a nominal value, or *current dollar value*, to real value, or *constant dollar* value, is

$$\text{Real} = \text{Nominal} \times (\text{Base Year Index} \div \text{Current Year Index})$$

To illustrate, nominal GDP in 2005 was $12,766.1 billion. The GDP deflator, having been 100 in 2000, was 113.49 in 2005. Real GDP for 2005 was therefore equal to $11,248.7 billion ($11,248.7 = $12,766.1 × [100 ÷ 113.49]) in real year 2000 dollars. Note that because the economy has faced some inflation—13.49% from 2000 to 2005—the nominal value of GDP has been reduced by this same amount to arrive at the real value.

The Consequences of Inflation

Why do so many policymakers, business people, and consumers dread inflation? Your attitude toward inflation will depend in large part on whether you live on a fixed income, whether you are a creditor or debtor, and whether you have properly anticipated inflation.

Many elderly people live on incomes that are fixed; only their Social Security payments are indexed to inflation. People on fixed incomes are harmed by inflation, since the purchasing power of their incomes declines. If people live long enough on fixed incomes, inflation can reduce them from comfortable living to poverty.

Creditors, meanwhile, are harmed by inflation because both the principal on loans and interest payments are usually fixed. Inflation reduces the real value of the payments they receive, while the value of the principal declines in real terms. This means that debtors benefit from inflation; the real value of their payments declines as their wages rise with inflation. Many homeowners in the 1970s and 1980s saw the value of their real estate rise from inflation. At the same time, their wages rose, again partly due to inflation, but their mortgage payment remained fixed. The result was that a smaller part of the typical family's income was needed to pay the mortgage, and thus the real value of mortgages had declined. Inflation thus redistributes income from creditors to debtors.

This result takes place, however, only if the inflation is unanticipated. If lenders foresee inflation, they will adjust the interest rates they offer to offset the inflation expected over the period of the loan. Suppose, for instance, the interest rate during zero inflation periods is roughly 3%. Now suppose a lender expects inflation to run 5% a year over the next 3 years, the life of a proposed loan. The lender will demand an 8% interest rate to adjust for the expected losses. Only when lenders fail to anticipate inflation does it harm them, to the benefit of debtors.

Note the adjustment costs that inflation brings on an economy. In times of low inflation, this inflation is virtually ignored. In times of rising or significant inflation, people start to worry about diminished purchasing power and a falling standard of living. Workers seek escalator clauses. Mortgage lenders seek inflation adjustments. In the early 1980s when inflation was in double digits in the United States, mortgage lenders decreased the amount of fixed-rate mortgages and offered adjustable-rate mortgages. Many potential borrowers faced a choice between 15% fixed-rate mortgages and 13% adjustable-rate mortgages with their annual uncertainty about what the interest rate would be. It is much better for everyone when inflation is low and does not have to be brought into every financial consideration.

Hyperinflation

Hyperinflation is an extremely high rate of inflation. Historically this was defined as an inflation rate of at least 50% a *month*. Today, however, most economists refer to an inflation rate above 100% a *year* as hyperinflation. But in most episodes of hyperinflation, the inflation rates dwarf 100% a year.

Hyperinflation is not new. It has been around since paper money and debt were invented. During our war of independence, the Continental Congress issued money until the phrase "not worth a continental" became part of the language. Germany experienced the first modern hyperinflation after World War I. The wholesale price index went from 100 in the summer of 1922 to nearly 200,000 in July 1923, then soared to nearly 800,000,000,000 three months later in November 1923.

The causes of hyperinflation are usually an excess of government spending over tax revenues (extremely high deficits) coupled with the printing of money to finance these deficits. Post–World War I Germany faced billions of dollars in war reparations that crippled the country. The German government found it difficult to collect enough taxes to pay the reparations (that were viewed by Germans as unfair), so it embarked on the forced taxation of hyperinflation. As more money was printed and circulated, the value of the currency fell as prices rose. Over time, financial assets in banks and pension accounts became worthless and were essentially taxed away.

When hyperinflation is at its worst, workers are paid hourly, and they or their families take the money and rush out and buy anything the money will purchase. Eventually, the monetary system breaks down and barter takes over. People no longer trust the money, so they are unwilling to accept it in exchange for goods or services. At the peak of hyperinflation in Germany, retail stores essentially closed and refused to part with their inventory except by barter. In the end, the economic system collapses.

Stopping hyperinflation requires restoring confidence in the government's ability to bring the budgetary process under control. It usually requires a change in regime and a new currency. However, a new administration and new currency are not sufficient unless the government is ready to rein in the deficit and reduce the growth of the money supply.

Hyperinflation is an extreme case, yet it shows how inflation can have detrimental effects on an economy. This is why it is important to keep track of inflation and, in turn, reveals the importance of having an accurate way to measure inflation.

Inflation is one important measure of the health of an economy. Another is employment and unemployment, to which we now turn.

Checkpoint   **Inflation**

REVIEW

- Inflation is a measure of the change in the cost of living.
- Inflation, a general rise in prices throughout the economy, is measured using price indexes, and is often quoted as a rate of inflation or the increase in prices over a 12-month period.

- Disinflation is a reduction in the rate of inflation, and deflation is a decline in overall prices in the economy.
- Hyperinflation is an extremely high rate of inflation.
- The consumer price index (CPI) measures inflation for urban consumers and is based on a survey of a fixed market basket of goods and services each month.
- The personal consumption expenditures index (PCE) is based on consumer expenditures in the GDP accounts. This index is a little more broadly based than the CPI.
- The producer price index (PPI) measures price changes for the output of domestic producers.
- The GDP deflator is the broadest measure of inflation and covers all goods and services in GDP.
- Escalator clauses adjust payments (wages, rents, and other payments) to account for inflation. Nominal values are adjusted to real (adjusted for inflation) values using price indexes. The formula is: real = nominal × (base year index ÷ current year index).
- Inflation affects people on fixed incomes and creditors negatively, but benefits debtors and those who anticipate inflation correctly.
- Hyperinflation is typically caused by excessive government spending that is financed by printing money and is especially devastating on a family's monetary assets. It can only be stopped when the government changes its spending regime and curtails the printing of money.

QUESTION

If you lived in a country where you saw the signs of a government beginning to spend excessively relative to its tax base and was funding this immense spending by printing new money, what would you do to protect yourself and your monetary assets?

Answers to the Checkpoint question can be found at the end of this chapter.

Unemployment

When people are unemployed, individual workers, their families, and the economy all suffer. Workers lose wages, and the economy loses what they could have produced. Consumer spending drops, moreover, and as we will see later, this drop in consumer spending can lead to other workers losing their jobs.

The Historical Record

The Census Bureau began collecting data on wages and earnings in the early 19th century, but it took the Great Depression to focus national attention on unemployment. By the 1940s, the Department of Labor began collecting employment data using monthly surveys to get a more detailed picture of the labor force. As the Bureau of Labor Statistics has noted,

> *To know about unemployment—the extent and nature of the problem—requires information. How many people are unemployed? How did they become unemployed? How long have they been unemployed? Are their numbers growing or declining? Are they men or women? Are they young or old? Are they white or black or of Hispanic origin? Are they skilled or unskilled? Are they the sole support of their families, or do other family members have jobs? Are they more concentrated in one area of the country than another?*[5]

---

[5]This is from the BLS Web site.

Once the BLS has collected and processed the current employment statistics, policymakers use this information to craft economic policies. Before we discuss how these statistics are defined, collected, used, and made accurate, let's briefly look at the historical record of unemployment and its composition.

Figure 3 shows unemployment rates for the last century. Unemployment has varied from a high of 25% of the labor force in the middle of the Great Depression to a low of just over 1% during World War II. Unemployment during the past 50 years has tended to hover around the 5–6% range, although it approached 10% during the 1981–83 recession.

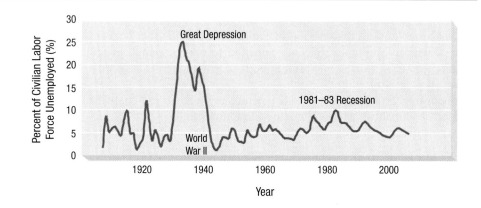

FIGURE 3

A Century of Unemployment (1907–2006)

Over the last century, unemployment has varied from a high of 25% of the labor force in the middle of the Great Depression to a low of just over 1% during World War II. Unemployment during the past 50 years has tended to hover around the 5–6% range, although it neared 10% during the 1981–83 recession.

Table 1 shows a breakdown of unemployment among various groups by age, race, gender, and education for 1980, 1990, and 2000. For all age groups, unemployment fell over this period, though some specific trends stick out. Young people, for instance—those under 24—had persistently higher unemployment rates

Table 1	Unemployment Rates by Age, Gender, Race, Education, Occupation, and Reason for Unemployment, 1980–2000		
	1980	**1990**	**2000**
Age			
Total unemployment	7.1	5.6	4.0
16 to 19 years old	17.8	15.5	13.1
20 to 24 years old	11.5	8.8	7.1
25 to 44 years old	6.0	4.9	3.3
45 to 64 years old	3.7	3.5	2.5
65 years and over	3.1	3.0	3.1
Gender			
Male	6.9	5.7	3.9
16 to 19 years old	18.3	16.3	14.0
20 to 24 years old	12.5	9.1	7.3
25 to 44 years old	5.6	4.8	3.1
45 to 64 years old	3.5	3.7	2.4
65 years and over	3.1	3.0	3.4

	1980	1990	2000
Female	7.4	5.5	4.1
16 to 19 years old	17.2	14.7	12.1
20 to 24 years old	10.4	8.5	7.0
25 to 44 years old	6.4	4.9	3.6
45 to 64 years old	4.0	3.2	2.5
65 years and over	3.1	3.1	2.8
Race and Ethnicity			
White	6.3	4.8	3.5
16 to 19 years old	15.5	13.5	11.4
20 to 24 years old	9.9	7.3	5.8
Black	14.3	11.4	7.6
16 to 19 years old	38.5	30.9	24.7
20 to 24 years old	23.6	19.9	15.0
Hispanic	10.1	8.2	5.7
16 to 19 years old	22.5	19.5	16.7
20 to 24 years old	12.1	9.1	7.5
Occupation			
Managerial and professional	2.5	2.1	1.7
Technical sales and administrative support	3.6	4.3	3.6
Operators, fabricators, and laborers	6.5	8.7	6.3
Education			
Less than high school diploma	8.4	9.6	7.9
High school graduates	5.1	4.9	3.8
Less than a bachelor's degree	4.3	3.7	3.0
College graduate	1.9	1.9	1.5
Reason Why Unemployed			
Job loser	3.6	2.7	1.8
Job leaver	0.8	0.8	0.5
Reentrant	1.8	1.5	1.4
New entrant	0.8	0.5	0.3

Source: U.S. Census Bureau, *Statistical Abstract of the United States 2001* (121st ed.), Washington, DC, 2001.

than older workers. Depending on the exact period, younger members of the labor force had unemployment rates three to four times higher than older workers.

Note that black unemployment has tended to be double the rate of white unemployment, and the unemployment rate for Hispanics has usually exceeded that for whites by roughly 50%. Unemployment for college graduates has consistently been extremely low, coming in at 1.5% in 2000. Roughly half of all unemployment is from job losses. The next largest group involves people who have not worked in some time and are looking to reenter the labor force. Finally, those people who quit their jobs or are new entrants into the labor force constitute a small percentage of the unemployed, about 20%.

Now that we have some idea of the composition of the unemployed, let us consider just how these numbers are compiled. First, we need to see how people get categorized as employed or unemployed.

The Household Survey

Every month the Census Bureau, as part of the Current Population Survey (CPS), contacts roughly 60,000 households to determine the economic activity of people during the calendar week in which the 12th day of the month falls. The sample group is drawn from over 700 geographical areas intended to represent the entire United States, including urban and rural areas. A quarter of the respondents in the sample are changed every month. More precisely, a family is interviewed for 4 consecutive months, then removed for 8 months, and finally put back into the sample for 4 more months before being removed permanently. In this way, the sample is kept from getting stale.

The Census Bureau does not directly ask interviewees if they are employed. Rather, it asks a series of factual questions designed to elicit information that permits the Bureau of Labor Statistics to determine by its own standards whether people are employed or unemployed, and whether they are in the labor force. After the BLS has processed the surveys, BLS publishes its findings, usually at the beginning of the following month.

Defining and Measuring Unemployment

The three major monthly numbers the BLS reports are the size of the labor force, number of people employed, and number unemployed. The unemployment rate is the number of people unemployed divided by the labor force.

Employed

People are counted as *employed* if they have done any work at all for pay or profit during the survey week. Regular full-time work, part-time work, and temporary work are all included. People who have a job, but are on vacation, ill, having child care problems, on maternity or paternity leave, on strike, prevented from working because of bad weather, or engaged in some family or personal obligation are treated as employed. These people are considered to be employed since they have jobs to return to once their temporary situations have been resolved.

One other group, called *unpaid family workers,* is considered to be employed. These are people who work 15 or more hours a week in a family enterprise; they usually show up in agriculture and retail. Unpaid family workers who work fewer than 15 hours a week are deemed not to be members of the labor force.

Unemployed

People are counted as *unemployed* if they do not have a job, but are available for work and have been *actively* seeking work for the previous 4 weeks. Actively looking for work means doing things like responding to help-wanted ads, sending off résumés, scheduling job interviews, visiting school placement centers, and contacting private or public employment agencies.

Note the emphasis on being active in the job search. A *passive* job search that merely involves looking in the want ads or talking to friends about jobs is not enough to characterize someone as unemployed. One exception involves workers who have been laid off but are expecting to be recalled; they do not need to seek other work to count as unemployed. Aside from the only other exception, that is, people suffering a temporary illness, individuals must be engaged in a job search to be counted as unemployed.

Labor Force

The **labor force** is the total number of those employed and unemployed. The unemployment rate is the number of unemployed divided by the labor force, expressed as a percent.

As the Bureau of Labor Statistics has noted,

> *Because of the complexities of the American economic system and the wide variety of job arrangements and job seeking efforts, the definitions of employment and unemployment must be specific so as to ensure uniformity of reporting at any given time and over any period of time. When all of the details are considered, definitions may seem rather complicated. The basic concepts, however, are still the same: people with jobs are employed, people who do not have jobs and are looking for jobs are unemployed, and people who meet neither labor market test are not in the labor force. The qualifying conditions are necessary to cover the wide range of labor force patterns and to provide an objective set of standards for consistent treatment of cases.*[6]

Labor force
The total number of those employed and unemployed. The unemployment rate is the unemployed divided by the labor force, expressed as a percent.

Problems with Unemployment Statistics

Trying to measure personal situations as complex as employment, unemployment, and job seeking can be expected to generate its share of controversy and criticism. When the Department of Labor announces its results each month, commentators often note that these numbers understate unemployment, since they do not include chronically unemployed workers who have grown so frustrated and discouraged they have dropped out of the labor force. Newspaper and television pundits agonize over the plight of discouraged workers or the underemployed while discussing the impact of the latest numbers on the stock market.

How unemployment is measured depends on the intended use of the resulting measurements. Various uses for unemployment statistics include (1) gauging the state of the economy, (2) determining the divergence of supply and demand in labor markets, and (3) assessing the distribution of unemployment and the extent to which people are suffering from being out of work. In the United States, most of our unemployment statistics have been developed to gauge the state of the economy. The Bureau of Labor Statistics does, however, publish data about underemployment and discouraged workers.

Underemployment and Discouraged Workers

It is not uncommon for people to take jobs that do not fully use their skills. In the early 1990s, many engineers and skilled workers who were employed in the defense industry saw their careers fall apart with the collapse of the Soviet Union. The "peace dividend" most of us enjoyed generated excess supplies in defense-related labor markets. More recently, the collapse of many Internet start-ups and telecommunications firms has thrown many highly skilled workers out of work.

The result of these shake-ups has been that many people are unable to find jobs that will enable them to duplicate their past standards of living. These individuals are *underemployed* in that they are forced to take jobs that do not fully—or in some cases even remotely—exploit their education, background, or skills.

Consider the following situation. After being laid off at the beginning of a recession, you spend several months looking for work, until finally you conclude that

---

[6]See BLS Web site.

landing a job in the current downturn is impossible. And so you give up looking for work. Are you still unemployed? Not according to official statistics. Clearly, you would like to resume working; you have simply despaired of doing so anytime soon. Sufficiently discouraged to have quit *actively seeking work*, the BLS classifies you as being out of the labor force; part of the leisure class.

The deeper a recession is, the more **discouraged workers** there will be. Today, the Census Bureau asks other questions of respondents to determine whether they fit into the discouraged worker category, listing these results separately.

Other countries have different definitions of actively seeking work, classifying individuals engaged in passive job searches as unemployed. Notably, Canada and Europe have more relaxed search standards than the United States.

Discouraged workers
To continue to be counted as unemployed, those without work must actively seek work (apply for jobs, interview, register with employment services, etc.). Discouraged workers are those who have given up actively looking for work and, as a result, are not counted as unemployed.

Checkpoint — Unemployment

REVIEW

- People are counted as employed if they worked for pay or profit during the survey week.
- People are unemployed if they do not have a job but are available for work and have been actively seeking work in the previous 4 weeks.
- The labor force is the sum of the employed and unemployed. The unemployment rate is the unemployed divided by the labor force.
- Unemployment statistics do not account for underemployed and discouraged workers.

QUESTIONS

Does it seem reasonable to require that to be counted as unemployed, a person must be actively seeking work? Why not simply count those who do not have a job but indicate they would like to work?

Answers to the Checkpoint questions can be found at the end of this chapter.

Unemployment and the Economy

Inevitably, our economy will contain some unemployment. People who are reentering the workforce or entering it for the first time will often find that landing their first job can take some time. Then they may find, moreover, that taking the first available job is not always in their best interests—that it might be better to take the time to search for another position better matching their skills and personality. Getting information and searching more extensively can extend the period people remain unemployed.

Unemployment can occur because wages are artificially set above the market clearing or equilibrium wage. Both minimum wage laws and union bargaining can have this effect, helping those workers who are employed to earn more, but shutting some potential workers out of jobs.

Employers often keep wages above market equilibrium to reduce turnover, boost morale, and increase employee productivity. These *efficiency wages* give employees an incentive to work hard and remain with their present employers, since at other jobs, they could get only market wages. These higher wages, however, can also prevent employers from hiring new workers, thus contributing to unemployment.

Changes in the business cycle will also generate unemployment. When the economy falls into a recession, sales decline, and employers are forced to lay off workers, so unemployment grows.

Separating different types of unemployment into distinct categories will help us apply unemployment figures to our analysis of the economy.

Types of Unemployment

There are three types of unemployment: frictional, structural, and cyclical. Each type has different policy ramifications.

Frictional Unemployment

Businesses and industries are born; sometimes they thrive, but just as often they waste away and die. At any given moment, some business is closing its doors, forcing its workers into unemployment. Similarly, there will always be some workers who are voluntarily quitting their jobs to search for better positions. In some cases, these people may already have other jobs, but it may still take several days or weeks before they can report to their new employers. In these cases, people moving from one job to the next are said to be frictionally unemployed.

Frictional unemployment is natural for our economy and, indeed, necessary and beneficial. People need time to search for new jobs, and employers need time to interview and evaluate potential new employees.

Frictional unemployment Natural unemployment for our economy; includes workers who voluntarily quit their jobs to search for better positions, or are moving to new jobs but may still take several days or weeks before they can report to their new employers.

Structural Unemployment

Structural unemployment is roughly the opposite of frictional unemployment. Whereas frictional unemployment is assumed to be of rather short duration, structural unemployment is usually associated with extended periods of unemployment.

Structural unemployment is caused by changes in the structure of consumer demands or technology. Most industries and products inevitably decline and become obsolete, and when they do, the skills honed by workers in these industries often become obsolete as well.

Declining demand for cigarettes, for instance, has changed the labor market for tobacco workers. Farm work, textile finishing, and many aspects of manufacturing have all changed drastically in the last several decades. Farms have become more productive, and many sewing and manufacturing jobs have moved overseas because of lower wages there. People who are structurally unemployed are often unemployed for long periods and then become discouraged workers.

To find new work, those who are structurally unemployed must often go through extended periods of retraining. The more educated those displaced are, the more likely they will be able to retrain easily and adjust to a new occupation. One benefit of a growing economy is that retraining is more easily obtained when labor markets are tight.

Structural unemployment Unemployment caused by changes in the structure of consumer demands or technology. It means that demand for some products declines and the skills of this industry's workers often become obsolete as well. This results in an extended bout of unemployment while new skills are developed.

Cyclical Unemployment

Cyclical unemployment is the result of changes in the business cycle. If, for example, business investment or consumer spending declines, we would expect the rate of economic growth to slow, in which case the economy would probably enter a recession, as we will examine in later chapters. Cyclical unemployment is the difference between the current unemployment rate and what it would be at full employment, defined below.

Frictional and structural unemployment are difficult problems, and macroeconomic policies provide only limited relief. Cyclical unemployment, most economists agree, is where public policymakers can have their greatest impact. By keeping the economy on a steady, low-inflationary, solid growth path, policymakers can minimize the costs of cyclical unemployment. Admittedly, this is easier said than done given the various shocks that can affect the economy. That said, since the early

Cyclical unemployment Unemployment that results from changes in the business cycle; where public policymakers can have their greatest impact by keeping the economy on a steady, low-inflationary, solid growth path.

1980s, American policymakers have done a remarkably good job of keeping the economy growing, ensuring a low unemployment rate, and keeping the inflation rate in check.

Defining Full Employment

Economists often describe the health of the economy by comparing its performance to *full employment*. We know full employment cannot be zero unemployment, since frictional and structural unemployment will always be present. Full employment today is generally taken to be equivalent to the natural rate of unemployment.

The Natural Rate of Unemployment

Natural rate of unemployment
That level of unemployment where price and wage decisions are consistent; a level at which the actual inflation rate is equal to people's inflationary expectations and where cyclical unemployment is zero.

The **natural rate of unemployment** has come to represent several ideas to economists. First, it is often defined as that level of unemployment where price and wage decisions are consistent—a level at which the actual inflation rate is equal to people's inflationary expectations. Natural unemployment is also considered to be the unemployment level where unemployment is only frictional and structural, or cyclical unemployment is zero.

Economists often refer to the natural rate of unemployment as the nonaccelerating inflation rate of unemployment (NAIRU). This is defined as the unemployment rate most consistent with a low rate of inflation. It is the unemployment level where inflationary pressures in the economy are at their minimum. We will discuss these issues in greater detail throughout the remainder of the book. For now, it is enough to remember that the natural rate of unemployment, or NAIRU, is the unemployment rate consistent with low inflation and low unemployment.

Full employment, or the natural rate of unemployment, is determined by such institutional factors as the presence or absence of employment agencies and their effectiveness. For many technology workers, Internet employment agencies like Monster.com represent efficient job search engines. Other factors might include the demographic makeup of the labor force and the incentives associated with various unemployment benefit programs.

Inflation, employment, unemployment, and gross domestic product (GDP) are the key macroeconomic indicators of our economic health. Our rising standards of living are closely tied to GDP growth. In the next chapter, we will investigate what causes our economy and living standards to grow over the long term.

Checkpoint

Unemployment and the Economy

REVIEW

- Frictional unemployment is inevitable and natural for any economy as people change jobs and businesses open and close.
- Structural unemployment is typically caused by changes in consumer demands or technology. It is often of long duration and often requires that the unemployed become retrained for new jobs.
- Cyclical unemployment is the result of changes in the business cycle. When a recession hits, unemployment rises, then falls when an expansion ensues.
- Macroeconomic policies have the most effect on cyclical unemployment.
- Full employment is typically defined as that level where cyclical unemployment is nil or that level associated with a low nonaccelerating inflation rate.

QUESTIONS

After the Berlin Wall fell and the Soviet Union split into several countries, the defense industry in the United States underwent a serious decline as part of the so-called peace dividend. Many high-skilled engineers and other workers became unemployed as the industry retrenched. For many, their skills were so specialized that they were unable to find new jobs at their old salaries. Were these people frictionally, structurally, or cyclically unemployed? What policies might the government implement to reduce the impact of this type of unemployment?

Answers to the Checkpoint questions can be found at the end of this chapter.

Job Gains and Losses: Establishment (or Payroll) Survey Versus Household Survey

As a final consideration of measurement issues, we turn to the issue of the *jobless recovery.* This term was bandied about in the 2004 presidential campaign. The U.S. economy went through a recession in 2001 and early 2002. It has since climbed out. We expect job loss in a recession and job creation in a recovery. It was claimed that this was a jobless recovery because job loss continued even after the recession ended. The claim was that 2.7 million jobs were lost between January 2001 and the end of 2003. In later chapters, we will look at the policies undertaken by the Bush administration and try to ascertain their effects. Right now, we want to consider this jobless recovery purely from a measurement point of view. Did the economy really lose 2.7 million jobs?[7]

A measurement issue arises because there are two ways of determining labor market employment, both undertaken by the Department of Labor. These are the Establishment (or Payroll) Survey and the Household Survey. They can give different readings.

The Establishment Survey focuses on roughly 400,000 manufacturing and service companies that are asked how many employees they currently have. If jobs are cut, this survey will immediately show a decrease in the number of employees. What happens to these former employees? If they find jobs with established companies, these new jobs will be counted immediately. If they find jobs with newly created companies, it will take time for the Department of Labor to discover these companies and include their employees. So the Establishment Survey will show job loss right away but will *undercount job creation* in newly created companies.

We can look at this issue another way. What happens when companies make large job cuts, such as offering people early retirement? The job might go away, but not the work. Either a company will hire new workers at lower wages, or it will outsource the work. If it outsources the work to established companies, these established companies will likely hire new workers, and this will show up in the Establishment Survey. However, if the outsourced work goes to new companies created just to do this work, job creation will not show up until the Department of Labor discovers the new company.

The result is that the Establishment Survey often overstates job loss. By how much? It all depends on job creation by new firms. One qualification: If work is outsourced overseas, this will be seen correctly as a job loss in the Establishment Survey. So the Establishment Survey overstates job loss, though not as much as first noted.

The second way of determining job loss is by the Household Survey. The Department of Labor interviews a sample of roughly 60,000 households about their employment. The Bureau of Labor Statistics then inflates the survey by the most recent estimate of the population.[8] It does not matter if someone is working at an established company or a new company or is self-employed. This survey, while smaller than the Establishment Survey, seems like a better source of actual employment data. Why not go right to the source—workers themselves—than to the firm?

---

[7]The following is based in part on the article by Allan H. Meltzer, "A Jobless Recovery?" *Wall Street Journal,* September 26, 2003, p. A8.

[8]Tao Wu, "Two Measures of Employment: How Different Are They?" *FRBSF Economic Letter,* August 27, 2004, p. 1.

The Household Survey provides a further benefit, though this is mitigated by some measurement issues. The Household Survey is better than the Establishment Survey in showing entrepreneurial activity. The person who leaves an established firm and starts a new business will show up as a job loss in the Establishment Survey but will not show up as employed in the same survey until the new company is recognized; however, the entrepreneur will show up immediately in the Household Survey, correctly showing no job loss. We can, however, wonder how much the Household Survey overcounts entrepreneurial activity: how many of these entrepreneurs would prefer to take a job in an established company rather than be on their own? Self-employment may simply be "a low-paying alternative to wage work," and when the unemployed become sufficiently discouraged, especially in a prolonged downturn, they turn to self-employment. Rising self-employment may simply reflect a weak economy. So the Household Survey may *overstate the robustness of the economy.*

Furthermore, the Household Survey may be overestimating job creation a bit.[9] Because the Household Survey is a sample, the Bureau of Labor Statistics has to multiply the result by an estimate of the total population. The estimated number of jobs will be too high if the population estimate is too high. In February 2004, the Federal Reserve Board thought the population estimate too high, and clung to the more pessimistic Establishment Survey.

What do these two surveys show? For the year ending in August 2003, the Establishment Survey showed a loss of 463,000 jobs, while the Household Survey showed a gain of 313,000 jobs. From the beginning of 2001, the Establishment Survey showed the 2.7 million job loss noted previously, while the Household Survey showed a loss of 220,000 jobs. This is much lower than the 2.7 million job loss jobless recovery number thrown about. In August 2005, the Household Survey showed 8.6 million more people employed than the Establishment Survey.

Figure 4 compares the two surveys over the last seven recessions by looking at employment increases 4 years after the trough of the recession. In five of the previous recessions before 2001, employment growth in the Establishment Survey exceeded that of the Household Survey. In the current recovery, the employment

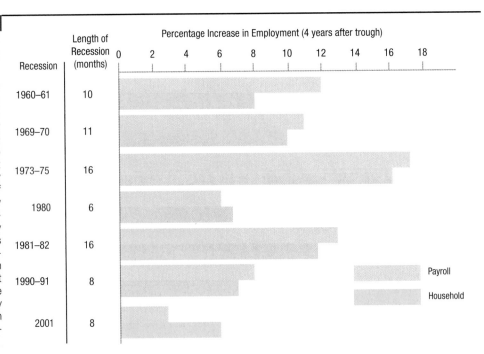

FIGURE 4

Comparing the Household and Establishment (Payroll) Employment Surveys

The Establishment Survey measures employment by surveying roughly 400,000 large businesses. The Household Survey interviews roughly 60,000 households each month to determine their employment status and is then adjusted by the most recent estimates of population. Employment in new firms and self-employed individuals are picked up more quickly with the Household Survey. As this figure illustrates, the recovery from the last recession (2001) has not been as robust as earlier recessions, and the Household Survey clearly shows a higher growth in employment than the Establishment Survey.

[9]For information in this paragraph, see Edmund L. Andrews, "Two Tales of American Jobs," *New York Times*, February 22, 2004, p. BU-6.

growth measured by the Household Survey has been double that found by the Establishment Survey, even though employment growth overall is considerably less than in prior recoveries. This slow growth may be the result of high productivity increases and the shift to self-employment by many high-tech workers laid off when the dot-com bubble burst in the late 1990s.

Which survey is closer to the truth? The Household Survey seems to be more accurate because it is closer to the source—workers themselves. Yet there is a lot of ambiguity to it. Against the Household Survey, the criticism of the Federal Reserve Board carries weight because the Establishment Survey is a much larger sample. Further, in 1998 BLS redesigned the Establishment Survey to make it more accurate.

Employment data do get adjusted over time. In 1992, it looked like the economy had faced a jobless recovery in 1991; benchmark revisions made several years later revealed a net *addition* of 900,000 jobs in 1991.[10]

As both surveys are continually updated and improved in the future, they should converge over time, but until then, knowing what each measures helps determine how to gauge a changing economy. Table 2 summarizes the essential differences in the two surveys.

Table 2	A Comparison of the Establishment Survey and the Household Survey

Establishment (payroll) Survey

- 400,000 business establishments surveyed
- Roughly one third of total nonfarm payroll employment
- Counts the number of jobs
- People with multiple jobs will be counted several times
- Only wage and salary workers on nonfarm payrolls counted
- Undercounts—some people losing jobs will find jobs in newly created companies that don't yet show up in the establishment survey
- Accurate count—work outsourced overseas

Household Survey

- 60,000 households surveyed
- BLS then adjusts survey for total population
- Counts the number of employed individuals
- People employed only counted once
- Covers all workers including self-employed
- Ambiguity—number of households is then inflated by the most recent estimate of the population—could be too high or too low
- Benefit—measures entrepreneurial activity
- Drawback—are entrepreneurs really entrepreneurs, or are they forced to be because they cannot find a full-time job?

Source: Mark Schweitzer and Guhan Venkatu, "Employment Surveys Are Telling the Same (Sad) Story," *Economic Commentary,* Federal Reserve Bank of Cleveland, May 15, 2004; and Tao Wu, "Two Measures of Employment: How Different Are They?" *Economic Letter,* Federal Reserve Bank of San Francisco, August 27, 2004.

---

[10]See Tim Kane, "Labor's Lost Jobs," *New York Times,* April 7, 2004, p. 19.

Note that the key is the measurement issue that sits behind this debate. Once we get the measurement issue out of the way, we can then discuss with more confidence whether the job loss number—higher or lower—is typical of a recession and a recovery. Different measurements lead to different conclusions about the significance of the job loss and can lead to different policies.

Key Concepts

Inflation, p. 140
Price level, p. 141
Disinflation, p. 141
Deflation, p. 141
Hyperinflation, p. 141
Consumer price index (CPI), p. 141
Personal consumption expenditures (PCE) index, p. 141

Producer price index (PPI), p. 141
GDP deflator, p. 141
Labor force, p. 143
Discouraged workers, p. 154
Frictional unemployment, p. 155
Structural unemployment, p. 155
Cyclical unemployment, p. 155
Natural rate of unemployment, p. 156

Chapter Summary

Inflation

Inflation is a general rise in prices throughout the economy. Disinflation is a reduction in the rate of inflation, whereas deflation is a decline in prices throughout the economy. Hyperinflation is an extremely high rate of inflation. Most economists refer to inflation above 100% a year as hyperinflation.

Four major price indexes are used to measure inflation in the United States. The consumer price index (CPI) is a measure of the average change in prices paid by urban consumers for a market basket of consumer goods and services. Every month, the Department of Labor's Bureau of Labor Statistics (BLS) surveys thousands of families and retail outlets to track changes in the prices of specific types of consumer goods and services. This market basket of goods, which is continually updated for changing consumer preferences, contains more than 200 categories, with each category containing over 200 items. The result of the monthly survey is the cost to purchase the fixed market basket of goods. This cost is then compared to the base period and put into percentage terms using the formula: CPI = (cost in current period ÷ cost in base period) × 100. The personal consumption expenditures index (PCE) measures the change in prices of consumption expenditures in the GDP accounts and is used by the Federal Reserve as its primary measure of inflation because it is broader than the CPI.

In similar fashion, the producer price index (PPI)—originally known as the wholesale price index (WPI)—measures the average change in prices received by domestic producers for their output. The PPI contains over 10,000 price indexes for specific products and product categories, over 3,200 commodity price indexes, nearly 1,000 indexes for specific outputs of industries in the services sector, and several major aggregate measures of price change.

The GDP deflator is the broadest measure of inflation; it is a measure of the average change in prices of the components in GDP, including consumer goods, investment goods, government goods and services, and exports. The prices of imports are excluded.

Price indexes are used for two primary purposes: escalation and deflation. An escalator agreement modifies future payments, usually increasing them, to take the effects of inflation into account. Deflating a series of data with an index involves adjusting some nominal (or money) value for the impact of inflation, thereby computing what economists refer to as the real (or adjusted for inflation) value.

People who live on fixed incomes and creditors are harmed by unanticipated inflation, since it decreases the purchasing power of their incoming funds. By the same token, inflation helps debtors: It decreases the real value of their debts. These effects are amplified during periods of hyperinflation.

Unemployment

Every month the Bureau of Labor Statistics contacts roughly 60,000 households to determine the economic activity of people during the calendar week in which the 12th day of the month falls. It asks a series of factual questions that permits the BLS to determine how large the labor force is and whether people are employed or unemployed.

People are counted as employed if they have done any work at all for pay or profit during the survey week. Regular full-time work, part-time work, and temporary work are all included.

People are counted as unemployed if they do not have a job, but are available for work and have been actively seeking work for the previous 4 weeks. Actively looking for work requires doing things such as sending off resumes, contacting employers directly, going on job interviews, visiting school placement centers, or contacting private or public employment agencies.

The labor force is the sum of those people employed and unemployed. It does not include people who may have lost their jobs and are not actively seeking work. The unemployment rate is the number of people unemployed divided by the labor force, expressed as a percent.

The Bureau of Labor Statistics also collects data on underemployed and discouraged workers. Underemployed workers are those individuals forced by weak economic conditions or changes in the job market to take jobs that do not fully use their education, background, and skills. Discouraged workers are unemployed individuals who have given up hope of finding a job and thus stopped actively seeking work. As a result, they are not classified as unemployed, because they are considered to be no longer in the labor force.

Unemployment and the Economy

Our economy will inevitably contain some unemployment. Unemployment results from wage levels that are sometimes kept artificially high to reduce turnover or improve morale. Unemployment is also caused by changes in the structure of an industry, downturns in the business cycle, and people entering the workforce or switching jobs and needing time to find work.

Unemployment is split into three types. When people are temporarily unemployed because they are switching jobs, they are said to be frictionally unemployed. Frictional unemployment is short term, and it exists because there are always some workers who are voluntarily or involuntarily changing jobs.

Structural unemployment is unemployment brought about by changes in the structure of consumer demands or technology. It is often long term, with workers requiring considerable retraining before they can find work again.

Cyclical unemployment is unemployment that arises because of downturns in the business cycle. This type of unemployment has the best chance of being affected by changes in government policy. By keeping the economy on a steady, low-inflationary, solid growth path, policymakers can minimize the costs of cyclical unemployment.

The natural rate of unemployment, or full employment, is that rate of unemployment where price and wage changes are consistent, and thus the inflation rate is equal to people's inflationary expectations. It is also where unemployment is only frictional and structural; cyclical unemployment is zero. Economists often refer to the natural rate of unemployment as the nonaccelerating inflation rate of unemployment (NAIRU). This is defined as the unemployment rate most consistent with a low rate of inflation.

Questions and Problems

1. In the beginning of a recovery after a recession, employment begins to rise and the news media report these data on job growth. Would such a report have an impact on the labor force? Would it affect the unemployment rate?

2. How could a decline in the unemployment rate actually reflect a deteriorating economy?

3. Since 1980, the U.S. population has grown 37%, while employment has risen by 44%, or nearly 20% faster than population. How can it be true that employment grows faster than population? Further, the number of people unemployed has only risen 5%. Are all of these indicators a sign of a strong or weak labor market?

4. In January 1980, the CPI stood at 77.8, and by January 2006, it was 198.3. By what percent have consumer prices increased over this period? Assume college graduates entering the job market were being paid on average $1,200 a month in 1980, and in January 2006, the average was $3,000. Are these newer graduates paid more or less after adjusting for inflation?

5. Why is frictional unemployment important to have in any economy?

6. Explain why hyperinflation has such a devastating impact on economies. Explain what it takes to stop hyperinflation.

7. Assume you just lost your job and you have decided to take a monthlong break to travel to Europe before looking for a new position. Just as you return home from your trip, you are interviewed by the Department of Labor about your employment status. How would you be classified (employed, unemployed, or not in the labor force)?

8. Describe the possible losses to our society and the economy when people are unemployed.

9. Why do teenagers and young people have high unemployment rates?

10. The Bureau of Labor categorizes unemployed people into several groups including job leavers, job losers, and discouraged workers. During a mild recession, which group would tend to increase the most? During a deep recession? During a boom?

11. Describe the three types of unemployment. What types of government programs would be most effective in combating each type of unemployment?

12. Describe the four measures of inflation in use today and the focus of each measure.

13. In 2000, median household income was $40,816. By 2004, it had grown to $44,389. The PCE for 2004 (2000 = 100) was 108.37. Has median household income, adjusted for inflation, grown or declined since 2000?

14. Describe who loses from unanticipated inflation.

15. What is required for a person to be considered unemployed? How is the unemployment rate computed?

16. Given the data for the United States between 1960 and 2000, complete the table below and answer the questions that follow.

Year	GDP (billions of dollars)	GDP Deflator (2000 = 100)	Real GDP (billions of 2000 dollars)	Population (millions)	Real GDP per Capita (billions of 2000 dollars)
1960	526.4	20.04	____	180.7	14,537
1970	1,038.5	____	3,772.3	205.1	____
1980	____	54.06	5,109.0	____	22,437
1990	____	81.61	____	250.1	28,432
2000	9,817.0	____	9,817.0	282.4	____

a. Between 1960 and 2000:
(1) GDP was how many times larger in 2000 than in 1960?
(2) The price level was how many times larger in 2000 than in 1960?
(3) Real GDP was how many times larger in 2000 than in 1960?
(4) What is the relationship between these values?
b. What was the percentage change in real GDP per capita between 1960 and 2000? Are people in the United States better off today than in 1960?
c. What are some of the problems associated with using real GDP per capita as a measure of our well-being?

CHECKPOINT: INFLATION

If you see the hyperinflation coming, you are in a position to protect monetary assets by purchasing hard or real assets such as real estate, gold, or diamonds. Early on, you might convert your monetary assets to the currency of other stable countries. If this is not possible, you would buy hard assets.

CHECKPOINT: UNEMPLOYMENT

The reason for the requirement that a person actively seek work is to empirically differentiate those who profess to want a job (at possibly a higher wage than they can earn in the market) from those who are actively trying to obtain work.

CHECKPOINT: UNEMPLOYMENT AND THE ECONOMY

Most would be structurally unemployed. Since many of these people have significant skills and education, retraining funds would go a long way to helping these people find new careers.

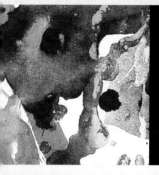

Economic Growth

*t*he quote by Nobel Prize winner Robert Lucas in 1988 argues that economic growth is of paramount importance. At that time Egypt's growth was over double that of India's, and India's GDP per capita was half of Egypt's. But a lot has happened in the last two decades: Egypt's growth rate faltered while India's accelerated. Today, India's growth rate is roughly twice that of Egypt and India's GDP per capita is nearly the same, but India's population at 1.13 billion people is 14 times that of Egypt. What has India done right and where has Egypt let down? That is a difficult question to answer, but we can try to answer it in this chapter by looking at many of the characteristics that promote long run economic growth.

In Chapter 1, we suggested that reducing real growth by 1 percentage point per year in the last century would result in our standard of living today equaling Mexico's. Alternatively, *adding* 1 percentage point to the annual economic growth rate over this same period would mean that our standard of living today would be *tripled*, resulting in a per capita GDP in excess of $100,000 and median family income over $120,000 annually. Clearly, the annual rate of economic growth is important.

For most of human history, per capita income was virtually unchanged. People lived a subsistence life and not a very long one at that. As Figure 1 on the next page shows and Angus Maddison noted, "From the year 1000 to 1820 the advance in per capita income was a slow crawl—the world average rose about 50 per cent. Most of the growth went to accommodate a fourfold increase in population."[1]

It has only been in the last century or so that standards of living have risen substantially and life expectancy has tripled. Even so, much of the world still leads a subsistence life. Looking at Figure 1 on the next page, it is clear that development has been uneven, even for neighbors.

Although standards of living have progressed nicely in the United States, Mexico lags way behind. Japan and Western Europe both made dramatic recoveries after

---

[1]Angus Maddison, *The World Economy, Vol. 1: A Millennial Perspective, Vol. 2: Historical Statistics* (Paris: Organisation for Economic Co-Operation and Development [OECD]), 2003, p. 9.

FIGURE 1

Per Capita GDP (1500–1998)

It has only been in the last century that economic growth and standards of living have shown significant improvement, but this improvement has been uneven. The United States and Western Europe have progressed nicely, while much of the rest of the world is still living at a subsistence level.

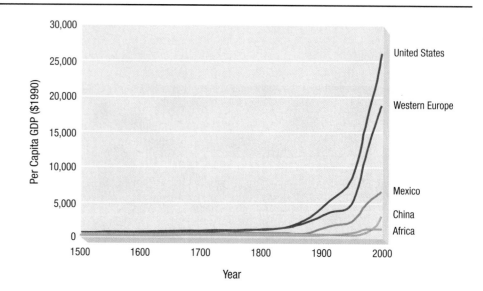

Economic growth
Usually measured by the annual percentage change in real GDP, reflecting an annual improvement in our standard of living.

World War II, whereas much of the Middle East and Africa did not. Understanding why these changes have taken place here and not everywhere else is one of the great challenges of macroeconomics. China, on the other hand, has made remarkable economic progress in the last several decades with its current annual growth rate exceeding 10%.

Much of macroeconomics is focused on the short-term goal of keeping the economy near full employment with low inflation. In the short run, individuals can improve their lives through human capital investments such as education and training. These investments make them more productive and have huge impacts on their wages and incomes. Also, in the short run, governments can provide safety nets for people, but if the safety nets become too extensive, they can have negative effects on the society's standard of living over the longer term.

In the short run, government policies cannot appreciably alter the standard of living of citizens. They can improve the quality of life at the margin through various policies such as free health care and education. Developing countries in the short run cannot expect to raise all citizens out of poverty and bring living standards up to those of Western Europe and the United States. Such changes require a combination of good policies, quite a lot of time, and often some luck.

This chapter focuses on long-term **economic growth** and describes the conditions needed to sustain economic growth and improve standards of living. In the long run, all variables in the economy can adjust to changing conditions. The models in this chapter are a good framework for evaluating policies meant to encourage economic growth in the long run. These models also suggest policies we should *not* undertake to deal with short-run fluctuations because their long-term effects are so deleterious. Having a good sense of what causes economic growth in the long run should help us later when we look at the economy in the short run.

The classical tradition of economic analysis began with Adam Smith's publication of *The Wealth of Nations* in 1776, and the classical model continued to be the dominant tool of economic analysis until the Great Depression. Classical economists took a long-run view of the economy that predicted relatively stable economic conditions around full employment.

In this chapter, we begin with a look at the classical model. We then turn to a broader view of the sources of economic growth, in particular a growing labor force, and we show why labor's productivity is so important. We take a close look at the role of technology in generating economic growth.

The last section looks at the role infrastructure plays in facilitating growth. Public infrastructure includes economy-wide attributes such as transportation facilities, communications networks, education systems, legal systems that protect property rights and freedom to contract, and stable financial institutions.

After studying this chapter you should be able to

- Describe the aggregate production function in terms of classical economic theory.
- Analyze labor supply and demand and the role of flexible wages.
- Explain Say's law.
- Use supply and demand to analyze the relationships among interest rates, savings, and investment.
- Describe the implications and limitations of classical economic theory.
- Describe the sources of long-term growth.
- Describe the sources of productivity growth.
- Describe modern growth theory.
- Define infrastructure and explain its importance.
- Describe the importance of tangible and intangible infrastructure.

The Classical Model

Early growth theory—the **classical model**—was based on the work of many famous economists including Adam Smith, Thomas Malthus, Alfred Marshall, and Karl Marx. Classical economists broke the aggregate economy into three markets: a product market, a labor market, and a capital market. All three markets were thought to be highly competitive, with product prices, wages for labor, and interest on loanable funds being set by the forces of supply and demand in each market. The competitive interaction of these three markets, according to classical economists, kept the economy operating near full employment.

We will employ a simple example of preparing invoices to be sent to customers, which in days past were done by individuals and typewriters. Today, computers spit these out by the thousands each hour. Keep in mind that our simple example (assuming that all activity is invoice preparing) can be expanded to cover all products and services produced in the economy.

Classical model
A model of the economy that relied on competitive conditions in product, labor, and capital markets, and flexible prices, wages, and interest rates to keep the economy operating around full employment. Anyone unemployed simply was unwilling to work at the prevailing real wage.

Aggregate Production Function

In Chapter 2, we briefly discussed production, the process by which individual firms turn inputs (factors)—land, labor, capital, and entrepreneurial ability—into goods and services. At this point, we consider aggregate production, or the production carried out by an entire economy.

Aggregate production function
An equation [Q = Af(K,L)], that relates aggregate output (Q) to technology (A) and to the quantities of inputs (K is capital, and L is labor) it uses in the production process (f).

An **aggregate production function** describes an economy's production by a simple formula:

$$Q = Af(K,L)$$

where
    Q = output or income
    A = an index of total factor productivity (technology)
    f = a function that relates output (Q) to inputs of capital (K) and labor (L)
    K = capital resources
    L = labor resources

This equation essentially tells us aggregate output is directly related to an economy's technology (A) and to the quantities of inputs it uses in the production process (f). If capital (K) and technology (A) are held constant, increasing labor inputs (L) will result in rising output. In the long run, these variables can change. As we will see later, this equation provides us with a simple approach for determining which policies will enhance growth in the long run. Note that land and entrepreneurship are not ignored, just assumed to be encapsulated in capital.

Product Markets

Classical economists focused on the microeconomics of markets applied to an aggregate economy. Consumer choices determine demand, and competitive markets determine supply, as we discussed in Chapter 3. This leads to a market equilibrium price and output for invoices as shown in Panel A of Figure 2. The market sets a price of $2.00 per invoice. The classical school argued that output and flexible prices from these competitive markets would absorb any changes in demand or supply.

FIGURE 2

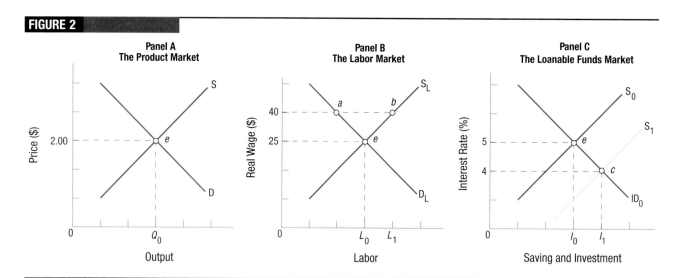

Classical Model of the Economy

Classical economists split the economy into three markets and argued that competitive forces would keep the economy at full employment (L_0). Supply and demand in the product and labor markets would ensure that all who wished to work at the prevailing real wage ($25 an hour in this case) would be employed. If consumers decided to save some of the earnings and consumption dropped, the capital market would adjust to lower interest rates (as saving increased to S_1) and business investment would take up the slack. These mechanisms tended to keep the economy at full employment.

Labor Markets

But how did classical economists get from product markets to the demand for and supply of labor? The product market determined that each invoice drafted, printed, and mailed is worth $2.00 to firms. If you can produce 100 letters in an 8-hour day, you will be worth $200.00 a day to your employer. Thus, your wage will be $200 a day, or $25.00 an hour, as shown in Panel B of Figure 2.

The demand for labor curve in Panel B reflects diminishing returns for much the same reasons that the production possibilities curves in Chapter 2 were bowed out from the origin. If more workers are hired and all are employed in the same office, each worker's output will fall, given that the firm's capital is fixed in the short term—printers become overloaded, workers get in each others' way or begin to gossip, and so forth. Now each worker produces less, so real wages must fall for the firm to be willing to hire more workers.

The supply of labor curve shown in Panel B shows the tradeoff workers face between working and leisure. Classical economists argued that workers will supply labor to the market on the basis of what their wages will buy. Workers are working for a real wage or nominal wages divided by the price level. The implication is that if money or nominal wages rise, but prices rise by the same percentage, workers will not be fooled by these higher nominal wages, and thus they will not offer more labor to the market because the new nominal wage will not buy more.

Equilibrium is at point e where firms hire workers up to the point where the demand for labor is equal to the supply of labor. At this point, all workers who want to work at this real wage rate ($200 a day or $25 per hour) are employed. Those who do not work are voluntarily unemployed; they could work but are unwilling to do so for the going wage.

Clearly, if real wages were higher, more people would be willing to work. Even so, given the supply of labor facing the market and the limits on labor productivity, L_0 represents full employment for this economy.

Flexible wages and prices keep this market in equilibrium at full employment. If real wages were somehow less than $25 per hour, there would be excess demand for labor and the market would quickly bid real wages back to $25 restoring the original equilibrium at point e in Panel B of Figure 2. Thus, changes in the price level or the nominal wage rate will lead to further changes in the wage rate or price level to keep real wages constant.

In the long run, L_0 will remain the equilibrium employment level unless technology improves or more capital is employed, increasing the demand for labor and shifting the curve to the right, increasing real wages. Alternatively, if the labor force grows, the supply of labor will shift to the right, increasing employment; but note that real wages would fall.

Notice also that all unemployment in this economy is voluntary. Classical economists recognized that if some artificial barrier were to keep wages above the equilibrium level, unemployment could result. In Panel B, for instance, persistent unemployment would result if real wages were artificially maintained at a wage of $320 a day through minimum wage laws or union collective bargaining, for example. In Panel B, at a wage of $40.00 ($320/8) an hour, unemployment would equal ab, since businesses would only be willing to hire to point a, but b workers would like to work. Before the Depression, however, minimum wage laws and unions were rare.

In summary, individuals supply labor to the market for real wages (what the money wages will purchase). Firms demand labor, hiring more when real wages are lower, resulting in equilibrium where business wants the same number of employees supplied. At this point, all those who want to work at the going real wage can, and those not working are voluntarily unemployed.

The classical school's assumption was that people worked for what wages would purchase and that all earnings would be translated into spending (demand). This

Say's law
The act of production produces income that leads to an equivalent amount of consumption spending; it is often paraphrased as "supply creates its own demand."

would ensure that there was no deficiency in consumption (demand), and that would guarantee full employment.

Jean Baptiste Say argued that workers offer their services to get incomes to spend on goods and services. Thus, **Say's law** suggests that

> *A product is no sooner created, than it, from that instant, affords a market for other products to the full extent of its own value . . . the mere circumstance of the creation of one product immediately opens a vent for other products.*[2]

Say argued, in other words, that there can be no deficiency in aggregate spending since the act of production also produces an income that leads to an equal amount of consumption. "Supply creates its own demand," as Say's law is often paraphrased.

But what about saving? Some people saved money from their income, and this offered the potential for underconsumption, which would lead to reduced incomes and employment below full employment. To counter this situation, classical economists turned to capital markets that equated saving by households with investment by business.

Capital Markets: Saving and Investment

In classical economics, saving and investment decisions are influenced primarily by interest rates. Saving reflects a willingness to abstain from current consumption; this abstention is then rewarded by the interest earned on saved funds. Higher interest rates represent higher rewards, and thus, consumers can be expected to save more as interest rates rise.

Panel C in Figure 2 portrays the market for loanable funds, or the capital market. The supply curve for loanable funds, S_0, is positively sloped, like most supply curves. As interest rates rise, the quantity of savings supplied rises as consumers choose to save more money rather than spend it.

Curve ID_0 represents the demand for loanable funds, or investment demand. As interest rates decline, the cost to investing falls, so borrowing for investment purposes will rise. We can think of the investment curve, ID_0, as an array of possible capital projects. When interest rates are 5%, investment projects up to I_0 will be undertaken, since they earn the required rate of return. As interest rates decline, more such projects become profitable.

But just how do saving and investment ward off insufficient demand to keep the economy at full employment? Assume the economy is initially at full employment in the labor market, and savings and investment are equal at $S_0 = ID_0$ (point e), and interest rates are at the equilibrium level (5%).

Suppose consumers decide to purchase fewer goods than before, so that consumption falls below the level needed to maintain full employment. The entire saving schedule now rises (shifts to the right) to S_1; at all interest rates, consumers want to spend less and save more.

Equilibrium moves to point c, where interest rates are lower (4%), but investment increases. This additional spending on business investment will increase demand throughout the economy, thereby moving the economy back to full employment. The increased spending by businesses has replaced the decrease in spending by consumers.

The result of classical analysis is that the economy will be at full employment all the time. Flexible wages, interest rates, and prices ensure that the economy hovers around full employment.

During the 18th and 19th centuries, as we have seen, per capita income rose very little. This led classical economists to be pessimistic about future standards of living. Most famous is Thomas Malthus, whose analysis that population would grow

[2]Say, Jean B., *A Treatise on Political Economy,* 1821, quoted in Brian Snowdon et al., *A Modern Guide to Macroeconomics: An Introduction to Competing Schools of Thought* (Brookfield, VT: Edward Elgar), 1994, p. 52.

Thomas Malthus (1766–1834)

*t*homas Carlyle called economics the "dismal science" after reading the famous essay by Thomas Malthus on the relationship between population growth and poverty, for which he is best known. Malthus also wrote extensively on Say's law.

Thomas Malthus was born in 1766 and raised in Surrey, England, the son of a philosophically inclined country gentleman who was a friend and admirer of Jean-Jacques Rousseau and David Hume. After attending Cambridge University, Malthus spent several years as a clergyman before accepting a teaching post in political economy at the college of the East India Company, the first position of its kind.

In 1793, the pamphleteer William Godwin published *Political Justice,* describing a utopian future with no war, poverty, crime, injustice, or disease. Malthus argued against the book's conclusions in a lengthy discussion with his father, who suggested he set down his ideas in print. The result was "An Essay on the Principle of Population as It Affects the Future Improvement of Society." Malthus took issue with Godwin, Rousseau, and Condorcet, who believed in social progress. Malthus argued that the origins of poverty were rooted in an unavoidable contradiction: population, when allowed to grow without limits, increased geometrically, while the food supply could only increase arithmetically. Any improvement in conditions of the poor would simply lead to population increases and to rising food prices and scarcities.

Malthus met David Ricardo in 1809 after the stockbroker-turned-economist wrote a series of articles criticizing protectionist agricultural policies. The two became lifelong friends and professional antagonists. One of their most significant debates was over Say's law, which held that a "general glut" in goods and services was a logical impossibility because supply will inevitably be matched by demand. Malthus, however, worried that insufficient demand might lead to a general glut and therefore an economic crisis. Ricardo countered by demonstrating with mathematical logic the validity of Say's law. Malthus deferred to Ricardo's logic but remained skeptical of his conclusions. His concern with general gluts, outlined in the *Principles of Political Economy* in 1820, would later bring praise from John Maynard Keynes. Malthus died in 1834.

substantially faster than the food supply has often been wrongly attributed to economics, causing it to be dubbed the "dismal science."

Implications for Economic Growth

If the economy is always operating at full employment, how does the economy grow? The implications for economic growth from classical economics are very straightforward using the aggregate production function we discussed earlier. Anything that improves the productivity of labor, the amount of capital employed with labor, or new productivity-enhancing technology will result in economic growth. This is very much like our conclusion on economic growth from production possibilities analysis in Chapter 2.

The primary limitations of classical analysis are its exclusive focus on the long run and its stylistic assumptions. In the real world, most of the politicians who are responsible for economic policy face reelection every few years. They will often support policies to assure their reelection, and not be as concerned with the long-run affects of short-term policies.

Second, as the Great Depression illustrated, high unemployment levels can last a long time. A long recession may be required before the mechanisms that classical economists envisioned bring the economy back to full employment. Consequently, a focus on shorter time frames is often needed.

Despite these limitations, most contemporary economists see the classical model as representative of the economy's long-run course. The classical model helps policymakers see the need to focus on increasing our long-run standard of living.

Checkpoint — **The Classical Model**

REVIEW

- Classical economists relied on competitive conditions in product, labor, and capital markets, and flexible prices, wages, and interest rates to keep the economy operating around full employment. Anyone unemployed simply was unwilling to work at the prevailing real wage.
- Economic growth in the classical model results from improvements in labor productivity, increases in capital, and productivity-enhancing technological change.

QUESTION

The classical model relies on competitive markets for labor, products, and capital to keep the economy near full employment and output. The United States has enjoyed nearly three decades of high employment, high growth, and low inflation, interrupted by two short and mild recessions. Has the recent growth in globalization and trade liberalization introduced more competition into labor, capital, and product markets, making our economy look and act like classical economists envisioned?

Answers to the Checkpoint question can be found at the end of this chapter.

Sources of Long-Run Economic Growth

The classical model states that economic growth can come from three sources: increases in capital, increases in labor, and improvements in technology. Communications and computers provide recent examples of industries that have experienced such high rates of technical change and improved productivity that prices have fallen off a cliff, even as output has ballooned. Both industries have powered the economic growth that we have seen over the last two decades.

Growth in the Labor Force

There can be little doubt that a big part of phenomenal economic growth of the United States over the past century can be tied to its population growth, and specifically to its immigration policies. Historically, U.S. immigration policies have been some of the most open of any country in the world. Immigration always gives rise to social tensions, but as *The Economist* has noted, our historic openness may be providential today:

> *For 50 years, America and the nations of Western Europe have been lumped together as rich countries, sharing the same basic demographic features: stable populations, low and declining fertility, increasing numbers of old people. For much of that period, this was true. But in the 1980s, the two sides began to diverge. The effect was muted at first, because demographic change is slow. But it is also remorseless, and is now beginning to show up.*
>
> *America's census in 2000 contained a shock. The population turned out to be rising faster than anyone had expected when the 1990 census was taken. There are disputes about exactly why this was. What is not in doubt is that a gap is beginning to open with Europe. America's fertility rate is rising. Europe's is falling. America's immigration outstrips Europe's and its immigrant population is reproducing faster than native-born Americans. America's population will soon be younger. Europe's is aging.[3]*

Over the last few decades, the U.S. labor force—those working and looking for work—has grown faster than the population. Women have entered the labor force in increasing numbers. The demand for their labor has led many companies to introduce more family-friendly policies such as day care, increased opportunities for job sharing, and more flexible working hours and locations, sometimes from home.

Government policies designed to enhance labor-force participation have included day care subsidies, enhanced protections for pension funds, support for retirement benefits, and tax incentives that make work more attractive. For instance, the progressivity of the income tax has been reduced over the past several decades. This raises the take-home pay of the second worker in the family, thereby increasing the benefits for both adults in a family from work.

A growing labor force is important for economic growth, and the **productivity** of that workforce is even more important.

Productivity
How effectively inputs are converted into outputs. Labor productivity is the ratio of the output of goods and services to the labor hours devoted to the production of that output. Higher productivity and higher living standards are closely related.

Productivity Is Important

As we saw earlier, the demand for labor and the equilibrium real wage is determined by the marginal productivity of labor. When worker productivity grows, real wages rise. The primary reason the American standard of living is so high is that American workers produce so much more per worker than do workers throughout most of the rest of the world. Many people in the developing world eke out a living using tools that would remind us of the 19th century. This lower productivity is reflected in their standard of living: Many of these people lead 19th-century lives.

The more you produce and the higher the value of the goods or services you produce, the higher will be your earnings and your standard of living. People whose skills are in high demand—entertainers, movie stars, and professional athletes—

[3]*The Economist,* August 24th, 2002, p. 19.

earn immense fortunes. The moment their star fades, however, whether because of age or changing public tastes, their incomes plummet. In the world of athletics or rock music, stars are often has-beens by age 35. Although their salaries are not as high as sports superstars, highly skilled executives, supercomputer systems programmers, and doctors all are highly productive, and their earnings reflect the value of their skills.

Higher productivity and higher standards of living similarly go hand in hand for nations as a whole. Highly productive places like the United States, Japan, and Europe are also places with high standards of living. At the opposite end of the spectrum, countries like Chad, Nigeria, and Pakistan have unproductive labor forces with low incomes, along with the problems this lower living standard entails.

Sources of Productivity Growth

Productivity growth raises wages and incomes. Let's look at some of the factors that increase labor productivity.

Increasing the Capital-to-Labor Ratio

Capital-to-labor ratio
The capital employed per worker. A higher ratio means higher labor productivity and, as a result, higher wages.

When a farmer in Nigeria plows his field with a crude plow hitched to a buffalo, the amount of land he can plant and harvest is miniscule. American farmers, in contrast, use farm equipment that allows them to plow, plant, fertilize, water, and harvest thousands of acres; they have a high **capital-to-labor ratio.** This raises U.S. farm productivity many orders of magnitude above that of poor Nigerian farmers. The ultimate result of this vastly superior productivity is that American farmers earn a far higher income than their counterparts in the developing world.

Developing countries have large labor forces, but little capital. Developed nations like the United States, on the other hand, have limited labor supplies, and each worker works with a large array of capital equipment. As a rule, the more capital employed with workers, the greater their productivity and the higher their earnings.

Increasing the Quality of the Labor Force

Investment in human capital
Improvements to the labor force from investments in improving skills, knowledge, and in any other way the quality of workers and their productivity.

A second source of productivity growth comes from improvements to the labor force from **investment in human capital.** Human capital is a term economists use to describe skills, knowledge, and quality of workers. On-the-job training and general education can improve the quality of labor by improving productivity. In many ways, increasing capital and a highly skilled labor force go together: Well-trained workers are needed to run the highly productive, often highly complex, machines. Unskilled workers are given the least important jobs and earn the lowest wages.

By investing in human capital, nations can ultimately raise their growth rates by improving worker productivity. Government programs that raise the literacy rate, such as universal public education, will also raise the rate of economic growth.

Improvements in Technology

Technological improvements can come from various sources and play a major role in improving productivity, our standard of living, and increasing economic growth. These include enterprising individuals who discover innovative new ways to produce a product, for example, Henry Ford and the assembly line, and the inventors of new products, such as Thomas Edison, who invented the lightbulb and hundreds of other products.

Over the past few decades, microcomputers and their associated software have improved productivity immensely. Hardly a business or government office exists today that does not use a computer to automate some office task. Spreadsheets and modern database programs have revolutionized the way businesses manage, plan, and keep track of their customers.

Tomorrow, the telecommunications industry and the Internet will further raise productivity by improving information flow and reducing the costs of producing and distributing products to consumers. Advances in biotech research will reduce the costs of developing new drugs and improve their efficacy. As researchers learn more about DNA, they may one day be able to target new drugs to specific individuals with unique genetic characteristics. This process will lower the cost of producing drugs, reduce the time needed for government approval, and enhance the healing power of the drugs.

Technological progress is the primary explanation for the extraordinary economic growth this country has enjoyed over the last century. The technologies that kept our economy expanding have also helped many other countries to grow. In the developing world, however, growth most often comes from foreign companies building factories that employ locals at low wages. These companies often pay more than workers could have hoped to earn on their own. These higher earnings become the grubstake to better education and earnings for their children.

Today, new technologies are helping many developing nations to jump-start their growth. Cheap cellular service has improved communications, inexpensive vaccinations and health education programs have reduced mortality rates, and the global movement of capital and production facilities has created new job opportunities. Trade liberalization has helped many countries to develop.

Modern Growth Theory

The seeds for modern growth theory were introduced by Nobel Prize winner Robert Solow in the 1950s by introducing a more robust production relationship and adding a relationship for technical progress that is determined outside of the model. These refinements led to the conclusion that technical change is an important driver of economic growth. Unfortunately, technology, an important element of growth, was not explained by the model.

Since the mid-1980s a new approach to understanding the process of technical change in economic growth has focused on increases in knowledge. Specifically, modern growth theory argues that economic growth is driven primarily by new knowledge produced by technical change.

In a groundbreaking 1986 article, Paul Romer focused on the "public good" characteristics of knowledge. He argued that research and development by one firm necessarily has positive spillovers on production in other firms. Examples include just-in-time inventory systems, which reduced operating costs and quickly spread throughout industry, and Netscape's development of the graphical Internet browser that revolutionized Internet communications, which nearly everyone takes for granted today. The crucial point is that many innovations developed by individual firms have these *public good* aspects, which mean that these firms are unable to completely internalize the benefits; some benefits spill over to the economy at large.

New knowledge discovered by one firm quickly becomes public, and in this way, the acquisition of capital (human and physical) exhibits increasing returns instead of the earlier assumption of diminishing returns. Instead of one firm exploiting its discovery or innovation, the benefits are shared among hundreds or thousands of firms, amplifying the returns to the economy. Again, modern consumer electronics are a clear example of this phenomenon, as new, more complex, and powerful products are released every year at lower and lower prices. Moore's law that computing power doubles every 18 months (and at lower prices) has been a driving force behind increasing returns in the digital revolution of so many products and industries. These forces have also been driving rising levels of labor productivity and our standard of living.

Notice that all of this is just the "unintentional by-product of capital accumulation by individual firms,"[4] but with millions of firms engaging in huge amounts of research and development, this adds up to a force that drives economic growth.

[4]Brian Snowdon and Howard Vane, *Modern Macroeconomics: Its Origins, Development and Current State* (Cheltenham, UK: Edward Elgar), 2005, p. 627.

Nobel Prize Robert Solow

*R*obert Solow won the Nobel Prize in Economic Sciences in 1987 for his work on developing realistic models for economic growth. He has also been praised for his contributions to empirical studies of the major factors behind growth and for his work in natural resources economics.

Solow was born in Brooklyn, New York, in 1924, the oldest of three children. He won a scholarship to Harvard University in 1940. A self-described "child of the depression," Solow gravitated toward sociology, anthropology, and later economics because he wanted to understand what "made society tick." Interrupting his undergraduate study, he joined the U.S. Army when he turned 18. After serving in North Africa and Sicily during World War II, he returned to Harvard in 1945 and then stayed there for graduate studies in economics.

Solow spent most of his career teaching at MIT. In the early 1960s, he served as chief economist on the Council of Economic Advisors. Working with leading economists Walter Heller and James Tobin, he was very influential in implementing Keynesian economic policies that predominated during the John F. Kennedy and Lyndon B. Johnson administrations.

In 1956, Solow published the first of several important papers, "A Contribution to the Theory of Economic Growth." In this study he proposed a mathematical model to understand growth. In "Technical Change and the Aggregate Production Function," he showed that not all economic growth resulted from changes in capital and labor. Another part of growth, which has come to be known as the "Solow residual," could be attributed to technological innovation. In "Investments and Technical Progress" (1960), he differentiated between the "vintages" of capital, suggesting that newer capital might be more valuable than older capital because of improvements in technology.

Once ideas and knowledge have been created, they can be spread to others for nearly nothing. In the digital world of software, instructions (computer code) can be used over and over, virtually for free.

As growth theories evolve, they lead economists to direct their attention to different reasons and sources of economic growth.

To summarize this section, economic growth comes from increases in capital, increases in labor, and improvements in technology. Increases in the capital-to-labor ratio tend to increase productivity. Increasing the size of the labor force and increasing the quality of the labor force turn directly into economic growth. And improvements in technology in this information age have led to the most dramatic increases in economic growth.

Sources of Long-Run Economic Growth

REVIEW

- The classical model states that growth can come from increases in capital or labor resources or from improvements in technology.
- Growth in labor is important, but the productivity of that labor is more important for growth and future standards of living.
- Increased productivity of labor can come from increases in the capital-to-labor ratio, improvements in the quality of the labor force, and improvements in technology.
- Modern growth theory suggests that research and development improve technology, which in turns drives economic growth through its huge public good aspects and positive spillovers.

QUESTION

In 2006, Warren Buffett, the world's second richest individual, announced that over the next few years he would be giving 85% of his wealth, over $30 billion, to the Bill & Melinda Gates Foundation. The foundation focuses on grants to developing nations, helping the poorest of the poor. What suggestions would you give the foundation to help these developing nations grow?

Answers to the Checkpoint question can be found at the end of this chapter.

Infrastructure and Economic Growth

What are the reasons that some nations are rich and others are poor? Economists have been struggling to answer this question for several centuries. Today, we know that part of the answer lies in the different infrastructure development among various countries. In essence, the focus on infrastructure means that there is something important that lies behind our aggregate production function: We just do not increase capital, increase labor, improve technology, and turn a crank to obtain economic growth.

Public Capital

Infrastructure is defined as a country's public capital. It includes dams, roads, and bridges; transportation networks, such as air and rail lines; power-generating plants and power transmission lines; telecommunications networks; and public education facilities. These items are tangible public goods that can easily be measured. All are crucial for economic growth.

Protection of Property Rights

Less tangible yet equally important national resources include a stable legal system that protects property rights. As mentioned in Chapter 4, many underdeveloped countries do not systematically record the ownership of real property: land and

Infrastructure
The public capital of a nation including transportation networks, power-generating plants and transmission facilities, public education institutions, and other intangible resources such as protection of property rights and a stable monetary environment.

buildings. Though ownership is often informally recognized, without express legal title, the capital locked up in these informal arrangements cannot be used to secure loans for entrepreneurial purposes. As a result, valuable capital sits idle; it cannot be leveraged for other productive purposes.[5]

Enforcement of Contracts

The legal enforcement of contract rights is another important component of an infrastructure that promotes economic growth and well-being. Patent and copyright laws that protect innovators for specified lengths of time are needed to promote invention and innovation. Every country has its innovators; the only question is whether these people are offered enough of an incentive to devote their efforts to coming up with the innovations that drive economic growth. In today's digital world, protecting copyrights is especially important, since the cost of duplicating digital products is nearly zero. Yet, without some sort of protection, producers of these goods would have little incentive to produce them.

Stable Financial System

Another important component of a nation's infrastructure is a stable and secure financial system. Such a financial system keeps the purchasing power of the currency stable, facilitates transactions, and permits credit institutions to arise. Bank runs, like those that caused major economic disruption in Uruguay and Argentina in 2001–02, are less likely when a nation's financial environment is stable.

Unanticipated inflations or deflations are both detrimental to economic growth. Consumers and businesses rely on the money prices they pay for goods and services for information about the state of the market. If these price signals are constantly being distorted by inflation or deflation, the quality of business and consumer decisions suffers. Unanticipated price changes further lead to a redistribution of income between creditors and debtors. Financial instability is harmful to improving standards of living and generating economic growth.

Economic Freedom Index

Because it is both tangible and intangible, a nation's infrastructure is difficult to measure. The country's roads, dams, and other public capital do not present much of a measurement problem, but trying to measure intangibles often requires subjective judgments. One reasonably objective measure for infrastructure is the economic freedom index.

This index is produced by the Fraser Institute, a nonprofit public policy research organization. It incorporates information from the following seven categories:[6]

- Size of government: consumption, transfers, and subsidies.
- Structure of the economy and use of markets: private markets or production and allocation through government mandate?
- Monetary policy and price stability: protection of money as a store of value and medium of exchange.
- Freedom to use alternative currencies.
- Legal structure and property rights: security of property rights and viability of contracts.
- International exchange: freedom to trade with foreigners.
- Freedom of exchange in capital and financial markets.

---

[5]For an extensive discussion of this issue, see Hernando de Soto, *The Mystery of Capital: Why Capitalism Triumphs in the West and Fails Everywhere Else* (New York: Basic Books), 2000.
[6]Ed Nosal and Peter Rupert, "Infrastructure and the Wealth of Nations," *Economic Commentary: Federal Reserve Bank of Cleveland,* January 15, 2002, p. 2.

Clearly, assigning some of these items a numeric value requires some subjective judgment. Even so, this index is one of the more reasonable approaches to measuring the infrastructure of a country.[7]

Figure 3 portrays the relationship among economic freedom, income, and economic growth. In both panels, economic freedom is split into quintiles, from the bottom 20% (least free) to the top 20% (most free). Panel A shows that those nations with the most economic freedom also have the highest GDP per capita adjusted for real purchasing power. Panel B shows that the growth in real per capita GDP during the 1990s was generally higher for those countries with higher levels of economic freedom.

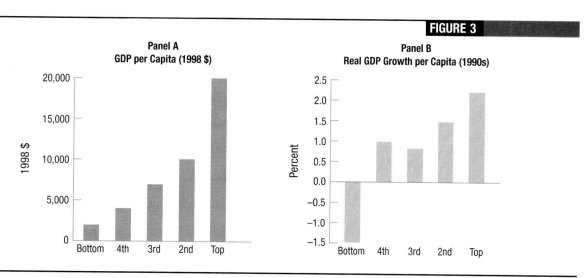

FIGURE 3

Panel A
GDP per Capita (1998 $)

Panel B
Real GDP Growth per Capita (1990s)

Economic Freedom, Income, and Economic Growth

The relationship among economic freedom, income, and economic growth is shown here. In both panels, economic freedom is split into quintiles, from the bottom 20% (least free) to the top 20% (most free). Panel A shows that those nations with the most economic freedom also have the highest real per capita GDP. Panel B shows that the growth in real per capita GDP during the 1990s was generally higher for those countries with higher levels of economic freedom.

This idea that economic freedom and economic development go hand in hand has not always been popular. After World War II, the dominant view was that richer countries should provide capital (foreign aid) to poorer countries, and that this capital, when spent by the governments of the poorer countries, would generate economic growth. This money, however, often went into large infrastructure projects such as dams and power plants that did little to stimulate growth, or else the money was siphoned off into the pockets of the powerful ruling elite.

One economist, Peter Bauer from the London School of Economics, argued that "opportunities for private profit, not government plans, held the key to development. Governments had the limited though crucial role of protecting property rights, enforcing contracts, treating everybody equally before the law, minimizing inflation and keeping taxes low. It was a tragedy that countries neglected this role."[8] Today, his ideas are part of a new conventional wisdom.

In this chapter, we have seen that the economy can be expected to hover around full employment in the long run. Over the long haul, that is, flexible prices, wages,

---

[7]See James Gwartney, Robert Lawson, and Walter Block, *Economic Freedom of the World 1975–1995* (Vancouver, Canada: Fraser Institute),1996, for a discussion of exactly how the index is constructed and a list of the numerous academic papers analyzing their approach.
[8]"Economic Focus: A Voice for the Poor," *The Economist*, May 4, 2002, p. 76.

and interest rates will tend to keep the economy operating near full employment. This simple model suggests that economic growth in the long run comes from growth of the labor force, improvements in labor's productivity, increases in capital, or improvements in technology. Investments in human capital and greater economic freedom also lead to higher growth rates and higher standards of living.

In the long run, the classical model is a reasonable picture of our economic system. Yet, what are we to do if the economy collapses in the shorter term? Classical theorists dismissed this possibility, arguing that a depressed economy would quickly return to full employment. The Great Depression of the 1930s was to prove their arguments wrong. We discuss this in the next chapter.

Checkpoint

Infrastructure and Economic Growth

REVIEW

- Infrastructure is a country's public capital including dams, roads, transportation networks, power generating plants, and public schools.
- Other less tangible infrastructure elements include protection of property rights, enforcement of contracts, and a stable financial system.
- The economic freedom index measures a country's infrastructure that supports economic growth.

QUESTION

Imagine a country with a "failed government" that can no longer enforce the law. Contracts are not upheld, and lawlessness is the order of the day. How could an economy operate and grow in this environment?

Answers to the Checkpoint question can be found at the end of this chapter.

The Changing Face of Innovation Waves

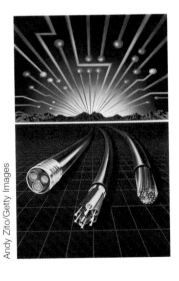

Andy Zito/Getty Images

As we saw in a previous chapter, Joseph Schumpeter viewed the economy as being hit with shocks of innovation over long periods of time. He referred to these waves of innovation as "creative destruction" in which a lone inventor creates a major new idea or process that propels the economy to ever greater heights, and once the innovation has spread across the economy, the economy begins a decline until another innovation occurs, and the economy booms again. These new ideas create a surge in investment that stimulates the business cycle and last—according to Schumpeter— roughly 50–60 years.

Before World War II, innovation came primarily from lone inventors and innovators, but after the war, business began establishing research and development departments that focused strictly on innovation. Bell Labs, a part of American Telephone and Telegraph (AT&T), was responsible for many innovations including the transistor that ushered in the digital age. Another was the Palo Alto Research Center (PARC), a subsidiary of Xerox Corporation that brought us technologies such as laser printing and the first graphical user interface (GUI), forerunner of the Mac and Windows operating systems.

It took 60 years to go from water power to steam power, then just 50 years to electricity as our major source of power. It took 50 years to get from steam to the internal combustion engine and 40 for commercial aviation to take its place in the transportation system. In the 1950s, electronic equipment became commonplace, and within 40 years, it was replaced by digital equipment, software, and the Internet. Since 1990, digital computing has spurred the development of biotechnology, sequencing of human DNA, and the development of nanotechnology. All of these may well become the next major innovation of the near future. All of this suggests that the time between waves of innovation is becoming shorter.[9] Figure 4 shows the important innovations during each wave and illustrates how the waves are becoming smaller. Why is this?

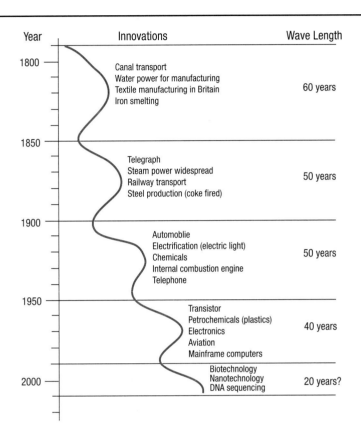

Year	Innovations	Wave Length
1800	Canal transport Water power for manufacturing Textile manufacturing in Britain Iron smelting	60 years
1850	Telegraph Steam power widespread Railway transport Steel production (coke fired)	50 years
1900	Automoblie Electrification (electric light) Chemicals Internal combustion engine Telephone	50 years
1950	Transistor Petrochemicals (plastics) Electronics Aviation Mainframe computers	40 years
2000	Biotechnology Nanotechnology DNA sequencing	20 years?

FIGURE 4

Are Innovation Waves Becoming Shorter?

In 60 years, economies went from water power to steam power and, in just 50 years, switched to electricity as the major source of power. It took 50 years to get from steam to the internal combustion engine and 40 years for commercial aviation to take its place in the transportation system. In the 1950s, electronic equipment held center stage, and within 40 years, it was replaced by digital equipment, software, and the Internet. Since 1990, digital computing has spurred the development of biotechnology, sequencing of human DNA, and the development of nanotechnology. These may represent the next major innovation wave. As the figure suggests, the time between waves of innovation seems to be getting shorter. Source: Based on a figure in "Catch the Wave: The Long Cycles of Industrial Innovation Are Becoming Shorter," *The Economist,* February 19, 1999.

Princeton economist William Baumol[10] suggests that capitalism's ability to produce a steady stream of new ideas and processes has made capitalism not only the most efficient growth machine but also the best economic system for generating economic growth. In his book *The Free-Market Innovation Machine,* he suggests that enforcement of contracts, protection of property (both physical and intellectual), and the rule of law all provide the right incentives to innovate. Further, he suggests that large oligopolistic (an industry with a few large companies) firms, especially high-tech firms, must innovate or die because "innovation [is] a prime competitive weapon." Clear examples of this competition are seen in computer chips (Intel and AMD), operating systems (Microsoft, Apple, and Linux), digital music players (iPod and other MP3 players), drug makers in their rush to bring new (patented) pharmaceuticals to the market, and movie companies with the use of more and better special effects.

Sony's new digital e-book Portable Reader with paperlike legibility along with Google's drive to put all books ever printed into an electronic database that can be searched and downloaded will introduce a new round of competition and innovation

[9]"Catch the Wave: The Long Cycles of Industrial Innovation Are Becoming Shorter," *The Economist,* February 19, 1999.
[10]William J. Baumol, *The Free-Market Innovation Machine: Analyzing the Growth Miracle of Capitalism* (Princeton, NJ: Princeton University Press), 2002.

with electronic book delivery. This will speed the pace of knowledge dissemination and increase the pace of new discoveries. Undoubtedly, innovation cycles will be reduced.

Baumol argues that innovation has become routine in large companies that want to survive, and the incentives established by patents and licensing have meant that firms often license their innovations to technology-exchange partnerships where cross licensing is the norm. He suggests that roughly 20% of the total economic benefits accrue to the original investors of the innovation, with the rest spilling over into the broader economy and society. For all of these reasons, the innovation cycle may be going from a long wave to a much shorter cycle. Would Schumpeter have been surprised by this?

Key Concepts

Economic growth, p. 166
Classical model, p. 167
Aggregate production function, p. 168
Say's law, p. 170

Productivity, p. 173
Capital-to-labor ratio, p. 174
Investment in human capital, p. 174
Infrastructure, p. 177

Chapter Summary

The Classical Model

Classical economists argued that competitive conditions in product, labor, and capital markets, combined with flexible prices, wages, and interest rates would keep the economy operating near full employment. Everyone willing to work at the prevailing real wage would be employed.

Economic growth and rising standards of living in the classical model results from improvements in the productivity of labor, increases in the capital stock, and technological change that improves productivity.

Sources of Long-Run Economic Growth

A key factor in American economic growth over the past century has been the expansion of its labor force from population growth and increased labor force participation. These trends have been encouraged by open immigration policies and increased incentives for entering the workforce, such as lower marginal tax rates.

The marginal productivity of labor is the most significant determinant of real wages, and high productivity is the primary reason our standard of living is so high. Sources of productivity growth include increases in the capital-to-labor ratio, increases in the quality of the labor force, and improvements in technology. Technological progress has been the most significant source of the enormous productivity gains the United States and many other countries have enjoyed over the past century.

Modern growth theories consider the growth in knowledge as key. Incentives for research and development result in processes that quickly spread to the entire economy. Knowledge has public good and spillover aspects that lead to increasing returns that drive modern economic growth.

Infrastructure and Economic Growth

One of the key reasons some nations are rich and others are poor is the different levels of infrastructure in various countries. Infrastructure is defined as a country's public capital. It includes not only tangible assets, such as dams, roads, and bridges, but also intangible goods, such as secure property rights, legally enforced contract rights, and a stable financial system.

Despite the difficulties of measuring infrastructure, the economic freedom index, produced by the Fraser Institute, is a fairly objective means of assessing a country's infrastructure. The index incorporates information from seven categories: size of government, structure of the economy and use of markets, monetary policy and price stability, freedom to use alternative currencies, legal structure and property rights, international exchange, and freedom of exchange in capital and financial markets.

Those countries with the most economic freedom also have the highest real per capita GDP. It is widely believed that investing in human capital and promoting greater economic freedom will lead to higher growth rates and higher standards of living in the developing world.

Questions and Problems

1. Describe how classical economists saw competitive markets keeping the economy near full employment.

2. Explain why the level of economic growth today is more important to your great grandchildren than to you.

3. The airline industry has struggled with unions in adapting to deregulation over the last two decades. Competitive pressures have resulted in lower wages for industry employees, but several airlines have had to invoke bankruptcy proceedings to eliminate their union contracts and reduce payroll costs. How do these activities square with the assumption of competitive labor markets and flexible wages assumed by classical economists?

4. The Chinese economy currently produces a GDP of roughly $10 trillion with over 1.3 billion people, so its GDP per capita is roughly $7,500. Contrast this with the United States, which produces over $13 trillion GDP with a population of roughly 300 million or nearly $44,000 per person. If an economy, adjusted for inflation, grows at 3% annually, it will be 4.4 times bigger in 50 years; at 5% growth, it will be 11.5 times bigger, and if it grows at 10% annually, it will be 117.4 times larger in 50 years. If the United States grows at an average annual rate of 3% over the next 50 years and China grows at 10%, will China's standard of living or per capita income catch up to that of the United States? Under what assumptions would China have a larger economy than the United States in 50 years? Answer the same questions if China only grows at a real rate of 5% and the United States grows at 3%. Considering the classical model in the chapter and the factors that contribute to long-run growth, is 10% or 5% growth for China more likely?

5. The standard of living we enjoy today is largely due to the investments of earlier generations of Americans. Do you agree? Why or why not?

6. Although abundant natural resources can be a blessing to a country, are they necessary to ensure economic growth and a prosperous economy?

7. In the quote that begins this chapter, Nobel Prize winner Robert Lucas in 1988 suggested that differences in growth rates between Egypt and India raise the most fundamental economic question of what causes economic growth. What makes this issue of growth so important? Is a long-term growth rate of 1.4% so different from 3.4%?

8. Why might a lack of economic freedom hold back development and keep living standards low?

9. What role might foreign investment play in helping developing nations improve their growth rate and increase income levels?

10. Higher levels of savings and investment lead to greater rates of economic growth. What can government do to encourage more savings and investment?

11. Per capita income (or output) is the general measure used to compare the standards of living between countries. If a country's population growth is higher than its economic growth, what happens to per capita income? What are some of the limitations to using per capita income as a measure to compare the well-being between countries?

12. One of the potential negative consequences of both economic and population growth is that we will eventually exhaust the Earth's natural resources, leading to our demise. What kind of activities might prevent this from happening?

13. Classical economists assumed that highly competitive labor and capital markets would keep the economy around full employment. Which of these two markets in our economy is the most like classical analysis? If these markets are not highly competitive, what might that mean for the conclusion by classical economists that full employment will typically prevail?

14. Why is investment in human capital good for both individuals and fostering economic growth for the economy as a whole?

15. Why is a stable financial system important to economic growth?

Answers to Checkpoint Questions

CHECKPOINT: THE CLASSICAL MODEL

A credible case could be made that globalization and trade liberalization have made world product, labor, and capital markets more competitive than ever before. The revolutions in communications, data processing, the Internet, and health care are introducing competitive pressures in all markets. In this way, the world economy may reflect the working of the classical model more today than in the past.

CHECKPOINT: SOURCES OF LONG-RUN ECONOMIC GROWTH

An organization like the Gates Foundation can help people improve their health (vaccinations, clean water, and sanitation) to enable them to improve their productivity and earning power. Then, focus on schools and improving education. All of this focus on human capital broadly can be accomplished with grants to communities or parents (subsidize them to send their kids to school) in developing nations.

CHECKPOINT: INFRASTRUCTURE AND ECONOMIC GROWTH

Not very well. Large-scale business that we are accustomed to could not exist. What's left is small individual businesses that serve small local populations. Growth is stymied, and everyone ekes out a small living. Countries like Somalia are in this no-win situation.

Keynesian Macroeconomics 8

re-Depression economic analysis essentially ignored the role of the government in macroeconomic stabilization. To be sure, the government was seen as providing the necessary framework in which the market could operate, maintaining competition, providing central banking services, providing for the national defense, administering the legal system, and so forth. But the government was not expected to play a role in promoting full employment, stabilizing prices, or stimulating economic growth—the economy was supposed to do this on its own. The prevailing thought of economists before the 1930s was that a *laissez-faire* (leave it alone) approach to the economy was the best approach for government. Competitive markets for labor, products, and financial assets would lead to flexible wages, prices, and interest rates that would keep the economy humming along near full employment, with only a minor recession here and there.

The Great Depression brought about a tsunami level change in political and economic thinking in this country. Before the Depression, government spending (federal, state, and local) was roughly 10% of the economy. Today, that figure has tripled to 30%. The government, moreover, has added a vast number of laws, rules, and regulations to the books.

Since the Depression, the U.S. population has more than doubled, growing from 121 million to nearly 300 million, yet over this same period, *real* gross domestic product has risen to nearly nine times its 1929 level. With government spending at 30% of this gross domestic product number today, our economy can truly be called a mixed economy where the government plays a huge role.

Most of the changes in post-Depression economic thinking can be traced back to one book, *The General Theory of Employment, Interest and Money,* by John Maynard Keynes, published in 1936. In this book, Keynes moved out of the classical framework, which had viewed the economy as three separate and distinct competitive markets, and focused his attention on the economy as a whole and on aggregate spending.

In this chapter, we are going to develop the Keynesian model that can be used to analyze short-run macroeconomic fluctuations. Keynes's focus is on aggregate expenditures. Keynes's operating assumption, given that he was writing to explain the economic consequences of the Great Depression, was that if consumers demanded a given level of output, it would be provided by business. Thus, consumer spending is a key component to explaining how the economy reaches short-term equilibrium employment, output, and income. Using this model, we will see why an economy can get stuck in an undesirable place. So let us get started with Keynes and his focus on aggregate expenditures.

After studying this chapter you should be able to

- Name the components of gross domestic product (GDP).

- Analyze consumption using the average propensity to consume (APC) and the marginal propensity to consume (MPC).

- Analyze savings using the average propensity to save (APS) and the marginal propensity to save (MPS).

- Describe the determinants of consumption, saving, and investment.

- Determine aggregate equilibrium in the simple Keynesian model of the private domestic economy.

- Explain why at equilibrium injections equal withdrawals in the economy.

- Explain the multiplier process, how it is computed, and why it operates in both directions.

- Describe macroeconomic equilibrium in the full Keynesian model when government and the foreign sectors are added.

- Explain why the balanced budget multiplier is equal to 1.

- Describe the differences between recessionary and inflationary gaps.

Aggregate Expenditures

Aggregate expenditures
Consist of consumer spending, business investment spending, government spending, and net foreign spending (exports minus imports): GDP = C + I + G + (X − M).

Recall that when we discussed measuring gross domestic product (GDP), we concluded that it could be computed by adding up either all spending or all income in the economy. We saw that the expenditures side consists of consumer spending, business investment spending, government spending, and net foreign spending (exports minus imports); thus, **aggregate expenditures** are equal to:

$$GDP = AE = C + I + G + (X - M)$$

Some Simplifying Assumptions

In this chapter, we first will focus on a simple model of the private economy that includes only consumers and businesses. Later in the chapter, we will incorporate government spending, taxes, and the foreign sector into our analysis. Second, we will assume, moreover, that all saving is personal saving. And since our initial model has no government sector at this point, GDP and national income, personal income and disposable personal income, are all regarded as equal because there are no taxes in this simple model.

Third, because Keynes was modeling a depression economy, we follow him in assuming that there is considerable slack in the economy. Unemployment is high and other resources are sitting idle. There is excess plant capacity, which means that if demand were to rise, business could quickly and without added cost increase output. We will assume, therefore, that the aggregate price level (the CPI, PCE, PPI, or GDP deflator) is fixed; output can grow without putting upward pressure on prices. With these assumptions in mind, let us begin by looking at consumption and saving.

Consumption and Saving

Personal consumption expenditures (C) represent nearly 70% of GDP, and for this reason **consumption** is a major ingredient in our model. Figure 1 shows personal consumption expenditures for the years since 1980. Notice how closely consumption parallels disposable income, and how it has consistently increased since 1980.

Consumption
Spending by individuals and households on both durable goods (e.g., autos, appliances, and electronic equipment) and nondurable goods (e.g., food, clothes, and entertainment).

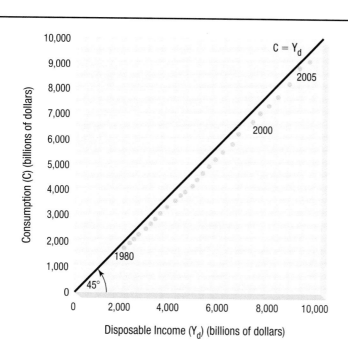

FIGURE 1

Consumption and Disposable Income

This graph shows personal consumption spending (C) for the years since 1980. The 45° line inserted in the figure represents the points where consumption is equal to disposable income (Y_d). If you spent your entire annual income, saving nothing, the 45° line would represent your consumption. Annual saving (S) is equal to the vertical difference between the 45° reference line and your annual consumption ($S = Y_d - C$).

The 45° line inserted in the figure represents all points where consumption is equal to disposable income (Y_d). If you spent your entire annual income, saving nothing, the 45° line would represent your consumption. Consequently, your annual **saving** (S) is equal to the vertical difference between the 45° reference line and your annual consumption ($S = Y_d - C$). After all, what can you do with income except spend it or save it?

Keynes began his theoretical examination of consumption by noting the following:

Saving
The difference between income and consumption; the amount of disposable income not spent.

The fundamental psychological law, upon which we are entitled to depend with great confidence both a priori from our knowledge of human nature and from the detailed facts of experience, is that men are disposed, as a rule and on the average, to increase their consumption as their income increases, but not by as much as the change in their income.[1]

---

[1] John Maynard Keynes, *The General Theory of Employment, Interest and Money* (New York: Harcourt Brace Jovanovich) 1936, p. 96.

John Maynard Keynes (1883–1946)

n 1935, John Maynard Keynes boasted in a letter to playwright George Bernard Shaw of a book he was writing that would revolutionize "the way the world thinks about economic problems." This was a brash prediction to make, even to a friend, but it was not an idle boast. His *General Theory of Employment, Interest and Money* did change the way the world looked at economics. Arguably, it changed the world.

Keynes belongs in a small class of economic earth-shakers such as Karl Marx and Adam Smith. His one-man war on classical theory launched a new field of study known as macroeconomics. His ideas would have a profound influence on theorists and government policies for decades to come. Keynes also led an enviable life outside of economics, achieving success as a speculator, theater impresario, journalist, public servant, and member of an exclusive literary circle, the Bloomsbury group.

Keynes grew up in the university town of Cambridge, England. His father, John Neville Keynes, was a leading economist; his mother, a former town mayor. He attended the best British schools, Eton and King's College, Cambridge.

During World War I, Keynes was assigned by the British Treasury to work on problems of wartime finances. Knowledgeable observers considered his contribution to have been indispensable to the war effort. Difficulties arose, however, after the peace, when Keynes was enlisted to advise the British government in negotiations over the Versailles Treaty. Strenuously objecting to the punitive financial terms imposed on Germany, Keynes resigned his position and published a brilliant diatribe called *The Economic Consequences of the Peace.*

During the world economic depression in the early 1930s, Keynes became alarmed when unemployment in England continued to rise after the first few years of the crisis. "I shall argue that the postulates of classical theory are applicable to a special case only and not to a general case," he wrote in the introduction to the *General Theory of Employment, Interest and Money.* "Moreover, the characteristics of the special case assumed by the classical theory happen not to be those of the economic society we live in." Keynes argued that *aggregate expenditures,* the sum of investment, consumption, government spending, and net exports determined the levels of economic output and employment. When aggregate expenditures were high, the economy would foster business expansion, higher incomes, and high levels of employment. With low aggregate spending, businesses would be unable to sell their inventories and would cut back on investment and production.

Consumption spending grows, in other words, as income grows, but not as fast. So, as income grows, saving will grow as a percentage of income. Notice that this approach to analyzing saving differs from the classical approach. Classical economists assumed that the *interest rate* is the principal determinant of saving and, by extension, one of the principal determinants of consumption. Keynes, in contrast, emphasized *income* as the main determinant of consumption and saving.

Table 1 portrays a hypothetical consumption function of the sort Keynes envisioned. As income grows from $4,000 to $4,200, consumption increases by $150 ($4,150–$4,000) and saving grows from 0 to $50. Thus, the *change* in income of $200 is divided between consumption ($150) and saving ($50). Note that at income levels below $4,000 saving is negative; people are spending more than their current income either by using credit or drawing on existing savings to support consumption.

Table 1	Hypothetical Consumption and Saving and Propensities to Consume and Save					
(1)	(2)	(3)	(4)	(5)	(6)	(7)
Income or Output Y	Consumption C	Saving S	APC C ÷ Y	APS S ÷ Y	MPC $\Delta C \div \Delta Y$	MPS $\Delta S \div \Delta Y$
3,000	3,250	−250	1.08	−0.08	0.75	0.25
3,200	3,400	−200	1.06	−0.06	0.75	0.25
3,400	3,550	−150	1.04	−0.04	0.75	0.25
3,600	3,700	−100	1.03	−0.03	0.75	0.25
3,800	3,850	−50	1.01	−0.01	0.75	0.25
4,000	4,000	0	1.00	0.00	0.75	0.25
4,200	4,150	50	0.99	0.01	0.75	0.25
4,400	4,300	100	0.98	0.02	0.75	0.25
4,600	4,450	150	0.97	0.03	0.75	0.25
4,800	4,600	200	0.96	0.04	0.75	0.25
5,000	4,750	250	0.95	0.05	0.75	0.25
5,200	4,900	300	0.94	0.06	0.75	0.25
5,400	5,050	350	0.94	0.06	0.75	0.25
5,600	5,200	400	0.93	0.07	0.75	0.25

Average Propensities to Consume and Save

The percentage of income that is consumed is known as the **average propensity to consume** (APC); it is listed in Column 4 of Table 1. It is calculated by dividing consumption spending by income (C/Y). For example, when income is $5,000 and consumption is $4,750, APC is 0.95, meaning that 95% of the income is spent.

The **average propensity to save** (APS) is equal to saving divided by income (S/Y); it is the percentage of income saved. Again, if income is $5,000 and saving is $250, APS is 0.05, or 5% is saved. The APS is shown in Column 5 of Table 1.

Average propensity to consume
The percentage of income that is consumed (C/Y).

Average propensity to save
The percentage of income that is saved (S/Y).

Notice that if you add Columns 4 and 5 in Table 1, the answer is always 1. That is because Y = C + S, so all income is either spent or saved. Similar logic dictates that the two percentages spent and saved must total 100%, or that APC + APS = 1.

Marginal Propensities to Consume and Save

Average propensities to consume and save represent the proportion of income that is consumed or saved. *Marginal* propensities measure what part of *additional* income will be either consumed or saved. This distinction is important because changing policies by government policymakers means that income changes and consumer's reactions to their *changing* incomes is what we will see later drives changes in the economy.

Marginal propensity to consume
The change in consumption associated with a given change in income (ΔC/ΔY).

The **marginal propensity to consume** (MPC) is equal to the change in consumption associated with a given change in income. Denoting change by the delta symbol (Δ), MPC = ΔC/ΔY. Thus, for example, when income grows from $5,000 to $5,200 (a $200 change), and consumption rises from $4,750 to $4,900 (a $150 change), MPC is equal to 0.75 ($150/$200).

Notice that this result is consistent with Keynes's fundamental psychological law quoted earlier, holding that, "men [and women] are disposed, as a rule and on the average, to increase their consumption as their income increases, but not by as much as the change in their income." In Table 1, the MPC for all changes in income is 0.75, as shown in Column 6.

Marginal propensity to save
The change in saving associated with a given change in income (ΔS/ΔY).

The **marginal propensity to save** (MPS) is equal to the change in saving associated with a given change in income; MPS = ΔS/ΔY. So, when income grows from $5,000 to $5,200, and saving grows from $250 to $300, MPS is equal to 0.25 ($50/$200). Column 7 lists MPS.

Note once again that the sum of the MPC and the MPS will always equal 1, since the only thing that can be done with a change in income is to spend or save it. A small word of warning, however: Though APC + APS = 1 and MPC + MPS = 1, most of the time APC + MPS ≠ 1 and APS + MPC ≠ 1. Try adding a few different columns from Table 1 and you will see that this is true. These little equations often show up on exams as wrong answers.

Figure 2 graphs the consumption and saving schedules from Table 1. The graph in Panel A extends the consumption schedule back to zero income, where consumption is equal to $1,000 and saving is equal to −$1,000. (Remember that Y = C + S, so if Y = 0 and C = $1,000, then S must equal −$1,000. This person is spending more than she earns, either borrowing money or drawing down her accumulated savings to stay alive.) The 45° line in Panel A is a reference line where Y = C. At the point where the consumption schedule crosses the reference line (point *a*, Y = $4,000), saving is zero, since consumption and income are equal.

The saving schedule in Panel B simply plots the difference between the 45° reference line (Y = C) and the consumption schedule in Panel A. For example, if income is $4,000, saving is zero (point *f*), and when income equals $5,000, saving equals $250 [line (*b* − *c*) in Panel A, point *g* in Panel B]. Saving is positively sloped, again reflecting Keynes's fundamental law; the more people earn, the greater percentage of income they will save (the average propensity to save rises as income rises). Make a mental note that the saving schedule shows how much people *desire* to save at various income levels.

How much people will *actually* save depends on equilibrium income, or how much income the economy is generating. We are getting a bit ahead of the story here, but planting this seed will help you when we get to the section where we determine equilibrium income in the economy.

Note finally that the consumption and saving schedules in our example are straight-line functions. This need not be the case, but it simplifies some of the relationships to graph them like this at this point. When the consumption and saving schedules are linear, the MPC is the slope of the consumption function, and the

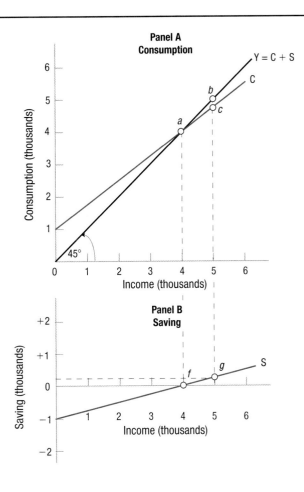

Panel A
Consumption

Panel B
Saving

FIGURE 2

Consumption and Saving

The consumption and saving schedules from Table 1 are put in graphical form here. Panel A extends the consumption schedule back to zero income, where consumption is equal to $1,000 and saving is equal to −$1,000. ($Y = C + S$, so if $Y = 0$ and $C = \$1,000$, then S must equal −$1,000.) The 45° line is a reference line where $Y = C$. At the point where the consumption schedule crosses the reference line (point a, $Y = \$4,000$), saving is zero, since consumption and income are equal. The saving schedule in Panel B simply plots the difference between the 45° reference line ($Y = C$) and the consumption schedule in Panel A. Thus, when income = $5,000, saving = $250 [line ($b − c$) in Panel A, point g in Panel B]. Note that saving is positively sloped: the more people earn, the greater the average propensity to save.

MPS is the slope of the saving schedule. In this case, MPC = 0.75 and MPS = 0.25, which tells us that every time income changes by $1,000, consumption will change by $750 and saving will change by $250.

Other Determinants of Consumption and Saving

Income is the principal determinant of consumption and saving, but other factors can shift the saving and consumption schedules. These factors include the wealth of a family, their expectations about the future of prices and income, family debt, and taxation.

Wealth. The more wealth a family has, the higher its consumption. When the stock market was soaring in the late 1990s, policymakers—most notably the Federal Reserve Board—were continually worried about the "wealth effect" the rising stock market might have on consumption spending. The concern was that, as many households saw their wealth dramatically expanding, rising consumption might have an adverse impact on the economy's inflation rate.

　　As it turned out, the stock market collapsed in 2000, and the economy moved into recession. Then, economists began worrying about the negative impact of this wealth effect. With $6–7 trillion of wealth evaporating from the stock market, the concern was that consumers would reduce their consumption even more than would otherwise be expected. To date, the impact of the wealth reduction seems to have been minimal, lending support to the Keynesian emphasis on income as the most important determinant of consumption and saving.

Expectations. Expectations about future prices and incomes help determine how much a family will spend today. If you anticipate that prices will rise next week, you will be more likely to purchase more products today. What are sales, after all, but temporary reductions in price designed to entice customers into the store today? Similarly, if you anticipate that your income will soon rise—perhaps you are about to graduate from medical school—you will be more inclined to incur debt today to purchase something you want, as was the case with high school student LeBron James, driving around in a Hummer, knowing that when he was drafted into the NBA, he would be making a fortune. Lotto winners who receive their winnings over a 20-year span often spend much of the money early on, running up debts. Few winners will spend their winnings evenly over the next 20 years.

Household Debt. The more debt a family has, the less it will spend in the current period. Though the household might want to spend more money on goods now, its debt level restricts its ability to get more credit.

Taxes. Taxes reduce disposable income, so taxes result in reduced consumption and saving. When taxes are increased, spendable income falls, so consumption is reduced by the MPC times the reduction in disposable income, and saving falls by the reduction in disposable income times the MPS. Tax reductions have the opposite impact.

Investment

Investment
Spending by business that adds to the productive capacity of the economy. Investment depends on factors such as its rate of return, the level of technology, and business expectations about the economy.

Though consumer spending, at 70%, is by far the largest component of GDP, it holds fairly steady from year to year. In contrast, *gross private domestic* **investment** (the "I" in the GDP equation), is volatile. The annual percentage changes in consumption and investment spending from 1980 to 2005 are shown in Figure 3.

Notice that although consumption seems to plod along with annual increases between 3% and 10%, investment spending has undergone annual fluctuations ranging from −10% to +30%. Investment constitutes roughly 17–18% of GDP, so its volatility often accounts for our recessions and booms.

The economic boom of the 1990s, for instance, was fueled by investments in information technology infrastructure, including massive investments in telecommunications. In the 1990s, people believed Internet traffic would grow by 1,000% a year, doubling every 3 months or so. This belief led many companies to lay mil-

---

FIGURE 3

Changes in Consumption and Gross Private Domestic Investment

The annual percentage changes in consumption and gross private domestic investment (GPDI) are shown here. Consumption is relatively stable and grows roughly 5% a year. Investment spending, on the other hand, has undergone annual fluctuations ranging from −10% to +30%.

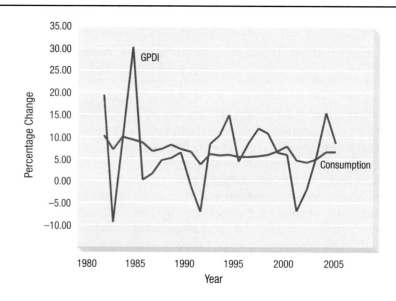

lions of miles of fiber optic cable. When the massive investments made in computer hardware and software over that same decade are taken into account, it is no wonder that the economy grew at a breakneck pace.

But this increase came to a halt in the early 2000s, when businesses—especially the telecoms—discovered they had built up a massive excess capacity, and thus bandwidth prices plummeted. Since 2000, bankruptcies and earnings restatements have occurred often, along with reductions in investment. This drop in investment spending rippled throughout the economy, leading to a recession. In 2004, business investment picked up, and the economy entered a recovery period.

Investment Demand

Investment levels depend mainly on the rate of return on capital. Investments earning a high rate of return are the investments undertaken first (assuming comparable risk), with those projects offering lower returns finding their way into the investment stream later. Interest rate levels also are important in determining how much investment occurs since much of business investment is financed through debt.

Figure 4 shows a hypothetical investment demand schedule, ID_0. When the interest rate is i_0, firms will invest an amount equal to I_0. When interest rates fall to i_1, investment rises to I_1 (a movement from point a to point b). As the rates for borrowing drop, more projects will become feasible, since the projected profit required to meet this lower interest rate is now less.

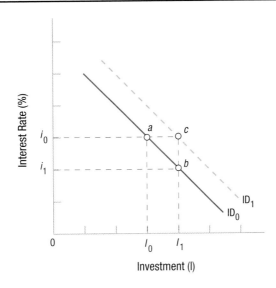

FIGURE 4

The Investment Demand Curve

Investment demand curve ID_0 illustrates that when the interest rate is i_0, firms will invest an amount equal to I_0, and when the rate falls to i_1, investment will rise to I_1. As the rates for borrowing drop, more investment projects become feasible, since the rate of return required to earn a profit declines. If business expectations improve, investment demand increases to ID_1.

Other Determinants of Investment Demand

The rate of return on investments is the main determinant of investment spending, but other factors shift the investment schedule shown in Figure 4.

Expectations. Projecting the rate of return on investment is not an easy task. Returns are forecasted over the life of a new piece of equipment or factory, yet many changes in the economic environment can alter the actual return on these investments. As business expectations improve, the investment schedule will shift to the right—businesses think returns will be going up, so they are willing to invest more at a given interest rate. Figure 4 illustrates such a scenario as a shift in the investment demand schedule from ID_0 to ID_1. Even though the interest rate is still equal to i_0, investment will be I_1 (point c).

Technological Change. It is clear (with the benefit of hindsight) that business expectations about technology and the Internet in the 1990s were exuberant. Technological innovations periodically spur investment. Electrification, automobiles, and phone service at the beginning of the 20th century and, most recently, microchips and the new products they have spawned are examples.

Producing brand new products requires massive investments in plant, equipment, and research and development. These investments often take a long time before their full potential is realized. Many economists expect that the investments in Internet and telecommunications technology are just in their beginning stages of boosting economic growth here and abroad.

Capital Goods on Hand and Operating Costs. The more capital goods a firm has on hand, including inventories of the products they sell, the less the firm will want to make new investments. Until existing capacity can be fully used, investing in more equipment and facilities will do little to help profits. When the costs of operating and maintaining machinery and equipment rise, the rate of return on capital equipment will decline and new investment will be postponed. Firms will wait until demand for their products grows enough to justify increasing production in the face of higher operating costs.

Aggregate Investment Schedule

To simplify our analysis, we will assume that rates of return and interest rates fully determine investment in the short run. But once that level of investment has been determined, it remains independent of income, or *autonomous*, as economists say. Therefore, in Figure 4, if interest rates are i_0 and investment demand is ID_0, investment will be I_0 in the short run (point a). Figure 5 shows the resulting aggregate investment schedule that plots investment spending with respect to income.

Because we have assumed that aggregate investment is I_0 at all income levels, the curve is a straight line. Investment is unaffected by different levels of income. This is a simplifying assumption that we will change in later chapters and look at the implications.

Our emphasis in this section has been on two important components of aggregate spending: consumption and investment. Consumption is 70% and investment is 18% of aggregate spending. Consumption is stable, but investment is volatile and especially sensitive to expectations about conditions in the economy. We have seen that on average some income is spent (APC) and some is saved (APS). But, it is that portion of *additional* income that is spent (MPC) and saved (MPS) that is most important for where the economy settles or where it reaches equilibrium, as we will see in the next section.

FIGURE 5

The Investment Schedule

In Figure 4, when interest rates were I_0 and investment demand was ID_0, short-run investment was I_0. The resulting aggregate investment schedule, relating investment spending to income, is shown here. Because aggregate investment is I_0 at all income levels, the curve is a straight line. This assumption simplifies the Keynesian model.

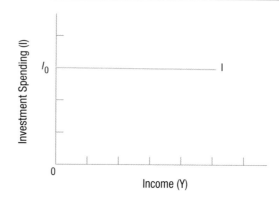

Checkpoint

REVIEW

- Classical economists looked at three primary markets and thought these markets would keep the economy operating around full employment. Keynes approached analysis of the economy by first looking at aggregate expenditures.
- Aggregate expenditures are equal to $C + I + G + (X - M)$, with consumption being roughly 70% of aggregate spending.
- Keynes argued that consumption spending grows with income but not as fast.
- Keynesian analysis suggested that consumption and saving were related to income.
- The average propensities to consume (APC) and save (APS) are equal to C/Y and S/Y, respectively.
- The marginal propensities to consume (MPC) and save (MPS) are equal to $\Delta C/\Delta Y$ and $\Delta S/\Delta Y$, respectively. They represent the change in consumption and saving associated with a change in income.
- Other factors affecting consumption and saving include wealth, expectations about future income and prices, the level of household debt, and taxes.
- Investment levels depend primarily on the rate of return on capital.
- Other determinants of investment demand include business expectations, technology change, operating costs, and the amount of capital goods on hand.
- Consumption is relatively stable, and investment is volatile.
- Together, consumption and investment represent 88% of aggregate expenditures (70% + 18%).

QUESTION

Figure 3 earlier illustrated that investment spending is much more volatile than consumption spending. Why is this?

Answers to the Checkpoint question can be found at the end of this chapter.

The Simple Keynesian Model

Since we have stripped the government and foreign sectors from our analysis at this point, aggregate expenditures (AE) will consist of the sum of consumer and business investment spending (AE = C + I). Aggregate expenditures based on the data in Table 1 are shown in Panel A of Figure 6 on the next page; Panel B shows the corresponding saving and investment schedules.

Let us take a moment to remind ourselves what these graphs represent. Point a in both panels is that level of income ($4,000) where saving is zero and all income is spent. Saving is, therefore, positive for income levels above $4,000 and negative at incomes below. The vertical distance ef in Panel A represents investment (I_0) of $100; it is equal to I_0 in Panel B. Note that the vertical axis of Panel B has a different scale from that of Panel A.

Equilibrium in the Keynesian Model

Ignoring government spending and net exports, aggregate expenditures (AE) consist of consumer spending and business investment (AE = C + I). Panel A shows aggregate spending; Panel B shows the corresponding saving and investment schedules. Point *a* in both panels shows where income equals consumption and saving is zero; all income is spent. Therefore, saving is positive for income levels above $4,000 and negative at incomes below $4,000. The vertical distance *ef* in Panel A represents investment ($100); it is equal to I_0 in Panel B. Equilibrium income and output is $4,400 (point *e*), since this is the level at which businesses are producing just what other businesses and consumers want to buy.

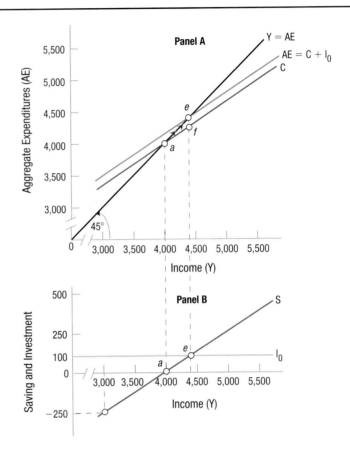

Macroeconomic Equilibrium in the Simple Model

The important question to ask is where this economy will come to rest. Or, in the language of economists, at what income will this economy reach **Keynesian macroeconomic equilibrium**? By equilibrium, economists mean that income at which there are no net pressures pushing the economy to move to a higher or lower level of income and output.

To find this equilibrium point, let's begin with the economy at an income level of $4,000. Are there pressures driving the economy to grow or decline? Looking at point *a* in Panel A of Figure 6, we see that the economy is producing $4,000 worth of goods and services and $4,000 in income. At this income level, however, consumers and businesses want to spend $4,100 ($4,000 in consumption and $100 in investment). Since aggregate expenditures (AE) exceed current income and output, there are more goods being demanded ($4,100) than are being supplied at $4,000. As a result, businesses will find it in their best interests to produce more, raising employment and income and moving the economy toward income and output level $4,400 (point *e*).

Once the economy has moved to $4,400, what consumers and businesses want to buy is exactly equal to the income and output being produced. Business is producing $4,400, aggregate expenditures are equal to $4,400, and there are no pressures on the economy to move away from point *e*. Income of $4,400, or point *e*, is an equilibrium point for our economy.

Panel B shows this same equilibrium, again as point *e*. Is it a coincidence that saving and investment are equal at this point where income and output are at equilibrium? The answer is no. In this simple private sector model, saving and investment will always be equal when the economy is in equilibrium.

Keynesian macroeconomic equilibrium
In the simple model, the economy is at rest; spending injections (investment) are equal to withdrawals (saving), and there are no net inducements for the economy to change the level of output or income. In the full model, all injections of spending must equal all withdrawals at equilibrium; I + G + X = S + T + M.

Remember that aggregate expenditures are equal to consumption plus business investment (AE = C + I). Recall also that *at equilibrium,* aggregate expenditures, income, and output are all equal; what is demanded is supplied (AE = Y). Finally, keep in mind that income can either be spent or saved (Y = C + S). By substitution, we know that, at equilibrium,

$$AE = Y = C + I$$

We also know that

$$Y = C + S$$

Substituting C + I for Y yields

$$C + I = C + S$$

Canceling the Cs, we find that, *at equilibrium,*

$$I = S$$

Thus, the location of point *e* in Panel B is not just coincidental; at equilibrium, actual saving and investment will always be equal. Note that at point *a*, saving is zero, yet investment spending is $100 at I_0. This difference means businesses desire to invest more than people desire to save. With *desired* investment exceeding *desired* saving, this cannot be an equilibrium point, since saving and investment must be equal for the economy to be at equilibrium. Indeed, income will rise until these two values are equal at point *e*.

What is important to take from this discussion? First, when intended (or desired) saving and investment differ, the economy will have to grow or shrink to achieve equilibrium. When desired saving exceeds desired investment—at income levels above $4,400 in Panel B—income will decline. When intended saving is below intended investment—at income levels below $4,400 — income will rise. Notice that we are using the words "intended" and "desired" interchangeably.

Second, at equilibrium all **injections** of spending (investment in this case) into the economy must equal all **withdrawals** (saving in this simple model). Spending injections increase aggregate income, while spending withdrawals reduce it. This fact will become important as we add government and the foreign sector to the model.

Injections
Increments of spending including investment, government spending, and exports.

Withdrawals
Activities that remove spending from the economy including saving, taxes, and imports.

The Multiplier Effect

Given an initial investment of $100 ($I_0$), equilibrium is at an output of $4,400 (point *e*). Remember that at equilibrium, what people *withdraw* from the economy (saving) is equal to what others are willing to *inject* into the spending system (investment). In this case both values equal $100. Point *e* is an equilibrium point because there are no pressures in the system to increase or decrease output; the spending desires of consumers and business are satisfied.

Table 2 and Figure 7 on the next page reproduce the important data from Table 1 and Panel B of Figure 6. As Keynes made clear, however, an equilibrium income (output) level of $4,400 (the shaded row in Table 2 where saving = investment = $100) might entail massive unemployment. He was writing during the Great Depression of the 1930s, when unemployment was over 20%, and he argued that given those conditions, business could not be expected to invest more. So, without some change in the behavior of consumers or businesses, the economy will remain at equilibrium point *e* indefinitely. There is no guarantee that the economy will automatically return to full employment if point *e* represents substantial unemployment.

Table 2	Keynesian Equilibrium Analysis with Different Investment Levels			
Income or Output (Y)	Consumption (C)	Saving (S)	Investment (I_0)	Investment (I_1)
3,000	3,250	−250	100	200
3,200	3,400	−200	100	200
3,400	3,550	−150	100	200
3,600	3,700	−100	100	200
3,800	3,850	−50	100	200
4,000	4,000	0	100	200
4,200	4,150	50	100	200
4,400	4,300	100	100	200
4,600	4,450	150	100	200
4,800	4,600	200	100	200
5,000	4,750	250	100	200
5,200	4,900	300	100	200
5,400	5,050	350	100	200
5,600	5,200	400	100	200

The Multiplier

Let us assume *full employment* occurs at output $4,800. How much would investment have to increase to move the economy out to full employment? As Figure 7 shows, investment must rise to $200 ($I_1$), an increase of $100. With this new investment, equilibrium output moves from point *e* to point *b*, and income rises from $4,400 to $4,800.

FIGURE 7

Saving and Investment

When investment is $100, equilibrium employment occurs at an output of $4,400 (point *e*). When investment rises to $200 ($I_1$), equilibrium output climbs to $4,800 (point *b*). Thus, $100 of added investment spending causes income to grow by $400. This is the multiplier at work.

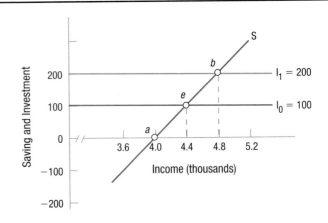

What is remarkable here is that a mere $100 of added spending (investment in this case) caused income to grow by $400. This phenomenon is known as the **multiplier** effect. Recognizing it was one of Keynes's major insights. How does it work?

In this simple example, we have assumed the marginal propensity to consume is 0.75. So, for each added dollar received by consumers, $0.75 is spent and $0.25 is saved. Thus, when business invests an added $100, the firms providing the machinery will spend $75 of this new income on more raw materials, while saving the remaining $25. The firms supplying the new raw materials have $75 of new income. These firms will spend $56.25 of this (0.75 × $75.00), while saving $18.75 ($56.25 + $18.75 = $75.00). This effect continues on until the added spending has been exhausted. As a result, income will increase by $100 + $75 + $56.25 + ... In the end, income rises by $400. Figure 8 outlines this multiplier process.

The general formula for the spending multiplier (k) is

$$k = 1/(1 - MPC)$$

Alternately, since MPC + MPS = 1, the MPS = 1 − MPC, so

$$k = 1/MPS$$

Thus, in our simple model, the simple multiplier is

$$1/(1 - .75) = 1/.25 = 4$$

As a result of the multiplier effect, new spending will raise equilibrium by four times the amount of new spending. Note that any change in spending (consumption, investment—and as we will see in the next section—government spending or changes in net exports) will also have this effect. Spending is spending. Note also—and this is important—the multiplier works in both directions.

Multiplier
Spending changes alter equilibrium income by the spending change times the multiplier. One person's spending becomes another's income, and that second person spends some (the MPC), which becomes income for another person, and so on, until income has changed by 1/(1 − MPC) = 1/MPS. The multiplier operates in both directions.

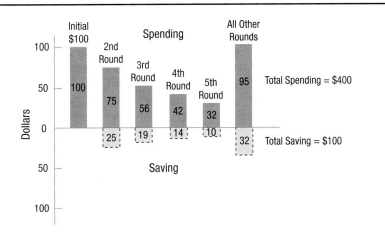

FIGURE 8

The Multiplier Process

An initial $100 of spending generates more spending because of the multiplier process shown in this figure. With an MPC = 0.75 in the second round, $75 is spent and $25 is saved. In the third round, $56.25 of the previous $75 is spent and $18.75 is saved, and so on. Total spending is $400, and total saving is $100 when all rounds are completed.

The Multiplier Works in Both Directions

If spending increases raise equilibrium income by the increase times the multiplier, a spending decrease will reduce income in corresponding fashion. In our simple economy, for instance, a $100 decline in investment or consumer spending will reduce income by $400.

This is one reason recession watchers are always concerned about consumer confidence. During a recession, income declines, or at least the rate of income growth falls. If consumers decide to increase their saving to guard against the possibility of job loss, they may inadvertently make the recession worse. As they pull more of their money out of the spending stream, *withdrawals* increase, and income is reduced by a multiplied amount as other agents in the economy feel the effects of this reduced spending. The result can be a more severe or longer-lasting recession.

REVIEW

- Ignoring both government and the foreign sector in our simple Keynesian model, macroeconomic equilibrium occurs when aggregate expenditures are just equal to what is being produced.
- At equilibrium, aggregate saving equals aggregate investment.
- The multiplier process amplifies new spending because some of the new spending is saved and some becomes additional spending. And some of that spending is saved and some is spent, and so on.
- The multiplier is equal to $1/(1 - MPC) = 1/MPS$.
- The multiplier works in both directions. Changes in spending are amplified, changing income by more than the initial change in spending.

QUESTION

Business journalists, pundits, economists and policymakers all pay attention to the results of the Conference Board's monthly survey of 5,000 households called the consumer confidence index. When the index is rising, this is good news for the economy, and when it is falling, concerns are often heard that it portends a recession. Why is this survey important as a tool in forecasting where the economy is headed in the near future?

Answers to the Checkpoint question can be found at the end of this chapter.

The Full Keynesian Model

With the simple Keynesian model of the domestic private sector (individual consumption and private business investment), we concluded that at equilibrium saving would equal investment, and that changes in spending changed income by more than the change in spending. This multiplier effect was an important insight by Keynes. To build the full Keynesian model, we now turn our attention to adding government spending and taxes and the impact of the foreign sector.

Adding Government Spending and Taxes

Although government spending and tax policy can get complex, for our purposes it will involve simple changes in government spending (G) or taxes (T). As we have seen in the previous section, any change in aggregate spending will cause income and output to rise or fall by the spending change times the multiplier.

Figure 9 illustrates a change in government spending. Initially, investment is $100, so equilibrium income is $4,400 (point *e*), just as in Figure 7 earlier. Rather than investment rising by $100, let's assume the government decides to spend an added $100 (on a power screwdriver?). As Figure 9 shows, the new equilibrium will be $4,800 (point *b*). This is a similar result as in Figure 7, confirming that spending is spending; the economy does not care where it comes from.

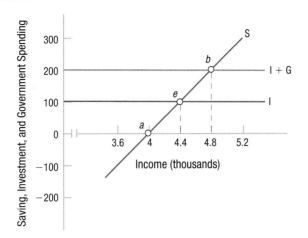

FIGURE 9

Saving, Investment, and Government Spending

A change in government spending (G) will cause income and output to rise or fall by the spending change times the multiplier. Here, investment is $100, so equilibrium income is $4,400 (point *e*), just as in Figure 7. Rather than investment rising by $100, the government decides to spend an additional $100. Equilibrium rises to $4,800 (point *b*), the same result again as in Figure 7. Thus, an increase in investment spending and an increase in government spending have the same effect on income and output.

A quick summary is now in order. Equilibrium income is reached when *injections* (here I + G = $200) equal *withdrawals* (in this case S = $200). It did not matter whether these injections came from investment alone or from investment and government spending together. The key is spending.

Changes in spending modify income by an amount equal to the change in spending times the multiplier. How, then, do changes in taxes affect the economy? The answers are not as simple in that case.

Tax Changes and Equilibrium

When taxes are increased, money is withdrawn from the economy's spending stream. When taxes are reduced, money is injected into the economy's spending stream because consumers and business have more to spend. Thus, taxes form a wedge between income and that part of income that can be spent, or disposable income. Disposable income (Y_d) is equal to income minus taxes ($Y_d = Y - T$). For simplicity, we will assume that all taxes are paid in a lump sum, thereby removing a certain fixed sum of money from the economy. This assumption does away with the need to worry now about the incentive effects of high or lower tax rates. These supply-side issues will be discussed in a later chapter.

Returning to the model of the economy we have been developing, consumer spending now relates to disposable income (Y − T) rather than just to income. Table 3 on the next page reflects this change, using disposable income to determine consumption. With government spending and taxes (fiscal policy) in the model, spending *injections* into the economy equal government spending plus business investment (G + I). *Withdrawals* from the system include saving and taxes (S + T).

Again, equilibrium requires that *injections* equal *withdrawals*, or in this case,

$$G + I = S + T$$

In our example, Table 3 shows that G + I = S + T at income level $4,500 (the shaded row in the table). If no tax had been imposed, equilibrium would have been at the point where S = G + I, and thus at an income of $4,800 (point *b* in Figure 9, not shown in Table 3). So imposing the tax reduces equilibrium income by $300. Because taxes represent a withdrawal of spending from the economy, we would expect equilibrium income to fall when a tax is imposed. Yet, why does equilibrium income fall by only $300, and not by the tax multiplied by the multiplier, which would be $400?

The answer is that consumers pay for this tax, in part, by *reducing* their saving. Specifically, with the MPC at 0.75, the $100 tax payment is split between con-

Table 3		Keynesian Equilibrium Analysis with Taxes				
Income or Output (Y)	Taxes (T)	Disposable Income Y_d	Consumption (C)	Saving (S)	Investment (I)	Government Spending (G)
4,000	100	3,900	3,925	−25	100	100
4,100	100	4,000	4,000	0	100	100
4,200	100	4,100	4,075	25	100	100
4,300	100	4,200	4,150	50	100	100
4,400	100	4,300	4,225	75	100	100
4,500	100	4,400	4,300	100	100	100
4,600	100	4,500	4,375	125	100	100
4,700	100	4,600	4,450	150	100	100
4,800	100	4,700	4,525	175	100	100
4,900	100	4,800	4,600	200	100	100
5,000	100	4,900	4,675	225	100	100

sumption, reduced by $75, and saving, reduced by $25. When this $75 decrease in consumption is multiplied by the multiplier, this yields a decline in income of $300 ($75 × 4). The *reduction* in saving of $25 *dampens* the impact of the tax on equilibrium income because those funds were previously withdrawn from the spending stream. Simply changing the withdrawal category from saving to taxes does not affect income: Both are withdrawals.

The result is that a tax increase (or decrease, for that matter) will have less of a direct impact on income, employment, and output than will an equivalent change in government spending.

The Balanced Budget Multiplier

By now you have probably noticed a curious thing. Our original equilibrium income was $4,400, with investment and saving equal at $100. When the government was introduced with a balanced budget (G = T = $100), income rose by $100 to $4,500, while equilibrium saving and investment remained constant at $100.

Balanced budget multiplier
Equal changes in government spending and taxation (a balanced budget) lead to an equal change in income (the balanced budget multiplier is equal to 1).

This has led to what economists call the **balanced budget multiplier.** Equal changes in government spending and taxation (a balanced budget) lead to an equal change in income. Equivalently, the balanced budget multiplier is equal to 1. If spending and taxes are increased by the same amount, income grows by this amount, hence a balanced budget multiplier equal to 1. Note that the balanced budget multiplier is 1 no matter what the values of MPC and MPS.

Adding Net Exports

Thus far we have essentially assumed a closed economy by avoiding adding foreign transactions: exports and imports. We now add the foreign sector to complete the Keynesian model.

The impact of the foreign sector in the Keynesian model is through net exports: Exports minus imports (X − M). Exports are *injections* of spending into the domestic economy, and imports are *withdrawals*. When Africans purchase grain from

American farmers, they are injecting new spending on grain into our economy. Conversely, when we purchase French wine, we are withdrawing spending (as saving does) and injecting these funds into the French economy.

Figure 10 adds net exports to Figure 9 with investment and government spending. Figure 10 adds $100 of net exports to the previous equilibrium at point b. This addition to spending boosts equilibrium to $5,200 (point c). Again, we see the multiplier at work as the $100 in net exports leads to a $400 increase in income.

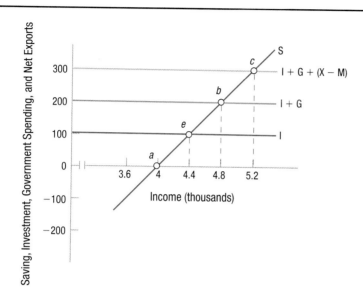

FIGURE 10

Saving, Investment, Government Spending, and Net Exports

Adding investment (I), government spending (G), and net exports (X − M) will cause income and output to rise or fall by the spending change times the multiplier. In this figure, we have added net exports (X − M) of $100 to the investment and government spending in Figure 9 to get I + G + (X − M). Thus, an increase in investment spending, government spending, and net exports have the same effect on income and output.

With the foreign sector included, all injections into the economy must equal all withdrawals, so at equilibrium,

$$I + G + X = S + T + M$$

Thus, if we import more and all other spending remains the same, equilibrium income will fall. This is one reason so may people focus on the trade deficit or net exports (X − M) figures each month. In later chapters, we will look more deeply into the relationship between the trade deficit (X − M), the budget deficit (G − T), as well as the impact on private savings and investment.

The Keynesian model illustrates the importance of spending in an economy. Investment, government spending, and exports all increase income, whereas saving, taxes, and imports reduce it. Further, the fact that consumers spend and save some of *changes* in income (MPC and MPS) gives rise to a spending multiplier that exaggerates the impact of changes in spending on the economy.

Recessionary and Inflationary Gaps

Keynesian analysis illustrated what was needed to get the economy out of the Great Depression: An increase in aggregate spending. Keynes argued that if consumers, businesses, and foreigners were unwilling to spend (their economic expectations were clearly dismal), government should. This, of course, led to the question of just how large would spending have to increase to return the economy to full employment?

Recessionary Gap

The **recessionary gap** is the increase in aggregate spending needed to bring a depressed economy back to full employment. Note that is not the difference between real GDP at full employment and current real GDP, which is called the GDP gap.

Recessionary gap
The increase in aggregate spending needed to bring a depressed economy back to full employment, equal to the GDP gap divided by the multiplier.

The recessionary gap is the added spending ($100) that when boosted by the multiplier (4 in this case) will close the GDP gap ($400).

Looking at Figure 11, the economy is at equilibrium at point e with equilibrium income or output (GDP) equal to Y_0. Full employment output is Y_f, so the GDP gap is $Y_f - Y_0$. Closing this GDP gap requires added spending that when multiplied brings the economy to full employment. The economy will reach full employment if spending increases by an amount equal to distance ab. It is also equal to the GDP gap divided by the multiplier $[(Y_f - Y_0) \div k]$. If the multiplier is 4 (MPC = .75) and the GDP gap is $400, a spending increase of $100 will bring the economy to full employment.

FIGURE 11

The Recessionary Gap

The recessionary gap is the increase in aggregate expenditures (length ab) that will move the economy to full employment (Y_f) from income level Y_0. It is also equal to the GDP gap ($Y_f - Y_0$) divided by the multiplier.

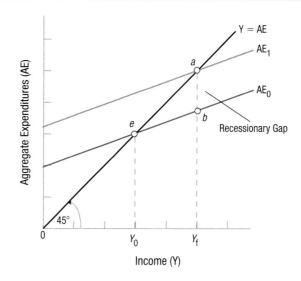

Inflationary Gap

If aggregate spending generates income above full employment levels, the economy will eventually heat up, creating inflationary pressures. Essentially, the economy is trying to produce more output and income than it can sustain for very long. Thus, the excess aggregate spending exceeding that necessary to result in full employment is the **inflationary gap.** Looking at Figure 12, AE_0, the initial level of aggre-

Inflationary gap
The spending reduction necessary (again when expanded by the multiplier) to bring an overheated economy back to full employment.

FIGURE 12

The Inflationary Gap

The inflationary gap is the reduction in aggregate expenditures (length ba) that will move the economy back to full employment (Y_f) from income level Y_0. It is also equal to the GDP gap ($Y_0 - Y_f$) divided by the multiplier.

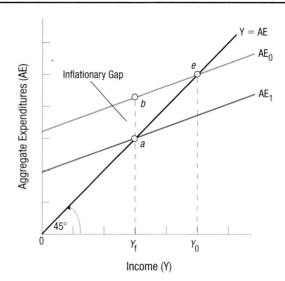

gate expenditures, exceeds that necessary for full employment by distance ba. Using our previous example, if full employment is an income of $4,400 and our current equilibrium, Y_0, is $4,800, a reduction in aggregate expenditures of $100 with a multiplier of 4 would bring the economy back to full employment at $4,400.

This Keynesian approach to analyzing aggregate spending revolutionized the way economists looked at the economy and led to the development of the modern macroeconomics you will study for the remainder of this course. In the next chapter, we extend our analysis to the aggregate demand and supply model, a modern extension of this Keynesian model to account for varying price levels and the supply side of the macroeconomy.

The Full Keynesian Model

REVIEW

- Government spending affects the economy in the same way as other spending.
- Tax increases withdraw money from the spending stream but do not affect the economy as much as spending reductions, because these tax increases are partly offset by decreases in saving.
- Tax decreases inject money into the economy but do not affect the economy as much as spending increases, because tax reductions are partly offset by increases in saving.
- Equal changes in government spending and taxes (a balanced budget) result in an equal change in income (a balanced budget multiplier of 1).
- A recessionary gap is the new spending required that, when expanded by the multiplier, moves the economy to full employment.
- An inflationary gap is the spending reduction necessary (again when expanded by the multiplier) to bring the economy back to full employment.

QUESTION

If the government is considering reducing taxes to stimulate the economy, does it matter if the MPS is .25 or .33?

Answers to the Checkpoint question can be found at the end of this chapter.

The Great Depression and Keynesian Analysis

There is little disagreement that the Great Depression was one of the most important events for the United States in modern history. Good aggregate data were not yet available, but President Roosevelt and Congressional leaders knew something was very wrong.

Within a couple of years, banks collapsed, farms and businesses were lost, the stock market fell to 1/10 of its value at the beginning of the decade, and soup kitchens fed a growing hoard as unemployment soared to nearly 25%, up from 3.2% in 1929. Worse, the Depression persisted: It did not look to be temporary; there was no end in sight.

The Keynesian model we have just studied provides some insight into the Depression. Figure 13 on the next page plots hypothetical saving and investment curves over the actual data for 1929 and 1933. Both government and the foreign sector were tiny at this time, so the basic Keynesian model effectively illustrates

Saving and Investment 1929–1933

Between 1929 and 1933, while government spending and net exports remained at roughly the same levels, investment dropped by over 90%. Income fell almost in half. The Keynesian model provides a good visual explanation for the Depression.

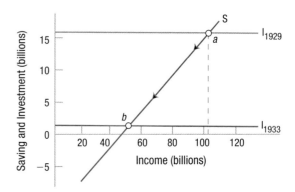

why the depression did not show signs of much improvement; by 1939, the unemployment rate was still over 17%.

Saving and investment were over $16 billion in 1929 or roughly a healthy 15% of GDP (point a). By 1933, investment collapsed to just over $1 billion (a 91% decline), and the economy was in equilibrium at an income of roughly half of that in 1929 (point b). Government spending remained at roughly the same levels while net exports, a small fraction of aggregate expenditures, fell by more than half their previous levels.

Keynes had it right: Unless something happened that would increase investment or exports (not likely given that the rest of the world was suffering a depression as well), the economy would remain mired in the Depression (point b). He suggested that government spending was needed. Ten years later (1943), the United States was in the middle of World War II, and aggregate expenditures swelled as government spending rose by a factor of 10. The Depression was history.

Key Concepts

Chapter Summary

Aggregate Expenditures

Gross domestic product (GDP) can be computed by adding up all spending or all income in the economy. The spending side consists of consumer spending (C), business investment spending (I), government spending (G), and net foreign spending, or exports minus imports, $(X - M)$. Hence, GDP = C + I + G + $(X - M)$.

Personal consumption expenditures represent roughly 70% of GDP. What consumers do not spend of their income, they save; thus, disposable income (Y_d) can be divided into consumption (C) and saving (S). Saving equals disposable income minus annual consumption ($S = Y_d - C$). Note that in our simple Keynesian model we initially eliminated government and the foreign sector, so disposable income was just income or GDP.

Keynes observed that as disposable income increases, consumption will increase, though not as fast as income. Consequently, as income grows, saving will grow as a percentage of income. This Keynesian approach to analyzing saving differs sharply from the classical approach, which assumed the interest rate to be the principal determinant of saving, and by extension, a principal determinant of consumption.

The percentage of income people consume is known as the average propensity to consume (APC). The average propensity to save (APS) is the percentage of income people save. Because income (Y) equals consumption plus saving (Y = C + S), APC + APS = 1.

The marginal propensity to consume (MPC) is the change in consumption associated with a given change in income; thus, MPC = $\Delta C/\Delta Y$. The marginal propensity to save (MPS) is the change in saving associated with a given change in income, MPS = $\Delta S/\Delta Y$. Again, because Y = C + S, MPC + MPS = 1.

Income is the main determinant of consumption and saving, but other factors can shift the entire saving and consumption schedules. These factors include family wealth, expectations about future changes in prices and income, family debt, and taxation.

Gross private domestic investment (the "I" in the GDP equation) accounts for roughly 17–18% of GDP. It is volatile, sometimes increasing by 30% or falling by 10%; these investment swings often account for booms and recessions.

Investment levels depend mainly on the rate of return. Investments earning a high rate of return are the investments undertaken first, assuming comparable risk, with projects offering lower returns being undertaken later. Interest rate levels also contribute to determining how much investment occurs, since most business investment is financed through debt. Some other determinants of investment spending include future expectations about returns, technological changes, the quantity of capital goods on hand, and operating costs. The aggregate investment schedule relates investment to income.

The Simple Keynesian Model

Ignoring government spending and net exports, aggregate expenditures (AE) are the sum of consumer and business investment spending: AE = C + I. When an economy is at equilibrium, aggregate expenditures, income, and output will all be equal; just what is demanded is supplied (AE = Y). And because income can be either spent or saved (Y = C + S), we can determine that, at equilibrium, investment equals saving (I = S). However, if *intended* saving and *intended* investment differ, the economy will have to grow or decline to achieve equilibrium.

The multiplier is equal to $1/(1 - MPC) = 1/MPS$. The multiplier process occurs because new spending sets up additional round-by-round spending based on the MPC that results in more total spending and income in the economy than the original change in spending. The multiplier expands the impact of both spending increases and decreases.

The Full Keynesian Model

Government spending affects the economy just like other spending. Tax changes have less of an impact than spending because some (the MPS) of tax changes come from or go into saving, reducing their multiplied effect. Equal doses of government spending and taxes (G = T) will increase income by the same amount, and vice versa for reductions in both. For this reason, the balanced budget multiplier is equal to 1.

The recessionary gap is the increase in aggregate spending (that is then multiplied) necessary to bring a depressed economy to full employment. When aggregate income exceeds full employment income, the inflationary gap is the reduction in aggregate expenditures (again expanded by the multiplier) needed to reduce income to full employment levels.

Questions and Problems

1. Describe the impact of rising interest rates on consumer spending.

2. Describe the important difference between the average propensity to consume (APC) and the marginal propensity to consume (MPC).

3. Using the aggregate expenditures table below, answer the questions that follow.

Income (Y)	Consumption (C)	Saving (S)
2,200	2,320	−120
2,300	2,380	−80
2,400	2,440	−40
2,500	2,500	0
2,600	2,560	40
2,700	2,620	80
2,800	2,680	120
2,900	2,740	160
3,000	2,800	200

   a. Compute the APC when income equals 2,300 and the APS when income equals 2,800.
   b. Compute the MPC and MPS.
   c. What does the simple Keynesian multiplier equal?
   d. If investment spending is equal to 120, what will be equilibrium income?
   e. Using the graph below, show saving, investment, and equilibrium income.

4. Explain why MPC + APS ≠ 1 and MPS + APC ≠ 1. Provide an example to show why.

5. Explain why we wouldn't expect investment to grow sufficiently to pull the economy out of a depression.

6. Define the simple Keynesian multiplier. Describe why a multiplier exists.

7. Explain why a $100 reduction in taxes does not have the same impact on output and employment as a $100 increase in government spending.

8. Assume a simple Keynesian depression economy with a multiplier of 4 and an initial equilibrium income of $3,000. Saving and investment equal $400, and assume full employment income is $4,000.
   a. What is the MPC equal to? The MPS?
   b. How much would government spending have to rise to move the economy to full employment?
   c. Assume the government plans to finance any government spending by raising taxes to cover the increase in spending (it intends to run a balanced budget). How much will government spending and taxes have to rise to move the economy to full employment?
   d. From the initial equilibrium, if investment grows by $100, what will be the new equilibrium level of income and savings?

9. Other than reductions in interest rates that increase the level of investment by businesses, what other factors would result in higher investment at existing interest rates?

10. The simple Keynesian model discussed in this chapter concluded that one form of spending was just as good as any other; increases in all types of spending leads to equal increases in income. Is there any reason to suspect that private investment might be better for the economy than government spending?

Use the figure below to answer questions 11–13.

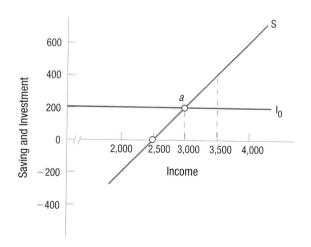

11. What are the MPC, the MPS, and the multiplier?

12. If the economy is currently in equilibrium at point *a* and full employment income is $4,000, how much in *additional* expenditures is needed to move this economy to full employment? What is this level of spending called?

13. Assume the economy is currently in equilibrium at point a and full employment income is $4,000. How much of a tax decrease would be required to move the economy to full employment?

14. Assume the economy is in equilibrium at $5,700, and full employment is $4,800. If the MPC is .67, how big is the inflationary gap?

15. How does the economy today differ from that of the Great Depression, the economy Keynes used as the basis for the macroeconomic model discussed in this chapter?

Answers to Checkpoint Questions

CHECKPOINT: AGGREGATE EXPENDITURES

Consumer spending, while four times larger in absolute size than investment spending, involves many small purchases by households that cannot vary from month to month such as rent (or mortgage payment), food, fuel, and others. Consumers change habits, but slowly. Business investment expenditures are typically on big-ticket items like new plant and equipment, if businesses have favorable expectations about the economy. Further, these investments are often undertaken (or not) by business when the group as a whole sees the economy going in the same direction. When expectations sour, investment typically falls by all firms.

CHECKPOINT: THE SIMPLE KEYNESIAN MODEL

When consumer confidence is declining, this may suggest that consumers are going to spend less and save more. Since consumer spending is roughly 70% of aggregate spending, a small decline represents a significant reduction in aggregate spending and may well mean that a recession is on the horizon. Relatively small changes in consumer spending coupled with the multiplier can mean relatively large changes in income, and therefore forecasters and policymakers should keep a close eye on consumer confidence.

CHECKPOINT: THE FULL KEYNESIAN MODEL

Yes, it does matter. If the tax reduction is going to be $100, for example, and the MPS is .25, the multiplier is 4, and the income increase will be $75 × 4 = $300. Keep in mind that in this case one fourth of the tax reduction will go into saving and will not be amplified by the multiplier. However, with a MPS of .33, the multiplier will be 3, and one third will not be multiplied (will go into saving), so the increase in income will be $67 × 3 = $201.

Aggregate Demand and Supply

9

t he Employment Act of 1946 charged policymakers with three goals: promoting economic growth, maintaining full employment, and achieving price level stability. This is a big charge for any administration.

Contrast two situations. First, imagine you are in an administration that takes office just as the stock market rallies because business investment spending has grown to new high levels in the race to implement new technologies, and the economy responds by producing ever greater employment opportunities without any real inflationary pressures. In this case, managing the economy looks easy. In contrast, if you join a new administration facing a collapse in the stock markets and the subsequent fall in consumer and business confidence that sends the economy into a recession, policymaking is not nearly as enjoyable.

Before the Great Depression in the 1930s, economists viewed the overall economy as simply a set of small competitive markets driven by consumer and business interests that Adam Smith's "invisible hand" kept working in the public interest. Wages, prices, and interest rates were determined in labor, product, and capital markets, and the government's role was to set appropriate competitive rules. This *laissez-faire* (leave it alone) view meant that the best government was minimal government. These markets were like those discussed in Chapter 3.

Furthermore, classical economists before the Depression argued that these competitive markets would ensure that the economy operated near full employment with recessions being relatively minor around the long-term growth trend. For example, if people started to save more and spend less because they were nervous about the economy, the increased savings would translate into lower interest rates, which would spur business investment. Adjustment would be relatively quick.

When the Depression hit in the United States, unemployment climbed to a quarter of the workforce. But because good data were unavailable at the time, economists continued to believe that the recovery was just around the corner. Figure 1 on the next page shows the extent of the Depression. Gross domestic product (GDP) fell nearly 40%, business investment fell by 80%, exports were cut nearly in half,

FIGURE 1

GDP, Investment, Exports, and Operating Banks 1929–1939

Data for GDP, business investment, exports, and the number of operating banks are indexed to 1929 (1929 = 100). All fell precipitously after 1929 and didn't recover to 1929 levels within the decade. Aggregate spending and income fell nearly one half between 1929 and 1933.

Source: U.S. Census Bureau, *Historical Statistics of the United States*, p. 1019; and Pedro Amaral and Jim MacGee, "The Great Depression in Canada and the United States: A Neoclassical Perspective," *Review of Economic Dynamics*, 2002, Data Appendix.

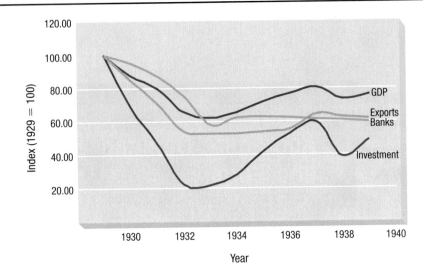

and almost half of the banks existing in 1929 failed by 1933, sending many families' life savings down the drain (there was no federal deposit insurance at that time).

The economy was clearly broken, and for a decade, it showed little sign of returning to prosperity. This brought a radical shift in economic thinking. This chapter develops a model of the macroeconomy based on the lessons learned in the 1930s.

British economist John Maynard Keynes convinced economists to turn away from focusing on individual competitive markets. Basing his analysis on a depression economy where there is immense slack (productive capacity), he argued that expenditures by consumers, business (in the form of investment), government, and foreigners (in the form of exports)—**aggregate expenditures,** also known as *aggregate spending*—was what determined employment and income.

Aggregate expenditures
Consist of consumer spending, business investment spending, government spending, and net foreign spending (exports minus imports), or GDP = C + I + G + (X − M).

His attention was drawn to the aggregate economy as a whole and not the individual markets that composed the basis for previous analysis. As such, Keynes created the beginnings of what we now call modern macroeconomics.

The Keynesian *fixed price* model we examined in the previous chapter essentially ignored aggregate supply since increasing production would occur without a rise in prices. Keynes's analysis was based on the facts of the Great Depression, in which significant industrial capacity was going unused, and unemployment was high. He concluded that any amount of spending (demand) could and would be supplied without any pressure on costs (the aggregate price level would not change). Clearly, more labor could be hired without having to raise wages; in fact, firms with just a few openings were mobbed with job applicants.

The lessons learned from the Depression and the insights from Keynes form the foundation of the demand side of the modern macroeconomic model we develop in this chapter. This modern approach looks a lot like the supply-demand model developed in Chapter 3, but extended to the aggregate (overall) economy. Whereas the Keynesian model assumed that the price level was fixed, the aggregate demand and supply model developed in this chapter is a *flexible price* model. The model also introduces additional complexities to the aggregate supply side of the economy.

The beauty of this approach is that it builds on concepts and skills you already have: defining demand curves, supply curves, and equilibrium; assessing changes in economic facts; and determining a new equilibrium.

After studying this chapter you should be able to

■ Describe why the aggregate demand curve has a negative slope.

■ Describe the effects of wealth, exports, and interest rates on the aggregate demand curve.

■ List the determinants of aggregate demand.

■ Analyze the aggregate supply curve and differentiate between the short run and long run.

■ Describe the determinants of an aggregate supply curve.

■ Define the multiplier and describe why it is important.

■ Describe demand-pull and cost-push inflation.

Aggregate Demand

The **aggregate demand** (AD) curve (or schedule) shows the output of goods and services (real GDP) demanded at different price levels.[1] The aggregate demand curve in Figure 2 looks like the product demand curves we studied earlier. Even so, these two curves and the reasons they slope downward are different.

Aggregate demand
The output of goods and services (real GDP) demanded at different price levels.

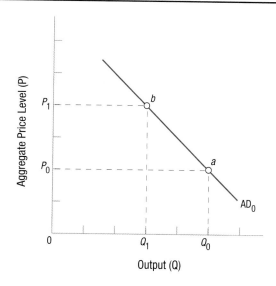

FIGURE 2

The Aggregate Demand Curve

The aggregate demand curve shows the amount of real goods and services (output = real GDP) that will be purchased at various price levels.

Why Is the Aggregate Demand Curve Negatively Sloped?

Product demand curves slope downward for two reasons. First, when the price of a given product declines, consumers' spendable income rises, because it takes less income to purchase the same quantity of the product as before; rising prices have an opposite impact. This is known, once again, as the *income effect*. Second, when

---

[1]The derivation using the Keynesian fixed price model is shown in the Appendix to this chapter.

the price of a product falls, consumers will purchase more of the product as they substitute it for other, higher-priced, goods—when the price of chicken declines, consumers substitute chicken for beef and other meats in their diets. This is known as the *substitution effect,* which was discussed in Chapter 3. Yet, these explanations for specific products will not suffice to explain the slope of the demand curve for the aggregate economy.

The Wealth Effect

One reason real output declines when the aggregate price level rises is the resulting reduction in household wealth, called the **wealth effect.** Families usually hold some of their wealth in financial assets such as savings accounts, bonds, and cash. A rising aggregate price level means that the purchasing power of this money wealth will decline. If for example, you have $5,000 in a savings account, and prices rise throughout the economy, that $5,000 will now purchase less than before. This reduction in household purchasing power means that some purchases are put on hold, thereby reducing output demanded. This is represented by a movement from point a to point b in Figure 2.

Wealth effect
Families usually hold some of their wealth in financial assets such as savings accounts, bonds, and cash, and a rising aggregate price level means that the purchasing power of this money wealth declines, reducing output demanded.

Impact on Exports

When the American aggregate price level rises, American goods become more expensive in the global marketplace. Higher prices mean that our goods are less competitive with the goods made in other countries. The result is that foreigners purchase fewer American products, and our exports decline. As exports drop, the quantity demanded of domestically produced goods and services (real GDP) also declines, resulting in lower real output.

Interest Rate Effects

Interest rates are the prices paid for the use of money. If we assume for a moment that the quantity of money is fixed, then as aggregate prices rise, people will need more money to carry out their economic transactions. As people demand more money, the cost of borrowing money—interest rates—will go up. Rising interest rates mean reduced business investment, which results in a drop in quantity demanded for real GDP, shown in Figure 2 as a movement from point a to b and falling real output.[2]

In summary, the aggregate demand curve is negatively sloped because of three factors. When the aggregate price level rises, this lowers household purchasing power because of the wealth effect. A rising aggregate price level also lowers the amount of exports because our goods are now more expensive. Furthermore, a rising aggregate price level increases the demand for money and so drives up interest rates. Rising interest rates reduce business investment and reduce the quantity demanded of real GDP. In each case, as aggregate prices rise from P_0 to P_1, quantity demanded of real GDP falls from Q_0 to Q_1.

Determinants of Aggregate Demand

We have seen that the aggregate demand curve is negatively sloped. Everything else held constant, a change in the aggregate price level will change the quantity of real GDP demanded along the aggregate demand curve. The *determinants* of aggregate demand are those factors that shift the entire aggregate demand curve when they change. They are the "everything else held constant." These include the components of GDP: consumption, investment, government spending, and net exports.

---

[2]The actual process is more complex than described here. Rising demand for money means individuals and businesses must sell bonds, reducing the price of bonds and raising interest rates. We will discuss this process in detail in future chapters.

If one of these components of aggregate spending changes, the aggregate demand curve will shift, as shown in Figure 3. At first, aggregate demand is AD_0, so a shift to AD_1 represents an increase in aggregate demand; more real output is demanded at the same price level, P_0. If for example, business decides to invest more in new technology, more real output is now demanded at the current price level, P_0. For similar reasons, a decline in aggregate demand to AD_2 means that less real output is being demanded. If consumers for some reason fear the onset of a recession and decide to reduce spending to increase their saving reserves, less output, Q_2, will be demanded.

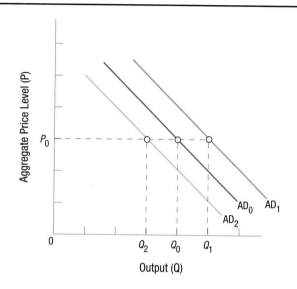

FIGURE 3

Shifts in the Aggregate Demand Curve

The determinants of aggregate demand include the components of GDP and aggregate spending: consumption, investment, government spending, and net exports. A change in one will shift the aggregate demand curve, as shown here. At first, aggregate demand is AD_0, so a shift to AD_1 represents an increase in aggregate demand; more real output is demanded at the same price level. A decline in aggregate demand to AD_2 means that less real output is being demanded.

Now let's consider what might cause the various components of aggregate expenditures to change.

Consumer Spending

Consumer spending is affected by four major factors: wealth, consumer confidence, household debt, and taxes. When any of these factors change, consumer spending patterns change. For example, when the technology-heavy NASDAQ stock market surged in the late 1990s, then—Federal Reserve Chairman Alan Greenspan became concerned that a consequent surge in consumer spending from the wealth effect, as we explained earlier, would increase aggregate demand and, as we will see near the end of this chapter, put upward pressure on prices and cause inflation. When the NASDAQ collapsed in the early 2000s, the Federal Reserve worried that sinking consumer confidence (caused by declining wealth) would reduce consumption spending, thereby adding to recession woes.

Consumer expectations and confidence about the economy play a significant role in determining the level of consumer spending. High confidence in the economy eases job security fears and stimulates consumer spending, shifting the aggregate demand curve to the right. High family debt ratios restrict access to future credit, reducing spending on high-ticket items often bought on credit. Increasing taxes reduces disposable income, reducing consumption, shifting the aggregate demand curve to the left.

Investment

Investment is determined mainly by interest rates and the expected rate of return on capital projects. When interest rates rise, investment will decline and the aggregate demand curve will shift to the left, and vice versa.

When business expectations become more favorable—perhaps some new technology is introduced, or excess capacity declines—investment will increase, and the aggregate demand curve will increase, or shift to the right. But if businesses see clouds on the horizon such as new regulations, higher taxes, restrictions on the use of technology, or excess capacity, investment will drop, and the aggregate demand curve will decline, shifting to the left.

Government Spending and Net Exports

Government spending and net exports have essentially the same impact on the aggregate economy as consumer and investment spending. When government spending or net exports rise, aggregate demand increases, and vice versa.

When the national income of a foreign country rises, this increases its demand for U.S. goods and services, thereby increasing our exports and our aggregate demand. A change in foreign exchange rates will also affect aggregate demand. An appreciation, or rise, in the value of the euro, for instance, will result in Europeans buying more U.S. goods since a euro will buy more. Again, this change increases American exports and aggregate demand.

A quick summary is now in order. The aggregate demand curve shows the quantities of real GDP demanded at different price levels. The aggregate demand curve slopes downward because of the wealth effect (the value of monetary assets declines when the price level rises), because exports fall as domestic prices rise, and because rising prices raise interest rates, which reduces investment. On the other hand, changes in one of the determinants of aggregate demand shift the aggregate demand curve. Table 1 summarizes the determinants of aggregate demand.

Table 1	Determinants of Aggregate Demand (aggregate demand curve shifts when these change)	
Determinant	**AD Increases**	**AD Decreases**
Consumer Spending		
• Wealth	Wealth increases	Wealth decreases
• Consumer expectations	Expectations improve	Expectations worsen
• Household debt	Debt falls	Debt rises
• Taxes	Taxes are cut	Taxes increase
Investment		
• Interests rates	Fall	Rise
• Expected rate of return on investment	Higher	Lower
Government Spending	Increases	Decreases
Net Exports	Increases	Declines
• Exports		
○ Income in other countries	Rising	Falling
○ Exchange rate changes	Depreciating dollar	Appreciating dollar
• Imports		
○ Income in the United States	Falling	Rising
○ Exchange rate changes	Depreciating dollar	Appreciating dollar

Again, the determinants of aggregate demand are those "other factors held constant": consumption, investment, government spending, and net exports. If one of those determinants changes, the entire aggregate demand curve will shift. Keep in mind that changes in the determinants are most important for policymaking. When a policy is enacted (say, lower tax rates), policymakers expect to stimulate consumer and investment spending, increasing aggregate demand, output, and employment.

But the aggregate demand curve only tells one part of the story. We have to consider the other part: aggregate supply.

REVIEW

■ The aggregate demand curve shows the relationship between real GDP and the price level.

■ The aggregate demand curve has a negative slope because of the wealth effect, the impact of the price level on exports, and the impact of the price level on interest rates.

■ The determinants of aggregate demand are consumer spending, investment spending, government expenditures, and net exports. Changes in any of these determinants will shift the aggregate demand curve.

QUESTION

Consumer spending is related to disposable personal income (income minus taxes). Describe how changing tax rates would affect consumption and aggregate demand.

Answers to the Checkpoint question can be found at the end of this chapter.

Aggregate Supply

The **aggregate supply** curve shows the real GDP that firms will produce at varying price levels. Even though the definition seems similar to that for aggregate demand, note that we have now moved from the spending side of the economy to the production side. We will consider three different possibilities for aggregate supply. The first possibility is a flat portion for aggregate supply, which might occur during a Depression. This is the basic Keynesian scenario discussed earlier. The second possibility illustrates the short run in which aggregate supply is positively sloped and prices rise when GDP grows. The last, long-run aggregate supply (LRAS), reflects the long-run state of the economy and is vertical. Growth occurs in the economy by shifting this vertical aggregate supply curve to the right.

Aggregate supply
The real GDP that firms will produce at varying price levels. During a depression, the economy has a lot of slack, and the aggregate supply curve will be flat. In the short run, aggregate supply is positively sloped because many input costs are slow to change, but in the long run, the aggregate supply curve is vertical at full employment since the economy has reached its capacity to produce.

Depression Period (Horizontal)

The flat part of the short-run aggregate supply (AS) curve, line segment P_0e in Figure 4 on the next page, represents the *depression period*. This flat section represents an economy with the type of excess capacity we have previously discussed. In such an economy, businesses can increase their output without having to face rising costs, because substantial numbers of machines and factories will be sitting idle, and many unemployed workers will be happy to accept any job offered.

FIGURE 4

Aggregate Supply

Three typical aggregate supply curves are shown here. During a depression the aggregate supply curve may become flat (range P_0 to point e) because the economy has so much excess capacity that businesses can increase their output without having to face rising costs. The short-run aggregate supply (AS) curve is positively sloped because many input costs are slow to change in the short run. The long-run aggregate supply (LRAS) curve is vertical, reflecting the assumptions of classical economic analysis. In the long run, all variables in the economy can adjust, and the economy will settle at full employment, shown at aggregate output Q_f.

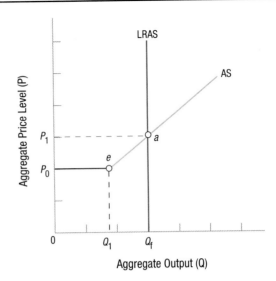

Aggregate Output (Q)

Circumstances do not have to be as extreme as just described for a flatter part of the aggregate supply curve to be in evidence, but that description provides a benchmark. If productivity is growing rapidly, for example, or raw material input prices are declining, the economy may be able to grow without price pressures. Often, the flat portion of the aggregate supply curve is more representative of the immediate period (a year or less) than of a longer term. The high economic and productivity growth quarters of the last 5 years are illustrative of this situation.

Short Run (Upward Sloping)

Short-run aggregate supply (AS) curve
The short-run aggregate supply curve is positively sloped because many input costs are slow to change in the short run.

As Figure 4 shows, the **short-run aggregate supply (AS) curve** is positively sloped because some input costs are slow to change in the short run. When prices rise, firms do not immediately see an increase in wages or rents since these are often fixed for a specified term; thus, profits will rise with the rising prices and firms will supply more output as their profits increase.

This situation, however, cannot last for long. As an entire industry or the economy as a whole increases its production, firms must start hiring more labor or paying overtime. As each firm seeks more employees, wages are driven up, increasing costs and forcing higher prices.

For the economy as a whole, a rise in real GDP results in higher employment and reduced unemployment. Lower unemployment rates mean a tightening of labor markets. This often leads to fierce collective bargaining by labor, followed by increases in wages, costs, and prices. The result is that a short-run increase in GDP will usually be accompanied by a rise in the price level.

Long Run (Vertical)

Long-run aggregate supply (LRAS) curve
The long-run aggregate supply curve is vertical at full employment because the economy has reached its capacity to produce.

The *vertical* **long-run aggregate supply (LRAS) curve** incorporates the assumptions of classical (pre-1930s) economic analysis. Classical analysis assumes that all variables are adjustable in the long run, where product prices, wages, and interest rates are flexible in the longer term. As a result, the economy will gravitate to the position of full employment shown as Q_f in Figure 4.

Full employment is often referred to as the *natural rate of output* or *the natural rate of unemployment* by economists. This long-run output is an equilibrium level where inflationary pressures are minimal. Once the economy has reached this level, further short-term increases in output are extremely difficult to achieve; there is simply no one else to operate more machines, and no more machines to operate. As we will see later, attempts to expand beyond this output level will simply produce higher prices and rising inflation.

In general terms, full employment is determined by the capital available, the size and quality of the labor force, and the technology employed. Remember from Chapter 2 that these are also the big three factors driving economic growth (shifting the LRAS curve to the right) once a suitable infrastructure has been put in place.

Determinants of Aggregate Supply

We have seen that, because the aggregate supply curve is positively sloped in the short run, a change in aggregate output, other things held constant, will result in a change in the aggregate price level. The determinants of aggregate supply—those other things held constant—include changes in input prices, productivity, taxes, regulation, the market power of firms, or business and inflationary expectations. When any of these determinants change, the entire AS curve shifts, as Figure 5 illustrates.

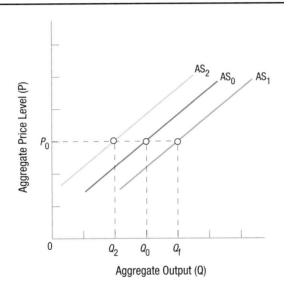

Input Prices

Changes in the cost of land, labor, capital, or entrepreneurship will change the output that firms are willing to provide to the market. As we have seen, when world crude oil prices rise, it is never long before gasoline prices rise at the pump. Rising input prices are quickly passed along to consumers, and the opposite is true, as well. New discoveries of raw materials result in falling input prices, causing the prices for products incorporating these inputs to drop. This means that more of these products can be produced at a price of P_0 in Figure 5 as aggregate supply shifts to AS_1, or now output Q_0 can be produced at a lower price on AS_1.

Productivity

Changes in productivity are another major determinant of aggregate supply. Rising productivity will shift the aggregate supply curve to the right—from AS_0 to AS_1 in Figure 5—and vice versa. This is why changes in technology that increase productivity are so important to the economy. Technological advances, moreover, often lead to new products that expand aggregate supply.

Taxes

Rising taxes or increased regulation can shift the aggregate supply curve to the left, from AS_0 to AS_2 in Figure 5. Excessively burdensome regulation, though it may provide some benefits, raises costs so much that the new costs exceed the benefits. This results in a decrease in aggregate supply. Often no one knows how much regulation has increased costs until some sort of deregulation is instituted.

Market Power of Firms

Monopoly firms charge more than competitive firms. So, a change in the market power of firms can increase prices for specific products, thereby reducing aggregate supply. When the Organization of Petroleum Exporting Countries (OPEC) finally coalesced in 1973, it formed an effective cartel and raised oil prices roughly 10-fold. Since at that time oil was an input into nearly all products, the AS curve shifted to the left.

Expectations

A change in business expectations can also change aggregate supply. If firms perceive that the business climate is declining, they may reduce their investments in capital equipment. This reduced investment results in reduced productivity, fewer new hires, or even the closing of marginally profitable plants, any of which can reduce aggregate supply in the short run.

A change in inflationary expectations by businesses, workers, or consumers can shift the aggregate supply curve. If, for example, workers believe that inflation is going to increase, they will bargain for higher wages to offset the expected losses to real wages. The intensified bargaining and resulting higher wages will reduce aggregate supply.

To summarize, there are three types of aggregate supply curves. In a Depression, the economy might face a horizontal aggregate supply curve, where capacity is so underused that production can be increased with negligible effects on the

Table 2	Determinants of Aggregate Supply (aggregate supply curve shifts when these change)		
Determinant		**AS Increases**	**AS Decreases**
Changes in Input Prices		Prices decline	Prices rise
Changes in Productivity			
• Technology		Improvements	Declines
• Changes in human capital		Improvements	Declines
Changes in Taxes and Regulations			
• Tax rates		Lower	Higher
• Subsidies		Higher	Lower
• Change in burdensome regulations		Reductions	Additions
Change in Market Power		Reductions	Increases
Changes in Business or Inflation Expectations			
• Business expectations		More positive	More negative
• Inflation expectations		Lower	Higher

aggregate price level. The short-run aggregate supply curve slopes upward because many input costs are slow to change in the short run. This AS curve will shift because of changes in input prices, the market power of firms, productivity, taxes, regulation, or business and inflationary expectations. Finally, the vertical long-run aggregate supply curve represents the full employment capacity of the economy. This output level depends on the amount of resources available for production and the available technology. Increases in resources or technology shift the LRAS curve to the right and represent economic growth. Table 2 summarizes the determinants of supply.

Checkpoint — Aggregate Supply

REVIEW

- The aggregate supply curve shows the real GDP that firms will produce at varying price levels.
- A horizontal aggregate supply curve represents a depression period in which the economy has significant slack and can increase output without pressure on prices.
- The short-run aggregate supply (AS) curve is upward sloping, reflecting rigidities in the economy since input and output prices are slow to change.
- The vertical long-run aggregate supply (LRAS) curve represents the long-run full-employment capacity of the economy.
- The determinants of aggregate supply include changes in input prices, the market power of firms, productivity, taxes, regulations, and business and inflationary expectations. Changes in these determinants will shift the aggregate supply curve.

QUESTION

In Europe nearly two thirds of wages are covered by union collective bargaining agreements; wage rates are determined (or fixed) for a given time period, typically 2 to 4 years. In the United States, only about one sixth of wages are covered. Unemployment rates in Germany, France, and Italy are typically double that (8–12%) of those in the United States (4–6%). Do higher unemployment rates in Germany, France, and Italy mean that their aggregate supply curves are flatter than ours in the United States?

Answers to the Checkpoint question can be found at the end of this chapter.

Macroeconomic Equilibrium

Let us now put together our aggregate demand and aggregate supply model. A *short-run* **macroeconomic equilibrium** occurs at the intersection of the aggregate supply and aggregate demand curves; see point *e* in Figure 6 on the next page. In this case, point *e* also represents *long-run macroeconomic equilibrium*, since the economy is operating at full employment, producing output Q_f.

Output level Q_f represents full employment. The AS curve assumes price level expectations equal to P_e, and thus Q_f is the natural rate of unemployment or output. Remember that the natural rate of unemployment is that unemployment level where inflation is low and consistent with inflationary expectations in the economy.

Macroeconomic equilibrium
Occurs at the intersection of the aggregate supply and aggregate demand curves. At this output level, there is no net pressures for the economy to expand or contract.

Macroeconomic Equilibrium

Point *e* represents a short-run macroeconomic equilibrium, the point at which the short-run aggregate supply and aggregate demand curves intersect. In this case, point *e* also represents a long-run macroeconomic equilibrium, since the economy is operating at full employment, producing output Q_f.

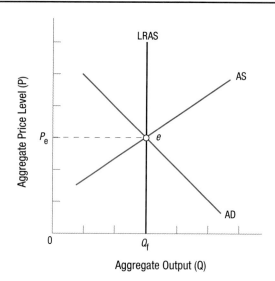

The Spending Multiplier

Multiplier
Spending changes alter equilibrium income by the spending change times the multiplier. One person's spending becomes another's income, and that second person spends some (the MPC), which becomes income for another person, and so on, until income has changed by $1/(1 - MPC) = 1/MPS$. The multiplier operates in both directions.

Marginal propensity to consume
The change in consumption associated with a given change in income ($\Delta C/\Delta Y$).

Marginal propensity to save
The change in saving associated with a given change in income ($\Delta S/\Delta Y$).

The spending **multiplier** is an important concept introduced into macroeconomics by John Maynard Keynes in 1936. The central idea is that new spending creates more spending, income, and output than just an amount equal to the new spending itself.

Let's assume, for example, consumers tend to spend three quarters and save one quarter of any new income they receive. If $100 of new spending is introduced into the economy, that initial spending adds $100 of new GDP (income to someone). Now $25 dollars of that new income will be saved, and $75 will be spent on additional products, creating $75 of new income to be spent and saved. Of this new $75 in income, $56.25 ($75 × 0.75) will be spent, creating still more income, and $18.75 ($75 × 0.25) will be saved, and so on, round-by-round.

Adding all of the new spending ($100 + $75 + 56.25 + . . .) from the initial $100 results in GDP increasing by $400. Adding up total new saving ($25 + 18.75 + . . .) equals $100, so that the initial $100 in new spending has increased savings by the same amount.

The proportion of *additional* income that consumers spend and save is known as the **marginal propensity to consume** and the **marginal propensity to save** (MPC and MPS). In our example, MPC = .75 and MPS = .25. The multiplier was equal to 4 given that $400 of new income was created with the introduction of $100 of new spending. The formula for the spending multiplier is equal to $1/(1 - MPC) = 1/MPS$ and, in this case, is $1/(1 - .75) = 1/.25 = 4$. This formula works as long as the price level is stable (the depression scenario). Let's see why.

Figure 7 shows how the multiplier varies depending on how variable the price level is to higher output. Let's begin with the economy initially at point *a*, with real output of Q_0 and aggregate demand equal to AD_0. If aggregate spending increases, aggregate demand shifts to AD_1, and equilibrium moves out to Q_1, a significant change in output, far greater than the initial increase in aggregate spending. This is the depression scenario where the price level does not increase as aggregate spending is increased, given the underused productive capacity in the economy.

Now when the economy starts moving up the AS curve in response to the same increase in aggregate spending, the story is different. Again assume that aggregate demand increases the same amount as before to AD_2 (the horizontal distance between AD_0 and AD_1 is the same as the change between AD_1 and AD_2). The new equilibrium is at point *e* with output Q_f. Notice that output has grown less than

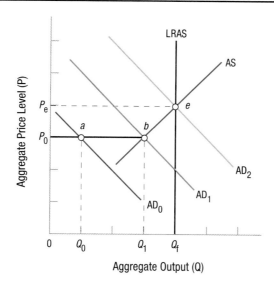

The Multiplier and Aggregate Demand and Supply

The spending multiplier magnifies new spending into greater levels of income and output because of round-by-round spending of a portion of each round of spending. Your spending becomes my income, and I spend some of that income, creating further income and consumption, and so on. Note that the multiplier effect depends on how much slack there is in the macroeconomy.

before: The distance from Q_1 to Q_f is less than the distance from Q_0 to Q_1. The reason is very straightforward: When the aggregate supply curve is flat (depression economy), the full impact of the spending multiplier occurs, but on the AS curve between Q_1 and Q_f, price increases or inflation eat up some of each spending round, so less real output results. Note that once aggregate demand is increased beyond AD_2, price increases soak up the entire increase in aggregate demand (along the LRAS curve) because real output cannot change.

Let's take a moment to summarize where we are before we begin to use this model to understand some important macroeconomic events. Macroeconomic equilibrium occurs at the intersection of AD and AS. It can also happen that this equilibrium represents long-run equilibrium, but not necessarily; equilibrium can occur at less than full employment. As we will see shortly, the Depression is one example. Increases in spending are multiplied and lead to greater changes in output than the original change in spending. For policymakers, this means that the difference between equilibrium real GDP and full-employment GDP (the GDP gap) can be closed with a smaller change in spending.

This leads us to the point where we can use the AD/AS model to analyze past macroeconomic events. By looking at these events through the AD/AS lens, we begin to see the options open to policymakers that become the focus of the next chapter. In this next section, we look at what happened during the Great Depression, then examine both demand-pull and cost-push inflation. Each type of inflation presents unique challenges for policymakers.

Using AD/AS: The Great Depression

Figure 6 conveniently showed the economy in long-run equilibrium and short-run equilibrium at the same point. The Great Depression demonstrated, however, that an economy can reach short-run equilibrium at output levels substantially below full employment.

The 1930s Depression was a graphic example of just such a situation. Real GDP dropped by nearly 30% between 1929 and 1933. Unemployment peaked at 25% in 1932 and never fell below 15% throughout the 1930s.

Figure 8 on the next page shows the actual data for the Depression with superimposed aggregate demand and supply curves for 1929 and 1933. Investment is the most volatile of the GDP components, and it fell over 80% during 1929 to 1933. This

---

FIGURE 8

Aggregate Demand, Supply, and the Investment Decline in the Depression

In this figure, aggregate demand and supply curves are superimposed on the real GDP and price level data for the Great Depression. Investment dropped over 80% and consumption declined nearly 20%. Together, these reductions in spending created a depression that was so deep that it took the massive spending for World War II to bring the economy back to full employment.

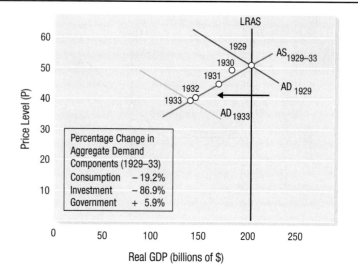

drop in investment reduced spending and therefore income and consumption, resulting in a deep depression. The increase in aggregate demand necessary to restore the economy back to 1929 levels was huge, and it was no wonder that only a 6% increase in government spending had virtually no impact on the Depression. It wasn't until the spending associated with waging World War II that the country popped out of the Depression.

Using AD/AS: Demand-Pull Inflation

Demand-pull inflation
Results when aggregate demand expands so much that equilibrium output exceeds full employment output and the price level rises.

Demand-pull inflation occurs when aggregate demand expands so much that equilibrium output exceeds full employment output. Turning to Figure 9, assume the economy is initially in long-run equilibrium at point e. If business becomes irrationally exuberant and expands investments in some area (again, like telecommunications in the late 1990s), this expansion will push aggregate demand out to AD_1. The economy moves to a short-run equilibrium beyond full employment (point a), and the price level rises to P_1.

FIGURE 9

Demand-Pull Inflation

Demand-pull inflation occurs when aggregate demand expands and equilibrium output (point a) exceeds full employment output (Q_f). Since the long-run aggregate supply (LRAS) curve has not shifted, the economy will in the end move into long-run equilibrium at point c. With the new aggregate demand at AD_1, prices have unexpectedly risen, so aggregate supply shifts to AS_2 as workers, for example, adjust their wage demands upward leaving prices permanently higher at P_2.

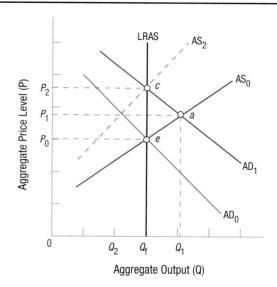

On a temporary basis, the economy can expand beyond full employment as workers incur overtime, temporary workers are added, and more shifts are employed. Yet, these activities increase costs and prices. And since long-run aggregate supply (LRAS) has not shifted, the economy will ultimately move to point c (if AD stays at AD_1), shifting aggregate supply to AS_2 and leaving prices permanently higher (at P_2). In the long run, the economy will gravitate to points like e and c. Policymakers could return the economy back to the original point e by instituting policies that reduce AD back to AD_0. This might include reduced government spending, higher taxes, or other policies that discourage investment, consumer spending, or exports.

Demand-pull inflation can continue for quite a while, especially if the economy begins on the AS curve well below full employment. Inflation often starts out slow and builds up steam.

Decade-long demand-pull inflation scenarios for the United States in the 1960s and for Japan in the last half of the 1980s and first half of the 1990s are shown in Figure 10.

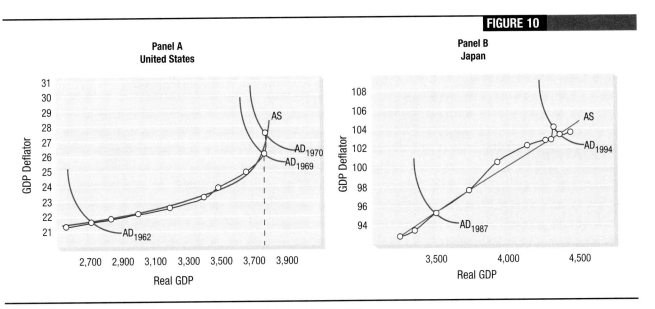

FIGURE 10

Demand-Pull Inflation United States (1960s) and Japan (1985–95)

This figure shows two examples of demand-pull inflation for the United States and Japan. Hypothetical aggregate demand and aggregate supply curves are superimposed over the data for the two time periods. The Vietnam conflict expanded aggregate demand in the 1960s, and the economy experienced inflation over the entire decade and faced rising inflation rates as the economy approached full employment in 1969. Japan experienced demand-pull inflation as it enjoyed a huge trade surplus and its exports expanded the economy. Japanese policymakers kept interest rates artificially low, fueling a real estate and stock bubble that collapsed in the 1990s, resulting in a decade-long recession.

For the United States, the slow escalation of the Vietnam conflict fueled a rising economy along the hypothetical aggregate supply curve placed over the data in Panel A. Early in the decade, the price level rose slowly as the economy expanded. But notice how the aggregate supply curve began to turn nearly vertical, and inflation rates rose as the economy approached full employment in 1969. Real output growth virtually halted between 1969 and 1970, but inflation was 5.3%. The economy reached its potential.

The Japanese economy during the 1985–95 period is a different example of demand-pull inflation. Panel B of Figure 10 shows a steadily growing economy with rising prices, throughout the 1980s and early 1990s. Japan was running huge trade surpluses and the yen was appreciating (becoming more valuable). A rising yen would eventually reduce exports (Japanese products would become too expensive).

To keep this from happening, the Japanese government kept interest rates artificially low, reducing the pressure on the yen and encouraging investment. But these policies fueled a huge real estate and stock bubble that began collapsing in the beginning of the 1990s and led to a decade-long recession from which Japan is still recovering.

Demand-pull inflation can often take a while to become a problem. But once the inflation spiral gains momentum, it can pose a serious problem for policymakers, as we will see in later chapters.

Using AD/AS: Cost-Push Inflation

Cost-push inflation
Results when a supply shock hits the economy, reducing aggregate supply, and thus reducing output and increasing the price level.

Cost-push inflation occurs when a supply shock hits the economy, shifting the aggregate supply curve leftward, as from AS_0 to AS_2 in Figure 11. The 1973 oil shock is a classic example. Because oil is a basic input in so many goods and services we enjoy, skyrocketing oil prices affected all parts of the economy. After a bout of cost-push inflation, in which rising resource costs push the economy from point a to point b in Figure 11, policymakers can increase demand to AD_1 and move the economy back to full employment at point c. For example, they might increase government spending, reduce taxes, or introduce policies that encourage consumption, investment, or net exports. But notice that this means an even higher price level. Alternatively, policymakers could reduce inflationary pressures by reducing aggregate demand, but this leads to an even deeper recession as output and employment fall further.

FIGURE 11

Cost-Push Inflation

Cost-push inflation is represented by an initial decline in aggregate supply from AS_0 to AS_2. Rising resource costs or inflationary expectations will reduce aggregate supply, resulting in a short-run movement from point e to point b. If policymakers wish to return the economy to full employment, they can increase aggregate demand to AD_1, but must accept higher prices as the economy moves to point c. Alternatively, they could reduce aggregate demand, but that would lead to lower output and employment.

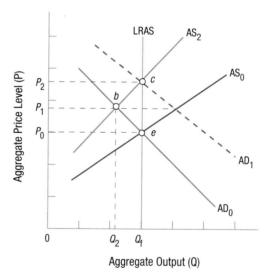

Figure 12 shows the striking leftward shift in equilibrium points for 1973–75. Output stood still, while prices rose as the economy adjusted to the new energy prices. Superimposed over the annual data are two hypothetical short-run aggregate supply curves. Notice that it took the economy roughly 3 years to absorb the oil shock. Only after the economy had adjusted to the new prices did it continue on a path roughly equivalent to the pre-1973 AS curve.

Before the Great Depression, economic analysis focused on the behavior of individuals, households, and businesses. Little attention was paid to the macroeconomic stabilization potential of government policies. The federal government had its responsibilities under the Constitution in areas such as national defense, the

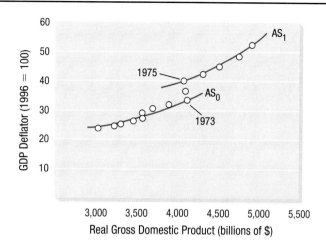

FIGURE 12

Cost-Push Inflation in the 1970s

The rise in equilibrium prices following the 1973 oil shocks was striking. From 1973 to 1975, prices rose, yet output stood still as the economy adjusted to the new energy prices. Superimposed over the actual annual data are two hypothetical short-run aggregate supply curves. Notice that it took the economy roughly 3 years to absorb the oil shock. Only after the economy had adjusted to the new prices did it continue on a path roughly equivalent to the pre-1973 short-run aggregate supply curve.

enforcement of contracts, and tax collection, but managing the economy was not among these.

The Great Depression of the 1930s and John Maynard Keynes's *The General Theory* drastically changed how economists viewed the role of the federal government. During the Depression, when unemployment reached 25% and bank failures wiped out personal savings—creating winding soup lines—federal intervention in the economy became imperative. After the 1930s, the federal government's role grew to encompass (1) expanded spending and taxation and the resulting exercise of fiscal policy, (2) extensive new regulation of business, and (3) expanded regulation of the banking sector, along with greater exercise of monetary policy.

The next chapter focuses on how government spending and taxation combine to expand or contract the macroeconomy. When the economy enters a recession, fiscal policy can be used to moderate the impact and prevent another depression. Later chapters will explore the monetary system and the use of monetary policy to stabilize the economy and the price level. As you read these chapters, keep in mind that the long-run goals of fiscal and monetary policy are economic growth, low unemployment, and modest inflationary pressures.

Checkpoint

Macroeconomic Equilibrium

REVIEW

- Macroeconomic equilibrium occurs where short-run aggregate demand and aggregate supply cross.
- The spending multiplier exists because new spending generates new round-by-round spending (based on the marginal propensities to consume and save) that creates additional income. Your new spending becomes my new income. Some (the MPC) is spent and thus becomes someone else's income, and some of that new income is also spent, and so on.
- The formula for the spending multiplier is $1/(1 - \text{MPC}) = 1/(\text{MPS})$.
- The multiplier is more effective when the economy has considerable slack.
- Policymakers can increase output by enacting policies that expand government spending, consumption, investment, or net exports, or reduce taxes.
- Demand-pull inflation occurs when aggregate demand expands beyond that necessary for full employment.

■ Cost-push inflation occurs when aggregate supply shifts to the left, causing the price level to rise along with rising unemployment.

QUESTIONS

Between 2004 and 2007, the price of petroleum products in the United States more than doubled, and gasoline and diesel fuel peaked at over $3.00 a gallon. Describe the impact of this price increase on aggregate supply. How might it affect employment, unemployment, and the price level? Would the impact depend on whether consumers and business thought the price increase was permanent?

Answers to the Checkpoint questions can be found at the end of this chapter.

Key Concepts

Aggregate expenditures, p. 212
Aggregate demand, p. 213
Wealth effect, p. 214
Aggregate supply, p. 217
Short-run aggregate supply (AS) curve,
  p. 218
Long-run aggregate supply (LRAS) curve,
  p. 218

Macroeconomic equilibrium, p. 221
Multiplier, p. 222
Marginal propensity to consume, p. 222
Marginal propensity to save, p. 222
Demand-pull inflation, p. 224
Cost-push inflation, p. 226

Chapter Summary

Aggregate Demand

The aggregate demand curve shows the quantities of goods and services (real GDP) demanded at different price levels.

The aggregate demand curve is downward sloping for several reasons. For one thing, when price levels rise, household wealth is reduced because the purchasing power of money held in savings accounts, bonds, and cash declines. Some purchases are thus put on hold, thereby reducing output demanded. This is known as the *wealth effect*. Second, when the country's aggregate price level rises, U.S. goods become more expensive in the global marketplace, so foreigners purchase fewer U.S. products, and thus exports decline. Third, as aggregate prices rise, people need more money to carry out transactions. This added demand for money drives up interest rates, which reduces business investment.

The determinants of aggregate demand include the components of aggregate spending—consumption, investment, government spending, and net exports. Changing any one of these aggregates will shift the aggregate demand curve.

Aggregate Supply

The aggregate supply curve shows the real GDP that firms will produce at varying price levels. The aggregate supply curve has three regions: a horizontal (depression) region, where output can be increased without increases in prices; a positively sloped section, where prices rise when GDP grows (AS curve); and a vertical region (LRAS curve), where output cannot grow.

A flat aggregate supply curve represents the depression period. It applies to an economy with so much excess capacity that businesses can increase their output without having to face rising costs; thus increased output does not lead to inflation.

The short-run aggregate supply (AS) curve is positively sloped because many input costs are slow to change in the short run. When prices rise, firms do not immediately need to increase wages or rents because these are often fixed for a specified term. However, as an industry or the economy as a whole increases its production, firms must start hiring more labor or paying overtime. As each firm seeks more employees, wages are driven up, increasing costs and forcing higher prices.

The vertical long-run aggregate supply (LRAS) curve reflects classical economic analysis. Over the long run, all variables in the economy, including prices, wages, and interest rates, can adjust. This means that an economy in the long run will gravitate to an equilibrium position at full employment.

The determinants of the aggregate supply curve include changes in input prices, the market power of firms, productivity, taxes, regulation, and business and inflationary expectations. If one of these determinants changes, the entire aggregate supply curve shifts.

Macroeconomic Equilibrium

A short-run macroeconomic equilibrium occurs at the intersection of the aggregate supply and aggregate demand curves. When an economy is operating at full employment, this also represents a point of long-run macroeconomic equilibrium. The Great Depression demonstrated, however, that an economy can reach short-run equilibrium at output levels substantially below full employment. Unless something happens to change aggregate demand or aggregate supply, the economy could remain mired in a recession.

The spending multiplier exists because new round-by-round spending generates more spending and income (based on the marginal propensities to consume and save) that creates additional income. Any new spending becomes someone's new income, and some of this new income (the MPC) is spent and this portion becomes someone else's income, of which some is spent, and so on.

Demand-pull inflation occurs when aggregate demand expands so much that equilibrium output exceeds full employment output. On a temporary basis, the economy can expand beyond full employment as workers incur overtime, temporary workers are added, and more shifts are added. All these components increase costs and prices. Without a reduction in aggregate demand, the economy will move to a new equilibrium where prices are permanently higher.

Cost-push inflation occurs when a supply shock hits the economy, shifting the aggregate supply curve leftward. The oil shock of the 1970s was a good example of cost-push inflation: Because of a sudden decrease in supply, prices rose dramatically, even as output held roughly constant. Cost-push inflation makes using policies to expand aggregate demand to restore full employment difficult because of the additional inflationary pressures added to the economy.

Questions and Problems

1. Describe the impact of rising interest rates on consumer spending.

2. There is little doubt that computers and the Internet have changed our economy. Information technology (IT) can boost efficiency in nearly everything: Markets are more efficient, IT is global, and IT improves the design, manufacture, and supply chain of products we produce. Use the aggregate demand and supply framework discussed in this chapter to show the impact of IT on the U.S. economy.

3. Unemployment can be caused by a reduction in aggregate demand or aggregate supply. Both changes are represented by leftward shifts in the curves. Does it matter whether the shift occurs in aggregate demand or aggregate supply? Use the AD/AS framework to show why or why not.

4. When the economy is operating at full employment, why is an increase in aggregate demand not helpful to the economy?

5. When the economy is hit with a supply shock, such as oil prices rising from $25 a barrel to $75, why is this doubly disruptive and harmful to the economy?

6. Explain why the aggregate supply curve is horizontal during a Keynesian depression period, positively sloped during the short run, and vertical in the long run.

7. In the figure below, the economy is initially in equilibrium at full employment at point e. Assume aggregate demand declines by 100 (shifts from AD_0 to AD_1).
   a. What will be the new short-run equilibrium?
   b. How large is the simple Keynesian multiplier in this case?

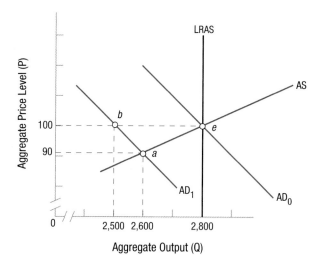

8. In the figure below, assume the economy is initially at full employment equilibrium at point e. Now assume that aggregate demand rises to AD_1, creating demand-pull inflation. Describe what happens to the economy in both the short run and the long run.

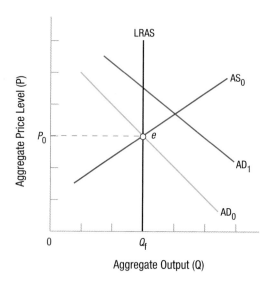

9. List some examples of factors that will shift the aggregate demand curve.

10. List some examples of factors that will shift the aggregate supply curve.

11. Use the table and grid below to answer the following questions:
    a. In the grid, graph the aggregate demand and aggregate supply curves (label them AD_0 and AS_0). What is equilibrium output and the price level?
    b. Assume aggregate demand grows by 100% (doubles; so that output doubles at each price level). Graph the new aggregate demand curve and label it AD_1. What is the new equilibrium output and price level?
    c. If full employment output is 600, what will be the long-run output and price level given the new aggregate demand curve?

Price Level	Output (aggregate supply)	Output (aggregate demand)
150	1,000	200
125	800	400
100	600	600
75	400	800
50	200	1,000

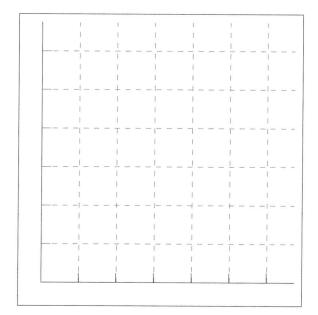

12. Why is cost-push inflation a more difficult problem for policymakers than demand-pull?

13. Why is consumer confidence so important in determining the equilibrium level of output and employment?

14. As the Japanese yen appreciated in value during the 1980s and 1990s, more Japanese auto companies built auto manufacturing plants in other parts of Asia and the United States. What impact did this have on net exports for the United States? Why did Japanese automakers build plants in the United States? Were the reasons similar to the reasons that American firms build plants (or outsource production) to China and other parts of Asia?

15. Some advocates have suggested that the United States should move to a universal health care plan paid for at the federal level like Medicare, which would be funded out of general tax revenues. Such a plan, it is argued, would guarantee quality health care to all. Ignoring all the controversy surrounding such a plan, would the introduction of universal health care paid for from general revenues have an impact on aggregate supply? Why or why not?

CHECKPOINT: AGGREGATE DEMAND

An increase in taxes (or tax rates) would reduce disposable income and consumption, shifting aggregate demand to the left. In a similar way, decreasing taxes would raise disposable income and shift aggregate demand to the right. Since government spending is an element of aggregate demand, what the government does with the revenue will also affect aggregate demand (more about this in later chapters).

CHECKPOINT: AGGREGATE SUPPLY

Probably not. Because of the greater extent of collective bargaining, European labor markets are less competitive, and "full employment" may be reached at higher unemployment levels than in the United States. Hiring additional workers in Europe costs more initially, and laying off workers is much harder by law. This added inflexibility in labor markets probably leads to a steeper aggregate supply curve in Europe than in the United States.

CHECKPOINT: MACROECONOMIC EQUILIBRIUM

Petroleum products are an important input in our economy. Higher oil prices will increase costs of transportation, and where oil is an important input (plastics), it will increase costs and reduce aggregate supply. Over time, these cost increases will show up as a higher price level, reduced employment, and higher unemployment. If the economy continues to grow, these impacts will be masked, but will simply reduce the growth numbers. After the oil price shocks in the 1970s, the United States became much more energy efficient, so today's price increases may not have quite the shock effect on the economy as was experienced in the 1970s. If the change is seen as permanent, consumers and businesses will begin making long-run adjustments to higher prices. For example, consumers will begin switching to more fuel-efficient cars (hybrids and smaller cars), and business will look at investing in energy-saving methods of distribution and production. If the price increases are just viewed as temporary, both groups might not adjust much at all.

Fiscal Policy

10

n the previous chapter, we constructed the aggregate demand and aggregate supply model of the macroeconomy. We used it to show that the economy could settle into equilibrium below full employment. Further, there was no guarantee that an economy in a deep recession or depression would automatically recover to its potential full employment level. Returning the economy to full employment often requires government action. This typically involves increased government spending because when the economy is well below full employment, consumers and business tighten their belts. Similarly, when the economy faces demand-pull or cost-push inflation, government policymakers can reduce the impact with appropriate policies.

In this chapter, we look at fiscal policy, which is one way the government tries to manage the economy and tame the business cycle. Fiscal policy involves adjusting government spending on goods and services, transfer payments, and taxes, with the express purpose of managing the macroeconomy. The following chapters will look at the other major way the government tries to manage the economy: through monetary policy.

In discussing fiscal policy, keep in mind that managing the economy is only one of the considerations guiding government decisions on taxing and spending. Many government operations have little to do with influencing aggregate output or the price level. Figure 1 on the next page shows the distribution of the nearly $3 trillion federal budget. The biggest source of revenues is individual income and Social Security taxes, which constitute over 80% of revenues; Social Security, national defense, and Medicare represent nearly two thirds of all spending.

The federal budget can be split into two distinct types of spending: discretionary and mandatory. Discretionary spending is the part of the budget that works its way through the appropriations process of Congress each year. **Discretionary spending** includes such programs as national defense (essentially the military), transportation, science, environment, income security (some welfare programs like

Discretionary spending
The part of the budget that works its way through the appropriations process of Congress each year and includes such programs as national defense, transportation, science, environment, and income security.

235

FIGURE 1

Federal Government Revenues and Outlays (2007)

The pie charts show the percentage distribution of the nearly $3 trillion of federal revenues and outlays. The bulk of revenues (80%) come from individual income taxes and Social Security payroll taxes. Spending is much more diversified, where most of the funds go to national defense, health, Social Security, education, and welfare.

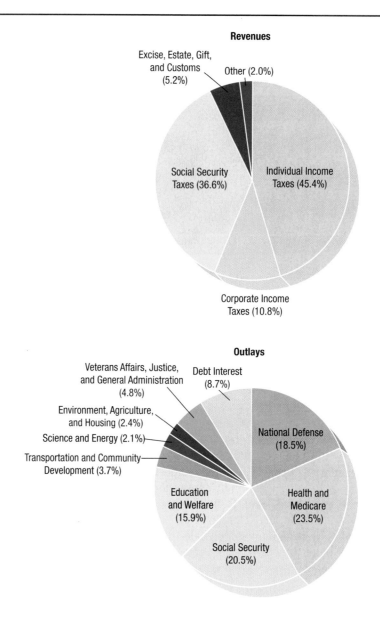

Revenues

Excise, Estate, Gift, and Customs (5.2%)
Other (2.0%)
Social Security Taxes (36.6%)
Individual Income Taxes (45.4%)
Corporate Income Taxes (10.8%)

Outlays

Veterans Affairs, Justice, and General Administration (4.8%)
Debt Interest (8.7%)
Environment, Agriculture, and Housing (2.4%)
Science and Energy (2.1%)
Transportation and Community Development (3.7%)
National Defense (18.5%)
Education and Welfare (15.9%)
Health and Medicare (23.5%)
Social Security (20.5%)

Mandatory spending
Authorized by permanent laws and does not go through the same appropriations process as discretionary spending. Mandatory spending includes such programs as Social Security, Medicare, and interest on the national debt.

Medicaid), education, and veterans benefits and services. As Figure 2 shows, discretionary spending is now under 40% and has steadily declined as a percent of the budget since the 1960s, when it was nearly 70% of the budget.

Mandatory spending is authorized by permanent laws and does not go through the same appropriations process as discretionary spending. To change one of the entitlements of mandatory spending, Congress must change the law. Mandatory spending includes such programs as Social Security, Medicare, interest on the national debt, and some means-tested income-security programs including food stamps and TANF (Temporary Assistance to Needy Families). This part of the budget has been growing, as Figure 2 illustrates, and now accounts for nearly two thirds of the budget.

Even though discretionary spending is only one third of the budget, this is still roughly $1 trillion and the capacity to alter this spending is a powerful force in the

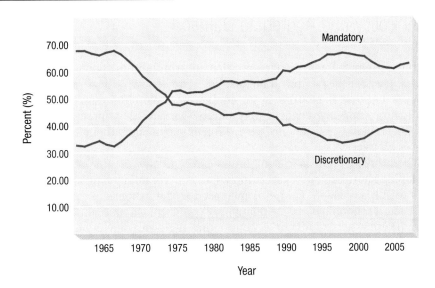

FIGURE 2

Discretionary and Mandatory Federal Spending

Mandatory spending includes programs authorized by law (also called entitlements) such as Social Security, Medicare, and food stamps. Mandatory programs do not go through the normal congressional appropriations process and have been growing. Discretionary programs are authorized each year by the appropriations process of Congress and include national defense, transportation, environment, and education spending. Discretionary spending has been steadily declining as a percent of the budget.

economy. Further, the two thirds of the budget that is on auto-pilot may well act as a stabilizing force that partly explains why the two short recessions in the last 25 years have been extremely mild.

We will look at three aspects of fiscal policy. First, we will examine government tools for influencing aggregate demand. Second, we look at how government can influence aggregate supply. You will use the aggregate demand and aggregate supply model in both of these sections. Finally, we will look at problems that come up in implementing the demand-side and supply-side policies that government believes necessary.

After studying this chapter you should be able to

- Describe the tools that governments use to influence aggregate demand.

- Describe mandatory and discretionary government spending.

- Describe the multiplier effect of increased government spending on the equilibrium output of an economy.

- Describe expansionary and contractionary fiscal policy.

- Describe why tax changes have a smaller impact on the economy than changes in government spending.

- Describe the fiscal policies that governments use to influence aggregate supply.

- Describe the impact of automatic stabilizers, lag effects, and the crowding out effects in fiscal policymaking.

- Describe the debate over the size of government and economic policy.

Fiscal Policy and Aggregate Demand

Government can influence aggregate demand through its spending on goods and services, transfer payments, and taxes. When an economy faces underutilization of resources because it is stuck in an equilibrium below full employment—when it faces a horizontal aggregate supply curve—we saw that increases in aggregate demand can move the economy toward full employment without affecting the price level.

When the economy is in equilibrium *below full employment* but faces a positive-sloping short-run aggregate supply (AS) curve, influencing aggregate demand brings with it a tradeoff: Output is increased at the expense of raising price levels.

When the economy is in an inflationary equilibrium *above full employment* and faces a positive-sloping AS curve, contracting aggregate demand brings about other tradeoffs: Decreasing output dampens inflation but leads to unemployment. We saw all of these in the previous chapter.

What is the mechanism whereby government influences aggregate demand? We mentioned government spending on goods and services, transfer payments, and taxes. We will go through these so you will see how government's actions can influence aggregate demand.

Discretionary Fiscal Policy

Discretionary fiscal policy
Involves adjusting government spending and tax policies with the express short-run goal of moving the economy toward full employment, expanding economic growth, or controlling inflation.

The exercise of **discretionary fiscal policy** involves adjusting government spending and tax policies with the express short-run goal of moving the economy toward full employment, encouraging economic growth, or controlling inflation.

Some examples of the use of discretionary fiscal policy include tax cuts enacted during the Kennedy, Reagan, and George W. Bush administrations. These tax cuts were designed to expand the economy, both in the near term and the long run—they were meant to influence both aggregate demand and aggregate supply. Tax increases were enacted under the George H. Bush and Clinton administrations in the interest of reducing the government deficit and interest rates. The Roosevelt administration used increased government spending, although small amounts by today's standards, to mitigate the impact of the Depression.

Government Spending

Though discretionary fiscal policy can get complex, the impact of changes in government spending is relatively simple. As we know, a change in government spending or other components of GDP will cause income and output to rise or fall by the spending change *times* the multiplier.

This is illustrated in Figure 3 with the economy initially in equilibrium at point *a*, with real output equaling $1,000. If government spending increases by $100, that $100 in new spending (after the round-by-round spending multiplication) will move the economy from real GDP of $1,000 to $1,400 (point *b*) with the price level held constant at P_0. Because the initial increase in government spending was $100 and equilibrium output rose by $400, we know that the multiplier is 4. This is the straightforward multiplier process of new spending that we discussed earlier, but now applied to government spending.

Note that when the economy reaches the positively sloped portion of the AS curve (along AS between points *b* and *c*) the value of the multiplier declines as some of the increase in output is absorbed into price increases. Once the economy reaches full employment (point *c*), further spending is not multiplied as the economy moves along the LRAS curve, and price increases absorb it all. Finally, keep in mind that the multiplier works in both directions.

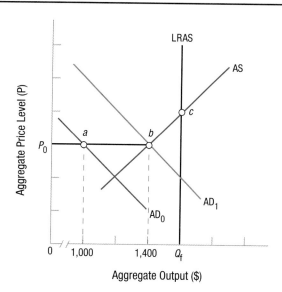

FIGURE 3

The Multiplier and Government Spending

The economy is initially in equilibrium at point *a*. Now government spending of $100 works it way through the economy round-by-round, both income and output are multiplied, and the new equilibrium is $1,400 (point *b*). Since $100 in new government spending generates $400 in new income and output, the multiplier must equal 4. Between points *b* and *c*, price increases absorb some of the increase in AD, so the multiplier is lower. Once the economy reaches full employment (point *c*), price increases absorb all of the increase in AD.

Taxes

Changes in government spending modify income by an amount equal to the change in spending *times* the multiplier. How, then, do changes in taxes affect the economy? The answer is not quite as simple. Let's begin with a reminder of what constitutes spending equilibrium.

When the economy is in equilibrium,

$$GDP = C + I + G + (X - M)$$

At equilibrium, all spending *injections* into the economy will equal all *withdrawals* of spending. To see why, let's simplify the above equation and begin with only a private economy, eliminating government (G) and the foreign sector, or net exports (X − M). Thus,

$$GDP = C + I$$

Gross domestic product (GDP) is equal to consumer plus business investment spending. Without government and taxes, GDP is just income (Y), so

$$Y = C + I$$

or

$$Y - C = I$$

Now, income minus consumption (Y − C) is just saving (S), so at equilibrium,

$$S = I$$

or

$$I = S$$

This simple equation represents a very important point: At equilibrium, *injections* (in this case, I) are just equal to *withdrawals* (S in this instance). Investment represents spending where saving is the removal of income from the spend-ing-income-spending stream.

Now, when we add government spending (G), taxes (T), and the foreign sector (X − M) to the equation, we have simply added some *injections* (G) and (X) and subtracted some *withdrawals* (T) and (M), so the equilibrium equation becomes

$$I + G + X = S + T + M$$

Now let's focus on taxes. When taxes are increased, money is withdrawn from the economy's spending stream. When taxes are reduced, consumers and business have more to spend. Thus, taxes form a wedge between income and the part of income that can be spent, or disposable income. Disposable income (Y_d) is equal to income minus taxes ($Y_d = Y − T$). For simplicity, we will assume that all taxes are paid in a lump sum, thereby removing a certain fixed sum of money from the economy. This assumption does away with the need to worry now about the incentive effects of higher or lower tax rates. These supply-side issues will be discussed later in the chapter.

Because taxes represent a withdrawal of spending from the economy, we would expect equilibrium income to fall when a tax is imposed. Consumers pay a tax increase, in part, by *reducing* their saving. If we initially increase taxes by $100, let's assume that consumers draw on their savings for $25 of the increase in taxes. Since this $25 in savings was already withdrawn from the economy, only the $75 in reduced spending gets multiplied, reducing income by $300 ($75 × 4). The *reduction* in saving of $25 dampens the effect of the tax on equilibrium income because those funds were previously withdrawn from the spending stream. Simply changing the withdrawal category from saving to taxes does not affect income. A tax decrease has a similar but opposite impact because only the MPC part is spent and multiplied, and the rest is withdrawn in the form of saving.

The result is that a tax increase (or decrease, for that matter) will have less of a direct impact on income, employment, and output than will an equivalent change in government spending.

Transfers

Transfer payments are money payments directly paid to individuals. These include payments for such items as Social Security, unemployment compensation, and welfare. In large measure, they represent our social safety net. We will ignore them as part of the discretionary fiscal policy, since most are paid as a matter of law, but we will see later in the chapter that they are very important as a way of stabilizing the economy.

Expansionary and Contractionary Fiscal Policy

Expansionary fiscal policy
Involves increasing government spending, increasing transfer payments, or decreasing taxes to increase aggregate demand to expand output and the economy.

Expansionary fiscal policy involves increasing government spending; increasing transfer payments such as Social Security, unemployment compensation, or welfare payments; or decreasing taxes—all to increase aggregate demand. These policies put more money into the hands of consumers and business. In theory, these additional funds should lead to higher spending. The precise effect expansionary fiscal policies will have depends, however, on whether the economy is at or below full employment.

When the economy is below full employment, an expansionary policy will move the economy to full employment, as Figure 4 shows. The economy begins at equilibrium at point *e*, below full employment. Expansionary fiscal policy increases aggregate demand from AD_0 to AD_1, and equilibrium output rises to Q_f (point *f*) as

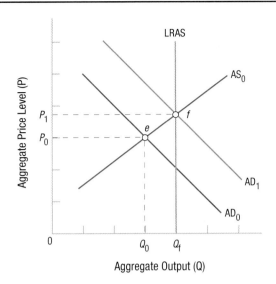

FIGURE 4

Expansionary Fiscal Policy Below Full Employment

When the economy is below full employment, expansionary policies move it to full employment. Here, the economy begins at equilibrium at point e, below full employment. Expansionary fiscal policy increases aggregate demand from AD_0 to AD_1, raising equilibrium output to Q_f and the price level to P_1 (point f).

the price level rises to P_1. In this case, one good outcome results—output rises to Q_f—though it is accompanied by one less desirable result, the price level rising to P_1.

Figure 5 shows what happens when the economy is at full employment: An expansionary policy raises prices without producing any long-run improvement in real GDP. In this figure, the initial equilibrium is already at full employment (point e), so increasing aggregate demand moves the economy to a new output level above full employment (point a), thereby raising prices to P_1. This higher output is only

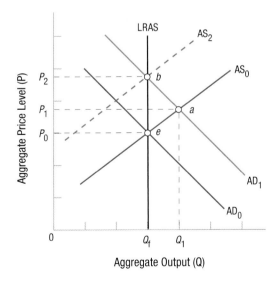

FIGURE 5

Expansionary Fiscal Policy at Full Employment

When an economy is already at full employment, expansionary policies lead to no long-run improvement in real GDP. Equilibrium is initially at price level P_0 (point e), with output at its full employment level. Increasing aggregate demand moves the economy to an output level above full employment (point a). This higher output is only temporary, however, as workers and suppliers adjust their expectations to the higher price level (P_1), thus shifting aggregate supply left toward AS_2. But this just pushes prices up further, until finally workers adjust their inflationary expectations, and the economy settles into a new equilibrium at point b. At this point, the economy is once again at full employment, but at a price level (P_2) that is higher than before.

temporary, however, as workers and suppliers adjust their expectations to the higher price level, thus shifting aggregate supply upwards to AS_2. Aggregate supply declines because workers and other resource suppliers realize the prices they are paying for products have risen; hence, they demand higher wages or prices for their services. This higher demand just pushes prices up further, until finally workers adjust their inflationary expectations and the economy settles into equilibrium at point b. At this point, the economy is again at full employment, but at a higher price level (P_2) than before.

When an economy moves to a point beyond full employment, as just described, economists say an *inflationary spiral* has set in. The explanation for this phenomenon was suggested earlier, but a later chapter will give it a more extensive treatment. Still, we can already see that one way to reduce such inflationary pressures is by a **contractionary fiscal policy**: reducing government spending, transfer payments, or raising taxes (increasing withdrawals from the economy). Figure 6 shows the result of contractionary policy. The economy is initially overheating at point e, with output above full employment. Contractionary policy reduces aggregate demand to AD_1, bringing the economy back to full employment at price level P_1. This policy reduces the inflationary pressures that had been mounting, thereby staving off an inflationary spiral, but the fall in aggregate output leads to an increase in unemployment.

Contractionary fiscal policy Involves increasing withdrawals from the economy by reducing government spending, transfer payments, or raising taxes to decrease aggregate demand to contract output and the economy.

FIGURE 6

Contractionary Fiscal Policy to Reduce Inflation

Inflationary pressures can be reduced by contractionary fiscal policies—by reducing government spending or transfer payments, or by raising taxes. In the figure, the economy is overheating at point e, with output above full employment at Q_0. Contractionary policies reduce aggregate demand to AD_1, bringing the economy back to full employment at price level P_1. These policies reduce the inflationary pressures that had been mounting, preventing an inflationary spiral, but the fall in aggregate output leads to an increase in unemployment.

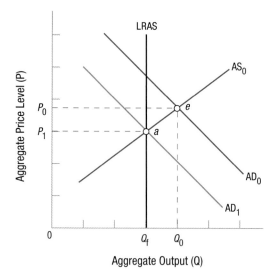

Exercising demand-side policy requires tradeoffs between increasing output at the expense of raising price levels, or else lowering price levels by accepting a lower output. When recession threatens, the public is often happy to trade higher prices for greater employment and output. One would think the opposite would be true when an inflationary spiral loomed on the horizon. Politicians, however, are loath to support contractionary policies that control inflation by reducing aggregate demand, since high unemployment can cost politicians their jobs. The demand-side fiscal policy tools—government spending, transfer payments, and taxes—remain unused. In these instances, politicians often look to the Federal Reserve to use its tools and influence to keep inflation in check. We will examine the Federal Reserve in the following chapters.

Checkpoint

Fiscal Policy and Aggregate Demand

REVIEW

■ Demand-side fiscal policy involves using government spending, transfer payments, and taxes to change aggregate demand and equilibrium income, output, and the price level in the economy.

■ Government spending raises income and output by the amount of spending times the multiplier. Tax reductions have a smaller impact on the economy than government spending because some of the reduction in taxes is added to saving and is therefore withdrawn from the economy.

■ Expansionary fiscal policy involves increasing government spending, increasing transfer payments, or decreasing taxes.

■ Contractionary fiscal policy involves decreasing government spending, decreasing transfer payments, or increasing taxes.

■ When an economy is at full employment, expansionary fiscal policy may lead to greater output in the short term, but will ultimately just lead to higher prices in the longer term.

QUESTION

Explain why cutting taxes represents expansionary fiscal policy.

Answers to the Checkpoint question can be found at the end of this chapter.

Fiscal Policy and Aggregate Supply

Fiscal policies that influence aggregate supply are different from policies that influence aggregate demand as they do not always require tradeoffs between price levels and output. That is the good news. The bad news is that **supply-side fiscal policies** require more time to work than do demand-side fiscal policies. The focus of fiscal policy and aggregate supply is on long-run economic growth.

Figure 7 on the next page shows the impact that fiscal policy can have on the economy over the long run. The goal of these fiscal policies is to shift the long-run aggregate supply curve to the right, here from $LRAS_0$ to $LRAS_1$. This shift moves the economy's full employment equilibrium from point a to point b, thereby expanding full-employment output while keeping inflation in check. In Figure 7, the price level declines as output expands. In practice, this would be an unusual, though by no means impossible, result of fiscal policies. If, for example, aggregate demand remained the same, the price level would fall. But this is rarely the case because AD typically expands as the economy grows, keeping prices from falling.

Figure 7 may well reflect what in general is happening in our current global economy. Improvements in technology and communications have increased productivity to the point that global aggregate supply has shifted outward. These changes, along with freer trade, have helped to keep interest rates and inflation low for several decades.

Just what fiscal policies will allow the economy to expand without generating price pressures? First, there are the government policies advocated by economists Lucas and Romer, the architects of modern growth theory we examined earlier that encourage investment in human capital (education) and policies that encourage the

Supply-side fiscal policies
Focus on shifting the long-run aggregate supply curve to the right, expanding the economy without increasing inflationary pressures. Unlike policies to increase aggregate demand, supply-side policies take longer to have an impact on the economy.

FIGURE 7

Fiscal Policy and Aggregate Supply

The ultimate goal of fiscal policy directed at aggregate supply is to shift the long-run aggregate supply curve from $LRAS_0$ to $LRAS_1$. This moves the economy's full employment equilibrium from point a to point b, expanding output while keeping inflation in check. With these fiscal policies the inflationary pressures are reduced as output expands, but these policies take a long time to have an impact.

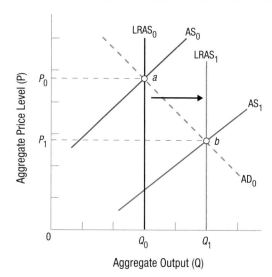

development and transfers of new technologies. Second, there are the fiscal policies that focus on reducing tax rates. Third, there are policies that promote investment in new capital equipment, encourage investment in research and development, and trim burdensome business regulations. These policies are intended to expand the supply curves of all businesses and industries.

Modern Growth Theory

Modern growth theory suggests there is a lot governments can do to create the right environment to encourage economic growth. We already have seen the benefits of building and maintaining a nation's infrastructure including roads, bridges, dams, and communications networks, or setting up a fair and efficient legal system and stable financial system. Economists Robert Lucas and Paul Romer have shown that the higher the levels of human capital and the easier technology is transferred to other firms and industries (the public good aspect of technology), the more robust is economic growth. Thus, they stress the long-run growth benefits of things such as higher education and research and development.

Reducing Tax Rates

Macroeconomics in its original sense has succeeded: Its central problem of depression prevention has been solved. . . . There remain important gains in welfare from better fiscal policies, but I argue that these are gains from providing people with better incentives to work and save, not from better fine-tuning of spending flows. Taking U.S. performance over the past 50 years as a benchmark, the potential for welfare gains from better long-run, supply-side policies exceeds *by far* the potential from further improvements in short-run demand management.

Robert Lucas, Jr. (2003)

The best summary of supply-side economics I know was uttered by Charles Schultze, who some of you will know as former Chairman of the Council of Economic Advisers, and a former director of the budget. He said, "There is absolutely nothing wrong with supply-side economics that dividing by ten wouldn't cure."

Robert Solow (2000)

Reducing tax rates has an impact on both aggregate demand and aggregate supply. Lower tax rates increase aggregate demand because households now have more money to spend. At the same time, lower tax rates mean that workers' take-home wages rise and this may encourage more work effort. At different times policymakers have lowered taxes to stimulate consumption: John F. Kennedy reduced tax rates in the early 1960s and George W. Bush in the early 2000s provided tax rebates equal to $300 per taxpayer as part of an economic stimulus package.

At other times, administrations have reduced marginal tax rates, the rate paid on the next dollar earned, with the express purpose of stimulating incentives to work and for business to take risks. President Kennedy reduced the top marginal rate from 70% to 50% and President Reagan reduced the top marginal rate from 50% to 28%.

Clearly, high marginal income tax rates can have adverse effects on the economy. When marginal income tax rates become too high, the incentives to work and for business to take on added risk can be harmed. This is the economic rationale for reducing tax rates. Unfortunately, this economic rationale has become clouded by a political dimension because "supply-side economics" became associated with a political movement in the 1980s.

As the quotes by the two Nobel Prize winners Robert Lucas and Robert Solow, leading off this section illustrate, there is still considerable controversy regarding the benefits of the supply-side approach to macroeconomic fiscal policy. The supply-side movement that resulted in the marginal tax rate reductions in the 1980s by the Reagan administration was partially driven by reference to a simple tax revenue curve drawn by economist Arthur Laffer.

The Laffer Curve

Economist Arthur Laffer first drew the curve in Figure 8 for a member of Congress to illustrate how reducing tax *rates* could increase tax *revenues*. The curve plots hypothetical tax revenues at various income tax rates and has become known as the **Laffer curve**. If tax rates are zero, tax revenues will be zero as well. If rates are 100%, revenues will again be zero, since there will be no incentive to earn income; everything just gets taxed away. In between these two extreme tax rates, tax revenues will be positive, reaching their maximum at point *b*.

The Laffer curve further suggests that if the economy is at point *a*, policymakers can increase tax revenues by raising tax rates. When Laffer developed the curve in the 1980s, however, he argued that the economy was found somewhere around point *c*, where further raising tax rates would reduce tax revenues. He felt that the

Laffer curve
Plots hypothetical tax revenues at various income tax rates. If tax rates are zero, tax revenues will be zero; if rates are 100%, revenues will also be zero. As tax rates rise from zero, revenues will rise, reach a maximum, and then decline.

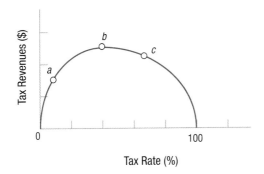

FIGURE 8

The Laffer Curve

The Laffer curve plots hypothetical tax revenues at various income tax rates. If tax rates are zero, tax revenue will be zero. If rates are 100%, revenue will also be zero, since there will be no incentive to earn income; it would just be taxed away. In between these two extremes, tax revenues will be positive, reaching their maximum at point *b*. If the economy is somewhere around point *c*, raising tax rates would reduce tax revenues, whereas lowering tax rates would increase tax revenues.

incentives to work and produce were being hampered by high federal marginal income tax rates, which topped 50% in some cases. If you already earn a high income, what incentive do you have to work more if Uncle Sam is going to take away 50% of your added earnings? (This is to say nothing about the state and local taxes you must pay plus Social Security taxes.)

The Laffer curve has something to say about the disincentive effects of high marginal tax rates. But critics zeroed in on two things. First, was the shape of the Laffer curve correct? If the curve were flatter, then the effects of lowering tax rates would be less. Second, how could we be sure where we were on the Laffer curve? These are tough questions to answer. Now throw in political considerations, with those on the political right looking for ways to limit government by reducing government revenue and those on the political left looking for ways to increase government spending and government revenue, and one can imagine how heated the discussion became in the 1980s.

High Marginal Income Tax Rates and the Labor Supply of Women

Once a family reaches high marginal income tax levels, additional dollars of income are so ferociously taxed that it may affect the decisions of women to enter the workforce. The Kennedy round of tax cuts in 1964 reduced the top marginal rate from 70% to 50% and the two Reagan tax cuts ultimately reduced the top rate from 50% to 28%. Women in the 1960s and 1970s married to successful men found it difficult to justify working when income taxes (state, local, and federal) and Social Security taxes claimed well over half of their entire salaries.

The Reagan Administration in the mid-1980s reduced top marginal income tax rates to 28% making second incomes more valuable. Two decades ago women were more likely to be secondary earners and not the primary earner in the household. Reducing marginal tax rates would have an impact on their decision on rather to work or not. This raised the incentive for married women to work. But how much did these lowered marginal tax rates lead to more women joining the work force?

Today, two people work in over half of all American families, and the labor force participation rate of women has risen markedly over the last several decades. How much of this resulted from reduced marginal income tax rates? Clearly, part of increase in the labor force participation rate of women has been due to changing social norms and expansion of educational and occupational opportunities for women. Also, the labor force participation rate for working age women has been steadily rising from 30% just after WWII to roughly 60% today. Economist Jonathan Gruber has summarized the evidence and concludes, "for secondary earners, each 1% rise in after-tax wages increases labor supply from 0.5% to 1%. Most of the response of secondary earners comes from the decision to work at all . . .".[1] The difficulty in determining the precise effects of the Reagan tax cuts on economic incentives has made it easier for these policies to become controversial.

Expanding Investment and Reducing Regulations

We have already seen how closely standards of living are tied to productivity. Investment will increase the capital with which labor works, thereby increasing productivity. Rising productivity will drive increased economic growth and raise the average standard of living, shifting the long-run aggregate supply curve to the right.

Investment can be encouraged by such policies as investment tax credits (direct reductions in taxes for new investment) and more rapid depreciation schedules for

[1]Jonathan Gruber, *Public Finance and Public Policy* (New York: Worth Publishers), 2005, p. 590.

plant and equipment. When a firm can expense (depreciate) its capital equipment over a shorter period of time, it cuts its taxes now rather than later, and so earns a higher return on the capital now. Similarly, government grants for basic research help firms increase their budgets for research and development, which results in new products and technologies brought to market.

Nowhere is this impact more evident than in the health care field. The Human Genome Project, largely supported by public funds, is already enabling new medicines to be developed at a much faster rate than previously. And beyond the obvious benefits this has for the people who require such medicines, investments of this sort pay dividends for the entire economy. As health care improves, workers stay on the job more and productivity rises.

Another way of increasing aggregate supply without raising prices involves repealing unnecessarily onerous regulations that simply hamper business and add to costs. Clearly, some regulation of business activities is needed. Still, these regulations should be subjected to rigorous cost-benefit analysis. Otherwise, excessive regulations end up simply adding to the costs of the products we buy, without yielding significant benefits. Examples of excessively regulated industries have included trucking and the airlines. When these industries were deregulated in the 1980s, prices fell and both industries expanded rapidly. Today, some economists argue that the Federal Drug Administration's drug approval process is too long and costly; bringing a new drug to market costs nearly one billion dollars.

Fiscal policies to increase aggregate supply are promoted mainly through the government's encouragement of human capital development and technology improvements, its power to tax, its ability to promote investment in infrastructure and research, and the degree and efficiency of regulation. Cutting marginal tax rates, offering investment tax credits, and offering grants for research are the favored policies. The political fervor of the 1980s supply-side movement has largely dissipated as marginal income tax rates have declined. But fiscal policies to encourage growth in aggregate supply are still an important part of the government's long-term fiscal policy arsenal.

Checkpoint
Fiscal Policy and Aggregate Supply

REVIEW

- The goal of fiscal policies that influence aggregate supply is to shift the long-run aggregate supply curve to the right.
- Modern growth theory stresses the importance of expanding aggregate supply through higher investments in human capital and a focus on technological infrastructure with "public good" benefits.
- The Laffer curve suggested that reducing tax rates could lead to higher revenues.
- Other fiscal policies to increase aggregate supply include providing incentives for business investment and reducing burdensome regulation.
- The major limitation of fiscal policies to influence aggregate supply is that they take a long time to have an impact on long-run aggregate supply.

QUESTIONS

In 1962 at a speech before the Economic Club of New York, President Kennedy argued that " . . . it is a paradoxical truth that taxes are too high today and tax revenues are too low—and the soundest way to raise revenues in the long run is to cut rates now." Is President Kennedy's argument consistent with supply side economics? Why or why not?

Answers to the Checkpoint questions can be found at the end of this chapter.

Implementing Fiscal Policy

Implementing fiscal policy is often a complex and time-consuming process. Three disparate groups—the Senate, House, and the executive branch—must collectively agree on specific spending and tax policies. Ideally, these decisions are made in the open with the public fully informed. The complexities of the budgeting process and its openness (not a bad thing in itself) give rise to several inherent difficulties. We will briefly consider some problems having to do with the timing of fiscal decisions and the crowding-out effect, after first looking at the automatic stabilization mechanisms contained in the federal budgeting process.

Automatic Stabilizers

Automatic stabilizers
Tax revenues and transfer payments automatically expand or contract in ways that reduce the intensity of business fluctuations without any overt action by Congress or other policymakers.

There is a certain degree of stability built into the U.S. macroeconomic system. Tax revenues and transfer payments are the two principal **automatic stabilizers**; without any overt action by Congress or other policymakers, these two components of the federal budget will expand or contract in ways that help counter movements of the business cycle.

When the economy is growing at a solid rate, tax receipts will rise, since individuals and firms are increasing their taxable incomes. At the same time, transfer payments will decline, because fewer people require welfare or unemployment assistance. Rising tax revenues and declining transfer payments have contractionary effects, so in this case, they act as a brake to slow the growth of GDP, thereby keeping the economy from overheating, or keeping it from generating inflationary pressures. When the economic boom ends, and the economy goes into a downturn, the opposite happens: Tax revenues decline and transfer payments rise. These added funds getting pumped into the economy help cushion the impact of the downturn, not just for the recipients of transfer payments, but for the economy as a whole.

The income tax is a powerful stabilizer because of its progressivity. When incomes fall, tax revenues fall faster since people do not just pay taxes on smaller incomes, but they pay taxes at lower rates as their incomes fall. Disposable income, in other words, falls more slowly than aggregate income. But when the economy is booming, tax revenues rise faster than income, thereby withdrawing spending from the economy. This helps to slow the growth in income, thus reducing the threat of an inflationary spiral.

The key point to remember here is that automatic stabilizers reduce the intensity of business fluctuations. Automatic stabilizers do not eliminate fluctuations in the business cycle, but they render business cycles smoother and less chaotic. Automatic stabilizers act on their own, whereas discretionary fiscal policy requires overt action by policymakers. This fact creates difficulties for implementing discretionary fiscal policy.

Fiscal Policy Timing Lags

Using discretionary fiscal policy to smooth the short-term business cycle is a challenge because of several lags associated with its implementation. First, most of the macroeconomic data that policymakers need to enact the proper fiscal policies are not available until at least one quarter (3 months) after the fact. Even then, key figures often get revised for the next quarter or two. The **data lag**, therefore, creates a 1- to 6-month period before informed policymaking can even begin.

Compounding this lag, even if the most recent data suggest the economy is trending into a recession, it may take several quarters to confirm this fact. Short-term (month-to-month or quarter-to-quarter) variations in key indicators are common and sometimes represent nothing more than randomness in the data. This **recognition lag** is one reason recessions and recoveries are often well under way before policymakers fully acknowledge a need for action on their parts.

Third, once policymakers recognize that the economy has turned downward, fiscal policy requires a long and often contentious legislative and implementation process. Not all legislators have the same goals for the economy, so any new government spending must first survive an arduous trip through the political sausage machine. Even then, once some new policy has become law, it often requires months of planning, budgeting, and the process needed to set up a new program. This process, the **implementation lag**, rarely consumes *less* than 18 to 24 months.[2]

The problem these lags pose is clear: By the time the fiscal stimulus meant to jump-start a sputtering economy kicks in, the economy may already be on the mend. And if so, the exercise of fiscal policy can compound the effects of the business cycle by overstimulating a patient that is already recovering. Some of these lags can be reduced by expediting spending already approved for existing programs rather than implementing new programs. Also, the lags associated with tax changes are much shorter, given that new rates can go into withholding tables and take effect within weeks of enactment. Therefore, policymakers tend to favor tax changes because of the problem of implementation lags.

Data lag
The time policymakers must wait for economic data to be collected, processed, and reported. Most macroeconomic data are not available until at least one quarter (3 months) after the fact.

Recognition lag
The time it takes for policymakers to confirm that the economy is trending in or out of a recession. Short-term variations in key economic indicators are typical and sometimes represent nothing more than randomness in the data.

Implementation lag
The time required to turn fiscal policy into law and eventually have an impact on the economy.

Crowding-Out Effect

The **crowding-out effect** of fiscal policy arises from deficit spending, which requires the government to borrow. This borrowing can drive up interest rates. A greater demand for loanable funds, whether by the government or the private sector, means higher interest rates. The result of these higher interest rates is often reduced consumer spending on durable goods such as cars or refrigerators, often bought on credit, and reduced business investment. While deficit spending is usually expansionary, its impact can be partially offset by reductions in private spending.

When an economy is at full employment and private borrowers are already competing vigorously for funds, we would expect the crowding-out effect to be large. In a severe recession, when consumers are not buying durable goods and firms do not feel much like borrowing for the sake of investing anyway, the crowding-out effect should be less pronounced. When crowding-out is minimal, fiscal policy is at its most powerful.

Crowding-out effect
Arises from deficit spending requiring the government to borrow, which drives up interest rates, which in turn reduces consumer spending and business investment.

The Size of Government Debate

Often, fiscal policy debates have little to do with the state of the macroeconomy. Underlying all the rhetoric about the economic benefits or dangers of tax cuts, budget deficits, and spending priorities lies a long-standing philosophical debate about the proper size of government. As a rule, those on the left of the political spectrum favor a larger and more active government, while those on the right are constantly looking for ways to limit the size and power of the government.

Figure 9 on the next page shows federal receipts and spending as a percentage of GDP from the 1950s through the present. Throughout the 1970s, the 1980s, and much of the 1990s, spending significantly exceeded tax receipts; spending was usually more than 20% of GDP, and taxes barely topped 18%. It was only the collapse

Dick Palulian/Getty Images

---

[2] Andrew Abel and Ben Bernanke, *Macroeconomics,* 3rd ed. (Reading, MA: Addison-Wesley), 1998, p. 584.

FIGURE 9

Federal Receipts and Expenditures as a Percent of GDP

This figure shows federal receipts and spending as a percentage of GDP from the 1950s to today. Throughout most of the last three decades, spending significantly exceeded tax receipts. Spending usually was more than 20% of GDP, with tax revenues just over 18%. The fall of the Soviet Union in the late 1980s permitted a drop in defense spending. The booming stock market of the late 1990s boosted federal capital gains tax revenues. The combination of these two events brought government spending back into line with tax receipts, until the recession of 2000 pushed them apart again.

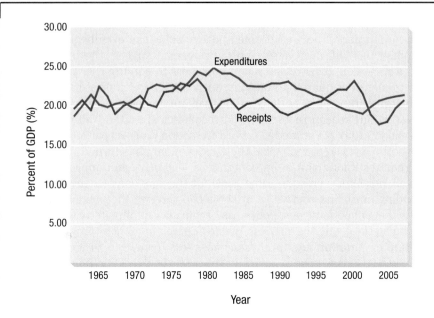

of the Soviet Bloc in the late 1980s, which permitted a decrease in defense spending, and the booming stock market of the late 1990s, which boosted federal capital gains tax revenues, that finally brought government spending back into line with tax receipts.

The resulting government surpluses were brief. The bull market collapsed in 2000, and along with tax rate cuts, caused a steep decline in tax revenues, while the mini-recession and national security concerns that dogged the opening years of this century increased the demand for government spending. The predictable result has been rising deficits. With the aging of the population, moreover, federal spending will undoubtedly grow as a percent of GDP as the proportion of the population receiving Social Security and Medicare increases, and the proportion of those of working age decreases.

One factor mitigating the budget deficits of the future is that the government has become a fellow investor in Individual Retirement Accounts (IRAs). When baby boomers retire and begin to draw on their IRAs, most of these funds will be taxed at ordinary income tax rates. These taxes will provide the federal government with growing revenues, which will help finance some of the future entitlements.

As clear as Figure 9 is, it may give a misleading view of fiscal policy. Government spending and receipts are given as a percentage of GDP. The figure suggests that high receipts generate pressure for tax cuts, as with the Reagan cuts in the early 1980s and the Bush cuts in 2001. It also suggests that government spending fluctuates.

Let's look at this situation another way and see what this implies for the fiscal policy tools of government spending and taxing. We saw that increases in government spending can help an economy during a recession, and an economy facing strong growth can afford to cut back in government spending. The actual magnitudes (the federal government spends nearly $3 trillion) qualify what we saw in Figure 9. From 1960 to the present, federal spending decreased in 1965—and this is the only year it did so. In other words, the federal government spent more money every year since 1960, year after year, except 1965. Of course, a growing economy may be able to accommodate this continual increase in spending. However, this history points to the federal government's tendency to spend more and more.

The reason is obvious: Some politicians can rail all they want against government spending, but when it gets down to it, what programs are going to be cut? Put another way, what voters are going to be hurt? So there is a natural tendency to spend more and more. The real question, year after year, is how much more? Government spending is often a blunter tool of fiscal policy than policymakers might hope.

How about the effectiveness of taxing as a fiscal policy tool? Looking at the magnitudes from 1960 to the present, federal revenues went down in four recession years: 1971, 1983, 1990, and 2001. The Reagan tax cuts were followed by immediate decreases in federal tax receipts, but the stimulative effects of these tax cuts soon changed this situation. Following the Bush tax cuts in 2001, Federal receipts fell through 2002, but have risen since then.

Furthermore, budget deficits constrain the government's ability to cut taxes. Again looking at magnitudes from 1960 to the present, the federal budget was in surplus in only 6 years: 1960, 1969, and 1998–2001. With current budget deficits in the hundreds of billions of dollars, the question is how much leeway fiscal policymakers have to cut taxes. Also, will they be forced to raise taxes regardless of the state of the economy? This action could have perverse effects if taxes are raised during a recession.

The purpose of these last paragraphs is to raise the possibility that fiscal policy is much more constrained now than it has been in the past. Luckily, fiscal policy provides just half the tool kit available to policymakers. As we will see in the next two chapters, the monetary system and monetary policy play an important role in giving fiscal policy room to work and reducing the effects of crowding-out.

Implementing Fiscal Policy

REVIEW

- Automatic stabilizers reduce the intensity of business fluctuations. When the economy is booming, tax revenues are rising, and unemployment compensation and welfare payments are falling, dampening the boom. When the economy enters a recession, tax revenues fall, and transfer payments rise, cushioning the decline. This happens automatically.
- Fiscal policymakers face data lags (the time it takes to collect, process, and provide data on the economy), recognition lags (the time required to see that a recession has in fact begun), and an implementation lag (the time required by Congress to decide on a policy, pass a law, and see it put in place).
- These lags can often result in government policy being mistimed. For example, expansionary policy taking effect when the economy is well into a recovery or failing to take effect when a recession is underway can make stabilization worse.
- Crowding-out occurs when the government runs a deficit and then sells bonds to finance the deficit. This drives interest rates up and reduces private investment. Lower investment now means reduced income and output in the future.

QUESTION

Unless the economy enters a deep recession, we rarely hear Congress discuss the budget in terms of fiscal policy; passing a spending and taxing package for macroeconomic purposes. Most of the discussion is on particular spending priorities for specific programs and bringing home projects for each politician's district. Has Congress essentially abandoned fiscal policy and left macroeconomic stabilization to the Federal Reserve and the setting of monetary policy?

Answers to the Checkpoint question can be found at the end of this chapter.

Chapter Summary

Fiscal Policy and Aggregate Demand

Governments try to influence aggregate demand by using fiscal policy. The government's main fiscal policy tools are spending on goods and services, transfer payments, and taxes.

Fiscal policy is powerful because of the multiplier effect. When aggregate spending increases by $1, the individuals or firms receiving this added dollar will spend part of it, saving the rest. Whatever part of the dollar is spent will be received by some other individual or firm, who will again spend part of the new earnings, saving the rest. This process continues until all the new spending has been exhausted. In this way, the initial $1 of spending can add considerably more aggregate output and income to the economy than just $1.

The multiplier tells us that added government spending will raise equilibrium income and output by the multiplier times the added spending and vice versa.

The exercise of discretionary fiscal policy involves changing government spending, transfer payments, or tax policies with the short-run goal of moving the economy toward full employment, encouraging economic growth, or controlling inflation.

When government fiscal policy is added to our model of the economy, equilibrium is achieved when government spending plus business investment (*injections*) into the economy equals saving plus taxes (*withdrawals*); thus, at equilibrium, G + I = S + T.

A change in government spending (G) will cause equilibrium income and output to rise or fall by the spending change times the multiplier. The effect of a change in taxes (T) on the economy is more complex. When taxes are increased, money is withdrawn from the economy's spending stream; when taxes are reduced, consumers and business have more to spend. Yet, a change in taxes will not change equilibrium income and output by the full change times the multiplier. People will put a part of a tax decrease into savings rather than spending it all. On the other hand, if there is a tax increase, people will "pay" for some of it by reducing savings.

Expansionary fiscal policies include increasing government spending; increasing transfer payments such as Social Security, unemployment compensation, and welfare payments; and decreasing taxes. These policies put more money into the hands of consumers and business. The opposite policies are contractionary, taking money out of the hands of consumers and business.

The multiplier will have its full effect when an economy is in depression. Price pressures are nil, and thus the effects of spending increases are multiplied throughout the economy, without being absorbed by higher prices. When the same economy begins to recover, its short-run aggregate supply curve will be positively sloped, and thus higher prices will absorb some of the effects of increased spending. When the economy reaches full employment, its long-run aggregate supply curve will be vertical. Spending increases will simply raise the price level without raising equilibrium income or output. When an economy moves beyond full employment, driving up wages and prices, an inflationary spiral sets in.

Exercising demand-side fiscal policy requires tradeoffs between output and price levels except when the economy is in a deep recession. Output can be increased, but only by raising the price level, or prices can be stabilized, but only by reducing output and increasing unemployment.

Fiscal Policy and Aggregate Supply

Supply-side policies do not require such tradeoffs; they can expand output without raising prices. Supply-side policies, however, take much longer to work than demand-side policies.

The goal of supply-side economics is to shift the long-run aggregate supply curve to the right, thereby expanding output without raising the price level, and perhaps even lowering prices. Some of the specific policies supply-side economists believe will help achieve this goal include reducing tax rates, encouraging investment in new capital equipment, encouraging investment in research and development, and ending burdensome regulations.

Economist Arthur Laffer has argued that high marginal tax rates discourage working. Lowering tax rates might increase tax revenues. Raising tax rates too high reduces tax revenues, because high marginal tax rates reduce the incentives to work and take risks.

Implementing Fiscal Policy

Without overt action by policymakers, tax revenues and transfer payments expand or contract in ways that help counteract the movements of the business cycle. These are called automatic stabilizers. When the economy is growing briskly, tax receipts rise and transfer payments sink, withdrawing spending from the economy. This decrease in spending acts as a brake to slow the growth of GDP, keeping the economy from overheating. When the economy goes into recession, the opposite occurs. Tax revenues decline and transfer payments rise. This increase pumps new funds into the economy, cushioning the impact of the downturn.

Using fiscal policy to smooth out the short-term business cycle is difficult because of several lags associated with implementing it. Most of the macroeconomic data policymakers need to enact fiscal policy is not available until 1 to 6 months after the fact; this is the data lag. And if recent data suggest an economic trend, it can take several quarters to confirm this trend; this is the recognition lag. Once lawmakers have recognized a need for action, it may require 18 to 24 months to plan, pass, and implement new economic policies; this is the implementation lag.

Consequently, by the time fiscal policy is enacted, the economy may well have moved to a different point in the business cycle, where the policy enacted could be detrimental.

The crowding-out effect arises when the government engages in deficit spending, thereby driving up interest rates. This action can reduce consumer spending on durable goods and business investment. Deficit spending has an expansionary effect on the economy, but this effect can be diminished by offsetting reductions in private spending.

Often, fiscal policy debates have little to do with the state of the macroeconomy. Underlying the rhetoric of the economic benefits or dangers of tax cuts, budget deficits, and specific spending priorities lies a long-standing philosophical debate about the proper size and role of government. The political left favors a larger and more active government, while the right argues for a more limited role for government.

Questions and Problems

1. A balanced budget amendment to the Constitution is introduced in Congress every so often. Congress would be required to balance the budget every year. What sort of problems would this introduce for policymakers and the economy? What would be the benefit of such an amendment?

2. At the beginning of the 2001 recession, Robert Dunn, writing in the August 19, 2001, issue of the *New York Times*, noted that, "An absurd debate is going on in Washington over who is to blame for the horrors of a declining federal budget surplus. The truth is that the fall in the surplus should be welcomed, given the current state of the economy, and politicians should be trying to take credit for it." Does Robert Dunn have it right? Why or why not?

3. In late 2004, economists Gregory Mankiw and Matthew Weinzierl, using dynamic scoring that accounts for the added economic growth from tax cuts on tax revenue, concluded that tax cuts can be partially self-financing. Roughly 17% of the cut in labor taxes and roughly half of the cuts in capital gains taxes are recouped through economic growth. Looking back to Figure 8 (the Laffer curve), is their study consistent with being at point *c* or point *a?*

4. The informal or underground economy operates off the books and typically for cash. Estimates of the underground economy in the United States are usually less than 10%. William Lewis, however, reports that half of Brazil's workers labor in the "informal" sector.[3] The Brazilian government represents nearly 40% of GDP, and corporations pay 85% of all taxes collected. Could lowering tax rates actually lead to higher tax revenues for the Brazilian government (a Laffer curve experiment)?

5. Explain why government spending gives a bigger boost to the economy than tax cuts.

6. Referring to the 2001 recession, an editorial in *The Economist* titled "Restoring the fiscal option" (January 17, 2002) argued that "In the United States, 9 months after the recession began, Republicans and Democrats are quarrelling over which ill-conceived measures to include in their stimulus package—as if to prove right those who say that fiscal expansion always come too late to be any use." Is that right? Is fiscal policy often too late to be helpful?

7. The macroeconomy has shown less variability in the last several decades—GDP has fluctuated, but less violently than in the past. Would the fact that nearly half of the federal budget goes to Social Security and Medicare have any impact on the variations in GDP? Why or why not?

8. Explain why increasing government purchases of goods and services is expansionary fiscal policy. Would increasing taxes or reducing transfer payments be contractionary or expansionary? Why?

9. One argument often heard against using fiscal policy to tame the business cycle is that the lags associated with getting a fiscal policy implemented are so long that when the program is finally passed and implemented, the business cycle has moved on to the next phase and the new program may not be

---

[3]William Lewis, *The Power of Productivity* (Chicago: University of Chicago Press), 2004.

necessary or even potentially destabilizing at that point. Does this argument seem reasonable? What counterarguments can you make in support of using fiscal policy?

10. As mandatory federal spending becomes increasingly a larger share of the budget, should we worry that the economic stabilization aspects of fiscal policy are becoming so limited as to be ineffective?

11. Individual income tax rates vary from zero (if your income is low enough) to 35% (for high-income individuals). Explain how this progressive tax structure acts as an automatic stabilizer for the economy.

12. Our current personal income tax system is progressive: Income tax rates rise with rising incomes and are lower for low-income individuals. Some policymakers often favor a "flat tax" as a replacement to our modestly progressive income tax system. Most exemptions and deductions would be eliminated, and a single low tax rate would be applied to personal income. Would such a change in the tax laws alter the automatic stabilization characteristics of the personal income tax?

13. In the 2000 presidential election, candidate Bush's platform included a promise to cut income taxes. The economy entered a recession just after he was elected in 2001. In early 2001, Congress passed a tax cut package that included tax rate reductions and $300–$600 rebates to all taxpayers. In general, was this an appropriate exercise of fiscal policy given that the economy was headed into a recession? Why?

14. Changes in tax rates affect both aggregate demand and aggregate supply. Explain why this is true.

15. During the late 1990s, the Clinton administration had very low deficits and actually ran 3 years of surpluses. As a result, interest rates were low and private investment was vibrant. When the government runs large deficits, as it has done since the early 2000s, interest rates inevitably rise, crowding out private investment. In the aggregate demand and supply model, spending is spending; income and output rise the same amount no matter whether the government spent on goods and services or business spent on investment. Why then are economists concerned with the crowding out of private investment?

Answers to Checkpoint Questions

CHECKPOINT: FISCAL POLICY AND AGGREGATE DEMAND

When tax rates are cut, the withholding tables are adjusted quickly and people see their take home pay increase. As a result, consumption rises, leading to increases in employment, income, and output.

CHECKPOINT: FISCAL POLICY AND AGGREGATE SUPPLY

In general President Kennedy's statement is consistent with the arguments of supply-siders who feel that any reduction in tax rates will yield higher revenues. When President Kennedy made his address, marginal tax rates were as high as 70%. Today, top marginal rates are 35% so it is less clear that rate reductions will lead to higher long-run revenues.

CHECKPOINT: IMPLEMENTING FISCAL POLICY

To some degree, Congress has left macroeconomic stabilization to monetary policy and the Federal Reserve, a subject left to the next few chapters. Congress mostly focuses on what programs and services are needed and funds those programs, generally ignoring macroeconomic conditions unless they are quite bad.

The Monetary System

11

*M*oney. Why are we so attached to money? Our dollar bills are simply pieces of paper with pictures of dead presidents (but not always: Hamilton is on the $10 bill, Franklin is on the $100 bill, and Salmon P. Chase is on the $10,000 bill) and printed with green ink. Yet, when the U.S. Treasury redesigned the $20 bill, how many of us could resist taking a good look at it? Even more, how many of us use old $20 bills and hold on to the new bills as long as we can? Why do we do this?— Old or new, they are worth the same.

How much are they worth? "Ay, there's the rub," as Hamlet said. These pieces of green paper are worth something because the government says they are "legal tender for all debts, public and private." You will find this phrase emblazoned on all U.S. dollar bills. It means you can take these green pieces of paper and use them to pay your debts—use your bills to pay your bills, in a manner of speaking.

These green pieces of paper are currency, just as coins are currency. Money is more than just currency. Think again about paying your bills. You probably do not gather together loads of dollar bills and then go to the gas company, electric company, telephone company, and bursar. Rather, you probably write a check. And most places accept checks, no questions asked; maybe an I.D. is required, but this says more about the possibility of fraud than the acceptability of checks in general. So checks serve the same function as currency, and thus are part of our definition of money, as you will see in a moment.

Money. In many ways, currency and checks are similar. We feel better when we have some of those green pieces of paper in our pockets. And we feel better when our checking account has a positive balance.

What may not be obvious is how governments can use money and monetary policy to manage the economy. We know in a general sense what governments can do—that is why we get apprehensive when government tampers with the currency. The specifics of what governments do are not so clear. It is now time to lift the veil and look at our monetary system.

In this chapter and the next, we will look at the roles money and monetary policy play in our economy. This chapter begins by considering the functions of money (it is not just used for buying goods and services), the definitions of money, and the process by which banks create money. The chapter then takes a first look at how the Federal Reserve System (often called *the Fed*) is organized and how it operates. The next chapter will then describe in greater detail the Fed's role in stabilizing the economy.

After studying this chapter you should be able to

- Describe the functions of money.
- Define the money supply, according to M1 and M2.
- Describe equilibrium in the money market.
- Describe the relationship between bonds and interest rates.
- Describe the functions of financial institutions and the money creation process.
- Describe the history and structure of the Federal Reserve System.
- List the Federal Reserve System's tools for conducting monetary policy.

What Is Money?

Money
Anything that is accepted in exchange for other goods and services or for the payment of debt.

Money is anything that is accepted in exchange for other goods and services or for the payment of debt. We are familiar with currency and coins; we use them every day. Over the ages, however, a wide variety of commodities has served as money—giant circular stones on the island of Yap, wampum (trinkets) among early Native Americans, and cigarettes in prisoner-of-war camps during World War II.

First, for a commodity to be used as money, its value must be easy to determine. Therefore, it must be easily standardized. Second, it must be divisible, so that people can make change. Third, money must be durable. It must be easy to carry (so much for the giant circular stones). Fourth, a commodity must be accepted by many people as money if it is to act as money. Money is so important that nearly every society has invented some form of money for its use. We begin our examination of money by looking at its functions.

The Functions of Money

Money has three primary functions in our economic system: as a medium of exchange, as a measure of value (unit of account), and as a store of value. These uses make money unique among commodities.

Medium of Exchange

Let us start with a primitive economy. There is no money. To survive, you have to produce everything yourself: food, clothing, housing. It is a fact that few of us can do all of these tasks equally well. Each one of us is better off specializing, providing those goods and services with which we are more efficient. Say I specialize in dairy products, and you specialize in blacksmithing. We can engage in **barter,** which is the direct exchange of goods and services. I can give you gallons of milk if you make me a pot for cooking. A *double coincidence of wants* occurs if, in a barter economy, I find someone who not only has something I want, but who also wants something I have. What happens if you, the blacksmith, are willing to make the cooking pot for me, but want clothing in return? Then I have to search out someone who is willing to give me clothing in exchange for my milk; I will then give you the clothing in exchange for the cooking pot. You can see that this system quickly becomes complicated. This is why barter is restricted to primitive economies.

Consider what happens when money is introduced. Everyone can spend their time producing goods and services, rather than running around trying to match up exchanges. Everyone can sell their products for money, then use this money to buy cooking pots, clothing, or whatever else they want. Thus, money's first and most important function is as a **medium of exchange**. Without money, economies remain primitive.

Unit of Account

Imagine the difficulties consumers would have in a barter economy in which every item were valued in terms of the other products offered—12 eggs were worth 1 shirt, 1 shirt equaled 3 gallons of gas, and so forth. A 10-product economy of this sort, assigning every product a value for every other product, would require 45 different prices. A 100-good economy would require 4,950 prices.[1] This is another reason why only the most primitive economies use barter.

Once again, money is able to solve a problem inherent in the barter economy. It reduces the number of prices consumers need to know to the number of products on the market; a 100-good economy will have 100 prices. Thus, money is a **unit of account**, or a measure of value. Dollar-prices give us a yardstick for measuring and comparing the values of a wide variety of goods and services.

Admittedly, ascribing a dollar-value to some things, such as human life, love, and clean air, can be difficult. Still, courts, businesses, and government agencies manage to do so every day. For example, if someone dies and the court determines this death was due to negligence, the court tries to determine the value of the life to the person's survivors—not a pleasant task, but one that has to be undertaken. Without a monetary standard, such valuations would be not just difficult, but impossible.

Store of Value

Using cherry tomatoes as a medium of exchange and unit of account might be handy, except that they have the bad habit of rotting. Money lasts, enabling people to save the money they earn today and use it to buy the goods and services they want tomorrow. Thus, money is a **store of value**. It is true that money is not unique in preserving its value. Many other commodities, including stocks, bonds, real estate, and jewelry are used to store wealth for future purchases. Indeed, some of these assets may rise in value, so they might be preferred to money as a store of value. Why, then, use money as a store of wealth at all?

The answer is that every other type of asset must be converted into money if it is to be spent or used to pay debts. Converting other assets into cash involves transaction costs, and for some assets, these costs are significant. An asset's **liquidity** is determined by how quickly, easily, and reliably it can be converted into cash.

Money is the most liquid asset because, as the medium of exchange, it requires no conversion. Stocks and bonds are also liquid, but they do require some time and often a commission fee to convert into cash. Recently, many investors found out that markets can and often do fluctuate, causing the real value of these assets to

---

Barter
The direct exchange of goods and services for other goods and services.

Medium of exchange
Money is a medium of exchange because goods and services are sold for money, then the money is used to purchase other goods and services.

Unit of account
Money provides a yardstick for measuring and comparing the values of a wide variety of goods and services. It eliminates the problem of double coincidence of wants associated with barter.

Store of value
The function that enables people to save the money they earn today and use it to buy the goods and services they want tomorrow.

Liquidity
How quickly, easily, and reliably an asset can be converted into cash.

---

[1]The formula for determining the number of prices needed when N goods are in an economy is $[N(N − 1)]/2$. Thus for 10 goods the result is $[10(10 − 1)]/2 = 90/2 = 45$.

be uncertain. Real estate requires considerable time to liquidate, with transaction costs that often approach 10% of a property's value. Household clutter once had no market value, but eBay has turned it into a more liquid asset.

Money differs from many other commodities in that its value does not deteriorate in the absence of inflation. When price levels do rise, however, the value of money will fall: If prices double, the value of money is cut in half. In times of inflation, most people will be unwilling to hold much of their wealth in money. If hyperinflation hits, money will quickly become worthless as the economy reverts to barter.

Money, then, is crucial for a well-functioning modern economy. All of its three primary functions are important: medium of exchange, unit of account, and store of value.

Defining the Money Supply

How much money is there in the U.S. economy? One of the tasks assigned to the Federal Reserve System is that of measuring our money supply. The Fed has developed several different measures of monetary aggregates, which it continually updates to reflect the innovative new financial instruments our financial system is constantly developing. The monetary aggregates the Fed uses most frequently are M1, the narrowest measure of money, and M2, a broader measure.

Up until March 2006, the Fed published another monetary aggregate called M3, which included M2 plus large denomination time deposits and other large deposits. The Fed indicated that it quit publication of M3 data because

> *M3 does not appear to convey any additional information about economic activity that is not already embodied in M2 and has not played a role in the monetary policy process for many years. Consequently, the Board judged that the costs of collecting the underlying data and publishing M3 outweigh the benefits.*

More specifically, the Fed defines M1 and M2 as follows:

M1 equals Currency
    + Travelers checks
    + Demand deposits
    + Other checkable deposits

M2 equals M1
    + Savings deposits
    + Money market deposit accounts
    + Small-denomination (less than $100,000) time deposits
    + Shares in retail money market mutual funds net of retirement accounts

M1
The narrowest definition of money; includes currency (coins and paper money), demand deposits (checks), and other accounts that have check-writing or debit capabilities, such as stock market and money market accounts.

M2
A broader definition of money that includes "near monies" that are not as liquid as cash, including deposits in savings accounts, money market accounts, and money market mutual fund accounts.

Narrowly Defined Money: M1

Since money is used mainly as a medium of exchange, when defined most narrowly, it includes currency (coins and paper money), demand deposits (checks), and other accounts that have check-writing or debit capabilities, such as stock market accounts. Currency represents roughly half of M1, with paper money constituting over 90% of currency; coins form only a small part of M1. Checking and other debit accounts represent the other half of the money supply, narrowly defined. Currently, M1 is equal to roughly $1.4 trillion. It is the most liquid part of the money supply.

Checking accounts can be opened at commercial banks and at a variety of other thrift institutions, including savings and loan institutions, mutual savings banks, and credit unions. Also, some brokerage houses offer checking services on brokerage accounts.

A Broader Definition: M2

A broader definition of money, M2, includes the "near monies"; money that cannot be drawn on instantaneously but is nonetheless accessible. This includes deposits in savings accounts, money market deposit accounts, and money market mutual fund accounts. Many of these accounts have check-writing features similar to demand deposits.

Certificates of deposits (CDs) and other small-denomination time deposits can usually be cashed in at any time, though they often carry heavy penalties for early liquidation. Thus, M2 includes the highly liquid assets in M1 and a variety of accounts that are less liquid, but still easy and inexpensive to access. This broader definition of money brings the current money supply up to nearly $7 trillion.

When economists speak of "the money supply," they are usually referring to M1, the narrowest definition. Even so, the other measure is sometimes used. For example, the index of leading economic indicators, for instance, uses M2, adjusted for inflation, to gauge the state of the economy. For the remainder of this book, the money supply will be considered to be M1 unless otherwise specified.

Where Did All the One-Dollar Coins Go?

When is the last time you got a Sacagawea or Susan B. Anthony dollar as change for some purchase?[2] For most of us the answer approaches never. Why don't dollar coins circulate in the United States?

The benefits to a dollar coin are clear: Coins last much longer than dollar bills, which tend to deteriorate within 18 months. Annual savings of coins over dollar bills run to a half billion dollars a year. This is why the Treasury has tried twice recently to introduce one-dollar coins. Production costs are higher, but coins circulate longer than bills, making total costs less for coins.

Introducing dollar coins faces a few serious hurdles. First, several industries will incur added costs. For example, banks will have additional costs to sort, store, and wrap the coins; and vending machines will have to be altered to accept the new coins. The coins cannot be too big, or the public will reject them as too heavy; this was the problem with the Kennedy half-dollar and the silver dollars of the past. But a small dollar, roughly the size of a quarter, generates confusion—is it a dollar or a quarter?—and again has been rejected by the public.

Other countries have successfully introduced dollar coins: Canada has $1 and $2 coins, and Britain has one- and two-pound coins. All are circulated widely. What do we need to do to launch a successful $1 coin in the United States?

After reviewing the experiences of other countries, the General Accounting Office (GAO) concluded that the successful introduction of a $1 coin would require that the government develop a substantial awareness campaign (a heavy, extended advertising campaign) to overcome initial public resistance. Second, the Treasury would have to mint sufficient coins for acceptance by the public. And third, and probably most important, the $1 bill would have to be eliminated. A key element in the general acceptance of the dollar coins in Canada was that the populace had no choice: The $1 bill was removed from circulation at the same time the dollar coins were introduced.

This being the case, one can ask why, did the Treasury try once again in 2007 to launch a dollar coin without removing the paper dollar from circulation? These $1 coins were based on the popularity of the state quarters program, in which each year five state quarters were released for general circulation. The new $1 coins released in 2007 started with an image of George Washington and eventually will contain images of all of the presidents. But these are more collector's items than

[2]See Sebastien Lotz and Guillaume Rocheteau, "The Fate of One-Dollar Coins in the U.S.," *Economic Commentary*, Federal Reserve Bank of Cleveland, October 15, 2004.

general issue—hence the continuance of the paper dollar bill. Could these eventually replace the paper dollar bill?

Given the potential annual savings, we will undoubtedly see further attempts at introducing a $1 coin in the United States in the near future until this coin is generally accepted.

What Is Money?

REVIEW

- Money is anything accepted in exchange for other goods and services and for the payment of debts.
- The functions of money include a medium of exchange, a unit of account, and a store of value.
- *Liquidity* refers to how quickly, easily, and reliably an asset can be converted to cash.
- M1 is currency plus demand deposits plus other checkable deposits.
- M2 is equal to M1 plus savings deposits plus other savings-like deposits.

QUESTIONS

Gresham's law says that bad money drives good money out of the marketplace. One example was the 1965 U.S. Coinage Act, which replaced silver quarters with "sandwich" coins made of a cheaper silver-nickel alloy. The pre-1965 quarters quickly vanished from circulation. Where did all the pre-1965 silver quarters go? Is Gresham's law much of a problem in today's economy with paper money and credit cards?

Answers to the Checkpoint questions can be found at the end of this chapter.

Money: Demand and Supply

Now that we have examined what money is and does, and how much money is available in the U.S. financial system, we will go on to look at the demand for money. We will then look at how banks can decrease or increase the supply of money.

The Market for Money and Bonds

We will consider the demand for money by focusing on the market for money and bonds. These markets are interrelated in complex ways.

The Demand for Money

The demand for money refers to the desire of individuals and firms to hold money as part of their asset portfolios. A complete personal portfolio of assets might include money, stocks, bonds, real estate, and other assets. Economists have identified three motives (demands) for holding money: a transactions demand, a liquidity or precautionary demand, and a speculative demand.

Because money is a medium of exchange, it is needed for buying and selling goods and services. So, individuals and firms need to hold a certain part of their wealth in money to be able to perform commercial transactions; this is the **transactions demand for money**. Individuals and firms, moreover, keep some of their

Transactions demand for money
That part of individual wealth held in money to perform commercial transactions (medium of exchange demand).

assets in money so they will be prepared for the unexpected—a car breaking down, an industrial accident, or a surge in business that requires input purchases on short notice. To some extent, credit cards have replaced cash balances as a means of preparing for the unexpected, thus dampening this liquidity, or the **precautionary demand for money**. Finally, some of most portfolios will be in money because other assets are risky. As long as inflation is not rampant, holding money for a short period is virtually risk free. This gives rise to the **speculative demand for money**.

Although the transactions and precautionary demands for money usually result in a constant portion of assets held as money, the speculative demand for money varies, and it is inversely related to the market interest rate. Holding assets in money has an opportunity cost: forgone interest. The higher interest rates go, the less money most people will want to hold, because the opportunity cost of not investing this money elsewhere is higher. Panel A of Figure 1 shows the demand for money as D_M. Clearly, as interest rates rise, the demand for money sinks, and vice versa. At interest rate i_e, a larger quantity of money is demanded than at the higher interest rate i_1.

Precautionary demand for money
That part of individual wealth held in money to handle unexpected events and expenses.

Speculative demand for money
When inflation is not a problem, holding money for a short period is virtually risk free, whereas holding other assets is more risky. The speculative demand for money varies inversely with interest rates since they are the opportunity costs of holding money in a portfolio.

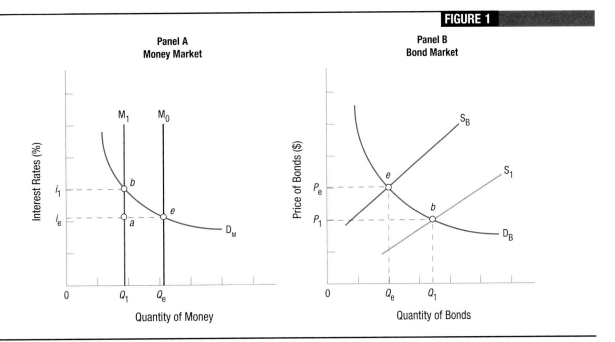

FIGURE 1

Money Supply, Bond Prices, and Interest Rates

Panel A shows the demand for money D_M; as interest rates rise, less money is demanded, and vice versa. The Fed initially sets the money supply at M_0. The market is in equilibrium at point *e*, with an equilibrium interest rate of i_e. Panel B shows the bond market. It is also initially in equilibrium at point *e*. Assume now that the Fed reduces the supply of money in the market, shifting the quantity of money to M_1 in Panel A. There is now a shortage of money in the market ($e - a$): people want to hold more money in their portfolios than is available and they will offer more of the bonds they hold for sale to generate cash. Panel B shows this increase in the supply of bonds as a rightward shift in the supply of bonds curve, to S_1. As a result, the price of bonds falls to P_1, and interest rates rise to i_1, where both markets are in equilibrium.

Equilibrium in the Money Market

By showing the money market in Panel A and the bond market in Panel B, Figure 1 shows how these two markets are interwoven. To examine this interaction, let us first assume in Panel A that the Fed has set the money supply at M_0. This puts the market into equilibrium at point *e*, with an equilibrium interest rate of i_e. The question of how the Fed determines the money supply will be put off until later in the chapter.

The bond market in Panel B begins in equilibrium at point e with quantity Q_e of bonds being sold at price P_e. The supply and demand for bonds operates like the supply and demand for anything else; as the price of bonds falls, a greater number are demanded, and if the price of bonds rises, more are offered for sale.

Assume the Fed decides to reduce the supply of money in the economy, shifting the quantity of money to M_1 in Panel A. Initially, there is a shortage of money in the market of $(e - a)$, since individuals and the money managers of large institutions want to hold more money in their portfolios than is available. Both groups will start offering more of the bonds they hold for sale to generate cash. Panel B shows this increase in the supply of bonds as a rightward shift in the supply of bonds curve, to S_1. The price of bonds falls to P_1, while the interest rate rises to i_1. At this new interest rate, people will want to hold money equal to Q_1—less than before—thus restoring the money market to equilibrium.

Note that an increase in the money supply would produce the opposite result, causing interest rates to fall. At this point, you may be wondering why interest rates rise when bond prices fall, and vice versa. Let us look more closely at why this is the case.

Bond Prices and Interest Rates

To see why bond prices and interest rates are inversely related, we need to analyze bond contracts more closely. A bond is a contract between a seller (the company issuing the bond) and a buyer that determines the following items:

- Coupon rate of the bond
- Maturity date of the bond
- Face value of the bond

The seller agrees to pay the buyer a fixed rate of interest (the coupon rate) on the face value of the bond (usually $1,000) until a future fixed date (the maturity date of the bond). So, if XYZ Company issues a bond with a face value of $1,000 at a coupon rate of 5%, it agrees to pay the bondholder $50 a year until the maturity date of the bond. Note that this $50 payment a year is fixed for the life of the bond.

Once a bond is issued, it is subject to the forces of the marketplace. As economic circumstances change, people may be willing to pay more or less for a bond originally sold for $1,000. The *yield* on a bond is the percentage return earned over the life of the bond. Yields change when bond prices change.

Assume, for instance, that when a $1,000 bond is issued, general interest rates are 5%, so that the bond yields an annual interest payment of $50. For simplicity, let's assume that the bond is a perpetuity bond, that is, the bond has no maturity date. The issuer of the bond has agreed to pay $50 a year *forever* for the use of this money.

Assume that market interest rates rise to 8%. Just how much would the typical investor now be willing to pay for a bond that returns $50 a year? We can approach this intuitively. If we can buy a $1,000 bond now that pays $80 per year, why would we pay $1,000 for a similar bond that pays only $50? Would we pay more or less for the $50-paying bond? Intuitively, if we can get an $80-paying bond for $1,000, we would pay *less* for a $50-paying bond.

There is a simple formula we can use:

$$\text{Yield} = \text{Interest Payment} \div \text{Price of Bond}$$

Or rearranging terms,

$$\text{Price of Bond} = \text{Interest Payment} \div \text{Yield}$$

The new price of the bond will be $625 ($50 ÷ .08 = $625). Clearly, as market interest rates go up, the price of this bond falls. Conversely, if interest rates were to fall, say, from 5% to 3%, the price of the bond would rise to $1,666.67 ($50 ÷ .03 = $1,666.67).

Let's summarize this important relationship between the bond market and interest rates. Returning to Figure 1, when the Federal Reserve decided to reduce the money supply, an initial shortage of money caused individuals and institutions to want more money in their portfolios. The supply of bonds rose in Panel B, causing the price of bonds to fall, and causing interest rates to rise in Panel A. When bond prices fall (rise), their interest rate will rise (fall).

When you are confronted with money and bond market issues in the following chapters, keep this simple analysis in the back of your mind. It will help you keep these issues straight when the analysis gets more complex.

What is important to remember here? We saw that there are three basic demands for money: a transactions demand, a precautionary demand, and a speculative demand. The transactions and precautionary demands are fairly stable, while the speculative demand is dependent on the interest rate. When the demand for money rises, individuals and business tend to satisfy this demand first by selling bonds for cash. So we can say that an increase in the demand for money can be actualized through the bond market. And the price of bonds is inversely related to the interest rate.

How Banks Create Money

Having considered the demand for money and how it relates to the bond market, let us look at the supply of money. How can financial institutions affect the money supply? They can do this by creating money.

The role banks and money play in our economy has a long history. Banks are essential for an economy to expand beyond the constraints of the barter system. The primary purpose of financial markets and institutions is to act as conduits for transferring funds from lenders to borrowers. By accepting deposits and making loans, however, banks and other financial institutions are also able to create money. Let us see how this happens.

Functions of Financial Institutions

Banks and other financial institutions offer consumers and businesses many services, including checking and savings accounts, ATM services, loans, estate management services, and safe deposit boxes. The most important of these is checking services, also known as *demand deposits,* since checking account balances are "due on demand."

As we have seen, money supply M1 includes currency and demand deposits, and other checkable deposits. This money supply splits roughly evenly between currency and checkable deposits. These checkable deposits are what allow banks and other financial institutions to create money through the issuance of loans. The whole process works because of a fractional reserve system.

Fractional Reserve System

Most of M1 is used for transactions purposes. A bank takes our deposits, say, when we get a paycheck, then disburses these funds to sellers as we write checks for various goods and services.

Banks loan money for consumer purchases and business investments. Assume you deposit $1,000 into your checking account, and the bank then loans this $1,000 to a local business to purchase some machinery. If you were to go to the bank the next day and ask to withdraw your funds, how would the bank pay you? The bank could not pay you if you were its only customer. Banks, however, have many customers, and the chance of all these customers wanting to withdraw their money on a given day is small. Such "runs on the bank" are rare, normally occurring only when banks or a country's currency are in trouble; the run by depositors on the Northern Rock Bank in Britain in late 2007 is one recent example.

Fractional reserve banking system
To prevent bank runs (all depositors demanding their deposits in cash at the same time), a portion of bank deposits must be held as vault cash, or else in an account with the regional Federal Reserve Bank.

It was the possibility of bank runs that led to the **fractional reserve banking system**. When someone deposits money into a bank account, the bank is required to hold a part of this deposit in its vault as cash, or else in an account with the regional Federal Reserve Bank. We will learn more about the Federal Reserve System at the end of this chapter, but for the moment, let us continue to concentrate on how fractional reserve banking permits banks to create money.

The Money Creation Process

Banks create money by lending their excess reserves. When money is loaned out, it eventually is deposited back into the original bank or some other bank. The bank will again hold some of these new deposits as reserves, loaning out the rest. The whole process continues until the entire initial deposit is held as reserves somewhere in the banking system.

To illustrate this process of money creation, we will use a stylized bank balance sheet that ignores the capital requirements necessary to open a bank. Under these simplified conditions, a bank balance sheet reads as follows:

Assets	Liabilities
Reserves	Deposits
Loans	

Liabilities are shown on the right side of the balance sheet. When you deposit money into the bank, it becomes a liability for the bank—the bank owes you money. Specifically, the bank is obliged to give you the deposited money on demand. To balance out this liability, however, the bank now has an asset consisting of the funds from your deposit. Assets are shown on the left side of the balance sheet. In our simple banking world, the bank can either put your funds into reserves or loan out part of this money to business or consumers. These loans become assets of the bank, since borrowers have an obligation to pay the bank back.

Assume that the Federal Reserve sets the reserve requirement at 20%. So, by law, banks must hold 20% of each deposit as reserves, whether in their vaults or in accounts with the regional Federal Reserve Bank. Now assume that you dig $1,000 out of your mattress at home and take it to Bank A. This bank puts 20% of your $1,000 into its vault and loans out the rest. Its balance sheet now reads:

Bank A	
Assets	**Liabilities**
Reserves = $200	Deposits = $1,000
Loans = $800	

As the balance sheet indicates, your $1,000 deposit is now a liability for Bank A. But the bank also has new assets, split between reserves and loans in the 20:80 ratio required by the Fed. (In each of the transactions that follow, we will assume banks become fully *loaned-up,* loaning out all they can and keeping in reserves just the amount required by law.)

Assuming that Bank A loans out the $800 it has in excess funds to a local gas station, this money will be deposited into Bank B. Bank B's balance sheet now reads:

Bank B	
Assets	**Liabilities**
Reserves = $160	Deposits = $800
Loans = $640	

Bank B, in other words, has new deposits totaling $800. Of this, the bank must put $160 into reserves; the remaining $640 it loans out to a local winery. The winery deposits these funds into its bank, Bank C. This bank's balance sheet shows:

Bank C	
Assets	**Liabilities**
Reserves = $128	Deposits = $640
Loans = $512	

This process continues until the entire $1,000 of the original deposit has been placed in reserves, thus raising total reserves by $1,000. By this point, all the banks together will have loaned out a total of $4,000. A summary balance sheet for all banks in the area reads:

All Banks	
Assets	**Liabilities**
Reserves = $1,000	Deposits = $5,000
Loans = $4,000	

Notice what has happened. Keeping in mind that demand deposits form part of the money supply, your original deposit of $1,000—new money injected into the banking system—has ended up increasing the money supply by $5,000. Bank reserves, in other words, have gone up by your initial deposit, but beyond this, an added $4,000 has been created. And this could happen because banks were allowed to loan a part of your deposit to consumers and business.

The Money Multiplier

We have just seen how banks create new money when they accept deposits. The **money multiplier** measures the potential or maximum amount the money supply can increase (or decrease) when new deposits enter (exit) the system. The money multiplier is defined as:

$$\text{Money Multiplier} = 1 \div \text{Reserve Requirement}$$

Thus, if the reserve requirement is 20%, as in our example, the money multiplier is $1/.20 = 5$. And so an initial deposit of $1,000 ends up creating $5,000 in money.

Notice that this formula gives us the *potential* money multiplier. The actual money multiplier will be less because of leakages from the system. For one thing, not all the money loaned out will be deposited back into banking accounts. Some people and businesses will want to keep some of their loans in cash for transactions purposes. This action diminishes their deposits, thus reducing the actual multiplier.

Similarly, banks will not always want to be loaned-up. At times, they may choose to keep some excess reserves, or reserves above the legally required amount. Again, this action will reduce the actual money multiplier, since issuing smaller loans recirculates less money back through the larger system.

Now that we have an idea of what determines the demand for money and how banks influence the supply of money because they can create money, let us turn to a brief survey of the Federal Reserve System. We will consider how it is organized, what purposes it serves, and what functions it has; the next chapter will take a closer look at the Fed in action.

Money multiplier
Measures the potential or maximum amount the money supply can increase (or decrease) when new deposits enter (exit) the system and is defined as: 1 ÷ reserve requirement. The actual money multiplier will be less since some banks will hold excess reserves.

Checkpoint

Money: Demand and Supply

REVIEW

- The demand for money consists of demand for transactions purposes, for liquidity or precautionary purposes, and for speculative purposes.
- The demand for money has a negative slope and the quantity demanded varies inversely with the interest rate. Higher interest rates represent a higher opportunity cost of holding money, hence we demand less money.
- Bond prices and interest rates are inversely related.
- The fractional reserve system permits banks to create money through their ability to accept deposits and make loans.
- The potential money multiplier is equal to 1 ÷ reserve requirement. This is the maximum value for the multiplier. The actual money multiplier is less, because some banks hold excess reserves, and not all of the funds from loans are deposited in the banking system.

QUESTIONS

If the Federal Reserve did not have any reserve requirements for member banks, would those banks hold zero reserves? Why or why not?

Answers to the Checkpoint questions can be found at the end of this chapter.

The Federal Reserve System

Federal Reserve System
The central bank of the United States.

The **Federal Reserve System** is the central bank of the United States. Early in the history of the United States, banks were private and chartered by the states. In the 1800s and early 1900s, bank panics were common. After an unusually severe banking crisis in 1907, Congress established the National Monetary Commission. This commission proposed one central bank with sweeping powers. But a powerful national bank became a political issue in the elections of 1912, and the commission's proposals gave way to a compromise that is today's Federal Reserve System.

The Federal Reserve Act of 1913 was a compromise between competing proposals for a huge central bank and for no central bank at all. The act declared that the Fed is "to provide for the establishment of Federal Reserve Banks, to furnish an elastic currency, to afford means of rediscounting commercial paper, to establish a more effective supervision of banking in the United States, and for other purposes."

Since 1913, other acts have further clarified and supplemented the original act, expanding the Fed's mission. These acts include the Employment Act of 1946, the International Banking Act of 1978, the Full Employment and Balanced Growth Act of 1978, the Depository Institutions Deregulation and Monetary Control Act of 1980, and the Federal Deposit Insurance Corporation Improvement Act of 1991.

The original Federal Reserve Act, the Employment Act of 1946, and the Full Employment and Balanced Growth Act of 1978 all mandate national economic objectives. These acts require the Fed to promote economic growth accompanied by full employment, stable prices, and moderate long-term interest rates. As we will see in the next chapter, meeting all of these objectives at once has often proved to be difficult, if not downright impossible.

The Federal Reserve is considered to be an independent central bank, in that its actions are not subject to executive branch control. The entire Federal Reserve

System is, however, subject to oversight from Congress. The Constitution invests Congress with the power to coin money and set its value, so the Federal Reserve Act delegated this power to the Fed, as subject to congressional oversight. Though several presidents have disagreed with Fed policy over the years, the Fed has always managed to maintain its independence from the executive branch.

Experience in this country and abroad suggests that independent central banks are better at fighting inflation than are politically controlled banks. The main reason for this, in the words of the Council of Economic Advisors, "is that an independent central bank is less vulnerable to short-term political pressures to inflate than are those with closer links to the government. During recessions, governments may try to rely on too much expansionary monetary policy to hasten a recovery."[3]

The Structure of the Federal Reserve

As noted earlier, the Federal Reserve System was a compromise between competing proposals for a massive central bank and no central bank at all. What Congress finally settled on were *regional* banks governed by a central authority. The intent was to provide the Fed with a broad perspective on the economy, with the regional Federal Reserve Banks contributing economic analysis from all parts of the nation, while still investing a central authority with the power to carry out a national monetary policy.

The Fed is composed of a central governing agency, the Board of Governors, located in Washington, D.C., and 12 regional Federal Reserve Banks in major cities around the nation. Figure 2 shows the 12 Fed districts and their bank locations.

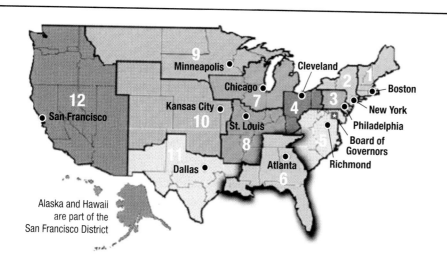

FIGURE 2

Regional Federal Reserve Districts

This figure shows the 12 regional Federal Reserve districts and their bank locations.

The Board of Governors

The Fed's Board of Governors consists of seven members who are appointed by the president and confirmed by the Senate. Board members serve terms of 14 years, after which they cannot be reappointed. Appointments to the Board are staggered so that one term expires on January 31 of every even-numbered year. The current chairman, Ben Bernanke, and the vice chairman of the Board must already be Board members; they are appointed to their leadership positions by the president, subject to Senate confirmation, for terms of 4 years. The Board of Governors staff of nearly two thousand people helps the Fed carry out its responsibilities for monetary policy, banking, and consumer credit regulation.

---

[3]*Economic Report of the President* (Washington D.C., U.S. Government Printing Office), 1993, p. 97.

Alan Greenspan

*a*lan Greenspan was first appointed chairman of the Federal Reserve Board in 1987. Greenspan shepherded the U.S. economy through good times and bad, weathering terrorist attacks and international financial crises and presiding over some of the lowest levels of unemployment and inflation in decades.

An inflation fighter by instinct, Greenspan also showed flexibility in his implementation of monetary policy, defying the conventional wisdom that a rapidly growing economy with low employment necessarily leads to high inflation. By allowing unemployment levels to drop, Greenspan helped make it possible for middle- and low-income workers to enjoy a greater share of the benefits of a buoyant American economy.

Business Week once dubbed Greenspan the "quintessential New Economist." During the Clinton years, he was a leading proponent of the view that the information age had changed the structure of the American economy. Although a conservative, he believed that productivity gains would allow the economy to grow faster than before without triggering inflation.

When the journalist Bob Woodward wrote a glowing biography of Greenspan, the title of the book was *Maestro,* a probable reference to Greenspan's masterly orchestration of monetary policy and his ability to find evidence of productivity gains in the economy that other economists overlooked. The technology bust of 2000, however, took some of the luster off of Greenspan's reputation. Some critics think Greenspan should have acted decisively to prevent the stock market bubble of the 1990s from growing beyond the bursting point. Greenspan argued that raising interest rates to depress the "irrational exuberance" of investors might have led to a worse economic crisis.

The performance of the economy in coming years will provide an important perspective on Greenspan's legacy and could influence the future path of Fed policy. If the economy recovers strongly, it may validate Greenspan's belief that improvements in data collection and processing information have made it possible for the Fed to make corrections more quickly and smoothly than in the past. Whatever the future holds, Greenspan, whose tenure ended in January 2006, was Fed chairman during stock market crashes, international financial crises, the boom of the Reagan recovery, the boom years of the 1990s, and the aftermath of 9/11. He has left an indelible imprint on the office of the chairman of the Federal Reserve Board.

Federal Reserve Banks

Twelve Federal Reserve Banks and their branches perform a variety of functions, including providing a nationwide payments system, distributing coins and currency, regulating and supervising member banks, and serving as the banker for the United States Treasury. Table 1 lists all regional banks and their branches. Each regional bank has a number and letter associated with it. If you look at the money in your wallet, you will see that all U.S. currency bears the designation of the regional bank where it was first issued, as shown in Table 1.

Table 1	Federal Reserve Regional Banks	

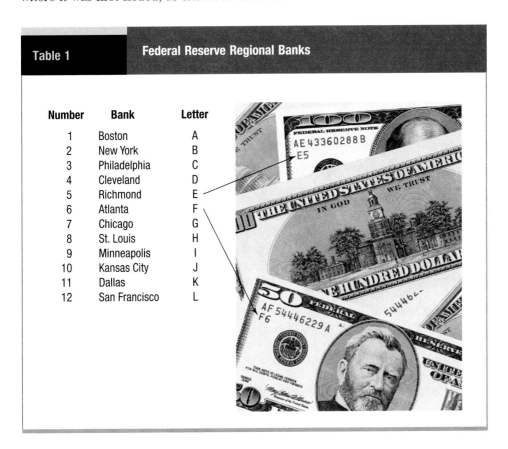

Number	Bank	Letter
1	Boston	A
2	New York	B
3	Philadelphia	C
4	Cleveland	D
5	Richmond	E
6	Atlanta	F
7	Chicago	G
8	St. Louis	H
9	Minneapolis	I
10	Kansas City	J
11	Dallas	K
12	San Francisco	L

Each regional bank also provides the Federal Reserve System and the Board of Governors with information on economic conditions in its home region. This information is compiled into a report detailing the economic conditions around the country—the *Beige Book,* as it is called. This report is provided to the Board a few weeks before policy decisions are required; later it is released to the public. The Board and the Federal Open Market Committee (FOMC) use the information in the *Beige Book* to determine the course of the nation's monetary policy.

Federal Open Market Committee (FOMC)

The **Federal Open Market Committee** (FOMC) oversees open market operations, the main tool of monetary policy. Open market operations involve buying and selling government securities. How these open market operations influence reserves available to banks and other thrift institutions will become clear at the end of this chapter and in the next chapter.

The FOMC is composed of the seven members of the Board of Governors and five of the regional Reserve Bank presidents. The president of the Federal Reserve Bank of New York is a permanent member. The other four members are represented for rotating 1-year terms by the other regional bank presidents. All regional presidents participate in FOMC deliberations, but only those serving on the committee

Federal Open Market Committee
This 12-member committee is composed of members of the Board of Governors of the Fed and selected presidents of the regional Federal Reserve Banks; it oversees open market operations (the buying and selling of government securities), the main tool of monetary policy.

can vote. Traditionally, the chairman of the Board of Governors has also served as the chairman of the FOMC.

The Tools of the Federal Reserve

The Federal Reserve has three primary tools at its disposal for conducting monetary policy:

- **Reserve Requirements**—The required ratio of funds that commercial banks and other depository institutions must hold in reserve against deposits.
- The **Discount Rate**—The interest rate the Federal Reserve charges commercial banks and other depository institutions to borrow reserves from a regional Federal Reserve Bank.
- **Open Market Operations**—The buying and selling on the open market of U.S. government securities, usually treasury bonds, to adjust reserves in the banking system.

Reserve Requirements

The Federal Reserve Act specifies that the Fed must establish a reserve requirement for all banks and other depository institutions. As we have seen, this law gives rise to a fractional reserve system that enables banks to create new money, expanding demand deposits through loans. The potential expansion depends on the money multiplier, which in turn depends on the reserve requirement ratio. By altering the reserve ratio, the Fed can alter reserves in the system and alter the supply of money in the economy.

Remember that banks hold two types of reserves: required reserves and excess reserves. Roughly 15,000 depository institutions, ranging from banks to thrift institutions, are bound by the Fed's reserve requirements. Reserves are kept as vault cash or in accounts with the regional Federal Reserve Bank. These accounts not only help satisfy reserve requirements but are also used to clear many financial transactions.

Banks are assessed a penalty if their accounts with the Fed are overdrawn at the end of the day. Given the unpredictability of the volume of transactions that may clear a bank's account on a given day, most banks choose to maintain excess reserves. Interest earned on these excess reserves is then used to pay the cost of Fed services, such as check clearing.

At the end of the day, banks and other depository institutions can loan one another reserves or trade reserves in the Federal Funds Market. One bank's surplus of reserves can become loans to another institution, earning interest (the federal funds rate). A change in the federal funds rate reflects changes in the market demand and supply of excess reserves. This rate is often viewed as a gauge of the prevailing monetary policy's tightness.

When banks hold excess reserves, they reduce the actual money multiplier. By raising or lowering the reserve ratio, the Fed can add reserves to the system or squeeze reserves from it, thereby altering the supply of money. Yet, changing the reserve requirement is almost like doing surgery with a bread knife. The impact of changing the reserve requirement is so massive and imprecise that the Fed rarely uses this tool.

When the Fed does resort to changing the reserve requirement, moreover, it usually does so to accomplish other, non-monetary-policy objectives. Economists Hein and Stewart studied the Fed's reserve requirement reductions in 1992 and concluded that the Fed acted "to ease the credit crunch of that time and improve the profitability of depository institutions without expanding the money supply or lowering interest rates."[4]

Reserve requirements
The required ratio of funds that commercial banks and other depository institutions must hold in reserve against deposits.

Discount rate
The interest rate the Federal Reserve charges commercial banks and other depository institutions to borrow reserves from a regional Federal Reserve Bank.

Open market operations
The buying and selling of U.S. government securities, usually treasury bonds, to adjust reserves in the banking system.

---

[4]See Scott Hein and Jonathan Stewart, "Reserve Requirements: A Modern Perspective," *Economic Review*, Federal Reserve Bank of Atlanta, Fourth Quarter, 2002, pp. 41–52.

Discount Rate

The discount rate is the rate regional Federal Reserve Banks charge depository institutions for short-term loans to shore up their reserves. The discount window also serves as a backup source of liquidity for individual depository institutions.[5]

The Fed extends discount rate credit to banks and other depository institutions in three categories. *Primary credit* is given to institutions in sound financial condition typically for overnight balancing of reserves. The rate charged is roughly one percentage point higher than the FOMC's target Federal Funds rate. *Secondary credit* is designated for those less-than-sound institutions and is extended with the expectation that the institution's problems will be quickly resolved. The rate for secondary credit is one-half a percentage point above the rate for primary credit. The Fed also extends credit on a *seasonal* basis where institutions have a clear record of seasonal needs.

In late 2007 the subprime mortgage market created a credit (liquidity) crunch that resulted in a very volatile stock market because institutions were unwilling to loan against mortgage collateral. The Fed used the discount window (lowered the discount rate) to encourage banks to borrow to inject liquidity into the financial system. This action by the Fed increased liquidity and took much of the extreme volatility out of the financial markets.

In the past, the Fed loaned banks money through the discount window at rates *below* what banks could get in the federal funds market. The Fed then relied on loan officers to restrict access to these below-market-priced funds. In January 2003, the Federal Reserve Banks raised their discount rates to levels *higher* than the federal funds rate. This change in operational procedure suggests the Fed intends to rely on above-market rates rather than more costly and less efficient administrative procedures to discourage loans.[6]

Neither the discount rate nor the reserve ratio, however, gives the Fed as much power to implement monetary policy as open market operations. Open market operations allow the Fed to alter the supply of money and system reserves by buying and selling government securities.

Open Market Operations

When one private financial institution buys a government bond from another, funds are simply redistributed around the economy; the transaction does not change reserves in the economy. When the Fed buys a government security, however, it pays some private financial institution for this bond; thus, it adds to aggregate reserves by putting new money into the financial system.

Open market operations are so powerful because of the dollar-for-dollar change in reserves that comes from buying or selling government securities. When the Open Market Committee buys a $100,000 bond, $100,000 of new reserves are instantly put into the banking system.

Once the reduced discount rate softened the liquidity crunch from the 2007 subprime mortgage meltdown, the Fed began to worry about the impact housing foreclosures might have on the new construction, the housing market, and the economy (remember that new construction is a component of gross private domestic investment). To minimize the impact of growing foreclosures the Fed lowered its target on the Federal Funds rate and used open market operations to reduce overall interest rates.

Monetary and banking systems are crucial elements of an economy. Most developed countries have central banks that perform functions similar to those of our Federal Reserve Banks. Many developing nations, however, lack adequate financial systems, and this deficiency can be their main impediment to economic growth.

[5]Board of Governors of the Federal Reserve System, *The Federal Reserve System: Purposes and Functions* (Washington, D.C.), 2005, p. 45.
[6]For greater detail on this issue, see Ed Stevens, "The New Discount Window," *Economic Commentary,* Federal Reserve Bank of Cleveland, May 15, 2003.

In the previous chapter, we saw how important fiscal policy can be for mitigating the impact of the business cycle. When recession sets in, governments can increase spending or reduce taxes to stimulate a recovery. During boom periods, meanwhile, policymakers can reduce spending or increase taxes to stave off inflation. Yet, because politicians are notoriously reluctant to take either of these two anti-inflationary measures, fiscal policymaking has an inflationary bias built into it.

Therefore, it is the nonpolitical Federal Reserve that has essentially been assigned responsibility for keeping the economy on a trajectory of solid growth, high employment, and stable prices. Simultaneously pursuing these goals is a difficult balancing act, and it often puts the Fed at odds with the Administration and Congress. The next chapter looks at implementing monetary policy.

Checkpoint

The Federal Reserve System

REVIEW

- The Federal Reserve is the central bank of the United States.
- The Federal Reserve System is structured around 12 regional banks and a central governing agency, the Board of Governors.
- The tools of the Federal Reserve include setting reserve requirements, setting the discount rate, and open market operations.
- The reserve requirement, while important, is rarely altered.
- The discount rate is normally set above the federal funds rate (the rate banks charge other banks who must borrow to maintain daily reserves).
- Open market operations consist of buying and selling government bonds on the open market. Buying bonds puts new reserves in the banking system and leads to increases in the money supply. The opposite is true when the Fed sells bonds.

QUESTIONS

The reserve requirement sets the required percent of vault cash plus deposits with the regional Federal Reserve Banks that banks must keep for their deposits. Many banks have widespread branches and automatic teller machines (ATMs). Would the existence of branches and ATMs affect the level of excess reserves (above those required) that banks hold? Why or why not? What would be the effect on the actual money multiplier?

Answers to the Checkpoint questions can be found at the end of this chapter.

Key Concepts

Money, p. 258
Barter, p. 259
Medium of exchange, p. 259
Unit of account, p. 259
Store of value, p. 259
Liquidity, p. 259
M1, p. 260
M2, p. 260
Transactions demand for money, p. 262

Precautionary demand for money, p. 263
Speculative demand for money, p. 263
Fractional reserve banking system, p. 266
Money multiplier, p. 267
Federal Reserve System, p. 268
Federal Open Market Committee, p. 271
Reserve requirements, p. 272
Discount rate, p. 272
Open market operations, p. 272

What Is Money?

Money is anything that is accepted in exchange for other goods and services or for the payment of debts. For a commodity to be used as money, it must be standardizable, so that its value is easy to determine; it must be divisible, so that people can make change; it must be durable; it must be easy to carry; and it must be widely accepted as money by large numbers of people.

Money has three primary functions in our economic system: as a medium of exchange, as a measure of value (unit of account), and as a store of value. Using money as a medium of exchange overcomes the problem of a double coincidence of wants that plagues barter economies. Similarly, using money as a measure of value drastically reduces the number of prices individuals must determine. Last, because money is a durable store of value, it allows people to save the money they earn today and use it to buy goods and services tomorrow.

An asset's liquidity is determined by how quickly, easily, and reliably it can be converted into cash. Money is the most liquid asset since it is the medium of exchange and requires no conversion.

The Federal Reserve System uses two different measures of the money supply. M1 includes currency (coins and paper money), demand deposits (checks), and other accounts that have check-writing capabilities, such as some brokerage accounts. M2 is composed of M1 plus the "near monies": money that cannot be drawn on instantaneously, but is nonetheless accessible, including savings accounts, money market deposit accounts, and money market mutual fund accounts.

Money: Demand and Supply

The demand for money refers to the desire of individuals and firms to hold money as part of their portfolio of assets. Money is held for several reasons. As a medium of exchange, it is needed for buying and selling goods and services; this is the transactions demand. Some money is held for precautionary reasons, or to prepare for unexpected expenses; this is the precautionary demand for money. Third, some part of most portfolios is held as money because other assets are risky. This speculative demand for money is inversely related to the interest rate: the higher the interest rate, the higher the opportunity cost of holding money.

The money and bond markets are closely interrelated. When the demand for money rises, individuals and businesses tend to satisfy this demand first by selling bonds for cash.

A bond is a contract between a seller (the company or government issuing the bond) and a buyer. The seller agrees to pay the buyer a fixed rate of interest (the coupon rate) on the face value of the bond (usually $1,000) until a fixed date (the maturity date of the bond). Once a bond is issued, its yield is subject to marketplace forces. As a general rule, as market interest rates rise, the value of bonds (paying fixed dollars of interest) will fall. Conversely, if interest rates drop, the price of bonds will rise.

Banks act as intermediaries, bringing together borrowers and lenders.

Banks operate under a fractional reserve system that allows them to create money. Banks accept deposits, and because bank runs are rare, they hold only a certain required fraction of these deposits, loaning out the rest. Most of the money loaned out will be deposited back into some other bank account. Part of these deposits will be held as new reserves; the rest will again be loaned out. This process continues until the entire initial deposit is held as reserves somewhere in the banking system. By this point, the new money in the economy has expanded to well beyond the size of the original deposit.

The money multiplier measures the potential or maximum amount the money supply can increase (or decrease) when new deposits enter (exit) the system. It is defined by the formula: money multiplier = 1 ÷ reserve requirement. Thus, if the reserve requirement is 20%, the money multiplier is equal to $1/.20 = 5$. This means an initial deposit of \$1,000 will end up creating \$5,000 in new money. The actual money multiplier is lower because of leakages. For instance, some people will hold cash for transactions, reducing the amount put back into the banking system, and some banks will hold excess reserves.

The Federal Reserve System

The Federal Reserve System is the central bank of the United States. It was established by the Federal Reserve Act of 1913 and has had its mission clarified and expanded by several acts since then. Today, the Fed is required by law to promote economic growth accompanied by full employment, stable prices, and moderate long-term interest rates.

The Federal Reserve is an independent central bank, in that its actions are not subject to executive branch oversight, although the entire Federal Reserve System is subject to oversight by Congress. Experience in this country and abroad suggests that independent central banks are better at fighting inflation than are politically controlled banks. Politicians are reluctant to enact the contractionary policies needed to stave off inflation.

The Fed is composed of a central governing agency—the Board of Governors—and 12 regional Federal Reserve Banks. The Board of Governors consists of seven members appointed by the president and confirmed by the Senate. Board members serve terms of 14 years, after which they cannot be reappointed. The chairman and vice chairman of the Board must already be Board members; they are appointed by the president, subject to Senate confirmation, for terms of 4 years.

The 12 regional Federal Reserve Banks and their branches provide a nationwide payments system, distribute coins and currency, regulate and supervise member banks, and serve as the banker for the U.S. Treasury. Each regional bank, moreover, provides the Federal Reserve System with information on economic conditions in its home region. This information is compiled in a report detailing the economic conditions around the country, the *Beige Book*, which the Board of Governors and the Federal Open Market Committee use to determine the course of monetary policy.

The Federal Open Market Committee (FOMC) oversees the Fed's open market operations, its primary tool of monetary policy. The FOMC is composed of the seven members of the Board of Governors, the president of the Federal Reserve Bank of New York, and four of the remaining 11 regional Reserve Bank presidents. Traditionally, the chairman of the Board of Governors also serves as the chairman of the FOMC.

The Federal Reserve has three primary tools at its disposal for conducting monetary policy. First, it can adjust the reserve requirement, the required ratio of funds commercial banks and other depository institutions must hold in reserve against deposits. By raising the reserve requirement, the Fed reduces the potential money multiplier, thus shrinking the supply of money in the economy. The Fed uses this policy tool infrequently, however, given that its impact is so massive and imprecise.

Second, the Fed can adjust the discount rate, the interest rate it charges commercial banks and other depository institutions to borrow reserves from a regional Federal Reserve Bank. When a bank's reserves fall below the required level, it must borrow money from the Fed or some other source to avoid penalty. Thus, a higher discount rate will encourage banks to hold more reserves. Most of these reserves, however, are borrowed from the Federal Funds Market. The Fed's discount window is a more expensive buffer against day-to-day fluctuations in reserves demand and supply.

The Fed's most powerful tool for conducting monetary policy involves open market operations. This involves buying and selling United States government securities on the open market to alter reserves in the banking system. When the Fed buys a government security, it pays some private financial institution for the bond, so it adds to aggregate reserves by injecting new money into the financial system. Open market operations are powerful because every dollar the Fed uses to buy up bonds puts a dollar of new reserves into the banking system.

Questions and Problems

1. Describe the three functions of money.

2. Describe why barter is inefficient and why no modern economy could exist on barter.

3. Besides being legal tender, what differentiates money from most of the goods we consume?

4. Describe the role required reserves play in determining how much money the banking system creates.

5. Why are checking accounts (demand deposits) considered a liability to the bank?

6. Explain why the actual money multiplier will be less than its potential ($1 \div$ reserve requirement).

7. The Federal Deposit Insurance Corporation (FDIC) insures individual bank accounts up to $100,000.00 per account. Does the existence of this insurance eliminate the need for reserve requirements? Does it essentially prevent "runs" on banks?

8. Explain the important difference between M1 and M2.

9. List the following assets from most liquid to least liquid: house (real estate), cash, 1-carat diamond, savings account, 100 shares of Google, Harley Davidson motorcycle, checking account, your old leather jacket.

10. What gives our money its value if there is no gold or silver backing the currency?

11. Many central banks in the world are independent in the sense that they are partially isolated from short-run political considerations and pressures. How is this independence attained? How important is this independence to policymaking at the Federal Reserve?

12. The president of what Federal Reserve Bank district is a permanent member on the Federal Open Market Committee? Why?

13. What tool does the Federal Reserve use most? Use least? Why?

14. Explain why bond prices and interest rates are inversely related.

15. Alan Greenspan, the past chairman of the Fed, noted that "the Federal Reserve has to be independent in its actions and as an institution, because if Federal Reserve independence is in any way compromised, it undercuts our capability of protecting the value of the currency in society." What is so important about protecting the value of the currency? How does Fed independence help?

16. Assume that First Purity Bank begins with a balance sheet below and is fully loaned up. Answer the questions that follow.

First Purity Bank	
Assets	**Liabilities**
Reserves = $700,000	Deposits = $2,000,000
Loans = $1,300,000	

    a. What is the reserve requirement equal to?
    b. If the bank receives a new deposit of $1 million, and the bank wants to remain fully loaned-up, how much of this new deposit will the bank loan out?
    c. When the new deposit to First Purity Bank works itself through the entire banking system (assume all banks keep fully loaned-up), what will total deposits, total loans, and total reserves be equal to?
    d. What is the potential money multiplier equal to?

Answers to Checkpoint Questions

CHECKPOINT: WHAT IS MONEY?

Most of the quarters were withdrawn from circulation by the Fed and hoarded by individuals. When silver prices rose, many were sold and melted for bullion. Gresham's law is not particularly important today since the money is fiat money—that is, money without intrinsic value.

CHECKPOINT: MONEY: DEMAND AND SUPPLY

If there were no reserve requirements, banks would still maintain reserves. They would need reserves for ATM and normal banking operations. Further, no bank wants to get a reputation for not being able to meet its depositor's needs—this could quickly drive a bank out of business.

CHECKPOINT: THE FEDERAL RESERVE SYSTEM

ATMs and branches require a lot of vault cash to maintain and might be expected to result in banks holding greater excess reserves. Thus, the actual money multiplier would be lower.

Monetary Policy

he Federal Reserve Act mandates that the Federal Reserve implement monetary policies that will promote economic growth accompanied by high employment, stable prices, and moderate long-term interest rates. In the previous chapter, we saw how banks create money using the fractional reserve system. We also saw the policy tools available to the Federal Reserve: reserve requirements, the discount rate, and open market operations. In this chapter, we will look at monetary policy: how the Federal Reserve (often called *the Fed*) uses these policy tools to change bank reserves and the money supply to pursue its mandated goals, as well as how the Federal Reserve balances these goals.

The first part of this chapter will consider several theories on how the effects of changes in reserves and the money supply filter through the rest of the economy. Such theories seek to identify what are usually called the *monetary transmission mechanisms* or *channels*. Our focus here will be on two of these channels. The first is the classical or *quantity theory channel*, where money is felt directly in the economy through purchases of goods and services. The second is the *interest rate channel*, which posits that the money supply affects interest rates, with changing interest rates then affecting other real variables in the economy.

A third monetary channel that should be noted here is the *expectations channel*, a transmission mechanism that arises because money affects inflationary expectations, and these changing expectations then have their own effects on the economy. A detailed discussion of expectations is left for a later chapter, which focuses on the dual challenge of controlling inflation and unemployment.

The second part of the chapter looks at the problem of lags in implementing monetary policy. These include lags between the time when monetary authorities receive information about the economy and the time required to recognize a problem and make decisions. Finally, time is required for a given policy to affect the economy. The existence of these lags means that the Fed is often making policy on an economy that is further on in the business cycle than anticipated and even further along when the selected policies take effect.

The final part of the chapter looks at how the Federal Reserve weighs its mandated goals when setting monetary policy. We have already seen how powerful and important the Federal Reserve is in influencing the economy. We will look at the Fed's short-run and long-run goals. Next, we will ask whether the Federal Reserve should be tied to specific rules or should have the discretion to formulate the policy it sees fit. If rules are best, what should they be? We end our discussion of monetary policy by looking at how open the Fed should be in explaining the reasons for its policy decisions.

Monetary policy is a key way that government influences the economy. It can be more effective at some times than others, as we will see. Furthermore, balancing the mandated goals is not an easy matter. Nevertheless, the Federal Reserve has been quite successful over the past 15 years in stabilizing the economy—just as it is supposed to do.

After studying this chapter you should be able to

- Describe the equation of exchange and its implications for monetary policy.
- Describe the classical monetary transmission mechanism.
- Describe Keynesian monetary analysis and the three motives for holding money.
- Describe the Keynesian monetary transmission mechanism and how it differs from classical theory.
- Describe the monetarist model of monetary theory.
- Describe the important differences in the three models of monetary theory and the implications of these differences for monetary policy.
- Describe the four lags that affect the implementation of monetary policy.
- Describe why the Fed targets price stability in the long run and inflation rates and output in the short run.
- Determine the effectiveness of monetary policy when demand or supply shocks occur.
- Describe controversy over whether the Fed should have discretion or be governed by simple monetary rules.

Monetary Theories

By changing reserves, the Fed can change not only the money supply but also the federal funds rate. As reserves increase, the excess reserves supplied to the federal funds market increase, so the federal funds rate declines, reducing interest rates. The increase in reserves means that banks have excess reserves, and some of these will find their way into loans and thus new money.

Assume for a moment that the economy enters a recession similar to the one that began in the first quarter of 2001. The Fed will want to increase excess reserves by

- lowering the reserve requirement ratio,
- lowering the discount rate, or
- purchasing government securities using open market operations.

These actions of the Fed are collectively called an **easy money or expansionary monetary policy**. All are designed to increase excess reserves and the money supply to stimulate the economy. Expansionary monetary policy, in other words, is intended to expand income and employment. The opposite of an expansionary policy is a **tight money, restrictive, or contractionary monetary policy**. Tight money policies are designed to shrink income and employment, usually in the interest of fighting inflation.

In the previous chapter, we saw that the Federal Reserve tends to favor the open market operations policy tool. The Federal Reserve will also use the discount rate, though not as often as open market operations. Changing reserve requirements is shunned because this tool is too blunt and its effects too murky.

Now that we know about the policy tools the Federal Reserve uses, we now want to look at what happens when these tools are used. How do increasing or decreasing excess reserves and the money supply translate into changes in economic activity? In this section, we will look at several theories of how changes in reserves, and thus changes in the money supply, alter income, employment, and prices. We begin with the classical or quantity theory channel.

The Long Run: Quantity Theory

The *quantity theory of money* is a product of the classical school of economics. As we saw in an earlier chapter, classical theory focuses on long-run adjustments in economic activity. Classical theory assumes that wages, prices, and interest rates are flexible in the long run, allowing the labor, product, and capital markets to adjust to keep the economy at full employment.

The Equation of Exchange

Classical economists defined money narrowly, limiting it to currency and coins, while assuming that money is for transactions purposes only. Money is held, this theory maintains, because spending and income do not occur at the same time: You receive income once or twice a month but spend that income over that entire period. The quantity theory was developed 300–400 years ago, a time of metallic currency when money was either gold or silver coins.

Quantity theory is defined by the **equation of exchange**:

$$M \times V = P \times Q$$

In this equation, M is the supply of money, V is the velocity of money, or the number of times it turns over in a year, P is the price level, and Q is the economy's output level. Note that in contemporary terms, the right side of the equation—the aggregate price level times the level of output—is equal to nominal gross domestic product (GDP). And if we define the money supply as M1, then the left side of the equation is equal to M1 times the average number of times per year M1 is spent on final goods and services.

To illustrate the use of the equation of exchange, for the year 2005, nominal GDP ($P \times Q$) was $12.601 trillion and M1 was $1.368 trillion. Consequently, the velocity of M1 was a little over 9 ($V = PQ/M = 12.601/1.368 = 9.21$). Clearly, the velocity of money will vary with different measures of money. In general, the more broadly defined the money supply, the lower the velocity will be. For example, M2 for the year 2005 was $6.627 trillion; thus M2 velocity was roughly 2 (i.e., $12.601/6.627 = 1.9$). Remember that M2 includes not only currency and demand deposits but also saving deposits, money market accounts, and various other small accounts.

For classical economists, the money supply consisted of currency, coins, and the beginnings of a banking sector. Velocity was determined by the quality of the prevailing monetary institutions and technology. Both of these were assumed to change slowly, meaning that velocity would also be slow to change.

Because classical economists assumed long-run full employment, the implications for monetary policy are straightforward. Since velocity (V) is assumed to be fixed by existing monetary institutions and the state of technology, and aggregate output (Q) is assumed to be fixed at full employment, any change in the money supply (M) will translate directly in a change in prices (P), or

$$\Delta M = \Delta P$$

In the long run, in other words, a change in the money supply will directly change the aggregate price level. Figure 1 illustrates this general proposition; it shows average monetary growth and inflation in 30 countries over the period 1970–2004. Notice the clear positive relationship between changes in the supply of money and inflation rates. This correlation is reasonably close over the entire period, confirming what Milton Friedman argued: "Inflation is always and everywhere a monetary phenomenon."

FIGURE 1

Money Growth and Inflation: 30 Countries From 1970 to 2004

The quantity theory predicts that $\Delta M = \Delta P$, or that in the long run a change in the money supply will bring about a directly proportionate change in the aggregate price level. Figure 1 illustrates this general proposition by showing monetary growth and inflation for 30 countries from 1970 to 2004.

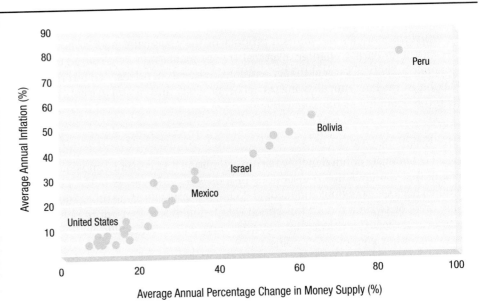

Classical Money Transmission Mechanism

Classical monetary transmission mechanism
Because money was assumed to be used only for transactions purposes, that the economy was operating at full employment (Q is fixed), and velocity (V) was dependent on banking technology and thus constant, the equation of exchange suggests the process is quite direct; any change in M will be felt directly in P.

What is the **classical money transmission mechanism**, or the channel through which changes in the money supply influence prices in classical theory? The equation of exchange suggests the process is quite direct; any change in M will be felt directly in P. This account is reasonable enough, given that the classical model was designed at a time when money was used almost exclusively for transactions purposes.

Still, explaining the quantity theory channel in the contemporary economy requires a subtler approach. Assume that, before an injection of new money, individual portfolios are in equilibrium: People hold just the money they need for their accustomed transactions. An increase in the money supply, holding the current price level steady, will therefore knock the supply of real money (M/P) out of balance. It ends up that $(M/P)_{\text{new}} > (M/P)_{\text{old}}$—people end up holding more money than they want or need.

Because individuals, consequently, want to lower M/P, and the only variable they control is M, they will start to spend more money on goods and services. The

Irving Fisher (1867–1947)

*I*rving Fisher was one of the ablest mathematical economists of the early 20th century. A staunch advocate of monetary reform, his theories influenced economists as different as John Maynard Keynes and Milton Friedman.

Born in upstate New York in 1867, Fisher studied mathematics, science, and philosophy at Yale University, receiving his B.A. in math in 1898 and his Ph.D. in economics—the first ever offered by the university—in 1901. For 3 years he taught mathematics at Yale, only switching to economics after the international success of his book, *Mathematical Investigations and the Theory of Value and Prices.* In the book, Fisher made important advances in mathematical economics and developed a theory to measure the utility of commodities. Fisher also designed a hydraulic "machine" to illustrate general equilibrium in a multimarket economy.

In 1906, he published *The Nature of Capital and Income,* which provided a theoretical basis for the science of accounting. Fisher defined capital as any stock of wealth that yields a flow of services over time. Income was the surplus of the flow of services above the amount necessary to maintain the stock of wealth. He suggested that the rate of interest was the link between capital and income, concluding that the value of capital was the present value of the future flow of income discounted at the going rate of interest.

Monetarists owe a great debt to Fisher's next great book, *The Purchasing Power of Money,* in which he offered an "equation of exchange:" $MV = PT$, where M is the amount of money in circulation, V is the velocity of circulation of that money, P is the average price level, and T is the number of transactions taking place. Classical economists have used variations of the formula to suggest that inflation is caused by increases in the money supply.

In 1898, Fisher contracted tuberculosis, which provoked a lifelong interest in health and nutrition. He became a vegetarian and wrote a best-selling self-help book called *How to Live: Rules for Healthful Living Based on Modern Science.* Among his many skills and interests, Fisher was a successful inventor and businessman. In 1925, he patented the "visible card index" system, which was an early version of the rolodex, and earned a fortune when his firm merged with another company, which came to be known as Sperry Rand. Unfortunately, within a few years he would lose everything in the stock market crash of 1929, an event that he famously failed to predict.

In fact, Fisher's belief that the market had reached a "permanently high plateau" a few weeks before the crash and his insistence on an imminent recovery throughout the early Depression years caused irreparable damage to a well-earned reputation as one of the greatest American economists. Fisher taught at Yale until his retirement in 1935.

He died in 1947.

economy, however, is already at full employment, Q being fixed, so prices will rise until real money balances return to equilibrium. In the end, prices will rise in exact proportion to the rise in the money supply.

Figure 2 illustrates how the quantity theory works within an aggregate demand and supply context. The economy is initially in equilibrium at point a, with price level P_0 and real output Q_0. The aggregate supply curve is vertical, reflecting the classical assumption of full employment, and the aggregate demand curve reflects an initial money level of M_0. Increasing the money supply to M_1 shifts aggregate demand upward to AD $(M = M_1)$, resulting in a new equilibrium at point b where prices increase to P_1, yet real output remains constant at Q_0.

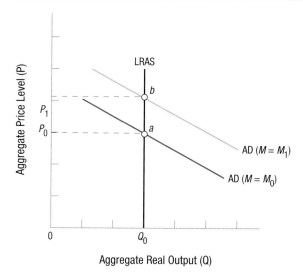

Quantity theory and the equation of exchange provide an adequate explanation of the effects of the money supply on the larger economy as long as money is limited to currency and coins. Indeed, when European explorers discovered massive new sources of gold and silver in the New World, economists accurately predicted what would happen: massive inflation. And even today, as Figure 1 illustrates, quantity theory still provides a good explanation of the long-run impact of monetary growth.

Yet, because the quantity theory is based on the classical model and has a long-run focus, it is of little use for explaining or offsetting short-run shocks in aggregate supply and aggregate demand. Long-run explanations of economic trends spanning decades are important, but policymakers often demand theories that offer them short-run policies that will counter unforeseen shocks to the economy. For this sort of short-run analysis, we need to turn to transmission mechanisms that work through interest rates.

The Short Run: Interest Rate Channels

We begin our discussion of short-run monetary policy channels with a look at Keynesian monetary theory. Developed during the Great Depression of the 1930s, Keynesian analysis had a profound effect on policymakers in the 1950s and 1960s. As we shall see, Keynes saw little benefit to tinkering with monetary policy when an economy was in the midst of a serious downturn.

The Keynesian view of monetary policy dominated economic thinking well into the 1960s, when Nobel Prize economist Milton Friedman challenged the orthodoxy with his monetarist approach to monetary policy and economic stabilization. Keynesian analysis was so ingrained in the economics profession that his efforts initially met with skepticism, but Friedman was not deterred. His perseverance and immense analytical skills eventually persuaded nearly all economists that monetary policy is extremely important.

As we shall see, both the Keynesian and monetarist approaches rely on changes in interest rates to bring about changes in investment, consumption, and the prices of other assets. Keynesian analysis made a significant break from prior classical analysis. Monetarism, on the other hand, returns to the long tradition of classical analysis in many ways. Monetarists see the economy as self-stabilizing around full employment in the long run. In contrast to classical economists, however, monetarists do see a need for the government to conduct monetary policy in the short run.

Keynesian Monetary Analysis

Writing during the Great Depression, John Maynard Keynes was forced to take a different approach to the economy than his classical predecessors. For one thing, with so many people unemployed for so long (U.S. unemployment was at 25% in 1933), he found it difficult to assert that the economy was simply fluctuating around full employment.

Keynes further argued that wages are inflexible ("sticky") downward, because workers and unions are unwilling to accept lower wages, even as an economy softens. As we saw in an earlier chapter, Keynesian analyses of saving and consumption and the propensities to consume and save led to the multiplier, and an economy stuck at equilibrium income below full employment.

In our earlier analysis of the Keynesian model, we ignored the relationship between the rate of interest and investment by assuming investment levels to be fixed. In this section, we will introduce the monetary side of Keynesian analysis.

Motives for Holding Money. Keynes identified three motives that people have for holding money rather than holding their wealth in other assets. Although covered in the previous chapter, it is worthwhile mentioning all three again to put Keynes's insight in context. Keynes acknowledged the *transactions motive* that formed the basis of classical monetary analysis. To this he added the *precautionary motive*. Beyond holding money to consummate transactions, Keynes believed people would hold money balances to accommodate unforeseen circumstances. These balances permit individuals to take advantage of unanticipated opportunities and to have cash on hand for emergencies. Both of these components of the demand for money are related, Keynes argued, to income levels. At higher income levels, more money is kept in hand for transactions and precautionary purposes.

The third motive for holding money is the *speculative motive*. This insight represents a major Keynesian innovation. Keynes asked why individuals would choose to hold money balances rather than holding their wealth in bonds, where it would earn interest. The answer is that people sometimes hold money for speculation against changes in interest rates or the price level.

When would money be a better investment than a bond? First, when interest rates have fallen to low levels. The expectation, after all, is that interest rates will eventually rise again. And when interest rates do rise, the price of bonds will fall, so bondholders will suffer capital losses that quickly wipe out the interest they receive.

Second, when the price level in the economy *falls,* money becomes a more valuable asset since its purchasing power increases. If a decline in prices is predicted, it is a good time to hold cash.

Keynesian Monetary Transmission Mechanism. Panel A of Figure 3 shows the Keynesian demand for money, along with the supply of money, initially equal to MS_0. This results in an interest rate of i_0. As we saw happen in the last chapter, when the money supply grows to MS_1, interest rates fall to i_1.

FIGURE 3

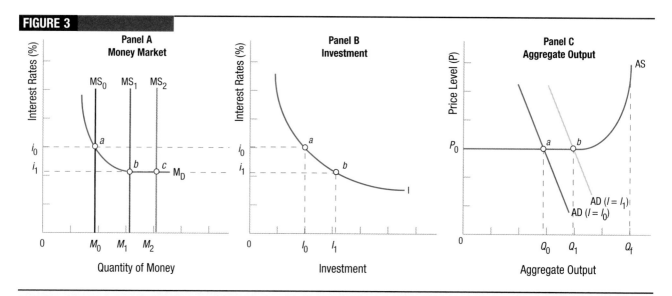

Keynesian Monetary Transmission Mechanism

This figure shows how Keynes predicted money would affect the economy. The economy begins in equilibrium with a money supply, MS_0 (point *a* in Panel A). This translates into investment equal to I_0 in Panel B. Investment I_0 generates an equilibrium output equal to Q_0 (point *a* in Panel C). When the money supply grows to MS_1, interest rates fall to i_1 and investment grows to I_1 (points *b* in Panels A and B). This translates into a higher income and output level Q_1 (point *b* in Panel C).

Increased money in the market means that people will want to convert more of it to interest-earning assets (bonds), causing the price of bonds to rise and the interest rate to fall (point *b*). Notice that when the money supply further grows to MS_2, people start simply hoarding money balances (point *c*). Keynes referred to this phenomenon as the **liquidity trap**. Once interest rates sink so low that people start to believe they can only go up, they hold onto all the money they can, rather than investing in bonds.

Figure 3 shows how Keynes predicted money would affect the economy. The economy is initially at equilibrium at money supply MS_0 (point *a* in Panel A). This translates into investment equal to I_0 in Panel B. Investment I_0 generates an equilibrium output equal to Q_0. This is shown in the aggregate demand and supply curves in Panel C (point *a*). When the money supply grows to MS_1, interest rates fall to i_1 and investment grows to I_1. This is shown as points *b* in Panels A and B. This translates into a higher income and output level Q_1, as shown at point *b* in Panel C.

To summarize, the **Keynesian monetary transmission mechanism** for money added into the economy is as follows:

$$\uparrow M \rightarrow \ \downarrow i \rightarrow \ \uparrow I \rightarrow \ \uparrow AD \rightarrow \ \uparrow Y \rightarrow \ \uparrow Q$$

Thus, an increase in the money supply should lower interest rates, leading to an increase in investment. This expands aggregate demand, which increases income, output, and employment. A decrease in the money supply would act in the opposite fashion.

Notice that once the economy falls into a liquidity trap, an increase in money has no effect on the economy. Interest rates do not fall because the added money is simply kept in cash balances and the economy goes nowhere. This was one reason Keynes argued that fiscal policy—not monetary policy—was needed to get the economy out of the Depression.

Comparing Keynes and the Classical Economists. We might take a moment to contrast the Keynesian approach to that of the classical equation of exchange. Keynesian analysis emphasizes the role of the speculative demand for money, whereas classical economists focused on the transactions demand. In the Keynesian model, changes in money affect the economy only indirectly through changes in interest rates and investment. Contrast this analysis with the classical approach, where monetary changes directly affect the price level.

In the liquidity trap, an increase in money is hoarded, and there is no change in the interest rate and, thus, no change in income, output, or employment. Monetary policy is totally ineffective. Another way to see this is with the equation of exchange ($M \times V = P \times Q$). As money is hoarded rather than circulated about the economy, an increase in M will be absorbed fully in V (as M goes up, V goes down), such that $P \times Q$ does not change.

Monetarist Model

Monetarism is most closely associated with the work of Milton Friedman. Keynesian analysis was the dominant theoretical analysis from the time the *General Theory of Employment, Interest and Money* was published in 1936 until the beginning of the 1970s. Already by the 1960s, however, studies of the influence of monetary policy had begun to appear.

The most famous of these was *A Monetary History of the United States, 1867–1960,* written by Friedman and Anna Schwartz and published in 1963. This study and others showed statistically that monetary variables play an important role in determining income and employment levels, as well as inflation. Although the studies of Friedman and Schwartz were often contested, they forced economists of all stripes to reconsider the role money plays in the economy.

Monetarist Innovations. Friedman pioneered the notion that consumption is not only based on income, but also that wealth plays a role. Two people with the same income but different levels of wealth, Friedman observed, will presumably consume at different levels; common sense says the wealthier individual will consume more.

Because empirical data on wealth and consumption were unavailable at the time, however, Friedman had to look for some proxy. To Friedman, wealth was composed of money, bonds, equities, real assets, and human capital. He developed the concept of *permanent income,* which is the present value of an individual's future stream of labor income. Friedman eventually settled on a weighted average of past incomes to define permanent income, the proxy for wealth embedded in human capital.

Friedman altered the demand for money to include wealth (using permanent income) and other variables. A simplified version of Friedman's demand function for real money balances is

$$M_d/P = f(W,\ r,\ p_e,\ u)$$

Nobel Prize Milton Friedman

*M*ilton Friedman may be the best-known economist of the latter half of the 20th century. During the 1980s, his advocacy of free market economics and "monetarist" theories had a dramatic impact on policymakers, notably President Ronald Reagan and British Prime Minister Margaret Thatcher. His book, *A Monetary History of the United States, 1867–1960,* coauthored with Anna Schwartz, is considered a modern classic of economics. He also made important contributions to consumption analysis, exchange rates, and economic stabilization policy.

Born in 1912 in Brooklyn, New York, Friedman's parents were immigrants who struggled to make ends meet. Awarded a scholarship to Rutgers University, Friedman paid for his additional expenses by waiting on tables and clerking in a store. At Rutgers, Friedman studied under future Federal Reserve Board Chairman Arthur Burns.

In 1932, he entered the University of Chicago as a graduate student in economics. Thanks to economist Harry Hotelling, Friedman was offered a fellowship to study at Columbia University, where he honed his analysis of mathematical statistics. Professors Wesley Mitchell and John M. Clark introduced him to an empirical approach and view of theory that differed from the Chicago school.

In 1946, he accepted a professorship at the University of Chicago. At the same time, he accepted a position from Arthur Burns at the National Bureau of Economic Research, delving into the role of money in business cycles. At Chicago, Friedman established a "Workshop in Money and Banking." In 1950, Friedman worked in Paris for the Marshall Plan, studying a precursor to the Common Market. He came to believe in the importance of flexible exchange rates between members of the European Community.

In 1956, Friedman published *Studies in the Quantity Theory of Money,* which laid out his views on the importance of money and monetary policy in determining the level of economic activity. His views were explicitly counter to the Keynesian belief in a range of activist government policies to stabilize the economy. Friedman advocated a consistent policy of steady growth in the money supply to encourage stability and economic growth.

Friedman was awarded the Nobel Prize in Economics in 1976. The prize givers acknowledged his monetary theories but emphasized his work on rethinking Keynes's theory of the "consumption function," the tendency of people to save rather than spend a higher proportion of money when they reached higher income levels.

The theory was important to the Keynesian explanation for economic downturns. Friedman's work suggested that people based their saving habits on "permanent income," that is, the typical amount they earn instead of on increases or decreases they may view as temporary.

Milton Friedman died in 2006.

where

M_d/P = real money demand (M_d = nominal money demanded; P = the aggregate price level)
W = permanent income (a proxy for wealth)
r = the return on financial assets
p_e = the expected inflation rate
u = a variable representing the individual's tastes and preferences[1]

Friedman's analysis suggests that the demand for real money balances will be higher if (1) wealth or permanent income is higher, (2) the rate of return on other assets is lower, and (3) the expected rate of inflation is lower. We will ignore the effects of the expected inflation rate until a later chapter.

Monetarist Transmission Mechanism. Friedman assumed that utility-maximizing individuals will allocate their wealth among various assets until their marginal rates of return are equal. This approach treats money as just one more asset within a generalized portfolio of assets that might include bonds, real estate, fine art, or consumer durables. Contrast this view with the approach of Keynes, who essentially viewed money as a substitute for bonds.

With Friedman's approach, when the money supply increases, more money will be held than is desired because the additional supply of money decreases the return on money. Excess money balances will thus be exchanged for other financial and real assets, including bonds, real estate, and consumer durables such as cars and houses. In the end, portfolios will rebalance, and markets will return to equilibrium.

The **monetarist transmission mechanism** can be symbolically described as follows:

$$\uparrow M \rightarrow \downarrow i \rightarrow (\uparrow I \text{ and/or } \uparrow C) \rightarrow \uparrow \text{AD} \rightarrow \uparrow Y \text{ and/or } \uparrow P$$

An increase in money will reduce interest rates as portfolios rebalance. This leads to a rise in investment or consumption, which leads to an increase in aggregate demand and, thus, ultimately an increase in income, output, or the price level. Monetarists, incidentally, assume that velocity is constant, so—with reference to the equation of exchange—any increase in M will change either P or Q, or both.

In the short run, either output or the price level can change. In the long run, however, an increase in money will ultimately increase prices. Figure 4 on the next page illustrates the monetarist approach that a change in output will operate only in the short run; in the long run, the economy will move back to its natural rate of unemployment (full employment output Q_f).

This economy is initially in equilibrium at point a, with price level P_0 and output equal to the long-run natural rate of output, Q_f. An increase in the money supply will shift the aggregate demand curve from AD_0 to AD_1, raising output to Q_1 and prices to P_1 (point b). Over time, for reasons we will detail in a later chapter,

Monetarist transmission mechanism
An increase in money will reduce interest rates as portfolios rebalance, leading to a rise in investment or consumption and resulting in an increase in aggregate demand and thus an increase in income, output, or the price level.

---

[1]See Brian Snowdon and Howard Vane, *Modern Macroeconomics: Its Origins, Development and Current State* (Northampton, MA: Edward Elgar), 2005, p. 167.

FIGURE 4

Monetarist Transmission Mechanism

Monetarists argue that a change in output will last only for the short run; in the long run, the economy will move back to its natural rate of unemployment. The economy begins in equilibrium at point *a*, with price level P_0 and output equal to the long-run natural rate of output Q_f. An increase in the money supply shifts the aggregate demand curve from AD_0 to AD_1, thus resulting in higher output Q_1 and higher prices P_1 (point *b*). Over time, the economy will move back to its natural rate Q_f, increasing prices in the long run to P_2. The long-run aggregate supply curve is therefore vertical at Q_f, as classical economics suggests.

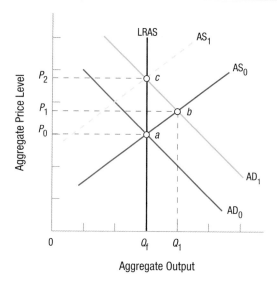

the economy will move back to its natural output (Q_f), raising prices in the long run to P_2. The long-run aggregate supply curve is therefore vertical at Q_f, as classical economics suggests.

We can put all three of these monetary theories together. In the short run, changes in the money supply affect output or the price level, unless the economy faces a Keynesian liquidity trap. In the long run, changes in the money supply will affect price only. What is clear from this is that monetary policy can be effective in the short run, again unless the economy is stuck in a liquidity trap.

Checkpoint

Monetary Theories

REVIEW

■ Expansionary monetary policy increases reserves and the money supply to stimulate the economy. Contractionary policy reduces reserves and the money supply and is designed to shrink output and income.

■ The equation of exchange is equal to $M \times V = P \times Q$. Classical economists assumed that velocity (V) was set by institutional and technical considerations, and that the economy hovered around full employment so that output (Q) was fixed. Money (M) and the price level (P) were directly related such that changes in the supply of money translated into changes in the price level: $\Delta M = \Delta P$.

■ Keynesian monetary theory suggested three motives for holding money: transactions, precautionary, and speculative.

■ In the short run, Keynesian monetary analysis suggests that changes in the money supply change interest rates, leading to a change in investment, changing aggregate demand, which in turn changes income, employment, and output.

■ Monetarists suggest that the economy functions more as the classical economists argued, but by focusing on the demand for money, they see monetary policy affecting investment and consumption in the short run. Money supply changes affect interest rates, which in turn change either investment or consumption, changing aggregate demand and thus affecting output or the price level.

QUESTION

Of the three motives for holding money, which one is most important for monetary policy?

Answers to the Checkpoint question can be found at the end of this chapter.

Monetary Policy Lags

At this point, it should seem clear how monetary policy should be used. When the economy goes into a recession, the Fed should use expansionary monetary policy to bring the economy back to full employment. Conversely, when the economy is running hot—the economy is operating above full employment and inflation is a problem—the Fed should use restrictive monetary policy to rein in the economy. Unfortunately, what seems so simple and obvious is fraught with many subtle problems.

First, the Fed must implement policies designed to accomplish these goals in timely enough fashion to have the desired effect. Here monetary policymakers face their first problem: various time lags in the data they receive, as well as several other associated lags.

Monetary policy is subject to four major lags: information, recognition, decision, and implementation. The combination of these lags can make monetary policy's impact "long and variable," in the words of Friedman and Schwartz. Not only does the Fed face a moving bull's eye in terms of its economic targets, but often it can be difficult for the Fed to know when its own policies will take effect and what their effect will be.

Information Lags

As we saw when we discussed fiscal policy lags, economic data are available only after a lag of 1–3 months. This is an **information lag**. So when an economic event takes place, changes may ripple throughout the economy for up to 3 months before monetary authorities begin to see changes in their data. Many economic measures published by the government, moreover, are subject to future revision. It is not uncommon for these revisions to be so significant as to render the original number meaningless. Thus, it might take the Fed several quarters to clearly identify a changing trend in prices or output.

Information lag
The time policymakers must wait for economic data to be collected, processed, and reported. Most macroeconomic data are not available until at least one quarter (3 months) after the fact.

Recognition Lags

Simply seeing a decline in a variable in 1 month or quarter does not necessarily mean that a change in policy is warranted. Again, data revisions upward and downward are common. In the normal course of events, for instance, unemployment rates can fluctuate by small amounts, as can GDP. A 1-month decline in the rate of growth of GDP does not necessarily signal the beginning of a recession, although it could. Nor does a 1-month increase in GDP mean the economy has reached the bottom of a recession: Double-dip recessions are always a possibility.

These difficulties point to one problem policymakers face in attempting to diagnose an ailing economy and respond with the appropriate policy. Because of the **recognition lag**, policymakers are often unable to recognize problems when they first develop. In the economy, as in life, small problems are usually easier to solve before they become big problems.

Recognition lag
The time it takes for policymakers to confirm that the economy is trending in or out of a recession. Short-term variations in key economic indicators are typical and sometimes represent nothing more than randomness in the data.

Decision Lags

Decision lag
After a problem is recognized, it takes some time for the Fed to decide on a policy. Since the Fed meets monthly, the decision lag is relatively short.

The Federal Reserve Board meets roughly on a monthly basis to determine broad economic policy, so once a problem is recognized, decisions are forthcoming, so the **decision lag** is relatively short. Once a policy has been implemented by the Federal Open Market Committee (FOMC), however, there is another lag associated with the reaction of banks and financial markets.

Implementation Lags

Monetary policy affects bank reserves, interest rates, and decisions by businesses and households. As interest rates change, investment and buying decisions are altered, but often not with any great haste. Investment decisions hinge on more than just interest rate levels. Rules, regulations, permits, and future expectations all enter the decision-making process.

Implementation lag
The time required for monetary policy to have an impact on the economy.

When Friedman and Schwartz studied monetary history from 1867 to 1960, they found that "long and variable" lags in implementing monetary policy made it difficult to use monetary policy for countercyclical management of the economy.[2]

These **implementation lags** could be quite long. Friedman and Schwartz found that the average lag for restrictive monetary policy was 12 months, but that the lag could range from 6 months to 29 months. For expansionary policy, the average lag was 18 months, though it could range between 4 months and 22 months.[3] These long and variable lags led Friedman to conclude that discretionary monetary policy is doomed to fail, and to propose instead a *monetary rule,* discussed next.

More recent studies estimate that the average lag for monetary policy is between a year and 18 months, with a range varying between a little over one quarter to slightly over 2 years. Thus, the original Friedman and Schwartz estimates still appear to hold true today. Using monetary policy to fine-tune the economy requires not only skill but also possibly some luck.

Checkpoint

Monetary Policy Lags

REVIEW

- Monetary policy is subject to four major policy lags: information, recognition, decision, and implementation.
- Information lags occur because economic data are only available after an extended time period. Once policymakers get the data, it may take several quarters to recognize a problem is brewing.
- Once monetary authorities recognize a problem, it takes a short while to reach a decision on policy. But once a decision is reached and monetary policy is used to change reserves and interest rates, it takes time before the economy responds.
- Monetary policy lags vary anywhere between one quarter and 2 years.

QUESTION

Why are monetary policy lags important to the effectiveness of monetary policy?

Answers to the Checkpoint question can be found at the end of this chapter.

---

[2]Milton Friedman and Anna Schwartz, *A Monetary History of the United States, 1867–1960.* A Study by the National Bureau of Economic Research, New York (Princeton, NJ: Princeton University Press), 1963.
[3]Peter Bofinger, *Monetary Policy: Goals, Institutions, Strategies, and Instruments* (Oxford: Oxford University Press), 2001, p. 73.

Implementing Monetary Policy

Lags are just one of the problems facing monetary policymakers. Carl Walsh explains the general problem inherent in implementing policy:

> *In the lobby of the Federal Reserve Bank of San Francisco, visitors are exposed to the difficulties of implementing monetary policy through an electronic video game. The object is to time the release of a dart from a moving arm in order to hit the bull's-eye of a moving target. The moving bull's-eye reflects, in a graphic manner, the uncertainty that exists over the appropriate goals of monetary policy, and the changing values of these goals as a result of developments both in the economy and in our understanding of the economy.*[4]

Remember, monetary policymakers must weigh the various goals laid out by the Federal Reserve Act and set targets for the economy.

Monetary Policy Targets

To achieve its goals, should the Federal Reserve target the price level or income and output? Our earlier discussion of classical and Keynesian monetary theories, and monetarism suggests that these targets should be based on both short-run and long-run considerations. Classical theory suggests that inflation represents a reasonable long-run target, whereas income and output are more appropriate for the shorter term.

Long Run: Price Stability

Economists generally agree that, in the long run, the Fed should target price stability since low rates of inflation have been shown to create the best environment for long-run economic health.

We have seen from classical analysis and the equation of exchange that, in the long run, aggregate supply is vertical and fixed at full employment, and changes in the supply of money result directly in changes in the price level. The Federal Reserve does seem to target low inflation rates as its long-term goal and has argued that this is the best policy for long-run economic growth.

Short Run: Price Level and Income

In the short run, demand and supply shocks to the economy may require differing approaches to monetary policy. The direction of monetary policy and its extent depends on whether it targets the price level or income and output, and whether the shock to the economy comes from the demand or supply side.

Demand Shocks. Demand shocks to the economy can come from reductions in consumer demand, investment, government spending, or exports, or from an increase in imports. Turning to Figure 5 on the next page, let us consider an economy that is initially in full employment equilibrium at point e. A demand shock then reduces aggregate demand to AD_1. At the new equilibrium (point a), the price level and output fall, to P_1 and Q_1. Notice that one target, output, is worse off than before; the other, the price level, is better off.

An expansionary monetary policy will increase the money supply, shifting aggregate demand back to AD_0, restoring employment and output to full employment. In

---

[4]Carl Walsh, "A Primer on Monetary Policy, Part 1: Goals and Instruments," *FRBSF Economic Letter,* August 5, 1994, reprinted in Jack Rabin and Glenn Stevens, *Handbook of Monetary Policy* (New York: Marcel Dekker), 2002, p. 299.

FIGURE 5

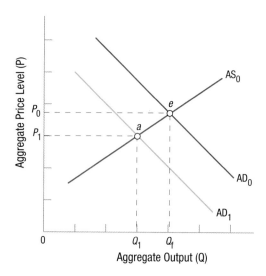

Demand Shocks and Monetary Policy

Monetary policy can be effective in counteracting a demand shock. The economy begins in full employment equilibrium at point *e*. Then a demand shock reduces aggregate demand to AD_1. At the new equilibrium (point *a*), the price level falls to P_1 and output falls to Q_1. An expansionary monetary policy will increase the money supply, shifting aggregate demand back to AD_0. This policy restores employment and output back to full employment, while restoring prices to their original level. Notice that whether the Fed targets price stability or full employment output, restoring either prices or output to their original levels requires increasing aggregate demand in a way that also restores the other variable to its original level.

this case, targeting either the original price level or the original income and output level will bring the economy back to the same point of equilibrium, point *e*. If the Fed targets the price level, increasing aggregate demand enough to restore the price level to P_0, full employment results. And if the Fed targets full employment output, raising aggregate demand sufficiently to restore output to level Q_f, this restores the price level to P_0.

A positive demand shock will produce a corresponding, though opposite, result. The positive demand shock will jolt output and the price level upward. Contractionary monetary policy will reduce both of them, restoring the economy to its original equilibrium.

For demand shocks, therefore, no conflict arises between the twin goals of monetary policy. Not only is the objective of full employment compatible with the objective of stable prices, but also by targeting either one of these objectives, the Fed takes steps that work to bring about the other.

Supply Shocks. Supply shocks can hit the economy for many reasons, including changes in resource costs such as a rise in oil prices, changes in inflationary expectations, or changes in technology. Looking at Figure 6, let us again consider an economy initially in full employment equilibrium at point *e*. Assume that a negative shock to the economy, say, an oil price spike, shifts aggregate supply from AS_0 to AS_1. The new equilibrium (point *a*) occurs at a higher price level (P_1) and lower output (Q_1).

Notice that not only has price level stability worsened, but so has output and income. Contrast this with the situation earlier, when a demand shock worsened the economy for one of its targets, but improved it for the other.

Supply shocks are virtually impossible to counteract because of their doubly negative results. Shifting AD_0 to AD_1 by increasing the money supply will restore

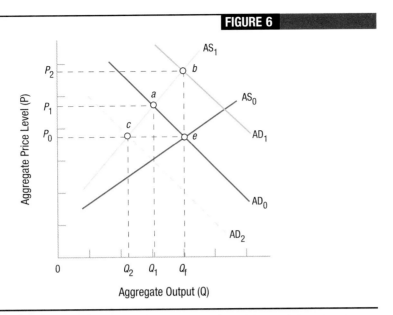

FIGURE 6

Supply Shocks and Monetary Policy

Monetary policy is less effective in counteracting a supply shock than a demand shock. The economy begins in full employment equilibrium at point e, until a negative supply shock shifts aggregate supply from AS_0 to AS_1. The new equilibrium (point a) is at a higher price level P_1 and lower output Q_1. This doubly negative result means a supply shock will be nearly impossible to counter. The Fed could increase the money supply to shift AD_0 to AD_1; this would restore the economy to full employment output Q_f. Yet, it also moves equilibrium to point b, where the price level is even higher, at P_2. Alternatively, the Fed could focus on price level stability, using contractionary monetary policy to shift aggregate demand to AD_2 and return prices to P_0. This results, however, in a reduction of output and income to Q_2, further deepening the recession.

the economy to full employment output Q_f. But at the same time, equilibrium moves to point b, where the price level is even higher, at P_2.

Alternatively, the Fed could focus on price level stability, using contractionary monetary policy to return the price level back to P_0 by shifting aggregate demand to AD_2. This results, however, in a reduction of output and income to Q_2. The decision to restore price stability makes the recession worse.

Implications for Short-Run Monetary Policy. Again, there is general agreement among economists that monetary policy should focus on price stability in the long run, while focusing on output or income in the short run. When a demand shock strikes, following this short-run policy course has the same effect as using price stability as the goal. When a supply shock occurs, however, targeting nominal income or output is preferable, since it permits the Fed to spread the shock's impact between income and output losses and price level increases. Figure 7 on the next page shows why.

In this figure, a supply shock has reduced output and income to Q_1 (point a). If the Fed targeted the price level, output would fall even further (point c), which could turn the recession into a depression.

The Fed can mitigate some of the effects of the supply shock, however, by using an expansionary policy that targets output and income. When aggregate demand is shifted to AD_1, the economy will suffer some added increase in the price level, which rises from P_1 to P_2. Yet, output will also rise from Q_1 to Q_2, and this reduces the severity of the recession. Notice that the Fed will not immediately try to push the economy back to full employment, since this action results in higher inflation (point b). Moving the economy back to full employment will be spread over several periods.

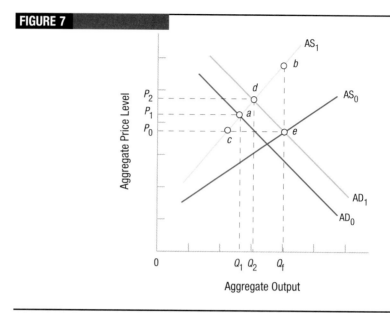

FIGURE 7

Targeting Output (income) and Supply Shocks

When a supply shock occurs, the Federal Reserve is best off targeting nominal income or output, since this permits the Fed to spread out the shock's impact between income and output losses and price level increases. This figure shows why. A supply shock has reduced output and income to Q_1 (point a). If the Fed targeted the price level, output would fall even further (point c), and the recession could turn into a depression. By using an expansionary policy that targets output and income, on the other hand, the Fed can mitigate some of the effects of the supply shock. Shifting aggregate demand to AD_1 raises the price level from P_1 to P_2, but also raises output from Q_1 to Q_2, reducing the severity of the recession. Notice that the Fed will not try to push the economy all the way back to full employment, since this would increase inflation (point b).

Rules or Discretion?

The Federal Reserve Act gives the Board of Governors significant discretion for conducting monetary policy. It sets out several goals—full employment, price stability, and reasonable interest rates—but leaves it up to the discretion of the Board how best to reach these objectives.

The complexities of monetary policy discussed above have led some economists, most notably Milton Friedman, to call for monetary rules that guide monetary policymakers. These procedural rules would essentially make policymakers "semiautomatons."

Other economists argue that modern economies are too complex to be managed by a few simple rules. Constantly changing institutions, economic behaviors, and technologies mean that some discretion, and perhaps even complete discretion, is essential for policymakers.

The performance of monetary authorities over the last two decades shows how effective discretionary monetary policy can be. Price stability has improved, unemployment and output levels have rebounded, interest rates have been low, and economic growth has been solid.

Nevertheless, the stock market retreat of 2000–02 and the modest recession that accompanied it remind us of the challenges that can still confront policymakers. Slow economic growth and technology-induced productivity increases caused reductions in employment. This gave rise to a situation many analysts dubbed "jobless growth" that seemingly made this last recession appear resistant to fiscal and monetary policy.

Simple Rules (Targets) to Guide Monetary Policy

Some economists argue that if policymakers used a simple and efficient rule on which to base successful monetary policy, they would have enough incentive to adopt it voluntarily, since it would guarantee success and their job would be much easier. If such a rule could be found, the case for mandatory legal rules to strictly guide the Fed would be weakened considerably. But what would such a voluntary rule look like?

It would have to be simple, direct, and unambiguous. The rule would therefore be fixed, meaning that reacting to unforeseen future circumstances would require changes in the rule. Given the complexities and uncertainties surrounding the monetary transmission channels and the economy, it is doubtful such a rule could cope with the various shocks that strike.

Peter Bofinger suggested that the difficulties in determining money's impact on the economy have made the key question for central banks the question of "how to frame their monetary policy so as to achieve the ultimate goal of low inflation while at the same time being flexible enough to accommodate supply shocks and to compensate demand shocks."[5] He added that this would not be an easy task.

Still, this does not mean that economists and Fed policymakers are not constantly searching for simple rules to guide monetary policy. Turning to a few of the proposals that have been suggested, we will begin with a look at monetary targeting, the practice of setting a fixed rate for the growth of the money supply. We will then consider inflation targeting, where policymakers set inflationary targets and take the necessary monetary actions needed to keep the economy in these ranges.

Monetary Targeting

Monetary targeting, as the name implies, aims to secure the steady growth of money stocks such as M1 or M2. In taking this approach, Fed policymakers use the equation of exchange, or quantity theory, to lay down a long-run path they would like to see the economy follow. The Fed then keeps a close eye on the economy's various monetary aggregates. If their growth is below the target level, the Board of Governors lowers interest rates or the FOMC buys bonds; if money stocks are growing too rapidly, the Fed enacts the opposite policies.

Friedman argued that variations in monetary growth are a major source of instability in the economy. To counter this problem, which is compounded by the long and variable lags in enacting discretionary monetary policy, Friedman advocated the adoption of monetary growth rules. Specifically, he proposed increasing the money supply by a set percentage every year, at a level consistent with long-term price stability and economic growth.

Remember that Friedman and other monetarists, like the classical economists before them, believe the economy to be inherently stable. If they are correct, then generating a steady increase in the money supply should reduce the destabilizing effects monetary policy can have on the economy. But how well would a rule such as Friedman's handle supply and demand shocks? Let us look at this issue.

Supply and Demand Shocks. Turning to Figure 8 on the next page, we begin once more with the economy at full employment equilibrium at point *e*. Assume now that the economy is hit with a negative demand shock, such as a reduction in exports. Aggregate demand declines to AD_1, and equilibrium moves to point *a*, where the price level and output are lower. Assuming Friedman's monetary growth rule is being observed, monetary policy keeps the money supply growing at a steady low rate. This action reduces interest rates, though not enough to move the economy back

Monetary targeting
Keeps the growth of money stocks such as M1 or M2 on a steady path, following the equation of exchange (or quantity theory), to set a long-run path for the economy that keeps inflation in check.

---

[5]Bofinger, *Monetary Policy*, p. 241.

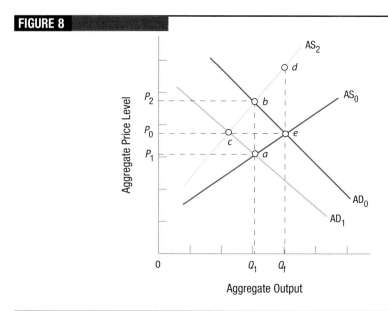

FIGURE 8

Supply and Demand Shocks and Monetary Policy

How well will a rule such as Friedman's monetary growth rule handle supply and demand shocks? In this figure, the economy begins in full employment equilibrium at point e, until it is hit with a negative demand shock. Aggregate demand declines to AD_1 and equilibrium moves to point a, where both the price level and output are lower. Assuming Friedman's monetary growth rule is observed, monetary policy will keep the money supply growing at a steady low rate. This reduces interest rates somewhat, though probably not enough to move the economy back to full employment in the short run. Only with time will adjustments in wages and prices return the economy to point e. Whether this result is acceptable to policymakers depends on the severity and duration of the recession.

Consider how Friedman's rule handles a negative supply shock; again, the beginning equilibrium is at point e. When the supply shock hits, equilibrium moves to point b, with higher prices, P_2. The monetary growth rule keeps aggregate demand constant at AD_0, which is better than policymakers' attempts to reduce inflation by reducing aggregate demand to AD_1. This would simply deepen the recession, moving the economy to point c. The monetary growth rule similarly keeps policymakers from attempting to restore full employment by increasing aggregate demand, which would simply move the economy to point d, thereby increasing inflation.

to full employment in the short run. Only over time will adjustments in wages and prices gradually return the economy to point e.

If the change in aggregate demand is small or temporary, a monetary growth rule will probably function well enough. But if the change is large, persistent, or continual, as was the case in the Great Depression, a discretionary monetary policy aimed at bringing the economy back to full employment more quickly would probably be preferred.

Consider a negative supply shock from, say, an increase in energy prices. Again, the initial equilibrium is at point e in Figure 8. When the supply shock hits, equilibrium will move to point b, with higher prices, P_2. The monetary growth rule keeps aggregate demand constant at AD_0. This is better than policymakers attempting to reduce inflation by reducing aggregate demand to AD_1, since this would simply deepen the recession, moving the economy to point c. The monetary growth rule similarly keeps policymakers from attempting to restore full employment by increasing aggregate demand, which would move the economy to point d, increasing inflation.

In some cases, a monetary rule keeps policymakers from making things worse by keeping them from doing anything. Yet, the monetary rule also prevents policymakers from aiding the economy when a policy change is needed. This would be especially helpful when the economy suffers modest demand shocks. When supply shocks hit, a monetary policy that moves the economy toward one target moves it away from the other. In this case, policymakers argue that they need to be able to balance one goal against another, rather than being tied down to strict rules that in the end do nothing.

In an interview in the *Financial Times,* on June 6, 2003, Milton Friedman noted that "the use of quantity of money as a target has not been a success," and "I'm not sure I would as of today push it as hard as I once did." Rather than money-supply targeting, more countries are committed to inflation targeting because of their universally positive experiences over the last two decades.

Inflation Targeting

Inflation targeting involves setting targets on the inflation rate, usually around 2% a year. If inflation (or the forecasted rate of inflation) exceeds the target, contractionary policy is employed, and vice versa. Inflation targeting has the virtue of explicitly reiterating that the long-run goal of monetary policy is price stability.[6]

Inflation targeting
Involves setting targets on the inflation rate, usually around 2% a year in recognition that the long-run goal of monetary policy is price stability.

Supply and Demand Shocks. Let us remain with Figure 8, again beginning in full employment equilibrium at point *e.* Again, assume that a negative demand shock hits the economy. Aggregate demand declines to AD_1 and equilibrium moves to point *a,* where both the price level and output are lower. Inflation targeting means that discretionary expansionary monetary policy will be used to bring the economy back to full employment at point *e.*

Now consider a negative supply shock from an increase in the price of energy or some other raw material. Equilibrium moves to point *b,* where the price level is higher, at P_2. Inflation targeting means that contractionary monetary policy should be used to return the economy to price level P_0. This reduces aggregate demand to AD_1, thus deepening the recession as the economy moves to point *c.* In reality, few monetary authorities would stick to an inflation targeting approach in this situation. They would be more likely to stimulate the economy slightly, hoping to move it back to Q_f with only a small increase in inflation.

The Fed's Performance

Determining how to measure the impact of the Federal Reserve policy on our huge complex economy is not easy. Figure 9 on the next page shows how three variables—unemployment, inflation, and interest rates—have fared during the tenure of the four Fed chairmen over the last three decades.

During the period when Arthur Burns headed the Fed, inflation was rising. The oil supply shock of 1973 was apparently met with a rather accommodative monetary policy as aggregate demand shifted out (look back at Figure 8). After the oil shock, the economy moved out toward point *d* from point *b.*

The economy was hit with a second oil price shock in the late 1970s and by the early 1980s, inflation had risen to double digits, peaking at nearly 14% in 1980. Paul Volcker, the new head of the Fed, decided to get very aggressive in fighting inflation. During his tenure, he used contractionary monetary policy to reduce inflation. By 1986, inflation had been reduced to slightly more than 2%, a remarkable feat.

During the 1990s, the Fed under Alan Greenspan alternated between encouraging output growth (mid 1990s) and fighting inflation (early and late 1990s). The Fed did a good job of keeping the economy near full employment. Interest rates trended down, and inflation was moderate during the 1990s and early 2000s. The most recent chairman, Ben Bernanke, took over in 2006.

Overall, the Fed has done a remarkable job of implementing monetary policy in the last three decades. Note how the high inflation-generated interest rates of

[6]For an extended discussion of inflation targeting, see Edwin Truman, *Inflation Targeting in the World Economy* (Washington D.C.: Institute for International Economics), 2003.

FIGURE 9

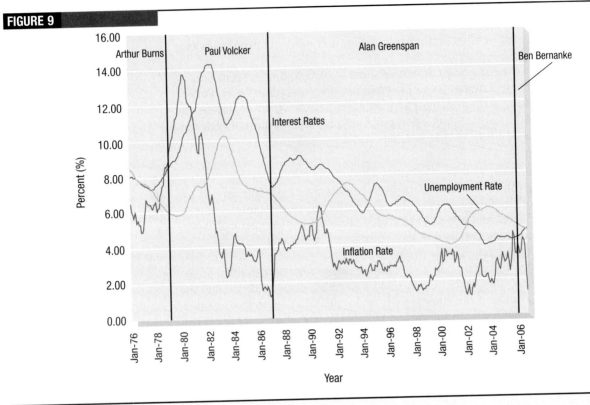

Inflation, Interest Rates, and Unemployment (1976–2006)

The Federal Reserve's record over the past 25 years has been admirable. After wringing inflation out of the system, the Fed has generally followed a low-interest rate policy that has paid off in steady economic growth.

the early 1980s have been wrung out of the system. The Fed has generally followed a low-interest rate policy once these inflation excesses were dampened. The dip in the GDP deflator below 2% during the late 1990s was followed by concerns of deflation. These fears were reduced in 2005 when a rebounding economy put the Fed on guard against gathering inflation. In addition, there has been reasonably steady growth over the past 20+ years, except for the short recessions in 1990–91 and 2001.

Even so, Fed policymaking has not always been smooth over the last 20 years. Look at interest rates in 1994, when the Fed raised interest rates seven times.[7] Its aggressive action caused turmoil in the financial markets, resulting in the default of Orange County, California, bonds, a run on the Mexican peso, and the failure of the Wall Street firm Kidder Peabody.

Based on our examination of the Fed's overall stellar record over the past 25 years and the turmoil in 1994, we can expect two things. First, the Fed likely will seek to continue this low-interest rate climate to stimulate sustained growth. Second, the Fed is likely to move more slowly and methodically in raising interest rates.

Monetary authorities use the discount rate, reserve requirements, and open market operations to implement monetary policy. In the longer term, increases in the money supply result in higher price levels. In the short run, however, increas-

---

[7]For the information on 1994, see Martin Crutsinger, "Fed Prepares to Hike Interest Rates—Gently," *Journal News,* May 3, 2004, p. 7A.

ing the supply of money can boost output, income, and the price level. In the next chapter, we will look at how budget deficits modify the effectiveness of monetary and fiscal policy.

Checkpoint

Implementing Monetary Policy

REVIEW

- In the long run, the Fed targets price stability. Low rates of inflation are most conducive to long-run economic health.
- In the short run, demand and supply shocks to the economy require different approaches to monetary policy.
- Monetary policy can target either the price level or output when the shock to the economy comes from the demand side. The objective of full employment is compatible with the objective of stable prices.
- Supply shocks present a more serious problem for monetary policy. A negative supply shock reduces output, but increases the price level. Expansionary monetary policy to increase output further increases the price level, and contractionary policy to reduce the price level worsens the recession. Targeting nominal income is preferable, since it permits the Fed to spread the shock's impact between income losses and price level increases.
- Monetary targeting focuses monetary policy on the rate of growth of the money supply. Inflation targeting involves setting targets on the inflation rate, usually around 2%. Both approaches have their plusses and minuses, but inflation targeting seems to be the trend today.

QUESTION

Explain why a negative supply shock such as rising oil prices is a difficult problem for monetary policy authorities to compensate for.

Answers to the Checkpoint question can be found at the end of this chapter.

Transparency and the Federal Reserve

How does the Fed convey information about its actions, and why is this important? For many years, the Fed took a "just trust us" approach to setting monetary policy. Decisions were made in secrecy, and often they were executed in secrecy: The public did not know that monetary policy was being changed. Since monetary policy affects the economy, the Fed's secrecy stimulated much speculation in financial markets about current and future Fed actions. Uncertainty led to various counterproductive actions by people guessing incorrectly. These activities were highly inefficient.

When Alan Greenspan became chairman of the Fed in 1987, this policy of secrecy started to change.[8] By 1994, the Fed released a policy statement each time it changed interest rates, and by 1998 it included a "tilt" statement forecasting what would probably happen in the next month or two. By 2000, the FOMC released a statement after each of its eight meetings even if policy remained the same.

Paul Anderson/Getty Images

---

[8]See the informative article by Greg Ip, "Fed's Big Question: Not What to Do, But What to Say," *Wall Street Journal,* October 27, 2003, p. A1.

This new openness has come about from the Fed's recognition that monetary policy is mitigated because financial actors may take counterproductive actions if they are uncertain what the Fed will do. A "just trust us" approach may be effective when the Fed generates broad confidence, but confidence can be a fleeting thing.[9] So the Fed's openness helps economic actors understand what the Fed is doing, and they can adjust their actions accordingly.

Yet this Fed "transparency," as it is called, is controversial within the Fed itself. It is not that Fed members want to go back to the "just trust us" approach. Rather, it has to do with two aspects of transparency, which can be called the "look back" and "look forward" approaches.[10]

There seems to be widespread agreement that the Fed should be transparent in a "look back" sense. By this is meant that the Fed should explain why it acted or failed to act. In the words of William Poole, president of the Federal Reserve Bank of St. Louis, Missouri:

> *Explaining a policy action—elucidating the considerations that led the FOMC to decide to adjust the intended funds rate, or to leave it unchanged—is worthwhile. Over time, the accumulation of such explanations helps the market, and perhaps the FOMC itself, to understand what the policy regularities are. It is also important to understand that many—perhaps most—policy actions have precedent value. . . . One of the advantages of public disclosure of the reasons for policy actions is that the required explanation forces the FOMC to think through what it is doing and why.*[11]

This is a clear statement that Fed transparency on why it took certain actions helps the market understand what is going on in the macroeconomy, what the Fed does in certain circumstances, and what the Fed is likely to do in similar future situations. It forces the Fed to act rationally. It brings in an element of predictability for the future, though it clearly does not tie the Fed's hands.

It is this tying of the Fed's hands that is at issue with the second aspect of transparency, which has to do with the looking-forward comments or tilt that are now included with the Fed's statements. A tilt statement could be "With inflation quite low and resource use slack, the Fed can be patient in removing its policy accommodation"; the phrase "can be patient" reveals the Fed's proclivities for the immediate future. One side thinks the Fed should do more of this. As Fed Chairman Ben Bernanke suggested, the Fed should say more about where the economy is headed and what the Fed will do because this affects the bond market and so strengthens monetary policy effects.[12] St. Louis Fed president William Poole, on the other hand, believes that revealing a tilt ties the Fed's hands because past pronouncements will make it harder for the Fed to change directions.[13]

Right now, the Fed's tilt is part of regular Fed statements and is likely to remain. Should opinions within the Fed diverge to the extent that Fed Chairman Bernanke finds it difficult to come up with a consensus, the tilt could disappear, but this is unlikely because it has become such a regular part of Fed's public utterings. Currently, with the debate going on inside the Fed itself about forward-looking transparency, it is unlikely that the tilt will become more detailed than it is now.

Some pundits have referred to deciphering what lies behind the tilt as "reading the tea leaves." This is likely to be the state of affairs for years to come. So there

---

[9]See the authors' response to the book review by James K. Galbraith of Ben Bernanke, Thomas Laubach, Frederic Mishkin, and Adam S. Posen, *Missing the Mark: The Truth About Inflation Targeting*, found in *Foreign Affairs*, September/October 1999, pp. 158–161.

[10]See William Poole, "Fed Transparency: How, Not Whether," The Federal Reserve Bank of St. Louis, *Review*, November/December 2003.

[11]Poole, "Fed Transparency," p. 5.

[12]Ip, "Fed's Big Question," p. A1.

[13]See William Poole, "FOMC Transparency," The Federal Reserve Bank of St. Louis *Review*, January/February 2005.

will still be a tension between strengthening the effect of monetary policy by conveying information on decision making to financial markets and tying the hands of monetary policymakers by revealing likely future courses of action.

Easy money or expansionary monetary policy, p. 281

Tight money, restrictive, or contractionary monetary policy, p. 281

Equation of exchange, p. 281

Classical monetary transmission mechanism, p. 282

Liquidity trap, p. 286

Keynesian monetary transmission mechanism, p. 286

Monetarist transmission mechanism, p. 289

Information lag, p. 291

Recognition lag, p. 291

Decision lag, p. 292

Implementation lag, p. 292

Monetary targeting, p. 297

Inflation targeting, p. 299

Monetary Theories

The quantity theory of money is a product of the classical school of economics. Classical economics focuses on long-run adjustments in economic activity and concludes that the economy will tend toward equilibrium at full employment in the long run.

Classical quantity theory is defined by the equation of exchange:

$$M \times V = P \times Q$$

In this equation, M is the supply of money, V is its velocity, P is the price level, and Q is the economy's output. Classical theorists considered the velocity of money to be limited by the prevailing monetary institutions and technology, and aggregate output to be fixed at full employment. The result is that a change in the money supply will translate directly in a change in prices, or that $\Delta M = \Delta P$. Thus, classical quantity theory predicts that, in the long run, changes in the money supply will bring about directly proportionate changes in the aggregate price level.

Keynesian monetary analysis was developed during the 1930s. It examines the short-run effects that changes in the money supply have on interest rates and subsequently on investment, consumption, and output.

Keynes identified three motives that people have for holding money in their portfolios. Individuals and firms need some money to buy and sell goods and services; this is the transactions motive for holding money. The precautionary motive reflects the desire most individuals and firms have to keep some money on hand to deal with unforeseen circumstances. Finally, Keynes recognized that people sometimes hold money rather than interest-bearing bonds to speculate against changes in interest rates or the price level; this is the speculative motive for holding money.

According to Keynesian analysis, an increase in the money supply causes the price of bonds to rise and the interest rate to fall. Falling interest rates boost investment, which raises aggregate demand and thus increases aggregate income, output, and employment.

Monetarism first arose in the 1960s as a response to Keynesian monetary analysis; it was pioneered by Milton Friedman. Monetarism focuses on the long run and assumes the economy will ultimately stabilize itself around full employment.

Friedman pioneered the notion that consumption levels are determined not only by income but also by wealth. This idea led him to develop the concept of permanent income, the present value of an individual's future stream of labor income as a proxy for wealth. Friedman then altered the demand for money to include wealth (permanent income) and other variables. Friedman's analysis suggests that the demand for real money balances will be higher if (1) wealth or permanent income is higher, (2) the rate of return on other assets is lower, and (3) the expected rate of inflation is lower.

Friedman assumed that utility-maximizing individuals will allocate their wealth among various assets until the marginal rates of return are equal. Thus, when the money supply increases, people will discover that they are holding more money than they desire, and the additional supply of money decreases the return on money. Excess money balances will thus be exchanged for other financial and real assets, including bonds, real estate, and consumer durables such as cars and houses. Eventually, portfolios will rebalance and markets will return to equilibrium.

Monetary Policy Lags

Monetary policy is subject to four major lags. The information lag refers to the time it takes—often 1 to 3 months—for monetary authorities to receive data that reflect events occurring in the economy. Because these data are often revised, and it can take some time before certain trends in the data become clear, policymakers face an even longer recognition lag before they can be certain they are facing a problem in the economy that demands a response.

There is then a decision lag as the Fed weighs the appropriate policy response, although this lag is usually minimal, given that the Board of Governors meets monthly. But there can be an implementation lag of months or even years before the effects of a monetary policy change begin to be felt throughout the economy.

Implementing Monetary Policy

In conducting monetary policy, the Fed has the broad option of targeting either a stable price level or full employment income and output. Most economists agree that, in the long run, the Fed should target price stability since low rates of inflation have been shown to provide the best environment for long-run economic growth.

In the short run, demand and supply shocks to the economy may need differing approaches to monetary policy. When a demand shock hits the economy, no conflict arises between the twin goals of monetary policy. Not only is the aim of full employment compatible with the objective of stable prices, but also in targeting either one of these objectives, the Fed will take steps that help to bring about the other.

When a supply shock hits the economy, in contrast, both price stability and output worsen. If the Fed then increases the money supply to restore the economy to full employment, this action only drives inflation up further, whereas if the Fed enacts a contractionary policy to stabilize prices, this move will just lead to a deeper recession. Most economists agree that when a supply shock occurs, an expansionary policy is best since it permits the Fed to spread the shock's impact between income and output losses and price level increases.

The complexities of monetary policy implementation have led some economists, notably Milton Friedman, to call for monetary rules to guide monetary policymakers. Other economists argue that modern economies are too complex to be managed by a few simple rules. Changing institutions, economic behaviors, and technologies require some discretion by policymakers.

Any monetary policymaking rule, whether legally binding or merely advisory, runs the risk of leaving policymakers unable to deal with quickly changing conditions. Economists and Fed policymakers are continually searching for simple rules to guide monetary policy. Most of the proposals that have been offered involve either monetary targeting or inflation targeting.

Monetary targeting aims to secure the steady growth of money stocks such as M1 or M2. In taking this approach, Fed policymakers use the equation of exchange, or quantity theory, to lay down a long-run path they would like to see the economy follow. The Fed then keeps a close eye on the economy's various monetary aggregates. If their growth is below the target level, the Fed uses expansionary policy; if money stocks are growing too rapidly, the Fed uses contractionary policy. Rules are least likely to be effective when a supply shock hits, given that promoting full employment under these conditions is likely to worsen inflation.

Inflation targeting involves setting targets on the inflation rate, usually of around 2% a year. If inflation (or the forecasted rate of inflation) then exceeds this target, the Fed implements a contractionary policy, and vice versa. Inflation targeting has the virtue of explicitly acknowledging that the long-run goal of monetary policy is price stability.

Questions and Problems

1. Consider the following quote:

   There are two forces that cause the economy to grow. One is real, the other is an illusion. The real force—entrepreneurial innovation and creativity— comes naturally as long as government policies do not drive it away. The artificial force is easy money. An increased supply of money, by creating an illusion of wealth, can increase spending in the short run, but this eventually turns into inflation. Printing money cannot possibly create wealth; if it could, counterfeiting would be legal.[14]

   Does this quote illustrate the short run versus the long-run aspects of monetary policy? Why or why not?

2. If oil (or energy) prices double, then remain steady at the new higher price, and the Fed *does nothing,* will inflation rise and continue at the new higher rate, or will it rise temporarily, then fall back to its former rate?

3. The *Financial Times* on June 8, 2006, reported that "the European Central Bank has lost patience with inflation that has remained persistently higher than its 2 per cent definition of price stability. It is almost certain to raise the cost of borrowing today, perhaps by 0.5 percentage points." Explain why increasing the "cost of borrowing" is an appropriate policy in this case.

4. It seems that each time the Fed raises interest rates, the stock market has an awful few days. Why do higher interest rates have such an impact on the stock market?

5. If the Fed persistently pursues an easy money policy, what is the likely outcome?

6. Why is it important for the Federal Reserve Board to be independent of the executive branch of the federal government?

7. What does the equation of exchange, $M \times V = P \times Q$, help explain?

[14]Brian Wesbury, "Economic Rehab," *Wall Street Journal*, June 7, 2006, p. A14.

8. Describe how open market operations alter the supply of money.

9. In 2002, when the Fed reduced the discount rate to around 1%, some commentators became concerned that the interest rate was so low that the Fed's ability to conduct monetary policy might be compromised. But Ben Bernanke, then a Fed governor, suggested

   > As I have mentioned, some observers have concluded that when the central bank's policy rate falls to zero—its practical minimum—monetary policy loses its ability to further stimulate aggregate demand and the economy. At a broad conceptual level, and in my view in practice as well, this conclusion is clearly mistaken. Indeed, under a fiat (that is, paper) money system, a government (in practice, the central bank in cooperation with other agencies) should always be able to generate increased nominal spending and inflation, even when the short-term nominal interest rate is at zero.

   Do you agree? Why or why not?

10. When the interest rate falls, people desire higher money balances. Why?

11. How is the impact of expansionary monetary policy different if the economy is considerably below full employment than when it is at full employment?

12. The May 13, 2006, issue of *The Economist* noted that "rather than worrying about being predictable—indicating to markets precisely what they are going to do next—central bankers ought to worry about being transparent—explaining how they think and why they choose their policies." How transparent can central banks be in explaining their reasoning for policy? Would it be easier for monetary authorities to be more transparent if they have an explicit framework such as inflation targeting?

13. Why are supply shocks so much harder than demand shocks for monetary policy to adjust to? Use the graph below to show your answer to this question.

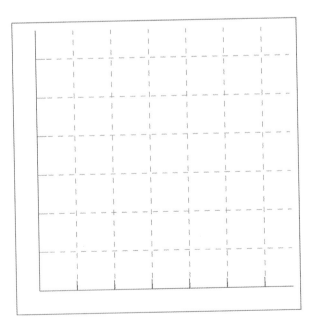

14. When NASA scientists were operating the Mars rovers, remotely driving them across the Martian landscape to collect and analyze rocks and crevices, the scientists complained that the 20-minute delay between when they issued a com-

mand and when the rovers responded made their job more challenging. Isn't this somewhat similar to what monetary policymakers face? How is it different?

15. William Poole, president of the Federal Reserve Bank of St. Louis, recently suggested, "We may face more inflation pressure than currently shows up in the formal data. . . . Statistical studies to detect pass-through from recent energy price increases have failed to show significant effects in U.S. price data. . . . But stories about widespread pass-through are becoming increasingly common." Another Fed policymaker, Randall Kroszner, concluded, "We want to try to look where inflation is going. We don't want to look in the rearview mirror at what has happened to inflation."[15] What policymaking problems are these two Fed members alluding to? Why are these problems important?

Answers to Checkpoint Questions

CHECKPOINT: MONETARY THEORIES

The speculative demand for money influences interest rates and is most important for monetary policy, because interest rates affect consumption and investment spending.

CHECKPOINT: MONETARY POLICY LAGS

Monetary policy lags are important because the economy is always changing. Policy lags often force policymakers to base policy decisions on forecasts, not where the economy is at the time of the decision. Once policy is made, the economy may change so much (or the data may be revised) between the time of decision and implementation that what was right for the economy 6 months ago is not right for it today.

CHECKPOINT: IMPLEMENTING MONETARY POLICY

Negative supply shocks increase the price level and at the same time lead to a reduction in output and employment. Any monetary policy improves one variable but hurts the other. For example, expansionary monetary policy designed to increase output will lead to a higher price level. Alternatively, contractionary policy to reduce the price level will result in output and employment declining further.

---

[15]"Data May Not Fully Reflect Inflation, Fed Officials Say," *New York Times*, June 17, 2006.

Federal Deficits and Public Debt

13

Some people have
compared the federal
government to an infant: It
has a limitless appetite at
one end and no sense of
responsibility at the other.
— Todd Buchholz

lexander Hamilton, Secretary of the Treasury in George Washington's administration, fought to establish a National Bank and to allow the federal government to borrow funds. His goal was to establish a powerful central government that would manage the economy and the money supply, promote industrialization, and finance public infrastructure projects such as roads and canals.

Thomas Jefferson, on the other hand, viewed public debt as a serious threat to the country and proposed that a balanced budget amendment be added to the constitution.[1] Jefferson and other Democrats feared that deficit spending and a high national debt would encourage the national government to "subvert the national balance of society, by empowering the central administration to dole out financial favors that would enable it to dominate the legislature and to achieve, on behalf of itself and its allies in the moneyed aristocracy . . . a tyrannical preeminence over the rest of society."[2] A quick read of any newspaper is enough to see that two centuries later, American politicians are still divided into those who take Hamilton's view of deficit spending and those who follow in Jefferson's footsteps.

As federal deficits approach $300 billion per year, most of us have a little bit of Jefferson inside of us. We know that each of us cannot have our spending overwhelm our revenues year after year. There are recognized periods when we can run a deficit—going to college is one—yet each of us knows we cannot have such a spending imbalance for the rest of our lives. With our personal situations in mind, we tend to project this spending imbalance on the federal deficit. It makes most of us uneasy. How much is too much?

In this chapter, we are going to explore the issue of whether deficits and debt will eventually destroy the economy. First, we will define what the public debt is, look at why deficits are persistent in our government, and then show what follows from a call to balance the budget. Second, we will examine how deficits are financed,

[1]Arthur Benavie, *Deficit Hysteria: A Common Sense Look at America's Rush to Balance the Budget* (Westport, CT: Praeger), 1998, p. 16.
[2]Daniel Shaviro, *Do Deficits Matter?* (Chicago: University of Chicago Press), 1997, pp. 18–19.

exploring the implications of the methods used today. Finally, we will look at the burden of the public debt, especially on future generations. We will analyze the effect of rising public debt on fiscal and monetary policy, and examine the fiscal sustainability of the federal budget. By the time this chapter is finished, you should have a good sense of the effect that deficits and public debt have on the economy.

After studying this chapter you should be able to

- Define deficits and the national debt.
- Describe public choice analysis.
- Describe the various approaches to balancing budgets.
- Describe the role of the Federal Reserve in financing debt and deficits.
- Analyze the relationship between budget and trade deficits.
- Explain the difference between internally and externally held debt.
- Describe the crowding-out effect.
- Analyze the sustainability of federal deficits.

Financing the Federal Government

We saw in a previous chapter that discretionary fiscal policy may call for increased government spending or tax reductions during times of recession. When the economy is expanding so rapidly that it risks overheating, government spending cuts or a tax increase may be warranted.

In the late 1990s, some economists argued that spending should be reduced, taxes increased, or a contractionary monetary policy implemented to cool down an economy and stock market that were overheating. Their advice was partly heeded, in that tax rates were increased as the economy entered a boom, and the federal budget ended the 1990s in surplus. The recession of 2001, caused in part by the fall in the stock market and a reduction in investment, moved the budget back into deficit. Let's first define deficits, surpluses, and public debt, before going on to consider if our government is prone to deficits.

Defining Deficits and the National Debt

Deficit
The amount by which annual government spending exceeds tax revenues.

Surplus
The amount by which annual tax revenues exceed government expenditures.

Public debt
The total accumulation of past deficits and surpluses; it includes treasury bills, notes, and bonds, and U.S. savings bonds.

A **deficit** is the amount by which annual government spending exceeds tax revenues. A **surplus** is the amount by which annual tax revenues exceed government expenditures. In 2000, the budget surplus was $236.4 billion. By 2003, tax cuts, a recession, and new commitments for national defense and homeland security had turned the budget surpluses of 1998–2001 into deficits—a deficit of roughly $250 billion for fiscal year 2007.

The **public debt**, or *national debt*, is the total accumulation of past deficits and surpluses. Gross public debt in 2007 was just over $9 trillion, but public debt held by the public was a little over half of that amount ($5 trillion). Some agencies of government, such as the Social Security Administration, the Treasury Department, and the Federal Reserve, hold some debt; one agency of government owes money to another. Debt held by the public (including foreign governments) is debt that represents a claim on government assets, not simply intergovernmental transfers.

Figure 1 shows the public debt held by the public as a percentage of gross domestic product (GDP) since 1940. During World War II, public debt exceeded GDP. It then trended downward until the early 1980s, when public debt began to climb again. Public debt held by the public as a percentage of GDP fell from the mid-1990s until 2002, first because of growing budget surpluses in the late 1990s, then because of falling interest rates (what the government has to pay on the debt), but it has risen since then. Public debt held by the public (as opposed to government institutions) is now 37% of GDP.

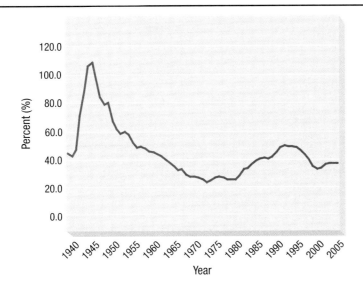

FIGURE 1

Public Debt Held by the Public as a Percent of GDP

The public debt as a percentage of GDP has varied considerably since 1940. During World War II, public debt exceeded GDP. It then trended downward until the early 1980s, when public debt began to climb again. Since the mid-1990s, public debt as a percentage of GDP has been falling, first because of budget surpluses at the turn of the century, then because of falling interest rates. Today, public debt held by the public (as opposed to government institutions) is 37% of GDP.

Public debt is held as U.S. Treasury securities including treasury bills, notes, bonds, and U.S. savings bonds. Treasury bills, or T-bills, as they are known, are short-term instruments with a maturity period of a year or less and pay a specific sum at maturity. T-bills do not pay interest. Rather, they are initially sold at a discount, and their yields are then determined by the time to maturity and the discount. T-bills are the most actively traded securities in the U.S. economy, and they are highly liquid, providing the closest thing there is to risk-free returns.

Treasury notes are financial instruments issued for periods ranging from 1 to 10 years, whereas treasury bonds have maturity periods exceeding 10 years. Both of these instruments have stated interest rates and are traded sometimes at discounts and sometimes at premiums. The discount or premium depends on interest rates and the coupon rates of the bonds. When market interest rates exceed the coupon rate, the note or bond will be discounted, and vice versa. Every week, the *Wall Street Journal* reports the various yields on treasuries and other securities; Table 1 on the next page provides an example.

Today, interest rates on the public debt are between 4% and 5% depending on the duration of the notes. This has not always been the case. In the early 1980s, interest rates varied from 11% to nearly 15%. Inflation was high and investors required high interest rates as compensation. When rates are high, government interest costs on the debt soar.

Interest on the debt as a percentage of GDP, as shown in Figure 2 on the next page, was steady from 1950 to 1980, hovering around 1.50%. This percentage more than doubled during the 1980s because of inflation, interest rates in the double digits, and rising budget deficits, along with a growing national debt. Since the

Table 1	Annualized Interest Rates on Certain Investments as Reported by the Federal Reserve Board on a Weekly Average Basis
	Week ended September 17, 2007
Treasury bills (90 day)	4.05
Commercial paper (financial, 90 day)	5.25
Commercial paper (nonfinancial, 90 day)	4.95
Certificates of deposit (resale 3 month)	5.52
Certificates of deposit (resale 6 month)	5.36
Federal funds (overnight)	5.33
Eurodollars (90 day)	5.60
Treasury bills (1 year)	4.23
Treasury notes (2 year)	4.08
Treasury notes (3 year)	4.11
Treasury notes (5 year)	4.21
Treasury notes (10 year)	4.48
Treasury bonds (20 year)	4.76

Source: The Federal Reserve.

mid-1980s, interest rates have dropped and deficits have fallen, even becoming surpluses for a short time. Consequently, interest as a percentage of GDP has declined to approach the level it was in the 1950s.

Now that we know what deficits and the public debt are, we can consider why deficits seem to persist in our government.

FIGURE 2

Public Debt Interest as a Percent of GDP

Interest on the debt as a percentage of GDP was steady from 1950 to 1980, hovering around 1.50%. This percentage more than doubled during the 1980s because of high inflation and high interest rates, along with growing budget deficits and a rising debt. Since the mid-1980s, interest rates have declined and deficits have fallen, even becoming surpluses for a short time. Therefore, interest as a percentage of GDP has declined to just above the level it was in the 1950s.

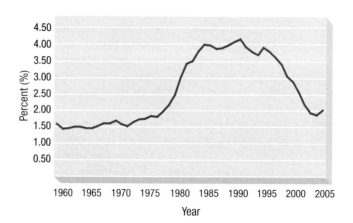

Public Choice Analysis

Why has deficit spending become almost endemic to our system of government? What impact do deficits have on the size and character of the federal government? These are the sorts of questions being asked by public choice economists.

Public choice theory involves the economic analysis of public and political decision making. It looks at such issues as voting, the relationship between voting and policy outcomes, the impact of election incentives on politicians, the influence of special interest groups, rent-seeking behaviors, and the effects of "rational ignorance" (Why do people take so much time and effort to vote when their votes count for so little?).

Public choice theorists often conclude that collective decision making is inherently flawed and inefficient. They view the government as a huge monopolist attempting to increase its size and power through higher taxes and other policies that end up devaluing its debt through unexpected inflation. Unanticipated inflation acts as a tax on debt holders as interest rates rise and bond values fall, creating capital losses.

James Buchanan, considered the father of public choice theory, essentially fused the disciplines of economics and political science. He was awarded the Nobel Prize in 1986 for "his development of the contractual and constitutional bases for the theory of economic and political decision making." Buchanan's analysis assumes that politicians and bureaucrats consider their own self-interest when making public policy. In this sense, they behave no differently than other economic actors, and this means our public policies may not always be guided by the "public interest."

As Robert Hershey noted, "Public choice can be considered the doctrine of the invisible foot; a negative analogue to Adam Smith's wealth-creating invisible hand."[3] Buchanan contrasted Adam Smith's description of social benefits that arise from private individuals acting in their own self-interest with the harm that frequently results from politicians doing the same thing. Competition among individuals and firms for jobs, customers, and profits creates wealth, and thus it benefits the entire society. Self-interested politicians, however, often instigate government interventions that are harmful to the larger economy. Driven by their own desire for reelection, politicians frequently cave in to pressure from special interest groups in ways that magnify market imperfections. Public choice analysis, therefore, suggests that government action should be limited.

Public choice economists like Buchanan argue that deficit spending reduces the perceived cost of current government operations. The result is that taxpayers permit some programs to exist that they would oppose if required to pay the full cost today. But this situation, public choice economists charge, amounts to shifting the cost of government to the next generation. And this intergenerational burden shifting, they argue, has led to the steady expansion of the federal government.

Public choice analysis helps us to understand why deficits seem inevitable: We do not pay the full costs of today's programs. Keep in mind the intergenerational issue as we examine the implications of balancing the budget.

Approaches to Federal Finance

Federal budget deficits have been the norm for the past 50 years, leading some observers to propose that the federal government, like state governments, should be required to balance its budget every year. Many economists argue that balancing the budget over the business cycle is a better approach, while still others have suggested that the federal government should focus on promoting full employment with stable prices, treating the budget deficit or surplus as a secondary concern. Let us examine each of these three approaches in greater detail.

Public choice theory
The economic analysis of public and political decision making, looking at issues such as voting, the impact of election incentives on politicians, the influence of special interest groups, and rent-seeking behaviors.

---

[3]Robert Hershey, " Man in the News; an Austere Scholar: James M. Buchanan", *New York Times*, October 17, 1986, p. D4.

Annually Balanced Budget

Annually balanced budget
Federal expenditures and taxes would have to be equal each year. Annually balanced budgets tend to be procyclical.

That the federal government should have an **annually balanced budget**, which means it would have to equate its revenues and expenditures every year, was the prevailing economic wisdom before the 1930s. The massive unemployment of the Great Depression, however, along with the appearance of Keynes's *General Theory* in 1936, caused many economists and policymakers to rethink their views. Today, we know that balancing the federal budget yearly would undercut fiscal policies aimed at maintaining full employment.

When an economy begins to fall into recession, output, income, and employment will all start to decline. Before long, tax revenues will begin to fall, even as government spending increases because of rising unemployment, which triggers increased payments for unemployment compensation. Both of these anticyclical automatic mechanisms tend to move the federal budget toward a deficit. But this is a welcome trend, since reducing taxes or increasing spending at the expense of running a deficit is often the best response to a looming recession. Such an expansionary fiscal policy is most likely to dampen the effects of the recession and restore the economy to its potential growth rate.

To insist on balancing the budget as recession looms by reducing spending or increasing taxes, would mandate a contractionary policy that would undoubtedly worsen the economic situation and thus ultimately increase the deficit. This is essentially what happened in the early 1930s. Many economists believe contractionary policies aimed at balancing the budget turned what probably would have been a modest recession into the global Depression.

As a result, few economists today favor annually balancing the federal budget, as the result would be incompatible with countercyclical fiscal policy.

Cyclically Balanced Budget

Cyclically balanced budget
Balancing the budget over the course of the business cycle by restricting spending or raising taxes when the economy is booming and using these surpluses to offset the deficits that occur during recessions.

To get around the procyclical aspects of annually balancing the budget, some economists have recommended having a **cyclically balanced budget**: balancing the budget over the course of the business cycle. The basic idea is to restrict spending or raise taxes when the economy is booming. By slowing spending growth or raising tax rates as the economy approaches the peak of the business cycle, overheating is reduced. These measures prevent inflationary pressures from taking hold, thereby heading off the need later to enact extreme contractionary policy measures. Surpluses, moreover, should accumulate during boom periods that can be used to offset deficits during downturns and recessions, when deficit spending is appropriate.

Balancing the budget over the business cycle is good in theory, and to an extent, this probably happens automatically as long as fiscal policy is held constant. When discretionary spending levels and tax rates are held reasonably stable, tax revenues will rise and spending will decline during booms, thereby creating either surpluses or smaller deficits. Conversely, tax revenues will fall and spending will rise during recessions, bringing on deficits. Automatic stabilizers, thus, tend to roughly equate spending and taxes over the course of the business cycle.

In practice, perfectly balancing the budget over the course of the business cycle is difficult and politically risky. Raising taxes during boom periods to create surpluses and dampen economic growth may be acceptable to the public and the political establishment, since everyone is more flexible during periods of economic expansion. Incomes are rising, so added taxes do not seem so onerous. And some of these added funds can be used to expand government services into areas of perceived need, while others are retained to build surpluses. But the political fact of life is that politicians are reluctant to raise taxes even when the economy is booming.

When recession arrives, however, the rhetorical knives are also sharpened and tax cuts and spending increases are called unfair, supposedly creating deficits "as far as the eye can see." What is naturally occurring and what is needed to correct the recession become the subject of rhetoric.

In addition, different phases of the business cycle are not of equal length or severity. Historically, booms tend to last longer than recessions. This complicates balancing the federal budget over a given cycle. Furthermore, forecasting turning points in business cycles along with their uncertain duration and extent is nearly impossible. Finally, and most problematic for a long-term balanced budget, politicians are always looking for new ways to serve their constituencies and find it difficult to ever cut spending.

Functional Finance

Economists who favor a **functional finance** approach to the federal budget believe the first priority of policymakers should be to keep the economy at full employment with stable prices. Whether the budget is in surplus or deficit is a secondary concern. Their view is that the government's primary macroeconomic responsibility is to foster economic growth and stable prices, while keeping the economy as close as possible to full employment.

Functional finance
Essentially ignores the impact of the budget on the business cycle and focuses on fostering economic growth and stable prices, while keeping the economy as close as possible to full employment.

The government's primary microeconomic job, meanwhile, is to provide those public goods and services that citizens want. These include national defense, a stable legal environment, and many other services we take for granted. Economists favoring a functional finance approach feel that if the government is successful in providing the right microeconomic mix and successful macroeconomic fiscal policies, deficits and surpluses will be unimportant. Rapidly growing and fully employed economies do not have significant public debt or deficit issues.

In sum, balancing the budget annually or over the business cycle may be either counterproductive or difficult to do. Furthermore, from public choice theory, we saw that balancing the budget is even more difficult when we consider politicians' incentives to spend and not raise taxes. Budget deficits begin to look like a normal occurrence in our political system.

Financing the Federal Government

REVIEW

- A deficit is the amount that government spending exceeds tax revenue in a particular year.
- The national debt is the total accumulation of past deficits and surpluses.
- Public choice analysis suggests that collective decision making is inherently flawed and inefficient, and deficit spending reduces the perceived cost of the current government operations.
- Several approaches to financing the federal government have been suggested, including annually balancing the budget, balancing the budget over the business cycle, and ignoring the budget deficit and focusing on promoting full employment and stable prices.

QUESTION

Is the absolute size of the national debt or the national debt as a percent of GDP the best measure of its importance to our economy? Explain.

Answers to the Checkpoint question can be found at the end of this chapter.

Financing Debt and Deficits

Seeing as how deficits may tend to be persistent, we now turn to the methods used by the federal government to finance debt and deficits. How does the government deal with debt, and what does this imply for the economy?

Government deals with debt in two ways. It can either borrow or sell assets. In borrowing, government sells bonds to government agencies, the Federal Reserve, and the public.

The Government Budget Constraint

Government budget constraint
The government budget is limited by the fact that $G - T = \Delta M + \Delta B + \Delta A$, where G is government spending and T is tax revenues, thus $(G - T)$ is the federal budget deficit; ΔM is the change in the money supply; ΔB is the change in bonds held by public entities, domestic and foreign; and ΔA represents the sales of government assets.

Given its power to print money and collect taxes, the federal government cannot go bankrupt. But it does face what economists call a **government budget constraint**:

$$G - T = \Delta M + \Delta B + \Delta A$$

where
G = government spending
T = tax revenues, thus $(G - T)$ is the federal budget deficit
ΔM = the change in the money supply
ΔB = the change in bonds held by public entities, domestic and foreign
ΔA = the sales of government assets

The Role of the Federal Reserve

Since government bonds are held by government agencies and the Federal Reserve, when the Federal Reserve buys bonds, it is exchanging cash for bonds. This part of the government's debt is therefore "monetized." With the Federal Reserve pumping new money into the money supply, the government is financing the deficit by "printing money" ($\Delta M > 0$).

If the Federal Reserve does not purchase the bonds, they may be sold to the public, including corporations, banks, mutual funds, individuals, and foreign entities. This also has the effect of financing the government's deficit ($\Delta B > 0$).

Asset sales ($\Delta A > 0$) represent only a small fraction of government finance in the United States. These sales include auctioning of the telecommunications spectra and offshore oil leases. Europe and many developing nations have used asset sales, or privatization, in recent years to bolster sagging government revenues and to encourage efficiency and development in the case where a government-owned industry is sold.

Thus, when the government runs a deficit, it must borrow funds from somewhere, assuming it does not sell assets. If the government borrows from the public, the quantity of publicly held bonds will rise; if it borrows from the Federal Reserve, the quantity of money in circulation will rise.

Budget and Trade Deficits

In earlier chapters, we learned that when an economy is at equilibrium (using budget and national income accounting arithmetic), all injections and withdrawals will be equal, thus:

$$G + I + X = T + S + M$$

In other words, government spending plus investment plus exports equals taxes plus savings plus imports.

By subtracting T from each side, we get

$$G - T + X + I = S + M$$

Now subtracting I and X from both sides and regrouping, this leaves

$$G - T = (S - I) + (M - X)$$

If the economy is at equilibrium, therefore, budget deficits (a positive number on the left side of the equation) must be made up by private savings $(S > I)$ or a trade deficit $(M > X)$. **Budget and trade deficits** are linked.

Budget and trade deficits
These are related by the following equation: $G - T = (S - I) + (M - X)$. So budget deficits must be covered by net domestic saving (private + corporate) or by net foreign saving (in the form of foreigners buying U.S. government bonds).

Implications of Deficit Financing in an Open Economy

Assume for a moment that investment and saving are equal, such that $(S - I) = 0$. With this constraint in place, the link between budget deficits and trade deficits becomes clear. If $T > G$ (a surplus) then $(M - X)$ must also be in surplus $(X > M)$. Conversely, when the budget turns to deficit $(T < G)$, a trade deficit will follow $(X < M)$.

The intuition here is this: If the United States runs a budget deficit, who buys its bonds? If savings and investments are equal, then bond purchases have to come from abroad. When we import, we send dollars abroad to pay for the goods and services we obtain. These dollars held abroad wind up as bond purchases. For there to be a surplus of dollars held abroad to soak up these U.S. deficit bonds, imports must be greater than exports, which is the definition of a trade deficit. Thus, budget deficits and trade deficits are linked.

Next, assume that exports and imports are equal $(X = M)$ such that the trade balance is zero. Budget deficits $(G > T)$ must be met by higher private saving $(S > I)$. This illustrates the crowding-out effect of government deficits. If G grows, with T and S remaining constant, investment must fall. Increased deficit spending by the government, therefore, crowds out private investment.

All this tells us that rising federal deficits must be paid for with rising trade deficits, rising private savings, falling investment, or some combination of these three. For example, in 2000 the government ran a *surplus* of nearly $200 billion in the National Income and Product Accounts and the trade deficit was under $400 billion with investment exceeding saving by nearly $600 billion. Contrast this with 2005, when the government ran a $300 billion *deficit*, the trade deficit exceeded $700 billion and investment was just $400 billion more than saving. During this 5-year period, our federal deficit worsened, our trade deficit became larger, and our investment to saving ratio worsened, just as the simple equation above suggests.

We have seen two key ideas in this section. First, to finance the deficit, government can either borrow or sell assets, but it is limited by the budget constraint. Second, rising deficits must be paid for by a combination of rising trade deficits, rising private savings, and falling investment. Because savings have been fairly stable, this leaves rising deficits dependent on rising trade deficits and falling investment—not a pleasant choice.

Checkpoint

Financing Debt and Deficits

REVIEW

- The federal government's deficit must be financed by selling bonds to the Federal Reserve ("printing money" or "monetizing the deficit"), by selling bonds to the public, or by selling government assets. This is known as the government budget constraint.

■ Budget deficits and trade deficits are related by the following equation: $G - T = (S - I) + (M - X)$. So budget deficits must be covered by net domestic saving (private + corporate) or by net foreign saving (in the form of foreigners buying U.S. government bonds).

QUESTION

Assume the federal government decided to increase spending and lower tax rates—running ever larger deficits—and got the Federal Reserve to agree to buy all of the new bonds that the treasury issued. What would be the impact on our economy?

Answers to the Checkpoint question can be found at the end of this chapter.

The Burden of the Public Debt

Politicians and other professional alarmists frequently warn that the federal government is going bankrupt, or that we are burdening future generations with our own enormous public debt. After all, total (gross) public debt exceeds $9 trillion and private debt held by the public totals $5 trillion, meaning that every baby born in the United States begins life saddled with over $16,000 in public debt. Such numbers are enough to scare anyone. Anyone but an economist, that is. Let's examine the burden of the public debt.

Internally Versus Externally Held Debt

The great advantage of citizens being creditors as well as debtors with relation to the public debt is obvious. Men readily perceive that they can not be much oppressed by a debt which they owe to themselves.

—*Abraham Lincoln (1864)*

Internally held debt
Public debt owned by U.S. banks, corporations, mutual funds, pension plans, and individuals.

Externally held debt
Public debt held by foreigners, roughly equal to half of the outstanding U.S. debt held by the public.

Consider first, as Abraham Lincoln noted in 1864, much of the national debt held by the public is owned by American banks, corporations, mutual funds, pension plans, and individuals. As a people, we essentially own this debt—this is **internally held debt**. Hence, the taxes collected from a wide swath of the American public to pay the interest on the debt are simply paid back out to yet another group of Americans. Foreigners do, however, now own over half of our national debt—this is **externally held debt**. Foreign entities hold roughly 25% of the total debt and just over 50% of the debt held by the public.

Of the interest paid on the $9 trillion gross public debt, roughly half goes to federal agencies holding this debt—the Social Security Administration, the Federal Reserve, and other federal agencies—25% goes to the American private sector, and roughly 25% goes to foreigners.

The interest paid on externally held debt represents a real claim on our goods and services, and thus can be a real burden on our economy. Figure 3 shows how real public debt held by the public has grown and how the portion of the debt held by foreigners has expanded. Until the mid-1990s foreigners held roughly 20% of publicly held debt.

Note that real debt rose dramatically just over a decade during Presidents Reagan and Bush senior's terms between 1982 and 1994. During this period the real debt tripled, rising from just over $1 trillion to nearly $3.5 trillion. Beginning in the middle of the 1990s, real debt fell back to $3 trillion and began expanding with the recession of 2001 and subsequent events.

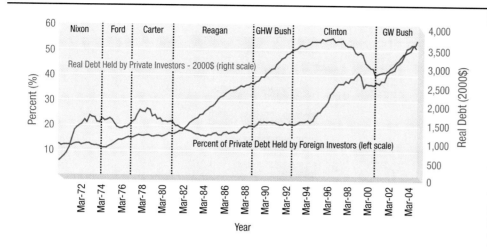

FIGURE 3

Real Public Debt Held by Private and Foreign Investors

This figure shows how real public debt held by private investors has grown since 1970. Real debt started growing rapidly at the beginning of the Reagan Administration in 1983. It fell during the Clinton Administration and has been growing during the G. W. Bush Administration. The share of privately held public debt held by foreigners grew rapidly during the Clinton Administration and has continued to grow.

Traditionally much of the U.S. debt is held internally, but this is changing. In just a decade, foreign holdings have doubled to just over 50% of debt held by the public, and over half of this is held by Asian (Japan, China, Korea, Taiwan, and Singapore) countries. Why such a rapid expansion of foreign holdings since the 1990s? The reason seems to be that these countries are buying debt to keep their exchange rates constant or keep their currencies from rising relative to the dollar. When their currencies rise, their exports to America are more costly, and as a result sales fall, hurting their economies. Better to accumulate U.S. debt than see their export sectors suffer.

Interest Payments

The national debt held by the public is large (nearly $5 trillion), resulting in interest costs of just over $200 billion in 2006, representing roughly 8% of the federal budget. If the national debt is so enormous, wouldn't it be wise to simply pay the debt down or pay it off? Not necessarily so. Many people today "own" some small part of the public debt in their pension plans, but many others do not. If taxes were raised across the board to pay down the debt, those who did not own any public debt would be in a worse position than those who did.

Servicing the debt requires taxing the general public to pay interest to bondholders. Most people who own part of the national debt (or who indirectly own parts of entities that hold the debt) tend to be richer than those who do not. This means money is taken from those across the income or wealth distribution and given to those near the top. Still, the fact that taxes are mildly progressive mitigates some, and perhaps even all, of this reverse redistribution problem.

In contrast to internally held debt, externally held debt makes up the bulk of debt of many developing countries. But, these countries have discovered that relying on externally held public debt has its limits. The typical result of such policies has been that a country's debt as a percentage of GDP becomes so high that it can no longer service the debt; it can only pay the interest. In some developing nations, the entire public debt is held by foreigners. Many large banks invest in the public debt of small nations since the yields are high, given the high risk of default.

Figure 4 on the next page shows the debt of several developing nations. Argentina has a large debt relative to its GDP. After street demonstrations in late 2001, Adolfo Rodriguez Saa, one of five Argentinian presidents in a 2-week period, declared a default on $88 billion in debt. This debt was held by foreign bondholders, mostly Italian and other European retirees who bought the bonds in the 1990s

Government Debt as a Percent of GDP

The debt of several developing nations is shown here. Argentina's huge public debt (as a percent of GDP) led to a default. Additional loans then become difficult to obtain.

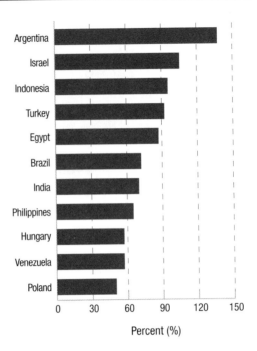

Percent (%)

to supplement their incomes.[4] In 2005, Argentina agreed to pay 25 cents on the dollar. Because of this default, obtaining further loans may be difficult (at least from Italian retirees).

Brazil's high debt combined with a vulnerable economy made it susceptible to political unrest. The 2002 presidential elections in Brazil, won by Luiz Inacio Lula da Silva, turned on Brazil's sluggish economy, rising unemployment rate, and the question of how to manage its huge public debt. Much of Brazil's problems stemmed from "inflation fears, which have a long history in Brazil, [and] are the main cause of its vicious cycle of capital flight, high interest rates, ballooning debt and fiscal imbalance."[5] Since 2002, Brazil's economy has rebounded due to reduced trade barriers, improved fiscal discipline, and improved monetary policy designed to reduce inflationary pressures. Today, investment in the economy is beginning to rebound. Brazil's situation highlights what happens when large deficits and the accompanying sales of government bonds and high interest rates crowd out private investment and stifle economic growth.

Crowding-Out Effect

As we saw in the budget constraint section above, when the government runs a deficit, it must sell bonds to either the public or the Federal Reserve. If it sells bonds to the Federal Reserve when the economy is near full employment, inflation will result. Panel A of Figure 5 shows why. At full employment, expansionary monetary policy results in a movement from point a to point c. As we will see in the next chapter, this may raise output to point b in the short run. But eventually the economy moves back to full employment at a higher price level (point c).

Alternatively, when the federal government spends more than tax revenues permit, it can sell bonds to the public. As the supply of bonds sold on the market rises, prices drop and interest rates rise. As interest rates rise in Panel B of Figure 5, pri-

---

[4]Matt Moffett, "After Huge Default, Argentina Squeezes Small Bondholders," *Wall Street Journal*, January 14, 2004, p. A1.

[5]*Wall Street Journal*, "What Lula Wants", October 28, 2002, p. A18.

FIGURE 5

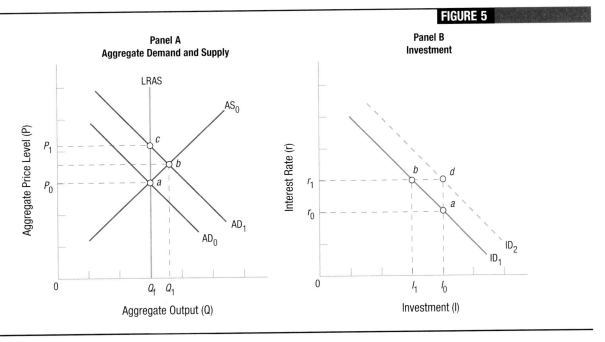

Panel A
Aggregate Demand and Supply

Panel B
Investment

The Crowding-Out Effect

When the government runs a deficit, it must sell bonds to either the public or the Federal Reserve. If it sells bonds to the Federal Reserve, when the economy is near full employment, inflation will result. Panel A shows such a policy as the movement from point *a* to point *c*. Output may grow in the short run to point *b*. But eventually price pressures will move the economy back to full employment at a higher price level (point *c*). Alternatively, the government can sell bonds to the public. As the supply of bonds sold on the market rises, prices drop and interest rates rise. As interest rates rise in Panel B, private investment drops from I_0 to I_1. The result is that future generations will be bequeathed a smaller and potentially less productive economy. This is the crowding-out effect of deficit spending.

vate investment drops from I_0 to I_1. The result is that future generations will be bequeathed a smaller and potentially less productive economy, resulting in a lower standard of living. This is the **crowding-out effect** of deficit spending.

Public Investment and Crowding Out

The crowding-out effect can be mitigated if the funds from deficit spending are used for public investment. Improvements in the nation's transportation infrastructure, education establishment, and research facilities, for instance, are all aimed at improving the economy's future productive capacity. Politicians have become adept, however, at labeling the most arcane pork barrel spending projects "investments." Many are no more investments than are family cars.

Think of the decision to run deficits and increase the national debt as an investment decision. When running a deficit, the government is borrowing money and spending it on a mix of public investments and consumption. The important question concerns how profitable the investments are for the economy. If the investments expand the nation's productive capacity enough, growth will be such that the debt-to-GDP ratio may fall. But if all or most of the deficit is spent on current consumption, growth in GDP may be weak and the debt-to-GDP ratio will most likely rise.

Some public investments are complementary with private investments. Cleaning up a superfund environmental disaster site using government funds, for example, may permit that site to be redeveloped using private funds. The result, as shown in Panel B of Figure 5, may be that investment demand rises to ID_2, thereby offsetting the crowding-out effect. In this example, expanding investment demand to ID_2 means that at the higher interest rates (r_1), investment returns to I_0 (point *d*).

Crowding-out effect
Arises from deficit spending requiring the government to borrow, thus driving up interest rates and reducing consumer spending and business investment.

Intergenerational Burdens of Fiscal Policy

John Kenneth Galbraith's greatest contribution to economics is the concept of the bezzle—the increment to wealth that occurs during the magic interval when a confidence trickster knows he has the money he has appropriated but the victim does not understand that he has lost it. The gross national bezzle has never been larger than in the past decade.

—*John Kay*[6]

The Enron, WorldCom, and other accounting scandals of the early 2000s caused an uproar among the media and the public. As these enterprises collapsed, and people lost their pension and retirement funds, cries rang out to extend prison terms for crooked executives. The Sarbanes-Oxley bill shot through Congress, adding stiffer penalties to corporate governance laws. Lawsuits began against the accounting firms that had audited the books of the collapsed companies in the hope of recovering some of the lost funds.

For all the vigor and indignation with which politicians and government prosecutors have pursued the wrongdoers in the latest wave of accounting scandals, many economists today suspect that federal accounting is no better than Enron's. Why is there not a similar outrage? In what follows, we look at the recent controversy surrounding federal budget accounting and look at some of the intergenerational burdens imposed by budgetary and fiscal policy. Our earlier discussion of public choice analysis will provide us with some help.

Economists, as usual, are debating how bad the present budget picture really is. One economist, Michael Boskin, has suggested that the government may underestimate future revenues by ignoring the future income from asset sales, including land and mineral rights, and the added tax revenues that are expected when baby boomers start drawing from their IRA accounts.[7] Boskin's estimates are controversial, but they suggest current revenue estimates may modestly understate reality.[8]

Other economists argue that future liabilities of the federal government far exceed projected revenues. This controversy has led to a new approach to budget analysis built around fiscal sustainability.

Fiscal Sustainability of the Federal Budget

Fiscal sustainability
A fiscal imbalance equal to zero.

Economists Jagadeesh Gokhale and Kent Smetters have proposed two different measures to assess the **fiscal sustainability** of the federal budget.[9] For a fiscal policy to be fiscally sustainable, the present value of all projected future revenues must be equal to the present value of projected future spending. By converting the estimates to present values, the sustainability of today's fiscal policies can be evaluated using estimates of current dollar imbalances.

Fiscal imbalance
The difference between the present value of future obligations and expected revenues, less government assets, assuming current policies remain unchanged.

Fiscal imbalance (FI), one of the measures Gokhale and Smetters propose, computes the difference between the present value of future obligations and expected revenues, assuming current policies remain unchanged. Fiscal imbalance is defined as follows:

$$FI = PVE - PVR - A$$

The present value of expenditures (PVE) and revenues (PVR) are discounted at the government's long-term interest rate to reflect the true values today. Assets of the government are represented by A. To be sustainable, FI must equal zero.

---

[6]John Kay, "America's Borrowing Bonanza Will End in Tears," *Financial Times*, May 26, 2004, p. 15.
[7]Unpublished paper cited by Peter Coy, "A Hidden Stash?" *Business Week*, June 30, 2003, pp. 34–36.
[8]Shortly after Boskin's estimates became public, other economists challenged them, and Boskin agreed that an error was made in the preliminary calculations. See Michael Mandel, "So I Was Off by a Few Trillion," *Business Week*, August 11, 2003, p. 30.
[9]J. Gokhale and K. Smetters, *Fiscal and Generational Imbalances: New Budget Measures for New Budget Priorities* (Washington, DC: AEI Press), 2003. Reprinted by the Federal Reserve Bank of Cleveland, December 2003.

Note that just because a given (or proposed) fiscal policy's fiscal imbalance is zero does not necessarily mean that it is sustainable. As *The Economist* has noted, "A law that lavished new spending on today's citizens, but fully paid for it by levying a 90% income tax on everybody born after this year, would have an FI of zero. It would not, however, be sustainable—future taxpayers would surely rebel—and it would also be monstrously unfair."[10]

Recognizing this, Gokhale and Smetters developed a second measure of sustainability, **generational imbalance** (GI), to estimate how much of the fiscal imbalance is being shifted to future generations. Clearly, some tax burden shifting is sensible. When current fiscal policy truly invests in the economy, future generations benefit, so some of the present costs may justifiably be shifted to them. Investments in infrastructure, education, research, national defense, and homeland security are good examples.

As Gokhale and Smetters point out,

> *suppose Congress creates a new Medicare benefit and finances it by raising payroll taxes such that each year's additional outlay is matched by additional revenue. By construction, this policy has no impact on Medicare's FI and, therefore, no impact on the federal government's total FI. . . . Nevertheless, this policy could potentially shift a substantial amount of resources away from future generations and toward current generations.*[11]

This feels a little like the recent Medicare drug benefit passed by Congress in late 2003.

Our current budget accounts measure and report debt and deficits on roughly a cash basis. These measures were developed and worked fine when government liabilities were mainly short-term projects such as road and dam building. Even military spending, agricultural price supports, and other programs of this sort were straightforward and short term enough to account for on a cash basis.

Today, the federal government has immense obligations that extend over long periods. Its two largest programs, Social Security and Medicare, account for one third of all federal spending. People entering their 60s, who are just beginning to enter retirement, can expect to live for two or three more decades. Add to this the fact that medical costs are growing at rates significantly higher than economic growth as new and more sophisticated treatments are developed and demanded.

So, you might ask, since we all get old and eventually need these services, how do these programs have an intergenerational impact? If each generation were to pay into a fund that accumulated enough to cover its own medical and Social Security costs, there would be no burden shifting. But that is not how these programs are structured.

Social Security and Medicare are pay-as-you-go programs. The current working generation, in other words, funds the older generation's benefits; there are no pooled funds waiting to be tapped as needed. Thus, these two programs represent huge unfunded liabilities to younger (and yet to be born) generations.

The two measures proposed by Gokhale and Smetters are designed "to reveal the consequences of current practices and to clarify the nature of the choices we face."

The current national debt held by the public is roughly $5 trillion. To most people, this is an immense amount—over $16,000 per person in America. And, indeed, the fiscal imbalance (FI) of the federal government is enormous when its liabilities of nearly $45 trillion are considered, nearly 10 times the current estimate of the public debt. Keep in mind that this is the present value of the government's liabilities, not just a sum of future dollar liabilities. A dollar of pension liability 75 years into the future has present value less than a nickel today. Moreover, FI grows by $1.6 trillion a year for every year it is not addressed.

Generational imbalance
An estimate of how much of any fiscal imbalance is being shifted to future generations.

---

[10]"Economic Focus: Hidden Dangers," *The Economist*, August 2, 2003, p. 65.
[11]Gokhale and Smetters, *Fiscal and Generational Imbalances*, p. 5.

What are the implications of this estimate for future budgeting? First, it means that bringing fiscal policy into sustainability today would require that the government "expropriate the nation's entire gross domestic product for the next four years to meet the Social Security and Medicare commitments it has already made."[12]

Second, it suggests that relying too heavily on present measures of deficits and public debt can mislead policymakers. Government accounting measures should help policymakers accurately see the real choices we face. If a program's future liabilities are seriously underestimated, future generations will get stuck with the bill.

Third, without some significant change in economic or demographic growth, taxes will have to be increased on a massive scale at some point, or else the benefits for Social Security and Medicare will have to be drastically cut. Gokhale and Smetters estimate that the 15.3% combined payroll tax would have to be doubled, or Medicare and Social Security benefits would need to be cut roughly in half.

If these estimates of fiscal imbalance are in the ballpark, fiscal policy is headed for a train wreck as the baby boomers begin retiring. The public choice analysis discussed above suggests that politicians will try to keep this issue off the agenda for as long as possible, one side fighting tax increases while the other resists benefit reductions. Clearly, given the magnitudes discussed here, this problem will be difficult to solve once it reaches crisis proportions.

The Burden of the Public Debt

REVIEW

- About half of the public debt held by the public is held by domestic individuals and institutions, and half is held by foreigners. The domestic half is internally held and represents transfers among individuals, but that part held by foreigners is a real claim on our resources.
- Interest on the debt approaches 10% of the federal budget, and these funds could have been spent on other programs. Again, half is paid domestically (as transfers among individuals), and half goes to foreigners—and this half is the real cost of the public debt.
- When the government pays for the deficit by selling bonds, interest rates rise, crowding out some private investment and reducing economic growth. To the extent that these funds are for public investment and not current consumption, this effect is mitigated.
- For fiscal policy to be fiscally sustainable, the present value of all projected future revenues must equal the present value of projected future spending.

QUESTION

Is crowding out an inevitable result of deficit spending if the Federal Reserve does not buy back an equivalent amount from the market?

Answers to the Checkpoint question can be found at the end of this chapter.

How Much Debt Can We Carry?

We started this chapter by talking about our individual uneasiness with personal debt, and projected this on to the federal government's position as a debtor run-

---

[12]Gokhale and Smetters, *Fiscal and Generational Imbalances*, p. vii.

ning large budget deficits. We saw that unlike individuals, the federal government has the ability to incur debt for some time because of its ability to print money and borrow from the public. Further, we saw that some of this debt is being financed by foreign entities through trade deficits. So the federal government can run up debts long after such magnitudes would sink individuals. Yet we did not try to quantify just how much debt the federal government could safely take on, though it is clear that it is far from that point at the present time. Some time down the road, this picture will change as Social Security and Medicare liabilities come home to roost. The implication is that we are better off dealing with this future problem now rather than later.

The curious thing is that Alan Greenspan, former chairman of the Federal Reserve Board, cautioned about the future threat from growing budget deficits, yet at other times he backed away from this.[13] This does not come from inconsistency on his part. He believed in the long-run fiscal problem discussed above. However, Greenspan seemed to have modified his view on how much debt individuals and the federal government could comfortably take on now. In other words, when we take our uneasiness over our personal debt situation and use it to determine some sense of the federal government's position, what happens when we gain more confidence that we personally can carry more debt? What happens is that we tend to push out that point, however indeterminate, when we think the federal government will be in trouble.

What is driving a notion that individuals and the federal government can better carry debt than at previous times? Two factors stand out: low interest rates and improved financial markets. Let us look at each one in turn.

Recently, interest rates were at 40-year lows. This led to improved personal balance sheets. For example, if the Smith family was carrying a 30-year mortgage at 7.5%, and mortgage rates had decreased to less than 5.5%, they would find it advantageous to refinance and lock in the lower rate. After paying their closing costs (transactions costs), they probably would wind up paying less monthly and so have extra money to spend. Now, consider the Jones family: If they had a similar type of mortgage, plus $15,000 in credit card debt at rates of 15–20%, they would find it beneficial to refinance their house at a higher balance (original mortgage plus credit card debt) and pay off the credit card debt. The Jones family would probably pay more per month than the original mortgage, but less than the original mortgage plus the credit card debt. And they would be more secure now paying a fixed 5.5% interest rate on the total debt rather than having that fluctuating high rate on their credit card debt.

As these two examples show, households can improve their balance sheets when interest rates are low. This is precisely what was done in the first five years of this century. When personal debt is more manageable, people feel more secure and confident about the future. It would be natural to think that the federal government is in the same position: With low interest rates, the deficit problem may not be as pressing. The danger point is moved out.

Improved financial markets help to explain the lack of panic about the ballooning U.S. trade deficit. If foreign entities believe that the U.S. trade deficit is too high, the dollar will drop in value. Foreigners simply will not want so many dollars. This, in fact, happened in early 2004. To restore equilibrium, the Federal Reserve could have raised interest rates. But it did not do so initially, though it raised interest rates later in 2004 and 2005 to fight inflation. Why did the Fed not raise interest rates in early 2004 to prop up the value of the dollar abroad? Alan Greenspan suggested that the United States can run large trade deficits because foreign investors have become less fixed to their home country's currency. Financial markets truly have become more global. A decline in this "home bias," in Greenspan's words, "has

---

[13]See Edmund Andrews, "Greenspan Shifts View on Deficits," *New York Times*, March 16, 2004, p. A1, for an excellent analysis of possible changing views on the dangers of deficits.

enabled the United States to incur and finance a much larger current account deficit than would have been feasible in earlier decades."[14]

If, in fact, we do believe now that we personally have a better capacity to take on debt, and by projection the federal government is in a better position, then we will not feel the same urgency about the looming fiscal problem. This might be a bad thing if we put off dealing with a future problem, though it might be good if we deal with the problem with more confidence about our ability to solve it. The bottom line: Even though our debt situation has improved, our future fiscal problem is not about to go away.

Key Concepts

Deficit, p. 310
Surplus, p. 310
Public debt, p. 310
Public choice theory, p. 313
Annually balanced budget, p. 314
Cyclically balanced budget, p. 314
Functional finance, p. 315
Government budget constraint, p. 316

Budget and trade deficits, p. 317
Internally held debt, p. 318
Externally held debt, p. 318
Crowding-out effect, p. 321
Fiscal sustainability, p. 322
Fiscal imbalance, p. 322
Generational imbalance, p. 323

Chapter Summary

Financing the Federal Government

A deficit is the amount by which annual government spending exceeds tax revenues. A surplus, when it occurs, is the amount by which the year's tax revenues exceed government spending.

The public debt, or national debt, is the total accumulation of past deficits and surpluses. Public debt consists of U.S. Treasury securities, including treasury bills, notes, and bonds, and U.S. savings bonds.

Treasury bills are short-term instruments with a maturity period of 1 year or less. They do not pay interest; rather, they are sold at a discount, and their yields are then determined by the time to maturity and the discount. Treasury notes are financial instruments issued for periods ranging from 1 to 10 years. Treasury bonds are federal bonds with a maturity period exceeding 10 years. Treasury notes and bonds have stated interest rates and are traded actively, sometimes at discounts and sometimes at premiums, depending on current interest rates and the coupon rates of the bonds.

Public choice theory involves the economic analysis of public and political decision making. It looks at such issues as voting, the relationship between voting and policy outcomes, the impact of election incentives on politicians, the influence of special interest groups, the analysis of rent-seeking behavior, and the effects of "rational ignorance." Public choice theorists often conclude that collective decision making is flawed and inefficient.

James Buchanan, considered the father of public choice theory, essentially fused the disciplines of economics and political science. Buchanan's analysis assumes that politicians and bureaucrats consider their own self-interest when making public policy. In this sense, they behave no differently than other economic actors. This means our public policies may not always be guided by the public interest.

---

[14]Andrews, "Greenspan Shifts View," as quoted on p. C2.

Public choice economists such as Buchanan argue that deficit spending reduces the perceived cost of current government operations. As a result, taxpayers permit some programs to exist that they would oppose if required to pay the full cost today. Public choice economists charge that this amounts to shifting the cost of government to the next generation.

Some observers believe the federal government, like state governments, should balance its budget every year. Others argue that balancing the budget over the business cycle is a better approach, while still others have suggested that the federal government should focus on promoting full employment with stable prices, treating the budget deficit or surplus as a secondary concern.

The prevailing economic wisdom before the 1930s was that the federal government should balance its budget annually. Today, we know that annually balancing the federal budget would undercut fiscal policies aimed at maintaining full employment. To insist on balancing the budget by reducing spending or increasing taxes when recession looms would require a contractionary policy that would worsen the economic situation and, in the end, increase the deficit.

Some economists have recommended balancing the budget over the course of the business cycle. The basic idea is to restrict spending or raise taxes when the economy is booming, to prevent inflationary pressures from taking hold. Surpluses, moreover, should accumulate during boom periods and be used to offset deficits during downturns and recessions. Balancing the budget over the business cycle is good in theory. In practice, however, balancing the budget over the course of the business cycle is extremely difficult and politically risky.

Economists who favor a functional finance approach to the federal budget believe the first priority of policymakers should be to keep the economy at full employment with stable prices; whether the budget is in surplus or deficit is only a secondary concern. These economists believe that if the government is successful in providing the appropriate microeconomic mix and successful macroeconomic fiscal policies, deficits and surpluses will be unimportant.

Financing Debt and Deficits

Given its power to print money and collect taxes, the federal government cannot go bankrupt. It does, however, face what economists call a budget constraint:

$$G - T = \Delta M + \Delta B + \Delta A,$$

where
  G = government spending
  T = tax revenues, thus $(G - T)$ is the federal budget deficit
ΔM = the change in the money supply
ΔB = the change in bonds held by public entities, domestic and foreign
ΔA = the sales of government assets

When the Federal Reserve buys bonds, it is exchanging cash for bonds. This part of the government's debt is, therefore, "monetized." With the Federal Reserve pumping new money into the money supply, the government is financing the deficit by "printing money" ($\Delta M > 0$).

If the Federal Reserve does not purchase the bonds, they must be sold to the public, including corporations, banks, mutual funds, individuals, and foreign entities. This also has the effect of financing the government's deficit ($\Delta B > 0$).

Asset sales ($\Delta A > 0$) represent only a small fraction of government finance in the United States.

When the government runs a deficit, it must borrow funds from somewhere, assuming it does not sell assets. If the government borrows from the public, the quantity of publicly held bonds will rise; if it borrows from the Federal Reserve, the quantity of money in circulation will rise.

When an economy is at equilibrium, all injections and withdrawals will be equal; thus $G + I + X = T + S + M$. By rearranging terms, we find that $G - T = (S - I) + (M - X)$. This tells us that if the economy is at equilibrium, budget deficits (a positive number on the left side of the equation) must be made up by private savings ($S > I$) or a trade deficit ($M > X$).

If investment and saving are equal, such that $S - I = 0$, the link between budget deficits and trade deficits becomes clear. If $T > G$ (a surplus), then $M - X$ must also be in surplus ($X > M$). Conversely, when the budget turns to deficit ($T < G$), a trade deficit will follow (X < M).

If exports and imports are equal ($X = M$), such that the trade balance is zero, budget deficits ($G > T$) must be met by higher private saving ($S > I$). This illustrates the crowding-out effect of government deficits. If G grows while T and S remain constant, investment (I) must fall. Increased deficit spending by the government ultimately crowds out private investment.

The Burden of the Public Debt

The vast bulk of the national debt held by the public is owned by U.S. banks, corporations, mutual funds, pension plans, and individuals. We essentially own this debt. Hence, the taxes collected from a wide array of Americans to pay the interest on this debt is simply paid back out to yet another group of Americans. Foreigners do own part of our national debt. The interest paid on externally held debt, in other words, the interest paid to foreigners, represents a real claim on our goods and services; it can thus be a real burden on our economy.

Many people today "own" some small part of the public debt in their pension plans, but many others do not. If taxes were raised to pay down the debt, those who did not own public debt would be in a worse position than those who did. Servicing the debt requires taxing the general public to pay interest to bondholders. People who own part of the national debt tend to be richer than those who do not. This means money is taken from those at the lower end of the income or wealth distribution and given to those near the top. Still, since taxes are mildly progressive, this mitigates some, and perhaps even all, of this reverse redistribution problem.

When the government runs a deficit, it must sell bonds to either the public or the Federal Reserve. If it sells bonds to the Federal Reserve (which monetizes the debt) when the economy is near full employment, inflation will result. Alternatively, the government can sell bonds to the public. As the supply of bonds sold on the market rises, prices drop and interest rates rise. The result is that future generations will be bequeathed a smaller and potentially less productive economy, resulting in a lower standard of living. This is the crowding-out effect of deficit spending.

The crowding-out effect can be mitigated if the funds from deficit spending are used for public investment. Improvements in the nation's transportation infrastructure, education establishment, and research facilities, for instance, are all aimed at improving the economy's future productive capacity.

Two measures have been proposed to assess the fiscal sustainability of the federal budget: fiscal imbalance and generational imbalance.

Fiscal imbalance (FI) computes the difference between the present value of future obligations and expected revenues, assuming that current policies remain unchanged. To be sustainable, FI must equal zero.

Generational imbalance (GI) estimates how much of the fiscal imbalance is being shifted to future generations. Clearly, some tax burden should be shifted. When current fiscal policy truly invests in the economy, future generations benefit, so some of the present costs may justifiably be shifted to them.

Today, the federal government has immense obligations that extend over long periods. Its two largest programs, Social Security and Medicare, account for one third of all federal spending. If each generation paid into a fund that accumulated enough to cover its own medical and Social Security costs, there would be no burden shifting. Yet, Social Security and Medicare are pay-as-you-go programs. The current working generation funds the older generation's benefits; there are no pooled funds waiting to be tapped when needed. These two programs represent huge unfunded liabilities to future generations.

Questions and Problems

1. Economists generally agree that Americans save too little, and if they saved more, net foreign borrowing would fall. Explain why this is true. What incentives might the government introduce to get people to save more?

2. President Reagan, in a speech, argued that inflation "has one cause and one cause alone: Government spending more than governments take in." Describe how deficits can cause inflation.

3. Daniel Altman wrote in the January 1, 2006, issue of the *New York Times*, that "one motivation for Mr. Reagan's tax cuts was a guess that the United States was on the right side of the [Laffer] curve—that is, lowering rates would actually yield more tax revenue overall." Tax rates on upper income individuals were 70% when Reagan took office. Do you think the United States is still on the right side of the Laffer curve today? Why or why not?

4. Robert Dunn, in the August 19, 2001, issue of the *New York Times* noted that "a federal budget surplus should decline in an economic downturn like this one, and attempts to "protect the surplus" by cutting expenditures, as some Republicans wish or by increasing taxes, as Democratic leaders in Congress have suggested, is madness." Is he right? Why or why not?

5. Since 1950 the federal government has run a surplus on average roughly 1 year in each decade. Why is it so difficult for the federal government to run a budget surplus?

6. What is one benefit to business when the government budget is in surplus?

7. What determines the inflationary impact of budget deficits?

8. Government accounting rules for corporations require that the present value of pensions and other long-term liabilities be included in their annual reports and on their balance sheets. Several airlines and steel companies became insolvent partly because of these liabilities and went through bankruptcy. In Fall of 2007, General Motors got the UAW to accept responsibility for GM's retiree health care fund to get this less than fully funded liability off GM's books. Why doesn't the federal government add the present value of its long-term liabilities for Social Security and Medicare to its budget reports each year?

9. If the economy (gross domestic product and income) are growing faster than the federal debt held by the public (both domestic and foreign), is a huge government debt any real problem?

10. In the late 1990s, along with the budget surpluses in 1999 and 2000 some policymakers were talking about retiring the entire federal debt outstanding (in private hands) by the early part of the next decade (2012–15). Today that discussion looks a little quaint. Leaving aside whether it is possible or not, is it a good idea to retire all federal debt held by the public?

11. Ben Stein wrote an open letter to Henry Paulson, just after Paulson was appointed U.S. Treasury Secretary in May 2006, arguing that America was facing a dire economic future:

   Just to give you an idea what you are up against, Standard & Poor's issued a warning not long ago. The caution was that if the United States government did not seriously alter fiscal policy, Treasury bonds would be downgraded to BBB, slightly above junk status, by 2020. This is a stunning piece of news for the world's most highly rated security denominated in its primary reserve currency. The S&P report said further that if the nation did not make serious changes after that, by 2025 Treasuries would be junk bonds, like the bonds of less successful emerging-markets nations.[15]

   What kind of problems implied here would reduce U.S. government bonds to "junk" status? What policies enacted today could eventually eliminate these problems?

12. When someone argues that the national debt is bankrupting the country, what arguments can you use to rebut this assertion?

13. How might interest paid on the national debt lead to greater income inequality?

14. Since balancing the budget over the business cycle seems like such a sensible idea, why haven't public policymakers (Congress and the executive branch) implemented a program to do this?

15. Assume that the U.S. balances its federal budget, and savings and investment remain where they are today. What impact would this have on the economies of Europe?

Answers to Checkpoint Questions

CHECKPOINT: FINANCING THE FEDERAL GOVERNMENT

The debt-to-GDP ratio is the measure that best illustrates the debt's impact. Gross domestic product represents the economy's earning (producing) potential and puts the debt relative to GDP in perspective. A small national debt alongside a smaller GDP would be much worse than our large debt associated with a huge economy.

CHECKPOINT: FINANCING DEBT AND DEFICITS

The Federal Reserve would be monetizing the debt. The impact would be to significantly increase the money supply and generate inflation. The added inflation would depend on how large the deficits were.

CHECKPOINT: THE BURDEN OF THE PUBLIC DEBT

No, it is not inevitable. When the economy is in a serious recession and investment spending is low due to unfavorable expectations by business, deficits are expansionary. As the economy approaches full employment levels of output, crowding out is a more serious issue.

---

[15]Ben Stein, "Everybody's Business: Note to the New Treasury Secretary: It's Time to Raise Taxes," *New York Times*, June 25, 2006, p. 3.

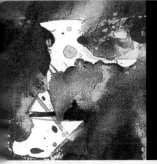

Macroeconomic Policy Challenges

14

*b*efore the 1930s, the common wisdom held that the economy was best left alone, since it would hover around full employment as flexible wages, prices, and interest rates kept business humming. The Great Depression, however, made mincemeat of the common wisdom. With the publication of Keynes's *General Theory*, the government's role in economic stabilization was substantially expanded. Today, the government routinely seeks to control the business cycle and the major macroeconomic variables of employment, unemployment, output, economic growth, and inflation.

The 1950s and 1960s provided economists with the nearest thing possible to a laboratory for testing Keynesian aggregate demand policies. In 1958, British economist A. W. Phillips found empirical evidence of a relatively stable negative correlation between changes in wages and unemployment. Later, a similar negative relationship between inflation and unemployment was discovered by U.S. economists, with lower rates of unemployment being associated with higher rates of inflation. This latter relationship has been dubbed the *Phillips curve* by economists.

This stable tradeoff between unemployment and inflation was soon translated into a menu of policy options among which policymakers could choose. Politicians would select a desired unemployment level, and economists could then tell them what inflation rate would be required.

In the late 1960s, however, Milton Friedman and Edmund Phelps advanced theoretical arguments maintaining that any direct relationship between inflation and unemployment would be short-lived. By the early 1970s, Friedman and Phelps had been proven correct, as something had gone terribly wrong with the economy and the Phillips curve predictions.

The breakdown of the stable Phillips curve led to the development of the concept of the *natural rate of unemployment*. Determined by such factors as technology, social and economic customs, regulations, and demographics, the natural rate of unemployment is that level of unemployment at which there are no inflationary pressures on the economy. If the economy might deviate from its natural level in the short run due to incorrect inflationary expectations, it should return to this level over the long run. The result, as Friedman and Phelps argued, is that there is no long-run tradeoff between inflation and unemployment. As for policymaking, this meant that any beneficial short-term effects would soon be dissipated and then show up as harmful long-term effects.

Before the 1970s were over, Robert Lucas, Thomas Sargent, and Neil Wallace were arguing that the *rational expectations* of economic actors (consumers and business) would eliminate even the short-run relationship thought to exist between inflation and unemployment. Taken to its logical conclusion, this *new classical* model suggests that public macroeconomic policy is totally ineffective, incapable of influencing either unemployment or output. No profession stands idly by as its very reason for being is logically assaulted from within. Thus, several *new Keynesian* economists challenged the rational expectations model, striking up a debate that continues to this day.

As the 1990s passed into the 2000s, globalization and the outsourcing of jobs to lower-wage countries became key political issues as many disparate groups combined to protest trade liberalization. As the economy moved out of the 2001 recession, recovery was anemic and job growth was nonexistent, thus earning it the label of a "jobless recovery."

In this chapter we consider modern challenges to macroeconomic policymaking. The first section focuses on the connection between inflation and real economic activity. This section explores Phillips curve analysis, along with the enhancements provided by Friedman and Phelps. Is there a tradeoff between inflation and unemployment?

The second section looks at the rational expectations debate and the new Keynesian response, coming face to face with the issue of whether macroeconomic policy can be effective at all.

The last section of this chapter briefly examines jobless recoveries, an issue vexing policymakers today. In a typical recovery, employment often grows rapidly. In the last two recessions, however, job growth was slow in coming. This slowness has forced economists to ask whether the business cycle has changed. The answer has important ramifications for the effectiveness of policy today.

After reading this chapter you should be able to

- Explain what Phillips curves are and what relationship they postulate between inflation and unemployment.
- Describe the natural rate of unemployment.
- Describe stagflation.
- Describe how inflationary expectations can take on a life of their own and stymie policymakers.
- Describe adaptive expectations and its major drawback.
- Describe rational expectations and its implications for policymakers.
- Critique the rational expectations theory.
- Describe what jobless recoveries are.
- Explain why jobless recoveries might arise.

Unemployment and Inflation: Phillips Curves

In his early work, A. W. Phillips[1] compared the rate of change in money wages to unemployment rates in Britain over the years 1861 to 1957. The nonlinear, negatively sloped curve shown in Figure 1 reflects his estimate of how these variables were related and has been called a **Phillips curve** in his honor. As you can see, when unemployment rises, wage rates fall.

Phillips curve
The original curve posited a negative relationship between wages and unemployment, but later versions related unemployment to inflation rates.

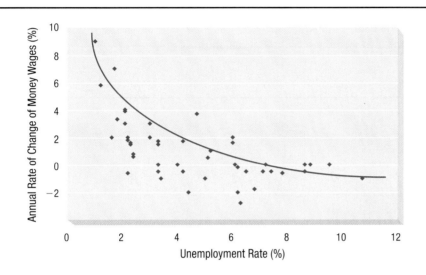

FIGURE 1

The Original Phillips Curve for Britain (1861–1957)

A. W. Phillips compared the rate of change in money wages to unemployment rates in Britain from 1861 to 1957. The resulting nonlinear, negatively sloped curve is the first example of a Phillips curve. When unemployment rises, wage rates fall, and vice versa. Note, some dots represent multiple years.

What explains this negative relationship between wages and unemployment? Labor costs or wages are typically a firm's largest cost component; in our economy, wages represent nearly three quarters of total costs. And as the demand for labor rises, labor markets will tighten, making it difficult for employers to fill vacant positions. Hence, when unemployment falls, wages go up as firms bid up the price of labor to attract more workers. The opposite happens when labor demand falls: unemployment rises and wages decline.

To illustrate this relationship, in the late 1990s, telecommunications workers were in short supply and many were earning six-figure salaries. For nearly 5 years, this labor market remained extremely tight; résumés flew around the Internet, and employees took the jobs of their choice. But when the dot-coms collapsed, resulting in excess capacity in the industry, unemployment in the telecommunications sector soared, and salaries plummeted for those workers lucky enough to find jobs.

The market relationship between wages and unemployment will clearly affect prices. But worker productivity also plays an important role in determining prices.

Productivity, Prices, and Wages

We might think that whenever wages rise, prices must also rise. Higher wages mean higher labor costs for employers—costs that businesses then pass along as higher prices. But this is not always the case. If worker productivity increases enough to

---

[1]A. W. Phillips, "The Relation Between Unemployment and the Rate of Change of Money Wages in the United Kingdom, 1861–1957," *Economica*, 1958, pp. 283–299.

offset the wage increase, then product prices can remain stable. The basic relationship among wages, prices, and productivity is

$$p = w - q$$

where:
p = rate of inflation
w = rate of increase in nominal wages
q = rate of increase in labor productivity

For example, when wages increase by 5% and productivity increases by 3%, inflation will increase by 2%.

Given this relationship, the Phillips curve can be adapted to relate productivity to inflation and unemployment, as shown in Figure 2.

FIGURE 2

The Phillips Curve

A rise in wages may cause a rise in prices, but if worker productivity increases sufficiently to offset the wage increase, product prices can remain stable. When the rates of change in productivity and wages are equal, inflation is zero (point a). This is the natural rate of unemployment. If policymakers want to use expansionary policy to reduce unemployment from u_n to u_1, they must be willing to accept inflation of p_1. Reducing unemployment further to u_2 would raise inflation to p_2 as labor markets tighten and wages rise more rapidly than productivity.

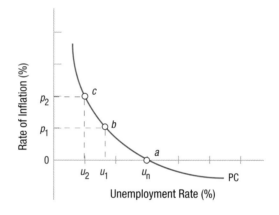

Natural rate of unemployment
The level of unemployment where price and wage decisions are consistent; a level at which the actual inflation rate is equal to people's inflationary expectations, and cyclical unemployment is zero.

Notice that when the rates of change in productivity and wages are equal ($w = q$), inflation is zero (point a). This level of unemployment is known as the **natural rate of unemployment**, the unemployment rate when inflationary pressures are nonexistent. This unemployment rate, for reasons that we will discuss below, is also known as the *nonaccelerating inflation rate of unemployment (NAIRU)*. Note that higher rates of productivity growth mean that for a given level of unemployment, inflation will be less (the Phillips curve would shift in toward the origin).

If policymakers want to use expansionary policy to reduce unemployment from u_n to u_1, then according to the curve shown in Figure 2, they must be willing to accept inflation of p_1. To reduce unemployment further to u_2 would raise inflation to p_2 as labor markets tightened and wages rose more rapidly.

Figure 3 shows the Phillips curve for the United States during the 1960s. Notice the nearly smooth negative relationship between the two variables, much like that in the last two figures. As unemployment fell, inflation rose. This empirical relationship led policymakers to believe that the economy presents them with a menu of choices. By accepting a minor rise in inflation, they could keep unemployment low. Alternately, by accepting a rise in unemployment, they could keep inflation near zero. Using the data found in Figure 3, policymakers concluded that an inflation rate of 3–4% was required to keep unemployment below 4%.

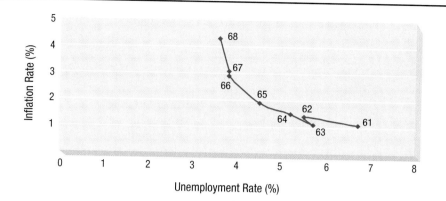

FIGURE 3

The Phillips Curve—1960s

The Phillips curve for the United States during the 1960s gives a smooth negative relationship between inflation and unemployment, much like that found in the last two figures. Using this relationship, policymakers concluded that an inflation rate of 3–4% was required to keep unemployment below 4%.

But just as policymakers were getting used to accepting moderate inflation in exchange for lower unemployment rates, the economy played a big trick on them. As Figure 4 shows, the entire Phillips curve began shifting outward during the early 1970s.

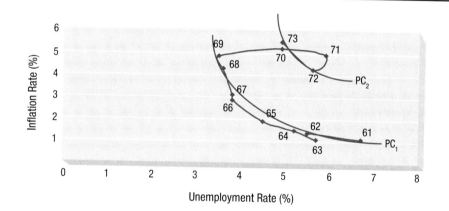

FIGURE 4

The Phillips Curve in 1961–73—Instability

Just as policymakers were getting used to accepting moderate inflation in exchange for lower unemployment rates, the economy surprised them. The entire Phillips curve began shifting outward during the early 1970s. Unemployment rates that, in the 1960s, had been associated with modest inflation of 2–3% quickly began requiring twice that rate.

What looked to be an easy task for those in charge—just select the desired rate of inflation and unemployment from the 1960s menu—turned into a nightmare. Unemployment rates that, in the 1960s, had been associated with modest inflation of 2–3% quickly began requiring twice that rate in the early 1970s, and as we will see in a few moments, by the late 1970s, these same unemployment rates were generating annual inflation rates approaching the double digits. The reason for these shifts turned out to be the oil supply shocks of the mid-1970s and the rising inflationary expectations that followed.

The Importance of Inflationary Expectations

As discussed in earlier chapters, workers do not work for the sake of earning a specific dollar amount, or a specific nominal wage. Rather, they work for the sake of earning what those wages will buy—for real wages. Consequently, when they bargain for wage increases, workers will take their past experiences with inflation into account. Furthermore, if workers failed to anticipate the inflation that occurred when they negotiated their previous contract, such that their real wages declined over the course of this contract, they will be looking to correct for this loss in the new contract—the new wages will have to make up the loss.

Taking **inflationary expectations** into account, wage increases can be connected to unemployment and expected inflation as follows:

$$w = f(u) + p^e$$

where

$$w = \text{wage increase}$$
$$f(u) \text{ (read "a function of unemployment")} = \text{relationship between unemployment and wage increases}$$
$$p^e = \text{inflationary expectations}$$

Combining this relationship with our previous equation, $p = w - q$, we get

$$p = f(u) + p^e - q$$

or

$$p = [f(u) - q] + p^e$$

The bracketed part of this equation represents a short-run Phillips curve that is now augmented by inflationary expectations p^e. This is the same tradeoff between inflation and unemployment that we saw before, but there is a unique tradeoff for each level of inflationary expectations.

For example, let's assume that when unemployment is 4%, inflation will normally be 5%. If productivity is growing at a 2% rate, then the Phillips curve part $[f(u) - q]$ will be 3%, similar to the inflation rate on Phillips curve PC_1 in Figure 4 for the 1960s. However, if inflationary expectations (p^e) grow to, say, 4%, the Phillips curve will shift to PC_2 in Figure 4, and the inflation rate now associated with 4% unemployment will be

$$p = [f(u) - q] + p^e = 3\% + 4\% = 7\%$$

Natural Rate of Unemployment

Panel B of Figure 5 shows a Phillips curve augmented by inflationary expectations. The economy begins in equilibrium at full employment with zero inflation (point a in Panel B). Panel A shows the aggregate demand and supply curves for this economy in equilibrium at point a in Panel A. Note that the economy is producing at full employment output of Q_f, and this translates to the natural rate of unemployment, u_n, in Panel B. (Keep in mind that the natural rate, or NAIRU, is that unemployment where inflation equals expected inflation, resulting in zero net price pressures in the economy.) The natural rate of unemployment is thought to be somewhere around 5%.

The Phillips curve in Panel B is initially PC_0 ($p^e = 0\%$). Thus, inflation is equal to zero and so are inflationary expectations (p^e).

Now assume, however, that policymakers are unhappy with the economy's performance and want to reduce unemployment below u_n. Using expansionary policies, they shift aggregate demand in Panel A from AD_0 to AD_1. This moves the economy to point b; real output and the price level rise, to Q_1 and P_1.

In Panel B, meanwhile, the unemployment rate has declined to u_1 (point b), but inflation has risen to something around 5%. Workers had anticipated zero inflation, or that prices would remain stable at P_0 in Panel A. As a result, inflation exceeds expected inflation. This *unanticipated inflation* means that real wages have fallen. Unionized workers will demand adjustments to their contracts to provide for higher nominal earnings. Workers who are not in unions will begin asking for raises, and

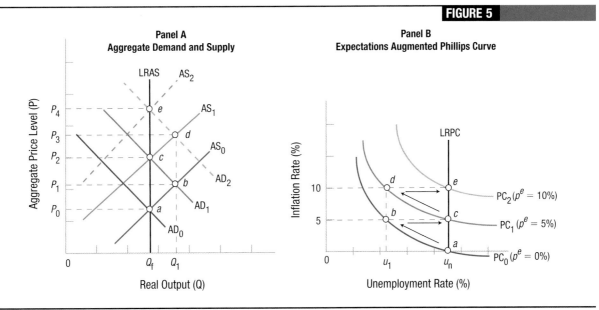

Aggregate Demand, Aggregate Supply, and the Expectations Augmented Phillips Curve

Panel A shows the economy's aggregate demand and supply curves, and Panel B shows the economy's Phillips curve, augmented by inflationary expectations. Using expansionary policies to reduce unemployment below u_n, policymakers shift aggregate demand in Panel A from AD_0 to AD_1. This moves the economy to point b, with real output and the price level rising to Q_1 and P_1. Unemployment declines to u_1 (point b in Panel B), but inflation rises to something approaching 5%. If policymakers attempt to hold unemployment below the natural rate, the economy will endure accelerating inflation. The long-run Phillips curve (LRPC) in Panel B shows the relationship between inflation and unemployment when the inflation rate is just equal to inflationary expectations.

employers wanting to keep turnover at a minimum may well begin offering higher wages.

The Long-Run Phillips Curve

The long-run Phillips curve (LRPC) shown in Panel B of Figure 5 as the vertical line at full employment (unemployment = u_n), shows the long-term relationship between inflation and unemployment when the inflation rate and the expected inflation rate are equal. The LRPC is the Phillips curve counterpart to the vertical long-run aggregate supply curve (LRAS) in Panel A.

Accelerating Inflation

As nominal wages rise, the result in Panel A is that, over time, the aggregate supply curve shifts leftward to AS_1, thus moving the economy back to full employment at point c. In Panel B, with inflation now running at 5%, the Phillips curve shifts outward to PC_1 ($p^e = 5\%$). Workers, however, now expect 5% inflation, and the economy moves back to point c. Unemployment has moved back to its natural rate, but inflationary expectations have risen to 5%. The aggregate price level, meanwhile, has risen from P_0 to P_2, or 5%.

By this point, however, policymakers are in trouble. To move the economy back to u_1 (or Q_1), policymakers must move along PC_1. Again, expanding aggregate demand in Panel A to AD_2 moves the economy to point d in Panel A and toward point d in Panel B. This causes output and inflation to rise, while dropping unemployment to u_1. But this time, the inflation rate rises toward 10%, with workers again failing to fully anticipate the rise in prices. Processes similar to those described previously will then move the economy back to the natural rate of unemployment (points e in both panels).

The end result is that workers now have inflationary expectations of 10%, and the economy settles on a new Phillips curve PC_2 ($p^e = 10\%$). Thus, policymakers are presented with the uncomfortable fact that the rate of inflation required to maintain unemployment below the natural rate keeps rising and rising.

The implications of this analysis for fiscal and monetary policymakers who want to fine-tune the economy and keep unemployment below the natural rate are not pleasant. For one thing, it means that if policymakers want to keep unemployment below the natural rate, they must continually increase aggregate demand so that inflation will always exceed what is expected. Thus, policymakers must be willing to incur a permanently *accelerating* rate of inflation—hardly a popular idea.

In 1968, Friedman and Phelps predicted such trends of accelerating inflation and outward-shifting Phillips curves. These predictions proved accurate, as Figure 6 shows. The inflation-unemployment tradeoff worsened throughout the 1970s and into the early 1980s, largely because of the oil price shocks and rising inflationary expectations. Inflation and unemployment continued to rise, creating what economists call **stagflation**. Where under the original Phillips curve the conclusion was that rising unemployment would be met by *falling* inflation, the 1970s witnessed rising unemployment and *rising* inflation (stagflation).

Stagflation
Simultaneous occurrence of rising inflation and rising unemployment.

FIGURE 6

The Phillips Curve in 1972–81—Supply Shocks

In 1968, Friedman and Phelps predicted accelerating inflation and outward-shifting Phillips curves. These predictions proved accurate, as this figure shows. The inflation-unemployment trade-off worsened throughout the 1970s and into the early 1980s, largely due to oil price shocks and rising inflationary expectations. Inflation and unemployment continued to rise, creating stagflation. By 1980, annual inflation was over 9%, and unemployment was over 7%.

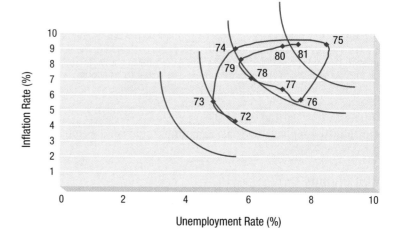

Stagflation is the simultaneous occurrence of inflation and unemployment, with both approaching double digits. By 1980, as Figure 6 shows, annual inflation was over 9%, and unemployment was over 7%. This bout of stagflation probably cost President Carter his reelection bid in 1980, and solving the problem kept President Reagan occupied until well into his presidency.

Phillips Curves and Disinflation

To eliminate inflationary pressures when they arise, policymakers must be willing to curtail growth in aggregate demand and accept the resulting higher rates of unemployment for a certain transition period. How long it takes to reduce inflation and return to the natural rate of unemployment will depend on how rapidly the economy adjusts its inflationary expectations. Policymakers can speed this process along and reduce the transition costs by ensuring their policies are credible, for instance, by issuing public announcements that are consistent with contractionary policies in both the monetary and fiscal realms.

Figure 7 illustrates how inflationary expectations are reduced to bring about a more favorable tradeoff. Initially, the economy is in equilibrium at point a, with the economy at natural rate of unemployment u_n and inflation at p_2.

To reduce inflationary expectations, policymakers must be willing to reduce aggregate demand and push the economy into a recession, thereby increasing unemployment to u_2. As aggregate demand slumps, wage and price pressures will soften, reducing inflationary expectations. As these expectations decline, the Phillips curve shifts inward, from PC_2 to PC_1, and if the process goes on long enough, the Phillips curve will eventually shift back to PC_0. The arrows in Figure 7 show the path the economy must take back to lower inflation rates. How fast this occurs will depend on the severity of the recession and confidence the public has that policymakers will be willing to stay the course.

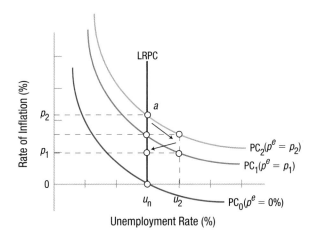

FIGURE 7

Phillips Curves and Disinflation

In the disinflation process, the economy initially is in equilibrium at point a, natural rate of unemployment u_n, and an inflation rate p_2. To reduce inflationary expectations, policymakers must reduce aggregate demand and push the economy into a recession, increasing unemployment to u_2. As aggregate demand slumps, wage and price pressures soften, reducing inflationary expectations. As these expectations decline, the Phillips curve shifts inward, from PC_2 to PC_1. If the process goes on long enough, the Phillips curve will shift back to PC_0. The arrows here show the path the economy must take back to roughly stable prices at the natural unemployment rate.

In 1981, the Reagan administration launched a long-term program designed to increase economic growth and reduce inflation. The long-term nature of the program and the reasons for it were summarized in the 1982 *Economic Report of the President*. "The major failure of the late 1960s and 1970s was to give insufficient weight to the long-term effects of economic policies. For example, the so-called Phillips curve . . . and its implication that a tradeoff was possible was one of the key notions relied on by economic advisors."

The Reagan administration took the view that stagflation had arisen from a "substantial increase in the Federal Government's role in the economy." Administration officials lamented that federal spending and taxes were absorbing a growing share of national output, that federal regulations had been growing in scope and burden, and that the money supply was growing at too rapid a rate.

The key points of the Reagan administration's long-term plan to increase economic growth and reduce inflation were to do the following:

- Reduce the rate of growth of government spending.
- Reduce income tax rates and accelerate depreciation charges for business investment in plant and equipment.

■ Reduce burdensome regulations.
■ Work with the Federal Reserve to reduce inflation and bring order to financial markets.

This aggressive plan of wringing stagflation out of the U.S. economy took the better part of the 1980s, as Panel A of Figure 8 shows. The movement of equilibrium points is consistent with the theoretical model we saw depicted in Figure 7: Inflation that took over a decade to develop required nearly another decade to be resolved. After the recession of 1982–83, which was the deepest since the Great Depression (unemployment exceeded 10%), inflationary pressures were heading downward. Federal Reserve Chairman Paul Volcker, who insisted on keeping interest rates high in the face of fierce public opposition, deserves much of the credit for this triumph over inflation, which was also a victory for the theories of Friedman and Phelps.

FIGURE 8

The Phillips Curve in the 1980s and 1990s— Disinflation

Wringing stagflation out of the American economy took the better part of the 1980s and 1990s, as shown here. The movement of equilibrium points is consistent with the theoretical model depicted in Figure 7: Inflation that took over a decade to develop required several decades to be resolved.

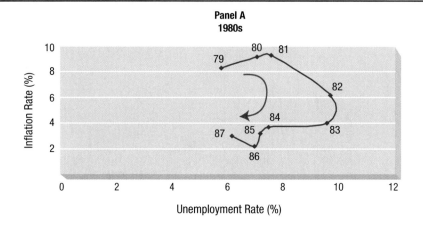

Panel A
1980s

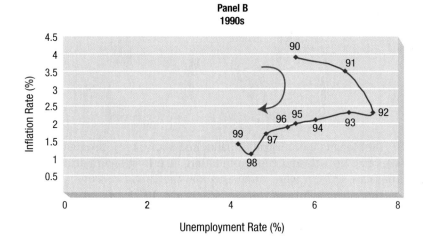

Panel B
1990s

This lesson about the importance of restraining monetary growth and focusing on stable prices was not lost on the next Federal Reserve chairman, Alan Greenspan. Throughout the decade of the 1990s, the Federal Reserve maintained a tight watch on inflation, and as Panel B of Figure 8 shows reduced inflation from around 4% to near 1%. Even today, with inflation hovering in the 3% range, the Fed is reluctant to permit even a short-term rise in inflation to stimulate the economy.

Recently, some economists have begun calling for a policy of pushing unemployment below the natural rate on a temporary or experimental basis; if inflation should then begin to accelerate, this policy could be reversed quickly. These economists suggest that the long-term benefits of the short-run increases in investment that usually accompany boom periods would more than offset the cost of a little inflation today.[2]

The legacy of the Reagan plan in the early 1980s, except for the failure to reduce government spending, has been followed over the last two decades and extends to policymaking today. The natural rate analysis just discussed assumes that inflation expectations adjust with a noticeable lag. Some economists, however, argue that consumers and business adapt their expectations so rapidly that their behavior tends to nullify much of policymakers' actions. We turn to this critique in the next section.

Checkpoint
Unemployment and Inflation: Phillips Curves

REVIEW

- The Phillips curve represents the negative relationship between the unemployment rate and the inflation rate. When the unemployment rate goes up, inflation goes down, and vice versa.
- The natural rate of unemployment is that level where inflation or inflationary pressures are nonexistent.
- Phillips curves are affected by inflationary expectations. Rising inflationary expectations by the public would be reflected in a shift in the Phillips curve to the right, worsening the tradeoff between inflation and unemployment.
- If policymakers use monetary and fiscal policy to attempt to keep unemployment continually below the natural rate, they will face accelerating inflation.
- This inflation requires that policymakers curtail aggregate demand and accept higher rates of unemployment during the transition period back to low inflation.

QUESTION

In the last decade, productivity growth has been unusually high, arguably because of technical advances in microcomputers, cellular phones, and Internet service. Have these advances made it easier for the Federal Reserve to contain inflationary pressures?

Answers to the Checkpoint question can be found at the end of this chapter.

Rational Expectations and Policy Formation

The use of expectations in economic analysis is nothing new. Keynes devoted a chapter to expectations in the *General Theory*, focusing on investors. In his usual colorful way, he asserted, "A conventional valuation which is established as the outcome of the mass psychology of a large number of ignorant individuals is liable to change violently as the result of a sudden fluctuation of opinion due to factors which do not really make much difference to the prospective yield."[3]

Keynes believed that expectations are driven by emotions. In the passage just cited, he suggested investors in the stock market will jump on board trends without attempting to understand the underlying market dynamics. Keynes might well

---

[2]Robert M. Solow and John B. Taylor (eds.), *Inflation, Unemployment, and Monetary Policy* (Cambridge, MA: MIT Press), 1999.
[3]John Maynard Keynes, *The General Theory of Employment, Interest, and Money* (New York: Harcourt Brace Jovanovich), 1964 (first published in 1936), p. 154.

have smiled at the technical analysts who appear on CNN and CNBC today purporting to predict what the stock market will do by referring to such chart formations as "head-and-shoulders," "double tops," and "double bottoms."

Friedman developed his natural rate of unemployment theory using what are known as **adaptive expectations**. In this model of expectations, people are assumed to perform a simple extrapolation from past events. Workers, for example, are assumed to expect that past rates of inflation, averaged over some time period, will continue into the future. Other economists have developed far more complex formulations of adaptive expectations. The key point to note, however, is that adaptive expectations are represented by a *backward-looking* model of expectations, which contrasts with the rational expectations model.

Defining Rational Expectations

In 1961, John Muth suggested that "expectations since they are informed predictions of future events are essentially the same as the predictions of the relevant economic theory."[4] William Poole explained rational expectations by noting that "market outcomes have characteristics as if economic agents are acting on the basis of the correct model of how the world works and that they use all available information in deciding on their actions."[5]

In the **rational expectations** model developed by Robert Lucas, rational economic agents are assumed to make the best possible use of all publicly available information. Before reaching a decision, people are assumed to consider all relevant information before them, then make informed, rational judgments on what the future holds. This does not mean that every individual's expectations or predictions about the future will be correct. Those errors that do occur will be randomly distributed, such that the expectations of large numbers of people will average out to be correct.

To illustrate, assume the economy has been in an equilibrium state for several years with low inflation (2–3%) and low unemployment (5.5–6%). In such a stable environment, the average person would expect the inflation rate to stay right about where it is indefinitely. But now assume the Federal Reserve announces it is going to significantly increase the rate of growth of the money supply. Basic economic theory tells us an increase in the money supply will translate into higher prices, such that increasing the annual rate of growth of the money supply should bring about higher future inflation rates. Knowing this, households and businesses will revise their inflationary expectations upward.

As this simple example shows, people do not rely only on past experiences to formulate their expectations of the future, as adaptive expectations theory would suggest. Rather, people use all information available to them in judging what the future will hold. This information can include past data, but it will also include current policy announcements and all other information that give them reason to believe the future might hold certain changes. If adaptive expectations are backward looking, rational expectations are *forward looking*, in that they assume people will use all of the information available to them.

Policy Implications of Rational Expectations

Do economic actors really form their future expectations as the rational expectations hypothesis suggests? If so, the implications for macroeconomic policy would

Adaptive expectations
Inflationary expectations are formed from a simple extrapolation from past events.

Rational expectations
Rational economic agents are assumed to make the best possible use of all publicly available information, then make informed, rational judgments on what the future holds. Any errors in their forecasts will be randomly distributed.

---

[4]John Muth, "Rational Expectations and the Theory of Price Movements," *Econometrica*, July 1961, pp. 315–335.
[5]William Poole, "Expectations," *Review of the Federal Reserve Bank of St. Louis*, March–April 2001, pp. 1–10.

Nobel Prize Robert Lucas

n the 1970s, a series of articles by Robert E. Lucas changed the course of contemporary macroeconomic theory and profoundly influenced the economic policies of governments throughout the world. His development of the rational expectations theory challenged decades of assumptions about how individuals respond to changes in fiscal and monetary policies.

Lucas was born in 1937 in Yakima, Washington. His father was a welder, who advanced through the ranks to become president of a refrigeration company. Lucas was awarded a scholarship to the University of Chicago. He had wanted to be an engineer, but Chicago did not have an engineering school, so he studied history. He attained a Woodrow Wilson Doctoral Fellowship in history at the University of California, Berkeley. There he developed a strong interest in economics and returned to the University of Chicago, earning his Ph.D. in 1964. One of his professors was Nobel laureate Milton Friedman, whose skepticism about interventionist government policies influenced a generation of economists. Lucas began his teaching career at Carnegie-Mellon University and later became a professor of economics at the University of Chicago.

Before Lucas, economists accepted the Keynesian idea that inflationary policies could lower the unemployment rate. Lucas, however, argued that the rational expectations of individual workers and employers would adjust to the changing monetary conditions, and unemployment rates would rise again. Drawing on earlier work by the economist John Muth, Lucas developed mathematical models to show that temporarily cutting taxes to increase spending was not a sound policy because individuals would base their decisions on expectations about the future. In other words, individuals were rational, forward thinking, and perfectly able to adapt to changing economic information. He also suggested that the fluctuations of fiscal and monetary policy could have harmful effects on the economy.

When the Royal Swedish Academy of Sciences awarded Lucas the Nobel Prize in 1995, it credited Lucas with "the greatest influence on macroeconomic research since 1970." In recent years, Lucas has turned his attention to issues of demographics and understanding the dynamics of economic growth.

be enormous; indeed, it could leave macroeconomic policy ineffective. This was the proposition advanced by economists Thomas Sargent and Neil Wallace in the mid-1970s.[6]

To illustrate, let us assume that the economy in Figure 9 is operating at full employment at point a. Short-run aggregate supply curve AS_0 reflects inflationary expectations of P_0. Suppose the Federal Reserve announces it intends to increase the money supply (or to increase its rate of growth).

FIGURE 9

Rational Expectations: The Policy Ineffectiveness Hypothesis

Rational expectations theory suggests that macroeconomic policy will be ineffective, even in the short term. Assume the economy is operating at full employment (point a) and short-run aggregate supply curve AS_0 reflects inflationary expectations of P_0. Now suppose the Federal Reserve announces it intends to increase the money supply. Expanding the money supply will shift aggregate demand from AD_0 to AD_1, and this will increase the demand for labor and raise nominal wages. Yet, as soon as the Fed announces it is going to increase the money supply, rational economic agents will use this information to immediately raise their inflationary expectations. Thus, output will remain unchanged, though the price level rises immediately to P_2.

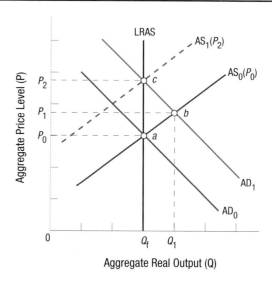

Expanding the money supply will shift aggregate demand from AD_0 to AD_1. This will increase the demand for labor and raise nominal wages. But what happens next?

Natural rate theorists, using adaptive expectations, would argue that workers will be fooled into thinking the increase in money wages represents a real raise, thus driving output and employment up to Q_1 (point b). After a time, however, workers will realize that real wages have not risen since prices have risen by at least as much as wages. Aggregate supply will then fall to AS_1 as price expectations climb to P_2, with the economy gradually moving back to full employment at a higher price level (point c). In this scenario, the Fed's policy succeeds in raising output and employment in the short term, but only at the expense of a long-term rise in the cost of living.

Contrast this with the picture rational expectations theorists paint of the same scenario. When the Federal Reserve announces it is going to increase the money supply, perfectly rational economic agents will heed this information and immediately raise their inflationary expectations. Since the model of the economy they use to determine their future expectations matches that shown in Figure 9, output will remain unchanged, but the price level will rise immediately to P_2. No one gets fooled

[6]Thomas Sargent and Neil Wallace, "Rational Expectations, the Optimal Monetary Instrument and the Optimal Money Supply Rule," *Journal of Political Economy*, April 1975; and "Rational Expectations and the Theory of Economic Policy," *Journal of Monetary Economics*, April 1976.

into temporarily increasing output or employment, even though the increase in the money supply still drives up prices.

In the rational expectations model, whenever the Federal Reserve announces a policy change, rational individuals and firms will anticipate the long-term results and move immediately to that new equilibrium, leaving the short-term aspects of the policy change ineffective. An example of how the Fed can use this phenomenon to its advantage arose in January 2004. The Fed did not change interest rates, but used a change in language to signal a potential willingness to raise interest rates. Note the subtle change in the tone of announcements from August 2003 to January 2004:

- August–October 2003: "Policy accommodation can be maintained for a considerable period."
- December 2003: "With inflation quite low and resource use slack . . . policy accommodation can be maintained for a considerable period."
- January 2004: "With inflation quite low and resource use slack, the (Fed) can be patient in removing its policy accommodation."[7]

By using this subtle shift in language, the Fed was hinting that a movement upward in interest rates might be forthcoming. The reaction of financial markets (the most efficient of all markets) was nearly instantaneous. After the Fed released its statement, the yield on 10-year treasury bonds rose from 4.08% to 4.17%, the Dow Jones Industrial Average dropped by nearly 200 points, and the dollar rose against the euro. This is precisely what rational expectations theory would have predicted. As soon as the Fed so much as hinted at a willingness to raise interest rates, markets reacted in much the same way as if the Fed had actually acted.

This suggests that if the Federal Reserve wants to use an increase in the money supply to raise output and employment in the short term, the only way it can do so is by *not* announcing its plans; it must essentially force economic actors to make decisions with substantially incomplete information. Rational expectations theory suggests that the Federal Reserve and other policymakers must fool the public if its policies are to have short-term benefits.

A Critique of Rational Expectations

To date, empirical assessments of Sargent and Wallace's policy ineffectiveness proposition have yielded mixed results. In general, these studies do not support the policy ineffectiveness proposition. That is, macroeconomic policies do have a real impact on the economy, and monetary policies are credited for reducing inflation over the past two decades.

New Keynesian economists have taken a different approach to critiquing rational expectations theory. Both the adaptive and the rational expectations models assume that labor and product markets are highly competitive, with wages and prices adjusting quickly to expansionary or contractionary policies. The new Keynesians point out, however, that labor markets are often beset with imperfect information, and that efficiency wages often bring about short-term wage stickiness.

Efficiency wage theory disputes the notion that labor markets are like commodity markets: highly competitive markets in which homogeneous goods are exchanged at market-clearing prices. For all labor is not equal. Just because people show up to work for 8 hours a day does not mean they all work equally hard. For this, people need incentives, and higher wages are one form of motivation. By paying their employees an efficiency wage, or a wage above the market-clearing level, employers can hope to improve morale and productivity, as well as create a

Efficiency wage theory
Employers often pay their workers wages above the market-clearing level to improve morale and productivity, reduce turnover, and create a disincentive for employees to shirk their duties.

[7]Greg Ip, "Fed Clears Way for Future Rise in Interest Rates," *Wall Street Journal*, January 29, 2004, p. A1.

disincentive for employees to shirk their duties. After all, if well-paid employees get caught shirking and are laid off, they would have to look for work elsewhere, most likely at lower, more competitive, market-clearing wage levels.

Nobel laureate George Akerlof noted,

Such wages [efficiency wages] cause rationing in the labor market. If employers pay above the market-clearing wage, more workers are going to apply for jobs than there are jobs available. Employers will pay such high wages for a variety of reasons. A leading reason comes from asymmetric information—that the employers cannot watch workers all the time and know everything they do. Employers cannot completely monitor them. So employers pay workers a higher wage so that, should they be caught shirking, they would lose something if they had to seek employment elsewhere.[8]

Imperfect information and efficiency wages suggest that wages and prices may be sticky and not instantly clear in the market. This means that neither workers nor firms can react quickly to changes in monetary or fiscal policy. And this would give such policies a chance of a short-term impact.

Though the policy ineffectiveness proposition has not found significant empirical support, rational expectations as a concept has profoundly affected how economists approach macroeconomic problems. Nearly all economists agree that policy changes will affect expectations, and that this will affect the behavior of economic agents. In turn, these expectations have the potential to reduce the effectiveness of monetary and fiscal policy.

So far, we have considered two challenges to the effectiveness of policy while taking the stylized model of the business cycle for granted. First, we looked at Phillips curves with the policymaker pressing a button, picking the amount of unemployment in column A and obtaining the amount of inflation in column B. We saw that this was overly optimistic, as Friedman's critique was to prove when stagflation hit in the 1970s. Second, we looked at rational expectations and showed how expectations could mitigate the effectiveness of policy. We now want to consider what would happen if our views about the business cycle were proven to be incorrect. If the nature of the business cycle is changing, this automatically questions whether policy will ever have the same impact. We look at this issue next.

Checkpoint
Rational Expectations and Policy Formation

REVIEW

- Adaptive expectations assume economic agents extrapolate from past events. It is a *backward-looking* model of expectations.
- Rational expectations assume economic agents make the best possible use of all publicly available information.
- Rational expectations are *forward looking*; economic agents use all available information to forecast the impact of public policy.
- Rational expectations analysis leads to the conclusion that policy changes will be ineffective in the short run because individuals will immediately adjust to the long-run consequences of the policy.

---

[8]"On Making Economics Realistic: Interview with George Akerlof," *Challenge*, November–December 2002, p. 11.

■ Market imperfections and asymmetric information are two reasons why the policy ineffectiveness conclusions of rational expectations analysis have met with mixed results empirically.

QUESTION

If efficiency wages are widespread throughout the economy but most workers feel they are significantly underpaid, will paying workers more prevent them from shirking?

Answers to the Checkpoint question can be found at the end of this chapter.

Are Recoveries Becoming "Jobless Recoveries"?

Globalization, new technologies, and improved business methods are making the jobs of policymakers much more difficult and may even be changing the nature of the business cycle. The two most recent recessions have deviated significantly from what has happened in past business cycles in that they have been followed by jobless recoveries.

Taming the business cycle has proven to be just as much art as science. Whenever economists believed they had finally gotten a handle on controlling the macroeconomy, some new event or transformation of the economy took place, humbling the profession. There is no doubt that, over the last two to three decades, the federal government and the Federal Reserve have done a remarkable job of keeping the economy on a steady, upward growth path, with only two minor recessions. The problem is, these recessions have not been normal.

The recoveries coming out of the last two recessions have been weak. It is true that the expansion of the 1990s was the longest on record, resulting in big increases in income and wealth and at one point giving rise to the term "the new economy." The recession of 2001, moreover, was mild compared to many past downturns. But the ensuing recovery, like that of 1990–91, was lackluster for those out of work and looking for a job.

Just what is a **jobless recovery**? When output begins to grow after a trough, employment usually starts to grow. But when output begins to rise, yet employment growth does not resume, the recovery is called a *jobless recovery*.[9]

We have already seen that business cycles vary dramatically in their depth and duration. The Great Depression was the worst downturn in U.S. history, and the most recent recession was one of the mildest. In this latest recession, the unemployment rate never rose above 6%, and real output actually increased throughout the downturn, though at a diminished rate. But if the recession was mild, the recovery was not as strong as in typical business cycles.

Figure 10 on the next page shows how the latest business cycle compares to previous cycles. It indexes real output for the current recession and recovery to those of previous business cycles. Specifically, real output for each business cycle is indexed to the trough of the cycle. This involves dividing each quarter's output by output at the trough. Thus, if one quarter after the trough, output has grown by 1%, the index would be 1.01 at that point. In this way, we can get a graphical picture of how output is doing throughout the course of each cycle.

Figure 10 on the next page shows that during the recession of 2001, output continued to grow throughout the cycle. In both of the last two recessions, however, once the trough had been reached, output grew much more slowly than in the previous

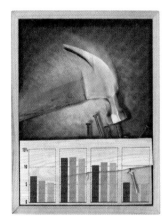

Russell Thurston/Getty Images

Jobless recovery
Takes place after a recession, when output begins to rise, but employment growth does not.

---

[9]Stacey Schreft and Aarti Singh, "A Closer Look at Jobless Recoveries," *Economic Review* (Kansas City, MO: Federal Reserve Bank of Kansas City), Second Quarter 2003, pp. 45–73. Figures 10 and 11 are adapted from this article.

FIGURE 10

Real GDP Growth Relative to Trough of Business Cycle

The last two business cycles are compared to previous cycles by indexing real output for the current recession and recovery to those of previous business cycles. For the recession of 2001, output continued to grow throughout the cycle. In both of the last two recessions, however, once the trough had been reached, output grew much more slowly than in previous recessions. One year after the trough, output in the last two recessions had grown only roughly half as much as in the typical recovery.

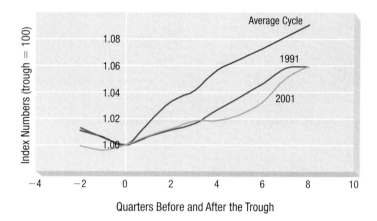

five recessions. One year (four quarters) after the low point in the cycle, output in the last two recessions had grown only roughly half as much as in the typical recovery—roughly 3% versus a typical 6%.

As noted in an earlier chapter, however, some of the employment sluggishness of the last two recoveries could be associated with the survey used to measure employment. The establishment survey (used here) shows limited employment gains, while the household survey shows considerable job creation over the recovery. Economists currently accept the establishment survey as more reliable.

Figure 11 presents the same type of indexed graph for employment, though indexing the figures monthly. Note that in the average cycle, employment falls to a trough, then grows steadily after that. Contrast this to what has happened in the last two recessions. Employment has declined into the trough, but then leveled out or even continued to decline. In both recessions, job growth was nil even 1 year after the trough had been reached.

FIGURE 11

Nonfarm Employment Growth Relative to Trough of Business Cycle

Employment in the last two recessions and recovery is indexed against previous business cycles, using monthly figures. Normally, employment falls to a trough, then grows steadily after that. But in the last two recessions, job growth leveled out or even continued to decline after the trough.

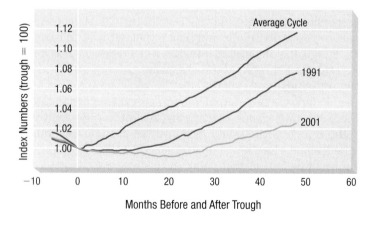

Because the last two recoveries have been slow to add jobs, it is possible that this will be the norm in the future. If this is what happens, policymakers will need to know why the business cycle has changed so that they can design policies that will work better. Several factors seem to be driving jobless recoveries: rapid increases in productivity, a change in employment patterns, and outsourcing. The latest recession and subsequent slow job growth may also have something to do with the over-investment that occurred during the previous boom, which has stifled investment during this recovery.

Productivity increases arising from computers, Internet services, and cellular phones make labor far more flexible than ever before. Now when the economy contracts, employers can more easily lay off workers and shift their responsibilities to the workers who remain. As a result, output may keep growing, or at least not drop much, even though fewer workers are employed. Then, when the market rebounds, increased productivity and flexibility permit firms to adjust to their rising orders without immediately hiring more people. This gives the firm more time to evaluate the recovery to ensure that hiring permanent employees is appropriate.

In addition, hiring practices have changed over the past few decades. Firms have begun substituting just-in-time (JIT) hiring practices for long-term permanent employees. This includes using more temporary and part-time workers, as well as adding overtime shifts for permanent employees. Again, by using temps, part-time workers, and overtime, a firm can increase its flexibility while limiting the higher costs associated with hiring permanent employees until it has time to evaluate the recovery and the demand for its products.

The massive investment that took place during the boom of the 1990s is probably responsible for much of the increased productivity we have seen lately. As Figure 12 shows, investment fell off during the 2001 recession far more than in previous cycles. This may partly explain why employers were slow to add employees during this recovery. Added investment in plant and equipment usually leads to more hiring. Without added investment, employers were able to fill their labor needs with temporary and part-time workers.

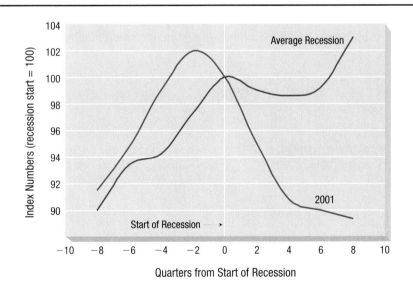

FIGURE 12

Real Business Fixed Investment Relative to the Start of the Recession

The massive investment that took place during the boom of the 1990s is largely responsible for the increased productivity we enjoy today. As this graph shows, investment fell off during the 2001 recession far more than in previous cycles. This may partly explain why employers were slow to add employees during this recovery. Added investment in plant and equipment typically leads to hiring. Without the added investment, employers were able to fill their labor needs with temporary and part-time workers.

Some observers have suggested that recent changes in employment patterns may just be a delayed reaction to the many laws and legal rulings that have restricted the flexibility of traditional labor resources. Firms are substituting less costly and more flexible labor for higher cost and less flexible permanent workers. Part-time and temporary employees rarely have benefits and can be added or terminated much more easily than permanent workers. Firms have benefited from being able to put off permanent hiring until they gained confidence that a recovery in the demand for their products can be sustained.

For employees, these changing labor patterns have brought both good and bad news. Workers have more options to work part-time or more flexible hours, and overtime can add to annual income. Most workers, however, would prefer permanent jobs to flexible—and uncertain—hours. Some workers who have permanent jobs, moreover, feel they must work overtime, not because they want the extra hours, but because they fear this is required to keep from losing their jobs.

Flexibility, though beneficial for the economy, can be hard on workers who are laid off and enduring long-term unemployment. Many workers are concerned with the growing ease at which firms can outsource jobs to developing nations, where wages are often only 10–20% of domestic wages. While less clear-cut, outsourcing may be contributing to a slower domestic demand for labor.

These explanations for the jobless recovery may be specific to this particular recovery, or they may portend basic changes in our view of the general business cycle and what policies might be effective. If basic changes are necessary, they may be substantial, but they will not become clear for some time yet. Note that even by the end of 2005, nearly 50 months after the trough, employment had only increased by 3%, an amount that the average recession is able to recoup in roughly 12 months.

One additional factor needs to be mentioned: globalization. The riots in Seattle in 1999 and Genoa in 2001 brought protests about globalization to the center of public attention. Meetings of the World Trade Organization (WTO) have brought together disparate groups who are against free trade. Globalism, the WTO, the World Bank, and the whole system of free trade are viewed as conspiracies designed to further the interests of multinational corporations at the expense of American workers, destroy the domestic manufacturing sector, ruin the environment, and exploit poor workers in developing countries. If these charges are valid, it is hard to imagine anyone but corporate executives supporting free trade.

But are the charges valid? Most economists think not. America opened its borders to trade after World War II, and we have prospered ever since. As Douglas Irwin asked, "Why was the economic prosperity of the 1990s accompanied by such hostility toward free trade?"[10] The last two chapters of this book discuss globalism, trade, and the impact of an open economy on macroeconomic policy.

Key Concepts

Chapter Summary

Unemployment and Inflation: Phillips Curves

In Britain, A. W. Phillips found a negative relationship between unemployment rates and money wages. As unemployment falls, wages rise as firms bid up the price of labor to attract more workers, and wages fall when unemployment rises. Unemployment was later connected to inflation, and the tradeoff between inflation and unemployment has become known as the Phillips curve.

A rise in wages may lead to a rise in prices, but if worker productivity increases enough to offset the wage increase, product prices can remain stable. The basic

---

[10]Douglas Irwin, *Free Trade Under Fire* (Princeton: Princeton University Press), 2002, p. 2.

relationship among wages, prices, and productivity is $p = w - q$, where p is the rate of inflation, w is the rate of increase in nominal wages, and q is the rate of increase in labor productivity.

The natural rate of unemployment is that unemployment rate at which inflationary expectations match inflation, and thus inflationary pressures in the economy are nonexistent. This unemployment rate is also known as the nonaccelerating inflation rate of unemployment (NAIRU), and it is often thought to be around 5%.

A negative relationship between unemployment and inflation is represented by the Phillips curve. It suggests that the economy presents policymakers with a menu of choices. By accepting modest inflation, they can keep unemployment low.

In the 1970s, however, policymakers and economists were stymied by the onset of stagflation, when unemployment and inflation rates approached double digits. Unlike the Phillips relationship, which postulated that unemployment would go down when inflation went up, unemployment and inflation both went up.

Workers do not work for the sake of earning a specific nominal wage, but for what this money will buy: a real wage. When bargaining for wage increases, workers will take their past experiences with inflation into account. Wage increases can be related to unemployment and expected inflation by the equation $w = f(u) + p^e$, where w is the wage increase, $f(u)$ is the relationship between unemployment and wage increases, and p^e is inflationary expectations.

If workers do not expect inflation and policymakers trigger inflation to stimulate output and reduce unemployment below its natural rate, output will rise, but real wages will fall as product prices rise. Workers will then start demanding contract revisions to raise their nominal wages, restoring output to its previous level, but at a higher price level.

If workers expect a certain rate of inflation when they negotiate their contracts, they will demand a higher nominal wage to account for the expected rise in prices. Thus, if policymakers want to raise output, they must raise inflation to a level even higher than workers had expected. This suggests that if policymakers want to keep unemployment consistently below its natural rate, they must be willing to accept a constantly accelerating rate of inflation.

If policymakers want to curtail inflationary pressures when they arise, they must be willing to curtail growth in aggregate demand and accept the resulting higher rates of unemployment for a transitional period. As aggregate demand slumps, wage and price pressures will soften, reducing inflationary expectations. As these expectations decline, the Phillips curve will shift leftward, returning the economy to lower inflation and unemployment rates.

Rational Expectations and Policy Formation

The adaptive expectations model assumes that people form their future expectations by performing a simple extrapolation from past events. Workers, for example, are assumed to expect that past rates of inflation, averaged over some time period, will continue into the future. Adaptive expectations theory is, therefore, a backward-looking model of expectations.

The rational expectations model assumes that rational economic agents will use all publicly available information in forming their expectations. This information can include past data, but will also include current policy announcements and all other relevant information. In this sense, rational expectations theory is a forward-looking model of expectations.

If the rational expectations hypothesis is correct, the implications for policymakers will be enormous. Specifically, it will mean that policymakers cannot stimulate output in the short run by raising inflation unless they keep their actions secret. Otherwise, workers would accurately predict the coming inflation and raise their wage demands immediately, thus raising prices without stimulating an increase in output.

The empirical record of rational expectations theory is mixed. New Keynesian economists have critiqued this theory on theoretical grounds, arguing that labor markets are often beset with imperfect information, and that efficiency wages often bring about short-term wage stickiness. (Efficiency wages are wages set above the market-clearing level to improve worker morale and productivity, and decrease turnover.) If wages are sticky, neither workers nor firms can react quickly to changes in monetary or fiscal policy, thus giving such policies a chance of having short-term impacts.

Questions and Problems

1. Ben Bernanke, the chairman of the Fed, recently noted that "in the 1970s the public had little confidence that the Fed would keep inflation low and stable." As a result, when oil prices rose, wages and prices quickly followed. This caused the Fed to have to sharply increase interest rates to curtail inflation. Is the same thing happening again today? Do people have a different perspective on the Fed than in the past?

2. The Phillips curve for the United States in the 1960s shown in Figure 3 becomes very steep after unemployment drops below 4%, and rather shallow as unemployment exceeds 6%. Why is a typical Phillips curve shaped this way?

3. Does the long-run Phillips curve make it difficult (if not impossible) for policymakers to increase output and employment beyond full employment in the long run?

4. Explain why inflation accelerates if policymakers use monetary and fiscal policy to keep unemployment below the natural rate.

5. Why would policymakers want to drive unemployment below the natural rate, given that inflation will result?

6. Does having rational expectations mean that all economic actors act rationally and are always correct?

7. Why couldn't the problems of inflation be solved by simply requiring that wages, rents, profits, product prices, and interest rates are subject to "cost-of-living" increases each year?

8. Explain why those who favor the rational expectations approach to modeling the economy do not favor discretionary policymaking.

9. In Canada, the consensus estimate of the natural rate of unemployment was 4.5% in 1970 and 7% in 2005. A minority view has claimed that the change to 7% is beyond explanation and must be too high. A similar change has taken place in the United States over this period, but the consensus estimate of the natural rate of unemployment is closer to 5% today. What would be the result if the Bank of Canada (the central bank in Canada) and the Federal Reserve in the United States assumed that the natural rate was 7% when it really was closer to 5%?

10. Why are inflationary expectations so important for policymakers to keep under control? When a supply shock such as an oil price spike hits the economy, does it matter how fast policymakers attempt to bring the economy back to full employment?

11. Would policymakers prefer a Phillips curve with a steep or shallow slope? Why?

12. A negative supply shock (a huge natural disaster or significant energy price spike) would do what to the short-run Phillips curve? To the long-run Phillips curve?

13. How are the long-run Phillips curve (LRPC) and the long-run aggregate supply (LRAS) curve related?

14. Would the credibility of policymakers' (Congress and the Fed) commitment to keeping inflation low have an effect on inflationary expectations when the economy is beset by a supply shock?

15. America's employment practices are much more flexible than most of those in the European countries. Does the fact that our labor markets are more flexible and more competitive than those of Europe make our Phillips curve tradeoffs more reasonable?

Answers to Checkpoint Questions

CHECKPOINT: UNEMPLOYMENT AND INFLATION: PHILLIPS CURVES

Since we have seen that $p = w - q$, if q is high, wage increases (w) can be high without any real pressures on inflation (p). High productivity growth along with globalization and lower wages in many other countries have helped to keep inflationary pressures in the United States in check.

CHECKPOINT: RATIONAL EXPECTATIONS AND POLICY FORMATION

If employees are convinced they are significantly underpaid (or they are worth more than they are paid), efficiency wages may have little impact on shirking, productivity, or turnover. If true, it probably doesn't do much for the rational expectations theory's effectiveness conclusion because there are a number of other inefficiencies in labor markets such as collective bargaining and information problems. Even those who think they are underpaid and begin looking for a new position often must face the reality that they are overpaid when no offers are forthcoming, or when information filters back to them about those who quit and ended up with lower-paying jobs.

International Trade

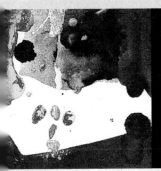

15

the world economy is becoming increasingly intertwined. Capital, labor, goods, and services all flow across borders. Most Americans wear foreign-made clothing, over half of us drive foreign cars, and even American cars contain many foreign components. Australian wines, Swiss watches, Chilean Sea Bass, and Brazilian coffee have become common in the United States; while overseas, Ford Escorts, Nike athletic shoes, and Intel Pentium computers with Microsoft Windows can be found in abundance. Trade is now part of the global landscape.

Worldwide foreign trade has quadrupled over the past 25 years. In the United States today, the combined value of exports and imports approaches $3 trillion a year. Twenty-five years ago, trade represented just over 15% of gross domestic product (GDP); today it accounts for more than a quarter of GDP. Nearly a 10th of American workers owe their jobs to foreign consumers. Figure 1 on the next page shows the current composition of U.S. exports and imports. Note that the United States imports and exports a lot of capital goods, that is, the equipment and machinery used to produce other goods. Also, we export nearly twice as many services as we import. Services include, for example, education and health care. Third, petroleum products represent nearly 12% of imports, totaling over $235 billion a year.

Improved communications and transportation technologies have worked together to promote global economic integration. In addition, most governments around the world have reduced their trade barriers in recent years. But free trade has not always been so popular.

In 1929–30, as the Great Depression was just beginning, many countries attempted to protect their domestic industries by imposing trade restrictions that discouraged imports. In 1930, the United States enacted the Smoot-Hawley tariffs, which imposed an average tax of 60% on imported goods. This move deeply hurt industries around the world, and it has been credited with adding to the severity of the global depression. Since World War II, in the wake of Smoot-Hawley's obvious failure, governments have steadily reduced trade barriers through a series of international agreements.

FIGURE 1

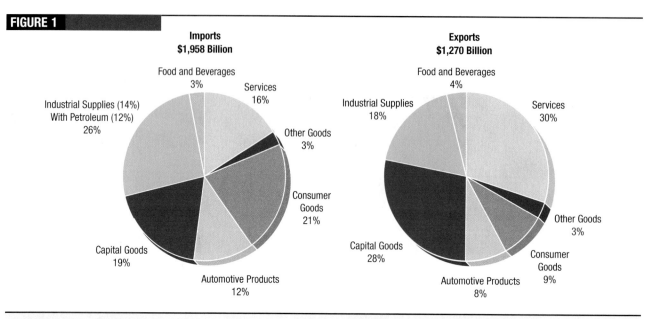

Imports
$1,958 Billion

Food and Beverages 3%
Services 16%
Industrial Supplies (14%) With Petroleum (12%) 26%
Other Goods 3%
Consumer Goods 21%
Capital Goods 19%
Automotive Products 12%

Exports
$1,270 Billion

Food and Beverages 4%
Industrial Supplies 18%
Services 30%
Other Goods 3%
Capital Goods 28%
Consumer Goods 9%
Automotive Products 8%

U.S. Trade by Sector (2005)

This figure shows trade by sector. The United States imports and exports large amounts of capital goods, the equipment and machinery used to produce other goods. Also, the United States exports nearly twice as many services as it imports.

Trade must yield significant benefits or it would not exist. After all, there are no laws requiring countries to trade, just agreements permitting trade and reducing impediments to it. This chapter begins with a discussion of why trade is beneficial. We look at the terms of trade between countries. We then look at the tariffs and quotas sometimes used to restrict trade, calculating their costs. Finally, we will consider some arguments critics have advanced against increased trade and globalization.

After studying this chapter you should be able to

- Describe the benefits of free trade.
- Distinguish between absolute and comparative advantage.
- Describe the economic impacts of trade.
- Describe the terms of trade.
- List the ways in which trade is restricted.
- Discuss the various arguments against free trade.
- Describe the issues surrounding increasing global economic integration.

The Gains from Trade

Economics studies voluntary exchange. People and nations do business with one another because they expect to gain through these transactions. Foreign trade is nearly as old as civilization. Centuries ago, European merchants were already sailing to the Far East to ply the spice trades. Today, people in the United States buy cars from Japan and electronics from South Korea, along with millions of other products from countries around the world.

Many people assume that trade between nations is a zero-sum game: a game in which, for one party to gain, the other party must lose. Poker games fit this description; one person's winnings must come from another player's losses. This is not true, however, of voluntary trade. Voluntary exchange and trade is a positive-sum game, meaning that both parties to a transaction can gain.

To understand how this works, and thus, why nations trade, we need to consider the concepts of absolute and comparative advantage. Note that nations per se do not trade; individuals in specific countries do. We will, however, refer to trade between nations, but recognize that individuals, not nations, actually engage in trade. We covered this earlier in Chapter 2, but it is worthwhile to go through it again.

Absolute and Comparative Advantage

Figure 2 shows hypothetical production possibilities curves for the United States and Canada. For simplicity, both countries are assumed to produce only beef and

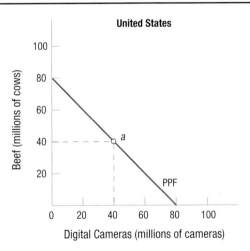

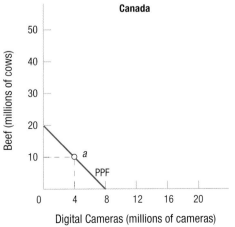

FIGURE 2

Production Possibilities for the United States and Canada

The production possibilities curves shown here assume that the United States and Canada produce only beef and digital cameras. In this example, the United States has an absolute advantage over Canada in producing both products; the United States can produce 4 times as many cattle and 10 times as many cameras as Canada. Canada nonetheless has a comparative advantage over the United States in producing beef.

Absolute advantage
One country can produce more
of a good than another country.

Comparative advantage
One country has a lower
opportunity cost of producing a
good than another country.

digital cameras. Given the production possibility frontiers (PPFs) in Figure 2, the United States has an absolute advantage over Canada in the production of both products. An **absolute advantage** exists when one country can produce more of a good than another country. In this case, the United States can produce 4 times as much beef and 10 times as many cameras as Canada.

At first glance, we may wonder why the United States would be willing to trade with Canada. Because the United States can produce so much more of both commodities, why not just produce its own cattle and cameras? The reason lies in comparative advantage.

One country enjoys a **comparative advantage** in producing some good if its opportunity costs to produce that good are lower than the other country's. In this example, Canada's comparative advantage is in producing cattle. As Figure 2 shows, the opportunity cost for the United States to produce another million cows is 1 million cameras; each added cow essentially costs 1 camera.

Contrast this with the situation in Canada. For every camera Canadian producers forgo producing, they can produce 2.5 more cows. This means cows cost only 0.4 camera in Canada (1/2.5 = 0.4). Canada's comparative advantage is in producing cattle, since a cow costs 0.4 camera in Canada, while the same cow costs an entire camera in the United States.

By the same token, the United States has a comparative advantage in producing cameras: 1 camera in the United States costs 1 cow, but the same camera in Canada costs 2.5 cows. These relative costs suggest that the United States should focus its resources on digital camera production and that Canada should specialize in beef.

Gains from Trade

To see how specialization and trade can benefit both countries even when one has an advantage in producing more of both goods, assume that the United States and Canada at first operate at point *a* in Figure 2, producing and consuming their own beef and digital cameras. As we can see, the United States produces and consumes 40 million cattle and 40 million digital cameras. Canada produces and consumes 10 million cattle and 4 million digital cameras. This initial position is similarly shown as points *a* in Figure 3.

Assume now that Canada specializes in producing cattle, producing all that it can, 20 million cows. We will assume the two countries want to continue consuming 50 million cows between them. This means the United States needs to produce only 30 million cattle, since Canada is now producing 20 million. This frees up some American resources to produce digital cameras. Since each cow in the United States costs a digital camera, reducing beef output by 10 million cattle means that 10 million more cameras can now be produced.

So, the United States is producing 30 million cattle and 50 million cameras. Canada is producing 20 million cattle and no cameras. The combined production of cattle remains the same, 50 million, but camera production has increased by 6 million (from 44 to 50 million).

The two countries can trade their surplus products, and will be better off. This is shown in Table 1. Assuming they agree to share the added 6 million cameras between them equally, Canada will trade 10 million cattle in exchange for 7 million digital cameras. Points *b* in Figure 3 show the resulting consumption patterns for each country. Each consume the same quantity of beef as before trading, but each country now has 3 million more digital cameras: 43 million for the United States and 7 million for Canada. This is shown in the final column of the table.

One important point to remember is that even when one country has an absolute advantage over another, countries will still benefit from trade. The gains are small in our example, but they will grow as the two countries approach one another in size and their comparative advantages become more pronounced.

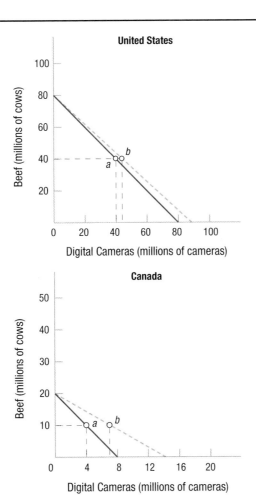

FIGURE 3

The Gains from Specialization and Trade to the United States and Canada

Assume Canada specializes in cattle. If the two countries want to continue consuming 50 million cows between them, the United States needs to produce only 30 million. This frees up resources for the United States to begin producing more digital cameras. Since each cow in the United States costs 1 camera to produce, reducing beef output by 10 million cattle means that 10 million more cameras can be produced. When the two countries trade their surplus products, both are better off than before.

There is one recent theoretical objection to this trade model. Nobel Prize winner Paul Samuelson has shown that under certain conditions outsourcing and trade could, on the whole, be negative for the United States.[1] Other economists have argued that while such an outcome is theoretically possible, empirically the chance

Table 1		The Gains from Trade		
Country and Product		**Before Specialization**	**After Specialization**	**After Trade**
United States	Cows	40 million	30 million	40 million
	Cameras	40 million	50 million	43 million
Canada	Cows	10 million	20 million	10 million
	Cameras	4 million	0	7 million

[1]Paul Samuelson, "Where Ricardo and Mill Rebut and Confirm Arguments of Mainstream Economists Supporting Globalization," *Journal of Economic Perspectives*, Summer 2004, pp. 135–146. If, for example, trading with the United States improves technology and productivity so much in developing nations that their greater output leads to a reduction in the price of U.S. exports, we might be worse off. This could even be the case despite cheaper consumer goods. The important point is that not just some industries and workers lose, but the economy as a whole could be a loser.

of trade not benefiting the United States in general is remote.[2] Nevertheless, his work adds a nuance to traditional trade analysis.

Practical Constraints on Trade

At this point, we should take a moment to note some practical constraints on trade. First, every transaction involves costs. These include transportation, communications, and the general costs of doing business. Over the last several decades, however, transportation and communication costs have declined all over the world, resulting in growing world trade.

Second, the production possibilities curves for nations are not linear; rather, they are governed by increasing costs and diminishing returns. Countries find it difficult to specialize only in one product. Indeed, specializing in one product is risky since the market for the product can always decline, new technology might replace it, or its production can be disrupted by changing weather patterns. This is a perennial problem for developing countries that often build their exports and trade around one agricultural commodity.

Although it is true that trading partners will benefit from trade, some individuals and groups within each country may lose. Individual workers in those industries at a comparative disadvantage are likely to lose their jobs, and thus may require retraining, relocation, or other help if they are to move smoothly into new occupations.

When the United States signed the North American Free Trade Agreement (NAFTA) with Canada and Mexico, many U.S. workers experienced this sort of dislocation. Some U.S. jobs went south to Mexico because of low wages. Still, by opening up more markets for U.S. products, NAFTA has stimulated the U.S. economy. The goal is that displaced workers, newly retrained, will end up with new and better jobs, although there is no guarantee this will happen.

Checkpoint

The Gains from Trade

REVIEW

- An absolute advantage exists when one country can produce more of a good than another country.
- A comparative advantage exists when one country can produce a good at a lower opportunity cost than another country.
- Both countries gain from trade when each specializes in producing goods in which they have a comparative advantage.
- Transaction costs, diminishing returns, and the risk associated with specialization all place some practical limits on trade.

QUESTIONS

In the 1990s, there was a surge of interest in sports memorabilia. In particular, baseball memorabilia shows witnessed lines of people willing to pay for a baseball player's autograph on a picture, baseball, or baseball card. All of this attention increased the interest of kids in buying baseball cards. A natural corollary of this is the trading of baseball cards. Assume you have a set of baseball cards for the current year but are

---

[2]Jagdish Bhagwati, Arvind Panagariya, and T. N. Srinivasan, "The Muddles Over Outsourcing," *Journal of Economic Perspectives*, Fall 2004, pp. 93–114.

missing some. In particular, you are a Cardinals fan and have all of the Cardinals cards except Albert Pujols. Would you trade for it? What would you want to give up for the Pujols card? What would the Pujols card holder expect in return? Who benefits from this trade?

Answers to the Checkpoint questions can be found at the end of this chapter.

The Terms of Trade

How much can a country charge when it sells its goods to another country? How much must it pay for imported goods? The terms of trade determine the prices of imports and exports.

To keep things simple, assume each country has only one export and one import, priced at P_x and P_m. The ratio of the price of the exported goods to the price of the imported goods, P_x/P_m, is the terms of trade. Thus, if a country exports computers and imports coffee, with two computers trading for a ton of coffee, the price of a computer must be one half the price of a ton of coffee.

When countries trade many commodities, the **terms of trade** are defined as the average price of exports divided by the average price of imports. This can get a bit complicated, given that the price of each import and export will be quoted in its own national currency, while the exchange rate between the two currencies may be constantly changing. We will ignore these complications by translating currencies into dollars, focusing our attention on how the terms of trade are determined and the impact of trade.

Terms of trade
The ratio of the price of exported goods to the price of imported goods (P_x/P_m).

Determining the Terms of Trade

To get a feel for how the terms of trade are determined, let us consider the trade in computers between the United States and Japan. We will assume the United States has a comparative advantage in producing computers; all prices are given in dollars.

Panel A of Figure 4 on the next page shows the demand and supply of computers in the United States. The upward sloping supply curve reflects increasing opportunity costs in computer production. As the United States continues to specialize in computer production, resources less suited to this purpose must be employed. Thus, ever-increasing amounts of other goods must be sacrificed, resulting in rising costs for computer production. Because of this rise in costs as ever more resources are shifted to computers, the United States will eventually lose its comparative advantage in computer production. This represents one limit on specialization and trade.

Let us assume the United States begins in pretrade equilibrium at point a, with the price of computers at P_1. Panel B shows Japan initially in equilibrium at point h, with a higher computer price of P_2. Since prices for computers from the United States are lower, when trade begins, Japanese consumers will begin buying U.S. computers.

American computer makers will increase production to meet this new demand. Japanese computer firms, conversely, will see the sales of their computers decline in Japan as prices begin to fall. For now, let us ignore transport costs, such that trade continues until prices reach P_e. At this point, U.S. exports ($Q_2 - Q_1$) are just equal to Japanese imports ($Q_4 - Q_3$). Both countries are now in equilibrium, with the price of computers somewhere between two pretrade equilibrium prices.

FIGURE 4

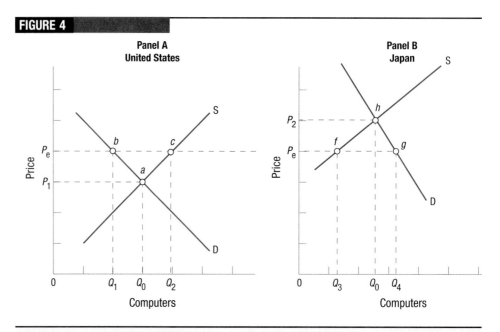

Panel A
United States

Panel B
Japan

Computers   Computers

Determining the Terms of Trade

Panel A shows the demand and supply of computers in the United States; the upward slope of the supply curve reflects increasing opportunity costs to produce more computers. The United States begins in pretrade equilibrium at point *a*, with the price of computers at P_1. Panel B shows Japan's initial equilibrium at point *h*, with a higher price of P_2. With trade, Japanese consumers will begin buying American computers because of their lower price. American computer makers will increase production to meet this new demand. Japanese computer firms will see sales of their computers decline as prices begin to fall. Ignoring transport costs, trade will continue until prices reach P_e. At this point, American exports $(Q_2 - Q_1)$ are just equal to Japanese imports $(Q_4 - Q_3)$. Both countries are in equilibrium, with the price of computers somewhere between two pretrade equilibrium prices.

Imagine this same process simultaneously working itself out with many other goods, including some at which the Japanese have a comparative advantage, such as cameras and electronic components. As each product settles into an equilibrium price like P_e, the terms of trade between these two countries get determined.

The Impact of Trade

Our examination of absolute and comparative advantage has thus far highlighted the blessings of trade. A closer look at Figure 4, however, shows that trade produces winners and losers.

Picking up on the previous example, computer producers in the United States are happy, having watched their sales rise from Q_0 to Q_2. Predictably, management and workers in this industry will favor even more trade with Japan and the rest of the world. Yet, domestic consumers of computers are worse off, since after trade they purchase only Q_1 computers at the higher equilibrium price of P_e. Computer users will likely oppose increased trade, and may even look to Congress to restrict trade.

Contrast this situation in the net exporting country, the United States, with that of the net importer, Japan. Japanese computer producers are worse off than before since the price of computers fell from P_2 to P_e, and their output was reduced to Q_3. Consequently, they must cut jobs, leaving workers and managers in the Japanese computer industry unhappy with its country's trade policies. Japanese consumers, however, are beneficiaries of this expanded trade, since they can purchase Q_4 computers at lower price P_e.

These results are not merely hypothetical. This is the story of free trade, which has been played out time and again: Some sectors of the economy win, and some lose. American consumers have been happy to purchase Japanese cameras such as Minolta and Nikon, given their high quality and low prices. American camera makers such as Kodak and Polaroid have not been so pleased, nor have their employees. These firms, watching their prices, sales, and employment decline, have had to adapt to the competition from abroad.

Similarly, the ranks of American textile workers have been decimated over the past two decades as domestic clothing producers have increasingly become nothing but designers and marketers of clothes, shifting their production overseas to countries where wages are lower. American-made clothing is now essentially a thing of the past.

To be sure, American consumers have enjoyed a substantial drop in the price of clothing, because labor forms a significant part of the cost of clothing production. Still, being able to purchase inexpensive T-shirts made in China is small consolation for the unemployed textile worker in North Carolina.

The undoubted pain suffered by the losers from trade often is translated into pressure put on politicians to restrict trade in one way or another. The pain is often felt more strongly than the "happiness" felt by those who benefit from trade.

How Trade Is Restricted

Trade restrictions can range from subsidies provided to domestic firms to protect them against lower-priced imports to embargoes in which the government bans any trade with a country. Between these two extremes are more intermediate policies, such as exchange controls that limit the amount of foreign currency available to importers or citizens who travel abroad. Regulation, licensing, and government purchasing policies are all frequently used to promote or ensure the purchase of domestic products. The main reason for these trade restrictions is simple: The industry and its employees actually feel the pain and lobby extensively for protection, while the huge benefits of lower prices are diffused among millions of customers whose benefits are each so small that fighting against a trade barrier isn't worth their time.

The most common forms of trade restrictions are tariffs and quotas. Panel A of Figure 5 on the next page shows the average U.S. tariff rates since 1900. Some economists have suggested that the tariff wars that erupted in the 1920s and culminated in the passage of the Smoot-Hawley Act in 1930 were an important factor underlying the severity of the Great Depression. Panel B shows the impact of higher tariffs on worldwide imports. The higher tariffs reduced trade, leading to a reduction in income, output, and employment, and added fuel to the worldwide depression. Since the 1930s, the United States has played a leading role in trade liberalization, with our average tariff rates declining to a current rate of roughly 5%.

Effects of Tariffs and Quotas

What exactly are the effects of tariffs and quotas? **Tariffs** are often ad valorem taxes. This means the product is taxed by a certain percentage of its price as it crosses the border. Other tariffs are unit taxes: A fixed tax per unit of the product is assessed at the border. Tariffs are designed to generate revenues and to drive a wedge between the domestic price of a product and its price on the world market. The effects of a tariff are shown in Figure 6.

Domestic supply and demand for the product are shown in Figure 6 as S and D. Assume that the product's world price P_W is lower than its domestic price P_0. Domestic quantity demanded Q_2 will consequently exceed domestic quantity supplied Q_1 at the world price of P_W. Imports to this country will therefore be $Q_2 - Q_1$.

Now assume that the firms and workers in the industry hurt by the lower world price lobby for a tariff and are successful. The country imposes a tariff (T) on this product. The results are clear. The product's price in this country rises to P_{W+T} and imports fall to $Q_4 - Q_3$. Domestic consumers consume less of the product at higher prices. Even so, the domestic industry is happy, since its prices and output have risen. The government, meanwhile, collects revenues equal to the shaded area

Tariff
A tax on imported products. When a country taxes imported products, it drives a wedge between the product's domestic price and its price on the world market.

FIGURE 5

Average U.S. Tariff Rates (1900–2004) and the Downward Spiral of World Imports, 1930–33

Tariffs and quotas are the most common forms of trade restrictions. Panel A shows that tariff rates in the United States peaked during the Great Depression. For the last several decades, tariffs have stayed at roughly a rate of 5%. When tariffs jumped with the passage of the Smoot-Hawley Act in 1930, world imports spiraled downward as shown in Panel B. As trade between nations declined, incomes, output, and employment also fell worldwide. In Panel B, total monthly imports in millions of U.S. dollars for 75 countries is shown spiraling downward from $2,738 million in January 1930 to $1,057 in March of 1933.

Source: Charles Kindleberger, *The World Depression 1929–1939* (Berkeley: University of California Press), 1986, p. 170.

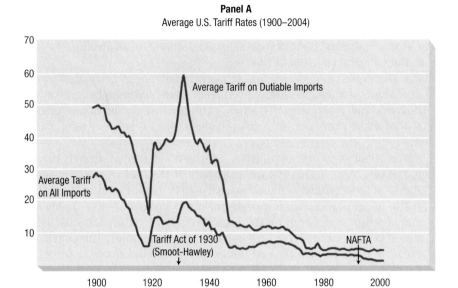

Panel A
Average U.S. Tariff Rates (1900–2004)

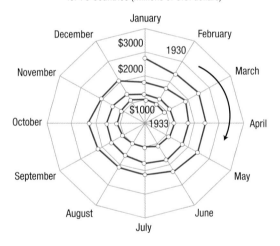

Panel B
The Downward Spiral of Total Imports for 75 Countries (millions of U.S. dollars)

Quota
A government-set limit on the quantity of imports into a country.

in Figure 6. These revenues can be significant: In the 1800s, tariffs were the federal government's dominant form of revenue. It is only in the last century that the federal government has come to rely more on other sources of revenue, including taxes on income, sales, and property.

Figure 7 shows the effects of a **quota.** They are similar to what we saw in Figure 6, except that the government restricts the quantity of imports into the country to $Q_4 - Q_3$. Imports fall to the quota level, and consumers again lose, because they must pay higher prices for less output. Producers and their employees gain as prices and employment in the domestic industry rise. For a quota, however, the government does not collect revenue. Then who gets this revenue? The foreign exporting company will get it, in the form of higher prices for its products. This explains why governments prefer tariffs over quotas.

The United States imposed quotas on Japanese automobiles in the 1980s. The primary effect of these quotas was initially to dramatically raise the minimum standard equipment and price for some Japanese cars and to increase ultimately the

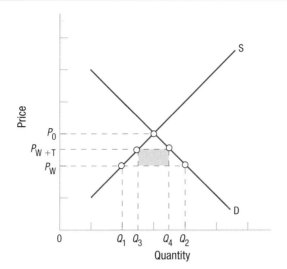

FIGURE 6

Effects of a Tariff

What are the effects of a typical tariff? Supply and demand curves S and D represent domestic supply and demand. Assume the product's world price P_W is lower than its domestic price P_0. Domestic quantity demanded Q_2 will consequently exceed domestic quantity supplied Q_1 at the world price of P_W. Imports will therefore be $Q_2 - Q_1$. If the country imposes a tariff (T) on this product, the domestic price rises to P_{W+T}, and imports fall to $Q_4 - Q_3$. Domestic consumers now consume less of the product at higher prices. However, the domestic industry is happy since its prices and output have risen. Also, the government collects revenues equal to the shaded area.

number of Japanese cars made in American factories. If a firm is limited in the number of vehicles it can sell, why not sell higher-priced ones where the profit margins are higher? The Toyota Land Cruiser, for instance, was originally a bare-bones SUV selling for under $15,000. With quotas, this vehicle became a $60,000 luxury behemoth with all the extras standard.

One problem with tariffs and quotas is that when they are imposed, large numbers of consumers pay just a small amount more for the targeted products. Few consumers are willing to spend time and effort lobbying Congress to end or forestall these trade barriers from being introduced. Producers, however, are often few in number, and they stand to gain tremendously from such trade barriers. It is no wonder that such firms have large lobbying budgets and provide campaign contributions to congressional candidates.

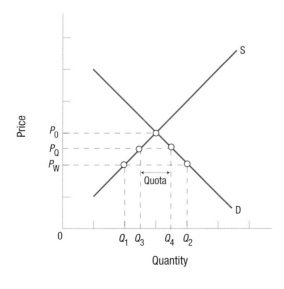

FIGURE 7

Effects of a Quota

What are the effects of a quota? They are similar to the effects of a tariff, except that the government restricts the quantity of imports into the country to $Q_4 - Q_3$. Imports fall to the quota level, and again consumers lose as they must pay higher prices for less output. Producers and their employees gain as prices and employment in the domestic industry rise. With a quota, however, the government does not collect revenues.

Checkpoint

The Terms of Trade

REVIEW

- The terms of trade are determined by the ratio of the price of exported goods to the price of imported goods.
- The terms of trade are set by the markets in each country and by exports and imports that eventually equalize the prices.
- Trade leads to winners and losers in each country and in each market.
- Trade restrictions vary from subsidies to domestic firms to government bans on the import of foreign products.
- Tariffs are taxes on imports that protect domestic producers and generate revenue.
- Quotas represent restrictions on the volume of particular imports that can come into a country. Quotas do not generate revenue for governments and are infrequently used.

QUESTION

When the government imposes a quota on a specific imported product, who benefits and who loses?

Answers to the Checkpoint question can be found at the end of this chapter.

Arguments Against Free Trade

"If goods do not cross borders, soldiers will."

Frédéric Bastiat

We have seen the benefits of trade, and have looked at how trade undoubtedly benefits some and harms others. Those who are harmed by trade often seek to restrict trade, primarily in the form of tariffs and quotas. Because trade leads to some loss, those who are harmed by trade have made arguments against free trade.

The arguments against free trade fall into two camps: traditional economic arguments including protection for infant industries, protection against dumping, low foreign wages, and support for industries judged vital for national defense. Second are globalization (social and economic) concerns that embody political-economy characteristics. These include domestic employment concerns, environmental concerns, and the impact of globalization on working conditions in developing nations. In what follows, we take a critical look at each of these arguments, showing that most of these arguments do not have a solid empirical basis.

Traditional Economic Arguments

Arguments against trade are not new. Despite the huge gains from trade, distortions (subsidies and trade barriers) continue, as Kym Anderson has noted, "largely because further trade liberalization and subsidy cuts redistribute jobs, income, and wealth in ways that those in government fear will reduce their chances of remaining in power."[3] In other words, changing current policies will hurt those dependent

---

[3]Kym Anderson, "Subsidies and Trade Barriers," in Bjorn Lomborg, *Global Crises, Global Solutions* (Cambridge, UK: Cambridge University Press), 2004, p. 542.

on subsidies and trade restrictions, and these firms and workers will show their displeasure at the voting booth. All of these traditional economic arguments against free trade seem reasonable on their face, but on closer examination, they look less attractive.

Infant Industry Argument

An **infant industry,** it is argued, is one that is too underdeveloped to achieve comparative advantage or perhaps even to survive in the global environment. Such an industry may be too small or undercapitalized, or its management and workers may be too inexperienced, to compete. Unless the industry's government provides it with some protection through tariffs, quotas, or subsidies, it might not survive in the face of foreign competition.

Infant industry
An industry so underdeveloped that protection is needed for it to become competitive on the world stage or to ensure its survival.

In theory, once the infant industry has been given this protection, it should be able to grow, acquiring the necessary capital and expertise needed to compete internationally. Germany and the United States used high tariffs to protect their infant manufacturing sectors in the 1800s, and Japan continued to maintain import restrictions up until the 1970s.

Though the infant industry argument sounds reasonable, it has several limitations. First, protecting an industry must be done in a way that makes the industry internationally competitive. Many countries coddle their firms, and these producers never seem to develop into "mature," internationally viable firms. And, once protection is provided (typically a protective tariff), it is difficult to remove after an industry has matured. The industry and its workers continue to convince policymakers of the need for continued protection.

Second, infant industry protection often tends to focus on capital manufacturing. Countries with huge labor supplies, however, would do better to develop their labor-intensive industries first, letting more capital-intensive industries develop over time. Every country, after all, should seek to exploit its comparative advantages, but it is difficult to determine which industries have a chance of developing a comparative advantage in the future and should be temporarily protected.

Third, many industries seem to be able to develop without protections, so countries may be wasting their resources and reducing their incomes by imposing protection measures.

Clearly, the infant industry argument is not valid for advanced economies such as the United States, much of Europe, and Japan. The evidence for developing nations shows some benefits but is mixed for the reasons noted above.

Antidumping

Dumping means that goods are sold at lower prices *below cost* abroad than in their home market. This often is a result of government subsidies.

Dumping
Selling goods abroad at lower prices than in home markets, and often below cost.

In the same way that price discrimination improves profits, firms can price discriminate between their home markets and foreign markets. Let's assume that costs of production are $100 a unit for all firms (domestic and foreign). A state subsidy of $30 a unit, for example, reduces domestic costs to $70 a unit and permits the firm to sell its product in world markets at these lower prices. Since home and foreign markets can be segregated and often have different elasticities of demand, this price discrimination raises profits if the price in the foreign markets is greater than $70 a unit. These state subsidies give these firms a cost advantage in foreign markets.

Firms can use dumping as a form of predatory pricing, using higher prices in their domestic markets to support unrealistically low prices in foreign markets. The goal of predatory pricing is to drive foreign competitors out of business. When this occurs, the firm doing the dumping then comes back and imposes higher prices. In the long run, these higher prices thereby offset the company's short-term losses.

Dumping violates American trade laws. If the federal government determines that a foreign firm is dumping products onto the American market, it can impose antidumping tariffs on the offending products. The government, however, must distinguish among dumping, legitimate price discrimination, and legitimate instances of lower cost production arising from comparative advantage.

Low Foreign Wages

Some advocates of trade barriers maintain that domestic firms and their workers need to be protected from displacement by cheap foreign labor. Without this protection, it is argued, foreign manufacturers that pay their workers pennies an hour will flood the market with low-cost products. As we have already seen, this argument has something to it: Workers in advanced economies can be displaced by low-wage foreign workers. This is what has happened in the American textile industry.

Once a handful of American clothing manufacturers began moving their production facilities overseas, thereby undercutting domestic producers, other manufacturers were forced to follow them. American consumers have benefited from lower clothing prices, but many displaced textile workers are still trying to get retrained and adapt to work in other industries. More recently, many manufacturing jobs have drifted overseas, and high-technology firms today are shifting some help desk facilities and computer programming to foreign shores.

On balance, however, the benefits of lower-priced goods considerably exceed the costs of lost employment. The federal government has resisted imposing protection measures for the sake of protecting jobs, instead funding programs that help displaced workers transition to new lines of work.

National Defense Argument

In times of national crisis or war, the United States must be able to rely on key domestic industries, such as oil, steel, and the defense industry. Some have argued that these industries may require some protection even during peacetime to ensure that they are already well established when crisis strikes and importing key products may be impossible. Within limits, this argument is sound. Still, the United States has the capacity to produce such a wide variety of products that protections for specific industries would seem to be unjustified and unnecessary.

So what are we to make of these traditional arguments? Although they all seem reasonable, they all have deficiencies. Infant industries may be helped in the short run, but protections are often extended well beyond what is necessary, resulting in inefficient firms that are vulnerable on world markets. Dumping is clearly a potential problem, but distinguishing real cases of dumping and comparative advantage has often proven difficult in practice. Low foreign wages are often the only comparative advantage a developing nation has to offer the world economy, and typically, the benefits to consumers vastly outweigh the loss to a particular industry. Maintaining (protecting) industries for national defense has merit and may be appropriate for some countries, but for a country as huge and diversified as the United States, it is probably unnecessary.

Globalization Concerns

Expanded trade and globalization have provided the world's producers and consumers with many benefits. Some observers, however, have voiced concerns about globalization and its effects on domestic employment, the global environment, and working conditions in developing nations. Let's look at each one of these globalization concerns.

Trade and Domestic Employment

Some critics argue that increased trade and globalization spell job losses for domestic workers. We have seen that this can be true. Some firms, unable to compete with imports, will be forced to lay off workers or even close their doors. Even so, increased trade usually allows firms that are exporters to expand their operations and hire new workers. These will be firms in industries with comparative advantages. For the United States, these industries tend to be those that require a highly skilled workforce, resulting in higher wages for American workers.

Clearly, those industries that are adding workers, and those that are losing jobs are different industries. For workers who lose their jobs, switching industries can be difficult and time consuming, and often it requires new investments in human capital. American trade policy recognizes this problem, and the Trade Adjustment Assistance (TAA) program provides workers with job search assistance, job training, and some relocation allowances. In some industries sensitive to trade liberalization, including textiles and agriculture, trade policies are designed to proceed gradually, thus giving these industries and their workers some extra time to adjust.

Possible employment losses in some noncompetitive industries do not seem to provide enough justification for restricting trade. By imposing trade restrictions such as tariffs or quotas in one industry, employment opportunities in many other industries may be reduced. Open, competitive trade encourages producers to focus their production on those areas in which the country stands at a comparative advantage. Free trade puts competitive pressure on domestic firms, forcing them to be more productive and competitive, boosting the flow of information and technology across borders, and widening the availability of inputs for producers. At the end of the day, consumers benefit from these efficiencies, having more goods to choose from and enjoying a higher standard of living.

Trade and the Environment

Concerns about globalization, trade, and the environment usually take one of two forms. Some people are concerned that expanded trade and globalization will lead to increased environmental degradation as companies take advantage of lax environmental laws abroad, particularly in the developing world. Others worry that attempts by the government to strengthen environmental laws will be challenged by trading partners as disguised protectionism.

Domestic environmental regulations usually target a product or process that creates pollution or other environmental problems. One concern in establishing environmental regulations, however, is that they not unfairly discriminate against the products of another country. This is usually not a serious problem. Nearly all trade agreements, including the General Agreement on Tariffs and Trade (GATT) and the NAFTA, have provisions permitting countries to enforce measures "necessary to protect human, animal or plant life or health" or to conserve exhaustible natural resources. Nothing in our trade agreements prevents the United States from implementing environmental regulations as long as they do not unreasonably discriminate against our trading partners.

Will free trade come at the expense of the environment? Every action involves a tradeoff. Clearly, there can be cases where the benefits of trade accruing to large numbers of people result in harm to a more concentrated group. In 1995, however, President Clinton's Council of Economic Advisors concluded:

> *There are also complementarities between good trade policies and good environmental policies. Agricultural protection in industrialized countries is a case in point. The protection of developed-country agriculture leads to more intensive farming, often of lands that are of marginal use, causing unnecessary soil erosion, loss of biological diversity, and the excessive use of pesticides and chemicals. Liberalizing trade in agriculture and lowering agriculture production subsidies can lead to a pattern of world farming that causes less environmental damage.*

> *Also, high trade barriers to labor-intensive imports, such as clothing, from developing countries lead these countries instead to export products that are intensive in natural resources, causing environmental damage. In addition, high-value-added natural resource-based products such as wood or paper products often face high tariff barriers, whereas the raw natural resource itself does not; this forces developing countries to rely on exports of unprocessed natural resources while denying them the revenue gains from the downstream products.*[4]

We have seen that trade raises incomes in developed and developing countries. And environmental protection is an income elastic good: As incomes rise, the demand for environmental protections rises faster. Studies suggest that once a country's per capita income exceeds roughly $5,000, its environmental protection efforts begin to improve.

In poor, developing nations, environmental protection will not at first be a priority. Critics of globalization are concerned that because environmental and labor standards in many developing nations are well below those of the developed countries, there will be pressure to adopt these lower standards in rich nations due to trade and foreign direct investment. But as Bhagwati and Hudec argue, there has been no systematic "race to the bottom" and many corporations often have the highest environmental and labor standards in the developing world.[5] Also, it is worth noting that over time, as incomes rise, environmental protection takes on added importance even in poorer nations. On balance, trade probably benefits the environment over the longer term, as incomes grow in developing nations and environmental protections take on greater importance.

Trade and Its Effect on Working Conditions in Developing Nations

Some antiglobalization activists argue that for the United States to trade with developing countries where wages are low and working conditions are deplorable simply exploits workers in these developing countries. Clearly, such trade does hurt American workers in low-wage, low-skilled occupations who simply cannot compete with the even lower-wage workers overseas. But it is not clear that workers in developing countries would be helped if the United States were to cut off its trade with those countries that refuse to improve their wages or working conditions.

Restricting trade with countries that do not raise their wages to levels we think acceptable or bring working conditions up to our standards would probably do more harm than good. Low wages reflect, among other factors, the low investments in human capital, low productivity, and low living standards characteristic of developing nations. Blocking trade with these nations may deprive them of their key chance to grow and to improve in those areas where we would like to see change.

Liberalized trade policies, economic freedom, and a legal system that respects property rights and foreign capital investment probably provide the best recipe for rapid development, economic growth, environmental protection, and improved wages and working conditions.

In summary, trade does result in job losses in some industries, but the gain to consumers and the competitive pressures that trade puts on domestic companies is beneficial to the economy as a whole. Trade raises incomes in developing nations, resulting in a growing demand for more environmentally friendly production processes. Trade is not the reason for low environmental standards in developing

---

[4]*Economic Report of the President* (Washington, D.C.: U.S. Government Printing Office), 1995, p. 242.
[5]Jagdish Bhagwati and Robert Hudec (eds.), *Fair Trade and Harmonization, Vol. 1: Economic Analysis* (Cambridge, MA: MIT Press), 1996, cited in Anderson (see note 3).

countries; they result from low income, low standards of living, and poor governmental policies. Trade brings about higher levels of income and ultimately better working conditions.

REVIEW

- The infant industries argument claims that some industries are so underdeveloped that they need protection to survive in a global competitive environment.
- Dumping involves selling products at different prices in domestic and foreign markets, often with the help of subsidies from the government. This is a form of predatory pricing to gain market share in the foreign market.
- Some suggest that domestic workers need to be protected from the low wages in foreign countries. This puts the smaller aggregate loss to small groups ahead of the greater general gains from trade. Also, for many countries, a low wage is their primary comparative advantage.
- Some argue that select industries need protection to ensure they will exist for national defense reasons.
- Clearly, globalization has meant that some U.S. workers have lost jobs to foreign competition, and some advocates would restrict trade on these grounds alone. But, on net, trade has led to higher overall employment. The U.S. government recognizes these issues and has instituted a Trade Adjustment Assistance (TAA) program to help workers who lose their jobs transition to new employment.
- Concern about the environment is often a factor in trade negotiations. Those concerned about globalization want to ensure that firms do not move production to countries with lax environmental laws, while others are concerned that environmental regulation not be used to justify protectionism. Trade ultimately raises income and environmental awareness in developing nations.
- Some antiglobalization activists consider shifting production to countries with low wages as exploitation and demand that wages be increased in other countries. Globalization has typically resulted in higher wages in developing nations, but not up to the standards of developed nations.

QUESTION

"The biggest gains in exports, imports, employment, and wages all occurred during the 1990s which was one of our greatest periods of economic growth. Thus it is clear that trade benefits both consumers and the economy." Evaluate this statement.

Answers to the Checkpoint question can be found at the end of this chapter.

The Dynamics of Trade: Cashmere

As a way of bringing together many of the concepts discussed in this chapter, let us look at one particular industry for a moment. When we hear the word *cashmere*, most of us conjure up images of soft, classy sweaters and scarves, whether we own any of these expensive items or not. It is the cashmere industry we will look at here.

The modern cashmere industry rests on international trade. It began in the 19th century when British colonialists in India discovered the fancy shawls of the

Indian rulers.[6] The word *cashmere* comes from Kashmir, the home of the goats used to provide the special soft fleece. Since that time, the goat herders moved to Inner Mongolia, part of China. The modern cashmere industry began when British entrepreneurs acquired the cashmere fleece and sent it to Scotland for weaving. Scottish companies became the main producers of finished cashmere products to the world. There were some Italian producers of cashmere as well, though the Scottish firms predominated.

This is changing. Competition had been limited by worldwide regulation of the textile industry. This regulation was undertaken under the guise of the familiar "cheap foreign labor" argument. By the end of 2004, the World Trade Organization (WTO) removed the remaining quotas in the textile industry.

What potential competitor stands to gain from this freer trade? In the cashmere industry, the obvious first choice is the provider of the cashmere fleece (China). And when you hear *China,* what immediately pops into your mind? (plenty of cheap labor). So the question then becomes: Is it worthwhile for Chinese entrepreneurs to develop their own cashmere industry by relying on ready access to the raw materials and cheap labor, or are they better off selling the raw materials to the Scottish cashmere producers?

It turns out that in fact Chinese entrepreneurs have been developing their own cashmere manufacturing industry over the past 10 years. They have been helped in part by the low capital costs of entry, as well as the plentiful labor pool in China. The issue then becomes one of the build up in skills. The natural thing for Chinese firms to do is start on the low end of the cashmere market, building up skills over time. For example, a fledgling firm can start with solid color sweaters and move up to more elaborate patterns once the basic skills are down pat. This is exactly what the Chinese firms have done. A joint venture between a Scottish firm and a Chinese firm in the mid-1990s likely hastened the transfer of manufacturing skills from Scotland to China.

From your study of the concepts in this chapter, you should be able to predict the likely effect on Scottish cashmere producers. In fact, the Scottish cashmere industry was hit on the low end but not on the high end of its market. There has been a loss of Scottish jobs as lower-priced Chinese cashmere sweaters and scarves have driven out the low end of what was once almost an exclusive Scottish market.

Again, based on what you have learned in this chapter, you should be able to predict the Scottish response. If Scottish firms still have an advantage producing more elaborate patterns, we can expect these patterns to become even more intricate. This is one way to justify a higher price. Also, the pressure is on Scottish firms to innovate. A previous innovation, by the Scottish firm Pringle, was the creation of the twin set: matching sweater and cardigan both worn at the same time. Queen Elizabeth wears twin sets. This means two products are sold at once. We can expect further innovations like this one from Scottish firms.

We can ask whether the "Cashmere: Made in Scotland" label will keep its cachet or eventually fade away in the face of continual Chinese advances in the cashmere industry. Only time will tell. This chapter helps us make several predictions. First, as Chinese workers build up skills, Chinese firms will expand up market. As these skills improve, Chinese workers will witness an increase in wages. As Chinese firms produce more cashmere, market demand for cashmere in China is likely to grow. Second, Scottish firms will face continual pressure to cut costs and innovate. The current job loss is likely to increase. New products will come to market, though we cannot predict what the market reaction will be. Third, as the price of cashmere products falls in the lower part of the market, more of us consumers worldwide will be able to afford these soft sweaters and scarves. There may come a time when even at the high end, "Cashmere: Made in China" becomes equivalent to "Cashmere: Made in Scotland." Such is the dynamism of international trade.

---

[6]Alan Cowell, "Cashmere Moves on, and Scotland Feels a Chill," *New York Times,* March 27, 2004, p. C1.

Chapter Summary

The Gains from Trade

Worldwide foreign trade has quadrupled over the past 25 years. Improved communications and transportation technologies have worked together to promote global economic integration. Most governments around the world have reduced trade barriers in recent years.

Free trade has not always been popular. In 1929–30, many countries attempted to protect their domestic industries by imposing trade restrictions that discouraged imports. In 1930, the United States enacted the Smoot-Hawley tariffs, which imposed an average tax of 60% on imported goods. This hurt industries around the world and has been credited with adding to the depth of the global depression.

In a zero-sum game such as poker, for one party to gain, the other party must lose. Voluntary exchange and trade is a positive-sum game, meaning that both parties to a transaction can gain. These gains arise because of comparative advantage.

One country has an absolute advantage over another if it can produce more of some good than the other country. A country has a comparative advantage over another if its opportunity cost to produce some good is lower than the other country's. Even when one country has an absolute advantage over another, both stand to benefit from trade if each focuses its production on the goods or industries with a comparative advantage.

There are some practical constraints on trade. First, every transaction involves costs; and second, production is governed by increasing costs and diminishing returns. This makes it difficult for countries to specialize in the production of just one product. Indeed, specializing in one product is risky, since the market for a product can always decline or its production can be disrupted. Third, even though countries benefit from engaging in trade, some individuals and groups can be hurt by trade.

The Terms of Trade

The terms of trade determine the prices of imports and exports. If a country exports computers and imports coffee, with two computers trading for a ton of coffee, the price of a computer will be one half the price of a ton of coffee. When countries trade many commodities, the terms of trade are defined as the average price of exports divided by the average price of imports.

When two countries begin trading, the price charged for one good may be different in the two countries. As market forces lead each country to focus its production on the goods and industries at which it has a comparative advantage, that good's price will tend to equalize in the two countries, moving to an equilibrium level somewhere between the two original prices.

Though beneficial to both countries, trade can produce winners and losers. If the United States has a comparative advantage over Japan in the production of computers and it begins exporting more computers to Japan, American manufacturers and workers will benefit from this increased business. American consumers will be hurt, however, as the price of computers rises to meet the Japanese demand. In Japan, where computers had been more expensive, computer manufacturers and workers will be hurt by the competition from American computers, but Japanese consumers will benefit from falling computer prices.

The most common forms of trade restrictions are tariffs and quotas. A tariff is a tax on imports. Most tariffs are ad valorem taxes, meaning that a product is taxed by a certain percentage of its price as it crosses the border. Other tariffs are unit taxes, meaning that a fixed tax per unit of the product is assessed.

Tariffs generate revenues while driving a wedge between a product's domestic price and its price on the world market. When a tariff is imposed on a product, its price will rise. This benefits domestic producers, increasing their sales and the price they can charge, but the resulting price increase hurts domestic consumers. The government collects the tariff revenues.

Quotas restrict the quantity of imports into a country. Quotas have much the same effect as tariffs, except that they do not generate revenues for the government.

Arguments Against Free Trade

Despite the many benefits of free trade, arguments continue for restricting trade. One is that infant industries exist and require some protection to survive. These are industries that are too underdeveloped to achieve a comparative advantage or perhaps even to survive in the global marketplace. The problem is, when do these industries mature?

Some American trade laws target dumping, which occurs when a foreign firm sells its goods below cost in the United States or at a price below what it charges in its domestic market. One goal of such dumping may be to drive American firms out of business, thus allowing the foreign firm to come back and impose higher prices on American consumers in the long run. Another may just be to gain a foothold or market share in a foreign market. Also, dumping may simply be a form of subsidized price discrimination. If the federal government determines that a foreign firm is dumping products onto the American market, it can impose antidumping tariffs on the offending products.

Some advocates of trade barriers maintain that domestic firms and their workers need to be protected from displacement by cheap foreign labor. Without this protection, it is argued, foreign manufacturers that pay their workers low wages will flood the market with low-cost products. This has occurred. On balance, however, most economists estimate that the benefits of lower-priced imported goods exceed the costs of lost employment. The federal government has resisted imposing measures to protect jobs, instead funding programs that help displaced workers transition to new lines of work.

In times of national crisis or war, the United States must be able to rely on key domestic industries such as oil, steel, and the defense industry. Some argue that these industries require some protection even during peacetime to ensure that they exist when a crisis strikes and importing may be difficult.

Some critics argue that increased trade and globalization spells job losses for domestic workers. Firms unable to compete with imports will be forced to lay off workers or even close their doors. Increased trade, however, allows firms that are exporters to expand their operations and hire new workers. For workers who lose their jobs, switching industries can be difficult and time consuming, and often requires new investments in human capital. American trade policy recognizes this problem. The Trade Adjustment Assistance (TAA) program provides workers with job search assistance, job training, and some relocation allowances.

Concerns about globalization, trade, and the environment usually take one of two forms. Some people are concerned that expanded trade and globalization will lead to increased environmental degradation as companies take advantage of lax environmental laws abroad, particularly in the developing world. Others worry that attempts by the government to strengthen environmental laws will be challenged by trading partners as disguised protectionism. Environmental protection is an income elastic good: As incomes rise, the demand for environmental protections rises faster. And since trade increases incomes in developed and developing countries, free trade may further the cause of environmental protection.

Some antiglobalization activists argue that for the United States to trade with developing countries where wages are low and working conditions are deplorable simply exploits workers in these developing countries. But restricting trade with these countries would probably do more harm than good. Low wages reflect low investments in human capital, low productivity, and low living standards characteristic of developing nations. Blocking trade with these nations may deprive them of their only chance to grow and thus improve in these areas.

Questions and Problems

1. Brandeis University professor Stephen Cecchetti has argued that "if people understood the benefits of free trade as well as they do the rules of a favorite sport, there would be solid support for trade liberalization." Do you agree with Professor Cecchetti? Why or why not?

2. South Korean film production companies have been protected for half a century by policies enacted to protect an infant industry. But beginning in July 2006, the days that local films *must* be shown by any movie house was reduced to 73 from 146. South Korean film celebrities and the industry are fighting the changes even though local films command half the box office. Why would a country enact special protection for the local film industry? Who would be the major competitor threatening the South Korean film industry? If films made by the local industry must be shown 146 days a year, does the local industry have much incentive to develop good films and be competitive with the rest of the world?

3. Expanding trade in general benefits both countries, or they would not willingly engage in trade. But we also know that consumers and society often gain while particular industries or workers lose. Since society and consumers gain, why don't the many gainers compensate the few losers for their loss?

4. In a recent study, three economists estimated the benefits of trade to the American economy since 1950.[7] Looking at the benefits from comparative advantage, economies of scale, diffusion of production technology, and many other factors, they estimated that trade accounted for roughly 20% of the gains in GDP per person. With such gains from trade to the average household, why would so many people seem to be against trade and globalization?

5. Some activist groups are calling for "fair trade laws" in which other countries would be required to meet or approach our environmental standards and provide wage and working conditions approaching those of developed nations in order to be able to trade with us. Is this just another form of rent seeking by industries and unions for protection from overseas competition?

6. Is outsourcing another example of the benefits of trade, in this case, trade between two companies? Many of the opponents of outsourcing are fans of the "open source" software movement that farms programming out to "volunteer"

---

[7]Scott C. Bradford, Paul L. E. Grieco, and Gary Clyde Hufbauer, "The Payoff to America From Global Integration," in C. Fred Bergsten and the Institute for International Economics, *The United States and the World Economy* (Washington, D.C.: Institute for International Economics, 2005), Chap. 2.

programmers or firms around the world. These individuals or firms must give their changes to the software to the open source community (run by a few people) and cannot sell the software, but can charge for services such as a help desk, technical improvements, or other services. Does the open source concept seem like trade between individuals?

7. Why is there free trade between states in the United States but not necessarily between countries?

8. What is the difference between absolute and comparative advantage? Why would Michelle Wie, who is better than you at both golf and laundry, still hire you to do her wash?

9. Automobiles built by General Motors, Chrysler, and Ford have fallen out of favor with American consumers as evidenced by their falling market shares over the last several decades and the acceptance of buyouts in late 2006 and 2007 by over 100,000 current employees of GM and Ford. Several decades ago, at the behest of the United Auto Workers (UAW) union and the big three automakers, quotas were placed on the importation of Japanese cars to protect American auto manufacturers. Why didn't these quotas work? Would additional trade restrictions benefit American auto workers in the UAW? Would they benefit American consumers?

10. Remittances from developed countries are over $200 billion each year. These funds are sent to their home countries by migrants in developed nations. Is this similar to the gains from trade discussed in this chapter, or are these workers just taking jobs that workers in developed countries would be paid more to do in the absence of the migrants?

11. Who are the beneficiaries from a large U.S. tariff on French and German wine? Who are the losers?

12. The figure below shows the production possibilities frontiers (PPFs) for Italy and India for their domestic production of olives and tea. Without trade, assume that each is consuming olives and tea at point *a*.

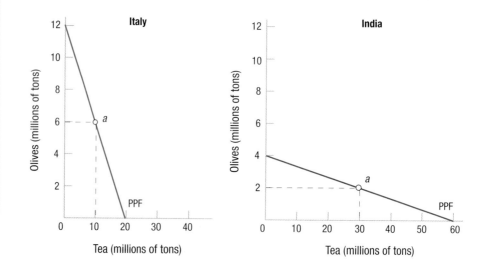

a. If Italy and India were to consider specialization and trade, what commodity would each specialize in? What is India's opportunity cost for tea and olives? What is Italy's opportunity cost for tea and olives?

b. Assume the two countries agree to specialize entirely in one product (Italy in olives and India in tea), and agree to split the total output between them. Complete the table below. Are both countries better off after trade?

Country and Product		Before Specialization	After Specialization	After Trade
Italy	Olives	6 million tons	_____	_____
	Tea	10 million tons	_____	_____
India	Olives	4 million tons	_____	_____
	Tea	30 million tons	_____	_____

13. The figure below shows the annual domestic demand and supply for 2GB compact flash cards for digital cameras.
    a. Assume the worldwide price of these 2GB cards is $10. What percent of United States sales would be imported?
    b. Assume the U.S. government puts a $5 tariff per card on imports. How many 2GB flash cards will be imported into the United States?
    c. Given the tariff in question *b*, how much revenue will the government collect from this tariff?
    d. Given the tariff in question *b*, how much more sales revenue will domestic companies enjoy as a result of the tariff?

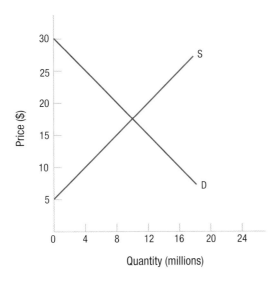

14. Why might protectionist trade barriers not save American jobs or benefit the economy?

15. Suppose Brazil developed a secret process that effectively quadrupled its output of coffee from its coffee plantations. This secret process enabled it to significantly undercut the prices of our domestic producers. Would domestic producers receive a sympathetic ear to calls for protection from Brazil's lower-cost coffee? How is this case different from that of protection against cheap foreign labor?

CHECKPOINT: THE GAINS FROM TRADE

Trading baseball cards is as old as the cards themselves. You would trade your extra cards for a Pujols card and others would do the same. Those with extra Pujols cards are your most likely trading partners. Clearly both parties benefit from trading cards in this instance. All *voluntary* exchange results in benefits to both parties or the trade would not take place.

CHECKPOINT: THE TERMS OF TRADE

When a quota is imposed, the first beneficiary is the domestic industry. Competition from foreign competition is limited. If the market is important enough (as we saw with automobiles), the foreign companies build new plants in the United States and compete as if they are domestic firms. A second beneficiary is foreign competition in that they can increase the price or complexity of their products and increase their margins. Losers are consumers and, to some extent, the government because a tariff could have accomplished the same reduction in imports, and the government would have collected some revenue.

CHECKPOINT: ARGUMENTS AGAINST FREE TRADE

Clearly the 1990s were a period of high growth in both trade and employment. The 1990s were also a time of heavy investment by businesses in technology and communications. Some industries and their employees were losers from trade, but the economy and other industries were clearly winners. Production employment has been on a steady decline over the last half century as services have become more important. When the most recent recession led to lost jobs and unemployment rose, more attention was focused on trade and outsourcing as a source of those lost jobs. But as the recession ended and our economy recovered, job gains have tended to quiet these voices.

Open Economy Macroeconomics

16

ou probably are aware of international finance if you have traveled abroad. To purchase goods and services in another country, you need to have an amount of that country's currency. True, you can use credit cards for major purchases, but you still need some currency for daily transactions. In Britain, you need to pay in British pounds; in France, you need euros. British and French shopkeepers and public transportation officials will not accept dollars. This means that sometime at the beginning of your trip, whether at the airport or a bank, you have to exchange your dollars for the currency of the country you are visiting. If you are like many of us, you will admit that you find these foreign currencies interesting; for example, what famous people are pictured on the banknotes? The key point, though, is that you need a certain amount of foreign currency when you travel abroad.

As with tourism, so with international trade. You may pay dollars for your Burberry scarf or Louis Vuitton handbag in a store in the United States, but eventually your dollars have to be converted to foreign currency when your payments make their way back to the host country. And if U.S. companies export goods abroad, they will want to bring dollars back to the United States, whether they get paid originally in the host country's currency or not.

Furthermore, in today's open economies, individuals can hold domestic and foreign financial assets. Your own financial portfolio might include foreign stocks, bonds, and currency, as well as domestic stocks and bonds. Buying and selling foreign securities and goods involves the buying and selling of foreign currency, also known as foreign exchange.

So, we can see that foreign exchange transactions for tourism, trade, and investment would seem to be large in number and amount. Yet, foreign exchange transactions dwarf the volume of exports and imports, often by as much as 30–40 times, in the same way that the annual value of all stock transactions far surpasses the market value of all companies on the New York Stock Exchange. Most foreign exchange transactions are conducted not for trade but for financial or speculative purposes. The social benefit to emerge from this speculation is a highly liquid foreign exchange market that ensures the possibility of trade. The large volume of speculative trade in currencies means that there will always be a market for international trade.

In this chapter, we want to look at foreign exchange markets to get a sense of how policymaking in the United States is affected by an open worldwide economy. We start with balance of payments accounts. Balance of payment accounts are to open economy macroeconomics what national income accounts are to an individual country's macroeconomic accounts. This accounting structure is the basis for open economy analysis. We then examine the foreign exchange market in detail, looking at both the trade and financial aspects of those common foreign currency events: currency appreciation and depreciation. Finally, we put this all together when we view fixed and flexible exchange rate systems and discuss how an open economy affects monetary and fiscal policymaking.

After studying this chapter you should be able to

- Define the current account and the capital account in the balance of payments between countries.

- Describe the difference between nominal and real exchange rates.

- Describe the effects of currency appreciation or depreciation on imports and exports.

- Describe the effects of changes in inflation rates, disposable income, and interest rates on exchange rates.

- Describe the differences between fixed and flexible exchange rate systems.

- Describe the implications for fiscal and monetary policies of fixed and flexible exchange rate systems.

The Balance of Payments

All open economies have balance of payments accounts. Open financial markets permit economies to run trade surpluses and deficits.

A simplified version of the U.S. balance of payments accounts for 2006 is shown in Table 1. These accounts were compiled by the Commerce Department's Bureau of Economic Analysis. The balance of payments represents all payments received from foreign countries and all payments made to them. Notice that the accounts are split into two broad divisions, the current account and the capital account.

The Current Account

Current account
Includes payments for imports and exports of goods and services, incomes flowing into and out of the country, and net transfers of money.

The **current account** includes payments for imports and exports of goods and services, incomes flowing into and out of the country, and net transfers of money.

Imports and Exports

In 2006, U.S. exports were $1,445.7 billion, with imports totaling $2,204.2 billion. This exchange produced a trade deficit of −$758.5 billion because we imported more than we exported. Some balance of payments accounts break exports and imports into separate categories of goods and services; here they are combined. This component of the current account is known as the balance of trade.

Table 1	The Balance of Payments 2006 (billions of U.S. dollars)	
Current Account		
Exports	1,445.7	
Imports	−2,204.2	
Trade balance		−758.5
Income received (inflow)	650.4	
Income payments (outflow)	−613.8	
Balance on income		36.6
Net transfers		−89.6
Current account balance		−811.5
Capital Account Balance		
Increase in foreign-owned assets in the United States	1,859.6	
Increase in U.S.-owned assets abroad	−1,055.2	
Net increase in foreign-owned holdings		804.4
Statistical discrepancy		7.1
Capital account		811.5

Income

Another source of foreign payments to the United States comprises income flows, which include wages, rents, interest, and profits that Americans earn abroad ($650.4 billion in 2006) minus the corresponding income foreigners earn in the United States ($613.8 billion). On balance, foreigners earned $36.6 billion less in the United States than U.S. citizens and corporations earned abroad in 2006.

Transfers

Direct transfers of money also take place between the United States and other countries. These transfers includes foreign aid, funds sent to such international organizations as the United Nations, and stipends paid directly to foreign students studying in the United States or U.S. students studying abroad. These transfers also include the money that people working in the United States send back to their families in foreign countries. Net transfers for 2006 totaled $89.6 billion.

Adding all current account categories for 2006 yields a current account deficit of $811.5 billion, equal to 6% of gross domestic product (GDP). In 2006, the United States paid out over three quarters of a trillion dollars more than it received. So, the United States had to borrow $811.5 billion from the rest of the world, or the net holdings of U.S. assets by foreigners must have increased by that same amount, or some combination of the two.

The Capital Account

The **capital account** summarizes the flow of money into and out of domestic and foreign assets. This account includes investments by foreign companies in domestic

Capital account
Summarizes the flow of money into and out of domestic and foreign assets, including investments by foreign companies in domestic plants or subsidiaries, and other foreign holdings of U.S. assets, including mutual funds, stock, bonds, and deposits in U.S. banks. Also included are U.S. investors' holdings of foreign financial assets, production facilities, and other assets in foreign countries.

plants or subsidiaries—a Toyota truck plant in Tennessee, for example. Note that the profits from such investments flow abroad, and thus they are in the income payments (outflow) category of the current account. Other foreign holdings of U.S. assets include portfolio investments such as mutual funds, stock, and bonds, and deposits in U.S. banks. American investors hold foreign financial assets in their portfolios, including foreign stocks and bonds. And American companies own plants and other assets in foreign countries.

Since the United States ran a current account deficit in 2006, it must run a capital account surplus. Capital inflows into the United States must equal over three quarters of a trillion dollars to offset the current account deficit. Indeed, foreign-owned assets in the United States rose by $1,859.5 billion, while U.S. ownership of foreign assets increased by only $1,055.2 billion, resulting in a net inflow of capital of $804.4 billion.

Theoretically, the net inflow of capital should precisely equal the current account deficit. The data in this area, however, are imperfect. Collecting data on a global scale from so many varied sources inevitably leads to many errors—which often cancel one another out, but not always. Though imperfect, modern trade data are surprisingly accurate. For 2006, the statistical discrepancy of $7.1 billion is not enough to alter the basic picture of the U.S. balance of payments.

Figure 1 shows the current and capital accounts as a percent of world GDP for the United States, China, fuel exporters, and other advanced and developing nations.

FIGURE 1

Current Account Balances and Net Foreign Asset Position (percent of world GDP)

This figure shows the current account balances and net foreign asset positions as a percent of world GDP (the World Bank's estimate of total world GDP—a summation of all countries) for the United States, China, fuel exporters, and other advanced and developing nations. The United States has been running large current account deficits since the mid-1990s and has become a huge debtor nation.

Source: *World Economic Outlook: Globalization and Inflation*, April 2006, International Monetary Fund, p. 28.

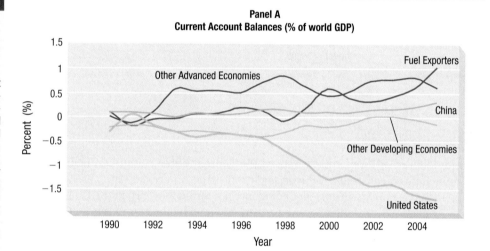

Panel A
Current Account Balances (% of world GDP)

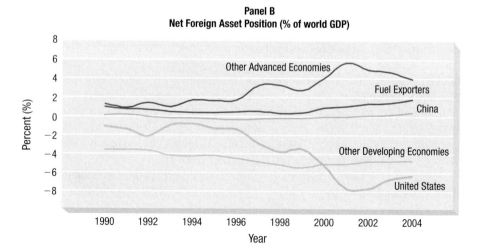

Panel B
Net Foreign Asset Position (% of world GDP)

Panel A shows most of our deficit going to China and fuel-exporting countries. The United States began in the mid-1990s to run large current account deficits that now exceed $800 billion a year. Panel B shows that we have become the world's largest debtor nation, and most of the liabilities are to other developed nations (Europe and Japan), as well as to the fuel exporters. High government deficits, a relatively low savings rate, high demand for imports, and oil price shocks have fueled these rising current account deficits.

The key point to remember is that balance of payments accounts have to show a balance: A deficit in the current account must be offset by a corresponding surplus in the capital account, and vice versa. Keep this point in mind as we go on to look at foreign exchange and policy implications of an open economy.

The Balance of Payments

REVIEW

- The balance of payments represents all payments received from foreign countries and all payments made to them.
- The balance of payments is split into two categories: current and capital accounts.
- The current account includes payment for exports and imports, income flows, and net transfers of money.
- The capital account summarizes flows of money into and out of domestic and foreign assets.
- The sum of the current and capital account balances must equal zero.

QUESTION

Ronald McKinnon, in the April 20, 2006, issue of the *Wall Street Journal*, noted, "China's saving is even higher than its own extraordinary high domestic investment of 40% of GDP. . . . The result is that China (like many other countries in Asia) naturally runs an overall current account surplus." Why would this be true? (*Hint:* Look back at the discussion on the relationship between federal and trade deficits in the chapter on "Deficits and the Public Debt".)

Answers to the Checkpoint question can be found at the end of this chapter.

Exchange Rates

As we saw in the introduction to this chapter, if you wish to go abroad or buy a product directly from a foreign firm, you will need to exchange dollars for foreign currency. Today, credit cards will automatically convert currencies for you, making the transaction more convenient. This conversion does not, however, alter the transaction's underlying structure.

Defining Exchange Rates

The **exchange rate** defines the rate at which one currency, say, U.S. dollars, can be exchanged for another, such as British pounds. The exchange rate is nothing more than the price of one currency for another. Table 2 on the next page shows exchange rates for selected countries for a specific date (September 28, 2007), as reported in the *Wall Street Journal*. Traditionally, exchange rates were always

Exchange rate
The rate at which one currency can be exchanged for another, or just the price of one currency for another.

Table 2	Exchange Rates and Key Currency Cross Rates (January 26, 2007)	
	Exchange Rates	
	U.S. Dollars	Currency Per U.S. Dollar
Argentina (peso)	.3175	3.15
Australia (dollar)	.8874	1.13
Brazil (real)	.5456	1.83
Britain (pound)	2.0461	.49
Canada (dollar)	1.0055	.9945
Japan (yen)	.0087	114.88
Mexico (peso)	.0914	10.94
Peru (new sol)	.3242	3.09
Russia (ruble)	.0402	24.86

Key Currency Cross Rates				
	Dollar	Pound	Peso	Cdn Dlr
Canada	.99	2.0349	.0909	—
Mexico	10.94	22.3862	—	11.0011
United Kingdom	.49	—	.0447	.4914
United States	—	2.0461	.0914	1.0055

Source: The Wall Street Journal.

quoted as the number of units of a foreign currency required to purchase one unit of domestic currency. As Table 2 illustrates, however, exchange rates are often listed from both perspectives.

Nominal Exchange Rates

According to Table 2, 1 British pound will buy 2.05 dollars. Equivalently, 1 dollar will purchase 0.49 pound. These numbers are reciprocal measures of each other ($1 \div 2.05 = 0.49$).

International exchange rates remain consistent even when we consider transactions involving many currencies. To illustrate this point, we need to look at the "Key Currency Cross Rates" subsection of Table 2. The exchange rates in the bottom half of Table 2 are exchange rates between several countries.

Ignoring transactions costs, let us first exchange 1 U.S. dollar for 1.0055 Canadian dollars. Next, we trade these Canadian dollars for 10.49 Mexican pesos (.9945 × 11.0011 = 10.94). As the table shows, this is precisely the number of Mexican pesos we need to buy 1 U.S. dollar. This shows that *currency arbitrage* is impossible; simultaneously buying and selling different currencies will not result in a profit.

Nobel Prize Robert Mundell

*a*warded the Nobel Prize in 1999, Robert Mundell is best known for his groundbreaking work in international economics and for his contribution to the development of supply-side economic theory. Born in Canada in 1932, he attended the University of British Columbia as an undergraduate and studied at the University of Washington and the London School of Economics before earning his Ph.D. from the Massachusetts Institute of Technology in 1956. For a year he served as a postdoctoral fellow at the University of Chicago, where he met the economist Arthur Laffer, his collaborator in the development of supply-side theory.

Supply-side economists advocated reductions in marginal tax rates and stabilization of the international monetary system in an effort to overcome *stagflation,* the persistent combination of economic stagnation and inflation that plagued the United States and other countries during the 1970s. This approach was distinct from the two dominant schools of economic thought, Keynesianism and Milton Friedman's monetarism, though it shared some ideas with both. Mundell's work had a major influence on the economic policies of President Ronald Reagan, who cut taxes to spark an economic recovery, and then Federal Reserve Chairman Paul Volcker, whose tight money policies helped curb inflation.

Mundell's early research focused on exchange rates and the movement of international capital. In a series of papers in the 1960s that proved to be prophetic, he speculated about the impacts of monetary and fiscal policy if exchange rates were allowed to float, emphasizing the importance of central banks acting independently of governments to promote price stability. At the time, his work may have seemed purely academic. Within 10 years, however, the Bretton Woods system of fixed exchange rates tied to the dollar broke down, exchange rates became more flexible, capital markets opened up, and Mundell's ideas were borne out.

In another feat of near-prophecy, Mundell wrote about the potential benefits and disadvantages of a group of countries adopting a single currency, anticipating the development of the European currency, the euro, by many years. Since 1974, Mundell has taught at Columbia University.

Nominal exchange rate
The rate at which one currency can be exchanged for another.

Real exchange rate
The price of one country's currency for another when the price levels of both countries are taken into account; important when inflation is an issue in one country; it is equal to the nominal exchange rate multiplied by the ratio of the price levels of the two countries.

Real Exchange Rates

A **nominal exchange rate** is the price of one country's currency for another. The **real exchange rate** takes the price levels of both countries into account. Real exchange rates become important when inflation is an issue in one country. The real exchange rate between two countries is defined as

$$e_r = e_n \times (P_d/P_f),$$

where
e_r = the real exchange rate
e_n = the nominal exchange rate
P_d = the domestic price level
P_f = the foreign price level

The real exchange rate is simply the nominal exchange rate multiplied by the ratio of the price levels of the two countries. In a broad sense, the real exchange rate may be viewed as a measure of the price competitiveness between the two countries. When prices rise in one country, its products are not as competitive in world markets.

Let us take British and American cars as an example. Assume Britain suffers significant inflation, thus pushing the price of Land Rovers up by 15% in Britain. The United States, meanwhile, suffers no such inflation of its price level. If the dollar-to-pound exchange rate remains constant for the moment, the price of Land Rovers in the U.S. market will climb, while domestic auto prices remain constant.

Now Land Rovers are not as competitive as before, resulting in fewer sales. Note, however, that the resulting reduction in U.S. purchases of British cars and other items will reduce the demand for British pounds. This puts downward pressure on the pound, reducing its exchange value and restoring some competitiveness. Markets do adjust! We will look at this issue in more detail later in the chapter.

Purchasing Power Parity

Purchasing power parity
The rate of exchange that allows a specific amount of currency in one country to purchase the same quantity of goods in another country.

Purchasing power parity (PPP) is the rate of exchange that allows a specific amount of currency in one country to purchase the same quantity of goods in another country. Absolute purchasing power parity would mean that nominal exchange rates equaled the same purchasing power in each country. As a result, the real exchange rate would be equal to 1. For example, purchasing power parity would exist if 4 dollars bought a meal in the United States, and the same 4 dollars converted to British pounds (say, roughly 2 pounds) bought the same meal in London.

If you have traveled abroad, you know that purchasing power parity is not absolute. Some countries, such as Malaysia and Thailand, are known as cheap countries, while others can be expensive, such as Denmark and Israel. The *Economist* annually publishes a "Big Mac Index," a lighthearted attempt to capture the notion of purchasing power parity.

Table 3 presents some recent estimates of PPP and the Big Mac Index.[1] Keep in mind that the cost of a McDonald's Big Mac may be influenced by many unique local factors (trade barriers on beef, customs duties, taxes, competition), and therefore it may not reflect real purchasing power parity. Also, in some countries where beef is not consumed, chicken patties are substituted; and in still other countries, vegetarian patties are used. Note that a Big Mac is cheap in Canada and expensive in Denmark.

[1]The data on purchasing power parity are from the Penn World Tables, using surveys that include hundreds of individual items that encompass all of the expenditure components of a nation's gross domestic product. The Big Mac index is from *The Economist*. See Michael Pakko and Patricia Pollard, "Burgernomics: A Big Mac Guide to Purchasing Power Parity," *Review of the Federal Reserve Bank of St. Louis*, November/December 2003, pp. 9–27.

Table 3	Measures of Purchasing Power Parity in 2002	
Country	**PPP**	**Big Mac**
Argentina	66	100
Australia	75	61
Brazil	45	66
Canada	79	77
Chile	45	98
China	23	48
Denmark	107	123
France	91	104
Germany	95	94
Greece	69	83
Israel	92	143
Japan	145	111
Mexico	61	88
New Zealand	66	67
Russia	17	55
Spain	74	83
Sweden	105	108
Thailand	30	58
Turkey	40	50

Source: See footnote 1.

Although not perfect, changes in the Big Mac Index often are reflective of movements in true purchasing power parity, given that simultaneous changes in several of the factors that distort the index often reflect real changes in the economy.

Exchange Rate Determination

We have seen that people and institutions have two primary reasons for wanting foreign currency. The first is to purchase goods and services and conduct other transactions under the current account. The second is to purchase foreign investments under the capital account. These transactions create a demand for foreign currency and give rise to a supply of domestic currency available for foreign exchange.

A Market for Foreign Exchange

Figure 2 on the next page shows a representative market for foreign exchange. The horizontal axis measures the quantity of dollars available for foreign exchange, and the vertical axis measures the exchange rate in pounds per dollar (£ per $). The

The Foreign Exchange Market for Dollars

A market for foreign exchange is shown here. The horizontal axis measures the quantity of dollars available for foreign exchange, and the vertical axis measures the exchange rate in pounds per dollar (£ per $). If exchange rates are fully flexible, and the exchange rate is initially e_1, there is excess demand for dollars: Q_2 minus Q_1. The dollar will appreciate, and the exchange rate will move to e_0. Alternately, if the exchange rate is initially e_2, there is an excess supply of dollars. Since there are more dollars being offered than demanded, the dollar will depreciate. Eventually, the market will settle into an exchange rate of e_0, where precisely the quantity of dollars supplied is the quantity demanded.

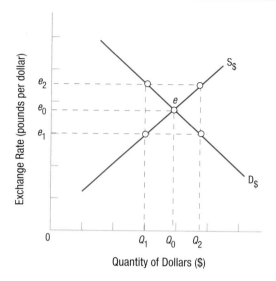

demand for dollars as foreign exchange is downward sloping; as the exchange rate falls, U.S. products become more attractive, and more dollars are desired.

Suppose, for example, that the exchange rate at first is $1 = £1, and that the U.S. game company Electronic Arts manufactures and sells its games at home and in Britain for $50 (£50). Then suppose the dollar *depreciates* by 50%, such that $1.00 = £0.50. If the dollar price of a game remains at $50 in the United States, the pound price of games in Britain will fall to £25 because of the reduction in the exchange rate. This reduction will increase the sales of games in Britain and increase the quantity of dollars British consumers need for foreign exchange. (Note that Figure 2 assumes a very elastic demand for games in Britain. Without this assumption, the analysis gets complicated, so we will assume highly elastic demands throughout this chapter.)

The supply of dollars available for foreign exchange reflects the demand for dollars, since to purchase pounds, U.S. firms or individuals must supply dollars. Not surprisingly, the supply curve for dollars is positively sloped. If the dollar were to *appreciate*, say, moving to $1 = £2, British goods bought in the United States would look attractive since their dollar price would be cut in half. As Americans purchased more British goods, the demand for pounds would grow, and the quantity of dollars supplied to the foreign exchange market would increase.

Flexible Exchange Rates

Assume that exchange rates are fully flexible, so the market determines the prevailing exchange rate, and that the exchange rate in Figure 2 is initially e_1. At this exchange rate, there is an excess demand for dollars since quantity Q_2 is demanded but only Q_1 is supplied. The dollar will **appreciate**, or rise in value relative to other currencies, and the exchange rate will move in the direction of e_0 (more pounds are required to purchase a dollar). As the dollar appreciates, it becomes more expensive for British consumers, thus reducing the demand for U.S. exports. Because of the appreciating dollar, British imports are more attractive for U.S. consumers, increasing U.S. imports. These forces work to move the exchange rate to e_0, closing the gap between Q_2 and Q_1.

Currency appreciation
When the value of a currency rises relative to other currencies.

Alternately, if the exchange rate begins at e_2, there will be an excess supply of dollars. Since more dollars are being offered than demanded, the value of dollars relative to British pounds will decline or **depreciate**. American goods are more attractive in Britain, increasing American exports and the demand for dollars, while British goods become more expensive for American consumers. Eventually, the market will settle into an exchange rate of e_0, at which precisely the quantity of dollars supplied is the quantity demanded.

Currency depreciation
When the value of a currency falls relative to other currencies.

Currency Appreciation and Depreciation

A currency appreciates when its value rises relative to other currencies and depreciates when its value falls. This concept is clear enough in theory, but it can get confusing when we start looking at charts or tables that show exchange rates. The key is to be certain which currency is being used to measure the value of other currencies. Does the table you are looking at show the pound price of the dollar or the dollar price of the pound?

Figure 3 shows the exchange markets for dollars and pounds. Panel A shows the market for dollars, where the price of dollars is denominated in pounds (£/$), just as in Figure 2. This market is in equilibrium at £0.56 per dollar (point e). Panel B shows the equivalent market for pounds; it is in equilibrium at $1.78 per pound (again at point e). Note that $1 \div 0.56 = 1.78$, so Panels A and B represent the same information, just from different viewpoints.

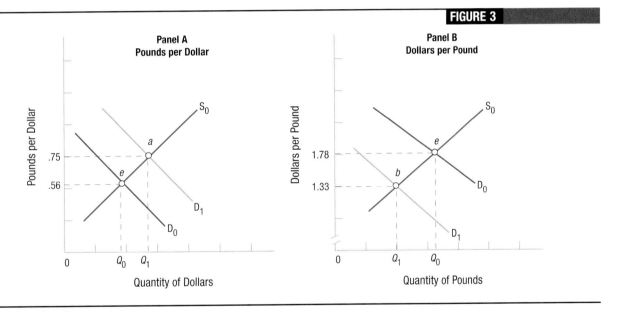

FIGURE 3

Panel A
Pounds per Dollar

Panel B
Dollars per Pound

The Foreign Exchange Market

Data for dollars and pounds are graphically represented here. Panel A shows a market for dollars in which the price of dollars is denominated in pounds (£/$). In Panel A, the market is in equilibrium at £0.56 per dollar (point e). Panel B shows the equivalent market for pounds in equilibrium at $1.78 per pound (again at point e). A rise in the demand for dollars means the dollar appreciates to £0.75 per dollar (point a in Panel A). Panel B shows that the corresponding decline in demand for pounds (from D_0 to D_1) leads to a depreciation of the pound as the exchange rate falls from $1.78 to $1.33 per pound (point b).

Note that a depreciating pound in Panel B indicates a decline in the exchange rate, but this simultaneously represents an appreciating dollar. Thus, graphs can be viewed as reflecting either appreciation or depreciation, depending on which currency is being used to establish the point of view.

Assume a rise in the demand for dollars. In Panel A, the dollar appreciates to £0.75 per dollar (point a), thus leading to a rise in the exchange rate. In Panel B, the corresponding decline in demand for pounds (from D_0 to D_1) leads to a depreciation of the pound and a fall in the exchange rate from \$1.78 to \$1.33 per pound (point *b*). Notice that the pound's depreciation in Panel B produces a decline in the exchange rate, but this decline simultaneously results in appreciation of the dollar. These graphs could be viewed as showing either an appreciation or a depreciation, depending on which currency represents your point of view.

For our purposes, we will try to use figures that show the exchange rate rising when the focus currency appreciates. Still, you need to be aware that exchange rates can be represented in two different ways. Exchange rate graphs are difficult and sometimes confusing, so you will need to think through each graph you encounter. We now turn our discussion to the impact of changing exchange rates on current and capital accounts.

Determinants of Exchange Rates

What sort of conditions will cause currencies to appreciate or depreciate? First, a change in our tastes and preferences as consumers for foreign goods will result in currency appreciation or depreciation. For example, if we desire to purchase more foreign goods, this will lead to an increase in the demand for foreign currency and result in the depreciation of the dollar.

Second, if our income growth exceeds that of other countries, our demand for imports will grow faster relative to the growth of other nations. This will lead again to an increase in demand for foreign currency, resulting in the depreciation of the dollar.

Third, rising inflation in the United States relative to foreign nations makes our goods and services relatively more expensive overseas and foreign goods more attractive here at home. This results in growing imports, reduced exports, and again leads to a depreciation of the dollar.

Fourth, falling interest rates in the United States relative to foreign countries makes financial investment in the United States less attractive. This reduces the demand for dollars, leading once again to a depreciation of the dollar. Note that if we reverse these stories in each case, the dollar will appreciate.

Exchange Rates and the Current Account

As we have already seen, the current account includes payments for imports and exports. Also included are changes in income flowing into and out of the country. In this section, we will focus on the effect that changes in real exchange rates have on both of these components of the current account. For our purposes, we will continue to assume that import and export demands are highly elastic for real exchange rates.

Changes in Inflation Rates

Let's assume inflation heats up in Britain, such that the British price level rises relative to U.S. prices, or the dollar appreciates relative to the pound. Production costs rise in Britain, so British goods are more expensive. American goods appear more attractive to British consumers, so exports of American goods will rise, improving the American current account. American consumers will purchase more domestic goods and fewer British imports because of rising British prices, further improving the American current account. The opposite is true for Britain: British imports rise and exports fall, hurting the British current account.

These results are dependent on our assumption that import and export demands are highly elastic with real exchange rates. Thus, when exchange rates change, exports and imports will change proportionally more than the change in exchange rates.

Changes in Domestic Disposable Income

If domestic disposable income rises, U.S. consumers will have more money to spend, and given existing exchange rates, imports will rise since some of this increased consumption will go to foreign products. As a result, the current account will worsen as imports rise. The opposite occurs when domestic income falls.

Exchange Rates and the Capital Account

The capital account summarizes flows of money or capital into and out of U.S. assets. Each day, foreign individuals, companies, and governments put $1.5 billion into treasury bonds, U.S. stocks, companies, and real estate.[2] Today, foreign and domestic assets are available to investors. Foreign investment possibilities include direct investment in projects undertaken by multinational firms, the sale and purchase of foreign stocks and bonds, and the short-term movement of assets in foreign bank accounts.

Because these transactions all involve capital, investors must balance their risks and returns. Two factors essentially incorporate both risk and return for international assets: interest rates and expected changes in exchange rates.

Interest Rate Changes

If the exchange rate is assumed to be constant, and the assets of two countries are *perfectly substitutable*, then an interest rate rise in one country will cause capital to flow into it from the other country. For example, a rise in interest rates in the United States will cause capital to flow from Britain, where interest rates have not changed, into the United States, where investors can earn a higher rate of return on their investments. Since the assets of both countries are assumed to be perfectly substitutable, this flow will continue until the interest rates (r) in Britain and the United States are equal, or

$$r_{\text{US}} = r_{\text{UK}}$$

Everything else being equal, we can expect capital to flow in the direction of the country that offers the highest interest rate, and thus, the highest return on capital. But "everything else" is rarely equal.

Exchange Rate Changes

Suppose that the exchange rate for U.S. currency is *expected to appreciate* ($\Delta \varepsilon > 0$). The relationship between the interest rates in the United States and Britain becomes

$$r_{\text{US}} = r_{\text{UK}} - \Delta \varepsilon$$

Investors demand a higher return in Britain to offset the expected depreciation of the U.K. pound relative to the U.S. dollar. Unless interest rates rise in Britain, capital will flow out of Britain and into the United States until U.S. interest rates fall enough to offset the expected appreciation of the dollar.

If capital is not perfectly mobile and substitutable between two countries, a *risk premium* can be added to the relationship just described; thus,

$$r_{\text{US}} = r_{\text{UK}} - \Delta \varepsilon + x$$

where x is the risk premium. Expected exchange rate changes and risk premium changes can produce enduring interest rate differentials between two countries.

In 2007, the dollar fell relative to the yen, the euro, and the British pound. This was a sign that foreign investors were not as enthusiastic about U.S. investments.

---

[2]Joel Millman et al., "Foreign Cash Flow Is Vital to U.S.—But Will It Last?" *Wall Street Journal*, January 15, 2004, p. A1.

Low interest rates and high deficits may have convinced foreign investors that it was not a good time to invest in the United States. The United States is more dependent on foreign capital than ever before. Today, more than half of U.S. Treasury debt held by the public is held by foreigners. Changes in inflation, interest rates, and expectations about exchange rates are important.

Exchange Rates and Aggregate Supply and Demand

How do changes in nominal exchange rates affect aggregate demand and aggregate supply? A change in nominal exchange rates will affect imports and exports. Consider what happens, for example, when the exchange rate for the dollar depreciates. The dollar is weaker, and thus the pound (or any other currency) will buy more dollars. American products become more attractive in foreign markets, so American exports increase and aggregate demand expands. Yet, because some inputs into the production process may be imported (raw materials, computer programming services, or call answering services), input costs will rise, causing aggregate supply to contract.

Let us take a more detailed look at this process by considering Figure 4. Assume the economy begins in equilibrium at point e, with full employment output Q_f and the price level at P_e. As the dollar depreciates, this will spur an increase in exports, thus shifting aggregate demand from AD_0 to AD_1 and raising prices to P_1 in the short run. Initially, output climbs to Q_1, but since some of the economy's inputs are imported, aggregate supply will decline, mitigating this rise in output. In the short run, the economy will expand beyond Q_f, and prices will rise.

FIGURE 4

Exchange Rates and Aggregate Demand and Supply

Assume the economy initially begins in equilibrium at point e, with full employment output Q_f and the price level at P_e. Assume the dollar depreciates. This will increase exports, shifting aggregate demand from AD_0 to AD_1 and raising prices to P_1 and output to Q_1 in the short run. In the long run, aggregate supply will shift from AS_0 to AS_1, as workers readjust their wage demands in the long run, thus moving the economy to point b. As the economy adjusts to a higher price level, the benefits from currency depreciation are greatly reduced.

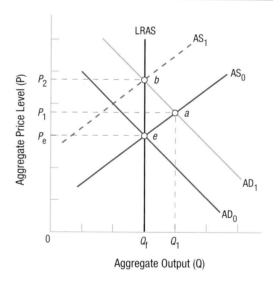

In the longer term, as domestic prices rise, workers will realize that their real wages do not purchase as much as before since import prices are higher. As a result, workers will start demanding higher wages just to bring them back to where they were originally. This shifts aggregate supply from AS_0 to AS_1, thereby moving the economy from point a in the short run to point b in the long run. As the economy adjusts to a higher price level, the original benefits accruing from currency depreciation will be greatly reduced.

Currency depreciation works because imports become more expensive and exports less so. When this happens, consumer income no longer goes as far, since the price of domestic goods does not change, but the cost of imports rises. In countries where imports form a substantial part of household spending, major depreciations in the national currency can produce significant declines in standards of living. Such depreciations (or devaluations) have occasioned strikes and, in some cases, even street riots; recent examples include Argentina, Brazil, Mexico, and Indonesia.

What are the implications of all this for policymakers? First, a currency depreciation or devaluation can, after a period, simply lead to inflation. In most cases, however, the causation probably goes the other way: Macroeconomic policies or economic events force currency depreciations.

Trade balances usually improve with an exchange rate depreciation. Policymakers can get improved current account balances without inflation by pursuing devaluation first, then pursuing fiscal contraction (reducing government spending or increasing taxes), and finally moving the economy back to point *e* in Figure 4. But, here again, the real long-run benefit is more stable monetary and fiscal policies.

Exchange Rates

REVIEW

- Nominal exchange rates define the rate at which one currency can be exchanged for another.
- Real exchange rates are the nominal exchange rates multiplied by the ratio of the price levels of the two countries.
- Purchasing power parity (PPP) is a rate of exchange that permits a given level of currency to purchase the same amount of goods and services in another country.
- A currency appreciates when its value rises relative to other currencies. Currency devaluation causes a currency to lose value relative to others.
- Inflation causes depreciation of a country's currency, worsening its current account. Rising domestic income typically results in rising imports and a deteriorating current account.
- Rising interest rates cause capital to flow into the country with the higher interest rate, and expectations about a future currency appreciation or depreciation affect the capital account.
- Currency appreciation and depreciation have an effect on aggregate supply and demand. For example, currency depreciation expands aggregate demand as exports increase, but some (now high-priced) imported inputs are inputs into production, reducing aggregate supply.

QUESTION

If China were to revalue its currency by 10%, so in effect the yuan appreciated by 10%, would this have an impact on the U.S. current account?

Answers to the Checkpoint question can be found at the end of this chapter.

Monetary and Fiscal Policy in an Open Economy

How monetary and fiscal policy is affected by international trade and finance depends on the type of exchange rate system in existence. There are several ways exchange rate systems can be organized. We will discuss the two major categories: fixed and flexible rates.

Fixed and Flexible Exchange Rate Systems

A **fixed exchange rate** system is one in which governments determine their exchange rates, then adjust macroeconomic policies to maintain these rates. A **flexible or floating exchange rate** system, in contrast, relies on currency markets to determine the exchange rates consistent with macroeconomic conditions.

Before the Great Depression, most of the world economies were on the gold standard. According to Peter Temin[3] the gold standard was characterized by "(1) the free flow of gold between individuals and countries, (2) the maintenance of fixed values of national currencies in terms of gold and therefore each other, and (3) the absence of an international coordinating organization."

Under the gold standard, each country had to maintain enough gold stocks to keep the value of its currency fixed to that of others. If a country's imports exceeded its exports, this balance of payments deficit had to come from its gold stocks. Since gold backed the national currency, the country would have to reduce the amount of money circulating in its economy, thereby reducing expenditures, output, and income. This reduction would lead to a decline in prices and wages, a rise in exports (which are getting cheaper), and a corresponding drop in imports (which are becoming more expensive). This process would continue until imports and exports were again equalized and the flow of gold ended.

In the early 1930s, the Federal Reserve in the United States pursued a contractionary monetary policy intended to cool off the overheated economy of the 1920s. This policy reduced imports and increased the flow of gold into the United States. With France pursuing a similar deflationary policy, by 1932 these two countries held more than 70% of the world's monetary gold. Other countries attempted to conserve their gold stocks by selling off assets, thereby spurring a worldwide monetary contraction. As other monetary authorities attempted to conserve their gold reserves, moreover, they reduced the liquidity available to their banks, thereby inadvertently causing bank failures. In this way, the depression in the United States spread worldwide.

As World War II came to an end, the allies met in Bretton Woods, New Hampshire, to design a new and less troublesome international monetary system. Exchange rates were set, and each country agreed to use its monetary authorities to buy and sell its own currency to maintain its exchange rate at fixed levels.

The Bretton Woods agreements created the International Monetary Fund to aid countries having trouble maintaining their exchange rates. In addition, the World Bank was established to loan money to countries for economic development. In the end, most countries were unwilling to make the tough adjustments required by a fixed rate system, and it collapsed in the early 1970s. Today, we operate on a flexible exchange rate system where each currency floats in the market.

Policies Under Fixed Exchange Rates

When the government engages in expansionary policy, aggregate demand will rise, resulting in output and price increases. Figure 5 shows the result of such a policy as an increase in aggregate demand from AD_0 to AD_1, with the economy moving from equilibrium at point a to point b in the short run and the price level rising from P_0 to P_1. A rising domestic price level means that U.S. exports will decline as they become more expensive. As incomes rise, imports will rise. Combined, these forces will worsen the current account, moving it into deficit or reducing a surplus, as net exports decline.

An expansionary monetary policy, combined with a fiscal policy that is neither expansionary nor contractionary, will result in a rising money supply and falling interest rates. In Figure 5, this causes aggregate demand to rise to AD_1. Lower inter-

---

[3]Peter Temin, *Lessons from the Great Depression: The Lionel Robbins Lectures for 1989* (Cambridge, MA: MIT Press), 1989, p. 8.

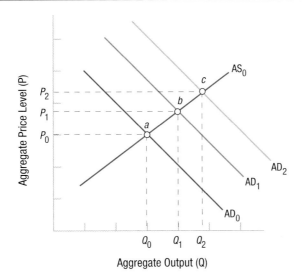

FIGURE 5

Monetary and Fiscal Policy in an Open Economy

When the government engages in expansionary policy, aggregate demand will rise, resulting in output and price increases. A rising domestic price level means that U.S. exports will decline as they become more expensive. As incomes rise, imports will rise. Combined, these forces will worsen the current account, moving it into deficit or reducing a surplus, as net exports decline.

An expansionary monetary policy, combined with a neutral fiscal policy, will result in a rising money supply and falling interest rates. Lower interest rates result in capital outflow. This reduces the domestic money supply. The greater the capital mobility, the more the money supply is reduced, and the more aggregate demand moves back in the direction of AD_0.

est rates result in capital flowing from the United States to other countries. This reduces the U.S. money supply.

The greater the capital mobility, the more the money supply is reduced, and the more aggregate demand moves back in the direction of AD_0. With perfect capital mobility, monetary policy would be ineffective. The amount of capital leaving the United States would be just equal to the increase in the money supply to begin with, and interest rates would be returned to their original international equilibrium.

Keeping exchange rates fixed and holding the money supply constant, an expansionary fiscal policy will produce an increase in interest rates. As income rises, there will be a greater transactions demand for money, resulting in higher interest rates. Higher interest rates mean that capital will flow into the United States.

As more capital flows into U.S. capital markets, interest rates will be reduced, adding to the expansionary impact of the original fiscal policy. Expansionary fiscal policy is reinforced by an open economy with fixed exchange rates as aggregate demand moves to AD_2.

Policies Under Flexible Exchange Rates

Expansionary monetary policy under a system of flexible exchange rates, again holding fiscal policy constant, will result in a growing money supply and falling interest rates. Lower interest rates lead to a capital outflow and a balance of payments deficit, or a declining surplus. With flexible exchange rates, consumers and investors will want more foreign currency; thus, the exchange rate will depreciate. As the dollar depreciates, exports increase; U.S. exports are more attractive to foreigners as their currency buys them more. The net result is that the international market works to reinforce an expansionary policy undertaken at home.

Permitting exchange rates to vary and holding the money supply constant, an expansionary fiscal policy will produce a rise in interest rates as rising incomes increase the transactions demand for money. Higher interest rates mean that capital will flow into the United States, generating a balance of payments surplus or a smaller deficit, causing the exchange rate to appreciate as foreigners value dollars more. As the dollar becomes more valuable, exports decline, moving aggregate demand back toward AD_0 in Figure 5. With flexible exchange rates, therefore, an open economy can hamper fiscal policy.

These movements are complex and go through several steps. Table 4 summarizes them for you. The key point to note is that under our flexible exchange rate system now, an open economy reinforces monetary policy and hampers fiscal policy. No wonder the Fed has become more important.

Table 4	Summary of the Effects of an Open Economy on Monetary and Fiscal Policy in a Fixed and Flexible Exchange Rate System	
	Flexible Exchange Rate	**Fixed Exchange Rate**
Monetary policy (fiscal policy constant)	Reinforced	Hampered
Fiscal policy (monetary policy constant)	Hampered	Reinforced

The beginning of the 21st century saw challenges to globalism, a falling dollar, and a U.S. economy with productivity and output growing at a historically rapid clip. High budget deficits again raised fears of rising interest rates and crowding out of private investment. Foreigners continued to plow funds into our economy, but concerns were being raised about their continuing capacity to pour investment into the United States.

Presidents and Congress several decades ago could adopt monetary and fiscal policies without much consideration of the rest of the world. Today, economies of the world are vastly more intertwined, and the macroeconomic policies of one country often have serious impacts on others. Today, open economy macroeconomics is more important, and good macroeconomic policymaking must account for changes in exchange rates and capital flows.

Checkpoint

Monetary and Fiscal Policy in an Open Economy

REVIEW

- A fixed exchange rate is one in which governments determine their exchange rates and then use macroeconomic policy to maintain these rates.
- Flexible exchange rates rely on markets to set the exchange rate given the country's macroeconomic policies.
- Fixed exchange rate systems hinder monetary policy, but reinforce fiscal policy.
- Flexible exchange rates hamper fiscal policy, but reinforce monetary policy.

QUESTION

The United States seems to rely more on monetary policy to maintain stable prices, low interest rates, low unemployment, and healthy economic growth. Do the facts that the United States has really embraced global trade (imports and exports combined are over 25% of GDP) and we have a flexible (floating) exchange rate help explain why monetary policy seems more important than fiscal policy?

Answers to the Checkpoint question can be found at the end of this chapter.

Chapter Summary

The Balance of Payments

The current account includes payments for imports and exports of goods and services, incomes flowing into and out of the country, and net transfers of money.

The capital account includes flows of money into and out of domestic and foreign assets. Foreign investment in the United States includes foreign ownership of domestic plants or subsidiaries; investments in mutual funds, stocks, and bonds; and deposits in U.S. banks. In a similar fashion, U.S. investors hold foreign financial assets in their portfolios and own interests in foreign facilities and companies.

Exchange Rates

The exchange rate defines the rate at which one currency can be exchanged for another. A nominal exchange rate is the price of one country's currency for another.

The real exchange rate takes price levels into account. The real exchange rate between two countries is defined as $e_r = e_n \times (P_d/P_f)$

where
e_r = the real exchange rate
e_n = the nominal exchange rate
P_d = the domestic price level
P_f = the foreign price level

Thus, the real exchange rate is the nominal exchange rate multiplied by the ratio of the price levels of the two countries.

The purchasing power parity of a currency is the rate of exchange at which some currency in one country can purchase the same goods in another country. Absolute purchasing power parity would mean that nominal exchange rates equalized the purchasing power in both countries. As a result, the real exchange rate would equal 1.

If exchange rates are fully flexible, markets determine the prevailing exchange rate. If there is an excess demand for dollars, the dollar will appreciate, or rise in value. As the dollar appreciates, it becomes more expensive for foreigners, reducing the demand for U.S. exports. An appreciating dollar makes foreign imports more attractive for American consumers, increasing imports.

If there is an excess supply of dollars, the value of dollars will decline or depreciate. American goods become more attractive to foreigners, increasing American exports and the demand for dollars. When the dollar falls, foreign goods become more expensive for American consumers, driving down American imports.

In looking at charts or tables showing exchange rates, it is important to keep in mind which currency is being used to measure the price of others. For example, does the table show the pound price of the dollar or the dollar price of the pound? Graphs can be viewed as showing either an appreciation or a depreciation, depending on which currency is being considered.

Real exchange rates affect the payments for imports and exports, and also affect the current account. If inflation heats up in Britain, production costs will rise in Britain. British goods become more expensive, and American goods more attractive to British consumers. American exports will rise, improving the American current account. The opposite occurs in Britain; British imports rise, and the British current accounts suffer.

Interest rates and exchange rate expectations affect the capital account. If the exchange rate is assumed to be constant, and the assets of two countries are perfectly substitutable, an interest rate rise in one country will cause capital to flow into it from the other country.

If, for example, U.S. currency is expected to appreciate, investors will demand a higher return in Britain to offset the expected depreciation of the U.K. pound relative to the U.S. dollar. Unless interest rates rise in Britain, capital will flow from Britain into the United States until U.S. interest rates fall enough to offset the expected appreciation of the dollar.

When capital is not perfectly mobile and substitutable between two countries, a risk premium will be added to interest rates. Expected exchange rate changes and risk premium changes can produce enduring interest rate differentials between two countries.

Monetary and Fiscal Policy in an Open Economy

There are several ways to organize an exchange rate system, including fixed and flexible rate systems. A fixed exchange rate system is one in which governments determine their exchange rates, then use macroeconomic adjustments to maintain these rates. A flexible or floating exchange rate system relies on currency markets to determine the exchange rates, given macroeconomic conditions.

Before the Great Depression, most of the world economies were on the gold standard. Countries had to maintain stocks of gold sufficient to keep the value of their currencies fixed relative to those of others. If a country's imports exceeded its exports, this balance of payments deficit had to come from its gold stocks. Since gold backed the national currency, the country would have to reduce the money circulating in its economy, thereby reducing spending, output, and income.

When exchange rates are fixed, an expansionary monetary policy combined with a neutral fiscal policy will result in a rising money supply and falling interest rates. The rise in the money supply leads to an initial rise in aggregate demand, but the lower interest rates cause capital to flow out of the United States to other countries, which reduces the money supply.

Keeping exchange rates fixed and holding the money supply constant, an expansionary fiscal policy will produce an increase in interest rates. As income rises, there will be a greater demand for money, resulting in higher interest rates. Higher interest rates mean that capital will flow into the United States. As more capital flows into these markets, interest rates will be reduced, adding to the expansionary impact of the original fiscal policy.

If exchange rates are flexible, an expansionary monetary policy with no change in fiscal policy will result in a rising money supply and falling interest rates. Lower interest rates lead to a capital outflow and a balance of payments deficit or declining surplus. With flexible exchange rates, consumers and investors will want more foreign currency; thus, there will be depreciation in the exchange rate. As the dollar depreciates, exports increase; U.S. exports look more attractive to foreigners as their currency buys more. The net result is that the international market works to reinforce an expansionary policy undertaken at home.

Allowing exchange rates to vary and holding the money supply constant, an expansionary fiscal policy with the money supply being held constant will produce a rise in interest rates. Rising income results in a greater demand for money, producing higher interest rates. Higher interest rates mean that capital will flow into the United States, generating a balance of payments surplus or a smaller deficit. This causes the exchange rate to appreciate as foreigners value the dollar more. As the dollar becomes more valuable, exports decline. With flexible exchange rates, an open economy can hamper fiscal policy.

Questions and Problems

1. Describe the balance of trade. What factors contribute to our trade deficit?

2. Mexican immigrants working in the United States often send money back home (known as remittances) to help their families or to add to their savings account for the future. Today, these remittances approach $20 billion a year. How are these transfers recorded in the balance of payments accounts?

3. What is the important difference between the current account and the capital account, given that they are equal to the same dollar amount?

4. How are most exchange rates determined?

5. If the euro appreciates by 30%, what will happen to imports of Mercedes-Benz automobiles in the United States?

6. Assume that global warming and especially high temperatures in Northern California have rendered it impossible for wine grapes in the Napa Valley (and all over California) to grow properly. Unable to get California wines, demand jumps dramatically for Australian wines. How would this affect the Australian dollar? Is this good for other Australian exports?

7. If the European economies begin having a serious bout of stagflation—high rates of both unemployment and inflation—will this affect the value of the dollar?

8. Describe the difference between fixed and flexible exchange rates.

9. Trace through the reasoning why monetary policy is enhanced by a flexible exchange rate system.

10. Assume the following exchange rates prevail:

(U.S. $ Equivalent)	
Argentina	.3253 (Peso)
Canada	.8812 (Dollar)
Mexico	.0914 (Peso)
Bahrain	2.6526 (Dinar)

How many Mexican pesos does it take to get one Bahrain Dinar? If you had 20 U.S. dollars, could you take a ferry ride in Canada if it cost $25 Canadian? If someone gave you 50 Argentinean pesos to settle a 150 Mexican pesos bet, would it be enough?

11. Zimbabwe devalued its currency in mid-2006 essentially turning a $20,000 Zimbabwe bill into a $20 bill. People were permitted only 3 weeks to turn in their old currency for new notes, individuals were limited to $150 a day, and companies were restricted to $7,000. Who do you think were the losers from this

devaluation, especially considering its limited turn-in period for the old currency?

12. When the world's economies are on a fixed gold standard and the discoveries of gold do not keep pace with the growing world GDP, what happens?

13. Exchange rates and purchasing power parity should be the same between countries. If it costs $300 to purchase an iPod in United States and 400 Australian dollars in Sydney, then the exchange rate between Australia and the United States should be 4:3. Why might purchasing power parity be different from the exchange rate?

14. Describe the difference between the nominal and real exchange rates. What does rising inflation do to that country's real exchange rate?

15. When the dollar gets stronger against the major foreign currencies, does the price of French wine rise or fall in the United States? Would this be a good time to travel to Australia? What happens to U.S. exports?

Answers to Checkpoint Questions

CHECKPOINT: THE BALANCE OF PAYMENTS

The equation $G - T = (S - I) + (M - X)$ provides the answer. For simplicity, assume a balanced budget $(G - T = 0)$. If $S > I$, then $X > M$ to balance the equation. Large private saving is balanced by fewer imports in comparison to exports. China is a net exporter, which shows up as a current account surplus in their balance of trade accounts.

CHECKPOINT: EXCHANGE RATES

Yes, a 10% appreciation in the yuan would make China's output more expensive in the United States, and we would import less from China, improving the U.S. current account.

CHECKPOINT: MONETARY AND FISCAL POLICY IN AN OPEN ECONOMY

As noted in this section, monetary policy is reinforced when exchange rates are flexible, while fiscal policy is hindered. This is probably only a partial explanation because fiscal policy today seems driven more by "events" and other priorities, and less by stabilization issues. Two decades of rather uninterrupted economic prosperity have resulted in a focus on interest rates, and monetary policy is the principal approach to macroeconomic stabilization.

Absolute advantage One country can produce more of a good than another country.

Adaptive expectations Inflationary expectations are formed from a simple extrapolation from past events.

Adverse selection Occurs when products of different qualities are sold at the same price because of asymmetric information. Insurance is a typical example because people know far more about their health and risk levels than the companies insuring them.

Aggregate demand The output of goods and services (real GDP) demanded at different price levels.

Aggregate expenditures Consist of consumer spending, business investment spending, government spending, and net foreign spending (exports minus imports): $GDP = C + I + G + (X - M)$.

Aggregate production function An equation $[Q = Af(K,L)]$, that relates aggregate output (Q) to technology (A) and to the quantities of inputs (K is capital, and L is labor) it uses in the production process (f).

Aggregate supply The real GDP that firms will produce at varying price levels. During a depression, the economy has a lot of slack, and the aggregate supply curve will be flat. In the short run, aggregate supply is positively sloped because many input costs are slow to change, but in the long run, the aggregate supply curve is vertical at full employment since the economy has reached its capacity to produce.

Allocative efficiency The mix of goods and services produced are just what individuals in society desire.

Annually balanced budget Federal expenditures and taxes would have to be equal each year. Annually balanced budgets tend to be procyclical.

Asymmetric information Occurs when one party to a transaction has significantly better information than another party.

Automatic stabilizers Tax revenues and transfer payments automatically expand or contract in ways that reduce the intensity of business fluctuations without any overt action by Congress or other policymakers.

Average propensity to consume The percentage of income that is consumed (C/Y).

Average propensity to save The percentage of income that is saved (S/Y).

Balanced budget multiplier Equal changes in government spending and taxation (a balanced budget) lead to an equal change in income (the balanced budget multiplier is equal to 1).

Barter The direct exchange of goods and services for other goods and services.

Budget and trade deficits These are related by the following equation: $G - T = (S - I) + (M - X)$. So budget deficits must be covered by net domestic saving (private + corporate) or by net foreign saving (in the form of foreigners buying U.S. government bonds).

Business cycles Alternating increases and decreases in economic activity that are typically punctuated by periods of downturn, recession, recovery, and boom.

Capital Includes manufactured products such as welding machines, computers and cellular phones that are used to produce other goods and services. The payment to capital is referred to as interest.

Capital account Summarizes the flow of money into and out of domestic and foreign assets, including investments by foreign companies in domestic plants or subsidiaries, and other foreign holdings of U.S. assets, including mutual funds, stock, bonds, and deposits in U.S. banks. Also included are U.S. investors' holdings of foreign financial assets, production facilities, and other assets in foreign countries.

Capital-to-labor ratio The capital employed per worker. A higher ratio means higher labor productivity and, as a result, higher wages.

Ceteris paribus Assumption used in economics (and other disciplines as well), where other relevant factors or variables are held constant.

Change in demand Occurs when one or more of the determinants of demand changes, shown as a shift in the entire demand curve.

Change in quantity demanded Occurs when the price of the product changes, and is shown as a movement along an existing demand curve.

Change in quantity supplied Occurs when the price of the product changes, and is shown as a movement along an existing supply curve.

Change in supply Occurs when one or more of the determinants of supply change, shown as a shift in the entire supply curve.

Circular flow diagram Illustrates how households and firms interact through product and resource markets and shows that economic aggregates can be determined by either examining spending flows or income flows to households.

Classical model A model of the economy that relied on competitive conditions in product, labor, and capital markets, and flexible prices, wages, and interest rates to keep the economy operating around full employment. Anyone unemployed simply was unwilling to work at the prevailing real wage.

Classical monetary transmission mechanism Because money was assumed to be used only for transactions purposes, that the economy was operating at full employment (Q is fixed), and velocity (V) was dependent on banking technology and thus constant, the equation of exchange suggests the process is quite direct; any change in M will be felt directly in P.

Common property resources Resources that are owned by the community at large (parks, ocean fish, and the atmosphere) and therefore tend to be overexploited because individuals have little incentive to use them in a sustainable fashion.

Comparative advantage One country has a lower opportunity cost of producing a good than another country.

Complementary goods Goods that are typically consumed together.

Consumer price index (CPI) A measure of the average change in prices paid by urban consumers for a typical market basket of consumer goods and services.

Consumer surplus The difference between market price and what consumers (as individuals or the market) would be willing to pay. It is equal to the area above market price and below the demand curve.

Consumption Spending by individuals and households on both durable goods (e.g., autos, appliances, and electronic equipment) and nondurable goods (e.g., food, clothes, and entertainment).

Contractionary fiscal policy Involves increasing withdrawals from the economy by reducing government spending, transfer payments, or raising taxes to decrease aggregate demand to contract output and the economy.

Cost-push inflation Results when a supply shock hits the economy, reducing aggregate supply, and thus reducing output and increasing the price level.

Crowding-out effect Arises from deficit spending requiring the government to borrow, which drives up interest rates, which in turn reduces consumer spending and business investment.

Currency appreciation When the value of a currency rises relative to other currencies.

Currency depreciation When the value of a currency falls relative to other currencies.

Current account Includes payments for imports and exports of goods and services, incomes flowing into and out of the country, and net transfers of money.

Cyclical unemployment Unemployment that results from changes in the business cycle; where public policymakers can have their greatest impact by keeping the economy on a steady, low-inflationary, solid growth path.

Cyclically balanced budget Balancing the budget over the course of the business cycle by restricting spending or raising taxes when the economy is booming and using these surpluses to offset the deficits that occur during recessions.

Data lag The time policymakers must wait for economic data to be collected, processed, and reported. Most macroeconomic data are not available until at least one quarter (3 months) after the fact.

Deadweight loss The loss in consumer and producer surplus due to inefficiency because some transactions cannot be made and therefore their value to society is lost.

Decision lag After a problem is recognized, it takes some time for the Fed to decide on a policy. Since the Fed meets monthly, the decision lag is relatively short.

Deficit The amount by which annual government spending exceeds tax revenues.

Deflation A decline in overall prices throughout the economy. This is the opposite of inflation.

Demand The maximum amount of a product that buyers are willing and able to purchase over some time period at various prices, holding all other relevant factors constant (the *ceteris paribus* condition).

Demand curve Demand schedule information translated to a graph.

Demand-pull inflation Results when aggregate demand expands so much that equilibrium output exceeds full employment output and the price level rises.

Determinants of demand Other nonprice factors that affect demand including tastes and preferences, income, prices of related goods, number of buyers, and expectations.

Determinants of supply Other nonprice factors that affect supply including production technology, costs of resources, prices of other commodities, expectations, number of sellers, and taxes and subsidies.

Discount rate The interest rate the Federal Reserve charges commercial banks and other depository institutions to borrow reserves from a regional Federal Reserve Bank.

Discouraged workers To continue to be counted as unemployed, those without work must actively seek work (apply for jobs, interview, register with employment services, etc.). Discouraged workers are those who have given up actively looking for work and, as a result, are not counted as unemployed.

Discretionary fiscal policy Involves adjusting government spending and tax policies with the express short-run goal of moving the economy toward full employment, expanding economic growth, or controlling inflation.

Discretionary spending The part of the budget that works its way through the appropriations process of Congress each year and includes such programs as national defense, transportation, science, environment, and income security.

Disinflation A reduction in the rate of inflation. An economy going through disinflation will typically still be facing inflation, but it will be at a declining rate.

Disposable personal income Personal income minus taxes.

Dumping Selling goods abroad at lower prices than in home markets, and often below cost.

Easy money or expansionary monetary policy Fed actions designed to increase excess reserves and the money supply to stimulate the economy (expand income and employment).

Economic growth Usually measured by the annual percentage change in real GDP, reflecting an annual improvement in our standard

Efficiency How well resources are used and allocated. Do people get the goods and services they want at the lowest possible resource cost? This is the chief focus of efficiency.

Efficiency wage theory Employers often pay their workers wages above the market-clearing level to improve morale and productivity, reduce turnover, and create a disincentive for employees to shirk their duties.

Entrepreneurs Entrepreneurs combine land, labor, and capital to produce goods and services. They absorb the risk of being in business, including the risk of bankruptcy and other liabilities associated with doing business. Entrepreneurs receive profits for this effort.

Equation of exchange The heart of classical monetary theory uses the equation $M \times V = P \times Q$, where M is the supply of money,

V is the velocity of money (or the number of times it turns over in a year), P is the price level, and Q is the economy's output level.

Equilibrium Market forces are in balance where the quantities demanded by consumers just equal quantities supplied by producers.

Equilibrium price Market equilibrium price is the price that results when quantity demanded is just equal to quantity supplied.

Equilibrium quantity Market equilibrium quantity is the output that results when quantity demanded is just equal to quantity supplied.

Equity The fairness of various issues and policies.

Exchange rate The rate at which one currency can be exchanged for another, or just the price of one currency for another.

Expansionary fiscal policy Involves increasing government spending, increasing transfer payments, or decreasing taxes to increase aggregate demand to expand output and the economy.

External benefits Positive externalities (also called spillovers) such as education and vaccinations. Private markets provide too little at too high a price of goods with external benefits.

External cost Occurs when a transaction between two parties has an impact on a third party not involved with the transaction. External costs are negative such as pollution or congestion. The market provides too much of the product with negative externalities at too low a cost.

Externally held debt Public debt held by foreigners, roughly equal to half of the outstanding U.S. debt held by the public.

Federal Open Market Committee This 12-member committee is composed of members of the Board of Governors of the Fed and selected presidents of the regional Federal Reserve Banks; it oversees open market operations (the buying and selling of

government securities), the main tool of monetary policy.

Federal Reserve System The central bank of the United States.

Fiscal imbalance The difference between the present value of future obligations and expected revenues, less government assets, assuming current policies remain unchanged.

Fiscal sustainability A fiscal imbalance equal to zero.

Fixed exchange rate Each government determines its exchange rate, then uses macroeconomic policy to maintain the rate.

Flexible or floating exchange rate A country's currency exchange rate is determined in international currency exchange markets, given the country's macroeconomic policies.

Fractional reserve banking system To prevent bank runs (all depositors demanding their deposits in cash at the same time), a portion of bank deposits must be held as vault cash, or else in an account with the regional Federal Reserve Bank.

Free rider When a public good is provided, consumers cannot be excluded from enjoying the product, so some consume the product without paying.

Frictional unemployment Natural unemployment for our economy; includes workers who voluntarily quit their jobs to search for better positions, or are moving to new jobs but may still take several days or weeks before they can report to their new employers.

Functional finance Essentially ignores the impact of the budget on the business cycle and focuses on fostering economic growth and stable prices, while keeping the economy as close as possible to full employment.

GDP deflator An index of the average prices for all goods and services in the economy, including consumer goods, investment goods, government goods and services, and exports. It is the broadest measure of inflation in the national income and product accounts (NIPA).

Generational imbalance An estimate of how much of any fiscal imbalance is being shifted to future generations.

Government budget constraint The government budget is limited by the fact that $G - T = \Delta M + \Delta B + \Delta A$, where G is government spending and T is tax revenues, thus $(G - T)$ is the federal budget deficit; ΔM is the change in the money supply; ΔB is the change in bonds held by public entities, domestic and foreign; and ΔA represents the sales of government assets.

Government spending Includes the wages and salaries of government employees (federal, state, and local); the purchase of products and services from private businesses and the rest of the world; and government purchases of new structures, equipment, and software.

Gross domestic product (GDP) A measure of the economy's total output; it is the most widely reported value in the national income and product accounts (NIPA) and is equal to the total market value of all final goods and services produced by resources in the United States.

Gross private domestic investment (GPDI) Investments in such things as structures (residential and nonresidential), equipment, and software, and changes in private business inventories.

Horizontal summation Market demand and supply curves are found by adding together how many units of the product will be purchased or supplied at each price.

Hyperinflation An extremely high rate of inflation; above 100% a year.

Implementation lag, fiscal policy The time required to turn fiscal policy into law and eventually have an impact on the economy.

Implementation lag, monetary policy The time required for monetary policy to have an impact on the economy.

Infant industry An industry so underdeveloped that protection is needed for it to become competitive on the world stage or to ensure its survival.

Inferior goods A good where an increase in income results in declining demand.

Inflation A measure of changes in the cost of living. A general rise in prices throughout the economy.

Inflation targeting Involves setting targets on the inflation rate, usually around 2% a year in recognition that the long-run goal of monetary policy is price stability.

Inflationary expectations The rate of inflation expected by workers for any given period. Workers do not work for a specific nominal wage but for what those wages will buy (real wages), so their inflationary expectations are an important determinant of what nominal wage they are willing to work for.

Inflationary gap The spending reduction necessary (again when expanded by the multiplier) to bring an overheated economy back to full employment.

Information lag The time policymakers must wait for economic data to be collected, processed, and reported. Most macroeconomic data are not available until at least one quarter (3 months) after the fact.

Infrastructure The public capital of a nation including transportation networks, power-generating plants and transmission facilities, public education institutions, and other intangible resources such as protection of property rights and a stable monetary environment.

Injections Increments of spending including investment, government spending, and exports.

Internally held debt Public debt owned by U.S. banks, corporations, mutual funds, pension plans, and individuals.

Investment Spending by business that adds to the productive capacity of the economy. Investment depends on factors such as

its rate of return, the level of technology, and business expectations about the economy.

Investment in human capital Improvements to the labor force from investments in improving skills, knowledge, and in any other way the quality of workers and their productivity.

Jobless recovery Takes place after a recession, when output begins to rise, but employment growth does not.

Keynesian macroeconomic equilibrium In the simple model, the economy is at rest; spending injections (investment) are equal to withdrawals (saving), and there are no net inducements for the economy to change the level of output or income. In the full model, all injections of spending must equal all withdrawals at equilibrium; I + G + X = S + T + M.

Keynesian monetary transmission mechanism An increase in the money supply lowers interest rates, thus increasing investment; expanding aggregate demand; and increasing income, output, and employment. The opposite occurs when the money supply is reduced.

Labor Includes the mental and physical talents of individuals that are used to produce products and services. Labor is paid wages.

Labor force The total number of those employed and unemployed. The unemployment rate is the unemployed divided by the labor force, expressed as a percent.

Laffer curve Plots hypothetical tax revenues at various income tax rates. If tax rates are zero, tax revenues will be zero; if rates are 100%, revenues will also be zero. As tax rates rise from zero, revenues will rise, reach a maximum, and then decline.

Land Includes natural resources such as mineral deposits, oil, natural gas, water, and land in the usual sense of the word. The payment to land as a resource is called rents.

Law of demand Holding all other relevant factors constant, as price increases, quantity demanded falls, and as price decreases, quantity demanded rises.

Law of supply Holding all other relevant factors constant, as price increases, quantity supplied will rise, and as price declines, quantity supplied will fall.

Liquidity How quickly, easily, and reliably an asset can be converted into cash.

Liquidity trap When interest rates are so low that people believe they can only rise, they hold onto money rather than investing in bonds and suffer the expected capital loss.

Long-run aggregate supply (LRAS) curve The long-run aggregate supply curve is vertical at full employment because the economy has reached its capacity to produce.

M1 The narrowest definition of money; includes currency (coins and paper money), demand deposits (checks), and other accounts that have check-writing or debit capabilities, such as stock market and money market accounts.

M2 A broader definition of money that includes "near monies" that are not as liquid as cash, including deposits in savings accounts, money market accounts, and money market mutual fund accounts.

Macroeconomic equilibrium Occurs at the intersection of the aggregate supply and aggregate demand curves. At this output level, there is no net pressures for the economy to expand or contract.

Macroeconomics Macroeconomics is concerned about the broader issues in the economy such as inflation, unemployment, and national output of goods and services.

Mandatory spending Authorized by permanent laws and does not go through the same appropriations process as discretionary spending. Mandatory spending includes such programs as Social Security, Medicare, and interest on the national debt.

Marginal propensity to consume The change in consumption associated with a given change in income ($\Delta C/\Delta Y$).

Marginal propensity to save The change in saving associated with a given change in income ($\Delta S/\Delta Y$).

Markets Institutions that bring buyers and sellers together so they can interact and transact with each other.

Medium of exchange Money is a medium of exchange because goods and services are sold for money, then the money is used to purchase other goods and services.

Microeconomics Microeconomics focuses on decision making by individuals, businesses, industries, and government.

Monetarist transmission mechanism An increase in money will reduce interest rates as portfolios rebalance, leading to a rise in investment or consumption and resulting in an increase in aggregate demand and thus an increase in income, output, or the price level.

Monetary targeting Keeps the growth of money stocks such as M1 or M2 on a steady path, following the equation of exchange (or quantity theory), to set a long-run path for the economy that keeps inflation in check.

Money Anything that is accepted in exchange for other goods and services or for the payment of debt.

Money multiplier Measures the potential or maximum amount the money supply can increase (or decrease) when new deposits enter (exit) the system and is defined as: 1 ÷ reserve requirement. The actual money multiplier will be less since some banks will hold excess reserves.

Moral hazard Asymmetric information problem that occurs when an insurance policy or some other arrangement changes the economic incentives and leads to a change in behavior.

Multiplier Spending changes alter equilibrium income by the spending change times the multiplier. One person's spending becomes another's income, and that second person spends some (the MPC), which becomes income for another person, and so on, until income has changed by $1/(1 - MPC) = 1/MPS$. The multiplier operates in both directions.

National income All income including wages, salaries and benefits, profits (for sole proprietors, partnerships, and corporations), rental income, and interest.

Natural rate of unemployment The level of unemployment where price and wage decisions are consistent; a level at which the actual inflation rate is equal to people's inflationary expectations, and cyclical unemployment is zero.

Net domestic product Gross domestic product minus depreciation or the capital consumption allowance.

Net exports Exports minus imports for the current period. Exports include all the items we sell overseas such as agricultural products, movies, and technology products, while imports are all those items we bring into the country such as vegetables from Mexico, wine from Italy, and cars from Germany.

Nominal exchange rate The rate at which one currency can be exchanged for another.

Normal goods A good where an increase in income results in rising demand.

Open market operations The buying and selling of U.S. government securities, usually treasury bonds, to adjust reserves in the banking system.

Opportunity costs The next best alternative; what you give up to do something or purchase something. For example, to watch a movie at a theater, there is not just the monetary cost of the tickets and refreshments, but the time involved in watching the movie. You could have been doing something else (knitting, golfing, hiking, or studying economics).

Personal consumption expenditures (PCE) Goods and services purchased by residents of the United States, whether individuals or businesses; they include durable goods, nondurable goods, and services.

Personal consumption expenditures (PCE) index A measure of the changes in consumer prices by focusing on consumer expenditures in the GDP accounts.

Personal income All income including wages, salaries, and other labor income; proprietors' income; rental income; personal interest and dividend income; and transfer payments (welfare and Social Security payments) received, with personal contributions for social insurance subtracted out.

Phillips curve The original curve posited a negative relationship between wages and unemployment, but later versions related unemployment to inflation rates.

Precautionary demand for money That part of individual wealth held in money to handle unexpected events and expenses.

Price ceiling A government-set maximum price that can be charged for a product or service. When the price ceiling is set below equilibrium, it leads to shortages. Rent control is an example.

Price floor A government-set minimum price that can be charged for a product or service. If the price floor is set above equilibrium price it leads to surpluses. Minimum wage legislation is an example.

Price level The absolute level of a price index, whether the consumer price index (CPI; retail prices), the producer price index (PPI; wholesale prices), or the GDP deflator (average price of all items in GDP).

Price system A name given to the market economy because prices provide considerable information to both buyers and sellers.

Producer price index (PPI) A measure of the average changes in the prices received by domestic producers for their output.

Producer surplus The difference between market price and the price that firms would be willing to supply the product. It is equal to the area below market price and above the supply curve.

Production The process of converting resources (factors of production)—land, labor, capital, and entrepreneurial ability—into goods and services.

Production efficiency Goods and services are produced at their lowest resource (opportunity) cost.

Production possibilities frontier (PPF) Shows the combinations of two goods that are possible for a society to produce at full employment. Points on or inside the PPF are feasible, and those outside of the frontier are unattainable.

Productivity How effectively inputs are converted into outputs. Labor productivity is the ratio of the output of goods and services to the labor hours devoted to the production of that output. Higher productivity and higher living standards are closely related.

Property rights The clear delineation of ownership of property backed by government enforcement.

Public choice theory The economic analysis of public and political decision making, looking at issues such as voting, the impact of election incentives on politicians, the influence of special interest groups, and rent-seeking behaviors.

Public debt The total accumulation of past deficits and surpluses; it includes treasury bills, notes, and bonds, and U.S. savings bonds.

Public goods Goods that, once provided, no one person can be excluded from consuming (nonexclusion), and one person's consumption does not diminish the benefit to others from consuming the good (nonrivalry).

Purchasing power parity The rate of exchange that allows a specific amount of currency in one country to purchase the same quantity of goods in another country.

Quota A government-set limit on the quantity of imports into a country.

Rational expectations Rational economic agents are assumed to make the best possible use of all publicly available information, then make informed, rational judgments on what the future holds. Any errors in their forecasts will be randomly distributed.

Real exchange rate The price of one country's currency for another when the price levels of both countries are taken into account; important when inflation is an issue in one country; it is equal to the nominal exchange rate multiplied by the ratio of the price levels of the two countries.

Recessionary gap The increase in aggregate spending needed to bring a depressed economy back to full employment, equal to the GDP gap divided by the multiplier.

Recognition lag The time it takes for policymakers to confirm that the economy is trending in or out of a recession. Short-term variations in key economic indicators are typical and sometimes represent nothing more than randomness in the data.

Reserve requirements The required ratio of funds that commercial banks and other depository institutions must hold in reserve against deposits.

Resources Productive resources include land (land and natural resources), labor (mental and physical talents of people), capital (manufactured products used to produce other products), and entrepreneurial ability (the combining of the other factors to produce products and assume the risk of the business).

Saving The difference between income and consumption; the amount of disposable income not spent.

Say's law The act of production produces income that leads to an equivalent amount of consumption spending; it is often paraphrased as "supply creates its own demand."

Scarcity Our unlimited wants clash with limited resources, leading to scarcity. Everyone faces scarcity (rich and poor) because, at a minimum, our time is limited on earth. Economics focuses on the allocation of scarce resources to satisfy unlimited wants.

Shortage Occurs when the price is below market equilibrium, and quantity demanded exceeds quantity supplied.

Short-run aggregate supply (AS) curve The short-run aggregate supply curve is positively sloped because many input costs are slow to change in the short run.

Speculative demand for money When inflation is not a problem, holding money for a short period is virtually risk free, whereas holding other assets is more risky. The speculative demand for money varies inversely with interest rates since they are the opportunity costs of holding money in a portfolio.

Stagflation Simultaneous occurrence of rising inflation and rising unemployment.

Store of value The function that enables people to save the money they earn today and use it to buy the goods and services they want tomorrow.

Structural unemployment Unemployment caused by changes in the structure of consumer demands or technology. It means that demand for some products

declines and the skills of this industry's workers often become obsolete as well. This results in an extended bout of unemployment while new skills are developed.

Substitute goods Goods consumers will substitute for one another depending on their relative prices.

Supply The maximum amount of a product that sellers are willing and able to provide for sale over some time period at various prices, holding all other relevant factors constant (the *ceteris paribus* condition).

Supply curve Supply schedule information translated to a graph.

Supply-side fiscal policies Focus on shifting the long-run aggregate supply curve to the right, expanding the economy without increasing inflationary pressures. Unlike policies to increase aggregate demand, supply-side policies take longer to have an impact on the economy.

Surplus Occurs when the price is above market equilibrium, and quantity supplied exceeds quantity demanded.

Surplus budgetary The amount by which annual tax revenues exceed government expenditures.

Tariff A tax on imported products. When a country taxes imported

products, it drives a wedge between the product's domestic price and its price on the world market.

Terms of trade The ratio of the price of exported goods to the price of imported goods (Px/Pm).

Tight money, restrictive, or contractionary monetary policy Fed actions designed to decrease excess reserves and the money supply to shrink income and employment, usually to fight inflation.

Transactions demand for money That part of individual wealth held in money to perform commercial transactions (medium of exchange demand).

Unit of account Money provides a yardstick for measuring and comparing the values of a wide variety of goods and services. It eliminates the problem of double coincidence of wants associated with barter.

Wealth effect Families usually hold some of their wealth in financial assets such as savings accounts, bonds, and cash, and a rising aggregate price level means that the purchasing power of this money wealth declines, reducing output demanded.

Withdrawals Activities that remove spending from the economy including saving, taxes, and imports.

Note: page numbers followed by f indicate figures; those followed by n indicate notes; those followed by t indicate tables.